Fodor's

FRANCE

FODOR'S
TRAVEL PUBLICATIONS

NEW YORK · TORONTO
LONDON · SYDNEY · AUCKLAND

WWW.FODORS.COM

CONTENTS

189

305

356

230

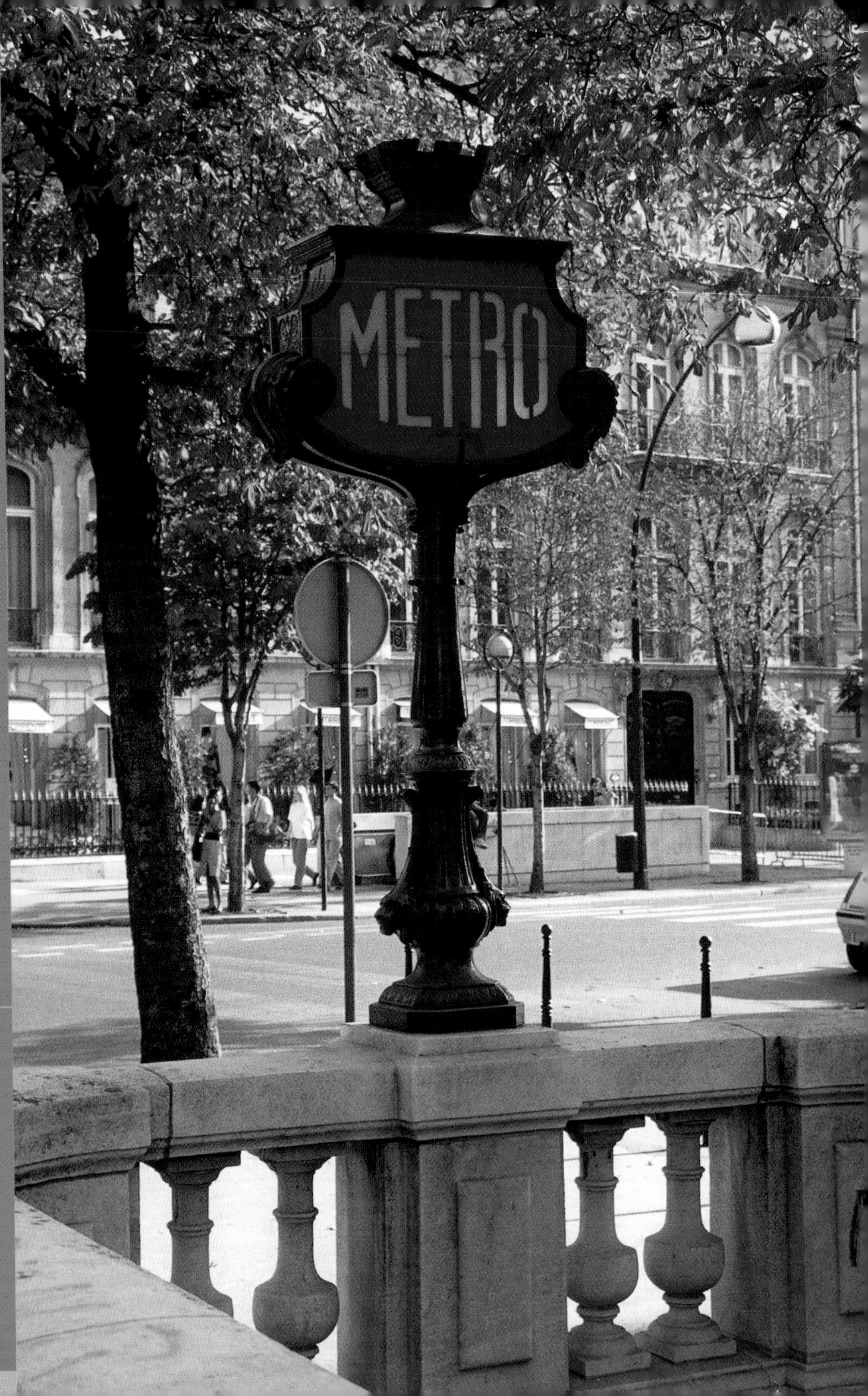
METRO

UNDERSTANDING FRANCE

Understanding France is an introduction to the country, its geography, economy, history and its people, giving a real insight into the nation. Living France gets under the skin of France today, while The Story of France takes you through the country's past.

UNDERSTANDING FRANCE

With memorable meals, world-renowned art collections and magnificent châteaux, France would be worth visiting even without the wonderful scenery. No wonder it is one of the world's most popular holiday destinations, clocking up more than 75 million visitors each year. It is the largest country in Western Europe and has a population of just over 63 million. Each part of the country has managed to retain its own character and this regional diversity can be seen especially in French food and wine, which inspire fierce local pride. The diversity is evident in the very landscape itself, with unending rows of vines in one region, followed by flocks of sheep, goats or cattle in the next, olive groves in the southeast and apple orchards in the northwest.

ECONOMY

France is the world's fifth largest economic power in terms of GDP, the sixth largest agricultural producer, the fifth largest provider of services and the fifth largest exporter of goods. It has a large and diverse economy with a sophisticated infrastructure of transportation and communications and a national electricity grid in which nuclear power plays a prominent part.

Until recently there was a strong division between France's wealthier cities and its poorer industrial and mining areas. But intelligent use of the high-speed rail network and budget air services has diluted the divide. Abandoned mining towns in the north are now home to many major international financial institutions, only an hour from Paris and within two hours of several European capitals. Likewise, workers in Paris now have the opportunity to buy homes near the Mediterranean and commute to the capital, injecting new blood and

new money into formerly run-down provincial villages. There has also been investment in discount shopping malls and low-rent business complexes far from the principal cities.

The country's best-known products are food and wine. Famously, former president Charles de Gaulle bemoaned the impossibility of governing a nation that produced more than 350 different cheeses. Bordeaux and Burgundy provide some of the world's top wines—and many of the more distinguished château estates are owned and managed by international financial institutions. The Champagne region is the source of the entire global supply of champagne, and the vast vineyards of Languedoc-Roussillon are Europe's principal suppliers of inexpensive and reliable supermarket table wines. Food is also a key lure to visitors, and restaurants and hotels pocket a fair share of the €37 billion spent annually by people coming from overseas.

POLITICS

The French president, both head of state and political leader, is elected once every five years, He—no woman has yet held the post—is a powerful figure who often manages to stamp his personality onto the country.

On 6 May 2007 Nicolas Sarkozy became the sixth President of France's Fifth Republic. A constitutional check is provided by separate elections for the *deputes*, the members of the National Assembly, from whose number the prime minister is appointed. Opposition to a president can be reflected in the election of a prime minister from a rival party. This leads to a period of 'cohabitation', a working compromise between two political agendas.

The other important elected official in France is the local mayor, whose powers are wide ranging. Even a village mayor can decide to reduce the working hours of local police, and personally intervene to stop house purchases, and Paris mayors are major political figures on the national stage.

LANGUAGE AND SOCIETY

France was originally many kingdoms and the regions retain the languages and cultures of other times. But there is fierce pride in the French language itself—remember the many campaigns to remove English words from the national vocabulary (*le weekend, le sandwich* and others). This pride is maintained by the Académie Française, who insist that email is called *mél*, with an accent to disguise its American origins.

Other tongues are fiercely defended in various corners of the country. Brittany celebrates its heritage with an annual gathering of Celts from Ireland, Wales, Scotland and even farther afield at the Interceltic fortnight in August. It is said that a Breton fisherman and his counterpart from Cornwall, England, can converse freely in their native tongues. In the southwest, French Basques are less volatile than the ETA activists across the Spanish border, but their language and rituals are celebrated with pride. On the southern side of the Pyrenees, another cross-border culture, Catalan, is almost a national identity in its own right. Across the southwest, bilingual road signs include place names in Occitan—the Langue d'Oc that gives a region its name.

The population of France includes sizeable ethnic minorities, in particular a large number of people of Arabic extraction. There has always been a national consensus that integration into mainstream French culture should be favoured over multiculturalism, and rigid secularism should be preferred to overt encouragement of religious expression. Occasionally social tensions—in which race is one ingredient—flare up in the cities and there is a continuing debate about how open to further immigration France can and should be. Particularly symptomatic of this is the issue of how to deal with *sans papiers* (the paperless) and their families—illegal immigrants who are working in France.

LANDSCAPE

France's distinctive borders give it the nickname The Hexagon. There are six mountain ranges (including the Alps, Jura, Vosges and Pyrenees) and 5,500km (3,418 miles) of coastline on the Channel, Atlantic and Mediterranean. Some dramatic river gorges cleave through the country and there are 15 million hectares (37 million acres) of forest. The landscape is both typically northern and typically southern European—lush hedgerows in Normandy, huge tracts of dusty scrubland in Languedoc, rich verdant undulating hills in Auvergne and heady fields of lavender in Provence.

VISITING FRANCE

France is a large country so don't be over-ambitious when deciding what to see during your visit. It is probably best to base yourself in one region—and they are all quite different—and really get to know it, rather than travel up and down the autoroutes ticking off as many sights as possible. In addition to the must-see sights, each region offers its own blend of leisure activities—do you want a weekend of culture and style in Paris or a week of walking in the Pyrenees, skiing in the Alps or relaxing on a beach on the Côte d'Azur?

If you're taking your car (▷ 51–55), it's a good idea to plan an overnight stop on longer drives. If you're moving around by train, consider buying a rail pass before you leave home, as this can save you money (▷ 57). Regions can vary greatly depending on the season, so bear this in mind when planning your trip. For example, Paris is quiet but stiflingly hot in August, while much of the south of France is packed with people and traffic; some of the trails in the Pyrenees are impassable during the colder months, while this, obviously, is an ideal time for skiing.

Opposite *A steep, cobbled lane in a Corsican village*
Below *Pinot Noir grapes*

FRANCE'S REGIONS

PARIS AND THE ÎLE DE FRANCE

Paris is a seductive capital, with its legendary style, romance, river, art and architecture. It is the heart of France's political, economic, social and cultural life and has a population of more than 2.1 million.

The Île de France region, with Paris at its heart, has a population of 11 million—and plenty of châteaux, including Versailles and Fontainebleau.

NORTHWEST FRANCE

Normandie (Normandy), west of Paris, has timbered manor houses, abbey ruins and seaside resorts. It is famous for Camembert, Calvados and its links with the Impressionists.

Bretagne (Brittany), the peninsula west of Normandy, has a long coastline of golden beaches, dotted with small fishing ports. The region's richly decorated churches are often surrounded by enclosed cemeteries with imposing gateways.

NORTH AND NORTHEAST FRANCE

Nord-Pas-de-Calais, at the northern tip of France, has the busy ports of Boulogne, Calais and Dunkerque, as well as Lille, capital of the north.

Picardie, south of Nord-Pas-de-Calais, has Amiens as its ancient capital, sitting on the banks of the Somme.

Champagne-Ardenne, to the east, shelters the chalk hills and escarpments of champagne country.

Lorraine, farther east, includes Nancy, former capital of the independent Duchy of Lorraine, and Metz, Lorraine's current capital.

Alsace borders Germany (and indeed belonged to Germany several times in its history) and you can see German influences in its food, wine and architecture. Strasbourg, the centre of the European Union, sits on its eastern edge.

THE LOIRE

Centre, south of Paris, is renowned for its Renaissance châteaux, historic towns, and the beautiful river and valley scenery.

Pays de la Loire, farther west, has the lively city of Nantes, a stretch of Atlantic coastline, and the towns of Angers, Saumur and Le Mans—famous for its 24-hour sports car race.

CENTRAL FRANCE AND THE ALPS

Franche-Comté, in the east of France and bordering Switzerland, has the Jura woods and mountains, which are popular with walkers and cross-country skiers.

Bourgogne (Burgundy) is a gastronomic hub known for mustard, *boeuf bourguignon* and snails. It has the wine towns of Dijon and Beaune.

Auvergne has the Massif Central mountain range, with its distinctive volcanic cones.

Rhône-Alpes includes Lyon, with its Renaissance old quarter. The region has the highest peak in Europe—Mont Blanc—and some of the best skiing.

SOUTHEAST FRANCE

Provence-Alpes-Côte-d'Azur borders Italy and has miles of Mediterranean coastline. There are the great cities of Marseille and Nice and the area's Roman past is evident in the amphitheatres and arches at Orange and Arles.

Languedoc-Roussillon also has a long Mediterranean coastline and its Roman legacy is the wonder of Roman engineering, the Pont du Gard. The main city, Montpellier, is vibrant and cosmopolitan.

Monaco is the tiny principality that thinks big.

SOUTHWEST FRANCE

Poitou-Charentes, north of Aquitaine, includes historic Poitiers, the sophisticated coastal town of La Rochelle

Left *A field of bright sunflowers*
Below *The game of boules is a popular pastime in France*
Opposite *French vineyards*

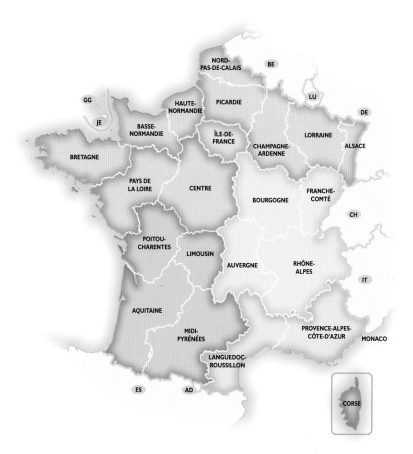

and the offshore islands of Ré and Oléron. There is also La Venise Verte—a huge area of greenery and waterways that is best explored by barque.

Limousin, east of Poitou-Charentes, is home to Limoges, famous for its fine porcelain.

Midi-Pyrénées, south of Limousin, shares its southern border with Spain and Andorra and includes part of the Pyrenees mountain range, the cultural city of Toulouse and the pilgrimage site of Lourdes.

Aquitaine, on the Atlantic seaboard, is famous for Bordeaux and its wine, the surrounding area, its sandy beaches and resorts, such as Biarritz, on the Atlantic coast, the caves and gastronomy—including foie gras and truffles—of the Dordogne area, and the Pyrenees mountains to the south.

CORSICA
This Mediterranean island lies off the coast of Provence. You can walk in the mountains, relax on the beach, spot the diverse birdlife and admire the architecture of Pisan and Genoese rulers.

THE BEST OF FRANCE

PARIS AND THE ÎLE DE FRANCE

Eiffel Tower (▷ 100–101): Test your nerves on the viewing platforms of this Paris landmark.

Musée du Louvre (▷ 90–91): One of the world's most famous art galleries.

Musée d'Orsay (▷ 93): A wonderful collection of Impressionist paintings and other art, in a former belle-époque train station.

Notre-Dame (▷ 95): Admire the cathedral's magnificent architecture, then climb the towers for wonderful views.

Fontainebleau (▷ 79): This château is just as lavish as Versailles but less crowded.

Fountains at Versailles (▷ 102–103): Pick a day when the famous fountains are flowing to experience Versailles at its best.

Views from Sacré-Cœur (▷ 99): Sunset is a great time to appreciate the breathtaking views from the front terrace of this basilica.

NORTHWEST FRANCE

Côte d'Albâtre (▷ 166–167): Start at Étretat for a cliff walk with breathtaking views along the Alabaster Coast, named after its chalky cliffs and milky waves.

Bayeux (▷ 126): See the famous 11th-century tapestry.

D-Day Beaches (▷ 133): Visit the beaches where Allied forces landed on 6 June 1944.

Honfleur (▷ 138): A picturesque fishing port and long-established artists' colony.

Mont St-Michel (▷ 140–143): Cross to this mystical abbey on its rocky mount and enjoy wonderful views of the bay.

Océanopolis (▷ 127): See 10,000 marine creatures at one of Europe's best aquariums.

Rouen (▷ 148–151): Normandy's capital has an attractive old town, good shopping and a cathedral famously painted by Monet.

Sables-d'Or-les-Pins (▷ 153): Relax on the golden sands of this beach, backed by pine trees.

St-Thégonnec (▷ 155): Brittany's most picturesque parish close.

NORTH AND NORTHEAST FRANCE

Battlefields of Picardie (▷ 187): See the fields where so many soldiers lost their lives during World War I and pay your respects at the immaculate war cemeteries.

Champagne-tasting (▷ 200–201): Visit a Maison du Champagne at Reims and remind yourself why bubbly has been prized for centuries.

Lille (▷ 194–197): France's fourth-largest city has a prestigious art gallery, vast shopping mall and 17th-century Citadelle.

Nancy (▷ 192): Immerse yourself in art nouveau architecture and fabulous glassware.

Nausicaà (▷ 188): An imaginative aquarium at Boulogne.

Strasbourg (▷ 202–205): This city, near the German border, is the seat of the European Parliament.

Sand sports on the Côte d'Opale (▷ 191, 218): Take a lesson in sand-yachting on the beaches of the Opal Coast north of Boulogne.

Troyes (▷ 199): An attractive village of half-timbered houses, cobbled streets and vivid stained-glass windows.

Above *A boat at Erbalunga village, on the eastern shore of Cap Corse*
Right *Canoeists gather on the shingle beneath the Pont-d'Arc, in the Gorges de l'Ardèche*
Opposite *Looking across to Mont St-Michel*

THE LOIRE

Chartres (▷ 230–231): See the awesome Notre-Dame-de-Chartres cathedral.

Châteaux of the Loire (▷ 226–235): This scenic region is dotted with fairy-tale châteaux.

Le Mans (▷ 236): Not just for car enthusiasts—as well as the racetrack and automobile museum there is a lovely old town, with cobbled streets, medieval timber-framed houses and a 12th-century cathedral.

Tours (▷ 239): A thriving city, between the Loire and Cher rivers, with a rich historical, cultural and architectural heritage.

Walking in the Loire Valley: For a walk around Langeais and the valley of the river Roumer, ▷ 240–241.

CENTRAL FRANCE AND THE ALPS

The Alps (▷ 283): The most exhilarating way to experience these mountains is on skis or a snowboard.

Dijon (▷ 264–265): This easily walkable, historic town is a hub of the Burgundy wine trade.

The Gorges de l'Ardèche (▷ 262): Canoe along the river and underneath the natural archway, the Pont-d'Arc.

Lac d'Annecy (▷ 259): For boat trips, water sports and outdoor activities in a beautiful mountain setting, Annecy is hard to beat.

Lyon (▷ 266–269): A must-see city, great for culture and nightlife.

Parc des Volcans: This park is ideal for walkers, with volcanic peaks such as the Puy de Dôme (▷ 270–271) giving views of the Auvergne.

SOUTHEAST FRANCE

Aix-en-Provence (▷ 298): An elegant town with fine Renaissance mansions and links with the painter Paul Cézanne.

Avignon (▷ 300): The main draws are the magnificent Palais des Papes, once the seat of the Pope, and the huge drama and dance festival held in July.

The Camargue delta (▷ 301, 326–327): Great for long, wild walks, peace and quiet, and birdwatching.

Cannes (▷ 303): Shop 'til you drop in Provence's most glamorous destination.

Gorges du Tarn (▷ 322–323): Drive, walk or take a boat along the river for spectacular gorge views.

Marseille (▷ 310–313): Soak up the history in the Vieux Port and Le Panier districts of this ancient city.

Montpellier (▷ 309): Visit in the summer to enjoy one of the city's many arts festivals.

Nice (▷ 316): Experience the city's hectic nightlife.

Nîmes and Pont du Gard (▷ 317, 319): Marvel at the Romans' engineering skills at the amphitheatre in Nîmes and at the Pont du Gard aqueduct.

SOUTHWEST FRANCE

Biarritz (▷ 354): A chic resort, with fantastic beaches.

Bordeaux (▷ 356–359): Sample the city's fine wines or enjoy its architecture.

Caves: See the prehistoric cave paintings at Lascaux (▷ 363) or Les Eyzies (▷ 361).

Drive through the vineyards of Bordeaux (▷ 376–377): Don't miss the picturesque wine town of St-Émilion.

Futuroscope (▷ 361): This leisure park, with its high-tech effects, has something to entertain the whole family.

Périgueux (▷ 366): Shop for truffles, foie gras, walnuts, wine and cheese in the markets—the biggest in the area.

La Rochelle (▷ 367): A sophisticated coastal resort, with lively cafés, interesting architecture and a vast marina.

Toulouse (▷ 372–373): Great for art and history.

CORSICA

Réserve Naturelle de Scandola (▷ 407): This coastal nature reserve has abundant birdlife.

Beaches: Take your pick from the island's many beaches.

Cap Corse (▷ 405): For white villages, sandy coves and peace and quiet, head to this mountainous peninsula.

TOP EXPERIENCES

Be cosmopolitan Take in one of France's great cities: Choose from Paris, Lille, Lyon, Bordeaux, Toulouse or Marseille.

Discover France's history Visit the Roman amphitheatre in Orange, the D-Day Landing beaches in Normandy or the megalithic standing stones at Filitosa, in Corsica.

Drink red wine from Bordeaux, champagne from Reims, Calvados from Normandy or beer from St-Omer.

Drive from château to château in the Loire, through the mountains in the Pyrenees or along the Mediterranean coastline (but not after drinking!).

Eat whatever the locals are eating, whether it's snails in Bourgogne, sauerkraut in Alsace or *bouillabaisse* in Provence.

Get on your bicycle Options include Bordeaux, a nature reserve in the Camargue or the vineyards of Champagne.

People-watch with a coffee in your hand at a town-square café.

Shop at a market, in a Parisian boutique or in a village *charcuterie*.

Ski, snowboard or simply enjoy a *vin chaud* in the Alps.

Swim in the sea. Try the Mediterranean in Corsica or Provence, or the Atlantic by Arcachon.

Take in some culture Try the Musée d'Orsay in Paris, Les Abattoirs in Toulouse or the Palais des Beaux-Arts in Lille.

Visit a cathedral and learn more about France's architectural history. Choices include Notre-Dame in Paris, Bordeaux's 1,000-year-old cathedral and Chartres.

Wander around a château For a fairy-tale Loire palace try the Château d'Ussé and for excess go to Versailles.

Walk in the countryside. Follow a mountain trail in the Alps, a coastal path in Brittany or a peaceful canal towpath such as the Canal de Bourgogne.

Watch sport The endurance event of the year is the Tour de France. International rugby or soccer matches take place at the Stade de France in Paris.

Above The Château de Fontainebleau, reflected in the lake in its extensive grounds
Below A skier weaves around the red-flagged gates in the slalom at La Tou

LIVING FRANCE

LIVING FRANCE

UNDERSTANDING

In a nation once made up of kingdoms and principalities, duchies and counties, there is no such thing as 'typically French'. The annual parades of model giants through the streets of the north would be as out of place in Provence as the traditional bullfighting of the south would be if it were transported to the Alps. Regional identity matters to the French—when a local talks patriotically of *mon pays* (my country) the reference is most likely to be the region rather than France itself. While food and drink most commonly define a region, games and traditions also play their part. Essentially, each area and its culture is determined by its landscape and geography. The story of how a rock or cave got its shape will provide cautionary bedtime tales for generations. Regions have their own slang, patois and even languages. Occitan (from Languedoc) and Breton (from Brittany) are languages that are being preserved and cultivated like endangered species. Even in conventional French-speaking towns, listen to older generations in conversation and you may find it hard to recognize the language of your school textbooks.

GYPSIES AND COWBOYS BY THE SEA

Gypsies dance with the Camargue's cowboys during one of the most lively events of the Provençal calendar, the Pèlerinage des Gitans (Gypsy Pilgrimage). The village of Les Saintes-Maries-de-la-Mer is where, legend has it, Maria Jacobé and Maria Salomé, half-sisters of the Virgin Mary, arrived with their maid Sarah, patron saint of gypsies. Every year in late May, gypsies from all over Europe make their pilgrimage to the coast. Dressed in vibrant, traditional costumes, gypsies and *gardiens* (local cowboys who look after wild black bulls) carry jewel-encrusted statues of St. Sarah and the Marias into the sea to be blessed. During the evening and into the night, the beach echoes to the sound of celebrations.

Clockwise from left to right *The abbey crowns Mont St-Michel; the azure Mediterranean viewed from Èze; gypsies during the Pèlerinage des Gitans in Les Saintes-Maries-de-la-Mer*

SILLY SKIING

The Olympic resorts in the Alps are known for serious sport, yet once a year, bathtubs are cooler than snowboards and scrap metal is sharper than skis. In late April, La Clusaz hosts the Défi-Foly waterslide challenge. Around 150 participants from across the region take part in the daredevil event around the Confins lake.

The fun begins at dawn as racers slide down the slope and try to cross the waters. In 2010, winner Philippe Troubat extended the record distance with a winning slide of 155m (508ft)

This inventive combination of downhill and waterskiing is then followed by the Unidentified Sliding Object contest to find the most bizarre object used on the course. Previous contestants have used car parts and baths to assist their passage gliding down the slopes to the waters.

PUFFED-UP PARADE

Should you feel a sudden gust of wind around your nether regions in Périgord Vert, don't worry—it means that you have been accepted as a local.

The worthy citizens of Nontron adorn themselves with clogs, masks and nightshirts, and take to the streets armed with a pair of bellows for the annual Soufflaculs parade, when residents joyfully shoot air up each others' nightshirts and pump up their petticoats to chase out evil spirits that might be lurking within.

The custom dates from an Ash Wednesday tradition at the nearby abbey of St-Sauveur, when monks used bellows to purify each nook and cranny before Lent. In the Middle Ages, townsfolk adopted the Bellows Festival as a cue for debauchery and licentiousness. The modern-day parade, however, is seen as a bit of harmless fun.

RIVIERA REVELS

Forget understated style—the Riviera has a gaudy party for a glorious fortnight, when the international visitors are looking the other way. Mardi Gras on the Riviera is the way to party out of winter and into spring sunshine. Shrove Tuesday ends more than two weeks of merrymaking. In Nice, massive papier mâché heads join the marching bands and dancing crowds following gigantic floats parading daily through the streets and along the Promenade des Anglais to the sea. The giant King of the Carnival reigns supreme until he is finally set alight and put to sea, bringing the carnival to its dramatic close.

Along the coast, the usually genteel folk of Menton provide a rival assault on the senses, with the added fragrance of citrus fruits when 130 tonnes of oranges and lemons are transformed into massive floats for the Fête du Citron.

SELF-BUILD CHÂTEAU

As if France doesn't have enough medieval châteaux, a brand new one is being built in Burgundy the old-fashioned way. Guédelon castle at Treigny (Yonne) is being laboriously raised from the bed of an abandoned quarry by a team of 50 craftsmen and women using only traditional building methods and materials found close to hand: wood, stone, earth, sand and clay. More than 300 volunteers are honing their skills working on site as artisans, or breaking sweat as labourers, to bring the project to fruition.

The project is the idea of Michel Guyot who had restored an ancient château and wanted to better understand the challenges and achievements of 13th-century builders. Work started in 1997 and the château won't be complete until around 2022, but even as a work in progress the site welcomes more than 340,000 visitors each year.

UNDERSTANDING LIVING FRANCE

15

There is a lot of talk in France about voter apathy, though this should not be confused with political apathy, as the French are prone to voicing their opinions. Even the most staid of weekly markets is likely to have at least one small protest somewhere. In the rural communities of the south, pamphlets and banners made from bedsheets issue dire warnings about the powers of the European Union, while in liberal university cities, foreign affairs will inspire a protest march or a well-mannered yet lively chorus will take up human rights and immigration issues. The downside is that strikes, official and unsanctioned, are a way of life. The French resign themselves to changing travel plans around railway strikes but get angry when industrial action affects their children's education. Politicians may not always get the votes, even if they can rely on popular support, but the ones who get it right have streets named after them for generations to come.

CITY OF PROTEST

Parisians feel it to be a matter of pride to pour into the streets to express their grievances by rallying, marching and erecting barricades. But while the Left demonstrates on the streets, when it is time to step into the polling booths it is the Right which has consistently won control of the capital. The election of a socialist mayor in 2001 meant that for the first time for nearly 100 years Paris was to be governed by the Left. After the election the mayor, Bertrand Delanoë, proudly declared 'For the first time since 1909, the forces for progress hold the majority. Paris is still the capital of the movement...a city that will neither conform nor submit.'

Clockwise from left to right *Cours Masséna market in Antibes; harvesting grapes by hand during the vendanges (grape picking) season; demonstrators in Dijon*

BOSS-NAPPING

As the economic crisis of 2008 tightened its grip and bank executives and hedge-fund managers became the people we loved to hate, French workers adopted a unique plan of action to protect their livelihoods. When senior executives came to visit and discuss possible redundancies and plant closures, they simply barred their retreat and took them hostage.

Luc Rousselet, the French Director of 3M, was held captive while staff negotiated better severance deals. So too were the bosses of Sony France, Siemens, Caterpillar and Hewlett-Packard. All of these situations took place in a spirit of good humour and the victims were seemingly well fed, including a dinner of fresh mussels for one executive.

A STREET HERO NAMED DÉSIR

Members of the European Parliament do not usually find their way to Strasbourg on a wave of support from an otherwise disaffected youth. However, Harlem Désir owes his parliamentary seat in part to his charismatic turning of the tide against the National Front racism of the 1980s, when attacks on cemeteries and offensive graffiti were rife. The organization SOS Racisme, once fronted by the media-friendly Monsieur Désir, celebrates the nation's multiculturalism with its simple logo, a yellow palm daubed with the words *Touche pas à mon pote* ('Hands off my mate'). What could otherwise have led to inner-city rioting has become a cause for partying in the streets, with jeering mob culture subdued by a cheering mass of humanity.

THANK YOU FOR THE MUSIC

Question: How does a politician transcend party lines to become a national institution? Answer: He gets the country singing. As corny as it may sound, in 1982 the then Minister for Culture, Jack Lang, did just that. Today, the Fête de la Musique that he founded is almost as important a part of summer as Bastille Day.

Amateurs and professionals stage 10,000 free concerts with many famous musicians returning to their home towns for the night of 21 June. In Paris, salsa bands and accordionists mingle with crowds, orchestras perform outside the Palais Royal, rock stars fill the place de la République and indie bands take over place Denfert-Rochereau. In every other city, town and village, musicians claim every spare paving stone and café terraces become stages for a night.

SACRE BLEUS

While most fans drown their sorrows over a couple of beers at the local bar when their team loses, the departure of the French football team, Les Bleus, from the World Cup in 2010—bottom of their group and amid player mutiny—provoked angst and moral crisis across the nation.

Not merely a bad run of poor form, the press and political classes see the affair as an insult to the very reputation of the country itself. Former Prime Minister Dominique de Villepin declared 'I do not want France to resemble our football team'.

A week after the team arrived back on French soil President Sarkozy ordered an official review of the debacle, led by Roselyne Bachelot, Sports Minister and French Olympian. Whether this high-level investigation will improve the team's results, only time will tell.

URBAN VS. RURAL

The arrival of the TGV (super-fast trains) cut journey times for travel around France. But move from the city to the countryside and your journey will still be measured in decades not hours. While cities such as Lille, Lyon, Toulouse and Montpellier vie with each other to outdo Paris as the ultimate contemporary city, rural France eschews the cult of internationalism, choosing instead a celebration of all things rural. People of all generations nod and bid each other a friendly *bonjour* or *bonsoir* when passing in the street or when entering a shop. Of course time does leave its mark, and those same fast trains that are making France smaller are nudging away at those differences. Paris is now only three hours from the Mediterranean, and as the local rail networks link up with TGVs, city families are finding it increasingly easy and attractive to move to the country. These families are buying houses in the country not simply for weekends and holidays (a trend that had seriously threatened many rural communities), but as their principal homes. They believe their children will receive a better education away from the metropolis, and so the breadwinner opts for a daily two-hour commute to the city, while the rest of the family lives the country life.

THE DAY THE SHEEP CAME TO TOWN

Spring sees the *transhumance*, when shepherds take their flocks from winter to summer grazing grounds. As the sheep are driven through the narrow streets of historic towns, it is a time for thanksgiving, music and wine. From little-known Vaucluse villages such as Jonquières to more established visitor destinations including St-Rémy-de-Provence and ski resorts in the Alps, thousands of sheep, dogs, donkeys and shepherds parade along the streets. Mass is said, tambourines are shaken and copious quantities of wine are quaffed until the animals are well on their way. Then, in autumn, the locals get ready for the return journey.

Clockwise from left to right *Hectic traffic on the avenue des Champs-Élysées, in Paris; high-speed TGV trains link cities across France; village life in Provence is slow paced*

14 JULY FESTIVITIES

Nothing highlights the difference between small country towns and big cities more than the different regional ways to celebrate the national holiday, Bastille Day, on 14 July. Paris lets its hair down with plenty of *bals publics* (free parties) hosted by the city's firemen, and in principal towns around France fireworks light up the sky.

However, in smaller towns the French Revolution knows its place, with local celebrations taking precedence. Villages in the *département* of Gard, in the south, celebrate the feast of Volo Biou, with dramatic processions based on the legend of a flying cow. The Hippodrome de Pompadour racecourse forsakes horses to become enamoured of an ass as the people of Corrèze, in the Limousin region of central France, celebrate the Day of the Donkey. Bastille Day is also celebrated in US cities.

A STROLL WITH YOUR SNORKEL

Ten per cent of France is protected parkland. However, should you fancy a ramble in the park of Port Cros, opposite Toulon, in a unique corner of Provence, don't forget your snorkel. The nature trail here, in Europe's most unusual national park, takes visitors underwater more than a third of a mile along the seabed.

This 700ha (1,729-acre) island nestles in amazingly clear waters and was designated as a national park in 1963, with the protected zone extending around the coast, some 600m (654 yards) out to sea. Signposted visitor trails continue from the island's pathways down into the unspoiled waters and to protect the wildlife, boats are not allowed to moor on the sandy beaches. Underwater guided tours from La Palud beach are free, but you should bring your own snorkel.

BEWARE OF THE BEAST

Just when parents in the Auvergne had finally dispelled their children's fears about the legendary Beast of Gévaudan, the *Brotherhood of the Wolf* (2001) was released. For city folk it was just a Gothic yarn, but locals still talk in hushed whispers about the creature that devoured at least 100 women and children between July 1764 and June 1767.

The attacks were so vicious that the Beast makes Conan Doyle's fictional Hound of the Baskervilles seem like a playful puppy. Yet, more than 200 years after his reign of terror, little is known about the creature. Was it a werewolf or a madman? Or had its reputation been enhanced simply as the result of mass hysteria? City scepticism and legend are explored in a *son et lumière* (sound and light show) at the Musée Fantastique de la Bête du Gévaudan, at Saugues.

AN ORIGINAL GALLERY

You don't need an urban gallery to create a contemporary art space, just a castle, a park and the help of a countess. At Drulon (www.drulon.com), in Centre-Val-de-Loire, Piet and Nanou Hendriks have transformed their château into a space to rival any city gallery. In 1998, the château and grounds were run down and overgrown, so the Hendriks married the skills of avant-garde artists with those of respected gardeners, such as Countess Alix de Saint-Venant, who designed the classical rose gardens and neatly laid-out formal borders.

You haven't seen a water feature until you come across strange figures rising through the marsh mists here. Nor will any other parterre or rose garden have prepared you for the lifelike figures, created by Martine Salavize and Djanashvili Amiran, emerging from bushes and wetlands.

UNDERSTANDING LIVING FRANCE

In most European countries and in the US, political leaders keep a close eye on the polls and an ear open for the latest whisper of public opinion. But in the 20th century, some French presidents instigated grand-scale projects with which their names would be associated long after any election result was forgotten. They thus followed the tradition set by the great French kings and emperors. Louis XIV dotted the country with buildings reflecting the glory of the Sun King and Napoleon commissioned an imperial statue on top of a column to commemorate his expected successful invasion of Britain, long before he called off the planned attack. So, after Charles de Gaulle's La Défense and President Georges Pompidou's Beaubourg, was it any wonder that François Mitterrand should have ended his reign with a cornucopia of *Grands Projets* that redrew the map of Paris in a manner hardly seen since Baron Haussmann laid out the boulevards? The most impressive project of the presidency of Jacques Chirac — although not particularly associated with him — is the Millau motorway suspension bridge in southern France.

Clockwise from left to right *The glistening stained glass of Paris's Sainte-Chapelle, commissioned by St. Louis in the 13th century; 20th-century pyramids at the Louvre; the ornate Château Royal de Blois; the famous 'inside-out' design of the Centre Georges Pompidou, in Paris*

MORE THAN A PINCH OF SALT

Modern presidential and mayoral schemes may be better known, but grand-scale utopian visions have been around for years. Listed by UNESCO, yet still hardly featuring among the best-known attractions in the land, are the royal salt works at Arc-et-Senans. It's hard to believe that Claude-Nicolas Ledoux's beautiful classical architecture was actually an industrial plant, but this monument, built between 1775 and 1779, was used to extract salt from the water from the old mines of Salins les Bains. The Saline Royale was more than merely a factory — it was a template for a new city, a vision of town planning, centuries ahead of its time.

TOO MUCH DESIGN?

The 21st century is the era of the designer hotel. Where once it was enough to have French designer Philippe Starck come up with a new chair or waiters' uniforms, France's newest hotels vie for the most outrageous concepts. In traditional Nice, the palatial elegance of the Negresco has a new rival in Matali Crasset's multiconcept Hi-hôtel on avenue des Fleurs, where you can choose the space that best suits your mood and personality. You can take a shower behind a plant screen in a room with an indoor terrace theme, relax on furniture created from computer monitors or sing along to the Sofablaster with its built-in music. Other options include a bathroom with a lava rock pool and, for total luxury, a champagne vending machine.

IDEAS ABOVE THEIR STATION

As the TGV stretches its superfast way across the country, linking up with similar high-speed rail networks in Germany, Belgium and Spain, the arrival of a dedicated train station in each town and city is cause for celebration.

When architect Rem Koolhaas created the futuristic Euralille district in Lille, with its famous 'ski-boot' Crédit Lyonnais skyscraper above the station, it was a case of history repeating itself. The old Flandres station along the road is in fact the original Gare du Nord from Paris, donated to the town when the 19th-century railway reached Lille. The people of Lille were unimpressed by the capital's hand-me-downs and commissioned a second level to the facade.

ANTIGONE WITHOUT THE ANTAGONISM

When a city has 1,000 years of cultural integration, building a brand new district risks upsetting the equilibrium of the place. France, like many other countries, has its share of the snaking concrete blight that mars the outskirts of many decent towns, creating social divisions and losing its lustre after just a couple of rainy winters. It helps when the architect and the politician creating the dream share the same vision. Thus architect Ricardo Bofill was perfectly able to reflect the harmonious aims of Mayor Georges Freche in his grand-scale Antigone district, which spills out of the Roman, medieval and belle-époque heart of Montpellier into a high-tech homage to Classical harmony. The district, with its ancient Greek-style lines and curves on an epic scale, is built for the future but celebrates the past.

UPSTAGING NATURE

The end of the 20th century saw a plethora of building projects with grand ideals. Surely the most ambitious must have been the dream of upstaging real volcanoes. The stunning green, panoramic landscape of the Auvergne is a living legacy to the great volcanoes that shaped the region.

The Parc des Volcans has long been a well-loved spot for those wishing to escape into lush and vibrant nature, but now man goes beyond nature with Vulcania, European Park of Volcanism, on a 57ha (141-acre) site at St-Ours-les-Roches. Here you can take a trip along simulated lava flows, burning rivers and ground that appears to crack beneath your feet. The attraction also presents a tour of the world's most beautiful volcanoes and even recreates momentous events like the eruption of Mount St. Helens in Washington state in May 1980.

Food and wine are not merely important to the French, they define the nation, its regions and its people. At its simplest level, the fresh produce of a village or a region is the essence of communication. Every wedding, confirmation, harvest festival or good-news day is likely to be celebrated with the uncorking of a bottle of the district's finest, be it champagne in Champagne, wine in the south or a potent Calvados in Normandy, served with the pick or catch of the day. On the coast, this might be a *bruscade* (seafood barbecue), in the east perhaps plums and *charcuterie* (cured pork). The best way to get to the heart of a region is to visit during one of the many hundreds of local food and wine festivals. An olive festival, for example, is an opportunity for the makers of cheeses, wines, pâtés and jams for miles around to offer tastings in the streets as much as for the olive growers to sell their oils and soaps. Food is the great equalizer in this republic, with budget, not class, determining who eats where. The rich may be able to afford to dine out every night of the year, but even those on low incomes will appreciate the rarer treat of a fine meal at a good restaurant. A gastronomic menu of five, six or seven courses in a decent restaurant may be beyond the budget of many, but the same establishment's inexpensive set *menu du terroir*, using good local ingredients, will be no less carefully considered and prepared.

A PROVENÇAL CHRISTMAS

If you dine out in Provence at the end of December you'll find that Christmas dinner is both a sweet and savoury occasion. The table is decked with symbolism and tradition in mind. The *Gros Souper* (Big Supper) on Christmas Eve is one of the South's most cherished rituals. With its 13 desserts, the meal is known for its abundance of sweets and, paradoxically, for its so-called austerity. Dishes include modest marinated vegetables, *anchoïade* (anchovy paste), salt-cod and *escargots à l'aioli* (snails in garlic), through to the finale of a spread of platters representing Christ and the apostles, with nougats, nuts and raisins, and plenty of fruit dishes, from delicious figs to sweet *confits* (candied fruits). The table is draped with three white cloths and set with bowls and candles symbolizing the Holy Trinity.

Clockwise from left to right *A traditional French bakery; a local specialty, Tarte Normande; bottles of red wine for sale in Galerie Vivienne in Paris*

VINE THERAPY

Au revoir to a diet of lettuce leaves, *adieu* to slimming pills and anti-wrinkle potions, and *bonjour* and *bienvenu* to the grape and its bounty. Doctors may concede that a glass of red wine can be beneficial, but in Bordeaux many locals extol the virtue of a bathtub full of grapey goodness for true well-being. *Vinothérapie* is a system of anti-ageing and slimming treatments based on vine and wine extracts, in particular grape seed polyphenols. The first *vinothérapie* facility, in the heart of the Graves vineyards, opened in 2000 and has inspired imitators at luxury spas. Half-day or week-long pampering sessions are available and after a grapeseed Jacuzzi in a barrel bath or a wine and honey wrap, you may feel ready to sample the stuff in the region's vineyards and wine cellars.

BASQUE-ING IN CHOCOLATE COUNTRY

The town that gave the world the bayonet and some of France's most celebrated cured hams, Bayonne, became a sanctuary for Jews fleeing the Spanish Inquisition. In return, the grateful refugees offered France the gift of chocolate.

The delights of the confection were unknown on the French side of the Pyrenees until the arrival of the refugees in the capital of the French Basque country, and people still come to Bayonne to taste the treats introduced by these Jewish chocolatiers. At quaint tea rooms on rue Neuf, chocolate is most popularly enjoyed as a mid-morning or mid-afternoon snack. However, the genteel nibble makes way for several days of chocoholic over-indulgence during the annual Chocolate Festival in midsummer.

ONE MAN AND HIS MELONS

Cavaillon, in the Vaucluse region, is the heart of melon country. One man who has more than a passing respect for the rich, succulent summer fruit is restaurateur Jean-Jacques Prévot. Not only does it feature on every menu from mid-May until the end of September (try the *melon cocotte* with lobster), but it is the heart of a local aperitif, *délice de melon*. Monsieur Prévot even makes paint from the pips and skins, and these contribute to the restaurant's exhibition of 600 melon-related arts and crafts.

The town itself hosts an annual melon parade in July, with music in the streets and melon-tasting.

WHAT A WHIFF!

It's official; the French produce the smelliest cheese in the world. Scientists in the UK invented an electronic 'nose' that assesses the odour given off by the cheese and after experimenting with hard, soft, goat milk, cow's milk and sheep's milk varieties from around Europe, it pronounced that Vieux Boulogne (also known as the Sablé du Boulonnais) is the most pungent.

This round cow's cheese, produced in the Pas de Calais in the far north of the country, has an orangey-red skin produced by washing the exterior in beer. It's the beer reacting with the enzymes in the cheese that produces the striking smell.

ARTS AND MEDIA

Every year in August the giants of contemporary music descend on an unlikely market town in rural Gascony to entertain the crowds packed into a temporary marquee. The Marciac Jazz Festival is merely one of many world-class festivals celebrated beyond the normal circuit of urban venues and it's an indication of how France embraces the arts. Almost every town takes pride in providing a programme of cultural events for the benefit of its inhabitants and visitors. Some events take place in atmospheric historic monuments: an international rock superstar might play the Roman arena of Nîmes or a talented local choir sing in the Romanesque church of some small village that you would otherwise never hear of. The high point of the arts year is the Avignon festival, when the world's art critics decamp to the walled city to report on what will be making headlines in Paris in the year to come, with each hotel lobby commandeered by the media as makeshift TV studios.

REIMS' SEASON

Around 120 free concerts between June and August make Reims a very special place to be in summer. Les Flâneries Musicales d'Été, established in 1990 by the late Yehudi Menuhin, provide many of the season's true delights.

Events take place in parks and public spaces around the city, with international performers such as Montserrat Caballé, Helen Merrill and Wilhelmenia Fernandez among the legends topping the bill in recent years. As effervescent as the fizz that made the city famous, the event offers an eclectic selection of concerts. You can expect to find jazz in a park, baroque on the street corner or even George Gershwin being sung on the cathedral steps.

Clockwise from left to right *The Europa Jazz Festival in Le Mans; detail of a painting by Rosso de Rossi in the Galerie de François I, at Fontainebleau; Rodin's famous* Le Penseur

WHEN ONE MOZART IS NOT ENOUGH

Some people can never have too much sun, nor too much Mozart. Thus Provence in summer reverberates to the sound of popular arias in historic settings. To add to Provence's festivals of music, such as the pageantry of Orange's epic productions and concerts at Aix-en-Provence's open-air theatre in the grounds of the archbishops' palace, a new venue arrived in 2002, when fashion designer Pierre Cardin launched his own opera festival in the ruins of Château Lacoste.

The opening star-studded production was Mozart's condemnation of loose morals and licentiousness, *Don Giovanni*. This was apt because the château's most famous resident before Pierre Cardin was the Marquis de Sade.

GETTING READY TO ROCK

While many children have to make do with a poster on the bedroom wall and a sticker on an exercise book, their French cousins are inducted into the world of live popular music at a young age.

France hosts Europe's premier outdoor rock festival aimed squarely at the under 12s. Rock Ici Mômes is a day-long music event for children whose tastes run more towards Glastonbury than computer games. Thousands of youngsters turn up at Sable-sur-Sarthe every July for six hours of rock and world music, face-painting and even an open-mike session.

Rock Ici Mômes is now more than 25 years old and its security and supervision have been honed to a fine art so that the children can enjoy the music in safety and their parents can relax

WHERE'S THE BEEF?

More vegetarians are venturing into the abattoirs of France than ever before as the city slaughterhouses turn away from carcasses in preference for the arts. Just as the meat-packing and processing halls of Calais are being turned into performance spaces, so the former abattoirs of Toulouse are bringing art lovers to the left bank of the Garonne.

Les Abattoirs is an exciting modern art gallery devoted to works from the second half of the 20th century, housed in Urbain Vitry's former slaughterhouses. Inside there are 2,000 works by 667 artists from 44 countries. From a slightly earlier period than the main collection, the gallery displays Pablo Picasso's massive stage backdrop for French dramatist Romain Rolland's play, *Le 14 Juillet*.

COMIC TALENTS

The English translation 'graphic novel' doesn't do justice to the phenomenon of the *bande dessinée* (known as BD) a hugely popular and profitable sector of Franco-Belgian publishing.

The Tintin and Astérix series may be the best known abroad but most BDs created today are intended for an adult audience, depicting explicit sex and violence where these are part of the story.

The name *bande dessinée* derives from the fact that the early drawings were created as a small strip or band. Today most BD editions—of which 4,863 titles were published in 2009—are sold as hard cover albums about A4 size.

The art of the BD is held in high critical regard and there is a prestigious international festival every year in Angoulême.

Sport follows wine and cheese a close third in the hearts of the French. Avid participators and supporters, they embrace mainstream and avant-garde activities with equal enthusiasm. The country has been the venue for a number of major sporting events. The Stade de France in St-Denis, Paris, built for the 1998 soccer World Cup, was the setting for the 2007 Rugby World Cup. When France hosts (and wins) major sporting events, the world soon knows about it, thanks to the sounds of car horns blaring down the Champs-Élysées. But one-off events apart, the nation has a packed sporting calendar, with the Le Mans 24-hour race and the French Open tennis tournament at the Roland Garros Stadium the best-known summer events. The Tour de France brings its own road show, making every stage of the route a day to remember for visitors. Golf is a popular participatory game and rugby and horse-racing are the principal topics of conversation at the Bar des Sports in every town. Other sports include skiing in the Alps, Massif Central and Pyrenees. At the local level, most towns and villages have sports facilities used by residents and visitors alike.

IRON LANES

Unique to the mountain regions, Via Ferrata work a little like marked footpaths. On a Via Ferrata, a series of metal rungs have been bolted into the rock face and gorges have been spanned by narrow steel rope bridges to create a set route. The existing foot and hand holds make it easier for non-mountaineers to enjoy the thrill of the climb, though ropes are still used for safety reasons. The routes are graded and some are specifically designed for children and those with no previous experience.

There are Via Ferrata throughout the French Alps, Pyrenees and the Massif Central but perhaps the most famous is the very difficult Ferrata de la Peille, in the mountains above Nice.

Clockwise from left to right *The arduous Tour de France bicycle race; high-speed action during the Monaco Grand Prix; France play England at rugby*

EXPANDING THE SPORTING ENVELOPE

When the Montgolfier brothers rose gently from French soil on their maiden balloon flight, little did they realize that they were inventing the 'adventure sports' business.

The French have been at the forefront of development in several adrenalin-pumping activities including parapenting (flying with a manoeuvrable parachute) and free climbing (climbing without ropes). Of course, the varied countryside makes a great playground but national boundaries haven't held back the sporting greats. The Paris–Dakar Rally (today the Dakar Rally), inaugurated in 1978 after its founder Thierry Sabine got lost in the desert and thought it would make a good location for a race, is now the world's most gruelling off-road event.

THE FRENCH SPIDERMAN

No one epitomizes the individual spirit of adventure more than Alain Robert. Born in Digoin in 1962, this urban legend has free-climbed more than 100 of the world's tallest skyscrapers.

His climbing career started at the age of 12 when he forgot his house keys and climbed eight floors to get into the apartment where he lived. His first skyscraper ascent was in Chicago in 1994. Robert has often found himself in the hands of police because not all his climbs are authorized by building owners. However, during his career, he's raised hundreds of thousands of dollars for charity.

He's also a champion rock climber despite suffering two falls that have left him 66 per cent disabled and suffering from vertigo.

JOUSTING ON WATER

Forget medieval re-enactments — the sport of jousting is alive and thriving on the waterways of Languedoc-Roussillon. Horses are unnecessary as the combatants ride on opposing boats, lances and shields at the ready, to do battle and topple the loser into the water.

While many summer challenges take place in towns and villages along the coastline, the sport's principal home is on the busy canals of the port of Sète, where water jousting has existed since Roman times and the present sport dates back to 1666. Hand-painted wooden *pavois* are both shields and trophies and local fishermen and dockers take the games very seriously. The water-jousting season opens on 29 June with weekend skirmishes on brightly painted barges, and ends with the celebrated St-Louis contest in late August.

STUNT OF THE CENTURY

The Tour de France has been going for more than a century—not bad for a marketing stunt. Staged in 1903 as a campaign to publicize *l'Auto* magazine, the first Tour saw 60 riders covering 2,500km (1,550 miles) over 19 days.

There were only six stages so riders had to pedal their boneshakers through the night, whereas these days, comfortable hotels are provided as standard, and tracts of the country are crossed by train or plane between stages.

The event has been dogged by intrigue almost since the first. Dirty tricks have included scattered nails and allegations of poisoning. More recently the focus has been on doping, though use of performance-enhancing substances is not new. In 1924, brothers Henri and Charles Pélissier claimed cocaine and chloroform kept them in the race.

Prêt-à-porter shows staged four times a year at the Carrousel du Louvre remind the world what real people will be wearing in the coming season, and the couture shows of Paris Fashion Week reveal what no one beyond the glare of a flashbulb would even think of wearing. Paris retains its rightful global reputation for chic, and France gets its own ideas as to how to keep one step ahead of the rest of the world. Every year another nation is hailed as the next world leader in fashion, but the glamour and style of the French are never really threatened. After all, when a new *enfant terrible* from outside the borders begins to steer international attention away from the country, the French fashion houses manage to lure the new talent.

Left to right *Vivid catwalk designs; you'll get noticed wearing these shoes*

THE BERET

The US baseball cap may have taken over the streets of the world, but France's stereotypical headgear, the beret, hasn't given up the battle to be cool. Worn in modern times by artists, revolutionaries and intellectuals, the beret drifts into and out of fashion and still makes an appearance on the catwalk in a postmodern way. The beret's authentic home is the Bearn, in southwest France, where a small museum in Nay, near Pau, will answer every question about the beret you have never thought to ask.

CHOCCY COUTURE

Between the prêt-à-porter shows and Paris Fashion Week, there is one event where all the critics agree that every item of clothing is good enough to eat. Edible couture is the highlight of the autumn *Salon du Chocolat* at the Porte de Versailles, a catwalk show combining the talents and skills of the finest chocolatiers with the city's more daring designers.

IN THE FAST LANE

The Champs-Élysées is packed with traffic, but once a month it closes to cars. To benefit, pack your in-line skates. Pari-Roller is the social event of the week in Paris, as tens of thousands gather near Montparnasse station on Friday evening. At 10pm the crowd becomes a parade and sets off. Strictly for experienced skaters, the route varies each week. Itineraries are posted on www.pari-roller.com. Once a month, two hours after the skaters have left the starting point, they turn into place Charles-de-Gaulle for the high-speed descent down the Champs-Élysées.

THE 21ST CENTURY MARIANNE

The seemingly effortless chic and confidence of the modern French woman is personified in Vanessa Paradis. A vocalist with seven hit albums, the face of Chanel, acclaimed actress and bagger of her own Hollywood legend—Johnny Depp—she's also a mother of two.

THE STORY OF FRANCE

Celtic tribes ruled Gaul from around 1500BC, but they fought each other so much that the Romans had little trouble adding their territories to the Empire. Julius Caesar's defeat of the Celtic leader Vercingetorix in 52BC consolidated Roman rule and 200 years of peace and prosperity followed. After the fall of the Roman Empire in the fifth century, a Germanic tribe called the Franks overran the country and renamed it Francia. The Merovingian dynasty ruled until the eighth century, with King Clovis making Paris his capital. He converted to Christianity in 497 and extended his influence over the Christian provinces. After Clovis, Merovingian power declined and it was the turn of the Carolingian kings to rise to power. In 754, Pepin the Short took the throne, although it was his son, Charlemagne, who became one of the most remarkable men in the history of France. His reign lasted for almost 40 years, during which time he advanced his country's culture and military power. In 800 he was crowned Holy Roman Emperor by the Pope, ruling territory equivalent to present-day Germany and France. But squabbles among Charlemagne's heirs split the Empire and the provincial counts and bishops appointed by Charlemagne became increasingly powerful. When the last Carolingian king died in 987, the counts elected one of their own as king, Hugh Capet, the founder of the dynasty that dominated France well into the Middle Ages.

Clockwise from left to right *The Roman amphitheatre in Arles; relief carving on a building in Arles; Corinthian capitals on the Maison Carrée in Nîmes*

VERCINGETORIX OR ASTERIX?

Vercingetorix is a French national hero, symbolizing resistance to tyranny. He led an uprising against the Romans in 52BC but was eventually captured and put to death in Rome by Julius Caesar. The legendary scene of Vercingetorix laying his arms at Caesar's feet is a key moment in French history, but in the hugely popular *Asterix* cartoon, Vercingetorix drops the lot with a clatter on Caesar's big toe and the Emperor hops about shrieking. In fact, René Goscinny and Albert Uderzo, the creators of *Asterix*, based their anarchic little hero on Vercingetorix. French myth has it that Vercingetorix escaped a terrible death in Rome and stayed behind to make life difficult for the occupiers, becoming a symbol of French resistance.

CROSSING THE RUBICON

Once Julius Caesar had subdued Gaul in 52BC, he was Governor of the whole province and a powerful man. Three years later, he was forced to take the greatest decision of his life—whether to stay, or leave Gaul and conquer his rival, Pompey, for control of the Roman Republic. Caesar gathered a force to invade and as he drew nearer to the Rubicon river, which separated Gaul from what is now Italy, he went more slowly and his doubts grew. He ordered a halt as he was undecided regarding what to do—stay where he was in Gaul or risk everything and continue to Rome. Then, with the famous words, 'Let the die be cast,' he crossed the river. Caesar left the fledgling state of Gaul behind him and led his army onwards towards Rome and his future as dictator.

URBICUS, BISHOP OF CLERMONT-FERRAND
c. AD250

Conversion to Christianity brought its own struggles and temptations for Urbicus, from a Roman senatorial family and the first Bishop of Clermont-Ferrand. After his conversion, he and his wife decided to live apart, in religious contemplation. But growing tired of this restraint, the bishop's wife ran to his church and started banging on the doors, demanding her conjugal rights. Urbicus let her in and she stayed the night. When Urbicus discovered that his wife was pregnant he was horrified and retreated to a monastery to ask forgiveness for his sin. But all went well as his new daughter became a nun like her mother, the bishop returned to his post, and in death they were all united by being buried in the same crypt.

CHARLEMAGNE AND THE FASTING BISHOP

A truly great king, Charlemagne chastized by example rather than punishing outright. A bishop staying at the palace once criticized him for eating early each day in Lent, which was not strictly allowed by the Church. Keeping calm, Charlemagne patiently told the bishop that he agreed with him and he was right, but then Charlemagne informed the bishop that he would henceforth be the last person to be served during his stay at the palace. At every meal the bishop had to wait until the nobles, the commanders, the courtiers and the officials had all been served before he was finally given his food. After many hungry days, Charlemagne asked the bishop, 'Do you now understand that I eat early not from greed, but in consideration for those who have to wait?'.

CAROLINGIAN MINUSCULE

Charlemagne tried hard to learn how to write but he left it very late. So it is extraordinary that the form of writing we still use today owes its existence to him. Until about AD800, writing was all in capital letters with no punctuation and with the words all running together, which created a great deal of confusion.

Under guidance from his teacher, Alcuin, Charlemagne set up writing schools in the monasteries. There, the monks developed Carolingian minuscule—capital and lower case letters, punctuation and separated words—the form of script you are reading at this moment.

The monks had to practise their new skills on something, and it's thanks to the writing schools that 90 per cent of the Latin works we now have survived at all.

The kings of the new Capetian dynasty had little real power and did not venture much beyond their stronghold of the Île de France. William of Normandy became their rival when he conquered England in 1066, and the marriage of Eleanor of Aquitaine to Henry II of England in 1152 provoked territorial wars that lasted for 300 years. However, the Capets gradually came to dominate France through a network of marriages and treaties. The Crusades, instituted in 1095 by Pope Urban II, benefited the dynasty when an internal crusade, the Albigensian Heresy, allowed them to crush their opponents in southern France. Many of the great cathedrals of France were constructed in the 13th century, the University of Paris opened and the country prospered. However, the 14th century witnessed the twin disasters of the Black Death (1348–49), which killed 30 per cent of the population, and the Hundred Years' War (1337–1453), provoked by English claims to the French throne, a legacy of Eleanor of Aquitaine's marriage to Henry II. The war went badly for the French and by 1422 Henry IV had been crowned King of France in Paris. Joan of Arc turned the fortunes of France, but was betrayed by Charles VII, who eventually drove the English out by 1453.

A MIRACULOUS CURE FOR BALDNESS

Bernard, a nobleman of the Auvergne, lost his hair after an illness and was so ashamed of his baldness that he hid himself away.

Around the year 1000, St. Foy came to him in a dream and told him to go to her shrine in Conques. She told Bernard to stand on the left side of the shrine and wait until the abbot had finished his prayers and washed his hands. The abbot would then wash Bernard's head with the water.

Putting his faith in this dream, Bernard rushed to Conques, where the abbot refused to do anything so silly. But Bernard wouldn't leave and the abbot gave in. Legend has it, the next day Bernard's head was covered in shiny curls.

Clockwise from left to right *French knights embark on a Crusade; construction of the Château de Luynes began in the 11th century on the site of a Roman citadel; Joan of Arc's arrival at the Château de Chinon*

CHRISTINE DE PISAN
1365–*c.*1430

Christine de Pisan was an Italian lady widowed in Paris in 1390. She had a family to support and, daringly for the time, decided to make her living by writing. Over the years she produced a number of biographies, histories and poetry, all on a heroic scale. De Pisan soon gathered a list of wealthy patrons and became one of the most popular writers in France. As the lone female voice of the time, she protected women from attacks by male writers, particularly in the debate on *The Romance of the Rose*, a famously misogynistic poem. 'Why do you hate women?' she asked simply. 'You have mothers and wives. Are they evil?'

JOAN OF ARC

A peasant girl called Joan wrote to the King of England in 1429 with breathtaking confidence and in the words of a born leader: 'Duke of Bedford, who call yourself the regent of France for the King of England, the Maid asks you not to make her destroy you,' she said. Joan of Arc broke down the boundaries of gender and class, in an age when women were subservient to men. But a more creative act of hers was the idea of patriotism. She gave her country a sense of itself as a nation. 'You have no rights in France from God,' she lectured Bedford, '…go home to your own country.' As Europe emerged from the Middle Ages others followed her example.

THE POPES AT AVIGNON
1309–1418

After years of violence at the hands of the citizens of Rome, the papacy fled to the safety of Avignon in 1309, after an invitation from King Philip, who lusted after papal money and influence on French soil.

The popes lived in a fortress-like palace, which the poet Petrarch called 'a sewer where all the filth of the universe had gathered', and by 1377 the court was so threatened by thieves and swindlers that Gregory XI returned to Rome. The sovereigns of Europe then sponsored their own candidates, and by 1414, there was the spectacle of three popes, each vying for pre-eminence. The prelates of the Sorbonne, among others, put a stop to this, and in 1418 a sole pope again sat in Rome.

THE RULES OF
COURTLY LOVE

Eleanor of Aquitiane and her daughter Marie de Champagne had a great influence on medieval notions of love.

Noble marriages were used to cement dynastic power but affairs of the heart were common. With courts full of young, unmarried men, elaborate rules existed to restrain them.

Iin the 12th century Andreas Capellanus gave us *De Arte Honeste Amadi (The Art of Courtly Love)*, the most comprehensive guide to the complex art, with 31 rules including a warning, 'When made public love rarely endures'; A knight was supposed to love his lady with the same feudal obedience he paid to his lord, so though affairs were passionate they were usually chaste.

France's long war with Italy lasted from 1494 to 1559 and was an attempt to curb the power of the Habsburg Empire. It had one fortunate result: the influx of ideas and art from the Italian Renaissance. The kings, especially François I, imported artists and architects, jewels and art works to add to the glory of the French monarchy. Some of France's finest châteaux, books and paintings were created during this period. Alongside this spectacular flowering of culture, Protestantism grew quickly after the Reformation of the 1530s. It was strengthened by the influence of the exiled John Calvin, and became a powerful force in the country. Catholic-Protestant wars, eight in all between 1562 and 1598, soon split the state, and their cruelty and violence brought it to breaking point. One of the worst incidents was the St. Bartholomew's Day Massacre of 1572, when nearly 3,000 Protestants were murdered in Paris and up to 20,000 more throughout the country. After assassinations and the threat of civil war, the troubles started to diminish only when the protestant Henry IV converted to Catholicism to gain entry to Paris in 1593. The Edict of Nantes of 1598, which granted rights and protection to Protestants, brought about an uneasy truce.

FRANÇOIS RABELAIS

In his fantasy epics *Gargantua* and *Pantagruel*, recounting the adventures of a father and son, comic genius François Rabelais symbolizes the energy of the French Renaissance. As a doctor, monk, writer and student of botany, astrology, philosophy, archaeology and history, who invented new devices for setting fractures while creating two immortal characters in world literature, Rabelais was a Renaissance man. His writings are funny and raunchy, but more importantly they come out of the humanist tradition of the times and are daring in their criticism of the Church and of the powerful people in the State. No one was spared from his satire and in the process he wrote some of the greatest works in French literature.

Clockwise from left to right *Sheep grazing in the grounds of the Château de Miromesnil; Leonardo da Vinci's Mona Lisa hangs in the Louvre; the moated Château d'O*

DIANE DE POITIERS

Diane de Poitiers, the mistress and great love of Henri II, was a remarkable woman in looks and mind. In an age when teeth blackened and wrinkles formed early, Diane kept her beauty intact well into her fifties, a fact attributed to her enjoyment of equine sports and the drinking of edible gold. She was a strong influence on Henri during his reign and was instrumental in ending the war with Italy in 1559.

However, it was in Henri's relations with his wife, Catherine de Medici, that Diane revealed her true mettle and cunning. On agreed nights, Henri would spend the first hours with his mistress, then go to his wife. After a while with Catherine, Henri would return to his beloved Diane. Catherine, not unreasonably, hated her rival even more.

LEONARDO DA VINCI IN FRANCE

François I was a collector of paintings, jewels and châteaux, but his great prize was Leonardo da Vinci. In 1516 the King lured the 70-year-old Leonardo to Amboise, where he treated the artist and inventor with true respect. Leonardo was given a house and a generous pension and, although he was paralysed in his left arm, he designed court entertainments, made drawings, investigated anatomy and the nature of water, and invented machines. He didn't stop until he died, perhaps, as legend has it, in the King's arms. François I certainly had a real affection for the old man and in return received a magnificent gift from Leonardo. He had brought the *Mona Lisa* with him from Italy and it still hangs in the Louvre today.

FRENCH CUISINE

Great French cuisine owes its existence in part to Catherine de Medici, who brought Florentine chefs to France when she married the Dauphin Henri in 1533. French cooking was still medieval, heavy and limited, but Catherine's chefs used delicate sauces instead of thick spices, refined sugar instead of honey and a wide variety of pastries, vegetables and fowl until then unknown in France.

Catherine also brought with her the fork, although the French resisted the use of this for a century. She expected richly dressed ladies to join banquets, and set her table with crystal and gold.

Under her influence, feasting became a spectacle. Catherine's kinswoman, Marie de Medici, arrived from Italy in 1600, bringing with her the recipe for puff pastry which has resulted in that most famous of French foods, the croissant.

THE ESSAYIST

Michel de Montaigne (1533–92) created the essay as a literary form. Born near Bordeaux into a wealthy family, Montaigne was educated in Latin and French as well as the arts. He studied law, and while involved in the Bordeaux *parlement* he was hugely influenced by his friend Etienne La Boétie.

Etienne's own work *Discours de la servitude volontaire* is an outspoken attack on absolute monarchy. La Boétie's death in 1563 in his early 30s troubled Montaigne and in 1570 he moved to the château he inherited from his father. There he lived with his wife and started writing his *Essais*. The first collection of essays was published in 1580 and covered an eclectic range of subjects while demonstrating tolerance, wit and wisdom. Montaigne was elected mayor of Bordeaux in 1581. He died at home in 1592.

This period was dominated by two great men, Cardinal Richelieu (1585–1642), minister to Louis XIII, and the Sun King himself, Louis XIV (ruled 1643–1715). Richelieu set about centralizing power under the monarch. He crushed a revolt by Louis XIII's brother, destroyed the Protestant stronghold of La Rochelle and tried to protect France's borders. His wars with Holland, Austria and England continued throughout the 17th century. Richelieu built up the navy and the textile industry, creating a vibrant economy. Louis XIV was fortunate to be served by a brilliant finance minister, Jean-Baptiste Colbert (1619–83). He worked to reform France's chaotic tax system and managed to provide the economy with a surplus. Louis spent this freely on his twin obsessions, the Château de Versailles (the glory of France and the envy of other monarchs who tried to copy it) and foreign wars. However, Louis's belligerence and intolerance did not serve his country well when he revoked the Edict of Nantes in 1685, thereby losing France a huge population of hardworking Protestants. His wars drained the treasury, and although he gained the throne of Spain for his grandson, the war to achieve this did not help France's finances. In 1715, just two years after the war ended, Louis died.

RICHELIEU — THE ROOTS OF ROYAL POWER

Cardinal Richelieu was an extraordinary man who laid the foundations of royal authority that were later so ruthlessly perfected by Louis XIV. Richelieu dominated Louis XIII's reign, which still suffered from many of the problems of the medieval monarchy — ambitious nobles, a Catholic Church hungry for power, and belligerent Protestants, the Huguenots.

Richelieu set about establishing royal power by crushing the Huguenots and reducing the power of the Church, even making it pay taxes. The popular view, much of it drawn from Alexandre Dumas's novel *The Three Musketeers*, is that Richelieu was a devious and ruthless politician. While this may be true, he also rebuilt the Sorbonne and founded the Académie Française in 1634.

Clockwise from left to right *The palace of Versailles; Jean-Baptiste Colbert, foreign minister to Louis XIV; Château de Vaux-le-Vicomte is a masterpiece of 17th-century architecture*

LOUIS'S FRIEND, MOLIÈRE

Louis XIV liked and protected the playwright Molière (1622–73). He funded his plays, was godfather to his son and dined alone with him, which was unheard of at the time. No doubt Molière regarded this with some caution, as Claude Le Petit, a writer who satirized the King, had his hand cut off before being burned alive in 1662. When Molière's *Tartuffe* (1664), a satire on hypocrisy, was attacked by the Church and the Queen Mother, he quickly withdrew the play; it was restaged in 1669. Louis appeared unconcerned, but as a consummate politician, he let others do his dirty work—up to 60 censors worked on Molière's plays. The reworked version of *Tartuffe* ends with the King praised to the skies, and Molière kept his hand.

THREE DAUPHINS DIE WITHIN A YEAR

At the beginning of 1711, Louis XIV felt that the succession to the throne had never been so secure. His son was in good health and his grandson already had two sons of his own. However, within 12 months three generations would be dead. The Grand Dauphin died first, of smallpox, in April 1711. The Grand Dauphin's son, the new heir to the throne, was an intelligent young man, well-educated and the great hope of many courtiers, who saw in him a professional politician who might make the country work. However, he succumbed to measles in February 1712, along with his wife and eldest son. Only the sickly two-year-old younger son was left, the future Louis XV, who reigned for a long time, but to little effect for the country.

VAUX-LE-VICOMTE

On 17 August 1661, the young Louis XIV went to a house-warming party at the château of his finance minister, Nicolas Fouquet.

Vaux-le-Vicomte was a miniature palace, full of gold, silk and fine furniture, where guests received horses and diamond tiaras as gifts. The King was furious at Fouquet's impertinence and would not tolerate a subject building a power base with public money.

The château was certainly the model for Versailles, and Louis appropriated the furniture and silver, along with the architect Le Vau, the garden designer Le Nôtre and the painter Le Brun, a brilliant trio. They started work on Versailles immediately, and Louis started to make it clear who was the master of France.

VERSAILLES—A PALACE FIT FOR THE SUN KING

When the French think of a palace, they probably think of Versailles. It is the physical embodiment of Louis XIV's iron will, but only his monstrous ego makes sense of it. To build and run Versailles swallowed five per cent of the national tax revenue. Up to 20,000 staff serviced it, with the cooks and the gardeners inheriting their positions, like the princes above them.

Marie-Antoinette, wife of Louis XVI, was mistaken when she treated the palace as a playground; it had been the Sun King's seat of power for nearly 50 years. However, after Louis XIV, Versailles began to lose its power and the mediocre rulers who followed him could never impose themselves on France as he did.

This spectacular era in French history started with the long, stultifying reign of Louis XV (1715–74). He failed to notice the revolutionary ideas of the Enlightenment espoused by writer Voltaire (1694–1778) and philosopher Jean-Jacques Rousseau (1712–78), or to sympathize with a country languishing under a cumbersome, outdated government. Louis fought expensive wars, and French aid to the Americans in their War of Independence only helped spread ideas of revolution throughout the country. Under the hapless Louis XVI (ruled 1774–93) and Marie-Antoinette, the economy disintegrated and by the time Louis called a meeting of the Estates General in 1789, France was almost ungovernable. Royal authority collapsed and a succession of fanatical groups took control of the Revolution, with thousands of people executed during the Reign of Terrror in 1794. The more rational Directory followed, but the country was ripe for a coup d'état by young soldier Napoleon Bonaparte. He carried through the *Code Civil*, but his government was dependent on military victories. The French became disillusioned with his dictatorship when he started losing wars after the Moscow campaign of 1812. His downfall came three years later, and in 1815, Louis XVI's brother, Louis XVIII, was made king.

Clockwise from left to right *The palace of Versailles; the Montgolfier fire balloon; Le Hameau at Versailles was a village built for Marie-Antoinette*

LES MENUS PLAISIRS

To amuse Louis XV, his mistress, Madame de Pompadour, started to produce plays at Versailles in 1747. A little theatre was built and everyone at court had enormous fun.

Invitations to plays were highly sought after and all the entertainments were funded by *Les Menus Plaisirs*, which provided costumes, props, fireworks and orchestras. The theatre swallowed huge sums of public money and, not surprisingly, the public didn't like it.

When Madame de Pompadour went to Paris, people threw mud at her carriage and threatening crowds gathered—she soon stopped going.

FLYING OVER VERSAILLES

On 19 September 1783, from the courtyard at Versailles, Louis XVI and Marie-Antoinette witnessed one of the first balloon flights, organized by the Montgolfier brothers. The Montgolfiers were paper manufacturers and had only discovered the principles of flight the year before. By 1785, men were flying across the Channel, and balloons floated over France like visitors from the future. On that day in 1783, 100,000 citizens gathered at Versailles, not to see the King (royal etiquette and grandeur meant little to them), but to witness the powers of freedom and invention, hardly the stuff of the French monarchy. These crowds were sinister forebears of the crowds who arrived at Versailles six years later to put an end to royal authority.

MARIE-ANTOINETTE AND HER FOLLIES

The teenage Queen Marie-Antoinette felt stifled by the etiquette of Versailles—she was once left shivering while duchesses squabbled over who had the right to hand the queen her chemise. She rebelled and indulged herself by building a fantasy farm, Le Hameau, lined with silk and lit by diamond candelabra, where she played peasant in cotton dresses and straw hats, while cows were led past on ribbons and milked into fine Sèvres porcelain pots. Her excesses were costly but were dwarfed by the cost of wars at the time. Stuffy courtiers were shocked by the queen's antics and the people ridiculed her by calling her Madame Deficit. She played shepherdess while people, not far away on the streets of Paris, were starving to death.

PATRIOTE PALLOY AND THE BASTILLE

The Fall of the Bastille on 14 July 1789 was the symbolic start of the French Revolution. But in a large country like France, where news still moved slowly, the Revolution needed quick, entertaining propaganda. An enterprising businessman, Pierre-Francois Palloy, hit on the idea of revolutionary kits, objects made from the remains of the Bastille such as keys, medals and models of the prison itself, which could be taken to all corners of the country.

'Apostles of Liberty', unemployed actors, roamed over France, shouting out slogans and revolutionary tales while waving souvenirs taken from prisoners in the Bastille in front of the crowd. This novelty waned when the people had a new public spectacle to occupy them—the guillotine.

CODE CIVIL OF 1804

This set of laws is Napoleon's enduring achievement, in which he brought about one of the great aims of the Revolution—the equality of all citizens before a rational code of laws. Under the *ancien régime,* laws could vary from region to region, or were simply the will of the monarch. Napoleon ordered the Code to be drawn up in 1800 and it came into effect in 1804.

Under his influence, the Code destroyed feudalism and although it deliberately ignored the rights of women, it united a France on the verge of anarchy and was exported throughout the Napoleonic Empire. It is a civil, not a criminal, code and is the basis of modern notions of liberty and civil rights that have been adopted throughout much of the Western world.

MONTGOLFIER FIRE-BALLOON.

This century swung between royalty and Revolution. The Bourbon Louis XVIII and Charles X were caught in the struggles between vengeful monarchists and those determined to maintain the Revolution. Charles's attempts at repression resulted in the Revolution of 1830 and his nephew, the 'Citizen King' Louis-Philippe took the throne. In turn he was deposed in 1848, the year that revolutions swept Europe. The following presidential elections were won by Louis Napoleon Bonaparte, Napoleon's nephew. In 1851 he proclaimed himself Emperor Napoleon III, but corruption led to instability. War with Prussia in 1870 destroyed both him and the French monarchy. After the agonies of the Commune in 1871, a bloodbath that killed more than 20,000 people, France entered the stable Third Republic and the glorious years of the belle époque. The achievements of this era are magnificent: the construction of the Suez Canal, the scientific advances of Pasteur and the establishment of Paris as Europe's capital of pleasure. Worth and Paquin created haute couture, César Ritz invented the luxury hotel, Cartier and Boucheron covered Europe in jewels and Escoffier cooked up the cuisine that, although modified, still dominates. By 1900, France, although no longer the military power of Europe, was the heart of luxury, taste and art.

Clockwise from left to right *The Riviera began attracting visitors in the 19th century; the belle-époque Maxim's restaurant in Paris; a poster advertising winter in Nice*

LES MISÉRABLES

Victor Hugo chronicled 19th-century France the way Charles Dickens chronicled Victorian England, and his best-known novel, *Les Misérables* (1862), still has a hold on the public imagination. It sold out on the first day, plays and films followed, and the musical is still one of the most popular in the world.

As with all great stories, it meshes the personal (the struggles of Jean Valjean and Cosette) with the public (the 1830 Revolution). Hugo wrote his book not about the poor, but for them, and in so doing gave them a voice and dignity they did not have in real life. In return they loved him—Hugo's funeral in 1885 was attended by 3 million people, more than the population of Paris.

THE CÔTE D'AZUR

British people of a certain class in the 19th century often went on the Grand Tour in Europe. In 1834, Lord Brougham, a member of the English aristocracy, was forced to spend the night in the village of Cannes and loved the place so much he built a villa there. His wealthy friends soon followed him and over the years British aristocrats opened up the rest of the coast, resulting in a train line connecting London directly to Menton (via a ferry) by 1868.

Royalty were not averse to the Riviera's charms — Queen Victoria spent winters at Nice in the 1890s, away from the chills and fogs of England. Even today there is a little bit of Nice that is forever England — the waterfront is named Promenade des Anglais.

THE SALON DES REFUSÉS

If one single event blew apart the world of the arts it was this exhibition organized by Emperor Napoleon III in 1863. The Salon des Refusés or Exhibition of the Rejects featured paintings deemed not acceptable by the ultra-conservative Académie des Beaux-Arts.

The rejected artists in the 1863 exhibition — including Manet and Whistler — broke the mould in terms of subject and style. They were inspired by scenes from contemporary life, which they often painted on location to capture the light and colour. Napoleon's exhibition gave these artists some major exposure, and although the initial verdict was far from universally favourable the style was here to stay. We know it today as Impressionism.

LIFE AND DEATH BY LOUIS PASTEUR

Joseph Meister owed his life and his death to Louis Pasteur. Besides the famous discovery of pasteurization (the heating of milk to make it safe to drink), Pasteur discovered the cure for rabies in 1885. He had tested it only on dogs when, in July 1886, nine-year-old Joseph came to Pasteur's laboratory, badly mauled by a rabid dog. Joseph's mother pleaded with the reluctant scientist to treat her son. Pasteur eventually agreed, and Joseph made a complete recovery.

As Pasteur's fame grew and grew, Joseph remained attached to the Pasteur Institute and became its concierge. In 1940, during World War II, the occupying Germans ordered Joseph to open Pasteur's crypt; rather than commit this sacrilege, he committed suicide.

DIAMONDS AT MAXIM'S

The frivolity of the belle époque is summed up in this anecdote from Hugo, *maître d'hôtel* at the fashionable restaurant Maxim's.

La Belle Otero and Liane de Pougy were courtesans. As well as having many rich lovers, they owned splendid collections of jewellery and were great rivals. One evening Otero, determined to humiliate Liane, arrived at Maxim's wearing her entire, astonishing collection of jewels, including a bolero of diamonds. Later, Liane arrived dressed in severe black without even a ring on. Following behind her was her dowdy maid in a cloak that Liane dramatically ripped off with a swirl, to huge applause. The girl was wearing every piece of Liane's jewellery. Spitting and cursing, La Belle Otero was carried out by her supporters.

After a decade of prosperity, World War I brought devastation to France. With 1 million people dead, 3 million wounded and industrial output down by 60 per cent in 1918, the nation was vengeful and bitter. The inter-war years saw some Socialist gains, with the Front Populaire of 1936 frightening employers into agreeing to many reforms. During World War II, France was occupied from 1940 to 1944 by the Germans and this left its scars on society. When the war ended, General de Gaulle, the leader of the Free French forces during the conflict, returned to provide a unifying influence. The ensuing Fourth Republic witnessed an exhausted country grow and prosper hugely throughout the 1950s. The Republic collapsed in 1958, when the brutal colonial war in Algeria almost provoked a right-wing coup. De Gaulle was brought back to become President of the Fifth Republic. He dominated France in the 1960s, but the revolutionary events of 1968, which brought society to a standstill, showed how much dissatisfaction there was. In the final decades of the 20th century France, with Germany, was the driving force behind greater integration of the European Union states.

A MOVEABLE FEAST

'*J'ai deux amours, mon pays et Paris,*' sang Josephine Baker in the 1920s.

Many of her fellow Americans agreed. Wealthy ones, like Winaretta Singer, married French noblemen. When movie star Gloria Swanson brought her trophy husband, the Marquis de la Falaise, back to the US she telegraphed her studio 'Arrange the ovation'.

Ernest Hemingway found US dollars bought plenty of French wine and good food, but while he thrived, nervy F. Scott Fitzgerald was almost destroyed.

Gertrude Stein, who bought paintings by Paul Cézanne and Picasso while they were going cheap, dubbed her compatriots the Lost Generation. The fallout of the alcohol (banned in Prohibition America) and parties was often realized in insanity and burned-out careers.

Clockwise from left to right *Crowds at the Cannes Film Festival; the Musée d'Art Modern et d'Art Contemporain in Nice; Art Goût Beauté front cover, September 1922*

20TH-CENTURY LOGOS—CHANEL

Coco Chanel, quintessential Frenchwoman and fashion designer, created great clothes. She also invented the branding, corporate identity and core values practised in business today.

Chanel dreamed up a simple, instantly identifiable look that has hardly changed. Her list of successes is formidable: the little black dress, the tweed suit, the handbag, the perfume. Each of them carried her name, relentlessly repeated, until it was reduced to two interlinked Cs, one of the top 10 most recognized logos.

Chanel predicted what women wanted, then gave it to them with a sparkling finish. Today, the look is still effortlessly reproduced.

OCCUPATION AND RESISTANCE—THE VICHY GOVERNMENT

From 1940 to 1944, under the German Occupation, the Vichy Government of Marshal Pétain ran the southern part of France. Between 1942 and 1944 the infamous Klaus Barbie (the Butcher of Lyon) committed a number of war crimes. Vichy is remembered for deporting 75,000 French Jews to Nazi concentration camps.

It's a painful episode that still divides French society. But Vichy did not spring solely from Nazi Occupation. Far right politicians in 1930s France had spoken out against foreigners and pushed through the Family Code in 1939, setting down strict laws for women and sexual morality.

THE CANNES FILM FESTIVAL

Fights, booing and mass walkouts at screenings, scantily clad starlets posing on the beach, and anarchy in 1968 when Truffaut and Godard invaded the stage—these are all events that have made the Cannes Film Festival a uniquely French occasion.

The first festival, which was scheduled for September 1939 as a riposte to Benito Mussolini's fascist version in Venice, was halted by the outbreak of World War II. However, since 1947, it has been up there with the Oscars as one of the most exciting and infuential events in the gobal movie calendar.

As is always the case with the film industry, behind all the glitz and excess a great deal of hard-headed business is undertaken. From romantic comedy to art house, 50 per cent of all the movies in the world are bought and sold during the festival.

FRANGLAIS, QU'EST-CE QUE SAY?

In 1964, René Etiemble, author of *Parlez-Vous Franglais?*, recommended severe punishments for those attempting to degrade French with English words, as words such as *le cheeseburger* and *le rip-off* found their way into the French language. 'People were shot during the war for treason,' he added.

No one has been executed yet, but in 1992 the French parliament altered the constitution, solemnly informing the country that 'the language of the Republic is French'. Parliament passed a law in 1994 insisting that French be used all the time. But then the Constitutional Council informed the government that it couldn't tell people how to speak. As ever, official interference has resulted in confusion. *Un e-mail*, for example, is now supposed to be *un mél*, which doesn't exist in either French or English.

- Goût - Beauté

Robe en crêpe " Ida " plissé (plis ronds).

Crêpe " Ida " corail. Le panneau de devant brode ton sur ton.

(Deux créations Worth)

(Meubles de MERCIER Frères, 100, Faubourg Saint-Antoine, Paris.

In January 2002, France, along with 11 European Union partners, embraced the euro and the French franc became history. After 80 years of enmity, France and Germany now have a friendship more determined than affectionate, and it is generally admitted that they fuel much of the policy of the European Union.

SARKO TAKES OFFICE

In May 2007, the right-of-centre and often controversial former minister of the interior, Nicolas Sarkozy, was elected the sixth President of the Fifth Republic, to succeed Jacques Chirac. One of his electoral promises was to revitalize the French economy by introducing greater liberalism. His popularity slumped, however, when he began a highly public affair with the ex-model turned singer Carla Bruni, whom he married in February 2008.

Above *TGV trains at a station, waiting to speed away*

LE TRAIN À GRANDE VITESSE

The pride of French railways, the TGV high-speed train, broke the world record during a run on 3 April 2007, recording a speed of 574.8kph (356.2mph); its everyday operating speed is up to 320kph (200mph). The TGV was introduced in 1981 but has really come into its own since Europe's internal borders came down. It links Paris with cities in neighbouring countries to the north and east; connects with Eurostar for access to the UK and will eventually meet Spain's TGV network for onward travel to Barcelona and Madrid.

PARIS PLAGE

Paris Plage, the beach by the river Seine, has become a summer must-see in the city of Paris. From mid-July to mid-August, when most Parisians desert the city during their annual holiday, part of the Right Bank is transformed into a seaside. Palm trees (Parisian-style, in a chic row) sway over 100m (109 yards) of imported sand, along with 300 deckchairs, 150 parasols and striped changing tents. Paris Plage was introduced in summer 2002 and proved to be a great success so Mayor Bertrand Delanoë has promised that it will be around for years to come.

NATURE CAPITALE

In May 2010 the Champs-Élysées was transformed for two days when farmers discovered an unusual way to protest against their falling incomes and what they perceive as a lack of support for the industry.

To coincide with International Biodiversity Day, soil, plants, including 700 full sized trees, pigs, cows and sheep, were transported to the capital to cover the asphalt and paving stones of the Champs-Élysées and create a green lung in the city.

Nature Capitale was organized by the Young Farmers Union in conjunction with Gad Weil, and is said to have cost over €4 million. But 1.9 million people visited the spectacle and bought plants and produce, so expect more of these very French 'protests' in years to come.

ON THE MOVE

On the Move gives you detailed advice and information about the various options for travelling to France before explaining the best ways to get around the country once you are there. Handy tips help you with everything from buying tickets to renting a car.

ON THE MOVE | FRANCE

BY AIR

Many visitors to France arrive by air and the numbers are increasing with the availability of inexpensive flights and the popularity of short breaks from other European countries. Paris has two airports, Paris–Charles de Gaulle (sometimes called Roissy) and the smaller Paris–Orly, and is also served by Beauvais Tillé airport, 88km (55 miles) farther north. Other French cities with major airports include Marseille, Toulouse, Lyon, Strasbourg and Bordeaux.

» Paris's busiest airport is **Paris–Charles de Gaulle**, 23km (14 miles) from the heart of the city. It has three terminals: T1, T2 and T3. T2 is subdivided into 2A, 2B, 2C, 2D, 2E, 2F and 2G. Airlines operating out of T1 include: Aer Lingus, British Airways, bmibaby and United Airlines. T2 serves Air France, British Airways, easyJet, KLM and American Airlines, among others. Airlines using T3 include Jet2. Terminals can change, so always check·before setting off.

» You'll find information desks, shops, restaurants, banks, bureaux de change, car rental firms and a first-aid station in T1 and T2. T3 has shops, cafés, a bureau de change and car rental outlets. The private

Baggages du Monde have a secure left-luggage facility at the TGV-RER train station at T2 (tel: 01 34 38 58 90, open 6am–9.30pm).

» The smaller **Paris–Orly** airport, 14km (8.5 miles) south of central

GETTING TO THE CITY FROM THE AIRPORT

AIRPORT	TAXI	TRAINS
Paris–Charles de Gaulle (CDG) (Paris)	Cost: €50 plus 15per cent night weighting. Journey time: 30 min–1 hour.	RER line B takes you into the heart of Paris (Gare du Nord, Châtelet or St-Michel). Trains leave roughly every 10–15 min, from 5am to 11.56pm. Cost: €8.40. Journey time: 30 min (to Châtelet)
Paris–Orly (ORY) (Paris)	Cost: around €40. Journey time: 20–30 min.	The Orlyval train (6am–11pm) takes you two stops to Antony, where you pick up RER line B. Cost: €7.40. Journey time: 35 min.
Beauvais Tillé (BVA) (North of Paris)	Cost: around €140 (7am–9pm), €180 (9pm–7am) Journey time: 1 hour 20 min.	None.
Marseille-Provence, also called Marseille-Marignane (MRS)	Cost: around €40 day, €50 night. Journey time: 30 min.	Services to Vitrolles depart 6.18–8.45pm. Cost: €4.70, Journey time: 15 min.
Toulouse-Blagnac (TLS)	Cost: around €22 day, €25 night. Journey time: 20 min.	None.
Strasbourg (SXB)	Cost: around €30–€35 day, €40–€45 night. Journey time: 30 min.	Trains leave from Gare Entzheim, which is a 5-min walk from the airport. They run from 5.34am–8.47pm. Journey time: 15 min.
Lyon St-Exupéry (LYS)	Cost: around €45 day, €60 night. Journey time: 30 min.	None.
Bordeaux (BOD)	Cost: around €25 day, €35 night. Journey time: 40 min.	None.

AIRPORT CONTACTS

Paris–Charles de Gaulle	3950 within France www.adp.fr
Paris–Orly	3950 within France www.adp.fr
Beauvais Tillé	0892 682 066 www.aeroportbeauvais.com
Marseille-Provence	04 42 14 14 14 www.mrsairport.com
Toulouse-Blagnac	3950 within France www.toulouse.aeroport.fr
Strasbourg	03 88 64 67 67 www.strasbourg.aeroport.fr
Lyon St-Exupéry	0826 800 826 www.lyonaeroports.com
Bordeaux	05 56 34 50 50 www.bordeaux.aeroport.fr

OTHER USEFUL CONTACTS

	TELEPHONE	WEBSITE
Information on all French airports		www.aeroport.fr
Air France	0820 320 820	www.airfrance.fr
American Airlines	1 800 433 7300 (US number)	www.aa.com
British Airways	0844 493 0787 (UK number)	www.ba.com
BMI	0844 848 4888 (UK number)	www.flybmi.com
Delta	1 800 241 4141 (US number)	www.delta.com
easyJet	0871 244 2366 (UK number)	www.easyjet.com
Ryanair	0871 2460 000 (UK number)	www.ryanair.com
United	1 800 538 2929 (US number)	www.united.com
Orlybus	246	www.ratp.fr
Paris Métro and RER information	3246	www.ratp.fr
Air France bus to Paris	0892 350 820	www.cars-airfrance.com

Paris, has domestic flights and some international flights. Its two terminals—Orly Sud and Orly Ouest—are connected by shuttle buses and the Orlyval train. The airport has shops, restaurants, bureaux de change and car rental companies.

» **Beauvais Tillé** airport, 88km (55 miles) north of Paris, is used by low-cost airlines. Facilities include a newsstand, restaurant and car rental desks.

» **Marseille-Provence** airport is 30km (19 miles) northwest of the city. Terminals 1 and 4 have restaurants, cafés, shops and information desks. Terminal 1 also has a pharmacy, first-aid point and bureau de change and Terminal 4 has a bank and car rental desks.

» **Toulouse-Blagnac** airport is 8km (5 miles) northwest of the city. In Departures, halls 1 and 2 have a restaurant, a bar, shops and a bureau de change. In Arrivals there are car rental companies, a café and a bureau de change. Hall D (opened in 2010) caters to all flights to non-Schengen countries and has restaurants, shops and rental desks.

» **Strasbourg** airport is 12km (7 miles) southwest of the city. There is a restaurant and café in Departures and a first-aid point, car rental companies, a café, shops and an information desk in International Arrivals.

» **Lyon St-Exupéry** airport is 28km (17 miles) east of Lyon. Facilities include restaurants, bars, shops, a post office and a bureau de change.

» **Bordeaux** airport is 10km (6 miles) west of Bordeaux. In Departures there are shops, bars

BUS	CAR
The Air France bus runs from Terminals 1 and 2 to Montparnasse and Gare de Lyon every 30 min, 7am–9pm. Cost: €16.50. Journey time: 45 min–1 hour. Another Air France bus runs to the Arc de Triomphe every 15 min, 5.45am–11pm. Cost: €14. Journey time: 45 min–1 hour. The Roissybus runs every 15 min from Terminals 1, 2 and 3 to Opéra, 6am–11pm. Cost: €9. Journey time: 45–60 min. Routes 350 and 350 also link the capital with the airport	Take the A1 south to Paris. Journey time: 30 min–1 hour.
The Air France bus runs from Orly Sud and Ouest to Les Invalides and Gare Montparnasse every 15 min, 5am–11pm. Cost: €11.50. Journey time: 30 min. The Orlybus runs from Orly Sud and Ouest to Denfert-Rochereau Métro station every 15–20 min, 6am–11.30pm. Cost: €6.40. Journey time: 30 min.	Take the A106, then A6A or A6B into Paris. Journey time: 20–40 min.
Bus to Porte Maillot running to meet flights, departing from Porte Maillot 3 hours before scheduled departure. Cost: €15. Journey time: around 1 hour 15 min.	Take the N1, D901, A16, N1 then A1 to Paris. Journey time: 1 hour 20 min.
Buses to the Gare St-Charles train station run from 4.30am–11.30pm and leave every 20 min. After 10.50pm they coincide with flight arrivals. Cost: €8.50. Journey time: 30 min.	Take the D20, D9, then A7 to Marseille. Journey time: 30 min.
Buses leave every 20 min. They run Mon–Sat 7.35am–12.15am and Sun and public hols 9.15am–12.15am. Cost: €5. Journey time: 20 min.	Take the D901 then A620 ring road and follow the signs for 'centre ville'. Journey time: 20 min.
Buses to the Baggersee train station leave every 20 min; from there you can take tram line A to the city centre. Buses run Mon–Sat 5.40am–10.20pm, Sun 6.30am–11.40pm. Cost €3.60. Journey time: 30 min.	Take the D221 and then D392 to Strasbourg. Journey time: 15 min.
Buses leave every 20 min. They run daily from 6am–11.40pm from the airport to Gare Perrache. Cost: €8.90. Journey time: 45 min.	Take the A432, A43 then N383 to Lyon. Journey time: 35 min.
Buses leave from Terminal B every 45 min. Buses run from the airport to the city centre Mon–Fri 7.45am–10.45pm, Sat–Sun 8.30am–10pm. Cost: €7. Journey time: 45 min.	Take the N563 then D106 to Bordeaux. Journey time: 40 min.

ON THE MOVE ARRIVING

BY TRAIN

There are good train links between France and other European countries. From the UK, the Eurostar from London St. Pancras runs through the Channel Tunnel to Paris and Lille, where services to other destinations across France operate. The Eurostar also travels direct to Disneyland® Resort Paris, Bourg St-Maurice and Moutiers (during the ski season only), and Avignon (weekly in summer). The Channel Tunnel rail link has revolutionized travel to Paris, allowing you to reach Paris from London in around 2 hours 15 minutes, without leaving the ground or boarding a boat. The tunnel opened in 1994, the longest undersea tunnel in the world, with 39km (24 miles) of its 50km (31 miles) length under the Channel.

BOARDING EUROSTAR

» Up to 16 trains per day travel to Paris from London; some stop en route at Ebbsfleet International and Ashford International (UK) and Calais (France).
» Trains leave from St. Pancras mainline rail station in north London. St. Pancras is on the Northern, Victoria, Piccadilly, Circle, Hammersmith & City and Metropolitan underground lines. King's Cross station is adjacent and Euston is a short walk away.
» To check in, insert your ticket into the machine then walk through the gate with your baggage. You must check in at least 30 minutes before your train is due to depart.

» Before you reach the departure lounge you must go through airport-style security checks and passport control (French passport control is actually carried out at Waterloo). Once in the departure lounge there are newspaper and gift shops, cafés, toilets, internet points and a mailbox.
» Boarding begins 20 minutes before departure. Information screens tell you where and when to board. Each train has 18 carriages (cars) so you could face a long walk along the platform. Trolleys (carts) for luggage are available, although you need a £1 coin as a deposit. Porters are available at the main Eurostar terminals. Once on board, large cases must be stored on the luggage racks at the end of each carriage, but you can put smaller bags in the racks above your seat.

THE JOURNEY

» A buffet car serves drinks, snacks and light meals. There are toilets and designated baby changing facilities on board. The journey through the tunnel itself takes around 20 minutes and an announcement is made just before you enter.

ARRIVING

» When you arrive in Paris's Gare du Nord station you do not need to go through passport control as this has been carried out at St. Pancras. Watch for pickpockets at the station.
» The covered taxi stand is well signposted. Don't be too depressed at the long queue, as it moves fairly quickly. A taxi into the middle of Paris

costs between €12 and €15, although there are extra charges for each piece of luggage and for travel after 7pm and on Sundays.
» Gare du Nord is on Métro lines 4 (purple) and 5 (orange). Line 4 (direction Porte d'Orléans) will take you across the river to the Left Bank. If your hotel is on the Right Bank, you can change lines at Gare de l'Est, Strasbourg St-Denis, Réaumur Sébastopol or Châtelet. Line 5 (direction Place d'Italie) is handy if you're heading to the Bastille area.
» Gare du Nord is also on three RER lines, D (green), B (blue) and the less useful east–west E line. Line B takes you to Châtelet, then on to the Left Bank (St-Michel-Notre-Dame and Luxembourg). The RER can be a confusing train system to the uninitiated (▷ 63). If it's your first time in Paris, it may be better to take the Métro or a taxi.

Eurostar Contact Details
08432 186 186 (UK);
www.eurostar.com

TIPS

» You'll pay less for your Eurostar ticket if you reserve it in advance. It is highly recommended that you do this, since non-booked seats are limited. The train is split into Business Premier, Standard Premier and Standard class. The Premier classes give you a meal, extra legroom, a reclining seat and free newspapers. Business Premier tickets also allow admission to the business lounge at London St. Pancras and Gare du Nord.
» Remember that you need your passport to travel between Britain and France (▷ 417).
» The official luggage allowance is two suitcases and one piece of hand luggage. Luggage must be clearly labelled with your name and seat number.
» Trolleys (carts) are available on the platforms at St. Pancras and Gare du Nord, for a £1 or €1 coin (refundable). If you have a heavy case a trolley is a good idea as the walk along the platform can be long.

BY FERRY, CAR OR LONG-DISTANCE BUS

If you want to drive from the UK to France you can use either the Eurotunnel, which takes you to Calais, or a ferry, with a choice of ports on France's northwestern coast. Driving to France from countries in mainland Europe is straightforward.

BY FERRY

» Numerous ferries link France with the UK. The cost of crossings varies widely according to time, day and month of travel. Most companies require you to check in at least 30 minutes before departure, although extra security checks may mean you have to arrive earlier.
» P&O Ferries and Seafrance sail from Dover to Calais (journey time: 90 minutes). There is a selection of shops, cafés, a bureau de change and several lounges. Once you arrive in Calais, it takes around 3 hours 15 minutes to drive through France to Paris (for directions ▷ Eurotunnel).
» Norfolk Line operates from Dover to Dunquerque for motorists only (no foot passengers).
» LD Lines operates a Dover–Boulogne service (journey time: approximately 50 minutes) and Portsmouth–Le Havre (journey time: 3 hours 15 minutes).
» Brittany Ferries sails from Portsmouth to Caen (journey time: 6 hours).
» Brittany Ferries sails from Poole to Cherbourg (journey time: approximately 4 hours; high-speed services take 2 hours 15 minutes, summer only) and from Portsmouth to Cherbourg (journey time: 5 hours; high-speed services 3 hours, summer only).
» Brittany Ferries sails from Portsmouth to St-Malo (journey time: approximately 11 hours) and Plymouth to Roscoff (journey time: 6–8 hours).

FERRY CONTACT DETAILS

Brittany Ferries: 0871 244 0744 (UK); www.brittany-ferries.com
Norfolk Line: 0844 847 5042 (UK); www.norfolkline.com

P&O Ferries: 08716 642 121 (UK); www.poferries.com
Seafrance: 0871 423 7119 (UK); www.seafrance.com
LD Lines: 0844 576 8837 (UK); www.ldlines.co.uk

BY EUROTUNNEL

» Load your car onto the Shuttle train at Folkestone for the 35-minute journey under the Channel to Calais/ Coquelles.
» To reach the terminal at Folkestone, leave the M20 at junction 11A and follow signs to the Channel Tunnel.
» There are up to three departures every hour, for 24 hours a day, and the price is charged per car (you need to reserve ahead).
» French border controls take place on the UK side, saving time when you arrive in Calais.
» You stay with your car during the journey, although you can go to the toilet or walk about within the air-conditioned carriage (car). During the journey you can listen to the on-board radio station and staff are available if you need any help.
» To reach Paris from Calais you can take the A16 (E40) in the direction of Dunkerque, then join the A26 (E15). At the intersection with the A1, head south on the A1 (E15), which will take you all the way to Paris. You will have to pay *autoroute* tolls.
» If you are driving from Calais to the south of France allow at least 11 hours. The journey time will vary depending on traffic, season and weather conditions. It is probably best to break up the journey with an overnight stop. You will have to pay toll charges if you use the *autoroutes*.

» For more information on driving in France, ▷ 51–55.

Eurotunnel Contact Details
0844 335 3535 (UK); www.eurotunnel.com

BY LONG-DISTANCE BUS

» Going to France by long-distance bus can be a useful option if you're on a tight budget, although the journey from London to Paris takes eight hours minimum.
» Eurolines runs services from Victoria Coach Station to Paris up to five times a day, with pick-up points at Canterbury and Dover. They also serve more than 60 other destinations in France. The Channel crossing is made either by Eurotunnel or ferry.
» Youy will need to book your ticket at least 30 days in advance for the least expensive fares.

Eurolines Contact Details
08717 818 181 (UK); www.eurolines.co.uk

TIPS

» Look out for inexpensive ferry deals in British newspapers.
» It is often less expensive to book Eurotunnel tickets online rather than by telephone.
» Vehicles that run on liquefied petroleum gas (LPG) cannot use the Eurotunnel.
» The phone numbers given on this page are UK-based. To call from the US, dial 011 44, then omit the initial zero from the number. To call from European countries, dial 00 44, then omit the initial zero.

France is a relatively large country, but its excellent network of trains and *autoroutes* means you can usually travel between regions quickly and easily.

BY ROAD

Driving in France is made easier by the country's extensive network of *autoroutes* (motorways/expressways). However, you'll have to pay a toll to use most of them. Journey times can be affected by weather conditions, traffic and the season—the roads, especially in the south of France, can get very busy in the summer.

BY TRAIN

The train is one of the best ways of getting around France—it is fast, comfortable and usually runs on time. France's state railway, the Société Nationale des Chemins de Fer (SNCF), runs the services. The high-speed train service—the TGV *(Train à Grande Vitesse)*—links cities and principal towns across France, while TER *(Trains Express Régionaux)* trains operate on the regional routes.

BY BUS

Long-distance bus travel is not an ideal option for crossing the country. Buses are really only useful for short trips in areas not served by the rail network, such as some destinations in Brittany, Normandy and the Côte d'Azur. Long-distance bus stations *(gares routières)* are usually close to train stations and major train and bus services generally coincide. Smaller towns without train stations are usually linked by bus service to the nearest station. Bus services in cities are generally excellent and inexpensive, but rural areas tend to be less well served.

DOMESTIC FLIGHTS

The train system is so efficient in France that air travel is not

particularly time-saving, although the national airline, Air France, still has an extensive network of flights linking most large towns to Paris, as well as connections between regional towns.

Air France operates flights to 16 French destinations from Paris Roissy-Charles de Gaulle and 14 from Paris Orly airport. Most routes have several flights a day, with an average flight time of just one hour. For information and reservations on Air France contact agencies in France (tel 0820 320 820; www.airfrance. fr), the UK (tel 0871 663 3777; www. airfrance. co.uk) or in the US (tel 1 800 237 2747; www.airfrance.us). For

information on French airports see www.aeroport.fr.

MAPS

Good regional maps are invaluable in planning a trip. The Automobile Association (UK) publishes four France atlases as well as a series of France sheet maps. The Automobile Association website, www.theAA. com, has a helpful route planner.

You can find town and city maps *(plans)* in France at *maisons de la presse* news-stands and bookshops. Every city and town, and many villages, has an *office de tourisme*, *syndicat d'initiative* or town hall that will provide a local map.

DRIVING IN FRANCE

France has a comprehensive system of autoroutes (motorways/expressways) fanning out from Paris, enabling you to cross the country with relative ease. From the capital, the A1 leads to the north, the A13 to Normandy and the northwest, the A4 to the northeast of the country, the A6 to the Alps and the Riviera, and the A10 to the west and southwest.

Driving is the best way to tour smaller villages and towns, but is not so convenient in some of the bigger cities, especially Paris, where the traffic is heavy, the one-way systems confusing and parking difficult and expensive.

BRINGING YOUR OWN CAR
Legal Requirements

» Private vehicles registered in another country can be taken into France for a holiday without any customs formalities.

» You must always carry the following documentation: a current passport or national ID card, a full (not provisional), valid national driver's licence (even if you have an International Driving Permit), a certificate of motor insurance, and the vehicle's registration document (as well as a letter of authorization from the owner if the vehicle is not registered in your name).

» You should always tell your insurer before you take your car abroad.

Third-party motor insurance is the minimum requirement in France but fully comprehensive cover is strongly advised.

» Check that your insurance covers you against damage in transit, for example on the train or ferry when your car is not being driven.

» Spot checks on cars are carried out and you may be asked to produce your documents at any time. To avoid a police fine and/or confiscation of your car, ensure your papers are in order.

» Display an international sticker or distinguishing sign plate as near as possible to the national registration plate at the rear of your car. If you don't, you will risk an

Use the chart below to work out the distance in km (green) and estimated duration in hours and minutes (blue) of a car journey

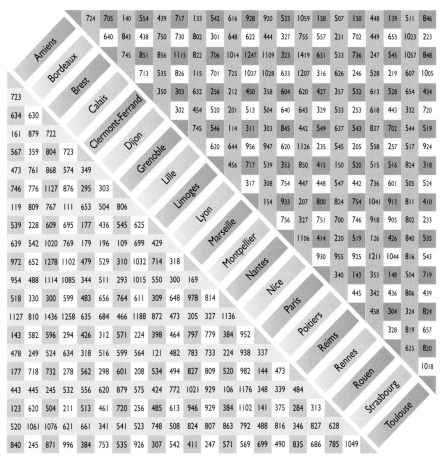

on-the-spot fine. Since Euro-plates (registration plates with the 12-star symbol of the European Union) were introduced in 2001, it has technically been unnecessary to display a conventional sticker when driving in the EU, but it is safer to display one.

» To avoid dazzling oncoming drivers you should adjust the headlights of left-hand-drive vehicles for driving on the right. On older cars, use the black headlamp beam converters that stick onto the glass. But don't use these on cars with halogen headlamps—check in your car handbook or with your dealer. If your vehicle has Xenon or High Intensity Discharge (HID) headlamps, check with your dealer who may need to make the adjustment.

» Remove the converters or have your headlamps reset as soon as you return home.

Breakdown Cover

If you are taking your own car, make sure you have adequate insurance to cover your expenses if your car breaks down during your trip to France. For information on Automobile Association breakdown cover, call 0800 085 2721 or visit www.theAA.com.

RENTING A CAR

» Most major car rental agencies have offices at airports, main train stations and in large towns and cities throughout France.

» Renting a car in France can be expensive due to high taxes. Arranging a fly-drive package through a tour operator or airline from home could be a less expensive option. SNCF, the national rail company, has inclusive train and car-rental deals from mainline stations.

» To be able to rent a car in France you must be at least 21 years old and have held a full driver's licence for at least a year. However, some companies either do not rent to, or else add a surcharge for, drivers under the age of 25. The maximum age limit varies, but the average is 70.

» You will have to show your licence and passport or national ID card.

» As a guide, companies should include the following in their rental agreement: unlimited mileage, comprehensive insurance cover, theft protection and 24-hour emergency roadside assistance.

» Some car rental agencies include all mileage in the cost but others may charge you extra above a certain distance, so check before you rent.

» Most international rental companies will let you return your car to other French cities, and even other countries, but there may be an extra charge for this. Always agree your drop-off point with the company first.

» Make sure you have adequate insurance and that you are aware of what you are covered for in the event of an accident.

» Bear in mind that low-cost operators may have an extremely high excess charge for damage to the vehicle.

» Most car rental companies supply vehicles with breakdown cover, so refer to your documentation or to the information regarding breakdowns in the car, which is often kept in the car's glove compartment or tucked under the sun visor.

» If your car breaks down on an autoroute, look for the emergency telephones which are provided on the roadside at regular intervals. You can contact the breakdown services from these telephones.

GENERAL DRIVING
Roads

» The autoroute is the French counterpart of the British motorway or American expressway and is marked by an 'A' on maps and road signs. A few sections, especially around key cities, are free of charge, but tolls are charged on the rest (autoroutes à péage). Tolls are expensive but are often worth it to get to destinations quickly. You can pay with cash or credit card. For information on autoroute conditions throughout France call 01 47 05 90 01 or look up www.autoroutes.fr.

» There is a comprehensive network of other roads, with surfaces that are generally good. A highway or trunk road is called a route nationale (N). The next level down is the route départementale (D), which can still be wide and fast. There are also quieter country roads.

Company	Telephone number	Website
CAR RENTAL COMPANIES		
Avis	0844 581 0147 (UK); 1 800 332 1212 (US)	www.avis.com
Budget	0845 544 3407 (UK); 1 800 472 3325 (US)	www.budget.com
Europcar	08713 849 847 (UK)	www.europcar.com
Hertz	08708 448 844 (UK); 1 800 645 3001 (US)	www.hertz.com
Sixt	0844 248 6620 (UK); 1 887 749 8227 (US)	www.sixt.com

The Law

» In France you drive on the right (*serrez à droite*).

» The minimum age to drive is 18, although to rent a car you must be at least 21.

» In built-up areas vehicles should give way to traffic coming from the right (*Priorité à droite*), unless signs advise otherwise. At roundabouts with signs saying *Cédez le passage* or *Vous n'avez pas la priorité*, traffic already on the roundabout has priority. On roundabouts without signs, traffic entering has priority. A priority road can also be shown by a white diamond-shaped sign with a yellow diamond within it. A black line through the diamond indicates the end of priority. A red-bordered triangle with a black cross on a white background, with the words *passage protégé*, also shows priority.

» Holders of EU driver's licences who exceed the speed limit by more than 25kph (16mph) can have their licences confiscated by the police on the spot.

» You must wear a seatbelt. Children under 10 must travel in the back, with a booster seat, except for babies under nine months with a specially adapted rear-facing front seat (but not in cars with airbags).

» Do not overtake where there is a solid single central line on the road.

» Expect harsh penalties if the level of blood alcohol is 0.05 per cent or more. If you drink, don't drive.

» You must always stop completely at STOP signs, or you may be fined.

Road Signs

» Road signs are split into three categories. Triangular signs with a red border are warnings, circular signs are mandatory (such as speed limits or No Entry) and square signs display text information.

» Signs include: *déviation* (diversion), *attention travaux* (roadworks), *sortie* (exit), *gravillons* (loose chippings), *chaussée déformée* (uneven road and temporary surface) and *nids de poule* (potholes).

» Before you take to the road, familiarize yourself with the French highway code (*code de la route*) on www.legifrance.gouv.fr.

» For more information on road signs check the website www.permisenligne.com.

Equipment

» Carry a red warning triangle in case you break down. Vehicles must have one reflective jacket and this must be worn by the driver when they exit the

SELECTED ROAD SIGNS

No entry except for buses and taxis

Road-toll pay station

A yellow diamond (top) indicates priority

Speed limits for various road types, in kph

Give way to traffic

Parking 150m to the left

Parking only for those with disabilities

No left turn

A town sign, with the road number displayed above

ROAD SIGNS

Allumez vos phares	Switch on your lights
Cédez le passage	Give way
Chantier	Roadworks
Péage	Toll
Priorité à droite/gauche	Give way to traffic from the right/left
Rappel	Reminder (the previous instruction still applies)
Route barrée	Road closed
Sens interdit	No entry
Sens unique	One way
Serrez à droite/gauche	Keep to the right/left
Stationnement interdit	No parking
Travaux	Roadworks

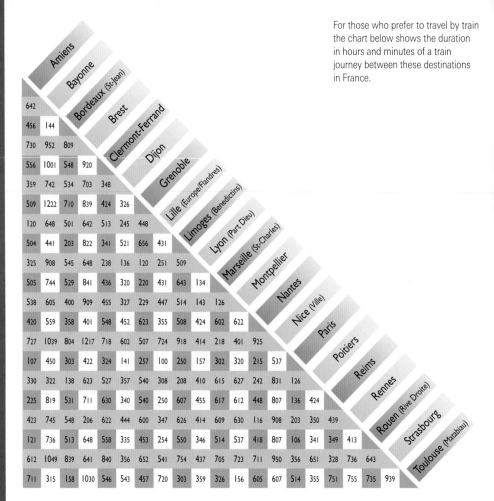

For those who prefer to travel by train the chart below shows the duration in hours and minutes of a train journey between these destinations in France.

vehicle in the event of an accident or breakdown.

» Keep a spare-bulb kit (buy before you go) to hand as it is illegal to drive with faulty lights.

» Snow chains must be fitted to vehicles using snow-covered roads, in compliance with road signs. You could be fined for non-compliance. Snow chains can be rented from most tyre specialists in France or you can buy them from hypermarkets, especially in mountain areas.

FUEL

» Fuel (essence) comes as unleaded (95 and 98 octane), lead replacement petrol (LRP or supercarburant), diesel (gasoil or gazole) and liquefied petroleum gas (LPG—GPL in France).

» Many filling stations close on Sundays and at 6pm the rest of the week. Most towns have an automatic 24-hour pump which works with a credit card.

» Prices are high at filling stations on autoroutes.

» Filling stations can be far apart in rural areas, so never let your tank get too low.

PARKING

» Authorized parking spaces are indicated by road markings (white dotted lines). In those marked Payant, you have to pay.

» Charges usually apply from 9am to 7pm, Monday to Saturday.

SPEED LIMITS	
Urban roads	50kph (31mph); 30kph (19mph) or 70kph (44mph) in some areas
Outside built-up areas	90kph (56mph); 80kph (49mph) in wet weather
Dual carriageways (divided highways), and non-toll motorways	110kph (68mph); 100kph (62mph) in wet weather
Toll motorways (autoroutes)	130kph (80mph); 110kph (68mph) in wet weather

Visiting drivers who have held a licence for less than three years are not allowed to exceed the wet-weather limits, even in good weather.

Sundays and holidays are generally free, but check the signs before parking your car.
» To pay for parking, buy a ticket from a machine at the side of the road and display it in your car.
» Some towns also have multi-level or underground parking areas.

CAR BREAKDOWN
» If your car breaks down on an autoroute, look for an emergency telephone along the roadside (at regular intervals) that will connect you with the breakdown services.
» If you break down on the Paris périphérique (ring road) or on an autoroute, you must call the police or the official breakdown service operating in that area, rather than contacting your own breakdown/insurance company.

ROAD CONDITIONS
» To find out about traffic conditions visit www.bison-fute.equipement.gouv.fr (in French only).
» For the National Road Information Centre (voice service in French) call 0800 100 200.
» For road conditions on autoroutes call 0892 681 077.

» For information on regional road conditions, call 0826 022 022.
» Autoroute FM (107.7) provides useful, up-to-date traffic bulletins.

HINTS FOR DRIVING AND PARKING IN PARIS
» The speed limit in central Paris is 50kph (31mph). On the ring road (périphérique) the limit is 80kph (49mph).
» Give way to traffic approaching from the right (priorité à droite), unless signs advise you otherwise.
» Don't use the bus lanes.
» Don't park or stop on any of the axes rouges (the key routes through the city).
» Avoid the rush hours (generally from 7 to 9.30am and 4.30 to 7.30pm, weekdays).
» The city's roads are least congested

in August, when many Parisians escape to the coast. However, be aware that August is also when most road repairs take place.
» The network of narrow streets in Paris can be confusing, so plan your route in advance.
» Useful maps include Maxi Paris and Maxi Banlieue by Editions L'Indispensable.
» On most of Paris's streets you must pay to park from 9am to 7pm Monday to Saturday.
» Parking tickets are usually dispensed by Pay-and-Display meters. They accept only the 'Paris Carte'. It is available in denominations from €10 to €30 and you can buy them in tobacconists. Two hours is the maximum stay period and hourly rates can vary from less than €1 up to €3.

USEFUL WEBSITES	
WEBSITE ADDRESS	WHAT YOU CAN FIND
www.iti.fr	Route planner
www.autoroutes.fr	Information on autoroutes
www.eveloppment-durable.gouv.fr	Road information
www.afp.com	French and international news
www.sytadin.tm.fr	Traffic reports around Paris
www.bison-fute.equipement.gouv.fr	Road conditions information

TRAINS

France has a good rail network and travel between cities and other European countries is relatively simple. The system is run by Société Nationale des Chemins de Fer (SNCF) which divides its services up into a series of brands, the most important of which are: TGV (the fastest trains on the network), Corail Intercités, Corail Teoz, Corail Lunéa (night services), Transilien (trains within the Île de France) and TER *(Trains Express Régionaux)*. Paris has six mainline stations, each serving different regions of France and the rest of Europe.

TICKETS

» Most trains have first and second classes, both of which are perfectly acceptable for travellers.
» Reduced-rate fares are generally available for normal travel on mainline routes by reserving well in advance.
» Ticket prices vary according to the level of comfort (first or second class; called Comfort 1 and Comfort 2 on Thalys trains, to and from northern Europe) and departure time. First-class fares are roughly 50 per cent more expensive than second-class.
» You can buy tickets in the stations, at SNCF offices and through some travel agents. Tickets for TGV trains must be reserved. You can do this up to a few minutes before departure, although in peak season it is best to reserve well in advance. Couchettes (sleeping berths) must be booked at least 75 minutes before the train leaves its first station.
» Make sure you stamp your ticket in the orange machines on the platforms before you start your journey. You'll risk a fine if you forget to do this. If leaving from a suburban train station in the Paris region to take a connection from one of the main Paris stations, you have to stamp your ticket twice, once at the suburban departure station and once when leaving Paris.
» If you are under 26, you can get a 25 per cent discount (called *Carte*

12–25) on some train travel. Seniors (aged over 60) also receive discounts (called *Carte Senior).*
» A variety of rail passes are available, which allow travel either within France only, or within France and certain other countries, or within the whole of Europe. You should buy these before you enter France, either through travel agents or Rail Europe (▷ 57).
» Ticket machines, with instructions in English, accept notes, coins and credit cards. They can also be used to collect tickets you have ordered on the internet, by telephone or Minitel (a videotex online service available only in France).

CATERING SERVICE

» Food—ranging from sandwiches and salads to hot meals—is available on most TGV and Corail services, but can be quite expensive.
» A benefit of first-class travel is that you can have food served at your seat during meal times on TGV trains travelling on the main routes. You'll need to reserve in advance.
» You can reserve meals when you purchase your train ticket. Ticket machines dispense meal vouchers.
» Hot and cold drinks and snacks are served on most trains.
» Overnight trains (and some day services) have vending machines dispensing hot and cold drinks and sweets (candy).

OVERNIGHT TRAINS

» Most overnight trains offer either reclining seats, couchette berths or a sleeper car.
» Reclining seats are available only in second class. They have adjustable head- and foot-rests and a reinforced foam seat for sleeping.
» In first class, the basic couchettes are in four-berth compartments while in second class they are in six-berth compartments.
» Sleeper car compartments are for up to two people in first class and up to three people in second class.
» Overnight trains operate between Paris Austerlitz and the Côte d'Azur (Nice and Vintimille); the Alps

(Bourg-St-Maurice, Saint-Gervais and Briançon); the Pyrenees (Tarbes, Luchon and Latour-de-Carol); Port-Bou (on the Spanish border south of Perpignan); Hendaye and Irun in the Basque Country; and Toulouse, Albi and the Gorges du Tarn. There are also overnight services between Alsace-Lorraine and the Côte d'Azur; northern France and the Côte d'Azur; the Basque Country and Bordeaux and the Riviera; the Basque Country and Geneva; Brittany and the Alps and Nantes and the Riviera.
» Trains also travel to other countries across Europe.

STATION ASSISTANCE
» Larger stations have an information kiosk, which is usually easy to find.
» If you need assistance, look for a member of the station staff, identifiable by their red waistcoats.
» You'll need a €1 deposit to use the luggage trolleys (carts).
» Porters, wearing red jackets and black or navy caps, can help with your luggage in main stations.

LEFT LUGGAGE
» Some stations have a left-luggage office or coin-operated lockers.

Electronic locks issue a printed ticket with a code number. You'll need to keep this ticket for when you return to collect your items.

» Don't store valuables in lockers.
» Security concerns mean that left-luggage facilities at stations are not always available.

UNDERSTANDING TRAIN TIMETABLES

» You can pick up free timetables *(horaires)* at stations or check train times online.
» SNCF timetables are usually published twice a year—the summer one applies from late May to late September, and the winter one from late September to late May.
» Be prepared to decipher French railway timetable terminology. Two rows of boxed numbers at the top refer to the *numéro de train* (train number) and to the *notes à consulter* (footnotes).
» Footnotes at the bottom explain when a particular train runs *(circule)*. *Tous les jours* means it runs every day; *sauf dimanche et fêtes* means it doesn't run on Sundays and holidays. *Jusqu'au*, followed by a date,

indicates the service runs only up until that date.

RAIL PASSES

» If you are staying in France for a long time, consider buying a rail pass *(Carte)* that is valid for a year. This entitles you to a 50 per cent discount with certain conditions and is available to those aged 12 to 25 *(Carte 12–25)*, those with a child under 12 *(Carte Enfant+)* and the over 60s *(Carte Senior)*. There is also a *Carte Escapades* for people aged 26–59, which gives a 40 per cent reduction for tickets.
» For foreign visitors using the rail network in France there are many attractively priced rail passes. You should buy these before you enter France. To buy certain passes you must have been resident in Europe for at least six months, and have a valid passport with you.
» Rail Europe sells a variety of rail passes (www.raileurope.com for US visitors; www.raileurope.co.uk for UK visitors).
» Once you are in France it may be difficult to change reservations that have been made abroad.

FASTEST JOURNEY TIMES FROM PARIS (APPROXIMATE)	
Amsterdam	4 hours 10 min
Bordeaux	3 hours
Brussels	1 hour 20 min
Lille	1 hour
Marseille	3 hours

INTERRAIL ONE COUNTRY PASS

Allows unlimited first- or second-class rail travel in France for three to eight days within one calendar month. A young person's (under 26) version is also available.

CAR TRANSPORTER SERVICES

» If you want to save several hours of driving time and, instead, relax on the train while your car is transported to your destination you have two options. SNCF's Auto/Train (www. voyages-sncf.com/guide/autotrain/ homepage_autotrain.htm) services operate between Paris and ten mainline stations in southern France, currently Avignon, Bordeaux, Brive-la-Gaillarde, Frejus St Raphael, Lyon, Marseille, Narbonne, Nice, Toulon and Toulouse. The service can also take motorcycles.

Accès aux Trains
Compostez votre billet

TIMETABLE, FARE AND OTHER INFORMATION

» Timetable, fare and service information is available from SNCF train stations, ticket outlets and travel agencies, by telephone (tel 3635; 24 hours; €0.34 per minute), the internet or Minitel.

» You can take a bicycle on most SNCF trains free of charge if storage is available (check in advance). Try to avoid travelling at peak periods. For security on long journeys, it is wise to dismantle your bike as far as you are able and preferably pack it in a purpose-made bag.
For more information see the website www.velo.sncf.com.

TIPS

» If you plan to travel by train during peak times (mid-June to early September, holiday periods and during rush hours), reserve your tickets well in advance.

» You must validate *(composter)* your ticket or travel pass before boarding the train.

» Bar and at-seat services on most long-distance trains are expensive. You may prefer to bring your own snacks.

» Pick-up and delivery of luggage from your hotel to your final destination can be arranged 24 hours in advance. Contact the SNCF Baggage Service (tel 3635). Luggage is picked up and delivered Monday to Friday from 8am to 5pm.

» If you wish to travel on a TGV on which all the seats have been reserved, you can be placed on standby. Your ticket entitles you to board the train but does not guarantee you a seat, so if all reserved passengers do take the train, you will have to stand.

» At most stations a layout diagram of your train will show you where your seat is located so you can stand on the correct part of the platform.

» Note that many carriages have a no mobile phone policy. Move to the ends of such carriages to make or receive calls.

LONG-DISTANCE BUSES AND TAXIS

France's excellent train service means that long-distance buses are not the most convenient option for moving from city to city. Eurolines operates services from Paris and other French cities to destinations in Europe, with stops en route in major French towns and cities. SNCF runs a bus service as an extension of rail links.

If you do wish to travel by bus, they are generally clean, comfortable and punctual. Large towns generally have a *gare routière* (bus station), which is often next to the *gare SNCF* (train station).

LONG-DISTANCE BUSES

» You can buy tickets for short distances on board, but for greater distances you will need to buy tickets in advance at the bus station. You must reserve your seat on most long-distance buses.
» Buses are slightly less expensive than trains, but significantly slower.
» If you are taking a bus operated by SNCF, you may be able to use an SNCF rail pass, if you have one. Check before you travel.
» Timetables tend to be constructed to suit working, market and school hours, so there is often one bus in the morning and one in the evening.
» For information on SNCF-run

buses, telephone 3635 (24 hours; €0.34 per minute).
» Few bus stations have a left-luggage office but some have information desks that can double as luggage rooms.

Eurolines Contact Details

Gare Routière Internationale de Paris Gallieni, 28 avenue du Général de Gaulle, Bagnolet, tel 0892 899 091; www.eurolines.fr

TAXIS

» A taxi is not the most cost-effective way of getting about but it can be convenient at times.
» There is a pick-up charge and a charge per kilometre (0.6 mile), plus an extra charge for luggage and journeys during the evening or on Sundays. All taxis use a meter (*compteur*).
» The best way to find a taxi is to head to a taxi stand, marked by a blue Taxis sign. You can phone for a taxi but this can be more expensive as the meter may start running when the taxi sets off to collect you.
» Smoking is allowed in some taxis—look for the sign.
» Always check the meter is reset when you enter the taxi.
» Some taxis accept bank cards, but it is best to have cash available. It is usual to leave a tip of around 10 per cent.

» If you want a receipt, ask the driver for *un reçu*.

Taxis in Paris

» You can hail a taxi in the street, if you can find one that is free. A white light on the roof indicates the taxi is available. When the light is off, the taxi is already occupied.
» Taxi charges are based on area and time—it is more expensive in the suburbs and at night. The tariff is shown on the meter.
» Journeys in central Paris average €10–€15. The meter starts at €2.20, with a minimum charge of €6.10. There is a surcharge of €1 for each piece of luggage and an extra €0.80 if you are picked up at a mainline station.
» Most drivers will not take more than three people; transport of a fourth person is charged at €2.95.
» If you have any complaints, contact the Préfecture de Police, Service des Taxis: 9 boulevard du Palais, 75195; tel 01 53 73 53 73.

Taxi companies in Paris include:

» Alpha Taxis: tel 01 45 85 85 85; www.alphataxis.fr
» Cab & Taxi: tel 01 40 40 78 36; www.cabettaxi.fr
» Taxis Bleus: tel 08 9170 10 10; www.taxis-bleus.com
» Taxi G7: tel 01 47 39 47 39; www.taxisg7.fr

GETTING AROUND IN PARIS

Paris has an efficient and relatively inexpensive transportation network and you should have few problems finding your way around the city. The Métro (subway) is the backbone of the network. Other useful options include buses, riverboats and the suburban RER trains and the Vélib cycle rental network. Finally, don't forget your own two feet—central Paris is compact and walking is a great way to get your bearings.

TICKETS

» The Métro and buses use the same tickets and travelcards, and these can also be used on the RER within central Paris.

» The city is divided into six fare zones. Most of the key sights are in Zone 1, although the Grande Arche is in Zone 3, Orly airport is in Zone 4 and Paris–Charles de Gaulle (Roissy) airport is in Zone 5.

» Buy tickets at Métro stations, on buses (one-way tickets only) and at some news-stands.

» Children under four travel free, and children between the ages of four and nine travel for half price.

VÉLIB

Paris has a network of communal automatic bike rental stations (www.velib.paris.fr) allowing you to cycle between attractions or rent a cycle for longer. Simply return the machine to the nearest cycle storage station when you've finished with it.

TICKETS

TYPE	PRICE	VALID	EXTRA INFORMATION
Single ticket	€1.60	Tickets are valid on the Métro, the RER (within central Paris) and most buses. You don't have to use them on the day of purchase, but once you have stamped a ticket (by slotting it through the automatic barrier at Métro stations or in the machine on buses) it is valid for that journey only.	You can change Métro and RER lines within one journey on the same ticket, but note that if you buy a ticket on a bus it doesn't permit changes.
Carnet	€11.60 for 10 single tickets	As single tickets, see above.	This is cost-efficient if you are planning eight journeys or more. If you are with a friend, you could buy 10 tickets and share them.
Mobilis	Zones 1–2: €5.90 Zones 1–3: €7.90 Zones 1–5: €13.20	Valid for one day on the Métro, buses and RER, within the relevant zones.	A less expensive option than the one-day Paris Visite card (see below).
Paris Visite, Zones 1–3	1 day : €9 2 days: €14.70 3 days: €20 5 days: €28.90 Children's passes (4–11 year olds) are roughly half-price	Valid for an unlimited number of journeys on the Métro, bus, RER and Transilien services, within zones 1–3. The ticket is valid from the first occasion you use it.	If you need to travel for one day only or if you are staying within zone 1, the Mobilis pass (see above) is a less expensive option. But with the Paris Visite card you also receive special offers for various sights. Buy the ticket at Paris tourist offices or at stations.
Paris Visite, Zones 1–6	1 day: €18.90 2 days: €28.90 3 days: €40.50 5 days: €49.40	Valid for an unlimited number of journeys on the Métro, bus, RER and Transilien services within zones 1–6 (including Versailles, Disneyland® Resort Paris and Orly and Paris-Charles de Gaulle airports).	An expensive option but gives discounted entry to some sights.
Le Passe Navigo Zones 1–2	€17.20	Valid for a week on the Métro, buses and RER within zones 1–2.	The card is officially intended for residents of the Île de France, and runs from Monday to Sunday. So the earlier in the week you purchase the card, the better value. You'll need a passport-size photo.

Travel Information

» You can pick up free Métro maps at every station.

» To speak to an adviser (in French only) call 3246. Lines open 24 hours a day, seven days per week. From outside France call (33 8 82 69 32 46). Lines open Monday–Friday 7am–9pm, Saturday–Sunday 9am–5pm.

» The major stations have information desks, although communication can sometimes be limited if you don't speak French.

» The RATP (Régie Autonome des Transports Parisiens) website (www.ratp.fr) has a helpful route planner and also gives up-to-date traffic and travel information.

How to survive the Métro

» When planning your route, don't confuse Métro lines with the suburban RER lines—both are usually shown on Métro maps. RER lines have letters rather than numbers and will usually flow off the map.

» To estimate your journey time, allow two minutes between each station. Bear in mind that it could take five minutes to walk from the station entrance to the actual platform (especially in warrens such as Châtelet).

» To save time, use the ticket machines rather than the manned ticket booths.

» Cash is more useful than credit cards when buying tickets.

» Always keep your ticket with you, in case you come across an inspector.

» If you need to change lines, don't exit the interchange station or you will invalidate your ticket.

» Keep your bags close to you and watch out for pickpockets.

» If you find you're going in the wrong direction, alight at the next station and double back. Follow directions to the correct platform, but be sure to stay within the automatic barriers or you'll invalidate your ticket.

» Street maps of the local areas are posted up in most station entrances.

» You may feel uncomfortable using the Métro alone late at night.

PARIS MÉTRO

» The Métro (Métropolitain) is the quickest way to travel for most journeys within the city. It runs from 5.30am to around 12.30am. On Fridays, Saturdays and the day before public holidays it runs until 2.15am.

» Each line is colour-coded and numbered (1–14, 3b and 7b).

» Stations are identified either by a large M or by the famous art nouveau Métro signs.

» Steps, or occasionally escalators, lead down into a lobby, where you can buy tickets from either a manned booth or a machine. Larger stations may also have shops and cafés.

» To reach the platforms, validate (composter) your ticket by slotting it into the machine at the automatic barrier, then collect it and keep it with you because inspectors make random checks.

» You'll often have a fairly long walk to the platform, so follow direction signs carefully. Signs will show the line number and colour. You also need to know the final destination of the train in the direction you wish to travel.

» Trains are frequent but get crowded during rush hour.

» An orange correspondance sign on the platform gives directions to connecting lines. Blue sortie signs show the exits.

BUSES

Paris has a comprehensive network of buses, with more than 1,300 vehicles fighting their way through the traffic. Taking the bus is a good idea if you want to see the streets and sights rather than simply passing under them on the Métro, but don't expect to get anywhere very quickly—the average speed is less than 13kph (8mph)!

» Most buses are painted easy-to-see white and turquoise and run from 5.30am to 8.30pm, although some continue into the evening, until around 12.30am. You're unlikely to have to wait more than 5 or 10 minutes from Monday to Saturday, but services are reduced or, on some routes, non-existent, on Sunday.

» The route number is displayed on the front of the bus, along with the final destination.

» Hold out your hand to stop the bus.

» If you need to buy a ticket, have the exact money ready as drivers don't carry much change.

» Enter at the front of the bus and show your travelcard or *carnet* ticket (▷ 60) to the driver. *Carnet* tickets or single tickets must be validated (stamped) in the machine next to the driver.

» In rush hour, it is unlikely that you will be able to get a seat. Be prepared for a long and uncomfortable stand.

» Just before your stop, press the red button to alert the driver that you want to get off. You'll see the *arrêt demandé* (stop requested) sign light up.

» Leave by the central doors.

Tickets

» Buses use the same tickets as the Métro. A single ticket is valid for most central routes but you are not allowed to change buses on one ticket.

» You can buy single tickets on board, but not travelcards or *carnets* of 10 tickets.

» Always stamp single tickets (including *carnet* tickets) in the machine near the driver, but not *Paris Visite*, *Mobilis* or *Carte Orange* passes. Keep your ticket until you have left the bus.

Finding Information

» The *Grand Plan Lignes et Rues*, available from Métro stations, has a useful bus map.

» www.ratp.fr has bus information in French and English, as well as a handy route planner.

» Call 246 to speak to an adviser (in French).

Night Buses

» The Noctilien network of buses runs through the night from just after midnight (12.30am) to 5.30am when normal buses come into service. The 47 nocturnal lines cover the centre and the suburbs. The two most useful routes are the circular N01 and N02 which connect the four principal interchange stations: Gare de l'Est, Gare St-Lazare, Gare de Lyon, Gare Montparnasse.

» RATP tickets and travelcards can be used on night buses. For more information see www.noctilien.fr.

TRAMS

Paris has four modern tram lines with a fifth planned. T1 runs from Gare de Saint-Denis to Noisy-le-Sec; T2 from La Défense to Issy-Val de Seine; T3 from Pont du Garigliano to Porte d'Ivry; and T4 from Bondy RER station to Aulnay-sous-Bois RER station.

TIPS

» Try to avoid the rush hour (roughly 7–9.30am and 4.30–7.30pm).

» Smoking is banned on buses, the Métro and the RER.

» Buying a *carnet* of 10 tickets is better value than buying tickets separately for each journey, and also saves time waiting in line at the ticket office.

RER

RER (Réseau Express Régional) trains travel through the city en route to the suburbs and can be a good time-saver if you are going from one side of town to the other. But reaching the correct platform can be a lengthy and confusing process, so for a short trip you're usually better off taking the Métro.

Tickets

» A single Métro ticket is valid for RER journeys in central Paris and you can change lines (including Métro lines) on the same ticket. For journeys farther afield, you'll need to buy a separate ticket valid for the destination.

» Travelcards (▷ 60) are valid as long as they cover all the zones you are going through.

» Keep hold of your ticket as you'll need to slot it through the automatic barrier to exit the station.

Using the RER

» Trains run from around 4.45am to 1.30am.

» The RER has five lines, named A to E. Each line breaks into offshoots, which bear a number after the letter.

» The RER lines in central Paris are on the Métro map, ▷ 75.

» Information screens in the lobby should tell you which platform you need to head to; or you could ask at the ticket desk.

» Slot your ticket into the automatic barrier and remember to retrieve it when it re-emerges after validation.

» An increasing number of platforms have screens with information on arrival times for the next five trains.

» When leaving the train, follow blue *sortie* signs if it is the end of your journey, or orange *correspondance* signs if you need to change to another RER or Métro line.

» You'll need to slot your ticket into the automatic barrier to leave the station.

TIPS

» Few visitors use the RER outside central Paris (unless they are going to Versailles, Disneyland® Resort Paris or to the airport) so you may feel conspicuous. Be aware that some of the suburbs the RER passes through are somewhat run-down, and the trains and platforms tend to have more graffiti than on the Métro. Outside peak periods, the trains may also be quite empty.

» Trains run fairly frequently in central Paris, but less so in the outlying areas.

GETTING AROUND IN MAJOR CITIES

Public transportation in large French cities is usually excellent, with a variety of modes available, from Métros and buses to trams and funiculars. If you decide to drive, you'll find that cars are often positively discouraged with high parking rates.

GETTING AROUND LYON
www.tcl.fr

Lyon is a manageable size and the network of buses, trams, funiculars and Métros, run by TCL (Transports en Commun Lyonnais) is extensive, easy to use and covers the city and the outlying districts. You can get a map *(plan du réseau)* from the tourist office or any TCL branch.

Métro

Lyon's four Métro lines—A (red), B (blue), C (orange) and the futuristic driverless line D (green)—criss-cross the middle of the city, stopping at 40 stations. They serve most major squares and streets and connect with buses, trams and funiculars. Trains run from 5am to shortly after midnight and are easy to use. The main Métro stations are Bellecour, Perrache and Part-Dieu. You'll need to stamp your ticket at the start of your journey.

Buses

Buses cover every corner of Lyon, with 120 routes, running generally from 5am to 9pm. Lyon also has 30 night routes with services running from Thursday to Saturday from 1am–4am (but check individual services). Stamp your ticket at the start of your journey.

Trams

There are three tram (streetcar) lines. T1 and T2, both start from Perrache SNCF and Métro station and T3 starts from Gare Part-Dieu. Trams run almost silently, so be careful when stepping into the street.

Funiculars

Two *funiculaires* (funiculars) depart every 10 minutes until 10pm from Vieux Lyon Métro station. One goes to Fourvière, to the hilltop basilica, and the other goes to Minimes, for the Roman ruins, or St-Just.

Tickets

You can use a one-hour ticket on the Métro, bus or tram. They cost €1.60 for one hour, €2.40 for two hours or €13.70 for a *carnet* of 10 tickets, although you can buy only one-hour tickets on the bus. A one-day travel pass, *Ticket Liberté*, costs €4.70 and gives unlimited access. The funicular costs €2.70 return.

GETTING AROUND MARSEILLE

Régie des Transports de Marseille (RTM) is responsible for the city's Métro. The main office is at Espace Infos, 6–8 rue des Fabres (Mon–Fri 8.30am–6pm, Sat 9am–5.30pm; tel 04 91 91 92 10; www.rtm.fr).

Métro

The city has two fast, well-maintained Métro lines. Métro 1 runs from La Fourragere in the eastern suburbs through the northeast suburbs to La Rose. Métro 2 runs roughly north to south, from Bougainville in the north to Sainte-Marguerite Dromel.

The Métro runs Monday to Thursday from 5am to 10.30pm, and on Friday to Sunday until 12.30am.

Tram

Marseille now has two tram routes T1 and T2 running east–west.

Tickets

Tickets cost €1.50 and can be used on any combination of Métro, bus and tram. Your ticket is valid for one hour after you have stamped it. There are no return tickets. Ther is a tourist card for bus and métro—one day costs €5, three days cost €10.50.

GETTING AROUND TOULOUSE
Métro
The Métro operates on two lines. Line A runs from Basso-Cambo to Balma-Gramont and line B runs from Borderouge to Ramonville. The lines intersect at Jean Jaurés (the stop serving place Wilson and the boulevards). The other two most useful Métro stations for visitors— both on line A—are Capitole (for the main square) and Marengo SNCF for the railway station.

The system operates from 5.15am to around midnight (12.42am on Fridays and Saturdays). Trains run every two minutes during the rush hour, and every six minutes outside the rush hour. Visit www.tisseo.fr for details.

Tickets
You can buy tickets at machines in Métro stations, which have instructions in English and give change. Many stations do not have a ticket office so make sure you have cash. Tickets cost €1.40, are valid for one hour and for a maximum of three transfers and can be used on both the Métro and buses.

GETTING AROUND LILLE
Métro
The VAL is a driverless two-line Métro system with trains that run both above and below ground. Visit www.transpole.fr for details.

Buses and trams
The regional bus network serves all districts of Lille and its surrounding towns, and even goes into Belgium. Many buses leave from the streets and squares around the two train stations (Lille-Flandres and Lille-

Europe, the Eurostar station). There is a limited night bus network.

Tickets
You can buy a one-way ticket (€1.30), a *carnet* of 10 (€10.60) or a one-day pass (€3.60), which you can use on the bus, tram (streetcar) and Métro. Services run from 6am to midnight; there is no service at all on 1 May. Get tickets and information at Lille-Flandres station or tel 0820 424 040.

GETTING AROUND STRASBOURG
www.cts-strasbourg.fr
Services are run by CTS (Compagnie des Transports Strasbourgeois). Call 03 88 77 70 70 for information.

Buses and trams
The city has five efficient, modern tram lines which run daily from 4.30am to 12.30am. There is also a good bus network.

Tickets
Tickets for buses (€1.40) and trams are the same and are valid for an hour. For unlimited travel, get a 24-hour ticket (€4 per day). You must stamp your ticket before your journey. For trams, insert your ticket into the machine on the platform. For buses, use the machine on board.

GETTING AROUND BORDEAUX
Buses and trams
The city has three state-of-the-art tram lines that run from 5am to 1am. Tickets are valid for both buses and trams and allow an hour for transfers. If you are arriving by car but want to avoid the traffic it's worth taking advantage of the *parc relais* system by which you leave your car in a secure car park and take the bus or tram. For information tel 05 57 57 88 88; www.infotbc.com.

Tickets
On the buses, a one-way ticket costs €1.40, five tickets €5.20 and a *carnet* of ten tickets costs €10.30. A one-day *Découverte* card costs €4.10 and gives unlimited travel. A seven-day *Télécarte* costs €10.10.

Getting around the country is becoming easier, thanks to improvements to buses and trains. Most airports have facilities for people with disabilities and Eurostar trains are accessible to wheelchair-users. But you'll still find challenges when getting around France, especially in historic towns, with their narrow, cobbled streets. Before you travel, it's worth checking what facilities are available at your arrival airport (look up www.aeroport.fr) and your hotel, as older buildings may not have an elevator.

ARRIVING IN FRANCE
BY AIR
In Paris, both Roissy–Charles de Gaulle and Orly airports are well equipped for people with reduced mobility. Shuttle buses between terminals have ramps for wheelchairs, as well as voice announcements for people with visual impairments. The terminals have adapted toilets, low-level telephones and reserved parking spaces. For more information on reduced mobility issues, contact Air France's SAPHIR service (tel 0820 01 24 24; UK tel 0870 160 0346 and US tel 1 800 210 6508; Mon–Fri 9–7, Sat 9–6). There are organizations that offer specialist services from the airports into Paris, which you'll need to reserve in advance.

If you are a wheelchair-user, inform your airline when you reserve your ticket.

BY TRAIN
Eurostar trains and terminals are wheelchair-friendly and wheelchair-users can also benefit from discounted tickets.

GETTING AROUND IN FRANCE
BY TRAIN
France's long-distance trains are equipped for people with reduced mobility. Most large stations have elevators or ramps to the platform. If you need assistance, request it at the time of reserving your ticket.

Facilities on regional trains tend to be more varied. Passengers with disabilities travelling on an SNCF train can take an able-bodied companion with them, either free or for a 50 per cent reduction depending on the train. The *Accès Plus* service offers assistance getting on and off trains. For information tel 0890 640 650 or see www.accessibilite.sncf.com.

IN PARIS
The Métro is virtually inaccessible to wheelchair-users, due to countless steps, a warren of passageways and inflexible automatic barriers. The exception is Line 14. Some RER stations on Lines A and B have elevators to the platforms, although some can be operated only by a member of staff (press the *Appel* button for assistance). Most stations have a ticket office fitted with induction loops for people with hearing impairments.

The RATP website has a list of stations with access facilities for people with disabilities.

Some buses have ramps for wheelchair-users and voice announcements of the next stop for passengers with impaired eyesight. Increasing numbers of buses are being made accessible to wheelchair-users.

USEFUL WEBSITES AND ORGANIZATIONS

Access Project
39 Bradley Gardens, West Ealing, London W13 8HE, UK
www.accessproject-phsp.org/paris
Advice on getting around in Paris.

Les Compagnons du Voyage
Tel 01 58 76 08 33
www.compagnons.com
An accompaniment service for the Métro, RER trains and buses in Paris.

Tourism for All
Tel 08451 249 971 (from UK)
www.tourisrmforall.org.uk
Travel and holiday information for people with disabilities.

RATP Mission Accessibilité
19 place Lachambaudie, 75570, Paris Cedex 12
Tel 3246; email: missionaccessibilite@ratp.fr
Set up by the Paris Métro operator RATP to improve access for people with disabilities.

Infomobi
Tel 08 10 64 64 64
www.infomobi.com
Travel information for people with disabilities in the Île de France area.

Maison de la France
www.franceguide.com
The website of the French tourist office has useful information for people with disabilities.

Mobile en Ville
www.mobile-en-ville.asso.fr
A website packed with information on disability access and related issues.

Mobility International USA
www.miusa.org
Promotes international travel and exchange schemes for people with disabilities.

Paris Tourist Office
25–27 rue des Pyramides, 75001
Tel 0892 683 000
www.parisinfo.com
Useful information about wheelchair access in the city's museums, on buses, the RER and at airports.

Society for Accessible Travel and Hospitality (SATH)
Tel 212 447 7284 (from US)
www.sath.org
A US-based organization offering advice for visitors with disabilities and promoting awareness of their travel requirements.

REGIONS

This chapter is divided into eight regions of France (▷ 8–9). Region names are for the purposes of this book only and places of interest are listed alphabetically in each region.

France's Regions 68–414

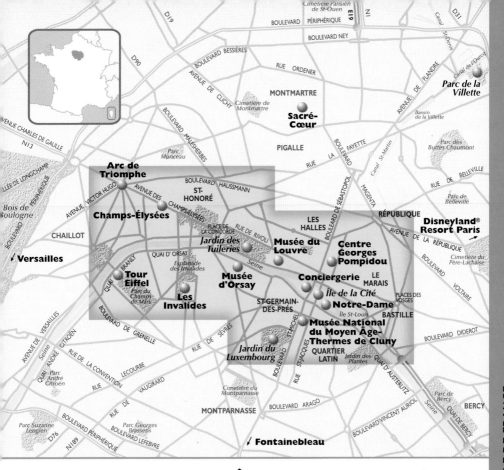

PARIS AND THE ÎLE DE FRANCE

France is a highly centralized nation, so it's no wonder that so many of its best attractions are packed into its capital. If you have only a few days here, you'll need to prioritize your sightseeing: Notre Dame cathedral, standing on an island in the Seine in the plumb centre of the city, is the place to get your bearings; the Eiffel Tower, soaring above the rooftops from whichever direction you look, gives the best view; a stroll along the Champs-Élysées to see the Arc de Triomphe is another must; and the Louvre museum needs at least half a day set aside to see its treasures. With time to do more, you won't run out of choice as the city has endless interesting museums, churches, streets and squares, and curious monuments to explore. If you just want to hop from pavement café to pavement café along picturesque streets—and walking is the best way to get around most parts of Paris—you'll want to plunge straight into the Latin Quarter or the village-within-a-city of Montmartre.

When you get tired of walking, Paris has a fast, efficient, inexpensive and well-structured system of public transportation to fall back on. It's worth taking a few minutes at the start of your stay to familiarize yourself with a plan of the Métro so that you can dip into and out of the system when needed.

Officially Paris forms part of the Île de France, a small administrative region made up of eight tiny *départements* which together cover a mere 2.2 per cent of national territory and accounts for 30 per cent of the country's GDP. Your only reason to venture into the suburbs, however, will be to visit the palaces of Fontainebleau and Versailles, or, if you have children in tow, to spend a day in at Europe's branch of Disneyland® at Disneyland® Resort Paris.

PARIS

250 m
250 yds

CHAILLOT

1

2

3

4

5

A   B   C

Argentine
Grande Arche
AVENUE DE LA GRANDE ARMÉE
Avenue Mac-Mahon
AVENUE DE WAGRAM
Musée Jacquemart André

Arc de Triomphe
Charles de Gaulle Étoile (+RER)
Charles de Gaulle Étoile (+RER)

AVENUE FOCH
Avenue Foch
Avenue Foch

VICTOR
HUGO
Kléber
KLÉBER
D'IÉNA

AVENUE DES CHAMPS-ÉLYSÉES

St-Philippe du Roule

Franklin D Roosevelt
Franklin D Roosevelt

Musée Baccarat

Boissière

Place des États-Unis
Place Amiral de Grasse

Musée National des Arts Asiatiques-Guimet

Musée Galliéra

AVENUE DU PRÉSIDENT WILSON

Iéna
Place d'Iéna

Musée d'Art Moderne de la Ville de Paris
Palais de Tokyo

Alma-Marceau

COURS   ALBERT   IER

Place du Trocadéro et du 11 Novembre
Trocadéro

Palais de Chaillot

Jardins du Trocadéro

NEW YORK

Seine

Pont de l'Alma (RER)
Les Égouts

Voie Sur Berge Rive Gauche
QUAI D'ORSAY

Place de la Résistance

Musée Marmottan Monet

BOULEVARD DELESSERT

Place de Varsovie

PONT D'IÉNA

QUAI BRANLY

Musée du quai Branly

Sq Alboni

VOIE GEORGES POMPIDOU

PONT DE BIR HAKEIM

Tour Eiffel

Champ de Mars-Tour Eiffel (RER)

Champ de Mars-Tour Eiffel (RER)

Bir-Hakeim

École Militaire

La Tour Maubourg

Parc du Champ de Mars

École Militaire
Place de l'École Militaire

AVENUE DE LA MOTTE-PICQUET

QUAI DE GRENELLE
BOULEVARD DE GRENELLE

SUFFREN

BOULEVARD HAUSSMANN

Miromesnil

-HONORÉ

Palais de l'Élysée

Champs-Élysées

Champs-Élysées-Clémenceau (Grand Palais)

AVENUE DES CHAMPS-ÉLYSÉES

Petit Palais

Grand Palais

ais de la couverte

COURS LA REINE

Port des Champs-Élysées

PONT ALEXANDRE III

QUAI D'ORSAY

Invalides (+RER)

Assemblée Nationale

Invalides (+RER)

Esplanade des Invalides

Place des Invalides

RUE DE GRENELLE

Les Invalides

Musée Rodin

INVALIDES

TOURVILLE Place Vauban

BOULEVARD DE BRETEUIL

St-Augustin

RUE DE LA PÉPINIÈRE

Lavoisier

BOULEVARD HAUSSMANN

Madeleine

Place de la Madeleine

BOULEVARD DE LA MADELEINE

Concorde

Place de la Concorde

Orangerie

Jeu de Paume

Jardin des Tuileries

72

Seine

Voie sur Berge Rive Gauche

QUAI DES TUILERIES

QUAI ANATOLE FRANCE

Assemblée Nationale

Musée d'Orsay (RER)

Musée d'Orsay

Solférino

ST-GERMAIN

Rue du Bac

Maison de Verre

St-Germain-des-Prés

Café de Flore & Les Deux Magots

RUE DE SEVRES

Sèvres-Babylone

St-Sulpice

Haussmann St-Lazare

Auber (RER)

Chaussée d'Antin-La Fayette

Opéra Palais Garnier

Opéra

CAPUCINES

Place de l'Opéra

Musée Fragonard

BOULEVARD DES CAPUCINES

Opéra

Place Vendôme

Place du Marché St-Honoré

Pyramides

RUE DE RIVOLI

Tuileries

Musée des Arts Décoratifs

RUE DE RIVOLI

Place du Carrousel

QUAI DU LOUVRE

QUAI VOLTAIRE

St-Germain-des-Prés

St-Sulpice

PARIS

250 m
250 yds

Jeu de Paume

Jardin des Tuileries

Tuileries

RUE DE RIVOLI

Musée des Arts Décoratifs

Palais Royale Musée du Louvre

Place du Carrousel

QUAI DES TUILERIES

Passerelle Léopold Sédar Senghor

Musée d'Orsay (RER)

Musée d'Orsay

Rue de Lille

Rue de Poitiers

QUAI VOLTAIRE

QUAI MALAQUAIS

Pont Royal

Pont du Carrousel

Port des Saints-Pères

QUAI DU LOUVRE

Seine

Musée du Louvre

Louvre-Rivoli

RUE DE RIVOLI

RUE DE RIVOLI

Pl du Louvre

St-Germain-l'Auxerrois

Pont des Arts

Institut de France

Musée des Beaux-Arts

Square du Vert-Galant

Pont Neuf (La Monnaie)

QUAI DE CONTI

Musée de la Monnaie

QUAI DES GRANDS AUGUSTINS

QUAI DES ORFÈVRES

QUAI DE LA MÉGISSERIE

Châtelet

Châtelet

Pl du Châtelet

PONT AU CHANGE

Place de l'Horloge

Palais de Justice

Conciergerie

Sainte-Chapelle

BOULEVARD DU PALAIS

Cité Cité

QUAI DU MARCHÉ NEUF

ST-GERMAIN-DES-PRÉS

Musée National Eugène Delacroix

St-Germain-des-Prés

St-Germain-des-Prés

Maison de Verre

Café de Flore & Les Deux Magots

Mabillon

BOULEVARD ST-GERMAIN

Odéon

Odéon

Mariage Frères

Rue St-André des Arts

St-Michel-Notre-Dame (RER)

St-Michel

Rue St-Séverin

St-Séverin

St-Michel-Notre-Dame (RER)

St-Ju le-Pa

Cluny La Sorbonne

Musée National du Moyen Age-Thermes de Cluny

La Sorbonne

ST-GERMAIN

BOULEVARD

Rue du Bac

St-Sulpice

St-Sulpice

Place St-Sulpice

RUE DE SÈVRES

Sèvres-Babylone

RASPAIL

BOULEVARD RASPAIL

Rennes

Rennes

Palais du Luxembourg

Jardin du Luxembourg

Luxembourg (RER)

Luxembourg (RER)

BOULEVARD SAINT-MICHEL

RUE SAINT-JACQUES

Panthéon

Pl du Panthéon

St-Placide

St-Placide

RUE DE RENNES

Place Pierre Lafue

Notre-Dame-des-Champs

Montparnasse Bienvenue

Jardin Marco Polo

RUE DES PETITS CHAMPS

Bibliothèque Nationale de France

Galerie Colbert

Galerie Vivienne

Place des Victoires

Jardin du Palais Royal

Galerie d'Orléans

Palais Royal

Galerie Véro-Dodat

St-Eustache

Les Halles

Jardin du Forum des Halles

Forum d Hall

Chât Les H (+F

Pyramides

L'OPÉRA

Place du Marché St-Honoré

72

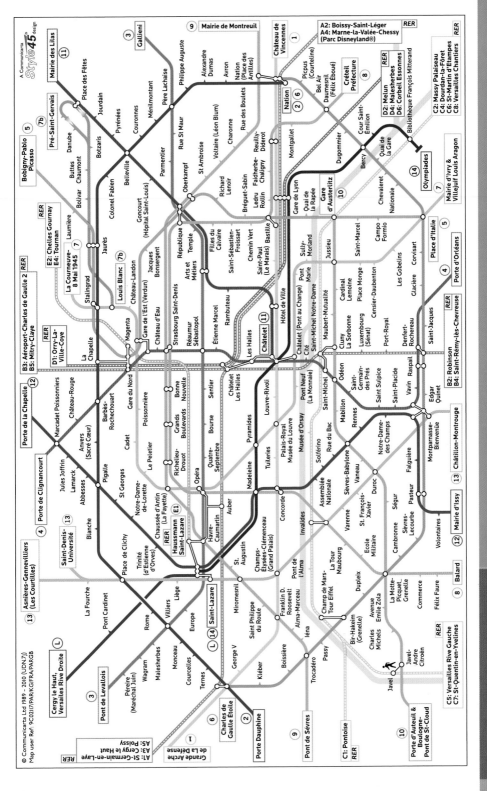

© Communicarta Ltd 1989 - 2010 (UDN7)
Map user Ref: 9C02I17/PAR/KG/FRA/PARGB

LE VAR
MONTEBELLO
LE MINCIO
CALDIERO

ARC DE TRIOMPHE AND CHAMPS-ÉLYSÉES

The wide, leafy Champs-Élysées is a focal point for the French nation, witness to momentous events such as De Gaulle's triumphal Liberation march in 1944 and the soccer World Cup celebrations in 1998. The bustling avenue, which is more than 2km (1.2 miles) long and 71m (232ft) wide, is packed with cinemas, shops, cafés and car showrooms. Go there on 14 July (Bastille Day) and most of the French army will roll past you. Another good time to visit is during the Christmas illuminations.

THE EARLY DAYS

The Champs-Élysées dates back to 1616, when Marie de Medici, second wife of the popular Henri IV, turned the area into a fashionable driveway. Then landscape designer André Le Nôtre (designer of the grounds of the Palace of Versailles) added alleys of trees and gardens, prompting the name 'Elysian Fields'. Walkways and fountains were installed in 1824 and the avenue soon became crowded with cafés, restaurants and a smart clientele.

ARC DE TRIOMPHE

The Arc de Triomphe crowns the western tip of the Champs-Élysées, standing on a hectic roundabout known as L'Étoile (the star). Within its grounds are the Tomb of the Unknown Soldier, installed in 1920 after World War I, and a poignant eternal Memorial Flame.

Napoleon I commissioned the arch in 1806, requiring an awesome memorial to the French army following their victory against the Russians and Austrians at the battle of Austerlitz. In 1810 a full-size model was installed to celebrate the emperor's marriage to Marie-Louise of Austria but the real thing was not ready until 1836, 15 years after Napoleon's death.

There are wonderful views from the rooftop of the monument, 50m (164ft) above street level. From here you can admire the geometry of Baron Haussmann's web-like street design and look along the Grand Axis towards the obelisk in place de la Concorde in one direction and the Grande Arche of La Défense in the other.

At night the city shimmers with lights. Back at ground level, save some time to admire the magnificent sculpted facade, the work of three different artists. Don't miss the fearsome winged figure of Liberty on François Rude's sculpture *La Marseillaise*, calling the French to defend their nation (northeastern pillar, facing the Champs-Élysées).

INFORMATION

Arc de Triomphe
www.monuments-nationaux.fr
✚ 70 B1 ✉ place Charles-de-Gaulle, 75008 ☎ 01 55 37 73 77 🕐 Apr–Sep daily 10am–11pm; Oct–Mar 10am–10.30pm ✋ Free to wander around the base. Rooftop: adult €9, all EU citizens and under 18 free 🚇 Charles de Gaulle–Étoile 🚌 22, 30, 31, 52, 73, 92 🚆 RER line A, Charles de Gaulle–Étoile 🎁 Gift shop 📙 €7 ☎ Call Monum on 01 44 54 19 30

Avenue des Champs-Élysées
✚ 71 D2 ✉ 75008 🚇 Charles de Gaulle–Étoile, Georges V, Franklin D. Roosevelt, Champs-Élysées-Clemenceau 🚌 32, 42, 73 and others 🚆 Charles de Gaulle–Étoile

TIPS

» It takes at least 30 minutes to walk from one end of the Champs-Élysées to the other and, with the heavy traffic, it is not a restful stroll. You may prefer to take the Métro—line 1 (yellow) runs underneath the entire length of the avenue.

» Most of the cafés and restaurants are at the Arc de Triomphe end, although you may find better-value places in the side streets.

Opposite *The Arc de Triomphe*
Above *The Champs-Élysées and the Arc de Triomphe at night*

PARIS AND THE ÎLE DE FRANCE • SIGHTS

REGIONS

INFORMATION

www.centrepompidou.fr

⊞ 73 J4 ✉ place Georges-Pompidou, 75004 ☎ 01 44 78 12 33 Ⓜ Centre Georges Pompidou: Wed–Mon 11–9. Musée National d'Art Moderne and exhibitions: Wed–Mon 11–9 (last ticket 8; late night Thu until 11pm for some exhibitions). Atelier Brancusi: Wed–Mon 2–6 ✋ Full ticket €12; Musée National d'Art Moderne, Atelier Brancusi and Children's Gallery: adult €10, under 18 free; free to all first Sun of month. Exhibitions: prices vary Ⓜ Rambuteau, Hôtel de Ville 🚌 29, 38, 47, 75 🚇 Châtelet-Les Halles ☕ Café on first floor 🍴 Georges restaurant on sixth floor 📖 Bookshops, boutique, post office 🎧 €19; downloadable audioguide for MP3 players €2.99

TIPS

» If you're a traditionalist when it comes to art, let yourself in to the Museum of Modern Art (relatively) gently by starting with the fifth floor (1905–1960) before tackling the more challenging fourth floor (1960 to the present day).

» If your mind is spinning from a day of modern art, enjoy a calming concert at the nearby church of St-Merri, Saturdays at 9pm and Sundays at 4pm.

Below *The bustling lobby of the Centre Georges Pompidou*

CENTRE GEORGES POMPIDOU

You'll either love or hate the brazen design of the Centre Georges Pompidou, and you may well feel the same about the contemporary art it contains. The venue has sparked controversy since it opened in 1977, gracing the historic heart of Paris with an incongruously modern building that resembles a giant air-conditioning system. But while its design may not please everyone, the arts complex attracts around 6 million visitors each year—roughly the same as the Louvre—with its canny, ever-changing mix of visual, performance and new-media art.

THE CONCEPT

Georges Pompidou, President of France from 1969 until his death in 1974, wanted a venue where people could enjoy contemporary film, drama, dance, music and visual art. The outlandish building took five years to construct and was a controversial addition to Beaubourg, a run-down district of 18th- and 19th-century town houses. Architects Renzo Piano and Richard Rogers turned the building 'inside out' by placing its 'guts' (all the piping) on the outside. This piping was coded: yellow for electrics, blue for air-conditioning, green for water and red for the elevators.

Pompidou did not live to see the opening of the building in 1977, but his vision proved sagacious—the venue was soon attracting 22,000 visitors a day, rivalling the Louvre in popularity. The site was closed for two years for extensive renovation work in the autumn of 1997, reopening just in time for the new millennium.

MUSÉE NATIONAL D'ART MODERNE

The Museum of Modern Art takes over where the Musée d'Orsay leaves off, featuring works from 1905 to the present day. Up to 2,000 pieces from the 50,000-strong collection are on display at any one time, ranging from Cubism by Georges Braque and Pablo Picasso to Pop Art by Andy Warhol and video art by Korean artist Nam June Paik.

The Centre Pompidou's temporary exhibitions, on the first and sixth floors, are as much of a draw as the permanent collections. Other attractions include children's activities, two cinemas and a library. The Brancusi workshop displays a magnificent collection of works by Constantin Brancusi, the Romanian abstract sculptor.

CHÂTEAU DE FONTAINEBLEAU

The Château de Fontainebleau rivals Versailles in grandeur and history but has the bonus of fewer crowds. What is now a vast palace grew in stages from a 12th-century royal hunting lodge, lost in what was then an immense forest. It owes most of its characteristic form and style to Francois I who transformed it into a sumptuous royal residence during the Renaissance, striving to create a 'New Rome'. He employed the cream of Italy's artists and craftsmen to decorate the interior. Subsequently the palace became a favourite residence of kings and emperors. Louis XIII was born here. Napoleon I had it refurbished at the height of his powers after the Revolution and, ironically, it was here that he was obliged to sign his declaration of abdication on 6 April 1814.

VISITING THE PALACE

You enter the château through the stately Cour du Cheval Blanc (Courtyard of the White Horse), also known as the Cour des Adieux. Napoleon Bonaparte bade farewell to his Imperial Guard at the horseshoe staircase here before being exiled to the island of Elba. Inside, your tour begins on the first floor. The dazzling Renaissance Salle de Bal (ballroom) has wood panels and frescoes, while the Galerie François I has frescoes painted by Rosso, a pupil of Michelangelo. Farther on, highlights in Les Grands Appartements des Souverains (Sovereigns' State Apartments) include the ornate Empress's Bedchamber, with a bed made for (although not used by) Marie-Antoinette, and Napoleon's extravagant Throne Room. L'Appartement Intérieur de l'Empereur (Napoleon I's Imperial Apartment) offers a glimpse into the emperor's personal life, although this is not his private apartment (Petits Appartements), which can be seen only on a guided tour, along with the Napoleon Museum. The Abdication Room has the table where Napoleon signed his deed of abdication.

THE GARDENS

Francois I had the estate around the palace laid out with gardens, lakes and canals. One surviving part of this is the Jardin de Diane, built around a fountain of Diana, one of several bronze statues. A century later the grounds were re-landscaped by André Le Nôtre, who also designed Versailles' stately grounds. His Grand Parterre, which extends southeast from the château, is considered the quintessence of French garden design of the time. The Jardin Anglais, was created after the Revolution, and is, as its name suggests, in the style of 18th-century English landscape gardening.

INFORMATION

www.musee-chateau-fontainebleau.fr
✚ 465 J5 ✉ Château de Fontainebleau 77300 ☎ 01 60 71 50 70 ❸ Renaissance Rooms, Sovereigns' State Apartments and Napoleon I's Imperial Apartment: Apr–Sep Wed–Mon 9.30–6; Oct–Mar Wed–Mon 9.30–5. Last admission 45 minutes before closing. Petits Appartements, L'Appartement des Chasses and Musée Napoleon I guided tour only. Gardens: May–Sep daily 9–7; Mar, Apr and Oct 9–6; Nov–Feb 9–5 👍 Adult €12.50, under 18 free, free to wander in the grounds; Petits Appartements, L'Appartement des Chasses and Musée Napoleon I: €6.50 per venue. Other rooms: adult €8, under 14 free 🚆 From Gare de Lyon to Fontainebleau-Avon; from here, the A/B bus takes you to the château 🚌 Take the A6 motorway from the Porte d'Orléans and leave at the Fontainebleau exit 🍴 Salon de Thé; picnics are allowed in the park, but not the gardens. See the noticeboard at the ticket desk for times. Audioguides free with general admission tickets 🛈 4 rue Royale (next to the Château de Fontainebleau bus stop) ☎ 01 60 74 99 99

TIP

» Holders of a Paris Museum Pass receive free entry to the château.

Above *Galerie François I overlooks the Cour de la Fontaine*

INFORMATION

www.monuments-nationaux.fr
✚ 72 H4 ✉ 2 boulevard du Palais, Île de la Cité, 75001 ☎ 01 53 40 60 93; 01 53 73 78 52 🕐 Mar–Oct daily 9.30–6; Nov–Feb 9–5 💶 Adult €7, under 18 and EU nationals aged 18–25 free 🚇 Cité, Châtelet 🚌 21, 24, 27, 38, 58, 81, 85, 96 🚉 RER line B, C St-Michel-Notre-Dame 📖 Bookshop 🎧 Daily guided tours in French, English, Italian and Spanish by reservation only, tel 01 44 54 19 30 🔎 €7

TIPS

» Signage in the rooms isn't particularly clear. Pick up a leaflet at the entrance to help navigate your way around.
» If you intend to visit the Sainte-Chapelle as well, buy a joint ticket at the Conciergerie.

Above *The Salles des Gens d'Armes*

CONCIERGERIE

Sailing past the Conciergerie's beautifully floodlit towers on an evening boat cruise, it is hard to imagine the fear that lurked within its walls for more than five centuries. The former palace played a gruesome role in the Revolution, housing more than 4,000 inmates, up to 600 at a time. Marie-Antoinette, wife of Louis XVI, was among the most famous prisoners and you can see a poignant recreation of her cell during your visit.

PALACE AND PRISON

The Conciergerie was originally a palace, part of a royal complex that included the Sainte-Chapelle and the Palais de Justice. The oldest parts of the building date from the early 14th century, although a governor's palace and fortress probably stood on the Île de la Cité as far back as Roman times. In the late 14th century, Charles V chose to live elsewhere, and the site became a law court and prison, with occasional use for royal functions. It was around this time that the Conciergerie gained its name, from the concierge who oversaw the site.

MEDIEVAL ORIGINS

Entering from the boulevard du Palais, you are plunged into semi-darkness in a vast Gothic chamber said to be Europe's oldest surviving medieval hall. The Salles des Gens d'Armes, 63m (206ft) long and 8.5m (28ft) high, dates back to the 14th century, when it formed the lower floor of the Grand'Salle. The king's staff ate in here, up to 2,000 of them at a time, while royal banquets and marriage celebrations were held upstairs. A spiral staircase leads up to the kitchens, where there are four walk-in fireplaces, each big enough to roast a couple of sheep.

DISNEYLAND® RESORT PARIS

Disneyland® Resort Paris attracts millions of visitors to its two theme parks—Disneyland® Park and Walt Disney Studios® Park. The resort, in the countryside east of Paris, opened in 1992 to a blaze of publicity.

DISNEYLAND® PARK

You can visit five different 'lands', each with its own themed rides, entertainment, restaurants and shops. Main Street U.S.A.® takes you back in time with its nostalgic scenes from an American town at the turn of the 19th century. Seasonal parades (check the website for dates and times) bring scenes from Disney's animated films to life with dancers and well-known characters. Fantasyland, especially popular with younger children, includes Sleeping Beauty Castle, the 'It's a Small World' ride, Peter Pan's Flight and the enchanting 'Le Pays de Contes de Fées' (Storybook Land) canal cruise. Adventureland boasts the swashbuckling Pirates of the Caribbean Adventure Isle and the high-speed 'Indiana Jones and the Temple of Peril' ride. Frontierland, with its canyons, gold mines and rivers, offers two thrill-seeker attractions—the 'Big Thunder Mountain' runaway train ride and the ghostly Phantom Manor. Discoveryland was inspired by Jules Verne's visions of the future, and the 'Mystery of the Nautilus' ride is based on the film *20,000 Leagues Under the Sea*. The 'Space Mountain: Mission 2' roller coaster is not for the faint-hearted. The spectacular Star Tours flight simulator whisks visitors on an interplanetary journey.

WALT DISNEY STUDIOS® PARK

The Walt Disney Studios® Park is based on Disney–MGM Studios in Florida. Four Production zones each aim to create the atmosphere of a film studio—Front Lot, Toon Studio with the new Toy Story Playland inspired by Disney® Pixar's *Toy Story*, Production Courtyard and Backlot. The 33m (108ft) water tower, crowned with Mickey Mouse's black ears, dominates the Front Lot. The Twilight Zone Tower of Terror™ is a free fall drop of 13 floors, while Stitch Live! is an interactive experience for all the family. You can take a ride on Crush's Coaster or Cars Race Rally or see the Moteurs…Action! Stunt Show Spectacular®.

DISNEY® VILLAGE

Between the two parks and the seven Disney® hotels you'll find the Disney® Village entertainment complex, open until the early hours and bustling with themed restaurants, bars, shops, street artists and cinemas.

©Disney

INFORMATION

www.disneylandparis.com

✚ 465 J5 ✉ BP 100, Marne-la-Vallée, 77777 Cedex 4 ☎ 08 25 30 02 22 in France; 0033 1 60 30 60 53 from abroad ⏱ Times vary 🚇 RER line A4 or Eurostar to Marne-la-Vallée/Chessy station 🚌 A4 motorway (Autoroute de l'Est), direction 'Metz/Nancy', and take exit 14 to Parc Disneyland ✋ 1-day 1 park ticket adult: €53, child €45; 1-day 2 park ticket adult €67, child €57. Prices may vary according to season 🅿 €8 per day; free if you are staying at a Disneyland® Resort Paris hotel 🛍 Shops and boutiques ❓ Height and age restrictions apply to some rides

TIPS

» Information points at City Hall in Disneyland® Park and Studio Services in Walt Disney Studios® Park provide maps and event details.

» A free FASTPASS time-saving system is available on some of the more popular rides, cutting down queuing time.

Below *Sleeping Beauty Castle*

REGIONS | **PARIS AND THE ÎLE DE FRANCE • SIGHTS**

CIMETIÈRE DU PÈRE-LACHAISE
www.pere-lachaise.com
Visit the graves of luminaries such as Frédéric Chopin, Marcel Proust and Oscar Wilde at this vast cemetery on the eastern edge of the city. Père-Lachaise covers 44ha (108 acres) and contains 70,000 tombs.

The cemetery is named after Louis XIV's confessor, Père La Chaise, who once owned the land here. It was designed by Brongniart in 1803 to echo the style of an English landscaped garden. At first, it was not popular, but once the graves of writers Molière and Jean de La Fontaine had been transferred here, it soon became the most fashionable place to be buried in Paris.

Now the cemetery has become a place of pilgrimage for many visitors to the city—among the famous people buried here are composers Frédéric Chopin and Georges Bizet, Paris town planner Baron Haussmann, artists Amedeo Modigliani and Eugène Delacroix, singers Edith Piaf and Maria Callas, writers Marcel Proust, Honoré de Balzac and Oscar Wilde, actresses Simone Signoret and Sarah Bernhardt, actor Yves Montand and dancer Isadora Duncan. One of the most visited graves is that of Jim Morrison, lead singer of The Doors, who died in Paris in 1971.

The Mur des Fédérés, in the eastern corner, marks the site of the Communards' tragic last stand in 1871, when the 147 survivors of the Commune were lined up against the wall and executed by a government firing squad.
➕ Off map 73 L2 ✉ boulevard de Ménilmontant, 75020 ☎ 01 55 25 82 10 🕐 Mon–Fri 8–6, Sat 8.30–6, Sun 9–6 (closes 5.30 early Nov to mid-Mar) ✋ Free 🚇 Père Lachaise, Gambetta 🚌 60, 69, 102 📧 For guided tours tel: 01 71 28 50 82

CONCIERGERIE
▷ 80.

DISNEYLAND® RESORT PARIS
▷ 81.

LES GALERIES
http://parisinconnu.com/passages
These elegant covered passageways, with their glass skylights and decorative floors, were the stylish shopping malls of early 19th-century Paris. Fewer than 30 of the original 140 passages survive—relics of pre-department store days. The elegant Galerie Vivienne, built in 1823, is one of the most fashionable, with its ornate cast-iron entrance gates, high glass roofs, chandeliers and splendid mosaic floors. Running parallel to it is the Galerie Colbert, dating from 1826. Others include the Passage des Panoramas, off boulevard Montmartre, and the Galerie Véro-Dodat, near the Louvre.
Galerie Vivienne ➕ 72 G2 ✉ 4 rue des Petits-Champs/6 rue Vivienne/5 rue de la Banque, 75002 🚇 Bourse
Galerie Colbert ➕ 72 G2 ✉ 6 rue des Petits-Champs, 75002 🚇 Bourse

GRAND PALAIS
www.palais-decouverte.fr
www.grandpalais.fr
The Grand Palais, with its soaring glass and iron domes, was built for the 1900 Universal Exhibition. A striking mix of art nouveau and neoclassical architecture, it hosts high-profile art exhibitions. On the western side of the Grand Palais, the Palais de la Découverte is a science museum, with a Planetarium.
Grand Palais ➕ 71 D3 ✉ avenue Winston-Churchill, 75008 ☎ 01 44 13 17 30; reservations 01 42 31 32 28 🕐 Variable.

Depends on the exhibition ✋ Varies 🚇 Champs-Élysées-Clemenceau 🚌 28, 42, 52, 72, 73, 80, 83, 93
Palais de la Découverte ➕ 71 D3 ✉ avenue Franklin D. Roosevelt, 75008 ☎ 01 56 43 20 21 🕐 Tue–Sat 9.30–6, Sun 10–7 ✋ Adult €7, child €4.50; €3.50 extra for Planetarium

GRANDE ARCHE
www.grandearche.com
Paris's most striking modern monument. The Grande Arche is best admired from below, looking up into the vast chasm that is greater than the height of Notre-Dame.

The futuristic monument-cum-office-block was designed as a symbolic western gateway to Paris and focal point of the new business district, La Défense. It was completed in 1989 in time for the bicentenary of the French Revolution.

Standing below the Grande Arche is a rather unnerving experience, as you look up at 300,000 tonnes of concrete, marble-cladding and glass rising 110m (360ft). But if you think that's daunting, wait until you take the glass elevator through the cavity of the arch on what looks simply like a piece of scaffolding.

At the top, walk outside to see the view, up some steps onto a viewing platform. The panorama is partly obscured by wire fencing and the office blocks of La Défense—if you climb only one of Paris's tall buildings, the Grande Arche is probably not the one to choose. However, if you have already seen the view from the Eiffel Tower and the Arc de Triomphe, the Grande Arche offers a new perspective.

The arch was the culmination of many unsuccessful attempts to find a nucleus for La Défense in the 1970s. The design, by Danish architect Johan Otto von Spreckelsen, was finally chosen in 1983.
➕ 70 off A1 ✉ 1 parvis de la Défense, 92044 Paris-La-Défense ☎ 01 49 07 27 27 🕐 Daily 10–7 (Apr–Sep until 8; last entry 30 min before closing) ✋ Adult €10, child (6–17) €8.50 🚇 Grande Arche de la Défense 🚌 73 🚈 RER line A, La Défense 🍴 🏛

ÎLE DE LA CITÉ

The Île de la Cité is where the Paris story began, when the Celtic Parisii tribe moved in more than 2,000 years ago. The Romans arrived 200 years later, and in the Middle Ages the island gained a royal palace (now the Palais de Justice and Conciergerie). Eight bridges connect the Île de la Cité to the left and right banks of the river. A ninth bridge leads on to the slightly smaller and calmer Île St-Louis (▷ 85).

THE ISLAND FROM THE SEINE

Today it is still a key part of the city, packed with visitors, traffic and fabulous architecture. One of the best ways to appreciate the beautiful buildings on the Île de la Cité is by boat, taking one of the trips that start from below the Pont Neuf, Paris's oldest bridge. From the water you'll see the elegant Notre-Dame rising high above the banks and the stern facade of the Conciergerie, once Paris's most notorious prison.

EXPLORING ON FOOT

On foot, the Île de la Cité's charms may be harder to appreciate at first, due to the heavy traffic and crowds of visitors. But persevere. When you have ticked off the don't-miss sights of Notre-Dame (▷ 95), the Conciergerie (▷ 80) and the Sainte-Chapelle (▷ 98) there are quieter spots where you can relax and enjoy the views.

The grassy square Jean XXIII is a good place to sit and admire the architecture of Notre-Dame, while square de l'Île de France, at the eastern tip of the island, gives lovely views of the Seine and the Île St-Louis. It is also home to the haunting Mémorial des Martyrs de la Déportation, commemorating the French citizens deported to concentration camps during World War II. The flower market in place Louis Lépine (Mon–Sat 8–7) sells anything from delicate blooms to trees 1.8m (6ft) high.

When your legs just won't take you any farther, give in and enjoy a coffee or crêpe in one of the cafés—although you may find yourself paying tourist prices for the privilege. The crowds thin out towards the northwestern extreme of the island. Place Dauphine is a handsome 17th-century square and beyond it square du Vert-Galant forms a green 'prow' from which there are good views downstream. Parisians often head to the riverbanks on this end of the island to sunbathe or eat a sandwich.

INFORMATION

✚ 70–71 H5 ✉ Île de la Cité, 75001 and 75004 Ⓜ Cité (also Pont Neuf, St-Michel, Châtelet, Hôtel de Ville)
🚌 21, 24, 27, 38, 47, 58, 70, 85, 96
🚆 RER line B, C, St-Michel-Notre-Dame
☕ A selection on Île de la Cité, as well as on the nearby Île St-Louis and in the Latin Quarter 🏛 A selection

Opposite *The grave of composer Rossini, in Père-Lachaise cemetery*
Below *The Île de la Cité*

PARIS AND THE ÎLE DE FRANCE • SIGHTS

REGIONS

INFORMATION

www.invalides.org

✚ 71 D5 ✉ Hôtel National des Invalides, 129 rue de Grenelle, 75007 ☎ 08 10 11 33 99 🕐 Apr–Sep Mon, Wed–Sat 10–6, Sun 10–3.30, Tue 10–9; Oct–Mar daily 10–5. Closed first Mon of each month 💰 Adult €9, under 18 and EU citizens aged 18–25 free 🚇 La-Tour-Maubourg, Invalides, Varenne 🚌 28, 63, 69, 80, 82, 83, 87, 92, 93 🚊 RER line C, Invalides 🛍 📖 Gift shop/bookshop 📖 €12 ☛ Guided tours available

TIPS

» The best way to appreciate the grandeur of Les Invalides is to approach the site from Pont Alexandre III.

» The Musée de l'Armée is busiest between 11am and 1pm.

» As an antidote to the war focus of Les Invalides, unwind in the nearby gardens of the Musée Rodin (▷ 94).

» The Musée de l'Armée is twinned with the Musée Rodin (▷ 94); you'll benefit from reductions on the entry ticket there if you present your entry ticket for the Army Museum.

Below *The golden Église du Dôme at Les Invalides*

LES INVALIDES

Although its architecture is pompous, severe and authoritarian, Les Invalides was actually built to house wounded and elderly soldiers. Louis XIV commissioned Libéral Bruant to design the imposing building, with its 195m (640ft) facade. In 1674 the first soldiers moved in and were welcomed by the king himself. It took another 32 years before the gold-encrusted Église du Dôme (Church of the Dome) was completed. Today, visitors come to see a later addition, the tomb of Napoleon I, as well as the impressive Musée de l'Armée (Army Museum). On entering the stately grounds you'll be following in the footsteps of many a military hero, including General de Gaulle and Winston Churchill.

REMEMBERING PAST CONFLICTS

The Musée de l'Armée is one of the largest of its kind in the world, and among the extensive collections of weapons, armour, flags, uniforms and paintings are some real gems. The museum is housed in three wings arranged around the *cour d'honneur*, to the north of the church. After a substantial renovation, the final galleries, the Hundred Days of Napoleon III, reopened in 2010.

As you would expect, Napoleon I features prominently, and you can see his frock coat, hat, coronation saddle and even his actual horse, Vizir (not for the squeamish). Don't miss the evocative World War II exhibition, which uses film footage, photos and day-to-day objects to convey the horrors of the war and the bravery of those who fought against Hitler. On the fourth floor the Musée des Plans-Reliefs displays huge scale models of fortresses and French towns, which were used to plan sieges in the 17th and 18th centuries.

ÉGLISE DU DÔME

The golden dome of this stunning church rises 107m (350ft) above the ground, a glistening monument to two of France's most influential and charismatic rulers, Louis XIV and Napoleon I. The church, dedicated to St. Louis, was designed by Versailles architect Jules Hardouin-Mansart and was completed in 1706. Its inauguration was a grand affair, attended by Louis XIV.

Napoleon's tomb is in a grandiose crypt directly below the dome. His remains were brought back to France in 1840, but it took another 21 years to create a mausoleum fit for an emperor.

Above left *Window-shopping on Île St-Louis*
Above *Wandering in the arcades of the Jardin du Palais Royal*

ÎLE ST-LOUIS

This peaceful, leafy island sits behind the Île de la Cité and offers wonderful views of Notre-Dame from its western tip. Visitors pack its main road, the narrow rue St-Louis-en-l'Île, to browse in the shops and try the famous ice cream at Maison Berthillon (closed Mon, Tue and Aug).

Architect Le Vau designed many of the town houses on the tiny island in the 17th century. Residents have included the poet and critic Charles Baudelaire, the sculptress Camille Claudel and the painter and caricaturist Honoré Daumier.

✚ 73 J5 ✉ Île St-Louis, 75004 🚇 Pont Marie, Sully Morland 🚌 67, 86, 87

INSTITUT DU MONDE ARABE

www.imarabe.org

The Arab World Institute is in a stunning aluminium and glass building that combines modern materials with the spirit of traditional Arab architecture. The southern facade consists of 240 metal panels, adjusted hourly to filter sunlight as it enters the building. Their design is inspired by traditional carved wooden screens called *moucharabiehs*.

The Institute, designed by Jean Nouvel, Pierre Soria, Gilbert Lezenes and Architecture Studio, opened in 1987. Exhibits in its museum range in origin from Spain to India and from prehistory to the 19th century. The views from the ninth floor are simply wonderful.

✚ 73 J6 ✉ 1 rue des Fossés-St-Bernard, 75005 ☎ 01 40 51 38 38 🕐 Tue–Sun 10–6 🎟 Adult €5, child (12–18) €4, under 12 free 🚇 Jussieu, Cardinal-Lemoine, Sully-Morland 🚌 24, 63, 67, 86, 87, 89 🍴 Le Ziryab panoramic restaurant ☕ Café Littéraire, Le Moucharabieh cafeteria 🎁

LES INVALIDES

▷ 84

JARDIN DU LUXEMBOURG

▷ 86.

JARDIN DU PALAIS ROYAL

This tranquil garden is the perfect place to recharge your batteries after a visit to the Louvre. The flower-filled enclave is separated from the 21st century by a cordon of handsome 18th-century arcades, sheltering quirky shops and *salons de thé*.

In good weather the garden is full of Parisians resting, reading and playing boules. Children roller-skate around the incongruous 280 black-and-white striped columns in the Cour d'Honneur, a controversial 1986 addition by artist Daniel Buren. You may like to throw a coin on a column and make a wish. The courtyard's sleek water features blend more easily with the rest of the garden.

It's worth walking through the arcades, with their small shops selling anything from art to silverware and model soldiers. There is a choice of places to stop for a drink.

The Palais Royal was commissioned by Louis XIII's adviser, Cardinal Richelieu, in the 17th century and was originally called the Palais-Cardinal. Louis XIV spent part of his childhood in the palace. Molière and his troupe of actors used to perform in the Théâtre du Petit Cardinal, which once stood at the southern corner of the palace. The nearby Comédie Française (▷ 110) still stages Molière's plays today.

The arcades and apartments surrounding the palace garden were constructed in the 18th century.

✚ 72 G3 ✉ place du Palais-Royal, 75001 🕐 Jun–Aug daily 7am–11pm; Apr–May 7am–10.15pm; Sep 7am–9.30pm; Oct–Mar 7.30am–8.30pm 🎟 Free 🚇 Palais Royal–Musée du Louvre 🚌 21, 48, 67, 69, 72, 81 🍴 Restaurants and tea rooms around the outside 🎁 Small shops in the arcades

INFORMATION
www.senat.fr

✚ 72 G6 ✉ rue de Vaugirard/rue de Médicis/boulevard St-Michel, 75006 ☎ Park: 01 42 34 23 89. Senate: 01 42 34 20 00. Musée du Luxembourg: 01 42 34 25 95 ⏲ Times vary depending on season; generally dawn to dusk ✋ Free ⓜ Odéon 🚌 21, 27, 38, 58, 82, 83, 84, 85, 89 🚈 RER line B, Luxembourg 🍴 Open-air cafés, kiosk restaurant 🏪 Kiosk ➡ Guided tours of the Palais du Luxembourg take place on the first Sat of each month. To reserve a place call or to sit in on a Senate debate call 01 42 34 20 00

JARDIN DU LUXEMBOURG

The Jardin du Luxembourg forms an attractive southern boundary to St-Germain and the Latin Quarter. Students come here to relax after lectures and visitors catch some breathing space between sightseeing. It is a popular haunt of chic Montparnasse residents and their offspring, who make the most of the many children's attractions.

ATTRACTIONS

The 24ha (60-acre) park has some of the most beautiful public flower displays in Paris and is landscaped in an appealing mixture of French, English and Italian styles. The focal point is a large octagonal pond, elegantly encircled by stone urns and statues of French queens and other notable women. On the northern side, the Italianate Palais du Luxembourg is a reminder of the park's Florentine origins and is now home to the French Senate. In good weather the park is full of Parisians sunbathing, playing boules or jogging along the shady paths. Other attractions include tennis courts, a bandstand and even a bee-keeping school. The Musée du Luxembourg, in the former orangery, stages temporary art exhibitions. The Fontaine Médicis is a popular romantic spot on the eastern side of the Palais du Luxembourg.

Children are well catered for, with donkey rides (during French school holidays), puppet shows in the Théâtre du Luxembourg (Wednesday, Saturday and Sunday from 2pm) and swings and slides. They can also rent remote-control yachts to sail on the pond.

MEMORIES OF HOME

Bored with the Louvre, Marie de Medici commissioned the gardens and palace in 1615, hoping for a reminder of her native Florence. She bought the land from Duke François of Luxembourg and asked architect Salomon de Brosse to use the Pitti Palace as inspiration. Work finished in the mid-1620s but Marie, widow of Henri IV, did not have long to enjoy it. She was exiled from France by the powerful Cardinal Richelieu and died penniless in Cologne.

During the Revolution, the Palais du Luxembourg was commandeered for use as a prison. After the Revolution, in 1799, it became the seat of France's Upper Chamber.

Below *Jardin du Luxembourg is especially popular on sunny days*

JARDIN DES TUILERIES

Paris's largest and oldest public garden is a delightful place to stroll around or relax in, and is much visited for the views it gives of the surrounding monuments. It is dominated at one end by the place de la Concorde and at the other by the mighty Louvre—there are also views of the Eiffel Tower, Arc de Triomphe and Musée d'Orsay.

The park runs alongside the Seine and the grandest way to enter is through the gilded gates at the Concorde end. This brings you to the first of the two large ponds. Two art galleries stand on terraces either side of this first pond. The Jeu de Paume is the sister gallery of the Hotel de Sully and is given over to exhibitions of photography and contemporary art. The Orangerie, as its name suggests, is a 19th-century greenhouse built for growing oranges but adapted in the 1920s to make an art gallery fit to display Claude Monet's series of waterlily pond paintings, the *Nymphéas*.

Follow the wide central avenue towards the Louvre and the gravel gradually gives way to grass and well-tended flower beds. You pass allegorical statues, open-air cafés and children's playgrounds. At the eastern end, the neoclassical Arc du Carrousel forms a symbolic gateway to the Louvre and is also the first arch in Paris's Grand Axis, the imaginary straight line linking the Louvre, the Arc de Triomphe and the Grande Arche.

HISTORY

The Tuileries was the inspiration of Catherine de Medici, who wanted an Italian-style garden to complement the palace built in 1564. Lavish balls, concerts and fireworks ensured her garden remained an important social venue.

The park as we know it today dates from 1649, when Louis XIV asked renowned landscape architect André Le Nôtre, who designed the gardens at Versailles and Fontainebleau, to redesign it in the formal French style. The palace went up in smoke at the hands of the Communards in 1871 but the garden survived. After years of neglect in the 20th century, it received a makeover in time for the new millennium.

INFORMATION

✚ 72 F3 ✉ place de la Concorde, 75001 ☎ 01 40 20 90 43 🕐 Apr–Sep daily 7am–9pm (also Jul–Aug 9–11pm); Oct–Mar 7.30am–7pm 🎟 Free 🚇 Tuileries, Concorde 🚌 21, 24, 27, 42, 68, 72, 73, 81, 84, 94, 95 ☕ Open-air cafés 📖 Bookshop at Concorde end

TIPS

» Children can rent model yachts to sail on the pond at the eastern end of the park.

» Free guided tours take place on Sunday afternoons during the summer months. For more information see the notice boards or call 01 49 26 07 59.

Above *The obelisk and the Arc de Triomphe are just two of the landmarks you can see from the Jardin des Tuileries*

MAISON EUROPÉENNE DE LA PHOTOGRAPHIE

www.mep-fr.org

The stylish Maison Européenne de la Photographie hosts dynamic exhibitions of contemporary photography. The galleries are spread over five floors of the 18th-century Hôtel Hénault de Cantobre, as well as occupying a newer wing that opened in 1996.

✚ 73 K5 ✉ 5–7 rue de Fourcy, 75004 ☎ 01 44 78 75 00 🕐 Wed–Sun 11–8. Closed during exhibition changeovers ✋ Adult €6.30, child €3.50, under 8 free; free to all Wed 5–8 🚇 St-Paul 🚌 67, 69, 76, 96 📷

LE MARAIS

The Marais district, on the eastern side of the Right Bank, has ornate architecture and trendy restaurants, boutiques and art galleries. There's a bustling Jewish quarter and Paris's oldest square—place des Vosges (▷ 98). The area was once low-lying marshland, hence its name *marais* (marsh). For two centuries sections were controlled by the powerful religious and military order, the Knights Templar. During the 17th century aristocrats competed to build the most elegant mansions, but the area later fell into neglect. Then, in 1962, restoration began. Many of these impressive buildings (called *hôtels)* now house museums, including the Musée Picasso (▷ 94), the Musée Carnavalet (▷ 89) and the Musée d'Art et d'Histoire du Judaïsme (▷ 88).

✚ 73 J4–K4 ✉ Le Marais 🚇 St-Paul, Rambuteau, Hôtel de Ville 🚌 29, 69, 75, 76, 96

MONTMARTRE

www.montmartrenet.com

This village within a city has cobbled streets, stunning views and the mighty Sacré-Cœur basilica.

Hilltop Montmartre, north of central Paris, has a split personality. There are the teeming tourist traps, including place du Tertre and the front steps of Sacré-Cœur, but venture a few minutes off the beaten track and you'll find quiet cobbled streets, whitewashed cottages and all the charm of a small village. It's hard to remember you are still in France's capital city.

The area earned an almost mythical status at the end of the 19th century, thanks to its community of artists and its raunchy nightlife. Henri de Toulouse-Lautrec immortalized scenes of dancing girls at the world-famous cabaret venue Moulin Rouge, where you can still see shows today.

Montmartre is crowned by the Sacré-Cœur basilica (▷ 99), a dazzling white creation that looks stunning against a blue sky. The nearby place du Tertre is the highest point in the city and swarms with visitors and street artists. Quieter, picturesque streets are nearby (▷ 104–105).

In Roman times, Montmartre's hill hosted a temple to Mercury. It was renamed Mont des Martyrs after the murder of Paris's first bishop, St. Denis, in the third century. He was said to have picked up his severed head and walked 10km (6 miles).

By the end of the 17th century around 30 windmills stood on the hill and Montmartre prospered with the production of wine, flour and gypsum (plaster of Paris). Only two of these windmills still stand.

✚ Off map 73 K2 ✉ 75018 🚇 Anvers, Abbesses, Blanche, Lamarck Caulaincourt 🚌 Montmartrobus (buses 30, 31, 54, 68, 74, 80, 85 have stops nearby) 🍴 Plenty of restaurants and cafés ☕ A selection ❓ For a Montmartre walk ▷ 104–105

MUSÉE DES ARTS DECORATIFS

www.ucad.fr

This museum displays decorative arts from the Middle Ages to the present day. The more than 150,000 items in the collection cover almost every aspect of the genre, from ceramics, glass and embroidery to wood and metalwork. Periods covered include the Middle Ages and Renaissance, art nouveau, art deco, Modern and Contemporary and there are a further five specialist departments: Glass, Toys, Drawings, Wallpaper and Jewellery.

✚ 72 F3 ✉ 107 rue de Rivoli, 75001 ☎ 01 44 55 57 50 🕐 Tue–Fri 11–6 (until 9pm on Wed), Sat, Sun 10–6 ✋ Adult €9, 18–25 €7.50, under 18 free 🚇 Palais-Royal–Musée du Louvre, Tuileries 🚌 21, 27, 39, 48, 69, 72, 81, 95 ☕

MUSÉE D'ART ET D'HISTOIRE DU JUDAÏSME

www.mahj.org

This museum paints a vibrant picture of the development of Jewish culture from the Middle Ages to the present day, both in France and throughout the rest of the world. It also highlights the contribution members of the Jewish community have made to European art.

The museum opened in 1998 in the Hôtel de St-Aignan, a restored 17th-century mansion that became home to Jewish immigrants from Eastern Europe in the 19th century.

✚ 73 J3 ✉ Hôtel de St-Aignan, 71 rue du Temple, 75003 ☎ 01 53 01 86 60 🕐 Mon–Fri 11–6, Sun 10–6 ✋ Adult €6.80, under 18 free 🚇 Rambuteau, Hôtel de Ville 🚌 29, 38, 47, 75 📷 ☕ Bookshop 📱 Audioguide included in entry price

Above *The Musée Carnavalet conveys the atmosphere of Paris in ages past*
Opposite *A Marais bookshop*

MUSÉE DES ARTS ET MÉTIERS

www.arts-et-metiers.net/

Art meets science at this quirky museum, with its collection of early scientific machinery, vintage cars and mechanical toys. Exhibits include a primitive calculating machine invented by Pascal and one of Edison's phonographs. Closer to today, a Formula 1 racing car sits incongruously in the former chapel. The museum, set up by the Revolutionary government back in 1794, is in a medieval priory with a 13th-century chapel.

➕ 73 J2 ✉ 60 rue Réaumur, 75003 ☎ 01 53 01 82 00 🕐 Tue–Sun 10–6 (Thu until 9.30pm) 💶 Adult €6.50, under 18 free 🚇 Arts et Métiers, Réaumur-Sébastopol 🚌 20, 38, 39, 47 🚻

MUSÉE CARNAVALET

www.carnavalet.paris.fr

Immerse yourself in the turbulent history of Paris at this intriguing museum, housed in two 16th- and 17th-century mansions. Paintings, memorabilia and sumptuous recreations of period rooms evoke the spirit of the city during the French Revolution and the reign of Napoleon I. The emphasis is on conveying an atmosphere rather than listing historical facts, so if you want a taste of the high life during Louis XV's rule or a glimpse of the terrors

of the Revolution, this is the place to come.

The main entrance takes you into the Hôtel Carnavalet, where exhibitions on two floors lead you up to the reign of Louis XVI. The adjoining Hôtel Le Peletier moves on to the Revolution (second floor), 19th century (ground and first floors) and 20th century (first floor).

➕ 73 K4 ✉ 23 rue de Sévigné, 75003 (also an entrance on rue des Francs-Bourgeois) ☎ 01 44 59 58 58 🕐 Tue–Sun 10–6 ✋ Free (except for temporary exhibitions) 🚇 St-Paul 🚌 29, 69, 76, 96 📖 Bookshop 🎧 In French and occasionally in English, call 01 44 59 58 31 for details

MUSÉE JACQUEMART ANDRÉ

www.musee-jacquemart-andre.com

Banker Edouard Jacquemart and his painter wife Nélie André were ardent art collectors and amassed an impressive collection. In 1875 they built a mansion on boulevard Haussmann to display the masterpieces. The mansion and its contents were donated to the Institut de France and opened as a museum in 1913. The collection includes paintings and sculptures by Italian artists (including Canaletto, Botticelli and Della Robbia), Flemish and Dutch masters (Van Dyck, Rembrandt and Frans Hals) and French artists (Boucher, David and Fragonard).

➕ 70 C1 ✉ 158 boulevard Haussmann, 75008 ☎ 01 45 62 11 59 🕐 Daily 10–6 💶 Adult €11, child €8.50, under 7 free, family 3 people pay, 4th person free 🍴 Daily 11.45–5.30 🚇 St-Philippe-du-Roule, Miromesnil 🚌 22, 28, 43, 52, 54, 80, 83, 84, 93 🚉 RER line A, Charles de Gaulle–Étoile

MUSÉE DU LOUVRE

▷ 90–93.

MUSÉE MARMOTTAN MONET

www.marmottan.com

It's a bit of a trek out to this museum in the leafy 16th *arrondissement* but you'll be rewarded with the world's largest collection of Monet paintings, and significant works by his contemporaries. The intimate setting in an elegant 19th-century town house makes a pleasant change from Paris's larger, more impersonal museums. And if the Impressionist works fail to satisfy your appetite, there are paintings and furniture from the Napoleonic period, as well as more than 300 illustrated pages from medieval and Renaissance manuscripts. It's a curious but compelling combination.

The main draw is the Monet collection, built up over the last 50 years from donations from the artist's son, Michel, and various other collectors. Many of the paintings are displayed in the purpose-built basement gallery, remarkably light and airy considering its underground location. Monet's *Impression—soleil levant* (c.1873) gave the Impressionist movement its name.

The museum takes its name from art historian Paul Marmottan, who left his house and collection of Empire paintings and furniture to the nation in 1932. The collection also includes paintings by Flemish, Italian and German primitives.

➕ Off map 70 A4 ✉ 2 rue Louis-Boilly, 75016 ☎ 01 44 96 50 33 🕐 Tue–Sun 11–6 (Wed until 9) 💶 Adult €9.50, child €5, under 8 free 🚇 La Muette (then a 10-minute walk; follow signs from the station) 🚌 22, 32, 52, 63 🚉 RER line C, Boulainvilliers 🛍 Gift shop/bookshop ♿ Wheelchair access to ground floor and basement only

MUSÉE DU LOUVRE

INFORMATION

www.louvre.fr

✚ 72 G4 ✉ 99 rue de Rivoli, 75001
☎ 01 40 20 50 50. Recorded information
in French and English: 01 40 20 53 17.
Auditorium: 01 40 20 55 55 🕐 Thu,
Sat–Mon 9–6, Wed, Fri 9am–10pm.
Closed Tue; some rooms closed in rotation
✋ Adult €9.50 (€6 after 6pm on Wed
and Fri), under 18 and EU nationals
(18–25) free. Tickets are valid all day,
so re-entry is allowed. Free first Sun of
month and 14 July. Temporary exhibitions
in the Hall Napoléon €11 🚇 Palais
Royal–Louvre 🚌 21, 24, 27, 39, 48,
69, 72, 81, 95 🚉 Châtelet-Les Halles
📖 Range of guidebooks on sale. Free
leaflet (in nine languages) available at
information desk to guide visitors around
the museum 🍴 Cafés and restaurants
📖 Large bookshop 🎫 A variety of
guided tours are available in English
and French, including *Visite-Découverte*
(Discovery Visits). Audiotours are available
in French, English, German, Spanish,
Italian and Japanese. Pick them up from
the entrances to the three wings of the
museum (€6)

INTRODUCTION

Charles V transformed Philippe-Auguste's 12th-century fortress on the Louvre
site into a medieval castle in the 14th century. The wily Renaissance king
François I ordered considerable rebuilding nearly two centuries later, and also
launched an art collection. During the Revolution, an art museum opened to
the public in the Grande Galerie. Napoleon celebrated his marriage to Marie-
Louise in the Louvre in 1810, and he set about creating a courtyard dominated
by the Arc du Carrousel and building a new wing. His victories overseas, and
the subsequent looting, added to the Louvre's stock. The 1980s and 1990s saw
extensive renovations to the galleries.

    The Louvre is one of the most famous art galleries in the world, with a vast
collection spanning thousands of years, from ancient civilizations to mid-
19th century European paintings. The main entrance is through I.M. Pei's
striking glass pyramid (1989) in the Cour Napoléon. Escalators take you to
a subterranean foyer, where you can pick up a museum plan. Don't be too
ambitious—there is no way you'll be able to see all 35,000 works on display in
one visit. If you don't know where to begin, you could take one of the *Visite-
Découverte* guided tours or rent an audioguide. When it's time for a break, the
museum has a choice of cafés and restaurants.

WHAT TO SEE
THE COLLECTIONS

The Louvre's collections divide into five parts: paintings, prints and drawings
from the 13th century to 1848 (for works after this date you need to go to the
Musée d'Orsay ▷ 93); medieval, Renaissance and modern sculpture; Islamic
art; decorative arts (jewellery, tapestries, ivories, bronzes, ceramics and furniture);
and oriental, Egyptian, Greek, Etruscan and Roman antiquities.

MONA LISA

When Leonardo da Vinci set up his easel in Florence in the early 16th century
to paint the *Mona Lisa*, little did he know he was creating what was to become

one of the world's most famous works of art. The diminutive painting, only 77cm (30in) tall and 53cm (20in) wide, is on the first floor of the Denon wing, surrounded by bullet-proof glass and a constant crowd of admirers. The identity of the woman is not known for certain, although she is believed to be the wife of Francesco del Giocondo, hence the portrait's other name, *La Gioconda*. Da Vinci painted the work between 1503 and 1506. François I obtained the painting soon after its completion. In 1911 an Italian stole the portrait, wanting to return it to its native Florence. It was recovered two years later, after a police hunt that won it worldwide fame.

VENUS DE MILO

The eternally serene *Venus de Milo* is the most famous of the Louvre's ancient Greek exhibits, discovered on the island of Melos in 1820. As Aphrodite, the goddess of love, she portrays the Greek image of perfect beauty. The marble statue was created around 100BC, during Greece's Hellenistic period, although its simple style harks back to Classical Greek sculpture.

THE EGYPTIAN COLLECTION

The Egyptian collection is the largest of its kind outside Egypt, containing 55,000 items, around 5,000 of which are on show. Don't miss the pink granite *Grand Sphinx*, part pharaoh, part lion, that once protected the corridors of a sacred shrine. Stylistic details suggest it could be more than 4,600 years old. The collections are presented thematically on the ground floor of the Sully wing, where topics include fishing, funerals, writing and jewellery. On the first floor the displays are chronological, starting with prehistory, tracing the rule of the pharaohs and ending just before the arrival of the Romans in 333BC. To see how Egyptian culture developed under Roman rule you can continue your tour in the lower floor of the Denon wing.

FRENCH HISTORICAL/ALLEGORICAL PAINTINGS

These vast paintings, on the first floor of the Denon wing, draw you into the action not only by their immense size but also the vivid detail. Look out for Delacroix's *Liberty Leading the People* (1830), where the presence of the allegorical figure of Liberty brings a sense of triumph to the destruction and chaos of the 1830 Uprising it portrays. David's neoclassical *The Coronation of Napoleon I* seems rather cold when set against the passion of Delacroix's work, although the detail is compelling. Almost 10m (33ft) wide, it was commissioned by the Emperor himself and completed in 1807.

TIPS
» The museum is least crowded first thing in the morning and during late-opening on Wednesdays and Fridays. Sunday is the busiest day.
» Remember the museum is closed on Tuesdays.
» The entrance fee is reduced after 6pm on Wednesdays and Fridays.
» To avoid queues, use a Paris Museum Pass or pre-book your ticket by phone or internet, through FNAC (tel 08 92 68 46 94; small commission charged) or at some department stores. This allows you to use the passage Richelieu entrance.
» Staff shortages mean that certain rooms are not open every day. If there are particular exhibits you want to see, check the website for the schedule of closures.
» Special tours are available for those with reduced mobility. Wheelchair loan is available on request. There is a special sculpture gallery for the blind. Ask for a leaflet at the information desk about disability access

Opposite *I.M. Pei's pyramid at the entrance to the Louvre museum*
Below left *Wandering past dramatic sculptures*
Below Mona Lisa, *by Leonardo da Vinci, is one of the must-see exhibits*

INFORMATION

www.musee-moyenage.fr

⊕ 72 H6 ✉ 6 place Paul-Painlevé,
rue du Sommerard, 75005 ☎ 01 53 73
78 16 🕐 Wed–Mon 9.15–5.45. Closed
public holidays 👆 Adult €8.50, 18–21
€6.50, under 18 and EU citizens (18–25)
free, free to all on first Sun of month
Ⓜ Cluny-La-Sorbonne 🚌 21, 27, 38, 63,
85, 86, 87, 96 🚇 RER line B, C St-Michel
📅 👆 Guided tours in English

TIPS

» Pick up a plan of the site at reception,
which highlights the key exhibits.
» You don't have to pay to enter the
Gothic courtyard off place Paul-Painlevé.
It's a calming spot to sit for a few minutes
and the turrets and gargoyles are worth
a look.
» After your visit, take a break in the
medieval gardens on the corner of
boulevards St-Michel and St-Germain.

Opposite *The Musée d'Orsay started life
as a belle-époque train station and the
ornate station clock still hangs in the
main hall*
Below *The facade of the Cluny Museum*

MUSÉE NATIONAL DU MOYEN ÂGE—THERMES DE CLUNY

Framed by the busy boulevards of Saint-Germain and Saint-Michel, the Cluny
Museum of the Middle Ages, in a 15th-century Gothic *hôtel* entered by a
handsome courtyard, is a good place to lose yourself for an hour or two in
contemplation of earlier, simpler times.

The name of the museum is slightly misleading as the collection begins in
antiquity and attached to the main building are the remains of a Gallo-Roman
frigidarium built between the first and third centuries. But the focus of the Cluny
is otherwise on exquisite Romanesque and Gothic art. The exhibits come from all
over Europe, from Saxony to Spain and England to Italy, and they are arranged
so that visitors can get close to them. The charm is often in the details that give
glimpses into everyday life hundreds of years ago.

Among the highlights of the museum are stained-glass windows, ivories,
altarpieces, Visigothic crowns, carved choir stalls, tapestries and embroideries,
and a surreal collection of stone heads knocked off 13th-century statues on
the west front of Notre-Dame by zealous Revolutionaries who thought they
represented French kings.

THE LADY AND THE UNICORN

Most visitors to the Cluny congregate in the circular room on the first floor
where a series of tapestries known as *La Dame à la Licorne* (The Lady and the
Unicorn) hang in a protective penumbra. The six tapestries were made in the
late 15th century and became famous after they were discovered in 1841 by
Prosper Mérimée in the Château de Boussac in the Creuse. Five of the pieces
depict the senses of touch, taste, smell, sight and hearing but the last stands
apart, being on a more inscrutable theme and dedicated to 'My Only Desire'. All
the tapestries are richly adorned with flowers and a variety of beasts, both real
and legendary, including the eponymous unicorn who, with the lady, makes an
appearance in each panel.

MUSÉE D'ORSAY

The collections here span 1848 to 1914, a crucial period in Western art that witnessed such giants as Monet, Renoir, Degas and Cézanne. Chronologically, the museum's collections fit neatly between those of the Louvre (▷ 90–91) and the Centre Georges Pompidou (▷ 78).

YOUR VISIT

Most people come to see the breathtaking Impressionist collection, which includes Monet's *Blue Waterlilies* (c.1916–19), Van Gogh's *The Church at Auvers-sur-Oise* (1890) and Renoir's *Ball at the Moulin de la Galette* (1876). But Impressionism forms less than a third of the vast display, which also includes sculpture, Symbolist and historical paintings, photography and art nouveau furniture. To see the works chronologically, start with the ground floor, then take the escalators to the Impressionist works on the upper floor, before finishing on the middle floor.

Even if your sole reason for visiting the museum is the Impressionist collection, don't leave without visiting the lavishly mirrored Salles des Fêtes (Room 51) or wandering through the central aisle on the ground floor, displaying 19th-century neoclassical sculpture. This is the best place to catch the feel of the building—part museum, part belle-époque train station—with its ornate clock and magnificent glass roof.

THE BUILDING

The imposing Orsay station and its accompanying hotel were built along the banks of the Seine in time for the Exposition Universelle in 1900. Victor Laloux designed the soaring glass and iron roof, together with the wildly ornate belle-époque restaurant and ballroom, all still intact. But in 1939 the advent of longer electric trains forced the station to close for long-distance travel (it was still used for suburban trains), less than 40 years after its completion. Public protest saved it from demolition, and approval was given to turn it into a museum in 1977. Italian architect Gae Aulenti masterminded the conversion of the interior, encasing both the walls and floors with stone, and President François Mitterrand opened the museum in December 1986.

INFORMATION

www.musee-orsay.fr
✚ 72 F4 ✉ 62 rue de Lille, 75007. Entrance on place de la Légion d'Honneur ☎ 01 40 49 48 14 🕓 Tue–Wed, Fri–Sun 9.30–6, Thu 9.30am–9.45pm. Last ticket 45 min before closing 🎫 Adult €9.50, 18–25 €7, under 18 and EU citizens (18–25) free, free to all on first Sun of month. Temporary exhibitions cost extra 🚇 Solférino 🚌 24, 63, 68, 73, 83, 84, 94 🚆 RER line C, Musée d'Orsay 🍴 On the middle level (11.45–2.45, 3.30–5.30; dinner 7–9.15 on Thu) ☕ Café des Hauteurs on upper level, with wonderful view of the old station clock; self-service café just above it 🛍 Gift shop and bookshop 🎧 Tours in English Tue–Sat 11.30 (€6.50). Audioguides (€5.50)

TIPS

» A Paris Museum Pass allows you to skip the queues, which can be long.
» Thursday evening is the quietest time to visit.
» The museum is closed on Mondays, unlike the Louvre and Centre Georges Pompidou, which close on Tuesdays.
» For more Impressionist paintings, visit the Musée Marmottan Monet (▷ 89).

MUSÉE PICASSO

www.musee-picasso.fr

The grand opening of this museum in 1985 put an end to 11 years of legal wrangling over Pablo Picasso's death duties. Thanks to a law allowing payment of these duties in the form of works of art, the French State received one quarter of Picasso's collection. The huge collection was enhanced even further after the death of his wife in 1990, and the museum now holds around 203 paintings, 158 sculptures, 16 collages and more than 1,500 drawings and prints. Also on display is Picasso's personal collection of works by his mentors and contemporaries, including Cézanne, Renoir, Miró, Braque and Matisse.

The museum is arranged chronologically, taking you on a journey from Picasso's early 1900s 'Blue' and 'Pink' periods through his years of Cubist experimentation with Braque and his classical period to the 1930s and beyond.

The collection is housed in the Hôtel Salé, a stunning 17th-century mansion in the heart of the Marais district, with a grand staircase, ornate chandeliers and beautiful old wooden doors. A small room dedicated to the history of the mansion displays black-and-white photographs and information about the building and its occupants over the years.

🚩 73 K4 ✉ Hôtel Salé, 5 rue de Thorigny, 75003 ☎ 01 42 71 25 21 🕐 Closed for renovations until 2012. Check website for opening hours after this time 🖐 Adult €7.70, under 18 free 🚇 St-Paul, Chemin Vert, St-Sébastien Froissart 🚌 29, 69, 75, 96 🎫 Guided tours: in French (1.5 hours), €6.50 per person 🍴 Summer café in the garden, open mid-Apr to mid-Oct 📚 Bookshop and gift shop

MUSÉE RODIN

www.musee-rodin.fr

This museum has soothing gardens, where you can wander past Rodin's sculptures or simply relax among the roses and admire the vibrant pink Rodin variety.

The Musée Rodin's open-air gallery, spread across nearly 3ha (7 acres) of beautifully landscaped gardens, makes a great escape from more intensive sightseeing. Once you've recharged your batteries strolling through the grounds, see more of Rodin's works in the airy 18th-century mansion where he once lived, the Hôtel Biron.

Outside in the sculpture garden, don't miss the brooding bronze *Le Penseur (The Thinker)*, supposedly representing the Italian poet Dante and originally placed outside the Panthéon, or the gruesome doorway *La Porte de l'Enfer (The Gates of Hell)*, inspired by Dante's *Divine Comedy*. *Les Bourgeois de Calais (The Burghers of Calais)* depicts six burghers who gave their lives to save their townsfolk during a siege by the English in the 14th century, while *Balzac* is, to some eyes, a rather unflattering portrayal of the writer in his dressing gown. There are few information boards, so rent an audioguide or pick up a free leaflet from the Hôtel Biron.

Inside the elegant rococo mansion, you can follow Rodin's artistic evolution chronologically, from his early academic sketches and paintings to his vigorous watercolours. The highlight is the passionate white marble *Le Baiser (The Kiss)*. There are also works by Rodin's contemporaries, including Camille Claudel, Renoir, Van Gogh and Monet.

🚩 71 D5 ✉ 77 rue de Varenne, 75007 ☎ 01 44 18 61 10 🕐 Tue–Sun 10–5.45. Later on Wed for some temporary exhibitions. Gardens open until 6 🖐 Adult €6, under 18 free. Garden only: €1 🚇 Varenne 🚌 69, 82, 87, 92 🚉 RER line C, Invalides 🍴 Garden café 📚 Book/gift shop 🎧 Audiotours €5. Guided tours once a week

Above left *The Musée Picasso*
Above right *Works at the Musée Rodin trace the evolution of the artist's work*

NOTRE-DAME

Notre-Dame is as famous a symbol of Paris as the Eiffel Tower and around 10 million people enter its doors each year. The crowds are smallest in the early morning, when the cathedral is also at its brightest. Save some time for wandering around the outside to admire the architecture, including the flying buttresses. One of the best views is from the Seine, on a boat trip that circles the Île de la Cité (▷ 83). Finally, if your legs will agree to it, there are wonderful views from the top of the 69m (226ft) towers.

HIGHLIGHTS INSIDE THE CATHEDRAL

The south rose window, in the transept, is especially glorious when the sun shines through, adding extra vibrancy to the purple hues. Christ stands in the heart of the 13m (42ft) diameter window, encircled by angels, apostles, martyrs and scenes from the New Testament. The intricately carved and painted choir screen, created in the 14th century and restored in the 1960s, has enchanting depictions of Gospel scenes. In contrast, the bronze altar at the heart of the cathedral is strikingly modern. It depicts the four evangelists, Matthew, Mark, Luke and John, as well as Old Testament prophets.

OUTSIDE AND UP THE TOWERS

The symmetrical west front is packed with statues and sculptures, originally painted and intended as a Bible for the illiterate. It's a tough climb, but it's well worth tackling the 69m (226ft) towers for views over Paris and a closer look at the grotesque gargoyles.

MORE THAN 800 YEARS OLD

Notre-Dame owes its existence to the 12th-century bishop Maurice de Sully, who decided that Paris needed its own cathedral. Pope Alexander III laid the foundation stone in 1163 and the choir was built in just under 20 years. Guilds of carpenters, stone-carvers, iron forgers and glass craftsmen worked on the grand project but it took almost 200 years to complete the building, which was finally ready in 1345.

By the time Napoleon I was crowned in the cathedral in 1804 the building was in a state of disrepair. Victor Hugo, author of *The Hunchback of Notre-Dame*, campaigned fervently for its restoration.

INFORMATION

www.monuments-nationaux.fr
www.notredameparis.fr

Cathedral

✚ 73 H5 ✉ place du Parvis Notre-Dame, 75004 ☎ 01 42 34 56 10 🕐 Mon–Fri 7.45–6.45, Sat–Sun 7.45–7.15 💷 Free 🚇 Cité, St-Michel, Châtelet 🚌 21, 24, 38, 47, 85, 96 🚆 RER lines B, C, St-Michel 🏛 In the cathedral and up the tower 🚻 Guided tours: French, English, Spanish and Russian by reservation only, tel 01 44 54 19 30 ❓ Organ recitals at 4.30pm on Sun

Towers

🕐 Jun–Aug Mon–Fri 10–6.30, Sat–Sun 10–11; Apr–May, Sep daily 10–6.30; Oct–Mar daily 10–5. Last admission 45 min before closing 💷 Adult €8, under 18 and EU nationals (18–25) free

TIP

» Try to visit just before a service, when you feel a sense of anticipation as lights are gradually turned on and people gather to worship.

Below *Notre-Dame at night, bathed in floodlights*

OPÉRA PALAIS GARNIER

www.operadeparis.fr

The sumptuous Opéra Palais Garnier was the largest theatre in the world when it opened in 1875. Charles Garnier beat 171 hopefuls in the competition to design the building. The stage can accommodate up to 450 performers and the opulent auditorium holds around 2,200 spectators under a domed ceiling painted by Marc Chagall in 1964. Even if you don't see one of the ballets staged here, take a look at the splendid marble and gilt Grand Staircase. Outside, notice Carrier-Belleuse's lamp-bearing statues and a copy of Carpeaux's sculpted group *La Danse*, to the right of the front arcade. A small museum explains the history of the Opéra house.

🚇 71 F1 ✉ place de l'Opéra, 75009 ☎ 0892 89 90 90 for all information 🕐 Daily 10–5. Closed during matinées; auditorium closed during rehearsals ✋ Adult €9, under 25 €5, under 10 free 🚇 Opéra 🚌 21, 22, 27, 29, 42, 53, 66, 68, 81, 95 🎧 Guided tours: adult €12,students (10–19) €9, child (under 10) €6

PALAIS DE CHAILLOT

www.theatre-chaillot.fr
www.musee-marine.fr
www.museedelhomme.fr

There are breathtaking views across the Seine to the Eiffel Tower from the terrace of the Palais de Chaillot. The colonnaded palace was built for the Exposition Universelle of 1937. Its curved wings are dotted with gleaming bronze statues, and its wide terraces overlook the fountains of the Jardins du Trocadéro. The palace houses the Théâtre National de Chaillot, the Musée National de la Marine and the Musée de l'Homme.

🚇 70 A3 ✉ 17 place du Trocadéro et du 11 Novembre, 75016 🚇 Trocadéro 🚌 22, 30, 32, 63, 72, 82

PANTHÉON

www.monuments-nationaux.fr

Originally a basilica, this striking monument is now the final resting place of some of France's greatest citizens. The neoclassical grandeur of the Panthéon is an arresting sight after you have wandered through the warren-like streets of the Latin Quarter to reach it.

The colossal mausoleum contains the tombs of many illustrious citizens, including writers Victor Hugo, Émile Zola and Voltaire, scientists Marie and Pierre Curie, Braille inventor Louis Braille, and World War II Resistance martyr Jean Moulin. Arguments still ignite periodically about who merits the honour of being buried here. The monument was commissioned by Louis XV as a basilica dedicated to St. Geneviève, patron saint of Paris, in thanks for his recovery from gout. The king laid the foundation stone in 1764 and work finally finished in 1790, by which time the original architect, Soufflot, had died. Only a year later, in 1791, the Revolutionaries seized the building, bricking up the windows and changing its function to a secular Temple of Fame.

You enter the building through an imposing columned area (peristyle), based on the grandiose frontage of Rome's Pantheon. Inside, the cross-shaped chamber feels austere.

To climb to the circular colonnade beneath the dome you must take a guided tour (and tackle 206 steps). But you'll be rewarded with panoramic views of the city from 35m (115ft) up. Downstairs in the huge, shadowy crypt you can see the tombs of Jean-Jacques Rousseau, Voltaire, Victor Hugo, Émile Zola, Marie Curie and others.

🚇 72 H6 ✉ place du Panthéon, 75005 ☎ 01 44 32 18 00 🕐 Apr–Sep daily 10–6.30; Oct–Mar 10–6. Last admission 45 minutes before closing ✋ Adult €8, 18–25 €5, under 18 and EU nationals free

🚇 Cardinal-Lemoine 🚌 21, 27, 84, 85, 89 🚊 RER B, Luxembourg 📚 Small bookshop/gift shop 🎧 Guided tours by reservation only. For tours in French, English, Spanish and Russian tel 01 44 54 19 30

PARC DE LA VILLETTE

▷ 97.

PLACE DE LA BASTILLE

Frenetic place de la Bastille, now bustling with street cafés and traffic, witnessed one of the pivotal events in France's history. Where in-line skaters and pedestrians now jostle for space, a Revolutionary mob stormed the Bastille prison in 1789 in a violent riot that signalled the start of the French Revolution.

The Bastille was built in 1380 as a fortress guarding the eastern entrance to Paris. It later became a jail for political prisoners. Nothing remains of the building, although paving stones mark its outline. A visual reminder of Paris's turbulent past is the Colonne de Juillet (July Column), which stands 50m (164ft) tall on place de la Bastille's busy roundabout. The ornate column was constructed in 1840 to commemorate victims of another revolt, the 1830 uprising, and is topped by the winged *Spirit of Liberty*.

Bastille has been spruced up and is now a lively nightspot, with bars and restaurants. During the day you can shop in the streets that radiate from the Colonne de Juillet. There is also a marina, galleries and the ultramodern Opéra Bastille, designed by Carlos Ott. Walk along the rue de Lyon and you'll arrive at the Viaduc des Arts, a railway viaduct converted into craft workshops and showrooms (9–129 avenue Daumesnil).

To escape the noise and traffic of the Bastille, head down rue St-Antoine, then turn right into the peaceful rue de Birague. Here, browse in the shops, then walk back in time through an archway to place des Vosges (▷ 98).

🚇 73 F5 ✉ place de la Bastille, 75004/75012 🚇 Bastille 🚌 20, 29, 65, 69, 76, 86, 87, 91 🍴 A good selection of cafés and restaurants

PARC DE LA VILLETTE

This ultramodern park, formerly the city abattoirs, was transformed in the 1980s into 55ha (136 acres) of water features, themed gardens, children's playgrounds and cultural venues. The site, northeast of central Paris, is dotted with trademark red metal follies and the Canal de l'Ourcq runs through the middle. The renovated former cattle hall, La Grande Halle, is now used for trade fairs, exhibitions and concerts and the Zénith concert hall, seating more than 6,000, hosts pop and rock events.

A covered walkway links the two main cultural venues at either end of the park, the Cité des Sciences et de l'Industrie to the north and the Cité de la Musique to the south.

CITÉ DES SCIENCES ET DE L'INDUSTRIE

The futuristic Cité des Sciences et de l'Industrie is a giant science and technology museum, packed with interactive displays. Highlights include the Explora exhibition, on levels 1 and 2, which has five main themes: The Universe, Water and the Earth, Challenges of the Living World, Industry and Communication. There is a planetarium (level 2) and the excellent Cité des Enfants, for three- to twelve-year-olds. The spherical Géode cinema is just south of the Cité des Sciences. This 400-seater cinema has a 1,000sq m (10,765sq ft) hemispherical screen, producing images that are 10 times larger than in a normal cinema.

CITÉ DE LA MUSIQUE

The Cité de la Musique opened in 1995 and is home to a concert hall, the Conservatoire National Supérieur de Musique de Paris and the Musée de la Musique. The museum covers music from the Middle Ages to the present day, including the music of cultures throughout the world. The Cité de la Musique also regularly hosts exhibitions.

INFORMATION

www.cite-sciences.fr
www.lageode.fr
www.cite-musique.fr

Cité des Sciences et de l'Industrie

Off map 73 K2 30 avenue Corentin-Cariou, 75019 01 40 05 80 00 General opening: Tue–Sat 9.30–6, Sun 9.30–9. Explora: Tue–Sat 10–6, Sun 10–7. Planetarium: Tue–Sun, shows every hour from 11–5 (except 1pm) Explora: adult €8, child €6, under 6 free. Planetarium: adult €3 plus admission to Explora, under 6 free Porte de la Villette 75, 152, PC2, PC3

Cité de la Musique

Off map 73 K2 221 avenue Jean-Jaurès, 75019 01 44 84 44 84 (information and reservations) Museum: adult €8, under 18 free Tue–Sat 12–6, Sun 10–6 (concert times vary) Porte de Pantin 75, 151, PC2, PC3

Above *Modern sculpture in the Parc de la Villette*
Opposite *The entrance to the Panthéon*

PLACE DE LA CONCORDE

Paris's largest square boasts the city's oldest monument and wonderful views of the Arc de Triomphe (▷ 77), the ornate gates of the Jardin des Tuileries (▷ 87), and across the river to the Assemblée Nationale and Eiffel Tower (▷ 100–101). In the Revolution, it witnessed the execution of more than 1,300 people.

The square, originally called place Louis XV, was designed by architect Jacques-Ange Gabriel and laid out between 1755 and 1775 to surround an equestrian statue of the king. During the Revolution it was renamed place de la Révolution, the statue of Louis XV was removed and the guillotine erected in its stead. With the cooling of Revolutionary passions, the square was renamed place de la Concorde, in the hope of a less troubled future. Coustou's magnificent *Chevaux de Marly* were added to the entrance of the Champs-Élysées (the horses you see today are replicas, the orginals are now in the Louvre).

The 230-tonne pink granite obelisk at the centre of the square is around 3,300 years old. It was presented to France by Mohammed Ali, Viceroy of Egypt, in 1883.

✚ 71 E3 ✉ place de la Concorde, 75008 Ⓜ Free Ⓠ Concorde 🚌 24, 42, 72, 73, 84, 94

PLACE DES VOSGES

Picturesque place des Vosges is only minutes from the busy Bastille district but a world away in character. Its charming arcades shelter galleries, boutiques and cafés where you can listen to the street musicians.

The square consists of a formal garden, with trees, a play area and a statue of Louis XIII, surrounded by 36 red-brick and stone-faced houses. The north and south facades each have a larger, central house, respectively the *Pavillon de la Reine* (Queen's Pavilion) and the *Pavillon du Roi* (King's Pavilion).

Place des Vosges was one of the first examples of town planning in Paris, when it was commissioned by Henri IV. It opened in 1612 amid

spectacular celebrations, under the name place Royale. In 1800, it was renamed place des Vosges in tribute to the first French *département* to pay its new taxes.

Princesses, duchesses, official mistresses, Cardinal Richelieu, the Duc de Sully, the writer Alphonse Daudet and, more recently, the painter Francis Bacon and the architect Richard Rogers have all lived here. Victor Hugo's home from 1832 to 1848 at No. 6 is now a museum.

✚ 73 K4 ✉ place des Vosges, 75004 Ⓠ Bastille, St-Paul, Chemin Vert 🚌 29, 96

QUARTIER LATIN

The Latin Quarter's picturesque side streets evoke the Middle Ages, while students give the area a refreshing vibrancy. No other district of Paris claims so many bookshops or colleges, and there are cinemas, jazz clubs, restaurants and historic churches. You'll find a relaxed and youthful atmosphere; the cliché of students and artists lingering for hours in cafés is actually true.

If you're arriving from the Right Bank or Île de la Cité, your first taste of the Latin Quarter is likely to be the chaotic place St-Michel, with its imposing fountain symbolizing St. Michael slaying a dragon. The busy boulevard St-Michel runs from here along the length of the district. Unless you want to browse in its clothes stores and bookshops it is best to venture into the winding, historic side streets.

Sights worth seeing include the mighty Panthéon (▷ 96) and the Musée National du Moyen Âge (▷ 92). The flower-filled Jardin du Luxembourg (▷ 86) is the perfect place to rest your aching feet.

The Latin Quarter is Paris's intellectual heart, a title it has held since the Middle Ages. It owes its scholarly, literary and artistic reputation to the founding of the Sorbonne University in the 13th century. Other colleges soon grew up around it and the area gained the new name of 'Latin Quarter', after the language used by the students.

✚ 73 H6 ✉ On the Left Bank, between Carrefour de l'Odéon and Jardin des Plantes, 75005 Ⓠ St-Michel, Cluny-La Sorbonne, Odéon 🚌 21, 24, 27, 38, 63, 84, 85, 86, 87, 89 🚊 RER line B, C, St-Michel-Notre-Dame 🍴 A wide selection of restaurants and cafés 🏬 Clothes stores and bookshops, including Shakespeare & Co (▷ 106)

SACRÉ-CŒUR
▷ 99.

SAINTE-CHAPELLE

www.monuments-nationaux.fr
Stunning stained-glass windows turn this 13th-century royal chapel into a shimmering jewel. The rays of blue, red and golden light streaming through the windows of Sainte-Chapelle seem out of this world. The chapel was commissioned by Louis IX (St. Louis) to house holy relics and to promote the king's authority as a divinely appointed leader. It was constructed within the royal palace complex (now the Palais de Justice). Fifteen windows, up to 15m (49ft) tall, and a glorious rose window depict more than 1,100 biblical scenes, from the Creation to the Apocalypse. The only downside is the crowds, which can detract from an awe-inspiring experience.

Before reaching the brilliance of the upper chapel you walk through the dark lower chapel, dedicated to the Virgin Mary. When you step into the upper chapel you are hit by colour from all directions, not only from the glorious windows but also from the patterned floor, the golden columns and the painted lower walls. Two thirds of the windows are 13th-century originals, the oldest stained glass in Paris. The panels start with Genesis in the window on the left as you enter and work round clockwise.

✚ 72 H5 ✉ 4 boulevard du Palais, Île de la Cité, 75001 ☎ 01 53 40 60 97 Ⓒ Mar–Oct Mon–Fri 9.30–12, 2–6, Sat–Sun 9.30–6; Nov–Feb Mon–Fri 9–12, 2–5, Sat–Sun 9–5 Ⓜ Adult €8, 18–25 €5, under 18 and EU nationals (18–25) free Ⓠ Cité, Châtelet 🚌 21, 27, 38, 85, 96 🚊 RER line B, C, St-Michel-Notre-Dame 🏬 🎧 Guided tours: by reservation only. For tours in French, English, Spanish and Russian tel 01 44 54 19 30

SACRÉ-CŒUR

The mighty Sacré-Cœur basilica is one of Paris's most prominent landmarks, shimmering at the top of Montmartre's hill. Its eastern-inspired dome is the second-highest point in the city and the views from the top stretch as far as 50km (30 miles). This sweeping panorama is the main attraction for many visitors. But walk into the hushed interior, especially during Mass, and it is an altogether more spiritual experience.

ATONEMENT

Sacré-Cœur was commissioned as atonement for the 58,000 people who died in the Franco-Prussian war of 1870–71 and the bloody events of the Commune. Citizens from across France donated the funds and the first stone was laid in 1875. Various problems hampered the project and the basilica was not completed until 1914. Then World War I intervened, and Parisians had to wait until 1919 for the consecration.

More than 140 years after the vow to build Sacré-Cœur, a team of priests still works in relays to maintain constant prayer for forgiveness for the horrors of war.

THE INTERIOR

Bronze equestrian statues of Joan of Arc and St. Louis guard the entrance to the basilica. A stone statue of Christ stands high above them, in an arched recess. Inside, the striking golden mosaic over the choir is one of the largest of its kind, covering 475sq m (5,113sq ft). Christ stands in the middle, with outstretched arms and a golden heart. The Virgin Mary, Joan of Arc, St. Michael, the Pope and a figure representing France are among those immediately surrounding him. God the Father and the Holy Spirit are represented on the ceiling.

INFORMATION

www.sacre-coeur-montmartre.com

✚ Off map 73 K2 ✉ place du Parvis du Sacré-Cœur ☎ 01 53 41 89 00
🕐 Basilica: daily 6am–10.30pm. Dome: Apr–Sep 9–7; Oct–Mar 9–6 💶 Basilica: free. Dome and crypt: €5 🚇 Anvers or Abbesses, then walk to base of funicular
🚌 Montmartrobus. Routes 30, 31, 80 and 85 pass the bottom of this hill where you can walk or catch the funicular.
🏪 Small bookshop/gift shop

TIP

» You'll get great views over Paris from the front terrace.
» If you have the time (and energy), it is worth climbing the dome for another panorama.
» The best view of the basilica itself is from below, in place St-Pierre.

Below *Sacre-Cœur basilica crowns the top of Montmartre*

REGIONS PARIS AND THE ÎLE DE FRANCE • SIGHTS

99

TOUR EIFFEL

The sleek iron silhouette of the Eiffel Tower, rising 324m (1,063ft) high, finds its way into many of the city's best views. Gustave Eiffel's extraordinary construction is a feat of late 19th-century engineering, weighing more than 10,000 tonnes and made up of 18,000 iron parts. It was a controversial addition to the city skyline in 1889 and was intended to last only 20 years. More than a century on, it has clocked up 200 million visitors.

VISITING THE TOWER

The view is the reason for climbing the Eiffel Tower, whether to take in the magnificent sweep across the city or to test your nerves peering down 120m (395ft) through the glass window on the floor of level 2. From the viewing gallery on level 3 you can see up to 75km (46 miles) on a clear day. If the vertigo-inducing top level is too much for you, the panoramas are equally stunning on level 2, where you can see the city in more detail. There is also a viewing gallery on level 1, with information boards.

The views are often at their best in the run-up to sunset, when the light is kinder to cameras. At night, a totally different picture unfolds, as hundreds of thousands of lights sketch out the city.

Once you have soaked up the view, you can learn more about the history of the tower from the short film shown at Cineiffel (level 1). Other attractions on the first floor include the Observatory, where you can monitor the sway at the top of the tower (measured at 9cm/3.5in during the storms of 1999), and the Feroscope, focusing on all things iron. You can also see the original hydraulic lift pump and a piece of the original spiral staircase, used by Monsieur Eiffel himself. If you want to boast of your whereabouts to your friends back home, you can ask to have your postcards franked with 'Tour Eiffel' at the post office on level 1 (daily 10–7.30).

CONSTRUCTION

Construction of the unconventional monument took only two years, finishing just in time for the Exposition Universelle of 1889. For 40 years the tower basked in the glory of being the highest structure in the world until New York's Chrysler Building usurped the title. It gained another 20m (66ft) in 1957 when television antennae were added.

INFORMATION

www.tour-eiffel.fr

➕ 70 B4 ✉ quai Branly, Champs de Mars, 75007 ☎ 0892 70 12 39 🕐 Mid-Jun to Aug daily 9am–midnight; Sep to mid-Jun 9.30am–11pm (stairs close at 6.30) 🛗 By elevator: level 1 adult €4.50, level 2 €8.10, level 3 €13.50, child (12–24) level 1 €3.50, level 2 €6.50, level 3 €11.50, child (3–11) level 1 €3, level 2 €4, level 3 €9. Stairs to levels 1 and 2 €3 all ages 🚇 Bir-Hakeim 🚌 42, 69, 72, 82, 87 🚆 RER line C, Champs-de-Mars/Tour Eiffel 🍴 58 Tour Eiffel on level 1, Jules Verne on level 2 ☕ Snack bars on ground floor, level 1 and level 2 🛍 Gift shops on levels 1 and 2. Post office on level 1 🎫 Visitex Autremont run guided tours. Prices start at €14.50. Tel 0825 05 44 03 or go to www.visitez-autrement.net to make a booking

TIP

» Reserve well ahead if you want to splash out at the plush Jules Verne restaurant on level 2.

Opposite *Looking across the Jardins du Trocadéro to the Eiffel Tower*
Below left *A view of the ironwork from underneath the tower*
Below *Souvenirs of Paris's most famous sight*

INFORMATION

www.chateauversailles.fr

✚ 465 J5 ✉ Versailles, 78000

☎ 01 30 83 78 00 ♿ Grands
Appartements: Apr–Oct Tue–Sun
9–6.30; Nov–Mar 9–5.30. Grand Trianon:
Apr–Oct daily 12–6.30; Nov–Mar 12–5.30.
Gardens: Apr–Oct daily 8am–8.30pm;
Nov–Mar 8–6. Fountains: early Apr–Oct
Sat–Sun 11–12, 3.30–5, (also other
occasional days). Park: daily 8 or 9–dusk

💷 Adult: State Apartments €15; Gardens
Apr–Oct €3, Nov–Mar free, €10 when
fountain show is on; Grand Trianon and
Petit Trianon €10; Passeport (combined
train travel and entrance ticket), Apr–Oct
€25; Nov–Mar €18, under 18 and EU
nationals (18–25) free. Nov–Mar free
most areas on first Sun of the month

🚆 RER line C to Versailles Rive-Gauche;
mainline train from Gare Montparnasse to
Versailles Chantiers; mainline train from
Gare St-Lazare to Versailles Rive Droite

🚌 Autoroute A13 to the Château de
Versailles exit, then follow signs 🍴 🛍

INTRODUCTION

More like a town than a mere palace, the Château de Versailles was the seat of
French power for more than 100 years, a self-contained world where members
of the royal family could be kept safely cushioned from their subjects in Paris,
20km (12.5 miles) away.

Versailles had relatively humble beginnings as a hunting lodge built for Louis
XIII in a deserted swamp. In 1661, Louis XIV decided to move his court here as
an astute way of isolating the nobility and his ministers while keeping an eye
on his not-too-distant capital. It was an ambitious project symbolic of the king's
absolute power—'Louis XIV took pleasure in subduing nature', as the Duc de
Saint-Simon put it—and building work continued right up to the Sun King's
death in 1715. The project put a severe strain on France's finances but the result
was the largest palace in Europe which awed both aristocracy and common
people with its extent and finery, and became a template for megalomaniac
monarchs everywhere. At its height, the court of Versailles consisted of around
20,000 people including statesmen, sycophants and schemers, royal mistresses
and an enormous retinue of staff at the beck and call of the actual and would-be
aristocrats who orbited around the king.

Versailles remained the seat of power of the French monarchy until 1789,
when the States General convened here and demanded a constitution. Louis
XVI's refusal to grant this led to the Revolution and in October the king was
ignominiously seized from his palace by a mob and forced to return to Paris,
ultimately to be deposed and executed.

A visit to Versailles can be divided into three parts: the palace itself, its
gardens and the park which includes the Domaine de Marie Antoinette. Rather
than trying to see everything a better policy is to limit yourself to a tour of the
Grands Appartements (State Apartments) and a stroll in the fountain-filled
gardens. To see all the buildings and rooms at Versailles would take two days.

WHAT TO SEE
THE PALACE
The State Apartments are on the first floor and are arranged around the Marble Courtyard, named after its marble paving. The chateau's masterpiece is the Galerie des Glaces (Hall of Mirrors) designed by Jules Hardouin-Mansart which is 73m (272ft) long, 10.5m (34ft) wide, and 12.3m (40ft) high. At opposing ends of it are the Salon of War and the Salon of Peace. Symbolically, the Treaty of Versailles was ratified here in 1919, ending World War I. Along the outer wall 17 windows give spectacular views over the gardens and fill the room with light in the afternoon. They are matched on the opposite wall by 17 large mirrors. On the ceiling are portraits of a triumphant Louis XIV.

Next to the Hall of Mirrors is the king's bedroom, placed at the exact centre of the palace and oriented towards the rising sun. It is connected to the queen's bedroom by the antechamber known as l'Oeil-de-Boeuf (Bull's Eye), where courtiers attended upon the king's ceremonial getting out of and going to bed.

Many rooms are on the theme of Greek deities. They include the Salon de Venus and the Salon d'Apollon (used as a throne room), which is dedicated to the god Apollo. In Europe, by the 17th century, Apollo had become equated with the sun god Helios, guarantor of world order, and Louis saw himself as his equivalent on earth, the Sun King.

Other parts of the palace worth seeing are the chapel, decked out in marble, and the opera house added to Versailles in 1770.

THE GROUNDS
The park was laid out by the king's preferred landscape architect, André Le Nôtre, and its various components make up the largest palace grounds in Europe. Closest to the palace are the formal French gardens laid out in geometric patterns, which are famous for their fountains. These are not always in motion and to catch them in full flow it's best to visit during one of the *Grandes Eaux Musicales* (weekends from April to September).

Beyond the gardens is the park where Louis XIV sailed a flotilla of ships and gondolas on the 1.6km (1-mile) Grand Canal. One large corner of the park, the Domaine de Marie-Antoinette, was, as it's name makes clear, reserved for the private pleasures of the queen. Two lesser palaces stand here, the Grand Trianon and the smaller Petit Trianon. The latter was built by Louis XV for Madame de Pompadour but she didn't live to see it completed.

Some way beyond the Trianons is a small lake besides which stand the surviving buildings of a hamlet built by Marie-Antoinette to provide rustic amusements for herself and her friends. The hamlet's farm supplied produce to Versailles' kitchens.

TIPS
» The busiest days at Versailles are Tuesdays, Sundays and holiday weekends. The palace is closed on Mondays.
» A Paris Museum Pass allows you to avoid some of the queues.

REGIONS PARIS AND THE ÎLE DE FRANCE • SIGHTS

Left *The palace of Versailles in all its glory*
Opposite *The Hall of Mirrors at Versailles, designed by Jules Hardouin-Mansart*

MONTMARTRE

There is so much more to Montmartre than the towering Sacré-Cœur basilica, impressive though this is. This walk shows you the lesser-known side of Paris's historic hilltop village, with its picturesque cottages, cobbled streets and panoramic views.

THE WALK

Distance: 3km (2 miles)
Allow: 2 hours
Start at: place Blanche
End at: place des Abbesses

HOW TO GET THERE

🚇 Blanche 🚌 30, 54, 68, 74

★ Starting from place Blanche, walk west along boulevard de Clichy, past the Moulin Rouge on your right.

❶ When the Moulin Rouge opened its doors in 1889, its cancan dancers were an immediate hit. The venue still stages cabaret shows.

From boulevard de Clichy turn right into avenue Rachel and continue to Cimetière de Montmartre.

❷ In the cemetery you can seek out the tombs of the writer Stendhal, composer Hector Berlioz and saxophone inventor Adolphe Sax.

Leave the cemetery the way you came in, at avenue Rachel, and then go up the steps on the right to rue Caulaincourt. Turn right onto this road and, at the end of the flyover, turn right along rue Joseph de Mastre. After a short way, turn sharp left up the steep and curving rue Lepic. Van Gogh lived at No. 54 from 1886 to 1888. Follow the curve, passing the Moulin de la Galette on the left.

❸ The Moulin de la Galette became a dance hall in the 19th century and inspired Renoir's painting *Le Bal au Moulin de la Galette*.

Turn left into rue Giardon, cross over avenue Junot/rue Novins and walk downhill to square Suzanne-Buisson, a gated garden on your left.

❹ The garden is named after a World War II heroine. The macabre statue is of the third-century bishop

St. Denis, who was beheaded by the Romans. Legend has it that he picked up his head and washed off the blood in a fountain here.

Walk through the garden and turn right just after the statue to take you down steps to place Casadesus. Climb the steps to your right into allée des Brouillards, a footpath named after 18th-century Château des Brouillards ('Mansion in the Mists') which stands back from it. The painter Pierre-Auguste Renoir lived in the château for a time in the 1890s and in another of the houses on the *allée* after that. At the end of Brouillards, cross place Dalida and up cobbled rue de l'Abreuvoir.

The road takes its name from the watering trough *(l'abreuvoir)* that stood at No. 15. No. 14 attracted many of the area's artists when it was the Café de l'Abreuvoir, while No. 12 was home to Camille Pissarro from

REGIONS PARIS AND THE ÎLE DE FRANCE • WALK

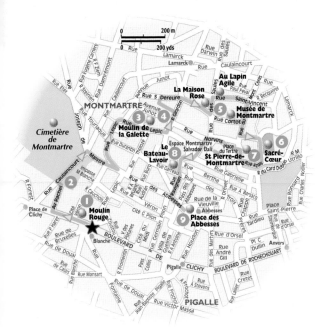

the corner into tree-shaded place Émile Goudeau.

8 On the right of place Émile Groudeau, look for Bâteau-Lavoir, where Picasso and Braque had studios and where Cubism was born. The original building burned down in 1970.

Leave the square by the small flight of steps at the bottom to continue down rue Ravignan. At the end, turn left into rue des Abbesses and from there to place des Abbesses.

9 In place des Abbesses take a look at the magnificent art nouveau Métro entrance and the unusual facade of the church of St-Jean-l'Évangéliste (1904), nicknamed St-Jean-des-Briques for its red bricks.

WHEN TO GO
During the day is best, as parts of Montmartre can be seedy at night.

WHERE TO EAT
Avoid the touristy restaurants in and around place du Tertre. There are quieter restaurants on rue Lepic but more choice on boulevard de Clichy and around place des Abbesses. La Maison Rose, on the route, has a modest menu.

PLACES TO VISIT
JARDIN SAUVAGE SAINT-VINCENT
www.paris.fr
✉ rue Saint-Vincent ☎ 01 71 28 50 56
🕐 Jul–Oct some Weds and Suns 💷 Free

MUSÉE DE MONTMARTRE
www.museedemontmartre.fr
✉ 12 rue Cortot, 76018 Paris ☎ 01 49 25 89 37 🕐 Jul–Aug Tue–Thu 11–6, Fri–Sun 11–7; Sep–Jun Tue–Sun 11–6 💷 Adult €8, child (12–25) €6

TIP
» For the classic view of Sacré-Cœur from below head down rue Yvonne le Tac from place des Abbesses, then rue Tardieu, past the funicular base station, to the bottom of square Louis Michel.

1888 to 1892. La Maison Rose is a good lunch stop.

Turn left at the corner after La Maison Rose and walk down the steep street past Montmartre's last bit of surviving vineyard. Turn right at the legendary cabaret Au Lapin Agile, and walk along rue Saint-Vincent. Next to the vineyard is a preserved woodland, the Jardin Sauvage Saint-Vincent (weekends only), which provides a glimpse of wilderness within the city.

Turn right up rue du Mont Cenis, once home to Hector Berlioz (No. 22). Four flights of steps take you up to the summit of Montmartre on which stands a bright white watertower with a small garden.

5 A short detour down the street opposite takes you to the Musée de Montmartre , the oldest house on the hill. The displays cover Montmartre's growth.

Continue on rue du Mont Cernis to the touristy part of Montmartre. Turn left down rue du Chevalier de la Barre and run the gauntlet of souvenir shops and portrait painters. Turn right along Cardinal Guibert, to reach Sacré-Cœur (▷ 99).

6 The neo-Byzantine basilica was commissioned as atonement for the 58,000 victims of the Franco-Prussian war (1870–71).

Turn right along rue Azaïs, with its views over the city. Turn right up rue St-Eleuthère to the church of St-Pierre-de-Montmartre on place Jean Marais.

7 Humbler than Sacré-Cœur, St-Pierre-de-Montmartre has a peaceful atmosphere. The church was originally part of the 12th-century abbey of Montmartre.

Leave place Jean Marais opposite the church and you immediately arrive at busy place du Tertre. Keep going in the same direction down rue Norvins. When you see a squat, ornate stone building (a former water cistern with a Renaissance fountain), turn left along the triangular place Jean-Baptiste Clément to reach rue Ravignan at the bottom. Turn right on this street and follow it round

Opposite *An ivy-clad house in Montmartre*

THE LITERARY LEFT BANK

Paris has always been a city to inspire writers and they have left their biographical and fictional traces everywhere. This walk links locations connected to writers in the Latin Quarter and St-Germain-des-Prés, and ends with a choice of three classic literary cafés.

THE WALK
Distance: 4km (2.5 miles)
Allow: Half a day, longer if you want to browse for books or linger in cafés
Start at: Notre-Dame
End at: place de St-Germain-des-Prés

HOW TO GET THERE
RER St-Michel-Notre-Dame

★ Start from the square in front of the cathedral of Notre-Dame.

❶ Notre-Dame was described by Victor Hugo in his 1831 novel *The Hunchback of Notre Dame*, the success of which shamed the city of Paris into taking more care of its famous monument.

Facing the cathedral, turn right and walk across Pont au Double. Cross the busy quai de Montebello, turn right and walk beside the gardens in front of the church of St-Julien-le-

Pauvre to reach rue de la Bûcherie, a street too short to be marked on many maps.

❷ If literary Paris had a spiritual home—at least for readers and writers of English—it has to be Shakespeare & Co bookshop. Opened by an American expat, George Whitman, in 1951 and run to his utopian ideals, it is an eccentric and welcoming place.

Walk to the end of the street and turn left up rue du Petit Pont. Across the road long gargoyles extend from St-Séverin over a narrow street. Turn left along the boulevard St-Germain and continue to place Maubert where there is a colourful street market each Tuesday, Thursday and Saturday. Turn right up rue des Carmes, which becomes rue Valette and climbs steadily to place Ste-Geneviève, beside the Panthéon.

To your left is the church of St-Etienne-du-Mont which has the remains of Racine and Pascal.

Turn right along the side of the Panthéon and enter the building from the front.

❸ Among the 70 distinguished people buried in the crypt of the Panthéon are Zola, Victor Hugo Voltaire and Rousseau.

From the Panthéon, head down rue Soufflot, cross rue St-Jacques and take the next turning right into rue Victor Cousin.

❹ A plaque on the wall of the Hôtel Cluny Sorbonne recalls the stay of the unruly Symbolist poet Arthur Rimbaud in room 62 in 1872 with a prosaic quotation: *'En ce moment, j'ai une chamber jolie'* ('I have a lovely room at the moment').

Rue Victor Cousin leads into the shady place Sorbonne, a good place to stop for a drink at a café, before continuing downhill beside the university. Turn left along rue des Écoles to emerge on boulevard St-Michel. Turn right and continue towards the river, crossing boulevard St-Germain. At place St-Michel cross the road, walk around the monumental fountain where two dragons spew water at the feet of St. Michael, and into pretty place St-André des Arts. Turn immediately right into rue St-André des Arts. After a short way, make a detour right up rue Git le Coeur.

❺ A nondescript hotel at No. 9 served as the 'Beat Hotel' in the 1950s. Here Allen Ginsberg wrote his poem 'Kaddish' and William Burroughs finished his controversial novel *The Naked Lunch*. The original establishment closed in 1963 but some photographs in the lobby of its replacement, the smart Relais-Hôtel du Vieux Paris, recall the site's earlier fame.

Return to rue St-André des Arts and turn right to continue in the direction you were going. Turn left down rue de l'Eperon and right into rue du Jardinet. Beyond the gate at the end you go through three courtyards which deliver you to the back door of Le Procope restaurant.

❻ Paris's oldest café, Le Procope (▷ 119), was founded 1686 and includes Molière and Voltaire among its former customers. Now restored, inside it is decorated with mirrors, chandeliers and shelves stacked with old books.

Turn right beside Le Procope (▷ 119) and walk through a short arcade to meet rue St-André des Arts again. Turn left. Over the crossroads, continue along rue de Buci. Turn right up rue de la Seine. Turn left down rue des Beaux Arts.

❼ L'Hôtel at No. 13 used to be known as the Hôtel d'Alsace and

it was here that Oscar Wilde died in 1900, aged 46, in exile, broken by prison and having converted to Catholicism. For a price, you can stay in the room in which he died.

At the end of rue des Beaux Arts is the École Nationale Superieur des Beaux Arts with a monumental courtyard. Turn left down rue Bonaparte to reach place St-Germain-des-Prés, which is presided over by the oldest church in Paris. Three famous *cafés littéraires* (literary cafés) stand nearby.

Across the square from the church is Les Deux Magots. On the next corner going away from the church is Café de Flore (▷ 110). Directly opposite Flore is Brasserie Lipp (▷ 115). Between them these three establishments have entertained many of the great writers of recent times, including Surrealists and the Existentialists. Their most famous regulars were Jean-Paul Sartre and Simone de Beauvoir. If you want to sit at a table and jot down your thoughts over a cup of coffee, you'll be in good company.

WHERE TO EAT
There are cafés and restaurants all along the route.

Above *Inside the Panthéon*
Opposite *Stacked paperbacks in a second-hand bookshop*

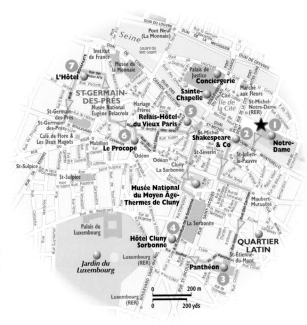

SHOPPING

AGNÈS B

www.agnesb.fr

Sober yet trendy, Agnès B's fashion is the epitome of young Parisian chic. Sharply cut items with original details are her signature, and her waistcoat with press studs is a classic. She sponsors budding designers.

✉ 6 rue du Jour, 75001 ☎ 01 45 08 56 56 🕐 Apr–Sep Mon–Sat 10.30–7.30; Oct–Mar 10–7 🚇 Les Halles

BARTHÉLÉMY (STÉ)

Established in 1904, this cheese-lover's paradise sells Brie, Mont d'Or (from Jura), Roquefort and much more. The old-fashioned shop supplies the Élysée Palace, home to France's president.

✉ 51 rue de Grenelle, 75007 ☎ 01 42 22 82 24 🕐 Tue–Sat 8–1, 4–7.15 🚇 Rue du Bac

BHV (BAZAR DE L'HÔTEL DE VILLE)

www.bhv.fr

The department store, City Hall Bazaar, has been operating since 1856 and is extremely well stocked. Clothes, furniture, home goods, electronics, home office—just about everything you could possibly need or think of has been gathered under one roof.

✉ 52 rue de la Verrerie, 75189 ☎ 01 42 74 90 00 🕐 Mon–Tue, Thu–Fri 9.30–7.30, Sat 9.30–8, Wed 9.30–9 🚇 Hôtel de Ville

LE BON MARCHÉ

www.lebonmarche.fr

The classiest brands and goods can be found at this department store and the Modernist interior design adds to the atmosphere. Don't miss the beauty parlour on the ground floor and the food hall, which stocks delicacies from around the world, in a nearby building.

✉ 24 rue de Sèvres, 75007 ☎ 01 44 39 80 00 🕐 Mon–Wed, Sat 10–8, Thu–Fri 10–9 🚇 Sèvres-Babylone, Vaneau

BOULANGERIE POILÂNE

www.poilane.fr

The legacy of artist bread-maker Lionel Poilâne lives on in what is often regarded as the best French bread, baked here from secret family recipes. The country nut-and-raisin bread is a must, but other delicacies include the traditional baguette, croissant and rye loaf.

✉ 8 rue du Cherche-Midi, 75006 ☎ 01 45 48 42 59 🕐 Mon–Sat 7.15am–8.15pm 🚇 Sèvres-Babylone, St-Sulpice

CHANEL

www.chanel.com

The tweed suit and the little black dress, Coco Chanel's signature outfits, keep on being reinvented by Karl Lagerfeld, head of this fashion house since 1984. Classic, sexy, feminine and chic, Chanel's designs embody Parisian elegance.

✉ 31 rue Cambon, 75001 ☎ 01 42 86 28 00 🕐 Mon–Sat 10–7 🚇 Madeleine

COLETTE

www.colette.fr

Paris's fashion heaven offers exclusive shopping par excellence. Come here for cutting-edge design from one of the industry's rising names, or for imported beauty products that are difficult to find

elsewhere. A glance at the press box will ensure you keep abreast of the trends. The water bar downstairs offers more than a hundred different brands of bottled water.
✉ 213 rue St-Honoré, 75001 ☎ 01 55 35 33 90 🕙 Mon–Sat 11–7 🚇 Tuileries, Pyramides

FAUCHON
www.fauchon.fr
This is the tastiest and probably the most expensive delicatessen in Paris. The best of French cuisine, including foie gras, fine condiments, chocolates and great wines, has been sold here since 1886. And not only French produce is on offer: You can find Beluga caviar, the best vintages of the finest spirits from all over the world, and many more exotic delicacies. Gift boxes are a good souvenir. There are also a pleasant tea room and caviar bar here.
✉ 26 place de la Madeleine, 75008 ☎ 01 70 39 38 00 🕙 Mon–Sat 9–9 🚇 Madeleine

GALERIE ELSA VANIER
www.elsa-vanier.fr
Producing avant-garde jewellery in step with the latest fashion collections, Elsa Vanier has a growing and loyal clientele. Pieces are fashioned in all kinds of metals and a range of precious and semi-precious stones designed by Elsa herself or by a range of other designers.
✉ 7 rue du Pré aux Clercs, 75007 ☎ 01 47 03 05 00 🕙 Tue, Thu–Sat 11.30–7, Wed by appointment 🚇 Rue de Bac

GALERIES LAFAYETTE
www.galerieslafayette.com
Opened in 1912, the main building of this grand old department store has an impressive stained-glass dome, balconies and gilded balustrades. It's a luxurious setting for the hundreds of brands and goods that are stocked here, including fashion and beauty items, accessories, home goods and fine foods.
✉ 40 boulevard Haussmann, 75009 ☎ 01 42 82 34 56 🕙 Mon–Wed, Fri–Sat 9.30–8, Thu 9.30–9 🚇 Chaussée d'Antin

ISABEL MARANT
www.isabelmarant.tm.fr
With her fashions regularly on the catwalk, Isabel Marant has updated Parisian elegance with a bit of a bohemian bourgeois twist. Silk paisley shirts, big woollen wrap-over tops: This is casual chic at its best.
✉ 16 rue de Charonne, 75011 ☎ 01 49 29 71 55 🕙 Mon–Sat 10.30–7.30 🚇 Bastille

LOLLIPOPS
www.lollipops.fr
Bags, scarves, hats and some jewellery form a collection that is both chic and playful, with interesting use of materials such as wool, suede and velvet. The range of products is displayed by shade, so it is easy to find matching pieces.
✉ 2 rue Rosiers, 75004 ☎ 01 42 77 43 75 🕙 Tue–Sat 10.30–7, Sun–Mon 1.30–7.30 🚇 Louvre-Rivoli

LOUIS VUITTON
www.vuitton.com
The beige and brown chequered pattern, and the interlaced LV initials are the house's signature and a symbol of designer chic. There's a wide range of co-ordinated leather goods, including suitcases, key rings, wallets, purses and shoes. There are also some high-quality clothes with prices to match.
✉ 101 avenue des Champs-Élysées, 75008 ☎ 01 53 57 52 00 🕙 Mon–Sat 10–8, Sun 11–7 🚇 George V

MARCHÉ BEAUVAU
This is one of Paris's liveliest markets—many restaurants send staff here to shop for fresh fruit and vegetables, fish and meat. Some merchants sell by auction, and everyone joyfully jostles everybody else—a truly Parisian experience.
✉ place d'Aligre, 75012 🕙 Tue–Fri 9–1, 3.30–7.30, Sun 8.30–1.30 🚇 Ledru-Rollin, Faidherbe Chaligny

MARCHÉ AUX FLEURS
This market is on an island in the Seine, close to Notre-Dame. There's a wide selection of plants and flowers, displayed on the banks of the river or in greenhouses, with a

Opposite *Boutiques in Le Marais*

couple of specialist stands (orchids and herb gardens).
✉ place Louis Lépine, Île de la Cité, 75004 🕙 Mon–Sat 8–7.30, Sun 8–7 🚇 Cité

MARCHÉ RASPAIL
The fruit and vegetables sold at this strictly organic market have been grown without pesticides, so they may not always look as good as those at the local supermarket, but they certainly have more taste. You will also find organic honey, bread and wine. Another organic market is held on boulevard des Batignolles on Saturday mornings.
✉ boulevard Raspail, 75006 🕙 Tue, Fri 7–2.30 🚇 Rennes

MAUREEN
www.maureenlesite.com
Maureen Vinot is one of the capital's most vibrant young designers, whose clothes and accessories have an up-to-date edge while retaining a soft, feminine touch. She sells directly from her small atelier (workshop).
✉ 2 rue Auguste Barbier, 75011 ☎ 09 52 36 89 17 🕙 Mon–Fri 12–7, Sat 2.30–7.30 🚇 Goncourt

PIERRE HERMÉ
www.pierreherme.com
Couture pastries? Chef Pierre Hermé works in association with a designer so his creations are as visually exciting as they are tasty. His gold-leaf ornamented chocolate cake is almost legendary. Be prepared for a wait at his small boutique, more like a jeweller's shop than a pâtisserie, but remember, satisfaction is at the other end of the line.
✉ 72 rue Bonaparte, 75006 ☎ 01 43 54 47 77 🕙 Mon–Fri, Sun 10–7, Sat 10–7.30 🚇 St-Sulpice, Mabillon

PRINTEMPS
www.printemps.com
Since 1865 it has been this store's ambition to be the most modern of its time. Under its main building's impressive stained-glass cupola, there are six floors dedicated to women's fashion, and Europe's

largest perfume department. There is also a men's store, and a department dedicated to home decoration.

✉ 64 boulevard Haussmann, 75009 ☎ 01 42 82 51 00 🕓 Mon–Wed, Fri–Sat 9.35–7, Thu 9.35am–10pm 🚇 Havre-Caumartin

XULY BËT

Malian designer Lamine Kouyate adds an ethnic twist to elegance. The distinctive patterned fabrics of his creations show the influence of his native Africa, but the sexy cuts are more reminiscent of a daring couture designer such as Versace, with some beautiful tight-fitting dresses, often with red stitching. Alongside the clothes, there is a collection of objects for the home, all handmade in Africa.

✉ 1 rue Pierre-Lescot, 75001 ☎ 01 42 33 50 40 🕓 Daily 11–2, 3–7 🚇 Les Halles

ENTERTAINMENT AND NIGHTLIFE

AUDITORIUM DU LOUVRE

www.louvre.fr

The impressive setting of this 420-seat auditorium, right beneath I.M. Pei's Louvre Pyramid, is matched by an excellent and varied schedule, including church music, film themes and recitals.

✉ Musée du Louvre, 75001 (entrance by the Pyramid) ☎ 01 40 20 55 00 🕓 Concerts: varies ⚡ €30 (8pm concert), €10 (12.30pm concert) 🚇 Louvre-Rivoli

AU P'TIT GARAGE

In a city not noted for its rock music, this American style bar stands out. The shabby-chic decor collected from

visits to local second-hand outlets, classic discs and the well-priced bar list add up to a popular draw with young, hip locals and expats.

✉ 61r Jean Pierre Timbaud, 75011 ☎ 01 43 14 00 24 🕓 Daily 6–2 🚇 Parmentier

BAZOOKA CAFÉ

This chic, trendy spot is near the Centre Georges Pompidou and close to the Marais, Paris's gay district. There is a good atmosphere here in the evening.

✉ 9 rue Nicolas Flamel, 75004 ☎ 01 42 74 45 82 🕓 Daily 3pm–2am 🚇 Châtelet

BUDDHA BAR

www.buddha-bar.com

A trend-setting cocktail bar and restaurant that attracts both fashionistas and curious tourists. An impressive 3.6m (12ft) Buddha presides over the place, a DJ plays the latest ambient sounds, and the service is super-cool.

✉ 8 rue Boissy d'Anglas, 75008 ☎ 01 53 05 90 00 🕓 Bar: Mon–Fri noon–2am, Sat–Sun 4pm–2am. Restaurant: daily 12–3, 7–9.30 🚇 Concorde

CAFÉ DE FLORE

www.cafedeflore.fr

Once the haunt of celebrated writers and philosophers (Jean-Paul Sartre used to be a regular), this café welcomes customers all day long, for a snack or a drink, in an elegant atmosphere.

✉ 172 boulevard St-Germain, 75006 ☎ 01 45 48 55 26 🕓 Daily 7am–2am 🚇 St-Germain-des-Prés

COMÉDIE FRANÇAISE/ SALLE RICHELIEU

www.comedie-francaise.fr

Despite its name, don't expect comedy at the Comédie Française, which was established in 1680 by playwright Molière. It is home to France's most prestigious troupe of actors. Classic works make up the repertoire, including works by Shakespeare, Chekov, Racine, Feydeau and, of course, Molière. There are three performance spaces.

✉ 2 rue de Richelieu, 75001 ☎ 0825 10 1680 🕓 Performance: daily 8.30pm, some matinées on Sat, Sun ⚡ From €11 🚇 Palais Royal-Louvre

CRAZY HORSE

www.lecrazyhorseparis.com

This Parisian institution was established in 1951. Its high-class 'Teasing' show presents dancers who, thanks to some clever lighting effects, appear to be almost nude. Dinner is served during the show.

✉ 12 avenue George V, 75008 ☎ 01 47 23 32 32 🕓 Shows: Sun–Fri 8.15, 10.45, Sat 7, 9.30, 11.45 ⚡ Show and dinner: from €175 🚇 Alma-Marceau, George V

LA DANSE

www.cafedeladanse.com

There's an intimate feel to this auditorium, with its small platform and exposed brick walls, and with room for up to 500 people. Pop, rock and world music dominate the bill, with some theatre and dance performances. There is a small bar on the premises. Credit cards are not accepted.

✉ 5 passage Louis-Philippe, 75011 ☎ 01 47 00 57 59 🕓 Performance: daily around 8pm ⚡ Around €20, but varies 🚇 Bastille

DUC DES LOMBARDS

www.ducdeslombards.com

This institution is where the most esteemed jazz musicians regularly warm the intimate atmosphere, their performances culminating in memorable jam sessions.

Left *Montmartre, in northern Paris, has many bars and clubs*

✉ 42 rue des Lombards, 75001 ☎ 01 42 33 22 88 🕙 Performance: Mon–Sat 9pm ✋ €19–25 🚇 Châtelet

ÉLYSÉE MONTMARTRE
www.elyseemontmartre.com
More than a century old, this establishment has retained its original retro-style interior and is now host to some of the best pop-rock concerts, staging international as well as French acts. It's also famous for its ball and techno nights.
✉ 72 boulevard Rochechouart, 75018 ☎ 01 44 92 45 36 🕙 Varies ✋ About €12–€45 (depending on performance) 🚇 Anvers

FOLIES-BERGÈRE
www.foliesbergere.com
A legendary venue, the Folies-Bergère has been in operation since 1869. Formerly famous for its risqué performances, it shows various productions from different companies and artists, including jazz ensembles.
✉ 32 rue Richer, 75009 ☎ Tickets: 0892 68 16 50; office: 01 44 79 98 60 🕙 Varies according to show ✋ Varies according to show 🚇 Cadet, Grands Boulevards

LA JAVA
www.la-java.fr
One of the capital's legendary venues—both Edith Piaf and Django Reinhardt appeared here—is now a little link to the past, though the contemporary schedule is very mixed, including comedy and poetry as well as music performances. There are dance sessions every Sunday afternoon.
✉ 105 rue du Faubourg du Temple, 75010 ☎ 01 42 02 20 52 🕙 Thu–Sun, concerts 9pm ✋ Varies 🚇 Goncourt

MAISON DE RADIO FRANCE
www.radiofrance.fr
Top-notch symphony orchestras, jazz concerts and operas are all presented here, either as live broadcasts or recorded for subsequent broadcasting.
✉ 116 avenue du Président-Kennedy, 75016 ☎ 01 56 40 15 16 🕙 Varies ✋ Free (or small charge) 🚇 Kennedy Radio France

MÉNAGERIE DE VERRE
www.menagerie-de-verre.org
A glass roof and concrete walls distinguish this former printing house. Expect modern dance performances and some multi-disciplinary festivals: video, dance and visual arts. Credit cards are not accepted.
✉ 12 rue Léchevin, 75011 ☎ 01 43 38 33 44 🕙 Performance: daily 8.30pm ✋ €13 🚇 Parmentier

MOULIN ROUGE
www.moulinrouge.fr
Established in 1889, and even more of an institution since the eponymous Hollywood movie. Admire the magnificent interior within an almost authentic red windmill, where fine food is served while you enjoy the titillating 'Féerie' show.
✉ 82 boulevard de Clichy, 75018 ☎ 01 53 09 82 82 🕙 Shows: daily 9pm, 11pm ✋ Show: from €80. Show and dinner: from €150 🚇 Blanche

LE NEW MORNING
www.newmorning.com/fr
Heaven for jazz fans, this famous club has welcomed the world's most prestigious musicians over the years. Bossa nova and salsa are also played.
✉ 7–9 rue des Petites-Écuries, 75010 ☎ 01 45 23 51 41 🕙 Concert: 9pm (days vary) ✋ Around €25 🚇 Château d'Eau

LE NOUVEAU CASINO
www.nouveaucasino.net
Opened in 2001, this club quickly developed a regular clientele. Excellent DJs, a beautiful interior, and a great location in a very busy district, are the keys to its success.
✉ 109 rue Oberkampf, 75011 ☎ 01 43 57 57 40 🕙 Thu–Sat midnight–6am; concerts most nights at 7.30 or 8pm ✋ Around €15 🚇 Parmentier, Ménilmontant, St-Maur

OPÉRA BASTILLE
www.operadeparis.fr
This massive modern auditorium, with its 2,700 seats, was inaugurated in 1989, amid much controversy. However, operas and symphony orchestras continue to benefit from the exceptional acoustics. There is

also some ballet. The website has a waiting system when it is busy.
✉ 120 rue de Lyon, 75012 ☎ 0892 899 090 🕙 Varies ✋ €10–130 🚇 Bastille

OPÉRA PALAIS GARNIER
www.operadeparis.fr
An architectural masterpiece, built during the 19th century by Charles Garnier, this venue offers a lavish and prestigious setting for visiting ballet and opera companies, as well as symphony orchestras.
✉ place de l'Opéra, 75009 ☎ 0892 899 090 🕙 Varies ✋ €10–130 🚇 Opéra

PALAIS OMNISPORTS PARIS BERCY
www.bercy.fr
The capital's biggest and loudest auditorium sees the world's biggest bands on stage—including Black Eyed Peas, Bon Jovi and Guns N' Roses in early 2010
✉ 8 boulevard de Bercy ☎ 01 40 02 60 60 ✋ Varies 🚇 Bercy

QUEEN
www.queen.fr
A prestigious address for this gay club, which is also the haunt of a trendy straight crowd. House and garage music are mixed by international DJs, with themes and atmospheres changing each night of the week.
✉ 102 avenue des Champs-Élysées, 75008 ☎ 01 53 89 08 90 🕙 Daily midnight–7am ✋ Mon €20; Tue–Thu, Sun €15; Fri–Sat €20 🚇 George V

SATELLIT CAFÉ
www.satellit-cafe.com
This centre for world music has room for 250 people. The schedule includes Latino, blues, African, Balkan and Mediterranean music.
✉ 44 rue de la Folie-Méricourt, 75011 ☎ 01 47 00 48 87 🕙 Concert: Wed–Fri 9. Dancing: Thu–Sat 10 ✋ Concerts €10, dancing €12 🚇 Oberkampf, St-Ambroise

THÉÂTRE DES CHAMPS-ÉLYSÉES
www.theatrechampselysees.fr
This grand auditorium, with red velvet seats and balconies, hosts

performances of opera, ballet, classical and chamber music, as well as jazz and solo variety singers.

✉ 15 avenue Montaigne, 75008 ☎ 01 49 52 50 50 ⏱ Performances: almost daily at around 8–8.30pm ✋ Varies Ⓜ Franklin D. Roosevelt, Alma-Marceau

THÉÂTRE NATIONAL DE CHAILLOT
www.theatre-chaillot.fr
This theatre is housed in the imposing neoclassical Palais de Chaillot. The largest auditorium can accommodate productions of all kinds, including top-quality contemporary works, as well as the usual classics.

✉ 1 place du Trocadéro, 75016 ☎ 01 53 65 30 00 ⏱ Performances: Tue–Sat 8pm, Sun 3pm ✋ €12–33 Ⓜ Trocadéro

THÉÂTRE DU PALAIS ROYAL
www.theatrepalaisroyal.com
A prestigious setting—within the gardens of the Palais Royal—adds to the attraction of this elegant theatre (containing red velvet seats and gilded panels) built in 1783. Plays and comedy acts dominate the schedule but there are also some classical music concerts.

✉ 38 rue de Montpensier, 75001 ☎ 01 42 97 40 00 ⏱ Performances: Tue–Fri 8.30pm, Sat 5pm and 9pm ✋ Varies Ⓜ Bourse, Palais Royal-Louvre

UGC CINÉ FORUM LES HALLES
www.ugc.fr
This 19-screen complex offers an extensive choice of films, all shown in their original language. Fantastic jumbo-sized photographic images of film stars are exhibited in the entrance hall.

✉ 7 place de la Rotonde, 75001 ☎ 0892 700 000, ext 21 ⏱ Daily 9am–10.30pm ✋ Adult €10, child €8 Ⓜ Châtelet-Les Halles

WAGG
www.wagg.fr
A compact dance floor (accommodating up to 350 people) gives this venue, in the heart of St-Germain-des-Prés, its welcoming atmosphere. The house and dance

music draws a trendy mid-20s to mid-30s crowd to this establishment.

✉ 62 rue Mazarine, 75006 ☎ 01 55 42 22 01 ⏱ Fri 11pm–dawn, Sat 10pm–dawn, Sun 5.30pm–2am ✋ €12 Ⓜ St-Germain-des-Prés, Odéon

SPORTS AND ACTIVITIES
AQUABOULEVARD
www.aquaboulevard.com
Alongside the aquapark, which has an inviting selection of waterslides and a wave machine, there activities designed for visitors who prefer to stay dry during their leisure time including squash courts, tennis courts, a putting range, restaurants and shops.

✉ 4–6 rue Louis Armand, 75015 ☎ 01 40 60 10 00 ⏱ Mon–Thu 9am–11pm, Fri 9am–midnight, Sat 8am–midnight, Sun 8am–11pm ✋ Aquapark: adult €25, child (3–11) €12 Ⓜ Balard, Porte de Versailles

COOK'N WITH CLASS
www.cooknwithclass.com
This small company runs gourmet classes and food shopping tours in Paris. All classes are in English and groups contain a maximum of six. You can discover the delights of fresh seasonal produce and how to turn the ingredients into delicious dishes.

✉ 21 rue Custine, 75018 ☎ 01 42 55 70 59 ✋ Group sessions from €125 Ⓜ Chateau-Rouge

FRANCE MONTGOLFIÈRES
www.franceballoons.com
These hot-air balloon tours let you discover Paris's surroundings, soaring

above villages, châteaux, rivers and forests. Take off is from the area around Fontainebleau.

✉ 63 boulevard de Ménilmontant, 75011 ☎ 08 10 60 01 53 ⏱ Tours from mid-Mar to Nov, on reservation ✋ From €205 for 3.5-hour tour Ⓜ Père Lachaise

GOLF DU BOIS DE BOULOGNE
www.golfduboisdeboulogne.com
Paris's largest golf course, in the middle of a race track, includes a course where you can practise your swing, a putting green and a crazy-golf area for practising shots, which has small greens with bunkers and watercourses.

✉ Hippodrome d'Auteuil, 75016 ☎ 01 44 30 70 00 ⏱ Daily 8–8 (closed on race days) ✋ €4 per bucket of balls, €5 per half-hour of crazy golf Ⓜ Porte d'Auteuil

PARC DES PRINCES
www.leparcdesprinces.fr
Inaugurated in 1972, the park has been home to Paris-St-Germain (PSG; www.psg.fr) soccer club since 1990. Within its boundaries you'll also find the Musée National du Sport (National Sport Museum), a shop and a restaurant.

✉ 24 rue du Commandant-Guilbaud, 75016 ☎ 3275 (touch 2) ⏱ Closed Fri and public hols ✋ From €6 Ⓜ Porte d'Auteuil, Porte de St-Cloud

HELIPARIS
www.helicoptere.com
Want to see everything in less than 30 minutes? Take a tour and monument-spot across Paris. Longer

tours are also available, for a bird's-eye view of the Château de Versailles and farther afield.

✉ 102 avenue des Champs-Elysées, 75008 ☎ 01 41 31 33 90 ⏰ By reservation 🎫 €219 for a 20-minute tour Ⓜ Étoile

RANDONNÉE EN ROLLERS
www.rollers-coquillages.org
In partnership with Nomades sports store, the Rollers and Coquillages Society organizes rollerblading through Paris every Sunday. The three-hour circuit changes regularly.
✉ Meet in front of Nomades: 37 boulevard Bourdon, 75004 ☎ 01 44 54 07 44 ⏰ Sun 2.30pm 🎫 Free Ⓜ Bastille

HEALTH AND BEAUTY
FASHION SHOW GALLERIES LAFAYETTE
www.galerieslafayette.com
To view the latest Continental styles book a place at the weekly fashion show at the Galeries Lafayette.
✉ 40 boulevard Haussmann, 75009 ☎ 01 42 82 34 56 ⏰ Fri 3pm 🎫 Free but by reservation only Ⓜ Chausée d'Antin

VILLA THALGO
www.thalgo.fr
At this classy institute the relaxing and energizing seven-hour session includes bodyscrub, seaweed wrap, balneotherapy, aquagym, jet shower and massages. There are also one-hour and half-day treatments.
✉ 8 avenue Raymond Poincare, 75016 ☎ 01 45 62 00 20 ⏰ Mon, Wed 8.30am–9pm, Tue, Thu–Fri 8.30am–8pm, Sat 9.30–8, Sun 10.30–6 🎫 Varies according to treatment Ⓜ Charles de Gaulle–Étoile

FOR CHILDREN
AQUABOULEVARD
▷ 112.

CITÉ DES SCIENCES ET DE L'INDUSTRIE
▷ 97.

DISNEYLAND® RESORT PARIS
▷ 81.

JARDIN D'ACCLIMATATION
www.jardindacclimatation.fr
With its ponds and tree-lined alleys,

FESTIVALS AND EVENTS

APRIL
MARATHON INTERNATIONAL DE PARIS
www.parismarathon.com
The marathon attracts more than 30,000 runners. It starts at the Champs-Élysées and finishes in avenue Foch.
☎ 01 41 33 15 68 ⏰ First or second Sunday in April Ⓜ Charles de Gaulle-Étoile)

MAY–JUNE
FRENCH TENNIS OPEN
www.rolandgarros.com
The prestigious French Tennis Open takes place over two-weeks.
✉ Stade Roland Garros, 2 avenue Gordon-Bennett, 75016 ☎ 01 47 43 48 00 Ⓜ Porte d'Auteuil

JUNE
FÊTE DE LA MUSIQUE
www.fetedelamusique.culture.fr
Free concerts are held all over the city, with everything from jazz and classical to techno and rap.
☎ 01 40 03 94 70 ⏰ 21 June

JUNE–JULY
PARIS JAZZ
www.parisjazzfestival.fr
The sound of jazz fills the Parc Floral, courtesy of musicians from Europe and America.
✉ Parc Floral, Route de la Pyramide, Bois de Vincennes, 75012 Ⓜ Château de Vincennes

JULY
BASTILLE DAY
Celebrations include fireworks and

fire station balls on 13 July, followed by the annual military parade down the Champs-Élysées on 14 July.
⏰ 14 July

TOUR DE FRANCE
www.letour.fr
The participants of this wildly popular bicycle race to cross the finish line on the Champs-Élysées.
☎ 01 41 33 14 00

JULY–AUGUST
FESTIVAL DE CINÉMA EN PLEIN AIR
www.villette.com
Open-air film festival.
✉ Parc de la Villette, 75019 ☎ 01 40 03 75 75 Ⓜ Porte de la Villette, Porte de Pantin

OCTOBER
NUIT BLANCHE
Concerts and other events take place in unusual venues across the city, through the night.
⏰ One night in October

this 'garden within a wood' is a walker's paradise. There are many activities to occupy the children including minigolf, playgrounds, bowling, wildlife and nature discovery, cookery and theatre trips, and sports. A trip on the little train is a good way to discover the area.
✉ Main entry: boulevard des Sablons,

Bois de Boulogne, 75016 ☎ 01 40 67 90 82 ⏰ Daily 10–7 (Oct–Apr closes 6pm) 🎫 Adult €2.90, children under 3 free Ⓜ Les Sablons

Above *The Jardin du Luxembourg is a fine venue for tennis*
Opposite *The Opéra Bastille benefits from outstanding acoustics*

PRICES AND SYMBOLS

The restaurants are listed alphabetically (excluding Le, La and Les). The prices given are the average for a two-course lunch (L) and a three-course dinner (D) for one person, without drinks. The wine price is for the least expensive bottle.

For a key to the symbols, ▷ 2.

ALCAZAR

www.alcazar.fr

Designer Terence Conran's bar-restaurant serves fish, as well as sophisticated non-fish dishes such as grilled lamb. There's a lounge bar, hosting international DJs, where you can enjoy pre-dinner drinks, and Sunday brunch is available.

✉ 62 rue Mazarine, 75006 St-Germain-des-Prés ☎ 01 53 10 19 99 🕐 Daily 12–2.30, 7pm–2am 🖐 L €27, D €40, Wine €23 🚇 Odéon

L'AMBASSADE D'AUVERGNE

www.ambassade-auvergne.com

Robust farmhouse cooking and wines featuring ingredients from the Auvergne, with dishes such as cabbage soup and cassoulet with Puy lentils.

✉ 22 rue du Grenier St-Lazare, 75003 Le Marais ☎ 01 42 72 31 22 🕐 Daily 12–2, 7.30–10 🖐 L €35, D €45, Wine €18 🚇 Rambuteau

AUBERGE CHEZ EUX

www.chezeux.com

Decorated in the style of a traditional Paris restaurant, this place near the Invalides has a good selection of salads and vegetarian dishes such as cold ratatouille. Worth ordering, if you do eat meat, is the *magret de canard* (breast of duck). For dessert try *mousse aux chocolat* (chocolate mousse) or the vanilla ice cream.

✉ 2 avenue Lowendal, 75007 Invalides ☎ 01 47 05 52 55 🕐 Daily 12–2, 7–10 🖐 L €55, D €65, Wine €30 🚇 École Militaire

L'AUBERGE DAB

www.gerard-joulie.com

Located in Porte Maillot, this restaurant is furnished with comfortable leather sofas and attractive fabrics making it elegant and warm and intimate at the same time. It serves generous seafood dishes using different varieties of oysters and other shellfish. The meat

and fish dishes are also excellent. The terrace usually opens around Easter.

✉ 161 avenue Malakoff, 75116 Paris ☎ 01 45 00 32 22 🕐 Daily 12–3, 7–2 🖐 L €45, D €65, Wine €19 🚇 Porte Maillot

L'AUBERGE DU MOUTON BLANC

www.gerard-joulie.com

This inn in the west of the city, now favoured by Parisians looking for peace and quiet, used to be a meeting point for Molière, Racine, Boileau, Chapelle and La Fontaine. On the wall is a picture of Molière reading his play *Le Misanthrope* here in 1666.

✉ 40 rue d'Auteuil, 75016 Paris ☎ 01 42 88 02 21 🕐 Daily 12–3, 7–11 🖐 L €30, D €40, Wine €18 🚇 Porte d'Auteuil

AU BOEUF COURONNE

www.gerard-joulie.com

Non-vegetarians only will be happy in this restaurant which calls itself the 'temple of meat'. With 16 different cuts of beef, no one could complain about the choice. You can order *le pavé des mandataires* (300g), *la pièce à la Charolaise* (500g) or the *côte de boeuf* (1.2kg). All come with the quality guarantee label of *Blonde d'Aquitaine*. Alternatively, there are traditional dishes featuring meat other than beef. You could try a main course such as *tête de veau* (calf's head), *rognon de veau entier grillé* (grilled whole veal kidney) and *carré d'agneau en persillade* (lamb in a parsley crust).

✉ 188 avenue Jean Jaurès, 75019 Paris ☎ 01 42 39 44 44 🕙 Daily 12–3, 7–12 🖐 L €40, D €55, Wine €19 🚇 Porte de Pantin

AU PIED DE CHAMEAU

www.aupieddechameau.fr
The Arabian Nights surroundings evoke a Moroccan souk, with performances by belly dancers, and Casablanca is the nightclub in the basement. The food reflects the North African feel with traditional tagine (meat and vegetable stew) and couscous.

✉ 20 rue Quincampoix, 75004 Les Halles ☎ 01 42 78 35 00 🕙 Daily 12–2, 8–1 🖐 L €30, D €45, Wine €17 🚇 Châtelet

AU PIED DE COCHON

www.pieddecochon.com
Open daily round the clock since it was established in 1946. Feast your eyes on the fresco-covered walls and your palate on one of France's regional dishes. The house dish, as its name suggests, is pig's trotters, the seafood is plentiful and the French onion soup a delight.

✉ 6 rue Coquillère, 75001 Les Halles ☎ 01 40 13 77 00 🕙 Daily 24 hours 🖐 L €25, D €50, Wine €17 🚇 Les Halles

AU TROU GASCON

This bistro with a turn-of-the-20th-century interior has excellent dishes from the southwest of France. The cassoulet, made with home-made sausages and beans from Tarbes, is one of the best on offer in Paris.

✉ 40 rue Taine, 75012 Bercy ☎ 01 43 44 34 26 🕙 Mon–Fri 12–2.30, 7.30–10.30. Closed Aug 🖐 L €45, D €60, Wine €19 🚇 Daumesnil

AU VIEUX COMPTOIR

www.au-vieux-comptoir.com
A popular, busy, little bistro run by Anne and Cyril who have gathered a comprehensive range of recipes from across the country. Dishes are on chalkboards around the dining room. Enjoy the regional wines and liqueurs in the late-evening atmosphere.

✉ 17 rue des Lavandieres-St-Opportune 75001 ☎ 01 45 08 53 08 🕙 Tue–Sat 10am–midnight 🖐 L €30, D €40, Wine €20 🚇 Châtelet

BISTRO ROMAIN

www.bistroromain.fr
One of a dozen across Paris, the decor at this Bistro Romain is reminiscent of an Italian opera house. The menu includes bowls of pasta. Those with big appetites will enjoy the carpaccio and the chocolate mousse, which come on an all-you-can-eat basis.

✉ 26 avenue des Champs-Élysées, 75008 Champs-Élysées ☎ 01 53 75 17 84 🕙 Daily 11.30am–1am 🖐 L €23, D €35, Wine €16.90 🚇 Franklin D. Roosevelt

BOFINGER

www.bofingerparis.com
The interior of this elegant restaurant is lavish art nouveau, with an impressive stained-glass ceiling, mirrors and carved wood everywhere. Fans of meat and fish will both find something to enjoy, with beautifully prepared traditional French dishes such as lobster, oysters, duck and sauerkraut on the menu.

✉ 3 rue de la Bastille, 75004 Bastille ☎ 01 42 72 87 82 🕙 Mon–Fri 12–3, 6.30–1, Sat–Sun 12–1 🖐 L €28, D €45, Wine €30 🚇 Bastille

BRASSERIE FLO

www.flobrasseries.com
A wonderful turn-of-the-century interior, with stained-glass panels, green leather booths and wood panels on the ceiling, sets the tone at this Parisian institution, established in 1886, which is now a listed building. Actress Sarah Bernhardt was once a regular. The menu includes foie gras, shellfish and

Alsatian dishes such as sauerkraut, but be sure to leave enough room for the delicious profiteroles.

✉ 7 cour des Petites Écuries, 75010 Grands Boulevards ☎ 01 47 70 13 59 🕙 Daily 12–3, 7–1.30 🖐 L €28, D €45, Wine €35 🚇 Château-d'Eau

BRASSERIE LIPP

www.brasserie-lipp.fr
Founded in 1880, this famous Parisian brasserie, the haunt of writers, politicians, and theatre and cinema stars, and a historic monument in its own right, has retained much of its authentic 1900 decor including ceramic tiles and mosaics of exotic plants. It serves brasserie-style French cuisine and some of its most popular dishes are *blanquette de veau à l'ancienne* (veal and vegetables cooked in a cream sauce), *escalope de saumon* (salmon fillet) and *sole meunière* (sole in a brown butter and lemon sauce).

✉ 151 boulevard de St-Germain, 75006 Paris ☎ 01 45 48 53 91 🕙 Daily 9am–1am 🖐 L €40, D €50, Wine from €18 🚇 St-Germain-des-Prés

BRASSERIE LA LORRAINE

www.brasserielalorraine.com
Although the menu is designed to be exploration of regional French cuisine, including sauerkraut and Burgundy snails, seafood is the primary attraction of this Parisian institution. For more than 70 years, fans of sea urchins and oysters have come here. There's also a takeout service at the seafood bar.

✉ 2 place des Ternes, 75008 Ternes ☎ 01 56 21 22 00 🕙 Daily 11.30am–12.30am 🖐 L €35, D €60, Wine €25 🚇 Ternes

CAFÉ CASSETTE

www.cafecassette.com
This modern establishment is good for a meal in all weathers; a large terrace, a veranda, and a bar and salon offering more comfort. The three menus offer restaurant meals (salmon tartare and grilled steak), café snacks (salads, club sandwiches) and drinks and desserts (try the pancakes and ice cream).

REGIONS | PARIS AND THE ÎLE DE FRANCE • EATING

✉ 73 rue de Rennes, 75006 St-Germain-des-Prés ☎ 01 45 48 53 78 🕓 Daily 7am–1am 🍴 L €30, D €45, Wine €18.50 🚇 St-Sulpice, Rennes

LE CHALET DES ÎLES
www.chalet-des-iles.com
In 1880, Napoleon III had a Swiss chalet dismantled and reconstructed on the edge of a lake in the Bois de Boulogne for the Empress Eugénie. The original burned down in 1910 and was rebuilt. It is now a romantic and secluded restaurant reached by a short ride in an old-fashioned row boat. The terrace is perfect for a summer evening's dining.
✉ Lac Inferieur du Bois de Boulogne, Porte de la Muette, 75016 Paris ☎ 01 42 88 04 69 🕓 Apr–Sep daily 12–2.30, 8–10.30; Oct–Mar Tue–Sat 12–2.30, 8–10.30, Sun 12–2.30 🍴 L €35, D €50, Wine €16 🚇 Rue de la Pompe

CHARTIER
www.restaurant-chartier.com
Founded in the late 19th century with the aim of serving a hot bowl of bouillon (meat and vegetables) at an affordable price to the blue-collar workers of the district, the Chartiers has preserved much of its original character, including its no-nonsense attitude to food, and is consequently something of a Parisian institution. The decor is brass, glass, mirrors and plain wood. The waiters dress in a traditional costume of rondin (a black waistcoat) and long white apron. The numbered drawers in wooden racks on the wall were for regular customers to store their napkins in.
✉ 7 rue Faubourg Montmartre, 75009 Paris ☎ 01 47 70 86 29 🕓 Daily 12–3, 7–10 🍴 L €22, D €28, Wine €12.50 🚇 Grands Boulevards

CHEZ ANDRÉ
This chic bistro near l'Étoile is a meeting point for business people, media types and fashion designers. It was opened in 1936 and has preserved its original atmosphere with shiny zinc bar counters. Chez André serves traditional but refined French cuisine. Among its specialities are cuisses de grenouilles (frogs'

legs), bouillabaisse du Chef (fish stew) or gigot d'agneau (roast leg of lamb). It has a good selection of wines served by the glass. From April you can eat on the terrace.
✉ 2 rue Marbeuf, 75008 Paris ☎ 01 47 20 59 57 🕓 Daily noon–1am 🍴 L €35, D €45, Wine €18 🚇 Alma-Marceau

CHEZ PAUL
www.chezpaul.com
One of a declining number of traditional basic Parisian bistros, Chez Paul offers the dining experience of yesteryear amid original early 1900s period decor. The menu is filled with excellent French staples including andouillette (entrail sausage) and pot au feu, though there are also steaks and fish options. Portions are generous. There is a good wine list.
✉ 13 rue de Charonne, 75011 Bastille ☎ 01 47 00 34 57 🕓 Mon–Fri 12–3, 7–12.30, Sat–Sun noon–12.30 🍴 L €30, D €40, Wine €18 🚇 Bastille

CITRUS ÉTOILE
www.citrusetoile.fr
Award-winning chef Gilles Epié has cooked for French presidents and the prices in his elegant restaurant near the Arc de Triomphe reflect his prestige. He likes adding Asiatic touches to his cooking. Another attraction is that he prepares virtually fat-free dishes.
✉ 6 rue Arsene Houssaye, 75008 Paris ☎ 01 42 89 15 51 🕓 Mon–Fri 12–2.30, 7.30–10.30 🍴 L €50, D €65, Wine €18 🚇 Charles de Gaulle-Étoile

CLEMENTINE
www.restaurantclementine.com
Gourmet French cuisine is served as ever in this authentic Parisian bistro founded in 1906 near the Bourse de Paris and the Grands Boulevards. Choice items on the menu include scallops in citronella cream, salmon fillet and pork chop in a prune sauce with orange butter. Dishes vary with seasonality of market produce. There is a good selection of wines.
✉ 5 rue St-Marc, 75002 Paris ☎ 01 40 41 05 65 🕓 Mon 12–2.30, Tue–Fri 12–2.30, 7–10 🍴 L €30, D €40, Wine €20 🚇 Rue Montmartre/Bourse

LE CONGRÈS MAILLOT
Located in the heart of the business quarter, near the Palais des Congrès, this is an ideal place for a business lunch or for a relaxed meal. It has a good selection of fresh fish, lobster and seafood but also a choice of meat dishes and desserts.
✉ 80 avenue de la Grande Armée, 75017 Paris ☎ 01 45 74 17 24 🕓 Daily 8am–2am 🍴 L €45, D €50, Wine €18 🚇 Porte Maillot

LA CORDONNERIE
www.restaurantlacordonnerie.com
This small family-owned restaurant sticks to traditional French dishes served to perfection at sensible prices. It's not pretentious, but cozy and welcoming—a neigbourhood joint in the heart of the city.
✉ 20 rue Saint-Roch, 75001 ☎ 01 42 60 17 42 🕓 Mon–Sat 12–2.30, 7.30–10.30 🍴 L €25, D €35, Wine €15 🚇 Pyramides

LA COUPOLE
www.flobrasseries.com
Follow in the footsteps of Pablo Picasso, Ernest Hemingway and Man Ray, and enjoy a meal at this elegant art deco brasserie, established in 1927. The bright and airy dining room has fresco-adorned pillars and Cubist floor tiles. All the brasserie classics are on the menu including seafood platters, sauerkraut and steak tartare.
✉ 102 boulevard du Montparnasse, 75014 Montparnasse ☎ 01 43 20 14 20 🕓 Sun–Fri 8.30am–1am, Sat 8.30am–1.30am 🍴 L €25, D €35, Wine €25 🚇 Vavin

DANS LE NOIR?
www.danslenoir.com
If you crave a new dining experience, this is the place to come. In this restaurant you eat in pitch dark, partly to savour the food without distractions but also to enhance the senses of taste and smell. You can choose what you are going to eat or be served a surprise meal. It is essential to reserve a table three to five days in advance. There is also a bar and lounge with a contrasting sunny terrace.

Opposite Le Ferme St-Simon offers a rustic menu

✉ 51 rue Quincampoix, 75004 Paris
☎ 01 42 77 98 04 🕐 Mon–Sat 7.45 or 8.15 and 10 or 10.30. No admission 45 minutes after the serving has started. Also open for lunch Sat 12.30 🍴 L €39, D €45, Wine €19 🚇 Les Halles

DRAGONS ÉLYSÉES
The high standard of service and the chic address make this restaurant perfect for a business or more formal lunch. There are both Chinese and Thai dishes such as stuffed crab, spring rolls and Peking-style pork. There is a gigantic underfoot aquarium, which contains more than 1,000 fish.
✉ 11 rue de Berri, 75008 Champs-Élysées ☎ 01 42 89 85 10 🕐 Daily 12–2.30, 7–1am 🍴 L €25, D €40, Wine €16 🚇 George V

L'EUROPÉEN
Opposite Gare de Lyon railway station, this brasserie dating from the 1900s has been beautifully renovated. It has different levels to create intimate spaces and is decorated with mirrors to lighten the interior. The English-style furniture gives it a cosy atmosphere but if you prefer to eat outside it has a terrace facing the station and its clock.
✉ 21 bis boulevard Diderot, 75012 Paris

☎ 01 43 43 99 70 🕐 Daily 7.30am–1am 🍴 L €35, D €45, Wine €18 🚇 Gare de Lyon

LA FERME ST-SIMON
www.fermestsimon.com
This 'farm' is decorated like an elegant country house. Chef Ali Iguedlane's' traditional French cuisine includes langoustines, prawns and his special dessert: soufflé au grand chocolat. There are also excellent wines.
✉ 6 rue de St-Simon, 75007 Invalides ☎ 01 45 48 35 74 🕐 Mon–Fri 12–4, 7.30–10, Sat 7.30–10 🍴 L €50, D €65, Wine €24 🚇 Rue du Bac

LE FLAUBERT
www.bistrotflaubert.com
This restaurant, part of a small chain created by chef Michel Rostang, serves up high-quality regional cooking. A chalkboard displays the daily specials, which vary according to what's available in the market. Hearty dishes include pig's trotters.
✉ 10 rue Gustave Flaubert, 75017 Ternes ☎ 01 42 67 05 81 🕐 Tue–Fri 12–2.30, 7–11, Sat 7–11 🍴 L €40, D €55, Wine €17.50 🚇 Courcelles

LE FLORIMOND
www.leflorimond.com
This is a small, chic bistro run with

panache by Pascal Gauillaumin. The menu gives a true picture of France with the finest regional ingredients served in contemporary style and it's a hit with discerning Parisians.
✉ 19 avenue de la Motte-Picquet, 75007 ☎ 01 45 55 40 38 🕐 Mon–Fri 12–2.30, 7.30–10.30, 2nd and 4th Sat of the month 7.30–10.30. Closed 1st and 3rd Sat of the month and every Sun. 🍴 L €30, D €45, Wine €19 🚇 École Militaire, Latour Maubourg

LE FRAMBOISY
www.leframboisy.com
An intimate bistro run by a dynamic young maître d' and chef, Le Framboisy aims to delight with its traditional touches and reasonable prices, but surprises with unusual elements such as the bio suggestions on the wine list. It is easy to find between Rivoli and the Marais.
✉ 6 rue Charlemagne 75004 ☎ 01 42 72 14 16 🕐 Tue, Thu 8–10, Wed 9am–10pm, Fri 8pm–10.30pm, Sat 11am–10.30pm 🍴 L €25, D €35, Wine €24 🚇 St Paul

LE GRAND CAFÉ
www.legrandcafe.com
Theatregoers, seafood-lovers and an eclectic flock of night owls make up the clientele of this restaurant, which is open day and night, every day of

the year. The interior is beautiful art nouveau, with an impressive stained-glass ceiling and fanciful furniture. Fish is king here and is served grilled, poached or *meunière* (in lemon and butter). The menu also includes some French meat dishes, such as fillet of Charolais beef with peppercorns.

✉ 4 boulevard des Capucines, 75009 Grands Boulevards ☎ 01 43 12 19 00 🕐 Daily 24 hours 🖐 L €30, D €45, Wine €18 🚇 Opéra

LES GRANDES MARCHES

www.lesgrandesmarches.com

The big steps that give the restaurant its name are those of the Opéra Bastille next door, although this building also has its own stylish staircase. It offers traditional rustic menus including *filet de boeuf, saumon rôti* and lamb. The restaurant is renowned for its seafood platters, and the views of place de la Bastille from the first floor.

✉ 6 place de la Bastille, 75012 Bastille ☎ 01 43 42 90 32 🕐 Daily 9pm–4am 🖐 L €30, D €50, Wine €19 🚇 Bastille

GUY SAVOY

www.guysavoy.com

Renowned chef Guy Savoy's motto is that cooking is 'the art of taking foodstuffs and transforming them into pure happiness'. The quality of the cuisine is high, with delicacies such as foie gras, truffles or Bresse chicken featuring on the menu. This tips a hat to classic cuisine but adds contemporary touches. Jackets must be worn.

✉ 18 rue Troyon, 75017 Champs-Élysées ☎ 01 43 80 40 61 🕐 Mon–Fri 12–2, 7–10.30, Sat 7–10.30 🖐 L €200, D €300, Wine €90 🚇 Charles de Gaulle–Étoile

LE HIDE

www.lehide.fr

This could be Paris's smallest restaurant, so it's best to make a reservation. The menu has five or six choices for each course and the classics are here. It's good French food at a bargain price created by a Japanese chef.

✉ 10 rue du Général Lanrezac, 75017 ☎ 01 45 74 15 81 🕐 Mon–Fri 12–3,

7.30–10.30, Sat 7.30–10.30 🖐 L €22, D €29, Wine €16 🚇 Charles de Gaulle–Étoile

LADURÉE

www.laduree.fr

Paris's first tea room, established in 1862, has a lavish 1871 interior. In these elegant surroundings you can sample wonderful teas and superb pastries. The macaroons are a must, with the original flavours (rose petal, Yunnan tea, apricot and ginger), changing seasonally. The meal menu ranges from breakfasts and sandwiches to omelettes, desserts and salads.

✉ 16 rue Royale, 75008 Madeleine ☎ 01 42 60 21 79 🕐 Mon–Thu 8.30–7.30, Fri–Sat 8.30–8, Sun 10–7 🖐 Tea €6.30, four macaroons €7.10, L €30, D €40, Wine €22 🚇 Concorde, Madeleine

LEMONI CAFÉ

You can choose the ingredients to make up your own menu in this health-conscious café, offering organic Mediterranean cuisine from Crete. Menus change daily according

to the best produce available in the market that day.

✉ 5 rue Hérold, 75001 Louvre/Palais Royal ☎ 01 45 08 49 84 ⏱ Mon–Fri 12–3 🍴 From €11 Ⓜ Sentier, Louvre-Rivoli, Les Halles

MARKET

www.jean-georges.com

Christian Liaigre designed this restaurant's sophisticated interior. The menu offers a raw bar, with a large choice of oysters, and fusion food by chef Jean-Georges Vongerichten. Try black truffle pizza or the 'black plate', an hors d'oeuvre selection including shrimps on a skewer, ginger lobster roll, raw tuna and spiced quail. There is also brunch at the weekend.

✉ 15 avenue Matignon, 75008 Champs-Élysées ☎ 01 56 43 40 90 ⏱ Mon–Fri 8–11, 12–3, 7–11.30, Sat 12–4.30, 7–11.20, Sun 12–4.30, 7–11.30 🍴 L €34, D €60, Wine €24 Ⓜ Franklin D. Roosevelt

MAXIM'S

www.maxims-de-paris.com

Established in 1893 by café waiter Maxime Gaillard, and acquired in 1981 by designer Pierre Cardin, this belle-époque restaurant is a temple of Parisian social life. Attentive service, refined French cuisine, live shows and a prestigious location add to Maxim's appeal.

✉ 3 rue Royale, 75008 Concorde ☎ 01 42 65 27 94 ⏱ Tue–Sat 12.30–2, 7.30–10.30, Sat 7.30–10.30 🍴 L €180, D €200, Wine €90 Ⓜ Concorde

LE MONTPARNASSE 1900

You can get a flavour of the belle époque in this authentic art nouveau restaurant, decorated with mirrors and balustrades, which is listed as a historic monument. It serves traditional French food and has a terrace for summer use.

✉ 59 boulevard du Montparnasse, 75006 Paris ☎ 01 45 49 19 00 ⏱ Daily 12–3, 7–12 🍴 L €35. D €45, Wine €17 Ⓜ Montparnasse–Bienvenüe

LE PETIT ZINC

www.petit-zinc.com

This art nouveau restaurant on the Left Bank, close to the St-Germain-des-Prés church, combines tradition with modernity and offers a calm atmosphere to rest during or after a day of sightseeing. Among its specialities are shoulder of lamb with pink garlic from Lautrec in the Tarn and *veau foie meunière* (veal liver in brown butter sauce). In good weather you can eat on the terrace.

✉ 11 rue St-Benoit, 75006 Paris ☎ 01 42 86 61 00 ⏱ Daily 12–12 🍴 L €35, D €50, Wine €18 Ⓜ St-Germain-des-Prés

LE PROCOPE

www.procope.com

This former Parisian café, now an elegant dining room, has quite a history, dating from 1686. The philosophers Voltaire and Rousseau were regulars. The food now on offer includes grilled beef and seafood platters.

✉ 13 rue de l'Ancienne-Comédie, 75006 St-Germain-des-Prés ☎ 01 40 46 79 00 ⏱ Daily noon–1am 🍴 L €30, D €50, Wine €19 Ⓜ Odéon

PRUNIER

www.prunier.com

The art nouveau interiors are so spectacular that the food has to be special to compete—and it doesn't disappoint. The seafood is particularly good and caviar is a speciality. Prunier is also famed for its professional service.

✉ 16 avenue Victor Hugo, 75016 ☎ 01 44 17 35 85 ⏱ Mon–Sat 12–2.30, 7–11 🍴 L €60, D €80, Wine €39 Ⓜ Charles de Gaulle–Étoile

LA RÔTISSERIE D'EN FACE

www.jacquescagna.com

This is the annexe of Jacques Cagna, the eponymous gastronomic restaurant across the street, where the celebrity chef mans the stoves. You can expect the same perfection here, with specials like sauteed scallops, spit-roasted chicken and suckling pig.

✉ 2 rue Christine, 75006 St-Germain-des-Prés ☎ 01 43 26 40 98 ⏱ Mon–Thu 12–2.30, 7–11, Fri 12–2.30, 7–11.30, Sat 7–11.30 🍴 L €30, D €46, Wine €20 Ⓜ St-Michel

SPOON FOOD AND WINE

www.spoon.tm.fr

Here you are in elegant, understated surroundings with sleek lines, deep purple walls and pastel cushions. Celebrated chef Alain Ducasse lets you choose the sauce and accompaniment to your meal from a list of French and Asian delicacies.

✉ 14 rue de Marignan, 75008 Champs-Élysées ☎ 01 40 76 34 44 ⏱ Mon–Fri 12–2.30, 7–10.30. Closed late Dec to early Jan 🍴 L €50, D €65, Wine €30 Ⓜ Franklin D. Roosevelt

TAILLEVENT

www.taillevent.com

A highly distinguished restaurant with a stylish decor where you can expect the best of French cuisine, with rich dishes such as foie gras, lobster and truffles. There is an exceptional wine cellar. Jackets are required.

✉ 15 rue Lamennais, 75008 Champs-Élysées ☎ 01 44 95 15 01 ⏱ Mon–Fri 12.15–2, 7.15–10. Closed 3–31 Aug 🍴 L €80, D €140, Wine €40 Ⓜ Charles de Gaulle–Étoile, George V

THOUMIEUX

www.thoumieux.com

Jean-François Piege and Thierry Costes have taken over this long-standing restaurant and given a modern twist to the brasserie menu.

✉ 79 rue St-Dominique, 75007 Invalides ☎ 01 47 05 49 75 ⏱ Daily 12–3.30, 7–11.30 🍴 L €35, D €50, Wine €18 Ⓜ Invalides

LE VERRE BOUTEILLE

www.leverrebouteille.com

This bistro, near the Arc de Triomphe, stays open until the small hours. Chef Patrick Ameline's aim is to satisfy with simple food cooked to perfection, and he succeeds. Try the warm goat's cheese, country-style *croque* and chocolate cake. There's also a good selection of wines.

✉ 85 avenue des Ternes, 75017 Étoile ☎ 01 45 74 01 02 ⏱ Tue–Sat 12–3, 7–4 🍴 L €25, D €31, Wine €19.80 Ⓜ Porte Maillot

Opposite *Try some southwestern French fare at Thoumieux*

PRICES AND SYMBOLS

Prices are the lowest and highest for a double room for one night including breakfast, unless otherwise stated. All the hotels listed accept credit cards unless otherwise stated. Note that rates vary widely throughout the year.

For a key to the symbols, ▷ 2.

ACADEMIES ET DES ARTS

www.hotel-des-academies.com
Don't come to this boutique hotel in Montparnasse unless you want to stay in a gallery of contemporary art. There are 'white bodies' by painter Jérôme Mesnager stamped on the facade and the interior walls, sculptures on the staircase and a dedicated video art room. Not so much a place to stay and a base for sightseeing as an affirmation that ultra-modern style is everything.
✉ 15 rue de la Grande Chaumière, 75006 St-Germain-des-Prés ☎ 01 43 26 66 44 💳 €189–€314, excluding breakfast (€12–€16) 🛈 20 ♿ 🚇 Vavin

LE D'ARTAGNAN

www.fuaj.org
This is France's largest youth hostel. Facilities include a bar open until 2am, a souvenir shop, four internet booths, electronic lockers, a cinema, TV lounge and automatic laundry. The rooms accommodate from three to eight people.
✉ 80 rue Vitruve, 75020 Ménilmontant ☎ 01 40 32 34 56 💳 €25 per person 🛈 435 beds 🚇 Porte de Bagnolet

L'ATELIER MONTPARNASSE

www.ateliermontparnasse.com
This three-star hotel pays tribute to 1930s Montparnasse. Facilities in the bedrooms include a laundry service, room service, cable TV, hairdryer and minibar. There is WiFi throughout the hotel..
✉ 49 rue Vavin, 75006 St-Germain-des-Prés ☎ 01 46 33 60 00 💳 €98–€167, excluding breakfast (€9) 🛈 17 ♿ 🚇 Vavin

AUBERGE DE JEUNESSE JULES FERRY

www.fuaj.org
The dormitories at this youth hostel have up to six beds and there are some bedrooms for couples. Facilities include an automatic laundry, electronic lockers and internet terminals. There is no kitchen although breakfast is included but there is a microwave that guests can use.
✉ 8 boulevard Jules Ferry, 75011 Canal St-Martin ☎ 01 43 57 55 60 💳 €23 per person 🛈 99 beds 🚇 République

GEORGE SAND

www.hotelgeorgesand.com
Between Madeleine and the Opéra close to the theatres and department stores, the George Sand is a short walk from the Louvre. The hotel is named after the 19th-century writer. The contemporary, renovated rooms are comfortable and have internet access, satellite televisions, air conditioning and soundproofing.
✉ 26 rue des Mathurins, 75009 Paris ☎ 01 47 42 63 47 💳 €180–€250, excluding breakfast (€13) 🛈 20 ♿ 🚇 Madeleine, Havre Caumartin

L'HÔTEL

www.l-hotel.com
A discreet, semi-luxurious hotel, which started life as a 'Pavillion d'Amour', on a quiet back street in St-Germain-des-Prés, convenient for visiting the Left Bank and the islands and sights across the river. The exuberantly elegant interior is by Jacques Garcia. If you want somewhere unique to stay, ask for the room in which Oscar Wilde died

Above *The bar area in L'Hôtel*

(▷ 107). The restaurant is closed on Sunday, Monday and during the month of August.

✉ 13 rue des Beaux-Arts, 75006 St-Germain-des-Prés ☎ 01 44 41 99 00 🛏 €255–€640, excluding breakfast (€16) 🛏 16 rooms, 4 suites 🔲 ▨ ▧ 🚇 St-Germain-des-Prés

HÔTEL CLUNY SORBONNE

www.hotel-cluny.fr

A small hotel on a quiet street facing the university of the Sorbonne, away from the noise of the grand boulevards. It has a modest claim to fame since the poet Rimbaud stayed here (▷ 106). Rooms have satellite TV and hair dryers, and guests have access to free WiFi. There is a pay car park not far from the hotel.

✉ 8 rue Victor Cousin, 75005 Paris ☎ 01 43 54 66 66 🛏 €8–€138 🛏 23 🚇 Cluny–La Sorbonne

HÔTEL FRANKLIN ROOSEVELT

www.hrroosevelt.com

This hotel has a warm atmosphere. For a bit of luxury, reserve the sixth-floor suite, which has a king-size bed and a Jacuzzi. Hotel facilities include a bar, a reading room and a winter garden.

✉ 18 rue Clément Marot, 75008 Champs-Élysées ☎ 01 53 57 49 50 🛏 €320–€360, excluding breakfast (€25) 🛏 48 🔲 🚇 Franklin D. Roosevelt, Alma Marceau 🚆 RER Pont-de-l'Alma

HOTEL GRAMONT

www.hotel-gramont-opera.com

Close to the Grands Boulevards and the Opéra, the renovated Gramont is a nicely decorated, well furnished and comfortable but unfussy property. There's a bar as well as a basement breakfast room on site. Free WiFi is available to guests.

✉ 22 rue Gramont 75002 ☎ 01 42 96 85 90 🛏 €145–€250 🛏 25 🔲 🚇 Opéra

HÔTEL DU JEU DE PAUME

www.jeudepaumehotel.com

A charming and romantic hotel on Île St-Louis in a 17th-century royal mansion incorporating a *jeu de paume* court. The hotel is centrally located for sightseeing.

✉ 54 rue Saint Louis en l'Île, Île St-Louis, 75004 ☎ 01 43 26 14 18 🛏 €285–€560, excluding breakfast (€18) 🛏 30 🚇 Pont Marie

HÔTEL DU PANTHÉON

www.hoteldupantheon.com

This three-star hotel is in the heart of the Latin Quarter. The rooms look onto the Panthéon and have cable TV and a minibar. There is also a laundry service and parking.

✉ 19 place du Panthéon, 75005 Latin Quarter ☎ 01 43 54 32 95 🛏 €90–€130 🛏 36 🔲 🚇 Cardinal Lemoine 🚆 RER Luxembourg

HÔTEL DU PARC MONTSOURIS

www.hotel-parc-montsouris.com

A little way from the main attractions, the quiet bedrooms at this two-star hotel have desks, cable TVs, free WiFi and hairdryers.

✉ 4 rue du Parc Montsouris, 75014 Denfert-Rochereau ☎ 01 45 89 09 72 🛏 €80–€90, excluding breakfast (€8) 🛏 35 🚇 Porte d'Orléans 🚆 RER Cité Universitaire

HÔTEL LE PETIT PARIS

www.hotelpetitparis.com

Designed and furnished by Sybille de Margerie, each room at the Petit Paris is individually and sumptuously furnished in striking style, taking inspiration from the major eras of the history of the city. It's in the heart of the stylish Latin Quarter—a very good address. Free WiFi.

✉ 214 rue Saint Jacques, 75005 ☎ 01 53 10 29 29 🛏 €240–€340 🛏 19 rooms, 1 suite 🚇 Luxembourg

HÔTEL ST-MERRY

www.hotelmarais.com

This three-star hotel was once the presbytery of the church of St-Merry. Built during the Renaissance, its interior also includes late-Gothic features. The suite and room nine are particularly distinctive. Guests have access to free WiFi.

✉ 78 rue de la Verrerie, 75004 Le Marais ☎ 01 42 78 14 15 🛏 €130–€250, excluding breakfast (€11) 🛏 11 rooms, 1 suite 🔲 🚇 Hôtel-de-Ville, Châtelet 🚆 RER Châtelet–Les-Halles

HÔTEL DE VARENNE

www.varenne-hotel-paris.com

A small. wood-panelled lobby with a feeling of yesteryear sets the scene for this welcoming budget option. Well placed for Musée Orsay, Musée Rodin and Les Invalides, the rooms are a little on the small side but nicely finished. A walled garden at the rear of the property is an extra bonus for outdoor relaxation.

✉ 44 rue de Bourgogne, 75007 ☎ 01 45 51 45 55 🛏 €130–€280 🛏 25 🚇 Varenne

PAVILLON DE LA REINE

www.pavillon-de-la-reine.com

This was the residence of Anne of Austria, Louis XIII's wife, and the exquisite interior retains many of its period features. Even the vaulted cellar where you can have breakfast has tapestries on the walls. Rooms have cable TV and some have canopy beds. Some bedrooms are in a second, more modern building.

✉ 28 place des Vosges, 75003 Le Marais ☎ 01 40 29 19 19 🛏 €380–€490, excluding breakfast (€28) 🛏 34 🔲 🚇 Bastille, St-Paul

RITZ

www.ritzparis.com

This world-famous hotel has been the epitome of luxury and elegance since its opening in 1898. The lavish interior is typical of French classicism, with antiques, chandeliers and heavy drapes. The hotel has a club, several restaurants, bars, private salons and the gourmet cookery school, Ritz-Escoffier.

✉ 15 place Vendôme, 75001 Opéra ☎ 01 43 16 30 30 🛏 €550–€870, excluding breakfast (€38–€67) 🛏 135 rooms, 40 suites 🔲 ▨ Indoor ▧ 🚇 Tuileries, Madeleine, Concorde

TERRASS HOTEL

www.terrass-hotel.com

Rooms are decorated in classical French style, and have satellite TV. The hotel has its own bar and restaurant as well as room service.

✉ 12 rue Joseph de Maistre, 75018 Montmartre ☎ 01 46 06 72 85 🛏 €170–€310 🛏 98 (2 non-smoking floors) 🚇 Place de Clichy, Blanche

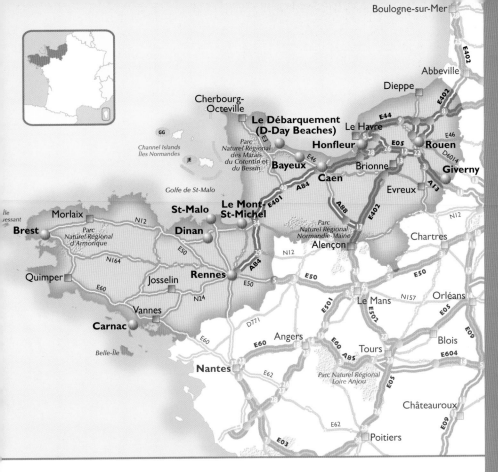

Boulogne-sur-Mer
Abbeville
Dieppe
Cherbourg-Octeville
Le Débarquement (D-Day Beaches)
Le Havre
Honfleur
Rouen
Giverny
Channel Islands Îles Normandes
GG
JE
Parc Naturel Régional des Marais du Cotentin et du Bessin
Bayeux
Brionne
Caen
Evreux
Golfe de St-Malo
St-Malo
Le Mont-St-Michel
Parc Naturel Régional Normandie-Maine
Chartres
Île d'Ouessant
Morlaix
Dinan
Alençon
Brest
Parc Naturel Régional d'Armorique
Quimper
Josselin
Rennes
Le Mans
Orléans
Vannes
Carnac
Angers
Tours
Blois
Belle-Île
Nantes
Parc Naturel Régional Loire Anjou
Châteauroux
Poitiers

E402, E44, E46, E05, D6014, A13, E401, A84, A88, E402, N12, N12, E50, N164, E60, N24, D771, E60, E60, A85, E604, E62, E501, E502, N157, E05, E09, E05, E09, E62, E03, D

NORTHWEST FRANCE

Two peninsulas give a distinctive shape to the western coast of France: one is Brittany, protruding 200km (120 miles) into the Atlantic; the other, Cotentin, belongs to neighbouring Normandy. Both of these regions have great individual character but what they have in common is the constant backdrop of the ocean, and it is often the coast that provides the greatest attractions. There are magnificent cliffs at Étretat on Normandy's Côte d'Albâtre (north of Le Havre) and at Pointe du Raz, the dramatic highlight of Brittany's Finistère, literally 'the end of the earth'. All the way along the coast there are beautiful beaches and holiday resorts popular among holidaymaking families from France and abroad.

Normandy's northern-looking beaches, however, have a sobering story to tell. On D-Day, 6 June 1944, thousands of fighting men came ashore on them to begin the liberation of occupied France, many losing their lives before they could make the beachhead.

The region's other attractions include ancient monuments such as the prehistoric alignments of standing stones at Carnac, the medieval town of Bayeux, where the famous tapestry of William the Conqueror's invasion of England is on display, or the atmospheric Mont St-Michel, rising out of a mesmerizing tidal bay between Brittany and Normandy.

The northwest has very few large cities, and while Caen, Rennes and Rouen are worth seeing, they are not unmissable. It is far better to travel the quiet country roads that link picturesque towns and villages, stopping perhaps to buy a fresh Camembert cheese or bottle of Calvados brandy (both specialities of Normandy) or to have a light lunch of crêpes, France's favourite fast food, which originated in Brittany. You'll probably find it hard to choose which places to leave out of your itinerary but don't miss the garden at Giverny where the Impressionist Claude Monet sat painting his large canvases of water lilies.

ALENÇON

www.paysdalencontourisme.com
www.ville-alencon.fr

Normandy's southern gateway is a handsomely restored old market town and the heart of the region's lace-making industry. Royal lace works were introduced here by Colbert, Louis XIV's finance minister, bringing together various lace-making techniques already established in the town. A museum pays homage to the craft. The Musée des Beaux-Arts et de la Dentelle (early Jul–early Sep Tue–Sun 10–6; early Sep–early Jul Tue–Sun 10–12, 2–6) is in a former Jesuit college in the Cour Carrée de la Dentelle. It illustrates the history of various European schools of lace-making, from the first to the 20th century. A small boutique at the entrance to the museum sells a range of high-quality examples.

Lace apart, there is plenty more to see in Alençon, including the Halle au Blé (corn exchange), opposite the town hall, with its stunning glass dome.

The town's religious heritage includes the birthplace of St. Thérèse of Lisieux, at 50 rue St-Blaise, and the Flamboyant Gothic Notre-Dame church, in place de la Magdeleine. The tourist office is in the Maison d'Ozé, a splendid turreted 16th-century house. Alençon's oldest building is believed to be the medieval Café des Sept Colonnes, in Grande Rue, a high-gabled, timbered building once home to the town executioner.

The library of the Musée des Beaux-Arts et de la Dentelle is a former chapel, with a wooden ship-shaped roof. The conservatory is filled with plants.

✚ 464 G5 ℹ Maison d'Ozé, place de la Magdeleine, 61003 ☎ 02 33 80 66 33 ◷ Jul–Sep Mon–Sat 9.30–7, Sun 10–12.30, 2–4.30; Apr–Jun Mon–Sat 9.30–12.30, 1.30–6.30; Oct–Mar Mon–Sat 9.30–12.30, 2–6 🚌 Alençon

Opposite *The village of Le Bec-Hellouin*
Right *Inspecting fishing boats alongside Barfleur's harbour*

BARFLEUR

www.ville-barfleur.fr

Just a short drive from the more commercial ferry port of Cherbourg (▷ 131), Barfleur sits on the eastern side of the Cotentin peninsula on a stretch known as the Viking coast. The town has been a port since the days of the Vikings and in the Middle Ages it was the peninsula's principal port. A plaque at the port entrance reminds you that the boat that took William the Conqueror to England in 1066 was built in Barfleur's shipyards. The town's tradition of supplying England with monarchs continued in 1194, when Richard the Lionheart set sail from here to be crowned king.

The prettiest and oldest district is Cour Sainte-Cathérine, with its arched stone entrance by the harbour. The post-Impressionist artist Paul Signac who is famed for his coastal scenes painted many views of Barfleur during the early 1930s.

A gentle stroll along the seaside paths takes in two small lighthouses, dwarfed by the Gatteville Lighthouse at Pointe de Barfleur, 4km (2.5 miles) north of the town, from which there are coastal views. At 75m (246ft) it is the second tallest in France; its light can be seen for 56km (35 miles). A small museum (closed mid-Nov to Jan) at the foot of the lighthouse tells its history and explains modern lighthouse technology.

Barfleur has France's first lifeboat station and there is a lifeboat museum at the harbour.

✚ 463 E3 ℹ 2 Rond-point Guillaume le Conquérant, 50760 ☎ 02 33 54 02 48 ✉ Jul–Aug daily 10–12.30, 2.30–7; May–Jun Mon–Sat 9.30–12.30 2.30–6.30, Sun 2.30–6.30; Feb–Apr, Sep–Nov Mon–Sat 10–12.30, 2.30–5.30; Dec–Jan Mon–Fri 10–12, 2–4. Closed 2 weeks Christmas 🚌 Regular service from Cherbourg

BAYEUX

▷ 126.

LE BEC-HELLOUIN

www.abbayedubec.com
www.monuments-nationaux.fr

The history of this village's peaceful walled abbey has been intertwined with England's for the best part of a millennium. The abbey was founded in the Middle Ages as a place of learning. Lanfranc, later Archbishop of Canterbury, taught here in the 11th century and his successor in England, Anselm, was another alumnus of Le Bec. The 15th-century St-Nicolas Tower is the abbey's only surviving medieval building. The abbey continued to maintain strong links with England even beyond Henry VIII's break with Rome in the 16th century.

During the French Revolution, the monks were expelled, books and tapestries looted and the 13th-century church and chapter house demolished. Even the bells were melted down. Monks returned in 1948 and the church today is in the former refectory wing of the newer 17th- and 18th-century buildings.

The central cloister remains calm and spiritual and the waterside Cour de France is another good place for quiet reflection. A walk through the tranquil grounds is revitalizing. The monks' workshop is famous for producing stylish tableware, including plates, bowls and vases, all brightly painted and for sale in the abbey shop.

The public are welcome to attend services at the abbey—Matins is daily at 7am.

✚ Abbaye du Bec-Hellouin ✚ 464 G4 ✉ 27800 ☎ 02 32 43 72 60 ◷ Daily 7am–9pm (except during services) ◷ Free 🚌 Jun–Sep Mon–Sat 10.30, 11, 3, 4, 5, Sun noon, 3, 4 and 6; Oct–May Mon–Sat 11, 3, 4, Sun noon, 3, 4 🎟 Adult €5, under 12 (or under 18 if visiting with a family) and all EU nationals 18–25 free

INFORMATION

www.bessin-normandie.com

✚ 463 F4 🛈 Pont St-Jean, 14400
☎ 02 31 51 28 28 🕐 Jun–Aug
Mon–Sat 9–7, Sun 9–1, 2–6; Jan–Mar,
Nov–Dec Mon–Sat 9.30–12.30, 2–5.30;
Apr–May, Sep–Oct daily 9.30–12.30, 2–6
🚆 Bayeux

Bayeux Tapestry

www.tapisserie-bayeux.fr

✉ Centre Guillaume Le Conquérant,
rue de Nesmond ☎ 02 31 51 25 50
🕐 May–Aug daily 9–7; mid-Mar to Apr,
Sep to mid-Nov 9–6.30; mid-Nov to mid-
Mar 9.30–12.30, 2–6. Ticket office closes
45 minutes before the museum 🎟 Adult
€7.80, child (10–18) €3.80, under 10 free

BAYEUX

Clean streets, timbered buildings and the gentle sound of watermills in the medieval quarter make Bayeux a welcome diversion on the Battle of Normandy route. The principal lure is, of course, the tapestry, but the place has more recent historical significance, being the first town liberated from German occupation in 1944. The Musée Mémorial de la Bataille de Normandie (May–Sep daily 9.30–6.30, film shown in English at 9.45, 11.15, 1, 2.45, 4.45, 5.35; Oct–Apr daily 10–12.30, 2–6, film shown in English 10.30, 2.45, 4.15. Ticket office closes one hour before the museum) focuses on the 1944 battle. Bayeux's less violent heritage is displayed in the Musée Baron Gérard in Hôtel du Doyen (show Bayeux Tapestry ticket for free entry; closed until Jun 2012), where you can see art, porcelain and lace exhibitions. The 11th- to 15th-century cathedral (Jul–Sep daily 9–7; Apr–Jun, Oct–Dec 9–6; Jan–Mar 9–5) has a carvings over the south entrance depicting the murder of Archbishop Thomas Becket in Canterbury by soldiers of England's King Henry II.

THE BAYEUX TAPESTRY

The tapestry, 70m (230ft) long but only 50cm (20in) high, is a masterpiece of political propaganda and cartoon storytelling. Commissioned by William the Conqueror's half-brother Odo, Bishop of Bayeux, it was stitched by nuns from 1070 to 1080. The frame-by-frame drama of how William, Duke of Normandy, won the crown of England in 1066 is punctuated by Latin captions, dramatic scenes of Halley's Comet, shipwrecks and banquets. The easiest way to interpret the tapestry is to listen to the commentary on the multilingual audioguide but this imposes a certain pace on the visit, even if you can linger in the exhibition hall at the end. Far better is to arrive prepared by a little background information and let your eyes explore the tapestry in a more relaxed way.

The story is told in 58 chronological scenes divided into three episodes: a visit by Harold, later claimant to the crown, to Normandy in 1064–66 (scenes 1–23); the death of Edward the Confessor on 5 January 1066 causing a crisis over the succession and preparations for the Norman invasion to be launched in the spring of 1066 (scenes 24–38); and as a climax, the landing in England on 28 September 1066 leading to the Battle of Hastings on 14 October 1066 (scenes 39–58) in which William defeats Harold. It's easy to become engrossed in the main narrative but don't ignore the historiated borders of the tapestry which are a veritable bestiary of animals as well as legendary creatures such as dragons.

Above A scene from the Bayeux Tapestry

BREST

Brest is one of France's largest cities and has been a significant settlement since Roman times. The city became an important seaport in the late 13th century and for 50 years in the 14th century it was held by the English. In 1631 Cardinal Richelieu recognized its strategic importance and developed it as a rudimentary naval base.

Over subsequent centuries its facilities and fortifications were improved and expanded. Its natural deep-water port makes it ideal as a submarine base. In 1941 the German navy built a bunker here from which U-boats could operate in the north Atlantic. The bunker was attacked 80 times by Allied bombers before Brest was liberated in 1944 causing surprisingly little damage. The French navy now uses Brest harbour as a base (along with Toulon) for its fleet of nuclear submarines. Despite its long history, the city is not particularly enticing—much of its older architecture was destroyed during World War II.

MAJOR SIGHTS

Inland from the waterfront, on the allée du Bot, the Conservatoire Botanique National de Brest is a fine botanical garden (garden: daily 9–6, free; greenhouses: Apr to mid-Sep Sun–Thu 2–5.30, small fee). The Musée des Beaux-Arts, at 24 rue Traverse (Wed–Sat, Mon 10–12, 2–6, Sun 2–6) is noted for its collection of works from the Pont-Aven school. The château, at the tip of the old town, has commanding views along the Rade de Brest and inland along the Elorn river. The Pont de Recouvrance is a huge lift-bridge said to be the highest in Europe. World War II in Finistère is remembered by a memorial museum in Fort Montbarey on allée Bir-Hakeim–route du Conquet (Mon–Fri 9–12, 2–6) where displays tell the story of the escape of free French naval forces, the Resistance, deportations and the German occupation of Brittany.

OCÉANOPOLIS

Brest's most important visitor attraction lies on the waterfront a little way out of the city heart. Océanopolis is a theme park on a Disneyesque scale, based on life in the oceans. More than 10,000 marine creatures live in aquariums varying in capacity from 50 litres (11 gallons) to 1 million litres (220,000 gallons).

The park is divided into three sections—Polar, Tropical and Temperate—and you'll see everything from octopuses and sharks to seahorses and electric eels. There are film shows and regular feeding displays, as well as a re-created penguin environment.

INFORMATION

www.brest-metropole-tourisme.fr

462 B5 place de la Liberté, 29210 02 98 44 24 96 Jul–Aug Mon–Sat 9.30–7, Sun and public hols 10–12; Sep–Jun Mon–Sat 9.30–6 The city bus system (BIBUS) is well organized. There are also bus services around the Brest region Ferry or pleasure boat links with the Crozon Peninsula from the Port du Commerce

Océanopolis

www.oceanopolis.com

Port de Plaisance du Moulin Blanc, BP411 02 98 34 40 40 Jul–Aug daily 9–7; early May–Jun, early to mid-Sep daily 9–6; mid-Sep to early May Tue–Fri 10–5, Sat–Sun 10–6 (also Mon 10–6 during French school hols) Adult €16.50, child (4–17) €11, under 4 free

Below *An aquarium at Brest's Océanopolis*

BELLE-ÎLE

www.belle-ile.com

Belle-Île is the largest of Brittany's islands and has wonderful scenery, especially on the Côte Sauvage in the west, where waves pound the cliffs. The island's capital and main port, Le Palais, is on the more sheltered eastern side, at the mouth of a small river. Sauzon, the second port, is smaller, with painted cottages and a harbour. Bicycle tracks make the island perfect to explore on two wheels. The landscape is dotted with prehistoric menhirs (standing stones). The view of Les Aiguilles de Port-Coton, a series of sharp rocks off the western cliffs, was painted by Monet.

⊞ 462 C7 ⓘ quai Bonnelle, BP30, 56360 ☎ 02 97 31 81 93 ⏱ Jul–Aug Mon–Sat 8.45–7, Sun 8.45–1; Sep–Jun Mon–Sat 9–12.30, 2–6, Sun 10–12.30 ⛴ From Quiberon ☎ 0820 056 000 Seasonal services from Lorient, Port-Navalo, La Turballe, Sauzon, La Trinité and Vannes. Boats: tel 0820 05 61 56 in France, 33 2 97 35 02 00 from abroad ⓘ Several shops in Le Palais rent out bicycles

BREST

▷ 127.

BRIONNE

www.tourismecantondebrionne.com

Brionne became part of Normandy in 1050 when William, Duke of Normandy's three-year siege ousted the Duke of Burgundy. The remains of a Norman keep stand high above the town, with good views over the river and valley. The remaining broad walls are an impressive reminder of William's military might.

The 15th-century Église St-Martin and the doll museum are also well worth visiting.

⊞ 464 G4 ⓘ 1 rue du Général de Gaulle, 27800 ☎ 02 32 45 70 51 ⏱ Jun–Sep Mon–Sat 9.30–12.30, 1.30–6, Sun 10.30–12.30; Apr–May Mon–Sat 9.30–12.30, 1.30–5.30, Sun 10.30–12.30; Oct–Mar Mon–Sat 9.30–12.30, 1.30–5.30

CAEN

▷ 129.

CANCALE

www.ville-cancale.fr
www.cancale-tourisme.fr

Cancale is Brittany's oyster capital and you can sample the shellfish at either a seaside stall or one of the finer restaurants in the port area (La Houle). The town's muddy beaches, on the western flank of the wide, shallow Baie du Mont-St-Michel, aren't ideal for seaside activities, but provide perfect conditions for oysters. The panoramic views of the nearby cliffs are typically Breton.

⊞ 463 E5 ⓘ 44 rue du Port, 35260 ☎ 02 99 89 63 72 ⏱ Jul–Aug Mon–Sat 9–7, Sun 9.30–1; Sep–Jun daily 9–1, 2.30–6 ⊟ TIV, the departmental bus line, runs to Cancale from St-Malo and Dol-de-Bretagne

CAP FRÉHEL

Cap Fréhel is one of Brittany's most dramatic promontories, offering spectacular views of the frothing waves below and the ragged scenery of the Emerald Coast. On a clear day you can see as far as the Channel Islands. Where land meets water, the red sandstone, porphyry and schist rocks break into jagged towers, battered by waves. The headland, 70m (230ft) above the sea, crowns 400ha (1,000 acres) of gorse and heather moorlands. This Fauconnière area is now a reserve, protecting the breeding grounds of several species of seabirds. The area is good for walking. You can visit the Cap Fréhel lighthouse (Jul, Aug daily 2–7).

The best views of the cliffs are from the water rather than the land. You can take boat trips around the cape starting from either St-Malo or Dinard. Fort La Latte (early Jul–Aug daily 10.30–7; Apr–early Jul, Sep daily 10.30–6.30) sits on the eastern promontory of the Anse de Sévignés opposing Cap Fréhel on the western flank. This castle took its current form between 1690 and 1715.

⊞ 463 D5 ⊟ The most picturesque approach to Cap Fréhel is along the D34 coast road

Left *The rugged coastline of Cap Fréhel*
Below *The harbour at Sauzon, Belle-Île*

CAEN

Caen is a working city with a busy river port and several top-class attractions, inevitably associated with tumultuous moments in history. After the massive bombardments of 1944 Caen rebuilt itself as a business-focused city; sadly what older architecture remains is now encircled with unimaginative concrete commercial estates.

REMEMBERING WORLD WAR II

The Mémorial de Caen, on esplanade Eisenhower, in the northwestern outskirts, immerses you in a century of global conflict (mid-Feb to 12 Nov daily 9–7; mid-Nov to mid-Feb 9.30–6; closed two weeks in Jan). The museum starts with the peace pledges of 1919, then moves through newsreels and scenes of daily life to the horrors of the Holocaust and German occupation. Multi-screen special effects recount the Battle of Normandy and a harrowing film, *Espérance*, hammers home the empty truth of post-war peace, with painful images of conflicts in Europe, Africa and the Middle East. Sections of the Berlin Wall mark out a huge Cold War exhibit, and an observatory reveals current locations of global disorder and suffering.

WILLIAM THE CONQUEROR

Highlights in Caen itself include the restored ramparts of the ducal castle, founded by William the Conqueror in the 11th century. Within the castle walls are the Musée des Beaux-Arts (Wed–Mon 9–6) and the Musée de Normandie (Jun–Oct daily 9.30–6, Nov–May Wed–Mon 9.30–6). The castle is flanked by two abbeys—St-Étienne for men and La Trinité for women—founded by William and his cousin-bride Matilda to help them to regain admission to the Church after being excommunicated following their incestuous marriage. These abbeys are known as the Abbaye-aux-Hommes and the Abbaye-aux-Dames.

You can see William the Conqueror's tomb at the Gothic-Renaissance abbey church of St-Étienne, although only his thighbone remains after a raid by Huguenots in the 16th century. The abbey itself is now the Hôtel de Ville, while the ladies' convent is home to the regional council. Guided tours allow you to see Matilda's tomb, the grand staircase and the cloister.

INFORMATION

www.ville-caen.fr
www.tourisme.caen.fr
✚ 464 F4 ℹ️ place St-Pierre, 14000
☎ 02 31 27 14 14 🕐 Jul–Aug Mon–Sat 9–7, Sun and public hols 10–1, 2–5; Sep–Mar Mon–Sat 9.30–1, 2–6; Apr Mon–Fri 9.30–1, 2–6, Sun 10–1 🍽️ The restaurants of the Vaugueux quarter are known for excellent seafood 🚌 Buses and a tramway 🚆 Caen ✈️ Caen-Carpiquet Airport, 9km (5.5 miles) west of the city

TIPS

» The Ticket 24h bus and tram pass costs €3.55 and is valid for 24 hours from the time of your first journey. It is sold on buses and trams.
» If you need some soothing surroundings after your visit to the Mémorial de Caen peace museum, head for the nearby avenue Amiral Mountbatten, where you'll find the Colline aux Oiseaux, a former rubbish tip reinvented as a floral park for the 50th anniversary of D-Day.

Above *A gargoyle on a city roof*

INFORMATION
www.ot-carnac.fr

✚ 462 C7 ℹ Carnac: place de l'Église; Carnac-Plage: 74 avenue des Druides ☎ 02 97 52 13 52 🕐 Carnac: Apr–Sep and French school hols Mon–Sat 9–1, 2–7, Sun 9–1. Carnac-Plage: Jul, Aug Mon–Sat 9–1, 2–7, Sun 2–7; Sep–Jun Mon–Sat 9–12, 2–6 🚌 No. 1 runs from Vannes. A bus connects Carnac-Plage and Carnac town with the main *alignements* several times a day, Jun–Sep 🚋 A *Petit-Train* links Carnac-Plage with Carnac *alignements* and La Trinité-sur-Mer in summer

CARNAC

The first sight of Carnac's fields of standing stones is breathtaking. There are more than 3,000 menhirs and other megalithic structures within a 4.5km (3-mile) radius and nobody knows for sure who put them there. What most experts agree is that the monuments—mostly long lines *(alignements)* of standing stones (menhirs)—were erected between 4500 and 1800BC and were used during a religious or ritual activity. It's possible that the *alignements* had some astronomical or calendrical function and that Carnac was once a place of pilgrimage comparable to Jerusalem or Mecca.

There are three main groups of *alignements* just north of the town. Ménec (closest to town), Kermario and Kerlescan, plus a smaller group, Petit Ménec, to the east and various other dolmens and prehistoric sites. Conservation measures mean it is no longer possible to wander at will among them. A Maison des Mégalithes (tel 02 97 52 29 81; Jul–Aug daily 9–8; May–Jun 9–7; Sep–Apr 10–5—times may vary) has been built in the parking area opposite the Ménec *alignements*, where guided tours can be arranged. There is also a small boutique and some explanation of the sites.

MORE PREHISTORIC FINDS

Le Musée de Préhistoire (10 place de l'Église; Jul–Aug daily 10–6; Apr–Jun, Sep Wed–Mon 10–12.30, 2–6; Oct–Mar Wed–Mon 10–12.30, 2–5; also open on Tue during French school hols; adult €5, child (8–18) €2.50) uses more than 6,000 prehistoric items to create a vivid picture of the people who may have erected the stones.

Some 300m (1,000ft) east of the town, the tumulus of St-Michel is a prehistoric burial mound that looks so much like a natural hill that a chapel was built on it in the 16th century. The mound, 12m (40ft) high, 125m (400ft) long and 60m (200ft) wide, is thought to date from around 4500BC.

CARNAC-PLAGE

As well as being France's megalithic capital, Carnac is also a holiday resort with a good beach (Carnac-Plage). The beach is linked by bus to the town centre and the *alignements* inland.

Opposite *Cherbourg's seafaring history continues to the present day*
Below *Standing stones or menhirs at Carnac*

CHÂTEAU DE KERJEAN
www.cdp29.fr

This fortified manor was built in the 16th century, when Louis Barbier decided to commission a home that would outdo that of his rival and one-time overlord at nearby Lanhouarneau. The building was damaged by fire in 1710 and suffered again during the Revolution, when the last feudal lord was guillotined. In 1911 it passed into state ownership and was restored and filled with antique furnishings.

In 20ha (50 acres) of parkland, it hosts a museum of Breton daily life. The lovely Renaissance well in the second courtyard comes complete with Corinthian columns.

✚ 462 B5 ✉ 29440 St-Vougay ☎ 02 98 69 93 69 🕐 Jul,–Aug daily 10–7; Jun, Sep Wed–Mon 1–6; Oct Wed–Mon 10–5; Nov–Dec, Feb–Mar Wed, Sun 2–5; Apr Wed–Mon 2–6. Also Wed–Mon during French school holidays, hours dependent on the month 💳 Adult €5, 18–25 €3.50, child (7–17) €1, under 7 free 🚗 The château is signposted off the D30 between Plouescat and Landivisiau 🎁 Gift shop with books and postcards

CHERBOURG
www.ot-cherbourg-cotentin.fr

Cherbourg has flourished as both a military and passenger port. Today the imposing art deco Gare Maritime Transatlantique passenger terminal has been reinvented as Cité de la Mer (Jul–Aug daily 9.30–7; Jun, Sep 9.30–6; Oct–Dec, Feb–Mar 10–6. Closed Jan), a celebration of Cherbourg's seafaring heritage. The biggest attraction is *Le Redoutable*, France's first nuclear submarine, and the largest submarine in the world open to the public. There's also a museum of naval history and an aquarium with an impressive 'undersea' trail that brings you face to face with marine life. Give yourself at least three hours to see everything.

Non-aquatic attractions in Cherbourg include the Musée de la Libération, in the Fort du Roule, with World War II exhibits (May–Sep Tue–Sat 10–12, 2–6, Sun–Mon 2–6; Oct–Apr Wed–Sun 2–6).

✚ 463 E3 ℹ 2 quai Alexandre III, 50100, ☎ 02 33 93 52 02 🕐 Mid-Jun to mid-Sep Mon–Sat 9.30–7, Sun 10–5; mid-Sep to mid-Jun Mon–Sat 10–12.30, 2–6 🚆 Cherbourg

COMBOURG
www.combourg.net
www.combourg.org

The château at lakeside Combourg is where the Romantic writer François-René de Chateaubriand (1768–1848) spent a short but gloomy period of his youth. The edifice rises above the maze of stone cottages surrounding it and there are lovely views from the château. Founded in the 11th century by the Archbishop of Dol (Dol-de-Bretagne), it underwent expansions and changes throughout the Middle Ages before coming into the hands of the Comte de Chateaubriand, father of the writer. The period the author spent here is recalled in his *Memoires d'Outre-Tombe*; in one room you can see his papers and furniture.

✚ 463 E5 ℹ Maison de la Lanterne, place Albert Parent, 35270 ☎ 02 99 73 13 93 🕐 Apr–Sep Mon–Sat 10–1, 2.30–6.30, Sun 10–12.30; Oct–Mar Mon–Sat 10–1, 2–6
Château ✉ 23 rue des Princes ☎ 02 99 73 22 95 🕐 Jul–Aug daily visits at 10.30 and 11.15, also 2–5.10; Apr–Jun, Sep–Oct 2–5. Gardens: Jul–Aug daily 9.30–12.30, 2–6; Apr–Jun, Sep Sun–Fri 9.30–12.30, 2–6; Oct Sun–Fri 10–12, 2–5

CONCARNEAU
www.concarneau.fr
www.tourismeconcarneau.fr

Concarneau combines all that is best about Brittany. It is one of France's key fishing ports and hosts great fish auctions (*criées*). The bustling town has plenty of shops and restaurants and a historic walled town (Ville

Close) is on an island within the port. There are beaches and boat trips.

The town was first fortified in the 11th century and was at its most formidable during the 14th century. The Ville Close, linked to the rest of the town by a bridge and gateway, was fortified by the military strategist Vauban during Louis XIV's reign. There are excellent views from its ramparts.

The main street, rue Vauban, is flanked by 16th- to 18th-century buildings filled with souvenir shops. The Musée de la Pêche (Fishing Museum) is at the start of this street (Jul–Aug daily 9.30–8 Apr–Jun, Sep–Oct 10–6; Feb–Mar 10–12, 2–6. Closed Nov–Jan except All Saints and Christmas holidays).

Concarneau's modern marina is on the seaward side of the Ville Close, while the main fishing port, with its utilitarian buildings, is on the land side. The fish auction at quai de la Criée (arrive by 6.30am) is the largest in Brittany and the catches are dispatched across France.

If you prefer to see live fish, visit the Marinarium, on the seafront at the place de la Croix. Much more than an aquarium, this is the showcase of the marine biology laboratory of Concarneau.

✚ 462 B6 ℹ quai d'Aiguillon, BP529, 29185 ☎ 02 98 97 01 44 🕐 Jul–Aug daily 9–7; Sep, May–Jun, early to mid-Sep Mon–Sat 9–12.30, 1.45–6.30, Sun 10–1; mid-Sep to Apr Mon–Sat 9–12, 2–6 🚌 20 to the main train line at Rosporden; 21 to Port Manech; 14A to Pont-Aven and Quimper; 15 to la Forêt-Fouesnant and Beg-Meil ⛴ To the Glénan Islands or along the Odet river with Vedettes Glenn ❓ The Blue Nets Festival is held in late Aug

LE CONQUET

www.leconquet.fr

Le Conquet is perhaps the prettiest of Brittany's coastal villages, with its whitewashed cottages hugging the hillside and its lively fishing harbour. There are beautiful beaches nearby: It is only a 2km (1-mile) walk from the harbour, via a footbridge, to the fine Plage des Blancs-Sablons. You can take a ferry to the islands of Ouessant and Molène. The square above the port is flanked by fishermen's stone cottages and is full of lobster pots, baskets and nets. Casting a protective eye over the port is La Maison des Seigneurs, part of a larger fortress dating from the 15th century and now a private home. Tiny but interesting Dom Michel chapel is at the top of rue Dom Michel le Noblezt.

Offshore lie the waters of the Parc Naturel Régional d'Armorique (Armorica Nature Reserve), now classed as a Biosphere Reserve by UNESCO. You can take trips by glass-bottomed boat.

➕ 462 A5 🛈 Parc de Beauséjour, 29217 ☎ 02 98 89 11 31 🕔 Mid-Jun to mid-Sep Mon–Sat 9.30–12.30, 2.30–7, Sun and public hols 9.30–12.30; Apr to mid-Jun Tue–Fri 9.30–12.30, 2.30–5.30, Sat 9.30–12.30; mid-Sep to Mar Tue–Sat 9.30–12.30 🚌 31 to Brest 🚢 To Molène and Ouessant

CÔTE D'ALBÂTRE

The Côte d'Albâtre (Alabaster Coast) from Le Havre to Le Tréport at the mouth of the Bresle river is named after its white cliffs which are most impressive at Étretat (▷ 166–167).

The largest town on the coast after Dieppe (▷ 135), is Fécamp where Benedictine liqueur is made in a distillery-cum-art gallery.

The prettiest place, meanwhile, is Veules-les-Roses, north of Saint-Valery-en-Caux, a holiday resort which claims to have the shortest river in France running through it. This gurgling stream flows for just over 1km (0.6 miles) from a source marked by watercress beds—flushed vivid green in winter—to the sea and is followed by a pleasant footpath.

➕ 464 G3 🛈 Offices at Le Havre, Étretat, Fécamp and Dieppe

CÔTE DE GRANIT ROSE

The Pink Granite Coast is one of the most dramatic stretches of Brittany's shoreline. Here, land meets sea in a spectacle of high cliffs, narrow inlets, fjord-like river valleys and sheltered coves. The name derives from the granite rocks—pinkish-brown in harsh sunlight, mellowing to a deep rosy hue at sunset.

The best places to see the rocks lie between Trébeurden in the west and Paimpol in the east. There is no easy route to follow along the coast for drivers. Narrow lanes carry you past tiny settlements to windblown promontories such as Pointe du Château or Le Gouffre.

The stretch around Ploumanac'h is good for walking, with the added benefit that you are never too far from a restaurant at Ploumanac'h or Perros-Guirec.

➕ 462 C4 🛈 Offices at Trébeurden, Perros-Guirec (▷ 145), Tréguier and Paimpol

COTENTIN PENINSULA

www.ot-cherbourg-cotentin.fr

This unspoiled peninsular landscape is far removed from Normandy's commercial towns and the fairy-tale quaintness of the hinterland. The Cotentin Peninsula offers visitors an authentic glimpse of French rural life, with farming and fishing to the fore.

On the west of the peninsula, the stark rugged coastline around Cap de La Hague and Nez de Jobourg is almost Breton in its craggy majesty, perfect for windswept walks and views out to the Channel Islands.

In contrast, the eastern side has a more verdant landscape. The fields and rich woodland around the Val de Saire stretch to the dunes of the D-Day beaches.

Highlights of the region include the view from Gatteville Lighthouse at Barfleur (▷ 125) and the island of Tatihou, with its Vauban fort, off the coast of the oyster fishing port of St-Vaast-la-Hougue. No more than 500 visitors a day are permitted. Arrive on foot at low tide or take the amphibious boat, included in the admission fee, to the fort and maritime museum.

➕ 463 E4 🛈 Cité de la Mer, Gare Maritime Transatlantique, 50100 Cherbourg-Octeville ☎ 02 33 20 26 26 🕔 Jul–Aug daily 9.30–7; Jun, Sep 9.30–6; Oct–Dec, Feb–Mar 10–6. Closed Jan 🚉 Cherbourg

COUTANCES

www.coutances.fr

Hailed as a masterpiece of Norman Gothic architecture, the cathedral at Coutances is grafted on to the remains of a Romanesque church. The 13th-century construction is well proportioned, with strong buttresses and elegant spires. Stained glass tells the story of St. Thomas Becket.

The nearby Jardin des Plantes is pleasant for a walk or picnic. In Ascension week, catch the jazz festival *Jazz sous les Pommiers*.

➕ 463 E4 🛈 place Georges Leclerc, 50200 Coutances ☎ 02 33 19 08 10 🕔 Jul–Aug Mon–Fri 9.30–6.30, Sat 10–12.30, 2–6, Sun 10–1; Sep–Jun Mon–Fri 9.30–12.30, 2–6, Sat 10–12.30, 2–5 🚉 Coutances

D-DAY BEACHES

Eight well-signposted routes take you through *Le Débarquement*—the invasion, battles and liberation of Normandy—and the beginning of the end of World War II. For veterans and their families, the respect with which the sacrifices of a generation are treated is uplifting. For younger people, the lessons of the past are recounted in a simple yet powerful way.

LIBERATION PLAN

A year before D-Day, Winston Churchill and Franklin D. Roosevelt began planning *Operation Overlord*, the Allied invasion of Normandy. On the night of 5 June 1944, 4,000 landing craft set sail from England for the Cotentin and Calvados coast in preparation for the dawn raids.

Aircraft silently targeted key defences at either end of the invasion front, with gliders and parachutists of the 6th Airborne Division taking Pegasus Bridge on the Caen-Ouestreham Canal at Benouville. Next, several hundred Rangers captured the Pointe du Hoc, before the landings at the five key beaches, where around 135,000 men and 20,000 vehicles came ashore from a large fleet of vessels between 6.30 and 7.30am.

British, French and Commonwealth forces, aiming to capture Caen, landed at beaches code-named Sword (Bella Riva, Lion-sur-Mer and St-Aubin), Juno (Bernières and Courseulles) and Gold (Ver-sur-Mer and Asnelles). Farther west, American troops landed at Omaha (St-Laurent, Colleville and Vierville) and Utah (the Cotentin coast towards Cherbourg). Losses were heavy, but the German forces lacked air support and the Allies won a vital toehold.

SEE WHERE IT HAPPENED

At Arromanches, remains of the prefabricated Mulberry Harbour towed across the Channel can still be seen offshore. Learn more about the landings at the Musée du Débarquement (late Jan–Dec daily) and the Arromanches 360-degree circular cinema. Pegasus Bridge sits in the grounds of the Mémorial Pegasus museum (Feb–Nov), in Ranville.

Rows of neatly tended war graves provide an indelible memory, whether the small plot of 40 British graves at Chouain, the classical Commonwealth memorial at Bayeux or the precision alignment of 9,387 white crosses of the American cemetery at Colleville-sur-Mer.

Quinéville's Le Mémorial de la Liberté Retrouvée (late Mar to mid-Nov daily) contains a street scene of life in occupied Normandy.

INFORMATION

www.calvados-tourisme.com
www.manchetourisme.com
www.ornetourisme.com
🔲 463 F4
Calvados 🔲 440 F4 🔲 8 rue Renoir, 14000 Caen ☎ 02 31 27 90 30 🕐 Mon–Fri 8.30–12.30, 1.30–5.30
Manche 🔲 Maison du Département, route de Villedieu, 50008, St-Lô ☎ 02 33 05 98 70 🕐 Mon–Fri 9–12, 2–5
Orne 🔲 440 G5 🔲 88 rue St-Blaise, 61002, Alençon ☎ 02 33 28 88 71 🕐 Mon–Fri 8.45–12, 1.30–5.30
❓ For the Mémorial de Caen, ▷ 129; for Bayeux's Musée Mémorial de la Bataille de Normandie, ▷ 126

TIPS

» Ask at the tourist office for the free booklet *The D-Day Landings and The Battle of Normandy*. If you buy a full-price ticket at any of the museums listed here, you can gain free entry to most of the others over the next 30 days.

» Many museums close from November to spring. During May and June, arrive early to avoid noisy school parties.

» Most museums have excellent access for people with disabilities.

Opposite *An artist perched above the beach at Barneville-Carteret, on the west coast of Normandy's Cotentin Peninsula*
Below *The ruins of a World War II bunker lapped by waves on Gold beach*

INFORMATION

www.dinan-tourisme.com

463 D5   9 rue du Château, 22105
02 96 87 69 76   Jul–Aug Mon–Sat
9–7, Sun 10–12.30, 2.30–6; Sep–Jun
Mon–Sat 9–12.30, 2–6   Dinan
From St-Malo

DINAN

Medieval Dinan is one of Brittany's best-preserved old towns. Many sections of the 600-year-old ramparts are walkable, such as Duchess Anne's Walk that brings you out into the Jardin Anglais, with panoramic views of the valley. There are also excellent views of the town and the Rance valley to be had from the Tour de l'Horloge.

LOCAL HISTORY

You can find out more about local history at the Château Musée, in the ruined 14th-century castle keep (Jun–Sep daily 10–6.30; Oct–May 1.30–5.30; closed Jan). In the 12th century, Dinan was an important centre for trade. A crusader Rivallon le Roux pledged that, if he survived, he would return to his home town and pay for a church dedicated to Christ. The Romanesque and Gothic St-Sauveur basilica (daily 10–5) was built between the 12th and 18th centuries. The basilica contains relics from many periods in the town's history, including the heart of another local knight, Bertrand du Guesclin, whose equestrian statue stands in place du Guesclin. This square hosts the local Thursday morning market.

EXPLORING THE OLD TOWN

The old town is perfect for exploring on foot. The narrow, cobbled rue du Petit-Fort winds its way (steeply) from the port to the heart of the town. It's lined with medieval merchants' houses, crêperies, arts and crafts shops and the Maison du Gouverneur, a spectacular three-storey, half-timbered house containing a display of regional furniture. Head to the place des Merciers to see the town's most beautiful half-timbered houses. The Gothic Église St-Malo has a superb English organ, dating from the Romantic period, and beautiful stained-glass windows illustrating great moments in the town's history. Every year the town hosts the Fêtes des Remparts in July attended by 500,000 locals and visitors.

A pleasant walk from central Dinan you'll find Léhon, a pretty hamlet with a ninth-century priory. You can take boat trips up the Rance from St-Malo to Dinan from April to September.

Above The Rance flows through the medieval town of Dinan

DEAUVILLE
www.deauville.org
Deauville is the summer playground of the north, with mock-Romanesque hotels and the weekend homes of rich Parisians. Popular pastimes include looking stylish on the seafront, betting on the races, gambling at the casino and seeing a cabaret. The season ends with an American Film Festival in September. The boardwalk is inscribed with names of stars who have graced the promenade. If it all seems very artificial, then that is the point—the resort is an upscale beach party.

🔢 464 G4 ℹ️ place de la Mairie, 14804 ☎️ 02 31 14 40 00 🕐 Jul–Aug (and during Festival du Cinema Americain) Mon–Sat 9–7, Sun 10–6; Sep–Jun Mon–Sat 10–6, Sun 10–1, 2–5 🚆 Deauville-Trouville

DIEPPE
www.dieppetourisme.com
Dieppe is a lively port town. The 15th-century Château-Musée (Jun–Sep daily 10–12, 2–6; Oct–May Mon, Wed–Sat 10–12, 2–5, Sun 10–12, 2–6) has paintings by Renoir, Boudin and Pissarro and an ivory collection, witness to the city's historic trade links with Africa. Other attractions include the timbered 17th-century Maison Miffant, the Cité de la Mer maritime museum and aquarium (daily 10–12, 2–6) and, on a clifftop above the port, the church of Notre-Dame-de-Bon-Secours, built in 1876 in memory of sailors lost at sea. For lunch, head for the quai Henry IV.

🔢 468 H3 ℹ️ Pont d'Ango BP152, 76204 ☎️ 02 32 14 40 60 🕐 Jul–Aug Mon–Thu 9–1, 2–8, Fri–Sat 9–1, 2–7, Sun 10–1, 2–5; May–Jun, Sep Mon–Sat 9–1, 2–6, Sun 10–1, 2–5; Oct–Apr Mon–Sat 9–12, 2–6 🚢 Dieppe ⛴️ From Newhaven, UK (4 hours); 2-hour fast ferry in summer

DINAN
▷ 134.

DINARD
www.ville-dinard.fr
www.ot-dinard.com
Dinard occupies a rocky outcrop across from St-Malo (▷ 154), and has several small, sandy beaches. High tides and sea breezes provide excellent yachting conditions, and the tempering effects of the Gulf Stream encourage subtropical vegetation.

Dinard was a Breton fishing port until the 19th century, when it was discovered by wealthy Americans and Britons. During the belle époque it was a place for yachting, gambling and other upper-class leisure activities. Today it is an upscale resort, popular with French visitors.

The Plage de l'Écluse, with its distinctive blue-and-white striped cotton beach huts, is the largest beach. Overlooking it is the Casino Barrière de Dinard (Gaming tables May–Sep Mon–Fri 9pm–3am, Sat–Sun 9pm–4am; Oct–Apr Wed–Thu, Sun 9pm–3am, Fri–Sat 9pm–4am. Slot machines Jul–Aug daily 11am–4am; Sep–Jun Sun–Thu 11am–2pm, Fri–Sat 11am–4am). Nearby are an Olympic-size, covered, heated seawater pool (French school hols daily 10–12.30, 3–7.30; rest of year Mon–Fri 10–12.30, 3–6.30, Sat 2–6.30, Sun 9–12.30) and the Palais des Arts et Festivals.

A footpath, the Chemin de Ronde, leads along the coast. The section from Plage du Prieuré to the Pointe du Mulinet, called Promenade du Clair de Lune, is popular for a stroll.

🔢 463 D5 ℹ️ 2 boulevard Féart, 35802 ☎️ 02 99 46 94 12 🕐 Mon–Sat 9.30–12.30, 2–6, Sun 10–12.15, 2.15–6 🚌 From St-Malo, La Richardais, St-Lunaire, St-Briac-sur-Mer and Lancieux. Nos. 7a, 11 link with Dinan ⛴️ From St-Malo ✈️ Dinard-Pleurtuit-St Malo airport is 6km (4 miles) south of the town ❓ During summer the Promenade du Clair de Lune is floodlit after dark and there are concerts in the gardens

DOMFRONT
www.domfront.com
Unrivalled views over the landscape of Lower Normandy make this pretty town an essential stop on a clear day. Dominated by the remnants of an 11th-century fortress perched high on the hilltop overlooking the Varenne river, the town has clusters of typical stone and timber houses lining its cobbled streets. At the foot of the hill stands the church of Notre-Dame-sur-l'Eau, where St. Thomas Becket is said to have celebrated Mass in 1166. In spring and summer brick-bordered flower beds, pots and hanging baskets justify Domfront's reputation as one of Normandy's *Villes Fleuries*. The town is in the heart of Camembert country and also produces the brandy Calvados Domfrontais (made with apples and pears), Pommeau, a fortified apple drink, and Poiré (perry). In spring, the blossom of the pear orchards outside Domfront is an unforgettable sight and scent.

🔢 463 F5 ℹ️ 12 place de la Roirie, 61700 ☎️ 02 33 38 53 97 🕐 Tue–Sat 10–12.30, 2–6 🚆 Flers, 23km (14 miles) away, then bus to Domfront ❓ In early Aug the town stages a medieval fair, with music, markets and feasting

Above *Dinard is a popular seaside resort*
Below *The chalk cliffs at Étretat*

mid-Jul, early Sep Mon–Sat 10–12.30, 2–6, Sun 10.45–12.45; early Apr to mid Apr, early Sep–Oct Mon–Sat 10–12.30, 2–6; Nov–Mar Mon–Sat 10–12.30, 2–5.30 🚌 Links to Quimper, Pont-Croix, Audierne and the Pointe du Raz ❓ Some beaches in the bay can be dangerous for swimming

ÉVREUX
www.grandevreuxtourisme.fr
Évreux has risen from the ashes many times over the years, most recently after the World War II air raids that melted its cathedral spire. A new spire topped with a golden rooster was installed in 1973. Parts of the church date from the 12th century, and the blend of Early and Flamboyant Gothic styles is testament to the town's rebuilding plans following each battle. Stained-glass windows from the 13th to 17th centuries are well worth a look. The Gothic Tour de l'Horloge chimes the hour from the last vestige of the medieval fortifications.
➕ 464 H4 ℹ️ place Général de Gaulle, 27000 ☎ 02 32 24 04 43 🕐 Mid-Jun to mid-Sep Mon–Sat 9.30–6.30, Sun 10–12.30; mid-Sep to mid-Jun Mon–Sat 9.30–6 🚆 Evreux

GIVERNY
▷ 137.

GRANVILLE
www.ville-granville.fr
On the bay of Mont St-Michel, this busy port and lively summer resort retains its 15th-century battlements. The main entrance to the upper town is via the original drawbridge of the Grande Porte. Climb to the Musée du Vieux Granville (Apr–Sep Wed–Mon, 10–12, 2–6; Oct–Mar Wed, Sat, Sun 2–6) to see local crafts and learn about the history of the fishing port. Modern art at the Musée Richard Anacréon (Jul–Sep Wed–Sun 2–6) includes works by Picasso.
The Musée Christian Dior is in the designer's childhood home (mid-May to Sep daily 10–6.30).
➕ 463 E5 ℹ️ 4 cours Jonville, 50400 ☎ 02 33 91 30 03 🕐 May–Sep Mon–Sat 9–1, 2–7, Sun 3–6; Oct–Apr Mon–Sat 9–12.30, 2–5.30 🚆 Granville

DOUARNENEZ
www.douarnenez-tourisme.com
Douarnenez is Brittany's second fishing town after Concarneau (▷ 131), but it lacks the refined air of its larger sibling. It was never touched by royalty; instead, its heritage is humble fishermen's cottages. The town has several sheltered harbours. You can learn more about links with the sea at the Port-Musée, in place de l'Enfer (Jul–Aug daily 10–7; early Feb–Jun, Sep–early Nov Tue–Sun 10–12.30, 2–6. In winter there's no access to the floating exhibits outside).
The town's history pre-dates Roman times. In the Dark Ages, Douarnenez was associated with King Mark and the Tristan legend and it is also one of the disputed sites of Brittany's mythical sixth-century Atlantis—the Lost City of Ys. In the 16th century, residents were plagued by the pirate La Fontenelle, who ransacked houses and stole stone to build his château on the Île d'Tristan.
There are excellent views over the eastern port from Les Plomarc'h, 500m (1,500ft) to the east.
➕ 462 B6 ℹ️ 1 rue du Dr Mével, BP216, 29172 ☎ 02 98 92 13 35 🕐 Mid-Jul to Aug Mon–Sat 10–7, Sun 10–6.30; mid-Apr to

GUIMILIAU
www.ot-paysdelandivisiau.com
This hamlet is named after St Miliau. The parish close with its Calvary and ornate gate is one of the finest in Brittany but the interior is equally beautifully decorated with detailed carvings on the retables, baptistry and porch. Some 3.5km (5.5 miles) to the northwest is Lampaul-Guimiliau with another fine parish close.
➕ 462 B5 ✉️ 14 avenue Foch, 29400 Landivisiau ☎ 02 98 68 33 33 🕐 Mon–Fri 9–12, 2–6

LE HAVRE
www.lehavretourisme.com
Le Havre is Normandy's premier industrial port, bounded by the English Channel and the Seine estuary. Claude Monet grew up here and his painting of boats in the harbour, *Impression—soleil levant* (c. 1873), gave the Impressionist movement its name. You can see works by Monet and many of his contemporaries at the Musée des Beaux-Arts André Malraux, on boulevard Clemenceau (Mon, Wed–Fri 11–6, Sat–Sun 11–7), as well as other art from the 17th to 20th centuries. The glass building is as close as an indoor space can get to bathing in the natural light that launched Impressionism. Two local artists represented in the gallery are Le Havre's Raoul Dufy and Honfleur's Eugène Boudin.
At the eastern edge of the town sits Harfleur, Normandy's major port until it silted up in the 16th century. In the pretty pedestrianized old town, the rue des 104 commemorates the 104 citizens who delivered the town from marauding Englishmen in 1435. The quayside walks and decorated barges also echo its maritime past.
➕ 464 G4 ℹ️ 186 boulevard Clemenceau, 76600 ☎ 02 32 74 04 04 🕐 Easter–Oct Mon–Sat 9–6.45, Sun 10–12.30, 2.30–5.45; Nov–Easter Mon–Sat 9–12.30, 2–6, Sun 10–1 🚆 Le Havre

Above *The Grande Porte, main entry to the upper town at Granville*
Opposite *Pink and red tulips in Monet's garden at Giverny*

GIVERNY

Thousands of visitors leave the main sightseeing trail in Normandy to visit this modest town in the Seine Valley. Ironically, there are no original works by Impressionist painter Claude Monet in the pretty pink-and-green house where he lived until his death in 1926. Plenty of prints and copies adorn the rooms, but it is the garden and the famous lily pond and bridge that lure the crowds. Gardeners keep the scene as close as possible to the way things were in Monet's day.

INSPIRATION

The painter bought the house in 1895, having rented it as a family home since 1883. It was here that he painted the irises and lily pond scenes that were his final obsessions. You can see his walled garden—Le Clos Normand—and the lily pond. A main road separates the gardens, but an underpass takes visitors safely to the pond. Wonderful though the gardens are, the press of people means they are not a place for quiet contemplation.

CONTINUING THE MONET TRAIL

The art trail spills over onto the nearby streets, and rue Claude Monet is filled with artists' workshops and galleries. The Musée des Impressionnismes (Apr–Oct daily 10–6) has works by Monet's American contemporaries in France. The Hôtel Baudy, a former boarding house and bar in rue Claude Monet, is where Monet met with Renoir, Sisley, Pissarro and Rodin and the American artists who followed them.

INFORMATION

www.giverny.org
www.fondation-monet.com

➕ 464 H4 🛈 Office de Tourisme de Vernon, 36 rue Carnot, 27201 ☎ 02 32 51 39 60 🕐 May–Sep Mon–Sat 9–12, 2–6, Sun 10–12, 2–6; Oct–Apr Mon–Sat 9–12.30, 2–5.30 🚉 Vernon station, then taxi or bicycle 5km (3 miles) to Giverny

Fondation Claude Monet

✉ rue Claude Monet, 27620 ☎ 02 32 51 28 21 🕐 Apr–Oct daily 9.30–6 💶 Adult €5.50 (house and garden), €6 (garden), €1.50 (house); child (8–11) €3.50; under 7 free

TIPS

» Arrive early to see the lily pond without the crowds.
» Visit in early summer to see the gardens at their very best.

INFORMATION
www.ot-honfleur.fr

✚ 464 G4 👤 quai Lepaulmier, 14602
☎ 02 31 89 23 30 🕐 Jul–Aug Mon–Sat
9.30–7, Sun 10–5; Easter–Jun, Sep
Mon–Sat 9.30–12.30, 2.30–6.30, Sun
10–12.30, 2–5; Oct–Easter Mon–Sat
9.30–12.30, 2–6, Sun 10–1 🚌 20 and 50
from Pont-l'Évêque

HONFLEUR

Honfleur is one of France's most attractive working ports and a familiar sight in
art galleries across the world. Painters who have captured the town on canvas
include J.M.W. Turner and local man Eugène Boudin. Honfleur continues to
attract artists seeking seascape inspiration, as well as visitors in search of a
seafood supper at the quayside.

SONS OF HONFLEUR

You can see some of the art inspired by the town at the Musée Eugène
Boudin (mid-Mar to Sep Wed–Mon 10–12, 2–6; Oct to mid-Mar Mon, Wed–Fri
2.30–5.30, Sat–Sun 10–12, 2.30–5.30; closed Jan to mid-Feb), in place Erik Satie.
The local painter's works are hung alongside pieces by Corot, Dufy and Boudin's
student, Monet. Less conventional, but highly stimulating is the Maisons Satie,
in boulevard Charles V (May–Sep Wed–Mon 10–7; Oct–Apr Wed–Mon 11–6;
closed Jan to mid-Feb). This modern museum experience celebrates the life and
work of another son of Honfleur, the eccentric composer and artist Erik Satie
(1866–1925). Art and music join forces as you walk past surreal images, while
headphones play Satie's music.

MARITIME TRADITION

The town also has a strong maritime tradition, as a plaque on the wall of the
16th-century Lieutenance building at the Vieux Bassin (Old Dock) reminds you:
It was from here that French pioneer Samuel de Champlain set sail for Quebec
in the early 17th century. The Vieux Bassin itself is packed with fishing boats and
pleasure craft. Tall, slate-fronted, oak-tiled and timber-framed buildings surround
the port—their ground floors now house ship's chandlers, art galleries and
restaurants. The 15th-century church of Ste-Cathérine, built by shipbuilders, has
its 18th-century bell tower built across the square as a precaution against fire.
Street musicians and craft stalls inhabit the pedestrian-only streets nearby.

Opposite *The haunting ruins of the
Abbaye de Jumièges*
Below *Honfleur's harbour*

ÎLE DE BRÉHAT

www.brehat-infos.fr

Île de Bréhat is a tiny traffic-free rural idyll, criss-crossed with dry-stone walls, granite cottages and myriad species of flowers. It makes a good day trip from the mainland and is ideal for walking or bicycling.

Only 2km (1 mile) off the north Brittany coastline, Bréhat is in fact two tiny islands connected by a 16th-century bridge. Each of the low-lying islands is less than 1km (0.6 mile) long and is surrounded by a ring of treacherous reefs which form a natural protection for its many bays and coves. Most of Bréhat's 470 residents live on the south island, where the mild Gulf Stream climate has encouraged a profusion of Mediterranean plants in the gardens of the pretty painted cottages. Ferries dock at tiny Port Clos, on the south coast. The Plage de Gerzido, the island's best beach, in the east, faces the mainland. From Port Clos it is a 500m (545-yard) walk north to the main village, Le Bourg. West of here is the Chapelle St-Michel from where there are lovely views. Nearby, the Moulin à Marée du Birlot (closed to visitors) is a restored 17th-century tidal watermill.

According to legend, fishermen of Île de Bréhat passed on their knowledge of sea routes to the New World to Christopher Columbus before his 'discovery' of those lands.

➕ 462 C5 ℹ️ Le Bourg, 22870 ☎ 02 96 20 04 15 🕐 Tue–Sat 10–12.30, 2–4.30 🚢 Vedettes de Bréhat operate year-round services from Pointe de l'Arcouest, just north of Paimpol. There are summer crossings from Binic, Erquy and St-Quay-Portrieux

ÎLE DE GROIX

This island, a 50-minute ferry ride from Lorient, is a raised plateau fringed by steep cliffs. The sheltered eastern coast has the best beaches, including the fine Plage des Grands Sables. The force of the Atlantic has left its mark on the western Côte Sauvage (wild coast).

The island, 8km (5 miles) by 2km (1 mile), has few visitor facilities, but there are 25km (15 miles) of

footpaths to explore. Rare minerals are found here and there is a geological reserve near Locmaria.

During the 1930s Groix had the largest tuna fishing fleet in France. You can learn more about the history of the fleet at the Écomusée (Jul–Aug daily 9.30–12, 3–7; May–Jun, Sep daily10–12.30, 2–5; Apr, Oct–Nov Tue–Sun 10–12.30, 2–5; Dec–Mar Wed, Sat–Sun 10–12.30, 2–5) at Port-Tudy. The last tuna fishing boat, the *Kevano*, sits in retirement in the port. Most of the island's 3,000 residents live in the capital, Groix.

➕ 462 C6 ℹ️ quai de Port-Tudy, 56590 ☎ 02 97 86 53 08 🕐 Jul–Aug daily 9.30–1, 2–7; Sep–Jun Mon–Fri 9–12, 2–5 🚢 From Lorient

JOSSELIN

www.paysdejosselin.com

This inland town has a medieval castle, whose rounded turrets make a memorable sight mirrored in the river Oust. The best views of the castle are from across the river in the Quartier Sainte-Croix.

The castle (mid-Jul to Aug daily 11–6; early Apr to mid-Jul, Sep 2–6; Oct Sat–Sun and school hols 2–5. Closed early Nov–early Apr) dates from the 14th century. It was restored in the 19th century. A sober wall of stone overlooks the river, with three circular towers topped by witch's-hat turrets. Once you enter the courtyard, the inland facade offers a riot of Renaissance detail on its 10 upper gables and exquisite

carving over each of its door and window openings on the lower floor. A magnificent carved frieze links the two elements at roof level. Inside, there is 17th- and 18th-century style decoration. Nearby, the Musée de Poupées has a family collection of around 600 dolls, dating from 1880.

A maze of cobbled alleyways links the courtyard to Josselin's main town square, where you'll find the late-15th-century Basilique Notre-Dame-du-Roncier.

➕ 462 D6 ℹ️ 4 rue Beaumanoir, 56210 ☎ 02 97 22 36 43 🕐 Mid-Jul to Aug daily 10–6; Apr to mid-Jul, Sep Mon–Sat 9.30–12, 2–6, Sun 2–6; Oct–Mar Mon–Fri 9.30–12, 2–5.30, Sat 9.30–12 🚌 From Pontivy, Rennes and Ploermel

JUMIÈGES

www.jumieges.fr

Jumièges was the greatest of the Seine Valley abbeys and its haunting ruins are worth a visit. The earliest remains, from the Église St-Pierre, date from the 10th century. The nearby (roofless) church of Notre-Dame, with its white twin towers, was built a century later. The abbey suffered in the 17th century, when much of its stone was used for other buildings. Its ruins stand in well-maintained parkland, and from April to September son-et-lumière shows add to the romantic atmosphere.

➕ 464 G4 ✉️ rue Guillaume le Conquérant ☎ 02 35 37 28 97 🕐 Apr–Sep daily 9–7; Oct–Mar 9.30–1, 2.30–5.30 ✋ Adult €4.60, under 18 free

MONT ST-MICHEL

INTRODUCTION

If the Eiffel Tower is one iconic silhouette of France, the other is Mont St-Michel with its elegant spire pointing skyward from an ancient abbey which looks seamlessly joined to the conical granite rock beneath it. Standing in a vast tidal bay and reached by a causeway, Mont St-Michel always stirs the imagination. Seen from the shore rising out of a mist, there is something distinctly otherworldy about it.

Even when the place is crowded in the height of summer it resonates with 1,300 years of its eventful history. In 708, St. Aubert, Bishop of Avranches, was inspired by repeated visions of the archangel Michael to build a modest chapel on the 79m (260ft) granite Mont Tombé (so named because it was believed to be an ancient graveyard).

Benedictine monks settled here in 966 at the invitation of the Duke of Normandy and a thriving village soon formed around them on the southeast side of the rock. A Romanesque church was constructed in the 11th century and work continued on other buildings over the following centuries. In the 13th century, the finest Gothic buildings, an ensemble known as La Merveille (The Marvel) were added to the abbey. Meanwhile, Mont St-Michel grew to be a famous place of medieval pilgrimage with pilgrims following roads called the 'paths to paradise'.

The Mount was fortified against attacks by the English during the Hundred Years' War (mid-14th to mid-15th centuries) and managed to withstand 30 years of siege. After the Revolution the shrine was rudely transformed into a prison. In 1874, the Mount's cultural and artistic merit was recognized and it was opened to visitors as a national monument. Three years later Emmanuel Frémlet's gilded statue of St. Michael was placed on top of a new steeple, 157m (515ft) high.

A monastic community returned to the site in 1966, the 1,000th anniversary of the installation of the original abbey and today ten members of the Fraternités Monastiques de Jerusalem continue to provide a spiritual counterbalance to what might otherwise be merely a hub of commercialism and tourism. Although 3.5 million visitors come to Mont St-Michel each year, the resident population is just 20. The Mount is now a UNESCO World Heritage Site.

If you're planning to visit during the peak summer months it's worth arriving very early (around 8am) or late in the day (after 5pm) to get a sense of the atmosphere of the place. Another option is to stay overnight in one of the four hotels in the village.

INFORMATION

www.ot-montsaintmichel.com
✚ 463 E5 ℹ BP4, Mont St-Michel 50170 ☎ 02 33 60 14 30 🕐 Jul, Aug daily 9–7; Apr–Jun, Sep Mon–Sat 9–12.30, 2–6.30, Sun 9–12, 2–6; Oct–Mar Mon–Sat 9–12, 2–6, Sun 10–12, 2–5

Le Mont

🍴 At La Mère Poulard, world-famous omelettes, beaten in age-old copper bowls, have fortified pilgrims and visitors alike for years 🚌 From Rennes, St-Malo 🚆 You could take the TGV to Rennes, which connects with a morning bus-link to the Mount. There is also a station at Pontorson, 9km (6 miles) from the Mount, from where you can take a bus 🅿 The visitors' parking alongside the present causeway is to be replaced with a large parking area 2km (1 mile) south of the coast road, on the mainland. Parking will cost €4, but a free eco-friendly shuttle-bus service (eventually to be replaced by a dedicated train line) will take visitors from their vehicles to the Mount ❓ Steep steps make the village difficult for visitor with disabilities

Opposite *Mont St-Michel at sunset*
Below *A distant Mont St-Michel shimmers above the water*

TIPS

» When the main street is packed with people, climb the steps to the less crowded ramparts to look down on the village and across the sea.

» Rather than pay the €8.50 admission charge to visit the abbey, you could time your visit to coincide with the midday Mass, when tickets are free. You can take your time walking through the monument after the service.

» *Son et lumière* shows are staged at the Mount in summer.

WHAT TO SEE

THE ABBEY

www.monuments-nationaux.fr

You can join a guided tour around the abbey and discover the huge treadmill in which prisoners once trudged to work a system of pulleys to haul building materials up the side of the Mount. The abbey is often referred to as La Merveille (The Wonder), but this epithet actually applies to a Gothic extension commissioned by King Philippe Auguste of France in the 13th century to celebrate his conquest of Normandy. The name reflected the amazing feat of the architects and builders who created it in just 20 years. La Merveille contains three floors of dining rooms for pilgrims (the Guests' Hall), nobles (the Knights' Hall) and monks (the Refectory). The Refectory is mysteriously lit by invisible windows. The whole edifice is topped by a tranquil cloister garden, with a window looking out to sea. The slim columns of the cloister are decorated with beasts and figures.

☎ 02 33 89 80 00 ⊙ May–Aug daily 9–7; Sep–Apr 9.30–6 ✋ Adult €8.50, 18–25 €5, under 18 and EU nationals (18–25) free 🎧 Audioguides €4.50

THE VILLAGE

You may be tempted to hurry through the village along the Grande Rue below the abbey, and you'll probably use it for its shops and restaurants, but it has several attractions of its own worth stopping for, including four museums, ramparts, gardens and a church. There are many flights of steps to negotiate so visitors with disabilities may find access difficult. The village may seem incongruously commercial for such a sacred spot, but its traders will tell you that they are merely continuing a medieval tradition. Hundreds of years ago, the final stretch of the pilgrimage route would be lined with souvenir stalls not all that different from those of today, and pilgrims would have to fight their way past hordes of beggars, pickpockets, touts and thieves as they wended their way up the hill to the abbey.

TIDES

The bay experiences the most extreme tidal movements in Europe. In exceptional low tide the sea withdraws 15km (9 miles) and the difference between the high- and low-water marks reaches 15m (50ft). The sea comes back in at a surprisingly fast pace although comparisons to a galloping horse are poetic exaggeration. The phenomenon of an incoming tide is worth witnessing at leisure from a good vantage point.

The most spectacular movements of water are the spring tides 36 to 48 hours after full and new moons, when the sun, earth and moon are in alignment. You need to be on the Mount a good two and a half hours before the high water mark is reached. Ask the tourist office for a tide table.

A plan is underway to reduce the silting up of the bay and thus reduce the extreme differences in high- and low-water marks. It is due for completion by 2012 and as part of it the causeway will be replaced with a pedestrian bridge.

Opposite *The abbey of Mont St-Michel towers over the village*

Below *This small side chapel in the abbey complex has beautiful stained-glass windows*

MAISONS DE LA BAIE

www.maison-baie.com

Back on the mainland, you can enjoy wonderful views of the Mount from the Maison de la Baie vantage points at Le Vivier-sur-Mer, Courtils and St-Léonard. These individually themed mini-museums offer a perspective on the daily life of the abbey in past times, along with excellent displays of local wildlife. They also organize escorted treks across the sands to the Mount, on foot and horseback, and guided tours of up to seven hours to explore the mussel and oyster beds and tidal shallows.

☎ Courtils: 02 33 89 66 00; Le Vivier-sur-Mer: 02 99 48 84 38; Vains: 02 33 89 06 06 ⊙ Summer daily 9–12.30, 2–6.30; winter Mon–Fri 9–12.30, 2–5.30

LISIEUX

www.lisieux-tourisme.com

Pilgrims flock here in summer to pay homage to St. Thérèse of Lisieux, whose touching autobiography proved particularly popular during the hard days of World War I.

Born Thérèse Martin, she moved with her family to Lisieux at the age of four. Throughout her childhood she begged her father to allow her to enter the Carmelite convent with her sister; aged only 15, Thérèse received papal dispensation to join the order. Always a frail young woman, she developed tuberculosis in the draughty convent. She died in 1897, aged just 24, shortly after completing her memoirs *History of a Soul*. She was canonized in 1925 and her relics are displayed in the Carmelite chapel.

In summer, a mini-train shuttles visitors between the chapel, Thérèse's family home at Les Buissonnets, and the domed basilica of Sainte-Thérèse.

The Gothic cathedral of St-Pierre contains the tomb of Bishop Cauchon, who oversaw the execution of Joan of Arc; it is also said to be where Eleanor of Aquitaine married England's Henry II. On Saturday morning (and Wednesdays in summer) you can buy delicious cheeses and cider at the town's market.

➕ 464 G4 ℹ 11 rue d'Alençon 14100 ☎ 02 31 48 18 10 🕐 Mid-Jun to Sep Mon–Sat 8.30–6.30, Sun 10–12.30, 2–5; Oct to mid-Jun 8.30–12, 1.30–6 🚉 Lisieux

LOCRONAN

www.locronan.org

Locronan is one of Brittany's prettiest towns, with its stone houses decked in flowers. It was a sacred site for druids, then a place of Christian pilgrimage after the death of the fifth-century Irish missionary St. Ronan. The town's golden age in the 17th century was based on the production of hemp sailcloth, but when Louis XIV abolished its monopoly in hemp, Locronan's economy collapsed. In the ensuing centuries, money was never available to update the buildings, leaving the architecture much as it was in the town's heyday.

The town square, place de l'Église, was used as a film set for *Tess* (1979). The 15th-century church of St-Ronan (daily 9–6) is in a style known as Ogival Flamboyant. It is surrounded by 17th- and 18th-century buildings, built by rich merchants, along with an office of the East India Company and the Canvas Office. Rue Moal, with humble weavers' homes, leads to the 15th- and 16th-century church of Notre-Dame-de-Bonne-Nouvelle (Our Lady of Good News; daily 9–6), with stained glass by Alfred Manessier (1911–93).

The Musée Municipal, in place de la Mairie, is a good venue to continue your historical explorations (open same hours as tourist office).

Surrealist painter Yves Tanguy (1900–55) lived on rue Lann, and potters, painters and sculptors work and have gallery space in the town.

➕ 462 B6 ℹ place de la Mairie, 29180 ☎ 02 98 91 70 14 🕐 Jul–Aug Mon–Sat 10–1, 2–6, Sun 2–6; Apr–Jun, Sep Mon–Sat 10–12, 2–6; Oct–Mar Mon–Fri 10–12, 2–5 🚌 Route 10 from Quimper to the Crozon peninsula runs through Locronan

MONT ST-MICHEL

▷ 140–143.

MORLAIX

www.tourisme.morlaix.fr

Morlaix sits in a ravine at the head of a large estuary, in the shadow of a towering viaduct. It was once Brittany's third city, prospering on shipbuilding, fishing, linen, paper and a little piracy. This made it a target for reprisals. The worst came in 1522, when the English attacked in retaliation for French corsairs' ransacking of Bristol. Morlaix's citizens took their revenge when they found the English sleeping off hangovers after helping themselves to the town's wine.

The railway viaduct was built in the 1860s. Below it, Morlaix rises up the valley sides. In the old town are *maisons à lanterne* (lantern houses), characterized by a central hall and a fireplace that carries through to the top of the house. You can visit the Maison à Pondalez, at 9 Grand Rue (Jul–Aug daily 10–12.30, 2–6.30; Apr–May, Sep Mon, Wed–Sat 10–12, 2–6, Sun 2–6; Oct–Mar, Jun Mon, Wed–Sat 10–12, 2–5). The Maison de la Duchesse Anne, in the rue du Mur, is where Anne of Brittany stayed in 1505 (Jun–Sep Mon–Sat 11–6; Oct–May Mon–Fri 11–6, Sat 11–5).

See Léon furniture and Breton paintings at the Musée Jacobin, in the Église Jacobin. The building is part of a 13th-century Dominican and Jacobin monastery, in place des Jacobins (Jul–Aug daily 10.30–12.30, 3–6.30; rest of year varies).

➕ 462 B5 ℹ place des Otages, 29600 ☎ 02 98 62 14 94 🕐 Mid-Jun to mid-Sep Mon–Sat 9–7, Sun 10–12.30, 3–8; mid-Sep to mid Jun Mon–Sat 9–12.30, 2–6 🚌 30 to Loccuirec; 52 and 61 to Huelgoat; 53 to Carantec-sur-Mer, St-Pol-de-Léon and Roscoff; 55 to Plougasnou and Le Diben 🚉 Morlaix

PARC NATUREL RÉGIONAL NORMANDIE-MAINE

www.parc-naturel-normandie-maine.fr
This huge area is one of 32 national parks that preserve 10 per cent of France's countryside from the ravages of modern life. Straddling two regions, Normandy and the Western Loire, the 134,000ha (331,130-acre) protected zone is home to 160,000 people as well as numerous winged and four-legged inhabitants. The forests of Écouves, Andaines, Perseigne and Sillé, covering 60,000ha (148,000 acres), shelter deer and boar.

Tributaries of the Orne river flow north towards the English Channel, while the waters of the Sarthe, Mayenne, Egrenne and Varenne head west to the Atlantic. In some places these seem little more than brooks; elsewhere, such as at Villiers, the natural gorges are dramatic. For height, head to the Mancelles Alps and the highest point in western France, Mont des Avaloirs. On lower ground the Passais country is lush farmland covered with apple and pear orchards, where the still of the night is punctuated by the sound of owls calling. Castles stand guard over this timeless region, some in ruins.

Forest rangers take escorted groups on nature rambles, mushroom hunts and deerstalking expeditions. Anglers fish for trout in the rivers and streams, while other visitors enjoy canoeing, hiking and climbing. The spa town of Bagnoles-de-l'Orne is a good base, as are Alençon (▷ 125), Sées, Carrouges, La Ferté-Macé or Domfront (▷ 135). Some hotels offer themed breaks.
🞦 463 F5 🛈 Maison du Parc, Le Capitre, 61320 Carrouges ☎ 02 33 81 13 33 🕐 Mon–Fri 9–12, 2–6

PERROS-GUIREC

www.perros-guirec.com
This is a good place for a family beach holiday or as a base for exploring. The town beaches—Plage de Trestraou and Plage de Trestrignel—and the scenic coastal paths are superb.

The resort encapsulates what is most attractive about Brittany's Pink Granite Coast (▷ 132), with fine sandy bays interspersed with rose granite rocky outcrops. The houses are made from the local rose granite, giving the town a beautiful pink hue, especially at sunset.

Just offshore are the Sept-Îles, which are among France's best bird sanctuaries.
🞦 462 C5 🛈 21 place de l'Hôtel de Ville 22700 ☎ 02 96 23 21 15 🕐 Jul–Aug Mon–Sat 9–7.30, Sun, public hols 10–12.30, 4–7; Sep–Jun Mon–Sat 9–12.30, 2–6 🚌 15 to Trégastel and Lannion 🚢 To the Sept-Îles (seasonal only), from the Gare Maritime at Plage de Trestraou or Port de Ploumanac'h

Above left *The lighthouse off the rugged coast at Pointe du Raz*
Above right *A shingled house with pretty window boxes in Morlaix*
Opposite *This square in Lisieux conjures up a quieter, less mechanized world*

POINTE DU RAZ

www.pointeduraz.com
Pointe du Raz is the most dramatic of Brittany's wild peninsulas. Here the land meets the untamed Atlantic Ocean in a crescendo of breaking waves, charging wind and screeching gulls. The point sits on the western tip of the Cap Sizun, and the views down to the sea and across to the Île de Sein are breathtaking. You can't drive to the tip, but you can park at a visitor centre with exhibition space, cafés and shops. In July and August a shuttle-bus takes you out to the tip, otherwise it is a walk of 1.5km (1 mile) along a paved footpath to the lighthouse.
🞦 462 A6 🛈 Maison de Site, Pointe du Raz ☎ 02 98 70 67 18 🕐 Jul–Aug daily 9.30–7.30; Apr–Jun, Sep daily 10.30–6; Oct–Mar Sun 2.30–5.30 (daily 10.30–6 in school hols) 🚌 7, 8 to Quimper

INFORMATION

www.tourisme-rennes.com

⊞ 463 E6 🚹 11 rue St-Yves, 35064
☎ 02 99 67 11 11 ⊕ Jul–Sep Mon–Sat
9–7, Sun 11–1, 2–6; Oct–Jun Mon 1–6,
Tue–Sat 10–6, Sun 11–1, 2–6 🍴 There
are plenty of bars around place Ste-
Anne; most close Sat lunch ⊕ Métro
system, with one line 🚌 Good bus links
🚊 Trains to St-Malo, Fougères, Dinan,
Vitré, Nantes

INTRODUCTION

Penetrate beyond the modern industrial shell of Brittany's capital and you'll find an old city worth spending a day getting to know. Rennes grew to be the most important town in eastern Brittany during the Middle Ages—vying for power with Nantes and Vannes. It finally became the undisputed Breton capital during the time of Anne of Brittany (1477–1514). Since then it has played a key role in Brittany's political and social struggles, including rebellions against the heavy taxation imposed during Louis XIV's reign, the Revolutionary Terror and the German occupation in World War II.

Although a great fire burned for more than a week in 1720, consuming much of old Rennes, the area between the market square (place des Lices) and the city's two waterways, the Ille and Vilaine rivers, escaped destruction. Following feverish conservation and restoration work in recent years, the streets in the centre are once again rich in architectural detail from various centuries. Rennes is particularly proud of its remaining tall and sometimes colourful timber-framed town houses.

The two main squares of the city are the place du Parlement de Bretagne, presided over by the sumptuous home of the Breton parliament, a regional court of justice originally built before Brittany was annexed to France in 1532 and the place de l'Hôtel de Ville, on which stands the town hall.

After exploring the old town, wander through the Parc du Thabor for a change of pace. These large gardens once formed the grounds of a Benedictine abbey on the site.

WHAT TO SEE

MUSÉE DES BEAUX-ARTS

www.mbar.org

This art gallery has paintings ranging from 14th-century Primitives to Impressionists and members of the Pont-Aven school. Artists represented include such luminaries as Leonardo da Vinci, Rubens, Paul Gauguin and Pablo Picasso. Look out for a powerful canvas by the 19th-century artist Luminais, depicting the legend of Ys (▷ 136). Exhibitions focus on Brittany's culture and history and range from archaeological finds to the *corsaires* (pirates).

✉ 20 quai Émile Zola, 35000 ☎ 02 23 62 17 45 ⊕ Tue 10–6, Wed–Sun 10–12, 2–6
⊕ République 🎫 Adult €5.72, under 18 free

CATHÉDRALE ST-PIERRE

Rennes's cavernous cathedral, with its vast dark marble pillars, dates from the 19th century. Don't miss the 16th-century Flemish retable in the fifth chapel on the right. Its 10 panels, full of human interest, depict scenes including the birth of Mary and the marriage of Mary and Joseph. The delightful rue de la Psalette, curving behind the cathedral, is a medley of beautiful half-timbered 15th-century houses. Psalette was the local word for the cathedral choir, and it is said that the street resounded with their singing.

✉ rue du Griffon 🕐 Daily 9.30–12, 3–6

PLACE DES LICES

This square once hosted jousts, although since the 17th century its main focus has been as a marketplace. Today, there's an open-air Saturday vegetable market (ends 1pm), and a meat market in the impressive covered hall. Near here, on the edge of the old town, is Porte Mordelaise, a fine gateway with a restored drawbridge. It dates from 1440, when the city walls were enlarged, and was intended as a ceremonial entrance into the city.

PLACE DE LA MAIRIE

In the spacious place de la Mairie you can admire the magnificent Hôtel de Ville (town hall), designed by Jacques Gabriel in the 18th century. The huge clock tower, known as Le Gros, links two curving side wings. From here, look down towards the elegant Palais de Commerce in place de la République.

MORE TO SEE

CHAPELLE ST-YVES

The converted Chapelle St-Yves now houses the tourist office, where you'll find a permanent exhibition on the history of Rennes and its trading links. It is also worth visiting for its impressive beams and the restored carvings in the chapel.

PALAIS DU PARLEMENT DE BRETAGNE

The former seat of the Breton parliament is north of place de la Mairie. Ironically, having survived the fire of 1720, it almost totally burned down in a fire in 1994. Restoration has now finished and its intricate timber-framed roof and beautiful coffered ceilings look as impressive as before. Look up to see the gilded figures that top the building.

TIPS

» Place Railier du Baty, a pleasant square near the cathedral, is a good place to sit and enjoy a coffee.
» Beware of traffic, even in streets or squares that appear to be pedestrian-only.

Opposite top *The 18th-century town hall, with its impressive clock tower*
Opposite bottom *A carved wooden figure on a house*
Below *A red timbered house adorned with wooden statues*

REGIONS NORTHWEST FRANCE • SIGHTS

147

INFORMATION

www.rouentourisme.com
✚ 464 H4 🛈 25 place de la Cathédrale,
BP 666, 76008 ☎ 02 32 08 32 40
🕐 May–Sep Mon–Sat 9–7, Sun and
public hols 9.30–12.30, 2–6; Oct–Apr
Mon–Sat 9.30–12.30, 1.30–6, Sun 10–1
🚊 Rouen: good connections to Paris

Above *The tower of St-Ouen, seen from rue Damiette*

INTRODUCTION

Rouen rises on the horizon as a blur of steeples above the grandly Gothic Notre-Dame Cathedral and nearby Abbey of St-Ouen. This makes for a memorable first view, especially if you are lucky enough to arrive at dawn or dusk. Don't be misled by the sprawling perimeter—the historic core is quite compact, worth seeking out and easily explored on foot.

The Romans established a settlement on the site of today's Rouen in the first century AD, calling it Rotomagus. In the Middle Ages, Rouen became the seat of the Dukes of Normandy, who won the English throne in 1066. Later, it was at the heart of the Hundred Years' War between the French and the English. One of the most defining—not to say traumatic—events in French history took place here during the war: on 30 May 1431 Joan of Arc was burned at the stake as a heretic in what is now place du Vieux Marché. Much later, in the 19th century, Gustave Flaubert immortalized the city of his birth by setting the scandalously realistic novel *Madame Bovary* in and around it.

Today, Rouen has one of the largest ports in France, despite being so far inland. The city lies on the Seine, 86km (53 miles) from the estuary at Le Havre. The contrast between the working docks along the river and the Gothic spires and quaint old streets of the city heart is striking.

Any tour of the centre should begin opposite the cathedral with a visit to the tourist office, housed in Rouen's oldest Renaissance building, the former tax collector's office, dating from 1509. Merchant trade has been key to Rouen's development over the centuries, funding many of the timbered and gabled tradesmen's houses in the city. Later buildings, including 19th-century stores, art deco shop fronts and post-World War II blocks, run down to the port. The city was heavily bombed during World War II and many historic buildings needed meticulous renovation.

WHAT TO SEE
CATHÉDRALE DE NOTRE-DAME
www.cathedrale-rouen.net
Rouen cathedral is one of the great churches of France, known across the world thanks to Impressionist painter Claude Monet's evocative *Cathédrales de Rouen* series (1892–93), studies of the cathedral at different times of day. Monet worked on the paintings from the second floor of what is now the tourist office. The cathedral's Gothic architecture spans 400 years, from the mid-12th to early 16th centuries. The dark, shadowy interior is offset by flashes of bright blue light through the stained-glass windows, dating from the 13th century. The choir contains tombs of many Dukes of Normandy, while the crypt holds the heart of Richard the Lionheart of England. The 151m (495ft) spire, the tallest in France, was built in the 19th century.
✠ 151 B3 ✉ place de la Cathédrale ⏰ Tue–Sat 7.30–7, Sun 8–6, Mon 2–6

AÎTRE ST-MACLOU
A short walk from the Gothic Église St-Maclou, in place Barthélemy, is its unusual annexe, the Aître St-Maclou. This pretty courtyard of timbered buildings is now home to the School of Fine Arts. A more macabre history is hinted at by the skulls that adorn the woodwork. This was a plague cemetery, built to house the remains of the victims of the Great Plague of 1348, which claimed the lives of 75 per cent of the population.
✠ 151 C2 ✉ rue Martainville ⏰ Église St-Maclou: mid-Mar to Oct daily 9–7; Nov to mid-Mar 9–6. Courtyard: daily 8–8 ✋ Free

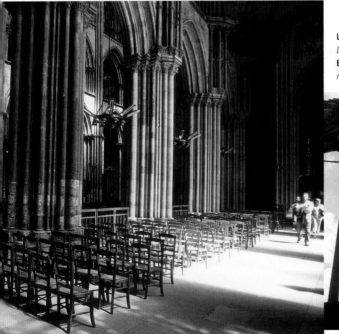

Left *Inside Rouen's Cathédral de Notre-Dame*
Below *Notre-Dame seen through the remains of the Bishop's Palace*

Above *A view across Rouen from a vista point*
Above right *Rouen's tall, timbered houses, with pretty flower displays*

L'ABBATIALE SAINT-OUEN

The main church of the Benedictine abbey that once stood on this site, this is a majestic flamboyant Gothic structure started in 1318. Intricate carved stonework is evident in the columns and buttresses of the exterior and the soaring vaults.
✚ 151 C2 ✉ place Général de Gaulle 🕐 Apr–Oct Tue–Thu, Sat–Sun 10–12, 2–5.30; Nov–Mar 10–12, 2–4.30

GROS HORLOGE

No visit to Rouen is complete without a stroll under the 14th-century Gros Horloge, a huge, one-handed, ornamental clock mounted on a sumptuously carved Renaissance arch straddling the road of the same name. Once part of a nearby belfry, the remarkable timepiece was moved to its present position in the 16th century, after locals complained that it was impossible to see its face in the narrow streets.
✚ 151 B3 ✉ rue du Gros-Horloge 🕐 Apr–Oct Tue–Sun 10–1, 2–7; Nov–Mar 2–6 (last admission 1 hour before) 💷 Adult €6, child (6–18) €3, under 6 free

JOAN OF ARC

This is the city of Joan of Arc (▷ 33), and the tales surrounding France's greatest folk heroine would alone be lure enough for visitors. On the place du Vieux Marché, a short stroll from the Gros Horloge, a large cross marks the spot where Joan of Arc was executed.

The nearby Église Jeanne-d'Arc (1981) is a stunning combination of modern slate and copper work on the outside, with light from Renaissance stained-glass windows within. The windows were salvaged from the earlier church of St-Vincent, destroyed during World War II. The wonderful contemporary sculpture was inspired by the martyr's pyre on which Joan of Arc was burned to death.

The remains of the two towers in which Joan was imprisoned from Christmas 1430 until her execution in 1431 can be seen on rue du Donjon. These vestiges of Philippe-Auguste's castle, built in 1204 and scene of Joan of Arc's trial, incorporate the Tour Jeanne d'Arc and traces of the Tour de la Pucelle. Learn more about the medieval heroine at the Musée Jeanne d'Arc, on place du Vieux Marché (mid-Apr to mid-Sep daily 9.30–7; mid-Sep to mid-Apr 10–12, 2–6.30).

LITERARY CONNECTIONS

There is the chance to pay homage to Rouen's literary heritage at museums dedicated to Gustave Flaubert (1821–80), author of *Madame Bovary*, and playwright Pierre Corneille (1606–84). The Musée Flaubert et d'Histoire de la

Médecine is in the house where Flaubert was born, at 51 rue de Lecat (Wed–Sat 10–12, 2–6, Tue 10–6). Flaubert's father was a surgeon and the museum contains not only displays about the novelist's life but also medical implements from the 19th century. The Musée Pierre Corneille is in the playwright's birthplace, at 4 rue de la Pie (Jul–Aug Wed–Sun 2–6; Sep–Jun Sat–Sun 2–6).

MUSÉE DES BEAUX-ARTS
This gallery has an impressive collection of paintings, drawings, sculptures and objets d'art from the 16th century to the present day. Highlights include Caravaggio's *Flagellation of Christ* and works by Renoir and Monet.
➕ 151 B2 ✉ esplanade Marcel-Duchamp ☎ 02 35 71 28 40 🕐 Wed–Sun 10–6 (second Sun of month until 10pm) ✋ Adult €5, child (under 18) free

MUSÉE DE LA CÉRAMIQUE
Learn more about the distinctive blue-patterned Rouen ware *(faïence)*, which rose to popularity in the 17th and 18th centuries. If you want to buy some, you'll also find it in the antiques quarter of the old town.
➕ 151 B2 ✉ 94 rue Jeanne d'Arc ☎ 02 35 07 31 74 🕐 Wed–Mon 10–1, 2–6 ✋ Adult €3, child (under 18) free

MORE TO SEE
JEWISH MONUMENT
The Jewish Monument, in the courtyard of the 16th-century Palais de Justice, is in fact the remains of the oldest surviving Jewish building in France. Believed to date from the 12th century, the site is the last vestige of the city's ghetto, destroyed after the expulsion of the Jews in 1306. Although it was originally thought to have been a synagogue, experts now believe it was a religious school.
➕ 151 B2 ✉ rue aux Juifs ❓ You can't enter the courtyard, but you can see the monument from outside

TIPS
» Visit Rouen during the last week in May to take part in the Joan of Arc festival, which usually coincides with the city's main cultural festival. On the Sunday closest to 30 May local children throw flowers into the Seine from Boïeldieu Bridge, the spot where Joan's ashes were scattered on the water.
» A good time to experience the Abbey of St-Ouen is during one of the many concerts held there. The organ is one of the most famous in France.
» Every five years (make a date for 2013) the world's greatest sailing ships gather along the quays for L'Armada, eight days of celebrations in June or July.

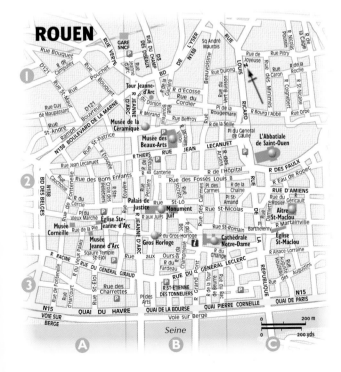

REGIONS · NORTHWEST FRANCE · SIGHTS

QUIBERON

www.quiberon.com

Quiberon is one of Brittany's most popular resorts, at the tip of a peninsula, with sandy beaches. It is a perfect base for exploring Belle-Île (▷ 128), offshore, and inland to Carnac (▷ 130) and Auray. But on a summer day it is the sands that have most pulling power—the one access road can be clogged with traffic.

Quiberon has long made a living from the sea. The port and ferry services are in the main town, while the marina is to the northeast.

✚ 462 C7 ➊ 14 rue de Verdun, 56174 ☎ 0825 13 56 00 🕓 Jun–Aug Mon–Sat 9–12.30, 2–6.30, Sun 10–1, 2–5; Sep–May Mon–Sat 9–12.30, 2–6 🚍 1 to Vannes. Quib'Bus links Quiberon with Vannes, Auray and Carnac (daily Jul–Aug and weekends in Jun and Sep) 🚉 In Jul and Aug the Quiberon line links with Auray, where there are regular trains to Vannes or Lorient ❓ Bathing is forbidden on the Côte Sauvage (the western coast) because of dangerous currents and sharp rocks

QUIMPER

www.quimper-tourisme.com

Quimper is a hub of Breton culture with a wonderful old quarter. It was an influential city throughout Brittany's independence but lost its power following union with France in 1532. The city suffered relatively little damage during World War II, despite its links with the French Resistance.

Today, the old quarter shelters half-timbered houses. Look out for the ornate Maison des Cariatides on rue Guéodet. The magnificent Cathédrale St-Corentin dates from the 13th to 19th centuries (May–Oct Mon–Sat 9.30–12, 1.30–6.30, Sun 1.30–6.30; Nov–Apr Mon–Sat 9–12, 1.30–6.30, Sun 1.30–6.30). Stained glass in the nave depicts Cornouaille nobility and their patron saints. The highlight of the Musée Départemental Breton, in rue du Roi Gradlon, are the Breton costumes (Jun–Sep daily 9–6; Oct–May Tue–Sat 9–12, 2–5, Sun 2–5). The Musée des Beaux-Arts, at 40 place St-Corentin, is one of the best art galleries in Brittany (Jul–Aug daily 10–7; Sep–Oct, Apr–Jun Wed–Mon 10–12, 2–6; Nov–Mar Mon–Sat 10–12, 2–6, Sun 2–6).

Quimper potters have produced *faïence* ceramics for three centuries. True Quimper ware, with its blue-and-yellow flower and bird pattern, is handmade. Examples are in the Musée de la Faïence, 14 rue J. B. Bousquet (closed for renovation).

✚ 462 B6 ➊ place de la Résistance, 29000 ☎ 02 98 53 04 05 🕓 Jul–Aug Mon–Sat 9–7, Sun 10–12.45, 3–5.45; Jun, early Sep Mon–Sat 9.30–12.30, 1.30–6.30, Sun 10–12.45; Apr–early Jun, Sep Mon–Sat 9.30–12.30, 1.30–6.30; Oct–Mar Mon–Sat 9.30–12.30, 1.30–6 🚍 1 to Brest via Plougastel-Daoulas, Le Faou, Pleyben and Châteaulin; 2A and 2B to Pont l'Abbé and Île-Tudy; 4 to Pont l'Abbé, Lechiagat and le Guilvinec; 9 to Pointe du Raz; 9 to Douarnenez; 10 to Camaret-sur-Mer, Locronan, Pentrez-Plage, Argol, Crozon and le Fret; 15 to Beg Meil; 16 to Bénodet

🚉 Quimper 🔆 The tourist office organizes guided tours of the cathedral and the old town ❓ The Festival de Cornouaille (Jul) attracts Celts from across Europe

REDON

www.tourisme-pays-redon.com

Rivers, roads, railways and a canal all converge at Redon, on the border of Brittany and the Pays de la Loire. The town is popular with boating people, who can sail along the river Vilaine or the Nantes–Brest canal, and the river Oust adds its own tortuous course. The Musée de la Batellerie (River Craft Museum), at quai Jean-Bart, documents canal life (mid-Jun to mid-Sep daily 10–12, 3–6; early Apr to mid-Jun, mid-Sep to mid-Nov Sat–Mon, Wed 2–6; closed mid-Nov to early Apr).

Redon lacks the charm of many Breton towns, but summer festivals are popular. It was settled in 832, with the founding of a Benedictine abbey. The town developed as a river port for Rennes and grew prosperous on trade. The Romanesque remains of Abbaye St-Sauveur include a nave and tower from the 12th century.

✚ 463 D6 ➊ place de la République, 35600 ☎ 02 99 71 06 04 🕓 Jul–Aug Mon–Sat 9.30–12.30, 1.30–6.30, Sun 10–12.30, 3–5.30; Sep–Jun Mon–Fri 9.30–12, 2–6, Sat 10–12.30, 3–5 (closed Tue 9.30–12); Sun 10–1, 4–6 🚍 10G to la Roche Bernard 🚉 Redon

RENNES

▷ 146–147.

Left *Boats moored in Redon*
Below *A timber-framed shop in Quimper*
Opposite left *The beach at St-Cast-le-Guildo*
Opposite right *Carving in Rochefort-en-Terre*

ROCHEFORT-EN-TERRE

www.golfedumorbihan.com
www.rochefort-en-terre.com

Rochefort-en-Terre is a small place with just 650 inhabitants, and wins award after award in 'most beautiful village' competitions. It is easy to see why. The setting is one of the most spectacular in Brittany, on a high spur overlooking the Arz valley and surrounded by dense woodland.

A maze of cobbled lanes tumbles down from the castle and you'll find interesting architectural details in every nook and cranny. The main street (in fact several streets linked by small squares) is lined with sturdy granite houses and halls, now home to souvenir shops, bookstores, restaurants and *crêperies*.

The castle was originally built on a slate promontory (the eponymous *roche forte*, or strong rock) in the Middle Ages, but was destroyed in the Revolution and rebuilt by two American brothers in the early 20th century (Jul–Aug daily 10–6.30; Jun, Sep daily 2–6.30; Apr–May Sat–Sun, public hols 2–6.30).

The church of Notre-Dame-de-la-Tronchaye, off rue du Pélican, has a facade of unusual Gothic windows under ornate gables. Inside you'll find one of the most important religious relics in Brittany—a highly revered statue of Our Lady of Tronchaye, discovered in a tree in the 12th century.

✚ 463 D6 🚹 place des Halles, 56220 ☎ 02 97 43 33 57 🕐 Mid-Jun to mid-Sep

Mon–Sat 10–1, 2–5 🚌 9 to Vannes ❓ The village is floodlit in the evenings (Apr–Sep nightly; Oct–Mar Sat only)

ROUEN

▷ 148–149.

SABLES-D'OR-LES-PINS

www.plurien-tourisme.com

The long stretches of golden sand and verdant pines that give this resort its name are the draw here. You can rent a beach buggy or take in a round of golf, but most people come to enjoy the beach. Sables-d'Or-les-Pins is essentially an artificial resort. Work began in the early 1920s but the project was abandoned after the financial crash of 1929, before it had been completed. As you arrive in town, a wide but neglected central boulevard hints at the grand design originally envisaged. This is flanked by ornate parades of shops and cafés. Just south of Sables-d'Or-les-Pins, the village of Plurien has a Knights Templar church and the remains of a Gallo-Roman villa.

✚ 463 D5 🚹 Manoir Montangué, 2240 Plurien ☎ 02 96 72 18 52 🕐 Jul–Aug Mon–Sat 9.30–12.30, 2–6.30, Sun 10–12; Sep–Jun Mon–Wed 9–12, Thu 9–12, 2.30–5.30, Fri 9–12, 3.30–5.30 ❓ Swimming in the sea can be dangerous because of strong currents

ST-CAST-LE-GUILDO

www.ot-st-cast-le-guildo.fr

This is one of the liveliest bucket-and-spade resorts on the Emerald Coast,

popular for its wide sandy beach. It is ideal for excursions to Dinard (▷ 135), Dinan (▷ 134) and St-Malo or for walks along the wild footpaths of Cap Fréhel (▷ 128).

The resort has several separate districts and its geography takes some fathoming. Le-Guildo is an old seaport on the Arguenon river. Its associated market town is called Notre-Dame. Here you'll find stone cottages set near the ocean, and the ruined chateau of Gilles de Bretagne overlooking the bay. St-Cast consists of L'Isle (the port), Les Mielles (the resort area, with a wide sandy beach) and Le Bourg (the administrative hub). L'Isle is a popular yacht stop in the summer, although the islets of Rocher de la Feuillade, Rocher du Bec Rond and Rocher de Canavez make navigation a challenge.

The Grande Plage (Large Beach) at Les Mielles has a fairground in summer, and a small square at the northern end has shops, bars and restaurants. The southern tip of the beach is marked by the small chapel of Notre-Dame-de-la-Garde, on a headland of the same name.

Between St-Cast and Le-Guildo is the tiny settlement of Pen-Guen, with its own beach. It is renowned in French golfing circles for its links course, one of the country's oldest.

✚ 463 D5 🚹 place Charles de Gaulle, BP 9, 22380 ☎ 02 96 41 81 52 🕐 Jul–Aug Mon–Sat 9–7, Sun 10–12.30, 3–6.30; Sep–Jun Mon–Sat 9–12, 2–6 🚌 1 to Lamballe; 14 to St-Malo; 13 to Dinan ❓ Fête de l'Huître (Oyster Festival) is at the end of Jun

INFORMATION

www.saint-malo-tourisme.com

⊕ 463 D5 🅸 esplanade St-Vincent, 35400 ☎ 08 25 13 52 00 🕐 Jul–Aug Mon–Sat 9–7.30, Sun 10–6; Apr–Jun, Sep Mon–Sat 9–1, 2–6.30, Sun 10–12.30, 2.30–6; Oct–Mar Mon–Sat 9–1, 2–6 🚉 St-Malo 🛈 Access to the ramparts is by steps only

TIPS

» Hotels and cafés within the Intra Muros are often more expensive than those outside.

» You can check tide times at the tourist office before walking the causeway to Grand Bé.

Opposite *The central square in the old quarter of Vitré*

Below *Pleasure boats at St-Malo*

ST-MALO

The Breton port of St-Malo has had a rumbustious nautical past, peopled by explorers, merchants, fishermen (the Newfoundland fishing fleets sailed from here in the 16th century) and ruthless *corsaires* (pirates). Today the port is quieter. Fishing and freight are still important to the economy, but the harbours also shelter pleasure craft.

CITADEL

The town's main attraction is its citadel, known as Intra Muros ('within the walls'), faithfully restored after destruction by bombs in 1944. Towering walls frame inviting glimpses of the elegant shopping streets and outdoor cafés within. Many of the streets are quite steep and paved with large cobbles. You can walk around the ramparts, originally constructed in the 14th century, with views of the sea on one side and the old town on the other.

Pass through a gap to cross the causeway to the island of Grand Bé to see the tomb of the writer Chateaubriand (1768–1848) and for great views of the islands, the mainland, the mountains and Dinard (▷ 135). Children are likely to enjoy this walk as there are rocks to clamber on and pools to explore. Don't get stranded by the tide: If you do, there's a six-hour wait before you can walk back!

Sights in the Intra Muros district include the Cathédrale St-Vincent (daily 8.30–7, except during religious services), with its modern stained-glass window and diamond-shaped mosaic commemorating Jacques Cartier's exploration of the interior of Canada in 1535. The aquarium concealed in the ramparts has an extraordinary range of tropical fish (mid-Jul to mid-Aug daily 9.30am–10pm; early Jul and late Aug 9.30–8; Apr–Jun, Sep 10–7; Oct–Mar 10–6; closed two weeks in mid Nov and first three weeks in Jan).

CASTLE MUSEUM

The Musée d'Histoire Château de St-Malo (Apr–early Nov daily 10–12, 2–6; early Nov–Mar Tue–Sun 10–12, 2–6), within St-Malo's old castle, has some fascinating exhibits. On the second floor, look out for the carved figurehead destined for the prow of a *corsaire* vessel, depicting a 17th-century sailor. One room describes the life of St-Malo fishermen in Newfoundland. Another floor deals with great men of St-Malo, including the naval commander Robert Surcouf (1773–1827) and the ubiquitous Chateaubriand (▷ 131).

The ruddy-faced figures are known as *Vannes et sa femme* (Vannes and his wife).
➕ 462 D6 🛈 quai Tebarly, 56000 ☎ 0825 13 56 10 🕐 Jul–Aug Mon–Sat 9–7, Sun 10–6; Sep–Jun Mon–Sat 9.30–12.30, 1.30–6 🍴 Cafés in place Gambetta 🚌 Links with Quimper, Carnac, Auray and surrounding towns in the Golfe du Morbihan 🚆 Vannes, links with Auray, Quimper, Brest, Rennes, Paris 🛈 The Office du Tourism runs several guided walks throughout the summer

VITRÉ

www.ot-vitre.fr

Half-timbered, slate-hung houses lurch in all directions on Vitré's hilly, cobbled streets, watched over by a turreted castle. The town is best seen from a viewpoint known as the Tertres Noirs, by the bank of the river Vilaine: a silhouette of bristling turrets, drum towers and ramparts.

The château played a vital role in the Middle Ages when Vitré sat on the border between Brittany and France and was a constant target (Apr–Sep daily 10.30–12.30, 2–6.30; Oct–Mar Wed–Sat, Mon 10–12.15, 2–5.30, Sun 2–5.30).

The church of Notre-Dame is within the town ramparts. Dating from the 15th and 16th centuries, its Flamboyant Gothic south facade contrasts with the plainer, late 16th-century west facade. Between the château and the church is the Poterne St-Pierre, leading to the remains of the city ramparts, a pleasant stroll with extensive views.

The 17th-century author Madame de Sévigné lived at 9 rue Sévigné. The Gothic manor Les Rochers-Sévigné, 7km (4 miles) southeast of town, was said to be her best-loved Breton residence (open same hours as château above).
➕ 463 E6 🛈 place Général de Gaulle, 35500 ☎ 02 99 75 04 46 🕐 Jul–Aug Mon–Sat 9.30–12.30, 2–6.30, Sun 10–12.30, 3–6; Apr–Jun, Sep Mon 2.30–6, Tue–Fri 9.30–12.30, 2.30–6, Sat 10–12.30, 3–5; Oct–Jun Mon–Tue 2.20–6, Wed–Fri 9.30–12.30, 2.30–6, Sat 10–12.30, 3–5 🚆 To Fougères and Rennes 🚆 Vitré 🛈 The tourist office organizes guided walking tours of the town in French only; audioguides in English

ST-THÉGONNEC

www.saint-thegonnec.fr

St-Thégonnec is the epitome of the Breton 'parish close', a highlight of this curiously specialized form of Breton art. In 16th- and 17th-century Brittany, as nowhere else in France, the buildings around the village graveyard developed into an elaborate architectural complex called the *enclos paroissial*. At first these were simple affairs, but as lower Brittany grew richer, they developed into highly ornate structures and their calvaries (the elaborate crucifix that stood outside the church) became the storybooks of the time.

St-Thégonnec was one of the richest parishes in Brittany during the 17th century. Its multi-branched calvary, constructed in 1610, shows Christ's tormentors carrying out their sadistic work with gusto (one was alleged to be the Protestant French king Henry IV), while angels mop up the Redeemer's blood. The little-known St. Thégonnec himself puts in an appearance on a low niche. The church interior is equally sumptuous, with statues adorning every nook, and altarpieces alive with detail. The tour de force is the wooden pulpit, encrusted with saints, angels, evangelists, Cardinal Virtues and God himself, giving Moses the tablets of stone inscribed with the Ten Commandments.
➕ 462 B5 🕐 Daily 9–6 (no visits during Sunday Mass at 10.30) 🚆 St-Thégonnec

VANNES

www.mairie-vannes.fr
www.tourisme-vannes.com

Vannes, on the western coast of the Golfe du Morbihan, has a wonderful old town full of 16th- and 17th-century architecture. Its narrow streets are perfect for strolling, and it has a livelier, more cosmopolitan feel than many Breton towns.

Throughout the Middle Ages Vannes shared the accolade of being the Breton capital with Nantes and Rennes. It is where Brittany was formally signed over to the French crown in 1532.

Its port played an important trading role in times past, but today it caters only for pleasure traffic. You can go on excursions from it around the Golfe du Morbihan.

The Cathédrale St-Pierre is a mixture of architectural styles from the 13th to the 19th centuries. The Rotunda Chapel contains the remains of the city's patron, St. Vincent-Ferrier. Almost opposite the cathedral, La Cohue dating from the 16th century, was once a market building and lawcourt. It now houses the Musée des Beaux-Arts (Jun–Sep daily 10–6; Oct–May Tue–Sun 1.30–6).

The Parc du Golfe, on the waterfront, has exhibition areas, a butterfly garden, aquarium, funfair and parkland for picnics.

A famous carved corbel peers out from the corner of rue du Rogues.

ST-MALO AND DINAN

No visitor to Brittany should miss the two north-coast towns of St-Malo and Dinan. Although very different in character—St-Malo is a busy port and Dinan a splendidly preserved medieval town—both are beautiful. The river Rance flows past Dinan and out to sea at St-Malo, and is barred on the way by a great tidal dam.

THE DRIVE
Distance: 90km (56 miles)
Allow: 1 day
Start/end at: St-Malo

★ St-Malo (▷ 154) is a ferry port, yachting base and commercial port, with a walled citadel well worth exploring. Walk the ramparts for views of the town, the sea and nearby islands.

Follow signs for Rennes through the suburb of St-Servan-sur-Mer and, keeping the estuary of the river Rance on your right, carry on past Tour Solidor.

❶ Medieval Tour Solidor, in the St-Servan district of St-Malo, was built in the late 14th century to protect shipping in the Rance from English pirates and Malouin *corsaires*. It was once the town jail and is now a museum with several model ships and information about St-Malo's seafaring tradition.

Follow signs for Dinard, following the road across the top of a huge dam, the Barrage de Rance, which generates electricity by harnessing the tidal current. Turn right onto the D266 into Dinard.

❷ Dinard (▷ 135) is a fashionable seaside town, a resort of the smart set since the turn of the 19th century, when the Prince of Wales used to holiday here. There are good views over a forest of yacht masts in the marina to the walls of St-Malo. From here you can go on a boat trip up the Rance to Dinan.

Return to the D266, following the signs for Dinan and Pleurtuit. Pass the aerodrome on the right and stay on this road, which becomes the D766, all the way into the middle of Dinan. Although the town is often crowded, it's usually possible to park in the Champ-Clos near to all the sights.

❸ With its half-timbered houses and the Jardin Anglais near St-Saveur, Dinan (▷ 134) is a place to explore on foot. Walk down to the banks of the Rance by rue du Jerzual, a steep

street lined with medieval houses, including a spectacular three-floor half-timbered building, the Maison du Gouverneur. The riverside is lined with restaurants, great for lunch or dinner.

From Dinan, follow signs to the suburb of Lanvallay, east of Dinan, and pick up the D676. Fork left onto the D29 and head north past Pleudihen-sur-Rance. Continue north via the D74 and D76, following signs for Le Port as you drive into Cancale.

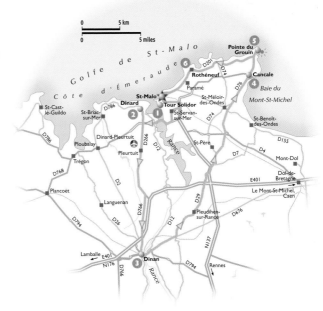

❹ The oyster port and seaside resort of Cancale (▷ 128) is tucked into a corner of the Baie du Mont-St-Michel. In good weather you should be able to see the Mont itself on the far side of the bay. Oysters are bred out in the bay and are gathered from the flat-bottomed boats that you can see moored in the harbour. There are plenty of small restaurant along the wharf, where the first course on any menu should be Cancale oysters.

From Cancale harbour, follow signs for Pointe du Grouin or St-Malo par la Côte, onto the D201 towards Pointe du Grouin, 7km (4.5 miles) farther on.

❺ Pointe du Grouin is a nature reserve and bird sanctuary, with marvellous views over the bay to Mont-St-Michel (▷ 140–143) and, to the south, to Mont-Dol near Dol-de-Bretagne. From the parking place there is a footpath up to the tip of the Pointe and from there another footpath leads along the coast to St-Malo.

Continue along the picturesque coast road past the Baie du Guesclin and through the suburb of Rothéneuf.

❻ Rothéneuf is a pleasant suburb of St-Malo, next to a wide beach. Sights here include the coastal rocks carved by the Abbé Foure in the 19th century and the manor house lived in by the 16th-century explorer and the discoverer of Canada, Jacques Cartier.

Pass through Paramé, and then along the waterfront and you reach the main gateway into St-Malo.

WHERE TO EAT
CHEZ LA MÈRE POUCEL
www.chezlamerepoucel.com
✉ 3 place des Merciers, Dinan
🕐 Lunch and dinner Mon–Sat, lunch Sun. Closed Apr–Oct Tue dinner, all day Wed and Sun dinner

INFORMATION
St-Malo
✉ Esplanade St-Vincent ☎ 08 25 13 52 00
Dinan
✉ 9 rue du Chateau ☎ 02 90 87 89 76

Left *Dinan Castle*
Opposite top *Cancale port*
Opposite bottom *A path leads between tree-shaded lawns to a cross and beyond to a domed building near Cancale*

REGIONS | NORTHWEST FRANCE • DRIVE

157

AROUND HUELGOAT

At the heart of inland Brittany, within the Parc Naturel Régional d'Armorique, Huelgoat is surrounded by magnificent countryside combining a lake, an unruly river and a forest scattered with rocks piled in curious formations. It is excellent hiking country and this walk takes you through many changes of scenery.

THE WALK

Distance: 5km (3 miles)
Allow: 2 hours
Start at: place Aristide Briand
End at: La Roche Cintrée

HOW TO GET THERE

The village is 25km (15 miles) south of Morlaix and the N12 motorway, in the northwest corner of Brittany.

★ Huelgoat (meaning high forest) lies beside a lake, and this position, together with the nearby wooded hills, makes it a popular summer resort and a good base for a range of activity holidays.

Start from place Aristide Briand at the heart of Huelgoat. Turn left at the northern end of the square, with the lake on your left. On the other side of the street, a well-marked path leads through the rocks.

❶ The huge boulders are piled in a chaotic formation because of the consistency of the granite: Soft inclusions crumble, isolating harder minerals, which eventually collapse onto one another. A Breton legend has it that the inhabitants of two nearby villages, wanting to settle a quarrel, hurled the stones at each other. Continue along the path.

❷ Along the way you'll see the Chaos du Moulin and the Grotte du Diable where you can descend a ladder and watch the river foaming and crashing against the rocks.

❸ On the other side of the river, the Roche Tremblante is a single boulder, weighing an estimated 100 tonnes, which rocks slightly when pushed. A little farther on, the Ménage de la Vierge consists of several rocks looking vaguely like everyday household utensils.

The pleasant allée Violette leads through the woods to the Pont Rouge and the D769A to Carhaix. Follow the road for approximately 100m (109 yards) and turn right onto a path in the form of a horseshoe, called Promenade du Fer à Cheval.

❹ The promenade dominates the Rivière d'Argent in a lovely setting before rejoining the road. Turn right and follow the road for another 300m (330 yards). A narrow staircase on the right goes down to Le Gouffre (the abyss) into which the river falls and disappears. Continue along the footpath past the Mare aux Fées (fairy pool), until you meet a gravel road where you turn right. Follow this road to the old mine, where information plaques indicate that you've found the right place.

❺ This is the site of an old silver mine, although there's little to see other than an open clearing with a stream running through it.

Cross the stream and take the footpath up the hill following the signs *Huelgoat par le canal*. Halfway up the hill the route splits. Keep left and continue to the top where you'll find a small hydroelectric station at the head of the canal.

❻ The canal is more of a channel, at just 1m (3ft) wide. It was created to bring water to silver mines in the area. The mines had been worked since Roman times but were abandoned at the end of the 19th century.

The Promenade du Canal follows the canal back to town, about 3.5km (2 miles) away.

❼ Just before you arrive, on the left, a road leads to La Roche Cintrée, with a good view of the town and the mountains.

WHERE TO EAT
AUBERGE MENEZ BRAS
www.auberge-menezbras.com
✉ 29690 Huelgoat ☎ 02 98 99 76 28
🕐 Tue–Sat lunch and dinner, Sun lunch

TOURIST INFORMATION
www.tourismehuelgoat.fr

Opposite *Wild flowers by a forest track*
Below *Large boulders by the waterside*

THE SUISSE NORMANDE AND ORNE VALLEY

This drive takes in some of the high points of the Suisse Normande, a pretty, hilly region south of Caen and bounded by the river Orne. The river runs beside the road for much of your drive. The roads are narrow, single-track in places, always winding and sometimes steep, so high speeds are not advisable. The route takes in attractive towns and villages and some good viewpoints.

THE DRIVE
Distance: 110km (68 miles)
Allow: 1 day
Start/end at: Caen

★ Caen (▷ 129) is the ancient capital of the dukes of Normandy and is full of interest. Sights include the castle, the Mémorial de Caen and the two abbeys—the Abbaye-aux-Hommes, built by William the Conqueror, and the Abbaye-aux-Dames, built by his wife Matilda.

Leave from below the castle, in the heart of town, and follow the *Toutes Directions* signs, then signs for Rennes-Granville as far as the racecourse at La Prairie. From there, pick up the D8, signed for Évrecy and Aunay-sur-Odon, and follow this road to Évrecy, passing a small group of World War II memorials on the left.

❶ The countryside around Caen is full of memorials to the bitter fighting of 1944. The one near Évrecy is dedicated to the men of the 43rd (Welsh) Division. There is a Churchill tank and a monument to Hill 112, declaring 'Whoever holds Hill 112 holds all of Normandy'.

Turn left at the church in Évrecy onto the D41. At Amayé-sur-Orne, turn right at the outskirts of the village onto the D212, signed for Thury-Harcourt. Turn left at the hamlet of Le Hom, crossing the river and an old rail track to reach the town of Thury-Harcourt.

❷ Thury-Harcourt is a market town and visitor base for the Suisse Normande and the Orne Valley. It is a pretty and prosperous town with a ruined moated château and a park. Two gatehouses, with strange beehive-shaped roofs, one wing and a bricked-up facade are all that can be seen of the château. A plaque on the park wall pays tribute to the British forces.

Leave Thury-Harcourt going south. Follow the D562 along the river for 13km (8 miles) then, at a large roadside cross, take the D133A down into the middle of Clécy.

❸ Clécy is set in one of the most attractive parts of the Orne Valley, at a point where the river is overlooked by high cliffs, and is popular as a base for walking and touring. It's a good place to stop for lunch and stroll around the town, admiring the fairy-tale architecture. Follow signs to the Pont du Vey, passing Clécy's miniature railway museum. Don't cross the bridge, but admire the watermill on the other side.

❹ There are fine views and walks along the Orne Valley from the Pont du Vey. The best way to see the river is from the footpath or the road that runs alongside it, overlooking the riverside hotels, the canoeists and the climbers who scramble on the cliffs by the old viaduct.

Follow the main road, signed for La Lande, round past a little art gallery on your right and several riverside cafés and restaurants on your left. Drive through Le Bô and Cossesseville, with their charming churches. (These roads may be flooded in winter.) With the river on your right, continue along the D167 through Pont d'Ouilly. At Le Bateau take the D18E towards the parking and picnic area by the viaduct. At the end of the viaduct turn sharp right under the arches on the D18A, signed St-Philbert, continuing to the top of the hill and the viewpoint at Roche d'Oëtre.

❺ The viewpoint at Roche d'Oëtre overlooks the river Rouvre. This 118m (387ft) precipice has no barrier, so heed the warning signs, be extra careful on wet or windy days, and keep control of small children.

Return the way you came, under the viaduct. Turn right back onto the D18 through Le Mesnil-Villemont. At

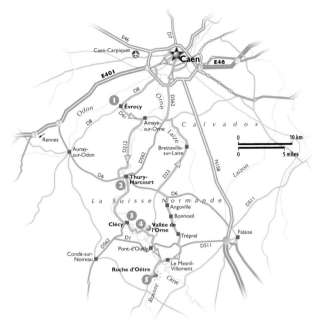

the T-junction turn left onto the D511, then right onto the D43. It's then a left turn onto the D241 to Tréprel. Continue on the D241 through farming country north to Bonnoeil and Angoville, then left onto the D6 to Meslay. Turn right onto the D23 to Bretteville-sur-Laize. Cross the river Laize and turn left onto the D132, along the Laize Valley to the D562. Turn right here to return to Caen through small suburban towns.

Opposite *Rue du Vaugueux, in Caen's old town*
Below *Caen War Memorial*

WHEN TO GO
Some roads on this tour may be flooded in winter.

WHERE TO EAT
AU SITE NORMAND
www.ausitenormand.com
✉ 1 rue des Châtelets, 14570 Clécy ☎ 02 31 69 71 05 ⏰ Closed mid-Dec to mid-Feb

Alternatively have a snack at one of the cafés by the Pont du Vey.

GIVERNY

The delightful riverside village of Giverny, spread across a hillside near Vernon, is the most visited place in Normandy. Crowds of art and garden lovers flock to see the home of Claude Monet and the world's most famous lily pond, immortalized in some of the artist's best-known paintings.

THE WALK
Distance: 9km (5.5 miles)
Allow: 2 hours 30 minutes
Start/end at: Fondation Claude Monet

HOW TO GET THERE

Giverny is near Vernon, off the D5, west of Paris (and possible as a day trip from the capital).

★ Start the walk outside the Fondation Claude Monet.

❶ In 1883 Monet moved into a pastel-pink house with grass-green shutters in Giverny (▷ 137), where he had worked with Renoir, Sisley and Manet for a number of years. He designed the gardens himself and created his famous water garden with its lilies and Japanese bridge. The main garden, with its 12 resident gardeners, still keeps to Monet's design and is a palette of changing hues from spring to autumn. Near the house, Monet's enormous studio is filled with huge copies of his works. (For the real thing, visit the Musée Marmottan Monet in Paris, ▷ 89.)

Head along rue Claude Monet, towards the Musée d'Art Américain. Take the lane to the right, called chemin Blanche-Hoschède, then go right again almost immediately up the narrow rue Hélène-Pillon, which curves left before becoming a dirt track. Follow this path along the backs of houses, running parallel to rue Claude Monet below, until you reach the end of the village. Turn left (signposted GR2 and marked with red-and-white paint markers) up a steep path, then turn right at the first intersection. The path snakes across meadowland towards the woods, with sweeping views over the Epte valley below.

At the next crossing of footpaths, go left and climb up through oak woods. At this point you leave the GR2 and the path is now marked in yellow. At the next crossroads, go right. At the edge of the woods, take the grassy path on the left, passing alongside pastureland then more woodland. As you reach the woods, turn right towards a small road. Turn

left onto the road, which runs steeply downhill. After 50m (55 yards), bear right, then right again along a track bordering the woods of La Réserve on the right, and flanked by fields on the left. When you come to a crossroads level with a small yellow house on the left, continue straight on, then go left along the fringe of the Garenne woods.

Turn to the right in the Garenne woods (once again following the red-and-white signs of GR2). Soon you will come to a promontory marked by a large cross, with a magnificent view of the Seine.

Continue down a very steep, narrow path leading to the hamlet of Manitaux. It comes out on a small lane bordered by cottages. Turn left, following the course of a former train track until you reach the edge of Giverny. Go along the grassy path behind the first houses in the village, until the path joins the Sente des Grosses Eaux and, soon afterwards, rue Claude Monet.

❷ Back on the main street of the village, proceed past the church, where Monet lies buried.

❸ Hôtel Baudy is an ancient boarding house and rendezvous of various painter friends of Monet, including Rodin, Sisley, Renoir,

Cézanne, Pissarro and various visiting American artists. It was also the site of the first studio and the first art exhibitions in the village.

❹ The Musée des Impressionismes, opened in 2009, has a permanent collection of works by Monet's American contemporaries in France and many temporary exhibitions.

Continue along rue Claude Monet, filled with artists' workshops and galleries, before returning to Claude Monet's house and garden at the far end of the village.

Above *An archway of greenery (left) and vivid flowers (right) in Monet's garden*
Below *Flowers in bloom in the summer*
Opposite *Monet's pond*

WHEN TO GO
Monet's gardens are closed on Mondays and November to March.

PLACE TO VISIT
MUSÉE DES IMPRESSIONNISMES
www.museedesimpressionnismesgiverny.com
✉ 99 rue Claude Monet, 27620 ☎ 02 32 51 94 65 🕐 Apr–Oct Tue–Sun 10–6 ✋ Adult €6.50, child (13–18) €4.50, (7–12) €3, under 7 free

THE EMERALD COAST

This drive takes in the fascinating Côte d'Émeraude, with its impressive cliffs, superb sandy beaches and the unforgettable Fort la Latte, on a barren promontory. Inland, the Forêt de la Hunaudaye and the surrounding area provide an interesting contrast.

THE DRIVE
Distance: 92km (57 miles)
Allow: Half to a full day
Start/end at: Lamballe

★ Lamballe, on a hillside beside a small river, is famous for its *haras national* (national stud farm), where you can take a guided tour. The Gothic Église Notre-Dame at the top of town has a finely carved rood screen and doorways.

Leave Lamballe eastwards by taking the D28, then bear right onto the D52A towards Plédéliac, 11km (7 miles) away. Turn left onto the D55 and drive for another 4km (2.5 miles), following the signs to Château de la Hunaudaye.

❶ The Château de la Hunaudaye dates back to the 12th century. It was battered into its present ruins during the Revolution. The most impressive parts are the Tour de la Glacière, the Renaissance manor house and the 15th-century keep, with a remarkable spiral staircase.

Turn left and left again along the D28 and drive through the Forêt de la Hunaudaye to the hamlet of St-Aubin, 6km (4 miles). Follow the D52 and turn right. Follow the D13 and D43 for 24km (15 miles) through Hénanbihen and Pléboulle to the Baie de la Frénaye and Fort la Latte.

❷ The medieval fortress of Fort la Latte (▷ 128) perches on a rocky promontory and offers magnificent views of Cap Fréhel to the west and the Côte d'Émeraude to the east. Two drawbridges span the deep cracks in the rock, which are filled by the sea at high tide. Inside the fortress, the oven heated cannonballs to set fire to enemy ships.

Drive round the Anse des Sévignés, 4km (2.5 miles), to Cap Fréhel (▷ 128), then follow the D34 to Sables-d'Or-les-Pins, 9km (5.5 miles). The scenic coast road winds through the wild Landes de Fréhel (Fréhel moors) to Pléhérel-Plage, with its beautiful beach.

❸ Most people come to Sables-d'Or-les-Pins (▷ 153) to walk on the long golden beach. Strong currents make it unsuitable for swimming.

Continue on the D34 and turn right onto the D786 towards Erquy, 8km (5 miles).

❹ This resort and fishing port is sheltered by the cliffs of Cap d'Erquy, 3km (2 miles) to the north, and is worth the detour. There are impressive views of the wide bay of St-Brieuc to Île de Bréhat (▷ 139).

Continue on the D786 towards Le Val-André for 5km (3 miles), past Château de Bienassis on your left.

BEAUSÉJOUR
www.beausejour-erquy.com
✉ 21 rue de la Corniche, Erquy ☎ 02 96
72 30 39 ⊘ Closed mid-Nov to mid-Mar

PLACES TO VISIT
CHÂTEAU DE LA HUNAUDAYE
www.la-hunaudaye.com
☎ 02 96 34 82 10 ⊘ Mid-Jun to mid-Sep
daily 10.30–6; Apr to mid-Jun, mid-Sep to
early Nov Wed, Sun 2.30–6

CHÂTEAU DE BIENASSIS
www.chateau-bienassis.com
☎ 02 96 72 22 03 ⊘ May to mid-Jun
Sat–Sun 2–5; mid-Jun to mid-Sep daily 2–5

Below *Cap Fréhel lighthouse*
Below left *Fishing boats moored in Erquy*
Opposite *Forte la Latte on its rocky perch*

❺ The late-medieval castle of Bienassis was rebuilt in the 17th century and furnished in Louis XIV and Breton Renaissance styles.

Continue on the D786 for 6km (4 miles) to Le Val-André.

❻ The beach at Le Val-André is one of Brittany's finest. A road running around the promontory has lovely views of the beach and of the Île du Verdelet, a bird sanctuary since the early 1970s and only accessible at low tide.

Follow the D34 to Planguenoual, then the D59 back to Lamballe.

WHEN TO GO
Both the Château de la Hunaudaye and Château de Bienassis are open in peak season only (see opening times, right).

AROUND ÉTRETAT

Immediately to the north and south of the small resort of Étretat, the cliffs of the Côte d'Albâtre are at their most spectacular, with sheer, white, striated walls plunging vertically into the breaking waves, a massive arch vaulting into the sea and a solitary needle of rock soaring to 70m (230ft) offshore. This coastal walk begins easily at the seafront of Étretat but it can be rough in places and it is advisable to wear sturdy non-slip footwear. If there is a little effort involved, the breathtaking panoramas make it worthwhile.

THE WALK

Distance: 6.5km (4 miles)
Allow: 2 hours 30 minutes
Start/end at: Étretat

HOW TO GET THERE

Étretat is on the Côte d'Albâtre, between Le Havre and Fécamp.

A modest fishing village for most of its history, Étretat lay in obscurity until the mid-19th century when the writers Guy de Maupassant and Alexandre Dumas discovered the delights of the pebbled beach enveloped by the cliffs, and the great artists of the day began to paint the scene. Fashionable visitors began to arrive from Paris and elsewhere, lured by the views reproduced by Delacroix, Boudin and Monet. In town, visit place du Maréchal Foch, with its wooden covered market built in 1926 amid a cluster of charming 16th-century town houses. For golfers, the 18-hole clifftop course is France's highest golf links, with fine views.

★ Start on the promenade. Walk to the eastern end, turn right, up 83 brick steps that open out onto a grassy clifftop pathway, past a children's theme park and to the top of the Porte (or Falaise) d'Amont and Chapelle Notre-Dame-de-la-Garde.

❶ On the Falaise d'Amont, stop by the sailors' chapel and admire the views of the western Falaise d'Aval across the beach, with a 70m (230ft) rock stack known as the Aiguille (needle) d'Étretat standing alongside. Inland from the chapel, a monument commemorates the lost aviators Nungesser and Coli, whose plane *L'Oiseau Blanc* was last seen flying over these cliffs in 1927 on its ill-fated bid to fly from Paris to New York. The aviators were presumed drowned in the Atlantic and their bodies were never recovered.

Continue along the cliff edge, past the chapel and go down some steps leading to the arch of Amont. A steep, slippery and narrow pathway, cut into the chalky stack, offers wonderful views of the white cliffs to the east. A wooden handrail and a ladder assist in the final descent to a small beach. Retrace your steps, past the chapel and back down the brick steps. Proceed along the promenade, a curve of café-lined concrete above the steep shingle beach. At the far end, another flight of steps, followed by a steep, well-trodden, flint-filled path, leads up beside a scenic golf course to Porte d'Aval. Bear right along the cliff edge, crossing a narrow bridge and onto the top of the cliff arch—not for those with a fear of heights.

2 From the cliff arch there are spectacular views over Étretat's slate roofs and to the Porte d'Amont

beyond. Legend has it that many centuries ago three beautiful sisters were imprisoned by an evil lord in a cave at the foot of these cliffs.

Continue along the windswept cliff edge, admiring the wild flowers, yellow gorse and purple sea cabbage, and on to a second arch, La Manne-Porte, with breathtaking views stretching as far as the port of Le Havre-Antifer. Just beyond the next headland, Pointe de la Courtine, follow a track inland (the GR21, marked with a red-and-white stripe), branching left, where two paths meet, to Valaine. At the next intersection, leave the GR21 and head down a narrow country lane, through the brick and stone farm buildings of Ferme le Valaine.

3 On the left, the lovely old farmhouse of Ferme le Valaine sells delicious home-produced cider, Calvados and goat's cheese.

Follow the road as it winds gently downhill, past grazing goats, until you reach the D940. Turn left back

into the middle of Étretat and left again back to the waterfront.

WHEN TO GO
Check weather reports before starting the cliff walk, as the wind may be strong and the steps slippery. Hardy visitors might like to join locals for the traditional New Year's Day swim!

WHERE TO EAT
Eat in Étretat or at the clifftop Dormy-House, at the end of the walk.
DORMY HOUSE
www.dormy-house.com
✉ route du Havre ☎ 02 35 27 07 88

INFORMATION
TOURIST INFORMATION
www.etretat.net
✉ place Maurice Guillard, 76790 Étretat
☎ 02 35 27 05 21 🕐 Mid-Jun to mid-Sep daily 9–7; mid-Mar to mid-Jun, mid-Sep to mid-Nov daily 10–12, 2–6; mid-Nov to mid-Mar Fri–Sat 10–12, 2–6

Opposite top *The Falaise d'Aval chalk cliff*
Opposite bottom *Chapelle Notre-Dame-de-la-Garde*
Below *A local brasserie in Étretat*

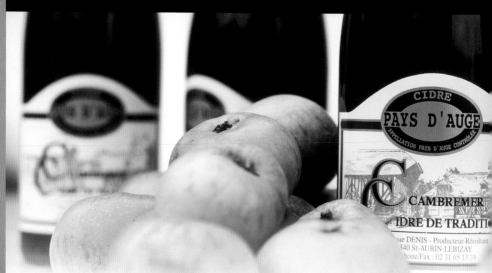

ARRADON
BELLE PLAISANCE
www.belleplaisance.com
On the Golfe du Morbihan you can rent beautifully restored sailing boats with a professional sailor to navigate and instruct. Decide where you want to go, or leave it to the experts. Make your reservation at least one week in advance and note that credit cards are not accepted.
✉ Nicolas Bourdy, 24 chemin de Gravellic, 56610 Arradon ☎ 02 97 44 80 91
🕐 Apr–Oct, by appointment 👆 €60 per person (whole day), €30 per person (half day), €30 6.30pm–8.30pm with apéritif, €30 8.30pm–10pm to watch sunset, all departing from Arradon port

LE BEC-HELLOUIN
ABBAYE NOTRE-DAME DU BEC
www.abbayedubec.com
The Benedictine monks here produce fine ceramics (tableware, dishes, vases and candlesticks), some of which use antique designs. Also for sale are a range of candles.
✉ 27800 Le Bec-Hellouin ☎ 02 32 43 72 60 🕐 Guided tours: Jun–Sep Mon–Sat, 10.30, 11, 3, 4, 5, Sun 12, 3, 4, 6; Oct–May Mon–Sat, 11, 3, 4, Sun 3, 4. Closed during services

Above *Local cider makes a good souvenir*

BLONVILLE-SUR-MER
LES PLANCHES
www.lesplanches.com
This nightclub has maritime-themed decorations and an outdoor pool. There are two dance floors and one is dedicated to retro tunes from the 1960s to the 1990s.
✉ Domaine du Bois Lauret, 14910 Blonville-sur-Mer ☎ 02 31 87 58 09 🕐 Jul–Aug daily 11pm–5am; Sep–Jun Fri–Sat 10pm–4am 👆 €12–€20

BREST
LE QUARTZ
www.lequartz.com
Inject a shot of culture into your visit to Brest. There are two performance halls, one seating 2,500, the other 400. This venue (take the bus to place de la Liberté) hosts plays, ballet, classical music, jazz, world music, opera and films.
✉ place Beethoven, 60 rue du Château, 91039 Brest ☎ 02 98 33 70 70
🕐 Performances: Sep–Jun Mon–Sat 8.30pm (check schedule) 👆 €8.50–€45

LE BREUIL-EN-AUGE
CHÂTEAU DU BREUIL
www.chateau-breuil.fr
Not many distilleries have such an elegant setting. This one occupies a stylish 17th-century château, where locally grown apples are turned into one of the region's most famous exports, the apple-based brandy, Calvados. Take a guided tour then choose from different vintages of Calvados or opt for derivatives such as *Pommeau* (Calvados and apple juice) or *Cœur du Breuil* (a Calvados-based liqueur).
✉ Les Jourdains, 14130 Le Breuil-en-Auge ☎ 02 31 65 60 00 🕐 Daily 9–12, 2–6 (sometimes closed Sun in winter) 👆 €3, under 18s free

CAEN
ZÉNITH DE CAEN
www.zenith-caen.fr
The auditorium can hold audiences of up to 7,000 for comedy, ballet, classical music concerts and more. There is no box office. Tickets can be purchased at the venue only on the evening of the performance, unless reserved beforehand through a ticket agency.
✉ rue Joseph Philippon, 14000 Caen
🕐 Performances usually start at 8.30pm

CAMEMBERT
FROMAGERIE DURAND
This farm produces authentic Camembert with an AOC quality standard. You can tour the *laiterie* to watch the process, try the cheese

and buy Durand label items, and other produce including fruit, vegetables, unpasteurised milk and cream, cider, apples and jam at the farm shop.

✉ Le Heronière, 61120 Camembert ☎ 02 33 39 08 08 ⏰ Mon–Sat 9–12, 3–6 ✋ Tours free, tasting €5

CAP FRÉHEL
PÂTISSIER-CHOCOLATIER R. JOUAULT

In this cottage-style building you can buy Breton pastries such as *far* and *élisa*. The bakery has won the European Lauriers d'Or trophy for its superb *kouignamann* (cake made with sugar, butter and almonds). Their special is *palet de Fréhel* (nougatine, almond and chocolate) with a depiction of Cap Fréhel.

✉ place de Chamblis, 22240 Fréhel ☎ 02 96 41 41 31 ⏰ Jul to mid-Sep daily 7.30–8; mid-Sep to Jun Sat–Sun 7.30–8

CARNAC
MAISON ARMORINE

www.maison-armorine.com

This sweet shop (candy store) sells 49 varieties of *niniche*, a long, thin lollipop, popular with Breton children. There is also lovely toffee made with salted butter.

✉ 7 avenue du Parc, 56340 Carnac ☎ 02 97 52 73 51 ⏰ Apr–Sep Mon–Sun 9.30–12.30, 2.30–7

CHERBOURG
L'ANTIDOTE

You can try wine by the glass from one of hundreds of vintages here. The bright interior is designer wood and brass and there's a pleasant terrace, open in fine weather.

✉ 41 rue au Blé, 50100 Cherbourg ☎ 02 33 78 01 28 ⏰ Bar: daily 10am–1am. Restaurant: summer daily 11.30–3, 6.30–11; winter Tue–Sat 11.30–3, 6.30–11

DEAUVILLE
CASINO DE DEAUVILLE

www.lucienbarriere.com

This casino and club is in a beautiful belle époque building on the shoreline. There are gaming tables, two bars, three restaurants and a nightclub; the dress code is formal.

✉ rue Edmond Blanc, BP 32400, 14802 Deauville ☎ 02 31 14 31 14 ⏰ Slot machines: Mon–Thu, Sun 10am–2am, Fri 10am–3am, Sat 10am–4am ✋ Free (must show a passport or identity card); cover charge for the game room

GOLF BARRIÈRE DE DEAUVILLE

www.lucienbarriere.com

You'll get beautiful views of the sea and the countryside from this 18-hole golf course on top of Mont Canisy, which offers fast greens and tough rough. Afterwards, have a drink in the clubhouse or browse in the shop.

✉ Mont Canisy St-Arnoult, BP 63500, 14803 Deauville ☎ 02 31 14 24 24 ⏰ Daily 9–6 ✋ €45–€95 green fee

DIEPPE
DIEPPE SCÈNE NATIONALE

www.dsn.asso.fr

This modern auditorium hosts plays and concerts. A cinema shows independent films and classics.

✉ quai Bérigny, 76374 Dieppe ☎ 02 35 82 04 43 ⏰ Daily 2–10 ✋ Films €6.50, live performances €20

DINAN
LA BOURBANSAIS

www.labourbansais.com

You'll find this zoo, with many protected species, in the grounds of Château de Bourbansais (which is worth a visit in its own right) east of Dinan. There is a playground with a bouncy castle, a tea room and a gift shop. Credit cards are not accepted.

✉ Domaine de la Bourbansais, 35720 Pleugueneuc ☎ 02 99 69 40 07 ⏰ Apr–Sep daily 10–7; Oct–Mar 1.30–5.30 ✋ Zoo: Adult €17, child (3–12) €12.50. Zoo and château: Adult €21.50, child (3–12) €15.50

CLUB CANOË KAYAK DE LA RANCE

www.nautismebretagne.fr

At Lanvallay, east of Dinan, this club rents out canoes and kayaks for trips on the Rance river lasting from one hour to one day. Take the bus to Le Port. Credit cards are not accepted.

✉ 13 rue du Four, 22100 Lanvallay ☎ 02 96 39 01 50 ⏰ Jul–Aug daily 9–7; Sep–Jun by appointment only ✋ Varies

DINARD
CASINO BARRIÈRE DE DINARD

www.lucienbarriere.com

Here you'll find roulette, blackjack, stud poker, and more than 100 one-armed bandits. The cocktail bar has a great view of the beach and there is a restaurant. Food is served all day and there's also live music.

✉ 4 boulevard Wilson, 35802 Dinard ☎ 02 99 16 30 30 ⏰ Gaming tables: May–Sep Mon–Fri 9pm–3am, Sat–Sun 9pm–4am; Oct–Apr Wed–Thu and Sun 9pm–3am, Fri–Sat 9pm–4am. Slot machines: Jul–Aug daily 11am–4am; Sep–Jun Sun–Thu 11am–2pm, Fri–Sat 11am–4am ✋ Free (over-18s only, must show a passport or identity card)

PISCINE MUNICIPALE

This Olympic-sized pool is filled with heated seawater. There is also a beach with activities for children. It's on bus circuit 3; ask for *Piscine*.

✉ 2 boulevard Wilson, 35800 Dinard ☎ 02 99 46 22 77 ⏰ Jul–Aug Mon–Fri 10–12.30, 3–7.30, Sat–Sun 10–12.30, 3–6; Sep–Jun Mon 3–6.30, Tue, Fri 5–8, Wed, Sat 2–6.30, Thu 12.15–1.30, 5–7.30, Sun 9–12.30. Extended hours during school holidays ✋ €4.50, child (5–18) €3.50

DOUARNENEZ
CHAR À VOILE PENTREZ

www.ffcv.org

Try sand yachting and kite surfing on this beach north of Douarnenez which, at low tide, is 3km (2 miles) long and 5km (3 miles) wide, giving you plenty of space. The minimum age for these activities is seven and it's a good idea to reserve your place in advance. Credit cards are not accepted.

✉ Pentrez Plage, 29550 St-Nic ☎ 02 98 26 55 27 ⏰ Jul–Aug daily 10–7; periods of school holidays Mon–Fri 10–12, 2–6, Sat–Sun 2–6; all other times Sat–Sun 2–6 ✋ Varies

DOUVRES-LA-DÉLIVRANDE
PÂTISSERIE DE LA BASILIQUE

You'll find this small village a stone's throw from the local beaches north of Caen. The pâtisserie itself is located in a pretty half-timbered house. For three generations, the

Jung family have been making Normandy specials such as *brasillés* (bread made with the local salted butter) and rich biscuits which are similar in taste and appearance to Scottish shortbread.

✉ 3 place de la Basilique, 14440 Douvres-la-Délivrande ☎ 02 31 37 29 74 🕐 Wed–Sun 7.45–12.45, 1.45–7.45

ÉTRETAT
VILLAGE ÉQUESTRE D'ÉTRETAT

www.etretat-equitation.fr

This equestrian venue, which welcomes beginners, is in a seaside resort. It offers guided rides through beautiful countryside and forest and on the cliffs of Étretat. There's a maximum of eight per group.

✉ 248–250 rue de la Sauvagère, 76790 Le Tilleul ☎ 02 35 27 04 22 🕐 Fri–Wed ✋ €25 per hour

GRANVILLE
STATION DE VOILE DE GRANVILLE

The water and beach sports on offer here include windsurfing, catamaran sailing, sea kayaking and sand yachting. The bay of Granville has very strong tides.

✉ 260 boulevard des Amiraux, 50400 Granville ☎ 02 33 91 83 72 🕐 Reserve ahead ✋ From €25.50 per session of catamaran sailing, windsurfing or kayaking

HONFLEUR
MARCHÉ TRADITIONNEL

This traditional market takes place on a charming square presided over by a 15th-century church and lined with cafés in half-timbered houses. Treat yourself to the locally caught fish and farm produce.

✉ place de l'Église Ste-Catherine, 14600 Honfleur 🕐 Sat 9.30–12.30

ÎLE D'OUESSANT
CENTRE EQUESTRE LES CALECHES DU PONANT

www.cheval-cdp-29.fr

Explore this island on a horse or Shetland pony. Several different routes pass beautiful spots and trek lengths vary from an hour to three days. Reserve in advance and note that credit cards are not accepted.

✉ Le Goubars, 29242 Ouessant ☎ 02 98 48 89 29 🕐 Daily 9–6 ✋ 1 hour €17.50, 2 hours €32 (min 3 people)

PERROS-GUIREC
GALERIE DE KER-ILIZ

www.produits-bretons-ker-iliz.com

This large mall sells products made or crafted in Brittany, such as Quimper *faïence,* Celtic jewellery, music, pottery, wooden items, biscuits and nautical clothing.

✉ 8 rue du Général de Gaulle, 22700 Perros-Guirec ☎ 02 96 91 00 96 🕐 Jul–Aug daily 10–12.30, 2.30–7.30; Sep–Jun closed Sun and Mon morning

QUIMPER
ARMOR LUX

www.armorlux.com

This store specializes in marine clothing and has been making the classic Breton striped sweaters for more than 60 years. Reserve ahead for a tour of the factory. In the shop, you'll find the latest designs as well as discontinued lines.

✉ 21 rue Louison Bobet, Kerdroniou Ouest, 29556 Quimper ☎ 02 98 90 05 29 🕐 Mon–Sat 9.30–7

RENNES
PÉNICHE SPECTACLE

www.penichespectacle.com

Two barges—*L'Arbre d'Eau* and *La Dame Blanche*—are now theatres presenting world music, jazz, cabaret and exhibitions. There are also performances for children.

✉ 30 quai St-Cyr, 35000 Rennes ☎ 02 99 59 35 38 🕐 Performance times vary ✋ Adult €13 concert, €9 cabaret

THÉÂTRE NATIONAL DE BRETAGNE (TNB)

www.t-n-b.fr

This theatre, at Gare on the Métro, has three separate performance halls for drama, dance, jazz and classical music. There's also a cinema which screens films in their original language. You can have lunch or dinner in the large restaurant and bar.

✉ 1 rue St-Hélier, 35040 Rennes ☎ 02 99 31 12 31 🕐 Ticket office: Tue–Fri 1–7, Sat 2–7 ✋ Tickets start at €24

ST-CAST-LE-GUILDO
CENTRE NAUTIQUE DE ST-CAST

www.centre-nautique-saint-cast.fr

At this water sports venue you can rent all kinds of sailing boats, windsurfers and kayaks, although for larger boats you'll need a permit. You can also have individual sailing lessons. Boat rental stops in November and restarts in April.

✉ Le Port, 22380 St-Cast-le-Guildo ☎ 02 96 41 86 42 and 02 96 41 71 71 🕐 Jul–Aug daily 10–7; Sep–Jun Tue–Sat 9–12, 2–5 ✋ Dinghy rental from €24 per hour

LA FERME DES LANDES

www.fermedeslandes.pays-de-matignon.net

A cider-lover's heaven with cider from different apple varieties, plus cider vinegar and apple juice, all home-brewed. Taste, buy and tour the farm (by appointment only). Every Friday afternoon in summer, there's a local farmers' market.

✉ Notre Dame du Guildo, 22380 St-Cast-le-Guildo ☎ 02 96 41 12 48 🕐 Jun, Aug daily 10–8; Apr–May, Sep Mon–Sat 2–7; Oct–Mar Fri–Sat 10–12, 2–6 🚗 Take the D786, the farm is just before Notre-Dame-du-Guildo coming from St-Cast-le-Guildo

GOLF CLUB DE PEN-GUEN

www.golf-st-cast.com

This superbly situated 18-hole golf course is 800m (850 yards) east of the town, with has access to the beach. There's a driving range and putting green. Call ahead to reserve.

✉ Route du Golfe, 22380 St-Cast-le-Guildo ☎ 02 96 41 91 20 🕐 Apr–Sep daily 7.30am–8pm; Oct–Mar 9–5.30 ✋ €55 in summer, €32–43 rest of year, trolley €4, clubs €8

TRÉGASTEL
CLUB HIPPIQUE DE TREGASTEL

www.equitation-tregastel.com

Go horseback riding through the Breton countryside, in a forest or along the seashore of the Côtes d'Armor region. You can also take lessons. Reserve in advance.

✉ 13 rue du Calvaire, 22730 Trégastel ☎ 02 96 23 86 14 🕐 Mon–Sat 9–12, 2–7; closed 2 weeks in Sep ✋ Adult €19 per hour

FESTIVALS AND EVENTS

MAY
JAZZ SOUS LES POMMIERS
www.jazzsouslespommiers.com
The musical year starts here with Maytime jazz sessions in bucolic cider country. Most concerts have a modest admission fee, but a festival pass gives free admission to many events.
✉ Coutances ☎ 02 33 76 78 50 (tourist office)

JULY
FÊTES HISTORIQUES
www.mairie-vannes.fr
Every year the citizens of Vannes go back in time for one week. The theme changes annually and could be anything from the Vikings to the early 1800s, with street performances, parades in original costumes and fireworks.
✉ Service d'Animation Culturelle, 31 rue Thiers, 56000 Vannes ☎ 02 97 01 62 40
⏰ Three days in mid-July

TOMBÉES DE LA NUIT
www.tdn.rennes.fr
Light shows and concerts are performed at dusk. Music and theatricals in the street are free; there is a small charge for shows in various venues.
✉ Rennes ☎ 02 99 32 56 56

FESTIVAL DES VIEILLES CHARRUES
www.vieillescharrues.asso.fr
One of France's biggest music festivals welcomes 150,000 music fans to watch bands playing everything from techno to folk. The three-day festival has a free campsite. To be sure of getting your ticket, buy it at least one month in advance.
✉ Association Les Vieilles Charrues, 29834 Carhaix ☎ 0820 890 066 or 02 98 93 04 42 (Carhaix tourist office)
🚌 Shuttle buses from train stations in Loudeac, Morlaix, Brest, Quimper, Crozon and Châteauneuf ⏰ Third weekend in July

FÊTE DES REMPARTS
One of the largest medieval festivals in Europe is held once every two years. During the last weekend of July Dinan is literally invaded by 800 actors and 3,000 extras in costume.
✉ Office de Tourisme, rue du Château, 22100 Dinan ☎ 02 96 87 69 76
⏰ Third weekend in July. Every two years (even years)

FESTIVAL DU JAZZ
www.mairie-vannes.fr/jazzavannes
Six days of evening jazz concerts begin with a free concert in front of the city hall. Three bands play per evening with some playing in the garden of Limur, and in the afternoons, amateur musicians play throughout the town.
✉ Service Animation Culturelle, 31 rue Thiers, 56000 Vannes ☎ 02 97 01 62 40
⏰ End of July

JULY–AUGUST
FESTIMUSICALES
Free concerts and performances all summer long. Expect jazz, African, reggae and Celtic music, folk dancing and street theatre.
✉ Espace Kernévéleck, 29170 Fouesnant ☎ 02 98 51 18 88 (tourist office)

AUGUST
FESTIVAL INTERCELTIQUE
www.festival-interceltique.com
For 10 days in August, Lorient is the scene of a large Celtic festival, with bagpipe and other traditional musical instrument contests, folk dancing demonstrations, Breton parties (festou-noz), cabaret, concerts across the city and street stands selling Celtic crafts.
✉ 8 rue Nayel, 56100 Lorient ☎ 02 97 21 24 29 ⏰ First two weeks in August

LA ROUTE DU ROCK
www.laroutedurock.com
This three-day popular music festival covers music from rock to techno. There's free camping in the moat

around the castle, free parking, a restaurant and bar, a left-luggage office, a supermarket and free shuttle from St-Malo train station.
✉ Fort St-Père or Office de tourisme de St-Malo, esplanade St-Vincent, 35400 St-Malo ☎ 02 99 54 01 11 (Fort St-Père) or 08 25 13 52 00 (tourist office) ⏰ Mid-August

FESTIVAL DE MUSIQUE CLASSIQUE DE DINARD– CÔTE D'ÉMERAUDE
www.festival-music-dinard.com
Dinard's three-week festival has exquisite classical music with many different styles on offer, from Beethoven to Gershwin and contemporary composers, all performed by well-known musicians and young talents. There's also a concert for children and the closing concert is free.
✉ Dinard tourist office, 2 boulevard Féart, 35802 Dinard ☎ 02 99 46 94 12 ⏰ Three weeks in August, first Sat to third Sun
✋ Varies

DECEMBER
TRANSMUSICALES ROCK FESTIVAL
www.transmusicales.com
Local bands play alongside international music legends at Brittany's music festival. Some concerts are free, while others have a small admission charge.
✉ Rennes ☎ 02 99 31 12 10

EATING

PRICES AND SYMBOLS

The restaurants are listed alphabetically (excluding Le, La and Les). The prices given are the average for a two-course lunch (L) and a three-course dinner (D) for one person, without drinks. The wine price is for the least expensive bottle.

For a key to the symbols, ▷ 2.

AUDRIEU
CHATEAU D'AUDRIEU

www.chateaudaudrieu.com
This listed historic manor with a gourmet restaurant makes a luxury retreat in the heart of D-Day country. Chef Olivier Barbarin makes full use of the superb local produce. Diners can select from the excellent entrées such as foie gras terrine with cocoa nibs and poached pears, iced watercress soup with oysters and salmon. Main dishes include gurnard, sea bass or duckling, pork and beef fillet. For dessert, there are figs cooked in red wine or plum tart. ✉ 14250 Audrieu ☎ 02 31 80 21 52 ⏰ Closed early Jan–early Feb ✋ L €53, D €71, Wine €32

Above *An assortment of locally caught seafood at a restaurant in Cancale*

ALENCON
PETIT VATEL

This stone house with flowery balconies is near the town centre and close to the Musée des Beaux-Arts et de la Dentelle. The dining room is decorated in pastel tones. The chef prepares refined French cuisine with the emphasis on Norman produce. ✉ 72 place du Commandant Desmeulles, 61000 Alençon ☎ 02 33 26 23 78 ⏰ Thu–Tue 12–1.45, 7.15–9.30. Closed Sun dinner, Tue dinner and mid-Jul to mid-Aug ✋ L €35, D €40, Wine €15

BARFLEUR
LE MODERNE

www.hotel-restaurant-moderne-barfleur.com
The restaurant of hotel Le Moderne specializes in traditional cuisine, especially fish and seafood. It's a good place to eat lobster (according to availability from the fishing harbour) roasted with butter, served Parisian-style with mayonnaise, or sautéed. There is also a good selection of meat dishes (lamb, tournedos of beef, or grilled steak). ✉ place du Général de Gaulle, 50760 Barfleur ☎ 02 33 23 12 44 ⏰ Wed–Mon 12–1.30, 7.30–9.30 ✋ L €40, D €55, Wine €17

BAYEUX
LE LION D'OR

www.liondor-bayeux.fr
Chef Patrick Mouilleau cooks dishes of the region. Try rabbit confit with sage and millefeuille of carrots, pan-sautéed salmon cooked in olive oil and thyme and served with thick slices of potato, or pigeon stuffed with foie gras and mushrooms. The desserts include delights such as roasted fig with honey and port. ✉ 71 rue St-Jean, 14400 Bayeux ☎ 02 31 92 06 90 ⏰ Daily 12–2.30, 7.30–10 except Sat lunch and Mon lunch. Closed Jan ✋ L €45, D €55, Wine €16

BELLE-ÎLE-EN-MER
LE MARIE-GALANTE

www.hotelgrandlarge.com
This restaurant with a terrace giving views of the ocean specializes in fresh fish and seafood but also includes other local products on the menu, notably *l'agneau de l'Île* (lamb cooked in a traditional way). Reservations are recommended. ✉ Hôtel Restaurant Le Grand Large Goulphar/Bangor, 56360 Belle-Île-en-Mer ☎ 02 97 31 80 92 ⏰ Daily 12–1.30, 7.30–9.30. Closed Tue lunch ✋ L €30, D €45, Wine €16

BREST

AMOUR DE POMME DE TERRE
www.amourdepommedeterre.fr
The formula is simple here: potatoes and every way they can be cooked. The *amour de pomme de terre* weighs in at 6kg (13lb). All plates are enormous and many come with an alcoholic drink. There are also special dishes for vegetarians and children and a good wine list.

✉ 23 rue des Halles, 29200 Brest
☎ 02 98 43 48 51 ⏱ Daily 12–2, 7–10
🖐 L €30, D €40, Wine €15

LA CHAUMIÈRE
www.restaurantlachaumierebrest.com
Dishes include fried sole with fresh mushrooms, *marmite du pêcheur* with four different fish, and a Thai-style veal escalope. Dishes for children and vegetarians are available on request.

✉ 2 rue Émile Zola, 29200 Brest
☎ 02 98 44 18 60 ⏱ Mon–Fri 12–2, 7.30–9.30, Sat 7.30–9.30. Closed Aug
🖐 L €18, D €30, Wine €13

RESTAURANT NAUTILUS
The restaurant is in the hotel Oceania. Dishes include steamed monkfish with artichoke ragout and black olives, tuna steaks, salmon carpaccio, and some lovely desserts.

✉ 82 rue de Siam, 29200 Brest ☎ 02 98 80 66 66 ⏱ Daily 12–2, 7–10.30 🖐 L €25, D €40, Wine €15

CAEN

LE CARLOTTA
www.lecarlotta.fr
If you are a fan of oysters or snails, you should find them served to your satisfaction here but there are other French specialities on the menu such as cassoulet, grilled steak, duck and terrines. The fixed-priced menus offer plenty of choice.

✉ 16 quai Vendeuvre, 14000 Caen ☎ 02 31 86 68 99 ⏱ Mon–Sat noon–11; food service 12.15–1.45, 7.30–10.45 🖐 L €27, D €40, Wine €19

LE PRÉLUDE
www.restaurantleprelude.com
The chef here serves a blend of traditional and innovative French cuisine from different regions of the country. Notable dishes are the foie gras, the *feuilleté de Saint-Jacques* (scallops in a puff pastry case) and the *gondole de magret de canard* (grilled duck breast with a compote of apricots).

✉ 102 rue Saint-Martin, 14000 Caen
☎ 02 31 85 35 99 ⏱ Mid-May to Aug Mon–Thu 12–3, Fri 12–2, 7–9.30; Sep to mid-May Mon–Fri 12–3, 7–9.30, Sat–Sun 7–9.30
🖐 L €9.50, D €19, Wine €11

CANCALE

CÔTE MER
www.restaurant-cotemer.fr
The seafront has numerous small family-run establishments serving oysters and seafood platters but if you are looking for something a little more refined head to Côte Mer. You still have the view across the bay and a more complex treatment of the fresh seafood landed daily.

✉ route de la Corniche, 4 rue Ernest Lamort, 35260 Cancale ☎ 02 99 89 66 08
⏱ Jul–Aug Thu–Tue 12–2, 7–10; Sep–Jun Mon, Thu–Sat 12–2, 7–10, Tue, Sun 12–2. Closed late Jun–early Jul 🖐 L €40, D €60, Wine €18

CARNAC

AUBERGE LE RATELIER
www.le-ratelier.com
This restaurant is in a 16th-century Breton farmhouse with beamed ceilings and a rustic decor. The cuisine is essentially based on seafood and fish from the evening's local catch, enhanced by the judicious use of light sauces.

✉ 4 chemin du Douet, 56340 Carnac
☎ 02 97 52 05 04 ⏱ Jul–Aug daily 12–2, 7–9.30; Sep–Jun closed Tue lunch, Wed lunch 🖐 L €30, D €40, Wine €18

CHAMPEAUX

AU MARQUIS DE TOMBELAINE
www.aumarquisdetombelaine.com
There are superb views from this restaurant standing on the cliffs of Champeux. The chef offers a varied selection of regional cooking combining traditional tastes with creative touches, as in his warm oysters with cider, *escalope de foie chaud sur tatin au miel* (liver on a honey tart) and *magret de canard au Camembert* (breast of duck with Camembert).

✉ 25 route des Falaises, 50530 Champeaux
☎ 02 33 61 85 94 ⏱ Thu–Mon 12–3.30, 6–10, Tue 12–3.30. Closed Tue dinner and Wed 🖐 L €30, D €45, Wine €15

CHERBOURG

CAFÉ DE PARIS
A long-established brasserie facing the fishing port of Cherbourg, Café de Paris is popular with both locals and visitors. It specializes in fresh fish and seafood (including poached oysters) and also serves some creative dishes.

✉ 40 quai Caligny, 50100 Cherbourg
☎ 02 33 43 12 36 ⏱ Mon–Sat 12–2, 7–10. Closed Sun 🖐 L €18, D €30, Wine €18

LA RÉGENCE
www.laregence.com
The menu includes regional specials, with an emphasis on seafood. There is a children's menu.

✉ 42 quai de Caligny, 50100 Cherbourg
☎ 02 33 43 05 16 ⏱ Mid-Jan to mid-Dec daily 12–2.30, 7.30–10. Closed mid-Dec to mid-Jan 🖐 L €20, D €40, Wine €16

CONCARNEAU

L'AMIRAL
www.restaurant-amiral.com
At this smart bar-restaurant the menu changes daily and there is always home-made bread. Reserve ahead during summer.

✉ 1 avenue Pierre Guéguin, 29900 Concarneau ☎ 02 98 60 55 23 ⏱ Jul–Aug daily 12–1.30, 7–9.30; Sep–Jun Tue–Sat 12–1.30, 7–9.30, Sun 12–1.30 🖐 L €25, D €40, Wine €15

HOTEL LES SABLES BLANCS
www.hotel-les-sables-blancs.com
The restaurant of this seaside hotel is a contemporary space with superb sea views. There is a range of set menus as well as good à la carte. As expected in this fishing town, the menus are strong on seafood, including crab, oysters and lobster. Meat dishes include pig' trotters, pigeon, lamb and duck.

✉ plage des Sables Blancs, 29900

Concarneau ☎ 02 98 50 10 12 🍴 L €23, D €65, Wine €21

CONCHES-EN-OUCHE
RESTAURANT ET HÔTEL DU CYGNE
www.lecygne.fr
This hotel/restaurant is located in a former coach house. Fresh regional produce is used and the menu changes with the season but always has French classics such as foie gras.
✉ 2 rue Paul Guilbaud, 27190 Conches-en-Ouche ☎ 02 32 30 20 60 🕐 Tue–Sat 12–2.30, 7.30–9.30, Sun 12–2.30 🍴 L €18, D €35, Wine €16

COSQUEVILLE
AU BOUQUET DE COSQUEVILLE
www.bouquetdecosqueville.com
The name comes from a kind of large prawn caught off the Normandy coasts and indicates the fish and seafood accent in the menu. Chef Stéphane Dieu bakes his own bread and uses vegetables from his garden.
✉ Hameau Remond, 50330 Cosqueville ☎ 02 33 54 32 81 🕐 Wed–Sun 12–2, 7.15–9 🍴 L €25, D €60, Wine €20

DEAUVILLE
AUGUSTO
www.restaurant-augusto.com
A chic bistro, Augusto claims to be the 'king of lobster'. The house special is served with a coral sauce and fresh pasta. Alternatives include a good selection of fish dishes, and meat choices such as chicken with morels and wild rice. For alfresco dining, there is a street terrace.
✉ 27 rue Désiré Le Hoc, 14800 Deauville ☎ 02 31 88 34 49 🕐 Thu–Mon 12–2.30, 7–10.30 🍴 L €30, D €50, Wine €23

DIEPPE
RESTAURANT DE L'HÔTEL WINDSOR
www.hotelwindsor.fr
The contemporary restaurant at the Hotel Windsor has panoramic sea views and serves local specials, with an emphasis on seafood. The fresh shellfish platter and the foie gras are highly recommended.
✉ 18 boulevard de Verdun, 76200 Dieppe ☎ 02 35 84 15 23 🕐 Mon–Fri 12–2,

7–9.30, Sat 7–9.30, Sun 2–4 (weekdays by reservation only) 🍴 L €30, D €50, Wine €24

DINAN
CHEZ LA MÈRE POURCEL
www.chezlamerepourcel.com
The exquisite 15th-century building is a listed monument. The restaurant specializes in lamb fresh from Mont St-Michel, which is available from April to September. Other temptations are lobster, local fish (including wild sea bass with a *sauce vierge*) and scallops in autumn and winter. A children's menu is available. Reservations are recommended.
✉ 3 place des Merciers, 22100 Dinan ☎ 02 96 39 03 80 🕐 May–Sep daily 12–2.30, 7–10; Oct–Apr Mon, Fri, Sat 12–2.30, 7–10, Tue, Sun 12–2.30 🍴 L €25, D €35, Wine €20

DINARD
DIDIER MÉRIL
www.restaurant-didier-meril.com
A 19th-century town house with a handsome conservatory is the home of Didier Méril's restaurant and boutique hotel. The menu concentrates on seafood including lobster and Cancale oysters, but still provides a choice of meat dishes. There are set drinks menus to match the set food menus, which helps those who are not sure what to order.
✉ 1 place Général de Gaulle, 35800 Dinard ☎ 02 99 46 95 74 🕐 Daily 12–2, 7.30–9 🍴 L €35, D €50, Wine €18

FÉCAMP
LA PLAISANCE
www.restaurant-la-plaisance-fecamp.com
This restaurant, with views over the port and the cliffs, specializes in fresh sea produce. There is a fixed-price, help-yourself buffet on Friday evenings where you can eat seafood as long as your appetite lasts.
✉ 33 quai Vicomté, 76400 Fécamp ☎ 02 35 29 38 14 🕐 Daily 12–2, 7–9.30 🍴 L €20, D €28, Wine €15.50

FOURGES
MOULIN DE FOURGES
www.moulin-de-fourges.com
This beautiful Romanesque mill, is right on the river just a couple of

miles away from Giverny. The food in the restaurant makes innovative use of the local produce, but isn't restricted to local recipes.
✉ 38 rue du Moulin, 27630 Fourges ☎ 02 32 52 12 12 🕐 Apr–early Nov Tue–Sat 12–2, 7–9.30, Sun 12–2; early Nov–Mar Tue–Thu, Sun 12–2, Fri–Sat 7–9.30 🍴 L €35, D €45, Wine €21

LE HAVRE
JEAN LUC TARTARIN
www.jeanluc-tartarin.com
You'll be dining among the Le Havre elite at Jean Luc Tartarin's restaurant. Suited businesspeople crowd the place at lunchtime to enjoy the refined cuisine that's season fresh. The smart steel chairs and concealed lighting have an office feel—so don't venture here if you want a rustic experience. The food and it's accompanying wine list is excellent.
✉ 73 avenue Foch, 76600 Le Havre ☎ 02 35 45 46 20 🕐 Tue–Sat 12–2, 7–9.30 🍴 L €50, D €75, Wine €22

HONFLEUR
L'ABSINTHE
www.absinthe.fr
The restaurant of the Hôtel Absinthe faces the fishing port and has two beautiful dining rooms with stone walls, fireplaces and beamed ceilings. One of them is a former English guardhouse dating from the Hundred Years War. The inventive gourmet cuisine makes use of fresh ingredients from the sea. There is a good selection of wines.
✉ 1 rue de la Ville, 14600 Honfleur ☎ 02 31 89 23 23 🕐 Daily 12–2, 7–9.30 🍴 L €50, D €70, Wine €27

LA FERME ST-SIMÉON
www.fermesaintsimeon.fr
In the 19th century this mansion was the haunt of artists of the Honfleur school, including Claude Monet. There is a hotel, restaurant and beauty spa with water treatments. The food features dishes such as langoustines and caviar, lobster risotto, oysters and mussels.

Opposite *Seafood is at the heart of almost every meal in Brittany and Normandy*

✉ rue Adolphe Marais, 14600 Honfleur
☎ 02 31 81 78 00 🕐 Daily 12.30–2,
7.30–9.30, Tue 7.30–9.30 ✋ L €65, D €129,
Wine €45

ÎLE DE BRÉHAT
L'OISEAU DES ÎLES
This popular crêperie is in a blue-shuttered building decorated with a large puffin. Inside, the bare pink granite walls complement the blue window and door frames and the white ceiling. The dining room has small square tables or you can eat on the terrace. All the basic crêpes are on offer (ham, cheese, mushroom) as well as specials such as *andouille* (Breton sausage) and salads. Reservations are recommended.
✉ rue du Port, 22870 Bréhat ☎ 02 96 20 00 53 🕐 Late Apr–Sep Sun–Fri 12–2, 7–10; mid-Oct to late Apr school hols only, hours as above ✋ L €12, D €16, Wine €9

JOSSELIN
LA MARINE
The crêpes reflect the seasons; for instance L'Automne has sweet chestnut purée and apple and pear jam. The local specialty crêpe, La Josselinoise, is filled with black pudding and fried apples. There is a special lunch menu for a crêpe-free meal (unless you want one for dessert), and there are vegetarian and children's options available. Make reservations in summer.
✉ 8 rue du Canal, 56120 Josselin
☎ 02 97 22 21 98 🕐 Jul–Aug daily 12–10; Sep–Jun Wed–Sun 12–2, 7–10. Closed 2 weeks in Nov ✋ L €12, D €18, Wine €11

JUMIÈGES
AUBERGE DES RUINES
www.aubergedesruines.fr
Located on a small square at the bottom of Jumièges abbey, this ancient inn has been renovated and decorated in a contemporary style but the original beams and the big fireplace have been retained. Chef Loic Henry, who is one the renowned Maîtres Cuisiniers de France, prepares Norman products with influences from Brittany.
✉ place de la Mairie, 76480 Jumièges
☎ 02 35 37 24 05 🕐 Daily 12–2, 7–9
✋ L €35, D €75, Wine €20

LAMPAUL-GUIMILIAU
L'ESCAPADE
The Escapade is the only real restaurant in town. The specials are goulash soup and Finistère ostrich steaks. They also serve crêpes, with unusual fillings such as prunes and smoked bacon or Le Forêt Noir (cherry, Amarena, chocolate and whipped cream).
✉ 8 place de Villiers, 29400 Lampaul-Guimiliau ☎ 02 98 68 61 27 🕐 Tue, Thu, Fri 12–1.30, 7–8.30, Wed 12–1.30, Sat, Sun 12–1.30, 7–9. Closed Mon, Feb and 3 weeks in Aug ✋ L €12, D €34, Wine €12

MONT ST-MICHEL
LE MOUTON BLANC
www.lemoutonblanc.fr
This historic hotel and restaurant below the abbey has been catering for pilgrims and other travellers for more than 100 years. The menu concentrates on Norman specialities from both land and sea and includes grills and roasts.
✉ Grande Rue, 50170 Le Mont Saint-Michel ☎ 02 33 60 14 08 🕐 Daily 12–2, 7–10 ✋ L €40, D €50, Wine €18

MORLAIX
BRASSERIE DE L'EUROPE
www.brasseriedeleurope.com
An elegant brasserie, in the hotel of the same name, it specializes in fish and seafood, with such dishes as cod in butter with herb and carrot tagliatelle and green lentils, or fried red mullet and foie gras with pineapple. Try the typically Breton *kouignamann* (a buttery cake) with apple marmalade for dessert. Reservations are recommended.
✉ place Émile Souvestre, 29600 Morlaix ☎ 02 98 88 81 15 🕐 Jul–Aug daily 8–10, 11–2, 7–9.30 for food, non-stop 8am–9.30pm for drinks. Closed Sun Sep–Jun 🍴 L €17, D €23, Wine €12

NASSANDRES
LE SOLEIL D'OR
www.manoirdusoleildor.com
The dining rooms of this old manor house with their oak floorboards and wooden panelling have the feel of a private country club. There are long-range views across the countryside from the terrace. The menu offers a taste of local dishes, though there are examples from around France. Try the local *andouillete* (small chitterling sausage) or the Calvados soufflé.
✉ 23 Côte de Paris, 27550 La Riviere Thibouville ☎ 02 32 44 90 31 🕐 Mon, Tue, Thu–Sat 12–1.30, 7–9.30, Sun 12–1.30 🍴 L €35, D €50, Wine €20

PERROS-GUIREC
LA CRÉMAILLÈRE
The two dining rooms are in a 17th-century building. The menu changes with the seasons and is based around fresh seafood and grilled meat. Dishes include scallop kebab with smoked duck breast, roast beef, and coffee tart with a citrus marmalade. In summer it's best to reserve a table.
✉ 13 place de l'Église, 22700 Perros-Guirec ☎ 02 96 23 22 08 🕐 Mon 7–10, Tue, Thu–Sun 12–2, 7–10 🍴 L €32, D €35, Wine €15

PLEYBEN
LA BLANCHE HERMINE
www.la-blanche-hermine.com
This Breton tavern is also a cookery school and it specializes in dishes prepared with cider such as Breton sauerkraut and beef with cider, but classic dishes are also available. There is also an extensive wine list and home-made pastries. It's essential to reserve in summer.
✉ 1 place Charles de Gaulle, 29190 Pleyben ☎ 02 98 26 61 29 🕐 14 Jul–20 Aug daily 11.30–3, 6.30–9.45; rest of year Thu–Tue 12–2.30, 7–9.45. Closed 15 Dec–Jan 🍴 L €20, D €28, Wine €12

PONT-ST-PIERRE
HOSTELLERIE LA BONNE MARMITE
www.la-bonne-marmite.com
A charming hotel and restaurant serving high-class cuisine using mainly produce from the sea. Chef Alexandre da Silva works in the Norman tradition and offers dishes such as lobster, turbot and *suprême de canard* (duck breast) There are two wine lists to choose from.
✉ 10 rue René-Raban, 27360 Pont-St-Pierre ☎ 02 32 49 70 24 🕐 Wed–Sat 12–2, 7.30–9, Sun 12–2, Tue 7.30–9 🍴 L €35, D €45, Wine €13

QUIMPER
LE CAFÉ DE L'EPÉE
www.quimper-lepee.com
The owners claim that this brasserie, in front of the *préfecture* on the banks of the river, is one of the oldest in France. Try the duck with sauerkraut and finish with one of their pies if you have room. On Saturday evenings there's an all-you-can-eat seafood buffet for €23.
✉ 14 rue du Parc, 29000 Quimper ☎ 02 98 95 28 97 🕐 Daily 10.30–midnight 🍴 L €25, D €35, Wine €15

QUIMPERLÉ
LE BISTRO DE LA TOUR
www.hotelvintage.com
This restaurant and wine cellar is on a street that is itself listed as a monument. There are two dining rooms. Dishes include oysters or the Breton cassoulet with *andouille* sausages. The wine list has more than 800 choices.
✉ 20 rue Dom-Morice, 29300 Quimperlé ☎ 02 98 39 29 58 🕐 Mid-Jul to Aug

Left *Chez la Mère Pourcel at Dinan*

Sat–Mon 7.30–9, Tue–Fri 12.15–1.45, 7.30–9; Sep to mid-Jul Tue–Fri 12.15–1.45, 7.30–9, Sat 7.30–9 ✋ L €34, D €58, Wine €15

RENNES
RESTAURANT LA COQUERIE
www.lecoq-gadby.com
Pierre Legrand, the chef at this gastronomic restaurant at Le Coq-Gadby boutique spa hotel has been awarded a Michelin star, so prepared to be indulged. The menu is concise and changes with the seasons.
✉ 156 rue d'Antrain, 35700 Rennes ☎ 02 99 38 05 55 🕐 Tue, Thu–Sat 12–1, 7–9, Wed 7–9 ✋ L €49, D €75, Wine €24

ROUEN
LE CATELIER
www.lecatelier-rouen.fr
Dine on local delicacies in this Norman house. Chef Marie-France Atinault specializes in seafood. Try scallops from Dieppe, turbot in a white wine sauce or lobster salad with cider-butter and fried apples. There are several prix-fixe options.
✉ 134 bis avenue des Martyrs de la Résistance, 76100 Rouen ☎ 02 35 72 59 90 🕐 Tue–Sat 12–2, 7–9. Closed first 3 weeks in Aug ✋ L €35, D €50, Wine €16

LA PÊCHERIE
www.lapecherie.fr
They serve generous platters of fish and shellfish, and less common combinations such as lobster in a cider reduction, at this friendly brasserie. A couple of meat dishes and some inventive desserts (spicy pineapple carpaccio and Earl-Grey-scented crème brûlée) complete the picture.
✉ 29 place de la Basse Vieille Tour, 76000 Rouen ☎ 02 35 88 71 00 🕐 Mon–Fri 12–2.30, 7.30–9.30, Sat 7.30–10 ✋ L €22.50, D €30.50, Wine €16

ST-MALO
LES EMBRUNS
www.restaurant-les-embruns.com
Seafood dishes are served here in a salmon-pink painted dining room. The menu follows the seasons, but some classics are fat scampi with mayonnaise, lightly salted salmon with asparagus and lamb's

kidneys with purple Brive mustard. Alternatively choose your meal from the lobster tank on display. The artwork on the walls is also for sale.
✉ 120 chaussée du Sillon, 35400 St-Malo ☎ 02 99 56 33 57 🕐 Tue–Sat 12–2, 7–10, Sun 12–2 ✋ L €25, D €35, Wine €16

ST-POL-DE-LÉON
AUBERGE LA POMME D'API
www.aubergelapommedapi.com
This 16th-century building houses a lovely country inn. The food is a treat, but you'd better brush up on your French as dishes are elaborately named: *dos de bar, cuit sur peau* (seabass), *légumes oubliés* (forgotten vegetables!) and *cèpes et saucisse de Morteau* (cep mushrooms and smoked sausage). Vegetarian and children's options are also available on request.
✉ 49 rue Verderel, 29250 St-Pol-de-Léon ☎ 02 98 69 04 36 🕐 Jul–Aug daily 12–2, 7.30–9; Sep–Jun Tue–Sat 12–2, 7.30–9, Sun 12–2. Closed last two weeks Nov ✋ L €35, D €45, Wine €20

TRÉBEURDEN
MANOIR DE LAN-KERELLEC
www.lankerellec.com
Set on the Granit Rose coast with exceptional views, the high ceilinged hotel dining room is a wonderful place for a gourmet dinner. Enjoy fois gras with spiced pineapple and lobster with gorgonzola and olive ravioli. The wine list represents most areas of France, with a selection of bottles from other parts of the world.
✉ allée centrale de Lan-Kerellac, 22560 Trébeurden ☎ 02 96 15 00 00 🕐 Closed mid-Nov to mid- Mar ✋ L €56, D €270, Wine €45

VAINS
À L'ABRI DU SAUNIER
www.abridusaunier.com
This restaurant in a very pretty village on Mont St-Michel bay, combines refined cooking with traditional cuisine. The menu varies with the seasons and the availability of fresh market produce. In summer you can dine on the terrace which gives access directly onto the garden. Try the *bœuf sauce Camembert* (beef

in Camembert sauce), *emincé de magret au vinaigre de framboise* (sliver of duck breast in raspberry vinegar), *tourtière de ris de veau farcie au foie gras* (flan of calf's sweetbreads stuffed with foie gras) or the *pavé de biche aux fruits rouges* (venison steak with red fruits).
✉ La Chaussée, Saint-Léonard, 50300 Vains ☎ 02 33 70 88 60 🕐 Mon–Sat 12–2, 7–9. Closed Wed ✋ L €24, D €30, Wine €13.50

VERNEUIL
HOSTELLERIE LE CLOS
www.hostellerieduclos.fr
This elegant hotel and restaurant is in a beautiful, fairy-tale-style manor house standing in its own parkland. The chef prepares seasonal dishes with market produce that are served in a grand dining room decorated with trompe l'oeil paintings.
✉ 98 rue de la Ferté-Vidame, 27130 Verneuil-sur-Avre ☎ 02 32 32 21 81 🕐 Wed–Sun 12.30–2, 7.30–9, Tue 7.30–9 ✋ L €50, D €70, Wine €28

VITRÉ
LE PICHET
www.lepichet.fr
Sit outside on the expansive covered decking to enjoy views of the gardens while you eat at Le Pichet. The menu stays close to the French staples of good meats—all of which have a provenance—and fresh seafood, along with well-presented and delicious desserts.
✉ 17 boulevard de Laval, 35500 Vitré ☎ 02 99 75 24 09 🕐 Mon–Fri 9–2.30, 6–9, Sat 9–2.30, 6–10, Sun 9–2.30. Closed Nov–Mar Wed, Thu and Sun lunch ✋ L €30, D €60, Wine €17

YVETOT
AUBERGE DU VAL AU CESNE
www.valaucesne.fr
This auberge has five small dining rooms to choose from. Out of the windows you can gaze on apple trees and cows grazing in the Norman countryside. The chef prepares seasonal dishes with regional market produce.
✉ Croix Mare, 76190 Yvetot ☎ 02 35 63 06 🕐 Wed–Sun 12–2, 7–9 ✋ L €40, D €55, Wine €15

PRICES AND SYMBOLS

The prices are the lowest and highest for a double room for one night including breakfast, unless otherwise stated. All the hotels listed accept credit cards unless otherwise stated. Note that rates can vary widely throughout the year.

For a key to the symbols, ▷ 2.

AVRANCHES
LA CROIX D'OR

www.hoteldelacroixdor.fr

In a peaceful, renovated 17th-century coaching inn in the town centre, this hotel is decorated with antiques and old copper objects. Bedrooms are light and airy and have views over the garden.

✉ 83 rue de la Constitution, 50300 Avranches ☎ 02 33 58 04 88 ✋ €68–€105, excluding breakfast (€9) 🛈 11

Above *A typical French breakfast of coffee and croissant*

LA RAMADE

www.laramade.fr

The Ramade is a lovingly decorated country house in its own grounds with a pretty conservatory and charming bedrooms. There is a gîte in the garden rented out by the weekend or by the week. The hotel is ideally located for visiting Mont St-Michel.

✉ 2–4 rue de la Côte, 50300 Marcey les Grèves ☎ 02 33 58 27 40 ✋ €69–€116, excluding breakfast (€10) 🛈 11

BAGNOLES DE L'ORNE
MANOIR DU LYS

www.manoir-du-lys.fr

This manor house is on the edge of the Andaine forest. Some rooms look out onto the orchard and some onto the park and are decorated in different styles—classic or modern. Alongside the manor are seven cabins on stilts, each with a sitting room, bedroom and bathroom—perfect for families. There are mountain bicycles for rent, a tennis court and a restaurant.

✉ route de Juvigny, La Croix Gauthier, 61140 Bagnoles de l'Orne ☎ 02 33 37 80 69 ⊗ Closed Jan ✋ €80–€220, excluding breakfast (€15) 🛈 23 rooms, 7 cabins 🏊 Outdoor heated

BARNEVILLE CARTERET
HOTEL DE LA MARINE

www.hotelmarine.com

Overlooking the yacht harbour at Carteret, the white Modernist architecture of the hotel is matched by a contemporary decor. Owned and operated by the Cesne family for five generations, the hotel has a seafood restaurant where chef Laurent Cesne presides; non-fishy Norman cuisine is also represented.

✉ 11 rue de Paris, 50270 Barneville-Carteret ☎ 02 33 53 83 31 ⊗ Closed late Dec–late Feb ✋ €90–€260, excluding breakfast (€15) 🛈 31 rooms, 2 suites

CABOURG

HÔTEL DU PARC
www.hotelduparc-cabourg.com
This hotel is close to the heart of the city and not too far from the beach. The simply furnished bedrooms are decorated in bright tones and have TV, telephone, alarm clock and hairdryer. Free parking is available for guests.

✉ 31–33 avenue Général Leclerc, 14390 Cabourg ☎ 02 31 91 00 82 💶 €56–€78, excluding breakfast (€8) 🛏 17

CAEN

IVAN VAUTIER
www.ivanvautier.com
A cool and contemporary spot with minimalist decor, this hotel makes a departure from the ornate classical French styling. Rooms are spacious and bathrooms are luxurious. The gastronomic Ivan Gaultier restaurant is on site.

✉ 3 avenue Henry Chéron, 14000 Caen ☎ 02 31 73 32 71 💶 €145–€220, excluding breakfast (€15) 🛏 19 🐾

CARNAC

HÔTEL DU TUMULUS
www.hotel-tumulus.com
Built in 1900 by the archaeologist Zacharie Le Rouzic as the first Welcome Centre at Carnac. The hotel, which been rebuilt and renovated and offers comfortable accommodation, is still run by the family. There's a restaurant on site, a spa and a pool in the garden.

✉ chemin de Tumulus, 56340 Carnac ☎ 02 97 52 08 21 🚫 Closed early Nov–early Feb 💶 €90–€215, excluding breakfast (€16) 🛏 23 🏊 Outdoor heated (in summer)

CHAMPEAUX

LES HERMELLES
www.hotel-leshermelles.com
Facing Mont St-Michel bay, this small hotel, on the Champeaux cliffs between Granville and Avranches, makes a good base from which to enjoy the seaside, visit sights in the area or go walking in the countryside.

✉ 18 route des Falaises, 50530 Champeaux ☎ 02 33 61 85 94 💶 €55–€62, excluding breakfast (€8) 🛏 6

CREPON

FERME DE LA RANCONNIERE
www.ranconniere.fr
This hotel in a quiet village is set in a fortified 18th-century farm. It has an inner courtyard, a garden and bedrooms decorated with antique Norman furniture. There are two types of bedroom to choose from: 2 or 3 stars depending on the level of comfort you prefer.

✉ route Creully-Arromanches, 14480 Crepon ☎ 02 31 22 21 73 💶 €55–€150, excluding breakfast (€12) 🛏 35

DEAUVILLE

HOSTELLERIE DE TOURGÉVILLE
www.hostellerie-de-tourgeville.fr
Originally built as a country estate by film director Claude Lelouch, this Norman-style complex of country houses is set in beautiful grounds. Facilities include sauna, tennis courts, swimming pool, beach and cinema.

✉ chemin de l'Orgueil Tourgéville, 14800 Deauville ☎ 02 31 14 48 68 🚫 Closed 2nd week of Feb to 1st week of Mar 💶 €130–€210, excluding breakfast (€18) 🛏 25 rooms, 35 suites 🏊 Outdoor 🍴

DIEPPE

LES ARCADES
www.lesarcades.fr
This historic building in the heart of town takes its name from its covered arcade. Rooms, which all have TV, are simply furnished and some have balconies. Hotel facilities include a sauna and internet access and the restaurant has a reputation for its excellent seafood.

✉ 1–3 arcade de la Bourse, 76200 Dieppe ☎ 02 35 84 14 12 💶 €63–€79, excluding breakfast (€8) 🛏 21

ÉTRETAT

DOMAINE SAINT CLAIR
www.hoteletretat.com
Le Donjon is stunningly set in a 19th-century Anglo-Norman-style château overlooking the village and cliffs of Étretat. Some rooms have a spa bathtub and all have satellite TV. There is also a restaurant.

✉ chemin St-Clair, 76790 Étretat ☎ 02 35 27 08 23 💶 €90–€340, excluding breakfast (€14) 🛏 21 🏊

DORMY HOUSE
www.dormy-house.com
Perched on top of the cliffs, some of the bedrooms mix period furniture with bright tones, while others are more country-style. The least expensive rooms are located in a separate villa. The hotel's restaurant (▷ 167) overlooks the sea.

✉ B.P. 2 route du Havre, 76790 Étretat ☎ 02 35 27 07 88 💶 €65–€190, excluding breakfast (€15.50) 🛏 61

FÉCAMP

HÔTEL NORMANDY
www.normandy-fecamp.com
The spacious, comfortable and modern rooms here all have satellite TV. There is an attractive restaurant, La Brasserie Maupassant, open for lunch and dinner. Parking is available for guests.

✉ 4 avenue Gambetta, 76400 Fécamp ☎ 02 35 29 55 11 💶 €58, excluding breakfast (€7) 🛏 33 (5 non-smoking)

GAILLON

CHÂTEAU CORNEILLE
www.chateau-corneille.fr
This is an 18th-century château in the Seine valley, standng in its own park and surrounded by meadows and forests. It is well located for visiting the D-Day beaches, Giverny, Rouen and Paris. The bedrooms are decorated in modern style and offer garden views. There is a gourmet restaurant in the old stables with a big, welcoming fireplace.

✉ 17 rue de l'Église Vieux Villez, 27600 Gaillon ☎ 02 32 77 44 77 💶 €106, excluding breakfast (€11) 🛏 20

LE HAVRE

VENT D'OUEST
www.ventdouest.fr
This hotel is conveniently in the heart of town. The lounge and some of the bedrooms have a nautical look, while others have countryside or mountain themes. There is WiFi throughout the hotel. There is no restaurant but a tea room serves snacks for guests. There is private parking.

✉ 4 rue Caligny, 76600 Le Havre ☎ 02 35 42 50 69 💶 €105–€135, excluding breakfast (€12) 🛏 33

HONFLEUR
L'ABSINTHE
www.absinthe.fr

In this 16th-century former presbytery all the the bedrooms have satellite TV and a Jacuzzi. The suite has the additional benefit of half-timbered walls. Some rooms are in a separate annex. The restaurant and Frog Brasserie are around the corner.

✉ 1 rue de la Ville, 14600 Honfleur ☎ 02 31 89 23 23 ✋ €115–€185, excluding breakfast (€12) ❶ 10 rooms, 2 suites

LISIEUX
HÔTEL DE LA COUPE D'OR
www.la-coupe-dor.com

This hotel has rooms which, although not very spacious, are pleasantly decorated in a rustic local style and have the additional benefit of cable and satellite TV. The restaurant's vast dining room serves local dishes.

✉ 49 rue Pont Mortain, 14100 Lisieux ☎ 02 31 31 16 84 ✋ €53–€60, excluding breakfast (€7.50) ❶ 16 (3 non-smoking)

LOCRONAN
HOSTELLERIE DU BOIS DU NÉVET
www.hostellerie-bois-nevet.com

This long, modern hotel snakes through the surrounding gardens. The comfortable rooms might lack charm, but all have TV, telephone and bathroom. Two rooms cater for guests with disabilities (including shower) and there are family rooms for up to five people. There is no restaurant but breakfast is served.

✉ route du Bois du Névet, 29180 Locronan ☎ 02 98 91 70 67 ⏰ Closed Nov–Easter ✋ €62–€71, excluding breakfast (€8.50) ❶ 35

LYONS-LA-FORÊT
LA LICORNE
www.hotel-licorne.com

This 17th-century inn has a quaint interior with rooms tastefully decorated and furnished with antiques. The dining room serves traditional regional dishes.

✉ 27 place Isaac Benserade, 27480 Lyons-la-Forêt ☎ 02 32 48 24 24 ✋ €95–€175, excluding breakfast (€12) ❶ 14, 7 suites (2 non-smoking)

MONTIGNY
LE RELAIS DE MONTIGNY
www.relais-de-montigny.com

At this modern hotel, rooms all have satellite TV, and some have a small terrace. There is also a restaurant.

✉ rue du Lieutenant Aubert, 76380 Montigny ☎ 02 35 36 05 97 ⏰ Closed end Dec–early Jan ✋ €86–€95, excluding breakfast (€12) ❶ 22

MORLAIX
HÔTEL DE L'EUROPE
www.hotel-europe-com.fr

This stylish, 200-year-old hotel is filled with antique furnishings. Rooms are large and soundproofed; suites sleep up to four people. A buffet breakfast is served in the dining room and the restaurant next door is connected to the hotel but independently run.

✉ 1 rue d'Aiguillon, 29600 Morlaix ☎ 02 98 62 11 99 ⏰ Closed 22 Dec–5 Jan ✋ €60–€150, excluding breakfast (€8) ❶ 60 rooms (10 non-smoking)

NOTRE-DAME-D'ESTRÉES
AU REPOS DES CHINEURS
www.au-repos-des-chineurs.com

This tea room and hotel occupies a former 17th-century coaching inn. *Chineurs* means 'bargain-hunters' and almost everything here is for sale. Some bathrooms have whirlpool tubs.

✉ chemin de l'Église, 14340 Notre-Dame-d'Estrées ☎ 02 31 63 72 51 ⏰ Closed Jan, Feb ✋ €75 ❶ 10 (2 suites)

PERROS-GUIREC
VILLA CYRNOS

This is one of the most expensive bed-and-breakfasts in town—but it's worth it. The spacious, comfortable rooms, which sleep up to four people, all have a TV. The friendly owner serves a formidable breakfast and there is parking.

✉ 10 rue de Sergent l'Héveder, 22700 Perros-Guirec ☎ 02 96 91 13 36 ⏰ Closed mid-Sep to Apr ✋ €70–€80 ❶ 5 (all non-smoking)

PORT-EN-BESSIN
LA CHENEVIÈRE
www.lacheneviere.com

This elegant 18th-century château has rooms decorated in classical style but with modern amenities such as TV and a minibar. Additional facilities include a laundry service, babysitting and internet access at reception. The gourmet restaurant, serving seasonal foods, is run by chef Didier Robin.

✉ Escures-Commes, 14520 Port-en-Bessin ☎ 02 31 51 25 25 ⏰ Closed Dec–Apr ✋ €202–€292, excluding breakfast (€21) ❶ 22

QUIMPER
HÔTEL DUPLEIX
www.hotel-dupleix.com

The spacious, modern rooms are quiet. There is a lounge and terrace. Three rooms have a terrace and there are family rooms for up to six people. Parking is available, but is not free.

✉ 35 boulevard Dupleix, 29000 Quimper ☎ 02 98 90 53 35 ✋ €69–€112, excluding breakfast (buffet breakfast €9) ❶ 29

RENNES
HÔTEL DES LICES
www.hotel-des-lices.com

A modern but not soulless hotel close to the heart of the old town. Nearly all rooms have their own balconies, are soundproofed and have satellite TV and telephone. A public car park is €2 per night.

✉ 7 place des Lices, 35000 Rennes ☎ 02 99 79 14 81 ✋ €64–€80, excluding breakfast (€9) ❶ 45 🚇 Sainte-Anne

ROUEN
HOTEL ERMITAGE BOUQUET
www.hotel-ermitagebouquet.com

A perfect diminutive bolt-hole in the heart of the city, a ten-minute walk to the historic sites, the Ermitage Bouquet offers modern touches in its 19th-century shell, including WiFi. Rooms are plain but serviceable with modern bathrooms.

✉ 58 rue Bouquet, 76000 Rouen ☎ 02 32 12 30 40 ✋ €94–€165, excluding breakfast (€12.50) ❶ 13 rooms, 3 suites

ST-CAST-LE-GUILDO
LES BLÉS D'OR
www.campinglesblesdor.fr

This pet-friendly campsite is close to the beach of St-Cast. There are large pitches, 30 of which have their own private shower, toilet and basin.

There are electricity hook-ups, a small launderette, a playground, table tennis and the site is close to a large supermarket. There are also some mobile homes and cottages available if you don't fancy camping.

✉ La Chapelle, 22380 St-Cast-le-Guildo ☎ 02 96 41 99 93 ✪ Closed Nov–Mar ✋ €16 (€26 with private bathroom) 🛏 135 pitches

ST-MALO
HÔTEL DES ABERS
www.abershotel.com
You'll find this hotel within the walls of the old city, behind a flowery 16th-century facade. All rooms have queen-sized beds, private bathroom, satellite TV, a hairdryer and a safe; some rooms are soundproofed. There are no family rooms, although baby beds are available. Tea and coffee are freely available in the lobby. There is an Indonesian restaurant attached to the hotel.

✉ 10 rue de la Corne-du-Cerf, 35400 St-Malo ☎ 02 99 40 85 60 ✋ €89–€130, excluding breakfast (Continental €13, English €18) 🛏 14 rooms

ST-THÉGONNEC
AR PRESBITAL KOZ
This 250-year-old former presbytery has a huge garden and six large, comfortable rooms with rustic furniture. All rooms have private bathrooms, but no TV. There is a small outdoor terrace for coffee. A Continental breakfast is included; if you reserve before noon, you can join the proprietors for dinner and drink all the wine you like for €22. Credit cards are not accepted.

✉ 18 rue du Lividic, 29410 St-Thégonnec ☎ 02 98 79 45 62 ✋ €56 🛏 6 rooms (all non-smoking)

ST-VAAST-LA-HOUGUE
HÔTEL DE FRANCE
www.france-fuchsias.com
A delightful country house hotel and restaurant near the harbour of St-Vaast. The rooms are tastefully furnished and most look onto a superb garden, with exotic plants such as banana trees, palm trees and mimosas, the setting for outdoor

chamber music concerts in August. Half-board packages (including dinner in the Restaurant des Fuchsias) are available.

✉ 20 rue du Maréchal-Foch, 50550 St-Vaast-la-Hougue ☎ 02 33 54 40 41 ✪ Closed Jan ✋ €52–€132, excluding breakfast (€11) 🛏 34

SULLY
CHÂTEAU DE SULLY
www.chateau-de-sully.com
Elements of this property date back to the 16th century though the main house was built in the 18th century. Set in well-kept lawns, ornamental gardens and woodland, it's a comfortable repose. There's a restaurant and covered, heated pool.

✉ route de Port-en-Bessin, 14400 Sully ☎ 02 31 22 29 48 ✪ Closed early Dec to mid-Jan ✋ €150–€190, excluding breakfast (€18) 🛏 23 🏊

VANNES
CAMPING MUNICIPAL DE CONLEAU
A comfortable campsite, 3km (2 miles) from the middle of town, in a good location near the sea with

trees to protect campers from the wind and sun. There are pitches for tents, caravans and camper vans (electricity hook-ups are available) and mobile homes for rent. Other facilities include table tennis, a playground and a launderette.

✉ 188 avenue du Maréchal-Juin, 56000 Vannes ☎ 02 97 63 13 88 ✪ Closed Oct–Mar ✋ €12–€20 per pitch (including 2 people) 🛏 247 pitches

VILLA KERASY HOTEL & SPA
www.villakerasy.com
This small hotel is elegance personified. Individually styled rooms are well furnished and take themes from traditional decor from lands that traded with the Compagnie des Indes (The French East India Company). Deluxe rooms have views over the Japanese gardens. The spa offers massage and other therapies.

✉ 20 avenue Favrel et Lincy, 56000 Vannes ☎ 02 97 68 36 83 ✪ Closed mid-Nov to mid-Dec ✋ €158–€250, excluding breakfast (€14) 🛏 15

Above *Camping Municipal de Conleau in Vannes*

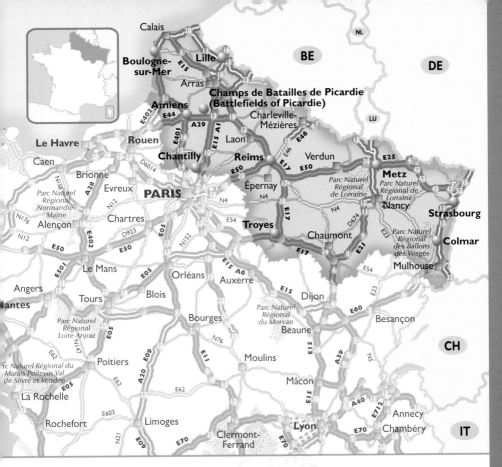

NORTH AND NORTHEAST FRANCE

The five regions that stretch from the English Channel coast to the river Rhine can best be described as frontier France. While Calais and Dunkerque are closer to London than Paris, French Flanders merges imperceptibly with southern Belgium, and Alsace and Lorraine, to the east, were for centuries the subject of a to-and-fro territorial dispute with Germany.

Many of the major battles of World War I were fought here and during World War II the north received the brunt of the invasion of France by the forces of Nazi Germany. Everywhere there are place names—Somme, Verdun—equated with battles and a visit to one of the many well-tended cemeteries, or the crumbling vestiges of a Maginot Line fort, part of France's pre-World War II eastern defences, is a moving experience.

But Northern France is much more than an international buffer zone and it is renowned for two achievements. In the Middle Ages, this was the birthplace of Gothic architecture, as the great cathedral at Amiens and many others testify. The other source of pride is the sparkling white wine of Champagne, which is made around Troyes and the historic city of Reims, where historically the kings of France were crowned.

Decades of peace and the virtual disappearance of borders facilitated by the European Union have enabled the north to reinvent itself and nowadays it could almost be thought of as 'internationalized France'. The Channel Tunnel has effectively joined the region of Nord-Pas-de-Calais to Kent in England, the city of Lille has replaced its heavy industry with a service sector built around the modern Eurostar/TGV rail junction, and Strasbourg is busy proclaiming itself as the quintessentially 21st-century European city, a cultural crossroads if ever there was one.

The north and northeast are more urban when compared with most of the rest of France but if you need a breath of fresh air there are two areas of upland clad with extensive forests to explore: the Ardennes (shared between France and Belgium) and the Vosges mountains in the far northeast.

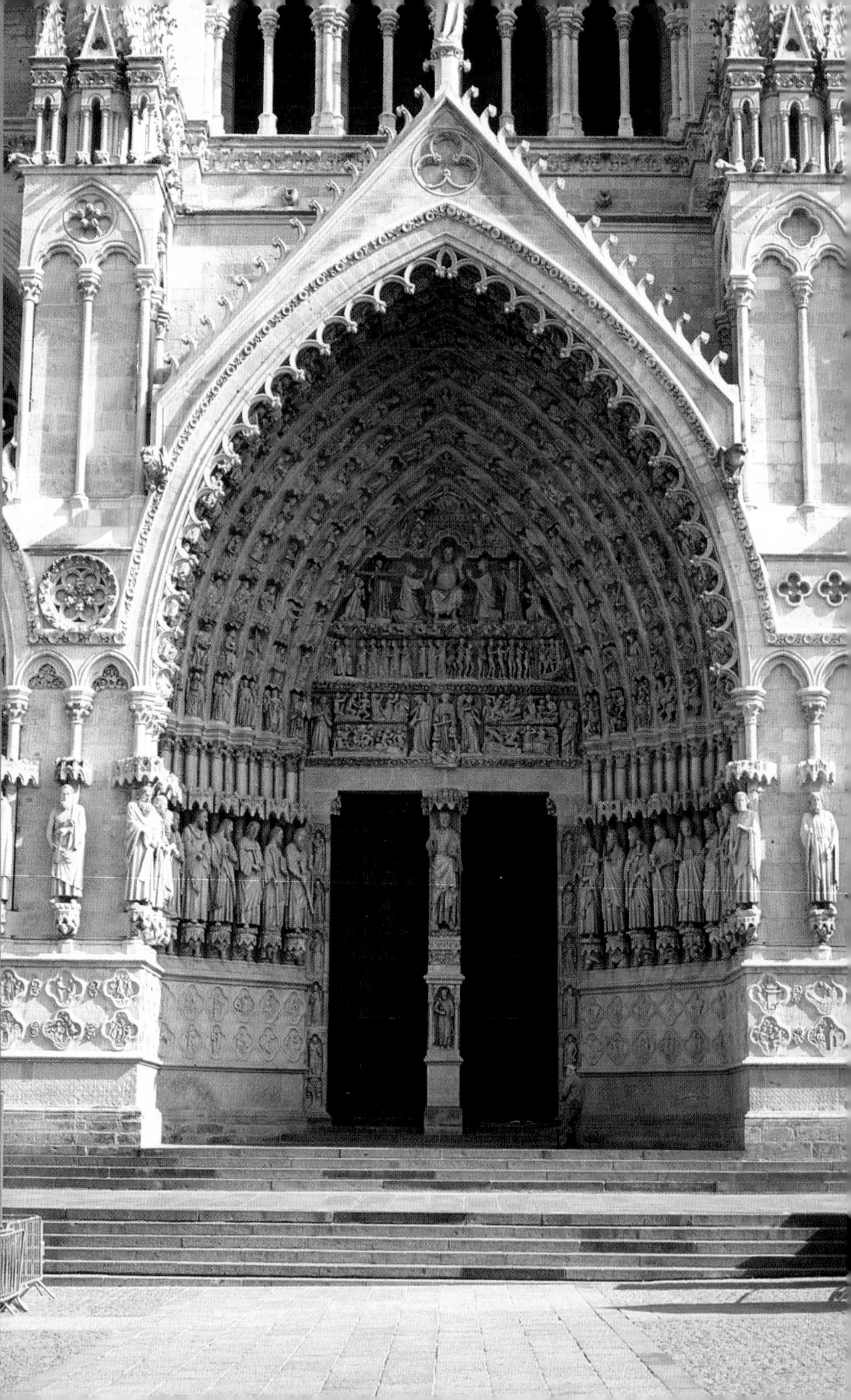

AMIENS

This lively city, the ancient capital of Picardie on the banks of the river Somme, suffered much damage in both world wars but has been extensively rebuilt. At its heart is the magnificent 13th-century Cathédrale Notre-Dame, now a World Heritage Site. The Gothic cathedral, 145m (476ft) long, 70m (230ft) wide and 42m (139ft) high, has a glorious west facade with a famous statue of Christ known as *Le Beau Dieu*. The serenely simple interior is enhanced by the richness of the 16th-century choir stalls. Southeast of the cathedral, in a 19th-century mansion in rue de la République, is the Musée de Picardie, displaying archaeological finds and 19th-century sculpture (Tue–Sun 10–12.30, 2–6). The Musée de l'Hôtel de Berny, in rue Victor Hugo, focuses on art and local history, including furniture representing the Louis XV and Louis XVI eras (closed for restoration until 2012).

You can still see shows at the 19th-century Cirque Municipal, on place Longueville, a curious drum-shaped building dedicated to the science fiction writer Jules Verne. Just east of here, the Maison de Jules Verne, in rue Charles-Dubois (mid-Apr to mid-Oct Mon, Wed–Fri 10–12.30, 2–6.30, Tue 2–6.30, Sat–Sun 11–6.30; mid-Oct to mid-Apr Mon, Wed–Fri 10–12.30, 2–6, Sat–Sun 2–6), was the writer's home for 18 years. Near the train station look out for La Tour Perret, 104m (341ft) high, built between 1948 and 1954.

AMIENS BY BOAT

Amiens's watery *hortillonnages*, in the flood plain of the Somme, form a strange area of market gardens threaded by little channels. You can reach parts on foot on the chemin de Halage (towpath) and others by boat (departing from 54 boulevard de Beauvillé; Apr–Oct daily from 2–5; may close earlier depending on visitor numbers). The picturesque Quartier St-Leu ('Little Venice of the North'), was once the weavers' and dyers' district. Here there are canals and narrow islands with painted leaning houses.

INFORMATION

www.amiens.com/tourisme

✚ 468 J3 🛈 40 place Notre-Dame, 80010 ☎ 03 22 71 60 50 🕓 Apr–Sep Mon–Sat 9.30–6.30, Sun 10–12, 2–5; Oct–Mar Mon–Sat 9.30–6, Sun 10–12, 2–5 🚊 Amiens

Opposite *Amiens' Cathédrale Notre-Dame*
Below *Canalside restaurants in Amiens*

REGIONS NORTH AND NORTHEAST FRANCE • SIGHTS

LES ARDENNES
www.ardennes.com

The densely wooded uplands of the Ardennes form a high plateau penetrated by the deep valley of the meandering river Meuse. They are a paradise for walkers and for hunters of deer or boar. A good way of exploring is by boat—you can take a *bateau-mouche* from Charleville-Mézières (▷ right) or Monthermé. There are fortresses at Rocroi, Sedan and Charleville-Mézières.

✚ 468 L3 ▮ Comité Départemental du Tourisme, 4 place Ducale, 08107 Charleville-Mézières ☎ 03 24 55 69 90 ◷ Jul–Aug daily 9.30–12, 1.30–7 (10 on Thu); Sep–Jun Mon–Sat 9.30–12, 1.30–6

ARRAS
www.ot-arras.fr

Arras has a Flemish feel, its houses embellished with curly gables. The town was renowned for its tapestries in the late Middle Ages and spent its wealth on its 16th-century town hall (rebuilt after World War I) and on adorning its two main squares with dignified town houses. The Grand' Place and the smaller Petite Place (or place des Héros) were created more than 800 years ago as market places. Underneath are the extensive cellars that sheltered local people during the bombardments of World War I. The British War Cemetery is on the western edge of town.

✚ 468 J2 ▮ Hôtel de Ville, place des Héros, 62000 ☎ 03 21 51 26 95 ◷ Apr to mid-Sep Mon–Sat 9–6.30, Sun 10–1, 2.30–6.30; mid-Sep to Mar Mon 10–12, 2–6, Tue–Sat 9–12, Sun 10–12.30, 2.30–6.30 ▯ Arras

BATTLEFIELDS OF PICARDIE
▷ 187.

BEAUVAIS
www.beauvaistourisme.fr

The medieval cathedral of Beauvais rises above the flat landscape. Work started in 1227 but soon after completion the choir area collapsed under its own weight. The 14th-century replacement remained roofless for two centuries. More disaster struck in 1573, when the new spire collapsed.

Much of the town was rebuilt after World War II, but you can see remains of the third-century Gallo-Roman town walls.

✚ 465 J4 ▮ 1 rue Beauregard, BP 537, 60005 ☎ 03 44 15 30 30 ◷ Apr–Sep Mon–Sat 9.30–12.30, 1.30–6 Sun 10–7; Oct–Mar Mon–Sat 9.30–12.30, 1.30–6 ▯ Beauvais

BOULOGNE-SUR-MER
▷ 188.

CALAIS
www.ot-calais.fr

The Hôtel de Ville belfry guides you to the town centre, and Auguste Rodin's sculpture *The Burghers of Calais*. Some of Rodin's bronzes are in the Musée des Beaux-Arts et de la Dentelle, in rue Richelieu (Apr–Oct Tue–Sat 10–12, 2–6, Sun 2–6; Nov–Mar Tue–Sat 10–12, 2–5, Sun 2–5). Plage-Blériot is named after Louis Blériot, who made the first flight across the English Channel, from Calais to Dover, in 1909. The Cité Europe shopping complex (▷ 219) offers excellent retail therapy.

✚ 468 H1 ▮ 12 boulevard Clémenceau, 62100 ☎ 03 21 96 62 40 ◷ Mid-Jun to mid-Sep daily 9–7; Apr to mid-Jun daily 10–7; mid-Sep to Mar Mon–Sat 10–6 ▯ Calais Ville for Paris; Calais Fréthun for Eurostar to London ⛴ To Dover, UK ▦ Shops close Sun, Mon; hypermarkets close Sun

CHANTILLY
▷ 189.

CHARLEVILLE-MÉZIÈRES
www.charleville-mezieres.org

Charleville-Mézières is a good base for touring the Ardennes (▷ left). Originally two towns, Charleville and Mézières, they merged in 1966. Mézières was a medieval trading town whereas Charleville, with its Renaissance square, is known internationally for puppetry; the Grand Marionnettiste clock on place Winston Churchill gives a puppet show on the hour. You can take boat trips on the river Meuse or head to quai Arthur Rimbaud to visit the museum dedicated to poet Arthur Rimbaud (1854–91), who was born here (Tue–Sun 10–12, 2–6).

✚ 468 L3 ▮ 4 place Ducale, Charleville-Mézières ☎ 03 24 55 69 90 ◷ Jul–Aug daily 9.30–12, 1.30–7 (10 on Thu); Sep–Jun Mon–Sat 9.30–12, 1.30–6 ▯ Charleville-Mézières

CHAUMONT
www.ville-chaumont.fr
www.tourisme-chaumont-champagne.com

Chaumont, capital of the Haute-Marne *département*, sits on a ridge in south Champagne. Its turreted stone houses are interspersed with modern buildings, and to the west a huge 19th-century railway viaduct crosses the Suize valley. The town began as a fortress built for the Counts of Champagne. All that remains of the castle is the 12th-century keep, where you can visit the Musée d'Art et d'Histoire and the Musée de la Crèche (summer Wed–Mon 2.30–6.30; rest of year Wed–Mon 2–6).

✚ 466 M6 ▮ place Général de Gaulle, 52000 ☎ 03 25 03 80 80 ◷ Mon–Sat 9.30–12.30, 2.30–6; Jun–Sep also Sun 10–12, 2–5 ▯ Chaumont

BATTLEFIELDS OF PICARDIE

The Champs de Batailles de Picardie (battlefields) were at the front line during World War I and now contain poignant war cemeteries and memorials. Many of the most dramatic struggles in French history have taken place in the Picardie region, whose gently rolling countryside offers few natural barriers to invasion from the northeast. The savage Battle of the Somme, in World War I, led to more than one million casualties. After the war, memorials arose all over the now silent battlefields to commemorate the unprecedented slaughter.

REMEMBRANCE TOUR

A good way to visit the key sites is to follow the 60km (37-mile) Circuit du Souvenir that starts at the rebuilt town of Albert. This tour takes you past timelessly serene war cemeteries, former battlefields and museums. Pick up a leaflet at a local tourist office or follow the roadside poppy symbols.

TRENCH LIFE

Before you set off, visit the underground Musée des Abris Somme 1916, in rue Anicet Godin, which recreates the conditions facing the soldiers in the trenches (Jun–Sep daily 9–6; Feb–May, Oct to mid-Dec 9–12, 2–6. Closed mid-Dec to Jan). A stretch of trenches has been preserved at Beaumont-Hamel, at the Mémorial Terre-Neuvien, watched over by a statue of a caribou, insignia of the Royal Newfoundland Regiment (tel 03 22 76 70 86; permanently open; visitor facility times vary). A rare semicircular concrete German shelter survives in a field outside Martinpuich.

MEMORIALS

At Thiepval, the imposing Mémorial Franco-Britannique (Franco-British Memorial) commemorates the 73,367 British and French men who died between July 1915 and March 1918 but have no known grave. The triumphal arch, 45m (150ft) high and designed by Sir Edwin Lutyens, can be seen for miles. Close by, the Tour d'Ulster (Ulster Tower) commemorates the soldiers from the 36th Ulster Division who lost their lives during the war. To the north of the Circuit du Souvenir, near Arras, the Canadian Vimy Parc Memorial dominates the hilltop at Vimy Ridge, scene of one of World War I's bloodiest battles.

INFORMATION

www.ville-albert.fr
www.somme-tourisme.com
Albert
➕ 468 J3 ℹ 9 rue Léon Gambetta, BP 82, 80300 ☎ 03 22 75 16 42
🕐 Apr–Sep Mon–Fri 9–12.30, 1.30–6.30, Sat 9–12, 2–6.30, Sun 10–12.30; Oct–Mar Mon–Sat 9–12.30, 1.30–5 🚆 Albert

Comité du Tourisme de La Somme
ℹ 21 rue Ernest-Cauvin, 80000 Amiens
☎ 03 22 71 22 71

TIPS

» Tourist offices provide useful leaflets, including *The Visitor's Guide to the Battlefields of the Somme*, *Le Circuit du Souvenir* and *The Somme Remembrance Tour of the Great War*.
» Remembrance ceremonies are held on 1 July, the date the Battle of the Somme began in 1916.
» Guided tours are available by reservation.

Above *A poignant reminder of the cost of war*
Opposite *A brass band plays in place des Héros, Arras*

INFORMATION

www.tourisme-boulognesurmer.com
✚ 468 H2 🛈 Forum Jean Noel, quai
de la Poste, 62200 ☎ 03 21 10 88 10
🕐 Jul–Aug daily 9–7; Apr–Jun 9–12.30,
1.30–6.30; Sep to mid-Nov 9.30–12.30,
1.30–6.30; mid-Nov to Mar 9.15–12.30,
1.45–6 🚊 Boulogne-Ville 🚢 LD
Lines operate between Dover (UK) and
Boulogne

TIPS

» Save money by buying a combined
ticket for Nausicaà and the Château-
Musée.
» Visitors with disabilities can telephone
Nausicaà in advance to arrange an
alternative circuit, avoiding steps and
crowds.
» France's premier fishing port offers the
freshest catch at its tables.
» Philippe Olivier's shop, on rue Thiers, is
a must for cheese-lovers.

Above *Boats in the harbour at Boulogne-
sur-Mer*

BOULOGNE-SUR-MER

This attractive Channel-port town is a treat for shoppers looking for something
different from the hypermarkets up the coast at Calais. Unlike Calais, the historic
heart of Boulogne emerged unscathed from World War II, although the port and
much of the lower town were devastated by bombs.

OLD TOWN

The narrow cobbled streets and historic buildings of the old town are enclosed
by 13th-century ramparts. The tree-lined walls make for a great summer stroll,
with views over the Channel. The medieval Château-Musée is linked to the
ramparts by a drawbridge and displays eclectic exhibits, from Egyptian mummies
to a bronze by Auguste Rodin; look out for the seascapes by Eugène Delacroix
(Mon, Wed–Sat 10–12, 2–5.30, Sun 10–12.30, 2.30–6). At the foot of the hill,
place Dalton hosts a bustling market on Wednesday and Saturday mornings.

The symbol of Boulogne, the slightly ungainly dome of the 19th-century
Basilica de Notre-Dame, replaced an earlier cathedral destroyed during the days
of the Revolution.

NAUSICAÀ AQUARIUM

The National Sea Centre on Boulogne's quayside (tel 03 21 30 99 99; Jul–Aug
daily 9.30–7.30; Sep–Jun 9.30–6.30; closed three weeks in Jan), which is named
after a Greek mythological character, aims to be more than an aquarium. In an
imaginative attempt to recreate the various habitats of the marine world (for
example, mangrove swamps, coral reefs) its constant theme is understanding
human interaction with the sea and the need to preserve the wonderful diversity
of aquatic life.

CHANTILLY

Famous for its forests, racecourses and whipped cream, Chantilly also has a fairy-tale château with outstanding art and a horse museum.

THE CHÂTEAU

The Château de Chantilly sits in forests north of Paris and has an appealing mix of architecture dating from the 14th to the 19th centuries. The Condé family became the owners in the mid-17th century and commissioned landscape architect André Le Nôtre to add lakes and canals to the grounds. During the Revolution, much of the château was destroyed and what remained was used as a prison. It was restored in the 19th century. The 115ha (285-acre) grounds are ideal for strolling, and in spring and summer you can travel on the canals in an electric boat or take a trip in a horse-drawn carriage.

MUSÉE CONDÉ

The museum opened in April 1898, and has a magnificent collection of art and furnishings from the Italian and French Renaissance to the 19th century. Look for works by Raphael, Fouquet, Fra Angelico, Poussin, Delacroix, Corot and Clouet, as well as a facsimile of the medieval *Les Très Riches Heures du Duc de Berry*.

GRANDES ÉCURIES

The stables (Apr–early Nov Wed–Mon 10–5; Dec Wed–Mon 2–6; Jan–Apr Wed–Mon 2–5. Horse shows and exhibitions will be held outside throughout the summer) were built for Louis-Henri, Duke of Bourbon, in the 18th century and could house 240 horses and more than 400 hounds. Today, they contain the Musée Vivant du Cheval (closed for renovation; for opening times check online at www.museevivantducheval.fr).

INFORMATION

www.chateaudechantilly.com

🕂 465 J4 ✉ Château de Chantilly/ Musée Condé, BP 70243, 60631 ☎ 03 44 27 31 80 🕐 Musée Condé: Apr–Aug Wed–Mon 10–6; Sep–Mar 10.30–5. Park: early Apr–early Nov Wed–Mon 10–8; early Nov–early Apr 10.30–6 ✋ Musée Condé and park: adult €12, under 18 free. Park only: adult €6, under 18 free 🚆 Chantilly-Gouvieux, then a 30-min walk 🚍 Autoroute du Nord (A1) and take the Survilliers-St-Witz exit. Alternatively take the N16 or N17 🎁 Gift shop 📖 Several to choose from, prices vary 🎧 Audioguide: €3. Guided tours need to be reserved in advance, tel 03 44 62 62 60

Below *The Château de Chantilly now houses the Musée Condé*

INFORMATION

www.ot-colmar.fr
✚ 467 P6 ℹ 4 rue Unterlinden, 68000
☎ 03 89 20 68 92 🌐 Jul–Aug Mon–Sat
9–7, Sun 10–1; Apr–Jun, Sep–Oct
Mon–Sat 9–6, Sun 10–1; Nov–Mar
Mon–Sat 9–12, 2–6, Sun 10–1. During
the Marchés de Noël (Christmas markets)
Mon–Sat 9–6, Sun 10–1 🚋 Colmar

TIPS

» Pick up a copy of the free *Discovery Trail*
leaflet from the tourist office to follow a
90-minute self-guided walking circuit of
the old town.
» Visit Colmar between late November
and the end of December for the town's
five Marchés de Noël (Christmas Markets)
at place des Dominicains, place de
l'Ancienne Douane, inside the Koïfhus
(place de l'Ancienne Douane), place
Jeanne d'Arc and the children's market in
Petite Venise.
» The old town is illuminated on Friday
and Saturday evenings and during special
events like the Festival International de
Colmar, Advent and Christmas.

Above *The waterways of Colmar's
Krutenau district*

COLMAR

Colmar lies at the southern tip of the wooded Vosges mountains and is the main
town in Alsace's vineyard-rich Rhine valley. It attracts large numbers of visitors to
its carefully restored old town and to the Musée d'Unterlinden, with the dramatic
Isenheim Altarpiece.

EXPLORE

It's a pleasure to stroll the narrow cobbled streets of the old town, with their
timber-framed houses and red-tinged Gothic churches. In place de l'Ancienne
Douane you'll see the striking Ancienne Douane or Koïfhus (Customs House),
once Colmar's economic and political hub. Colmar's oldest house, Maison
Adolph (*c.* 1350), is on place de la Cathédrale, to the north. Maison Pfister, on rue
des Marchands, is a bourgeois residence dating from 1537; its painted panels
depict emperors and biblical characters. On the same road, the Musée Bartholdi
is in the birthplace of 19th-century sculptor Frédéric Auguste Bartholdi, creator of
New York's Statue of Liberty (Mar–Dec Wed–Mon 10–12, 2–6).

The quartier des Krutenau is a picturesque area, where the pastels of old
fishing cottages are reflected in the river Lauch. The district, nicknamed La
Petite Venise (Little Venice), is where gardeners brought their produce in flat-
bottomed boats.

FINE ARTS MUSEUM

The town's greatest treasure is indoors, in the tranquil chapel of the Musée
d'Unterlinden, in rue d'Unterlinden (May–Oct daily 9–6; Nov–Apr Wed–Mon
9–12, 2–5). This museum, in a 13th-century Dominican convent, houses the
Isenheim Altarpiece, masterpiece of Matthias Grünewald (*c.* 1475–1528). The
eight panels of the altarpiece were painted between 1512 and 1516 for the
church of the Monastery of St. Anthony, at nearby Isenheim. They open to
reveal vivid religious scenes including the *Crucifixion* — the best-known panel,
with its emaciated, agonized Christ — the *Resurrection*, the *Angelic Concert* and
the *Temptation of St. Anthony*. Few fail to be gripped by its emotional impact. A
rather calmer view of the Christian story is seen in the *Orlier Altarpiece*, attributed
to Martin Schongauer (*c.* 1445–91). The museum also has local archaeological
finds, Alsatian folk art and decorative art.

COMPIÈGNE

www.mairie-compiegne.fr

The elegant town of Compiègne was a retreat for French kings from the 14th century. It is surrounded by the glorious Forêt de Compiègne and has one of France's largest castles. The Château de Compiègne (Wed–Mon 10–6) has more than 1,000 lavish rooms and Louis XIV threw some spectacular parties here. His successor, Louis XV, commissioned architect Jacques Gabriel to carry out rebuilding work in the 18th century, and Napoleon I and Napoleon III both spent time here. There are three museums within the grounds—the Museum of the Second Empire, the Museum of the Empress and the National Museum of the Car and Tourism.

In a clearing in the forest along the route de Soissons, at Rethondes, you can see the spot where the Armistice was signed on 11 November 1918, ending World War I. A railway carriage similar to the one in which the historic event took place, the Clarière de l'Armistice, houses a small museum (Apr to mid-Oct Wed–Mon 9–12.30, 2–6; mid-Oct to Mar Wed–Mon 9–12, 2–5.30).

465 J4 place de l'Hôtel de Ville, BP 9, 60200 03 44 40 01 00 Apr–Sep Mon–Sat 9.15–12.15, 1.45–6.15; Oct–Mar Mon 1.45–5.15, Tue–Sat 9.15–12.15, 1.45–5.15 (also Sun 10–12.30, 2–5, Easter–Oct) Compiègne

CÔTE D'OPALE

The cliffs, dunes and beaches of the Opal Coast stretch from the Belgian border down to the Bay of the Somme. The most visited section is between Calais and Boulogne-sur-Mer (▷ 188). On a clear day you can see the English coast from the top of the 45m (148ft) Cap Gris-Nez, midway between the two ports. The key resort is Le Touquet, nicknamed 'Paris-Plage' because of the stream of well-to-do Parisians who flocked here for hotel pampering at the beginning of the 20th century. The village of Wissant, 16km (10 miles) southwest of Calais, is famous for circular boats known as *flobarts*, from

which fishermen sell their catch in the market square. Many visitors drive inland or south from Calais, and so miss the Flemish final stretch of the Côte d'Opale, which is a pity as the port of Dunkerque (▷ right) is worth a visit.

468 H1 12 boulevard Clémenceau, 62100 Calais 03 21 96 62 40 Mid-Jun to mid-Sep daily 9–7; Apr to mid-Jun daily 10–7; mid-Sep to mid-Jun Mon–Sat 10–6 Calais Ville, Calais Fréthun Take the D940 coast road

DOUAI

www.ville-douai.fr

Douai was a prosperous town in the Middle Ages, thriving in textiles and cereals trade. In the 17th century, it became a refuge for English Roman Catholics during the English Civil War. Despite damage in both world wars, the town still has historic buildings, including the Gothic bell tower, 64m (210ft) tall. The Musée de la Chartreuse (Wed–Mon 10–12, 2–6), on rue des Chartreux, displays Flemish, Dutch and Italian paintings from the 15th to the 17th centuries and French works from the 18th and 19th centuries. Douai was the administrative town for France's northern coalfield; learn more about mining at the Centre Historique Minier in an old mine in nearby Lewarde (Mar–Oct daily 9–5.30; Nov–Feb Mon–Sat 1–5, Sun 10–5).

468 K2 place d'Armes 59500 03 27 88 26 79 Apr–Sep Mon–Sat 10–1, 2–6.30, Sun 3–6; Oct–Mar Mon–Sat 10–12.30, 2–6.30 Douai

DUNKERQUE

www.ot-dunkerque.fr

Once a fishing village, Dunkerque ('the church of the dunes') has become France's third-largest port. The Dutch, Spanish and English fought over it down the centuries, until France bought it back from England in the mid-17th century. For many, the name Dunkerque is synonymous with the events of 26 May to 3 June 1940, when 350,000 Allied troops, cut off by the German advance, were evacuated to England from the port and the beaches of nearby Malo-les-Bains. Learn more about this at the modest Mémorial du Souvenir, in rue des Chantiers de France (Apr–Sep daily 10–12, 2–5). Around 90 per cent of the town was destroyed near the end of World War II. The port's seafaring history, from privateers to conventional trade, is told in the Musée Portuaire, in a 19th-century tobacco warehouse on the quai de la Citadelle (Jul–Aug daily 10–6; Sep–Jun Wed–Mon 10–12.45, 1.30–6). You can take boat trips around the port and to the lighthouse (summer weekends only). The sandy beaches of Malo-les-Bains are a stroll from the port.

468 J1 rue de l'Amiral Ronarc'h, 59140 03 28 66 79 21 Mon–Sat 9.30–12.30, 1.30–6.30, Sun 10–12, 2–4 Dunkerque To Dover, UK

Below *Dinghies at the village of Ambleteuse on the Côte d'Opale*

ÉPERNAY

www.ot-epernay.fr

Épernay, surrounded by vine-covered hills, is a must for lovers of champagne. You can take a guided tour of some of the 28km (17 miles) of cellars belonging to Moët et Chandon, and sample their product at the *dégustation*, at 18 avenue de Champagne (Mar to mid-Nov daily 9.30–11.30, 2–4.30; closed mid-Nov to Feb). Champagne production began in Épernay in 1743 and the wealth it brought can be seen in the mansions along avenue de Champagne. Other *maisons de champagne* nearby include Mercier, at 70 avenue de Champagne (Mar to mid-Dec daily 9.30–11.30, 2–4.30; early Jan–Mar Thu–Mon 9.30–11.30, 2–4.30) and De Castellane, at 57 rue de Verdun (Apr–Nov daily 10–12, 2–6; Dec–Mar by appointment only).

🚺 466 L4 🚺 7 avenue de Champagne, 51201 ☎ 03 26 53 33 00 🕐 Mid-Apr to mid-Oct Mon–Sat 9.30–12.30, 1.30–7, Sun 11–4; mid-Oct to mid-Apr Mon–Sat 9.30–12.30, 1.30–5.30 🚉 Épernay

HAUT KŒNIGSBOURG

www.haut-koenigsbourg.net

The formidable silhouette of the pink sandstone Château du Haut-Kœnigsbourg rises over the forested slopes above Sélestat. It is the highest castle in Alsace, at more than 700m (2,300ft) above sea level. The castle was reconstructed in the early 20th century for Kaiser Wilhelm II, when Germany ruled Alsace.

🚺 467 P5 ✉ Château du Haut-Kœnigsbourg, 67600 Orschwiller ☎ 03 88 82 50 60 (information line in French) 🕐 Jun–Aug 9.15–6; Apr–May, Sep 9.15–5.15; Mar, Oct 9.30–5; Nov–Feb 9.30–12, 1–4.30 💳 Adult €7.50, under 18 free; free first Sun of month, Oct–Mar

LAON

www.ville-laon.fr

More than 80 of Laon's buildings have been classed as *Monuments Historiques* and there are proposals to make this walled city of winding medieval streets and sandstone architecture a UNESCO World Heritage Site. The city clings to a ridge more than 100m (330ft) above the plains of Picardie and Champagne. Two abbeys once stood here and so many churches sprang up that the site was named the Montagne Couronnée (Crowned Mountain). At one point it was capital of the Carolingian kingdom.

The picturesque Ville Haute (upper town) is surrounded by 7km (4 miles) of ramparts with splendid views. Above the rooftops are the five towers of the 12th- to 13th-century Cathédrale Notre-Dame, each 75m (245ft) high. The west front epitomizes the Gothic style; the interior has a simple grandeur. Look for figures of oxen high in the towers, commemorating the beasts that hauled the heavy stone uphill.

The Cité Médiévale district around the cathedral includes the Palais Épiscopal, now the law courts, and the 12th-century Hôtel-Dieu. The Musée Municipal de Laon, in rue Georges Ermant (Jun–Sep Tue–Sun 11–6; Oct–May Tue–Sun 2–6) has Classical antiquities and 18th-century earthenware.

The less scenic Ville Basse (lower town) is linked to the upper town by an overhead tram, the Poma.

🚺 465 K4 🚺 Hôtel-Dieu, place du Parvis Gauthier de Mortagne, 02000 ☎ 03 23 20 28 62 🕐 Easter–early Nov daily

9.30–1, 2–6.30; early Nov–Easter Mon–Sat 9.30–12.30, 2–5.30, Sun 2–5.30

🚉 Laon station is in the Ville Basse

LILLE

▷ 194.

METZ

▷ 193.

MULHOUSE

www.tourisme-mulhouse.com

Mulhouse, a dynamic industrial town near France's border with Germany and Switzerland, is home to the lofty Tour de l'Europe with its revolving restaurant, and some outstanding museums. Highlights include the Cité de l'Automobile (early Apr–Oct daily 10–6, early Feb–early Apr, Nov–Dec 10–5; Jan–early Feb Mon–Fri 2–5, Sat–Sun 10–5), on avenue de Colmar. At the open-air Écomusée d'Alsace, off the D430 to the north, traditional buildings show daily life in Alsace as it was in past years (Jul–Aug daily 10–7; Mar–Jun, Sep–early Nov 10–6).

🚺 467 P6 🚺 place de la Réunion ☎ 03 89 66 93 13 🕐 Jul–Aug, Dec daily 10–7; Sep–Jun Mon–Sat 10–6, Sun 10–12, 2–6 🚉 Mulhouse

NANCY

www.ot-nancy.fr

Nancy prides itself on its classical townscape, the product of the urban planning of its enlightened rulers. It was the capital of the Duchy of Lorraine before joining the kingdom of France on the death of the last duke, Stanislas, in the mid-18th century. Stanislas was responsible for the elegant place Stanislas, linking the then new town to the old.

You can learn more about Lorraine's history at the Musée Lorrain, in the Ducal Palace (Tue–Sun 10–12.30, 2–6). Nancy was an important place for art nouveau and you can see a collection of decorative arts in art nouveau style at the Musée de l'École de Nancy, on rue du Sergent Blandan (Wed–Mon 10–6).

🚺 467 N5 🚺 place Stanislas, BP 810, 54011 ☎ 03 83 35 22 41 🕐 Apr–Oct Mon–Sat 9–7, Sun 10–5; Nov–Mar Mon–Sat 9–6, Sun 10–1 🚉 Nancy

METZ

Metz (pronounced 'Mess') is the capital of Lorraine and the oldest city in the region. It is a picturesque settlement, on the banks of the rivers Moselle and Seille, with buildings in the dark yellow stone known as *pierre de jaumont*, and an abundance of parks.

There was a town here in Roman times, and during the Middle Ages Metz was a wealthy independent city-state. It became part of France in the mid-16th century but was taken by Germany in 1871 after the Franco-Prussian War, not returning to France until 1918. It has developed into a modern city and is now home to software and communications companies.

ARCHITECTURAL HERITAGE

You can see examples of German architecture in the area around the huge neo-Romanesque train station, but the city's Gothic Cathédrale St-Étienne is characteristically French, with a lofty interior and a vast amount of sumptuous stained glass. The windows cover an impressive 6,500sq m (70,000sq ft) and date from the 13th to the 20th centuries. Look for the biblical scenes by Marc Chagall in the north transept and ambulatory.

The cathedral dominates the 18th-century place d'Armes, also home to the Hôtel de Ville. On nearby rue du Haut-Poirier, a 17th-century convent houses three museums known as Les Musées de la Cour d'Or—the Musée Archéologique, Musée d'Architecture and Musée des Beaux-Arts (Mon, Wed–Fri 9–5; Sat–Sun 10–5). The Ancienne Église St-Pierre-aux-Nonnains, on rue de la Citadelle, is one of the oldest churches in France. The main shopping area is south of the cathedral, around place St-Louis.

RIVERSIDE

Metz's riverside is worth seeking out, not least for the formidable Porte des Allemands on boulevard Maginot. The four towers on this gateway guarded the eastern entrance to the medieval city. From Moyen Pont there are good views.

INFORMATION

www.mairie-metz.fr

✚ 467 N4 ℹ 2 place d'Armes, BP 80367, 57007 ☎ 03 87 55 53 76 ◷ Apr–Sep Mon–Sat 9–7, Sun 10–7; Oct–Mar Mon–Sat 9–7, Sun 10–3 🚉 Metz

Above *Metz, beautifully illuminated at night*
Opposite *A cobbled street leads to the Port d'Ardon in Laon*

193

REGIONS | NORTH AND NORTHEAST FRANCE • SIGHTS

INTRODUCTION

Capital of the Nord-Pas-de-Calais region and with a population of 1.5 million, Lille is the fourth largest city in France and a compelling blend of the old and new. It began life as a village surrounded by tributaries of the river Deûle, giving rise to its name (*l'île*—the island). Gradually, canals and a river port were created from the waterways, attracting merchants and prosperity to the burgeoning market town. From the Middle Ages onwards Lille passed from kingdom to kingdom, belonging to France, Spain, Burgundy, Flanders and the Netherlands. Louis XIV captured the city in 1667 and it was officially handed over to France as part of the Treaty of Utrecht in 1713.

In the 19th century its entrepreneurs grew rich from metalwork, chemicals and above all textiles but in the 1980s all these heavy industries were replaced by a service sector in which tourism plays an important role.

The arrival of the TGV from Paris and the Eurostar between Britain and Brussels, turned Lille into a self-styled 'crossroads of Europe', within reach of a day-trip from London, and indeed its immediate accessibility is one of is charms for the visitor.

Once there, it's easy to get around on the integrated Métro, bus and tram system. Attractions include the Palais des Beaux-Arts, the star-shaped Citadelle, the vast Centre Euralille shopping mall (for a city with such a mercantile past, shopping is second nature) and the warren of cobbled streets in the old town. Here, the 17th-century buildings are built of Lezennes white stone and Armentières brick, with intricately carved wheat sheaves and cherubs crowning the doorways. The heart of the city is the Grand Place, officially named the place du Général de Gaulle after the most famous local son. There are many bars and restaurants on the streets between here and nearby place Rihour and place du Théâtre. Lille's newer part is farther east, in the Euralille district.

When you are ready to stop for something to drink, forget wine and order a glass of *blanche de Lille*, the city's own pale beer.

INFORMATION

www.lilletourisme.com

⊞ 468 K2 🛈 Palais Rihour, place Rihour, BP 205, 59002 ☎ 03 59 57 94 00 (outside France) or 08 91 56 20 04

🕐 Mon–Sat 9.30–6.30, Sun 10–12, 2–5

🚇 Two Métro lines serve the city and surrounding area 🚌 Most buses leave from place des Buisses, between Lille's two train stations. There are also two tram routes 🚊 Lille-Europe station has Eurostar trains from London, Ebbsfleet and Ashford (UK), TGV trains from Paris and all over France, and Thalys trains from Brussels. Regional services arrive at Lille-Flandres station ✈ Lille Lesquin airport, 12km (7 miles) from the city centre, has international and domestic flights

Opposite *Cafés on place du Général de Gaulle*
Below *Christmas rides*

TIPS

» If you are using the Métro, buses or trams, remember to punch your ticket at the start of your journey.

» A City Pass gives you unlimited use of the buses, Métro and trams within Lille, as well as entry to some museums (1 day €20, 2 days €30, 3 days €45)

» For a weekend hotel bargain, contact the tourist office (at least eight days in advance) for details of the two-for-one Bon Weekend offers.

» Town stewards, wearing yellow jackets, give advice and directions to visitors.

Above *The Tour Crédit Lyonnais,* *nicknamed the 'ski-boot' building*
Below *Euralille shopping mall*

WHAT TO SEE

PALAIS DES BEAUX-ARTS

www.pba-lille.fr

This magnificent late 19th-century palace, which was enlarged by almost 50 per cent in the 1990s, houses France's second national museum after the Louvre in Paris, with a collection of masterpieces spanning more than 400 years. Artists represented range from Flemish and Dutch masters to the Impressionists, including Monet, Renoir and Van Gogh. There's 19th-century French sculpture in a hall on the ground floor, while the basement contains the medieval and Renaissance collection, including 40 sketches by Raphael and Donatello's bas-relief *Herod's Feast*.

Other highlights are 18th-century relief maps of northern France's fortified cities, and Vauban's models for his Citadelle. Look for the stained-glass windows near the main staircases. When it's time for a break, relax in the airy atrium with a coffee.

✚ 197 B2 ✉ place de la République ☎ 03 20 06 78 00 🕐 Mon 2–6, Wed–Sun 10–6. Closed first weekend in Sep 🚇 République 🚌 14 🖐 Adult €5.50, child (12–18) €3.80, under 12 free

CITADELLE

The architecture in Lille's historic heart is an appealing mix of Flemish and French, but the Citadelle, just outside Vieux Lille, is entirely French, built by Louis XIV's military engineer Vauban. The vast fortress—a mini-town—is in the shape of a five-pointed star and inspired the design for the US Pentagon. It was completed in 1670, after only three years of building work.

The main entrance, the Porte Royale, was intended to reflect the grandeur of Louis XIV, but security was another key concern—the gateway is at an angle to the drawbridge to avoid enemy fire and the walls are 4m (13ft) thick. The Citadelle is still home to 1,000 soldiers.

✚ 197 A1 ✉ avenue du 43ème Régiment d'Infantrie ☎ Tourist office: 03 59 57 94 00 🕐 Guided tours only, early Mar–Aug Thu, Fri, Sun at 3 and 4. You must reserve in advance at the tourist office 🚌 14 🖐 Adult €7, child (under 16) €5.50

EURALILLE

www.euralille.com

This futuristic shopping, business and leisure district opened in 1994 to coincide with the launch of the Eurostar rail service. It sits on 70ha (170 acres) of land on the eastern side of the city, sandwiched between Lille's two train stations, and was laid out by Dutch architect Rem Koolhaas.

You can choose from around 140 shops at the Centre Euralille mall or attend a concert in the 5,000-seat Grand Palais, and there are restaurants, a hypermarket, a hotel and holiday apartments. The modernistic Gare Lille-Europe is crowned by Christian de Portzampac's Tour Crédit Lyonnais, whose shape has led to it being popularly known as the 'ski boot'.

✚ 197 C1 ✉ avenue Le Corbusier ☎ 03 20 14 52 20 🕐 Euralille: Mon–Sat 10–8. Hypermarket: 9am–10pm. Restaurants: 9am–10pm 🚉 Gare Lille-Europe and Gare Lille-Flandres

MUSÉE DE L'HOSPICE COMTESSE

This former hospital takes you back to the 15th to 17th centuries, with French, Flemish and Dutch paintings, period furniture and rare musical instruments. Don't miss the tapestries by local weaver Guillaume Werniers and the kitchen decorated in Dutch style.

The museum sits discreetly behind the shopfronts of the rue de la Monnaie, one of Lille's oldest streets. A hospital was founded here in 1237 by Jeanne de Constantinople, Countess of Flanders.

✚ 197 B1 ✉ 32 rue de la Monnaie ☎ 03 28 36 84 00 🕐 Wed–Sun 10–12.30, 2–6, Mon 2–6 🚇 Rihour 🖐 Adult €3.50, child €2

WAZEMMES

There is a carnival atmosphere at the Sunday morning Wazemmes market, which is more an event than a shopping opportunity. The sound of accordions and the aroma of Sunday lunch waft past stands selling anything from puppies and kittens to bric-a-brac. You'll find the pet market near Gambetta Métro station and antiques and bric-a-brac on the streets around the church of St-Paul-et-St-Pierre. Toys, clothes, fruit and vegetables are sold on place de la Nouvelle Aventure, and cheese, meat and fish in the market hall.

✚ 197 A2 ✉ place de la Nouvelle Aventure ◷ Sun, Tue, Thu 7–2 🚇 Gambetta

MORE TO SEE

BOIS DE BOULOGNE

This park is wrapped around the Citadelle and bordered by the canal of the river Deûle. It is popular with bicyclists and joggers and there is also a zoo.

✚ 197 A1 ◷ Daily 🚌 14

MAISON NATALE DU GÉNÉRAL DE GAULLE

www.maison-natale-de-gaulle.org

War hero and first president of the Fifth French Republic, Charles de Gaulle was born here, in his grandmother's house, on 22 November 1890. It is now a museum of his life.

✚ Off map 197 B1 ✉ 9 rue Princesse ☎ 03 28 38 12 05 ◷ Wed–Sat 10–1, 2–6, Sun 1.30–5.30 (ticket office closes 1 hour earlier) 🚌 3, 6 ♿ Adult €6, child (10–18) €4

MUSÉE D'ART MODERNE

www.musee-lam.fr

The modern art museum, a short Métro and bus ride out from the city, displays works by Picasso, Modigliani, Braque and others in its light, airy galleries. Sculptures embellish the gardens.

✚ Off map 197 C1 ✉ 1 allée du Musée, Villeneuve d'Ascq ☎ 03 20 19 68 68 ◷ Wed–Mon 10–6. Call to check whether it has reopened following refurbishment 🚇 Pont de Bois, then bus 41 to Parc Urbain–Musée ♿ Adult €6.50, child (12–25) €1.50, under 12 free

VIEILLE BOURSE

The opulent 17th-century trading exchange is the most beautiful building in Lille, with its intricate carvings and cloistered courtyard. Merchants once traded here—today you browse the second-hand book market or watch chess players.

✚ 197 B1 ✉ place du Général de Gaulle ◷ Tue–Sun 1–7 🚇 Rihour ♿ Free

Above *Place du Général de Gaulle*

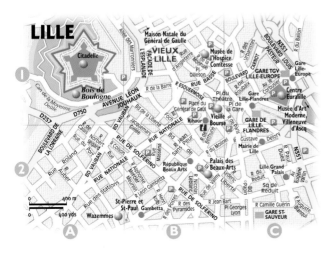

PARC ASTÉRIX
www.parcasterix.com
This witty, essentially French theme park has attractions based on the antics of the Gallic cartoon hero Astérix (▷ 30). The park, only 30km (19 miles) north of Paris, is packed with Roman related games, funfair rides and food. All the heroes are here, along with their enemies. Attractions include Zeus Thunder roller coaster, water rides and shows. At the Gauls' village, a scale model depicts Paris through the centuries. The park provides a lively day out.
✚ 465 J4 ✉ Parc Astérix, 60128 Plailly ☎ 08 26 30 10 40 🕓 Early Apr–Sep, school hols in Oct; mid Dec to early Jan, times vary 🖐 Adult €39, child (3–11) €29, under 3 free 🚇 RER Roissy-Pôle 🚌 A1 Paris-Lille Highway

REIMS
▷ 200.

RIQUEWIHR
www.ribeauville-riquewihr.com
Riquewihr is a picturesque village (can be crowded in summer) on the Alsace Route du Vin, with timbered houses, cobbled streets and surrounded by vineyards, 300m (1,000ft) above sea level. You can taste the delicious wines at many of the local bars and restaurants. The village dates from medieval times—two 13th-century gate towers and part of the old ramparts survive. In one of the gate towers, the Tour des Voleurs, you can see the reconstruction of a torture chamber (Jul–Aug daily 10.30–1, 2–6; Apr–Jun, Sep–Oct Sat–Sun 10.30–1, 2–6). The village has other museums on topics from stagecoaches to local history.
✚ 467 P6 ℹ 2 rue de la 1ière Armée, 68340 ☎ 03 89 73 23 23 🕓 Apr–Oct, Dec Mon–Sat 9.30–12, 2–6 (Tue opens 10am), Sun 10–1; Jan–Mar, Nov Mon–Sat 10–12, 2–5, Sun 10–1. Jan–Mar, Nov closed Sun

RONCHAMP
www.tourisme-ronchamp.fr.st
Ronchamp's highlight is the modern chapel on a hill to the northwest. Notre-Dame-du-Haut (Apr–Sep daily 9.30–6.30; Oct–Mar 10–4) was designed by Le Corbusier in 1955 and is as much a sculpture as a building. A billowing roof covers the interior and stained-glass windows are deeply set into the massive concrete walls. There are works by Marc Chagall and Henri Matisse inside. The chapel was built in memory of French soldiers killed here in 1944, replacing a church wrecked during the battle. From the hill, you can see the Jura and Vosges mountains. Ronchamp has a mining museum on place de la Mairie (Jun–Aug Wed–Mon 10–12, 2–7; Sep–May Wed–Mon 2–6).
✚ 467 N6 ℹ place du 14 Juillet, 70250 ☎ 03 84 63 50 82 🕓 Mon–Fri 10–12, 1.30–5.30, Sat 10–12

ST-OMER
www.tourisme.saintomer.com
This market town in the marshes has fine 17th- and 18th-century houses. You can take boat trips on its network of canals (watergangs). The 13th-century cathedral has a 16th-century white tower and an art collection including Rubens' Deposition of Christ. Beer is the town's best-known export. The German V2 rocket base at nearby Helfaut-Wizernes is now La Coupole, a museum of rocket science and occupied France (Jul–Aug daily 10–7; Sep–Jun 9–6).
✚ 468 J2 ℹ 4 rue du Lion d'Or, 62500 ☎ 03 21 98 08 51 🕓 Easter–Sep Mon–Sat 9–6, Sun 10–1; Sep–Easter Mon–Sat 9–12.30, 2–6 🚉 St-Omer

SÉLESTAT
www.selestat-tourisme.com
Among the medieval streets, the 12th-century Sainte-Foy church is one of the finest Romanesque buildings in Alsace (Sun–Fri 8–6, Sat 9–6). You can see books and manuscripts dating back to the seventh century in the Bibliothèque Humaniste, on rue de la Bibliothèque (Jul–Aug Mon, Wed–Fri 9–12, 2–6, Sat–Sun 2–5; Sep–Jun 9–12, 2–6). Find out about local bread-making at the Musée de la Maison du Pain on rue du Sel (Dec Mon–Fri 9.30–12.30, 2–6, Sat 9–12.30, 2–6, Sun 9–12.30, 2.30–6; Jan–Nov Tue–Fri 9.30–12.30, 2–6, Sat 9–12.30, 2–6, Sun 9–12.30, 2.30–6).
✚ 467 P5 ℹ Commanderie St-Jean, boulevard du Général Leclerc, BP 184, 67604 ☎ 03 88 58 87 20 🕓 Jul–Aug Mon–Fri 9.30–12.30, 1.30–6.30, Sat 9–12.30, 2–5, Sun 10.30–3; Apr–Jun, Sep–Dec Mon–Tue, Thu–Fri 9–12, 2–5.45, Wed 9.30–12, 2–5.45, Sat 1–12, 2–5; Jan–Mar Mon–Fri 10–12, 2–5.45, Sat 9–12, 2–5 🚉 Sélestat

STRASBOURG
▷ 202–205.

TROYES

A stroll around the old town in Troyes evokes the atmosphere of medieval times, when merchants came from all over Europe to attend the great fairs here. The city, on the banks of the Seine, was relatively unharmed during both world wars, so its medieval streets are still lined with half-timbered houses.

STAINED GLASS

Troyes has an exceptional heritage of stained-glass windows in its nine churches—so much so that it is known as the Ville Sainte du Vitrail ('blessed city of stained-glass windows'). The windows date from the 13th to 19th centuries and on-site restoration laboratories use methods that have hardly changed over the years. Troyes's last great master was the 17th-century Linard Gontier, who specialized in a technique of shading known as *grisaille*. You can see his work in the Église St-Martin-ès-Vignes on avenue Marie de Champagne. The Gothic Cathédrale St-Pierre-et-St-Paul (mid-Jul to mid-Sep daily 10.15–1, 2–6.45; mid-Sep to mid-Jul Tue–Sat 8.30–12, 1–5, Sun 2.15–4.45) is in the old Cité district, north of the Canal de la Haute Seine. One of the largest cathedrals in France, it is bathed in light streaming in through the magnificent stained-glass windows.

MUSEUMS

Troyes has almost as many museums as churches, all housed in venerable buildings. The Musée d'Art Moderne (Tue–Sun 10–1, 2–6), in the former bishop's palace next door to the cathedral, focuses on French art from 1850 to 1950, including works by Rodin, Soutine and Derain. South of the Cité district, in the Vauluisant *quartier*, the Église St-Pantaléon has a vast collection of statues rescued from various churches during the Revolution.

INFORMATION
www.tourisme-troyes.com
⊞ 466 L6 ⚑ 16 boulevard Carnot, BP 4082, 10000 (opposite train station)
☎ 03 25 82 62 70 🕓 Mon–Sat 9–12.30, 2–6.30 (also Sun 10–1 in summer)
🚉 Troyes

Opposite left *Half-timbered houses and pink sandstone towers in Riquewihr*
Opposite right *A canal boat at Claimarais, St-Omer*
Below *Cathédral St-Pierre-et-St-Paul*

REGIONS NORTH AND NORTHEAST FRANCE • SIGHTS

INFORMATION

www.reims-tourisme.com
✚ 466 L4 ℹ 2 rue Guillaume de
Machault, 51100 ☎ 08 92 70 13 51
🕐 May–Sep Mon–Sat 9–7, Sun 10–6;
Apr, Oct Mon–Sat 9–6, Sun 10–6; Mar
Mon–Sat 9–6, Sun 10–1; Nov–Feb
Mon–Sat 9–6, Sun 10–12 🚉 Reims

TIPS

» The tourist office rents out audioguides
that take you around the key sights.
» The Reims City Card (€15) offers free
or reduced admission fees for several
attractions.

INTRODUCTION

Now a modern, dynamic city, Reims (sometimes spelled Rheims in English)
played a pivotal role in early French history. It was here in 496 that St. Remigius
baptized Clovis I, the first king to unite all the Frankish tribes and bring the whole
of Roman Gaul under a single ruler, thus laying the foundation for the nation
of France. Subsequently, Reims became the venue for all royal coronations;
25 kings in all came here to be conferred with legitimacy. The most significant
ceremony took place in 1429 when Joan of Arc accompanied Charles VII on his
trek to Reims to prove that he was the right man to reunite the country and expel
the English from France.

The city was close to the front line during World War I and much of the
historic heart was reduced to rubble. More destruction followed in World War II
but it was also in Reims that the German army formally surrendered to the Allies
in 1945.

Nowadays, your first impression of Reims is likely to be of a large, industrial
city rather than a historical treasure but don't be put off. Head for the city centre,
where most of the sights are located. The cathedral, Palais du Tau and Basilique
St-Rémi are listed World Heritage Sites. Many visitors also come here to visit its
famous champagne producers.

WHAT TO SEE

CATHÉDRALE NOTRE-DAME

The 13th-century cathedral is the city's best-known monument. World War I
destroyed much of the Gothic building but it has been expertly restored, and now
has three beautiful stained-glass windows by Marc Chagall. The west front is
particularly inspiring, with its vivid rose window, Gallery of the Kings and famous
statue of the 'Smiling Angel'. Next to the cathedral, the late 17th-century Palais
du Tau was formerly the Archbishop's palace (early May–early Sep Tue–Sun
9.30–6.30; early Sep–early May Tue–Sun 9.30–12.30, 2–5.30). Now it contains
the cathedral museum, where you can see exhibits ranging from sculptures to
coronation paraphernalia. Look for the striking Salle du Tau, where lavish royal
banquets were held after coronations.
✉ place du Cardinal-Luçon 🕐 Daily 7.30am–7.30pm; no visits during services

Above *Hundreds of bottles in a Reims
champagne cellar*

BASILIQUE ST-RÉMI

The vast Romanesque St-Rémi Basilica dates from 1007 and shelters the tomb of St. Rémi and a wonderful collection of 12th-century stained-glass windows. Next to the basilica is the Musée St-Rémi (Mon–Fri 2–6.30, Sat–Sun 2–7), in the Benedictine abbey of St-Rémi. Exhibits here range from prehistory to the Renaissance.

✉ place du Chanoine Ladame 🕐 Daily 8–dusk or 7pm at the latest; no visits during services

CHAMPAGNE

Reims's status as a champagne producer owes much to the geology underlying the city. The chalk rock has been worn into caves, vast natural cellars for maturing and storing the precious sparkling wine that is synonymous with celebration. Dom Perignon, a 17th-century monk, invented the process that gives champagne its sparkle. No visit to Reims would be complete without a visit to a *maison du champagne* (champagne house), where you can tour the *caves* (cellars) and indulge in a *dégustation* (tasting). Most *maisons du champagne* have English-speaking guides, although at some you need to book tours in advance. Those that don't require pre-booking include Champagne Maxim's, Champagne G.H. Mumm & Cie, Champagne Piper-Heidsieck and Champagne Taittinger.

MUSÉE DES BEAUX-ARTS

This is the city's main arts museum, close to the cathedral in part of the 18th-century Abbaye St-Denis. Its collection ranges from the Renaissance to today. Highlights include 27 paintings by the 19th-century artist Corot.

✉ 8 rue Chanzy ☎ 03 26 35 36 00 🕐 Wed–Mon 10–12, 2–6 ✋ Adult €3, child (under 18) free, free to all first Sun of month

MORE TO SEE

MUSÉE-HÔTEL LE VERGEUR

This museum has a fascinating collection of decorative arts.

✉ 36 place du Forum ☎ 03 26 47 20 75 🕐 Tue–Sun 2–6 ✋ Adult €4, child (10–18) €1, under 10 free

MUSÉE DE LA REDDITION

See the room in Eisenhower's headquarters where the German army signed its surrender *(reddition)* on 7 May 1945. There is also a World War II exhibition.

✉ 12 rue Franklin Roosevelt ☎ 03 26 47 84 19 🕐 Wed–Mon 10–12, 2–6 ✋ Adult €3, under 16 free

CHAMPAGNE HOUSES

Champagne Maxim's

✉ 17 rue des Créneaux
☎ 03 26 82 70 67 🕐 Daily 10–7

Champagne G. H. Mumm & Cie

www.mumm.com
✉ 34 rue du Champ de Mars
☎ 03 26 49 69 87 🕐 Mar–Oct daily 9–11, 2–5; Nov–Feb Mon–Fri 9–11, 2–5 by appointment, Sat 9–11, 2–5, Sun 2–5

Champagne Taittinger

www.taittinger.fr
✉ 9 place St-Nicaise ☎ 03 26 85 84 33 🕐 Mid-Mar to mid-Nov daily 9.30–1, 2–5.30; mid-Nov to mid-Mar Mon–Fri 9.30–1, 2–5.30

Veuve Clicquot

www.veuve-clicquot.com
✉ 1 place des Droits de l'Homme
☎ 03 26 89 53 90 🕐 Apr–Oct 10–6 by appointment

Below *City statues*

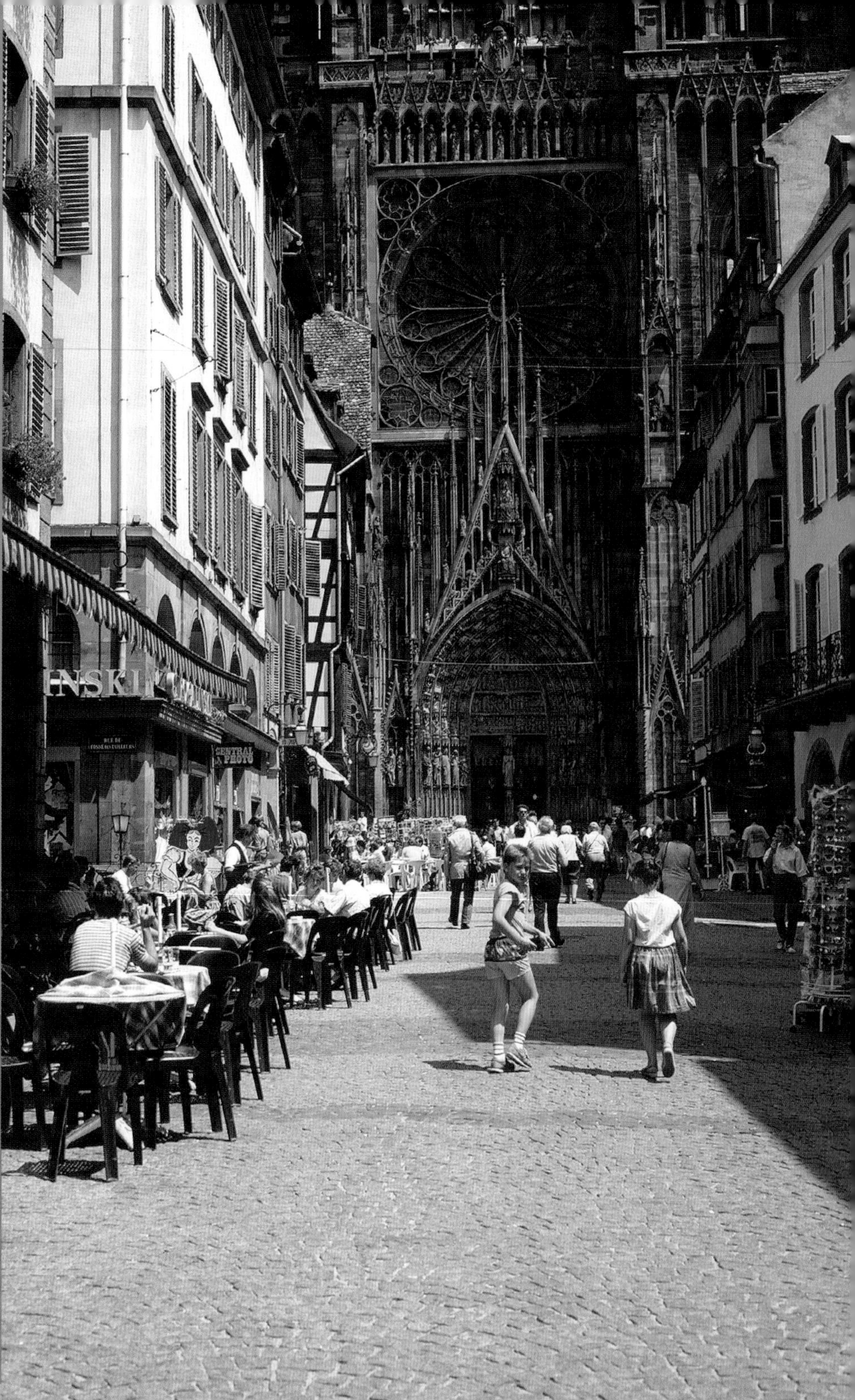
CENTRAL PHOTO

INTRODUCTION

Only three cities in the world are home to major international institutions without being national capitals: New York, Geneva and the 'European capital' of Strasbourg, which is the seat of the Council of Europe, the European Parliament and European Commission on Human Rights.

The city's location on the border with France and Germany is partly responsible for this new mediating role, but it was a source of conflict in the past. Strasbourg was forced to switch allegiances many times over the years. Hitherto, a Free City it joined France in the 17th century, but after the Franco-Prussian War (1870–71) became part of the German Empire's annexed territory of Elsass-Lothringen. The city moved back to France at the end of World War I, only to be reoccupied by Germany from 1940 until its liberation in 1944. A poignant war memorial in place de la République highlights the city's plight during this time—a mother mourns her two dying sons, one who fought for Germany and the other for France.

Now indisputably French, Strasbourg nevertheless retains reminders of its German connections. Its river port, on the Rhine, is one of the busiest in the country. The central part of the city is an island, encircled by the river Ill, and much of it is traffic-free, making it well suited to exploration on foot. It is dominated by the soaring spire of the medieval cathedral. Head to the western tip of the island to see the picturesque area of Petite France.

WHAT TO SEE

CATHÉDRALE DE NOTRE-DAME
www.cathedrale-strasbourg.fr

You can see the 142m (466ft) spire of Strasbourg's pink sandstone Gothic cathedral wherever you are in the heart of the city. The cathedral took more than 250 years to build, with work finishing in 1439. It is rich in sculptural decoration, especially the west facade. Inside, in the south transept, the three-tiered Pilier des Anges (Pillar of Angels) depicts the Last Judgement in a triumph of carving. Nearby, don't miss the 19th-century Horloge Astronomique, a vast, intricate astronomical clock. Be there at 12.30 to see the 12 Apostles parading before Christ. If you're feeling energetic, climb the 332 steps up the tower to the viewing platform (Apr–Sep daily 9–7.15; Oct–Mar 10–5.15; also Jun–Aug until 10pm on Fri–Sat).

➕ 205 C2 ✉ place de la Cathédrale ☎ 03 88 21 43 30 🕐 Daily 7–11.20, 12.35–7

HEART OF EUROPE

Strasbourg's location on the border between Western and Central Europe makes it an ideal base for various European institutions, clustered together in the Quartier Européen. The European Parliament has a purpose-built, curvaceous glass and steel home, constructed just in time for the new millennium. Opposite, the sizeable Palais de l'Europe is home to the Council of Europe (tel 03 88 41 20 29; one-hour visits for groups only, Mon–Fri, by reservation). The European Commission on Human Rights and the European Court of Human Rights are in the Palais des Droits de l'Homme, which overlooks the canal, designed by Sir Richard Rogers and opened in 1995.

MUSEUMS

South of the cathedral in place du Château, the Musée de l'Oeuvre Notre-Dame (Tue–Fri 12–6, Sat–Sun 10–6), displays cathedral-related sculptures, stained glass, paintings and furniture. These buildings were used by the cathedral architects in the 14th and 15th centuries.

INFORMATION
www.ot-strasbourg.fr

➕ 467 Q5 ℹ️ 17 place de la Cathédrale, 67082 ☎ 03 88 52 28 28 (also offices at place de la Gare and Pont de l'Europe)
🕐 Daily 9–7 🚍 Trams and buses
🚉 Strasbourg

Opposite *A narrow street leading to the cathedral*
Below *The Council of Europe*

TIPS

» Pick up a copy of the *All Strasbourg in your pocket*! leaflet from the tourist office.

» The Strasbourg-Pass, available from the tourist office, gives free admission and reductions at various sights over three days (€12.40).

» Christmas markets take place in late November and December in place Broglie, place de la Cathédrale and place de la Gare.

» For a break from city life, have a walk on the banks of the river Ill or take a boat trip.

Next door, the 18th-century Palais Rohan, built for the Bishop of Strasbourg, houses three key museums (all open Mon, Wed–Fri 12–6, Sat–Sun 10–6): In the Musée Archéologique, in the basement, you can learn more about life in Alsace from prehistory to AD800. On the ground floor, the Musée des Arts Decoratifs features the lavish apartments of the cardinals as well as decorative arts from the 17th to the 19th centuries. On the first floor, the Musée des Beaux-Arts displays European paintings from medieval times to the 19th century.

To the south, near the pont du Corbeau, is the Ancienne Boucherie (Old Butchery) housing the Musée Historique, which highlights Strasbourg's political, economic and military history. Nearby, the 14th-century former customs house is now the Galerie de l'Ancienne Douane, hosting temporary exhibitions. Across the bridge, three 17th- and 18th-century Alsatian houses on quai St-Nicolas form the Musée Alsacien (Wed–Mon 10–6), focusing on folk culture.

The Musée d'Art Moderne et Contemporain, in place Hans-Jean Arp (Tue, Wed, Fri 12–7, Thu 12–9, Sat–Sun 10–6) overlooks Vauban's Dam and includes works by Monet, Picasso and others, as well as photography and graphic art.

South of the Botanical Gardens, in the heart of the university campus, the Musée Zoologique (Mon, Wed–Fri 12–6, Sat–Sun 10–6) has lively exhibitions on animal-related topics.

PETITE FRANCE

The fishermen, millers and tanners who once worked in this area have been replaced by craftspeople. The winding streets, half-timbered houses and turreted bridges are best observed from the top of the 17th-century Barrage Vauban, a weir which formed part of the city's defences. Also in Petite France are the Ponts Couverts, built in the 13th century as wooden roofed bridges, but replaced by uncovered stone versions in the 19th century.

MORE TO SEE
ÉGLISE PROTESTANTE ST-THOMAS
www.fondation-saint-thomas.fr

Strasbourg's second-largest church was started in the 12th century and finally finished in the 16th, resulting in an exquisite piece of Alsatian Gothic architecture. Highlights include the mausoleum of Maréchal Maurice de Saxe, by 18th-century Parisian sculptor Jean-Baptiste Pigalle.

Above *The European Parliament building*

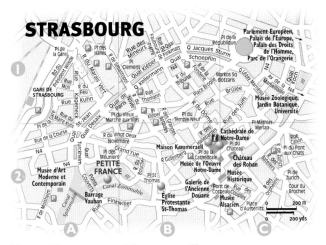

STRASBOURG

➕ 205 B2 ✉ place Saint-Thomas ☎ 03 88 32 14 46 🕐 Apr–Oct daily 10–6; May, Nov, Dec 10–5; Feb 2–5. No visits during services.

JARDIN BOTANIQUE

More than 6,000 species of plants grow in these 3.5ha (9-acre) botanical gardens. The former observatory is now a planetarium.

➕ Off map 205 C1 ✉ rue Goethe ☎ 03 90 24 18 65 🕐 Mon–Fri 8–12, 2–4 (closes later in summer); also open certain weekends 2–4 🚻 Free

MAISON KAMMERZELL

This is arguably the most beautiful house in Strasbourg. The half-timbered upper floors were added in the 16th century, where there is now a restaurant.

➕ 205 B2 ✉ place de la Cathédrale

PARC DE L'ORANGERIE

This leafy park has floral displays, a boating lake, waterfall, small zoo, children's playground, bowling alley and restaurants.

➕ Off map 205 C1 ✉ avenue de l'Europe/avenue du Président Edwards ☎ 03 88 60 90 90 🕐 Daily

Above *A local band entertaining diners*
Below *Strasbourg's Christmas market, outside the cathedral*

☎ 03 29 08 08 88 ☯ Apr–Oct Mon–Sat 9–6.30, Sun 10–1, 2–6; Nov–Mar Mon–Sat 9–12, 1.30–6 🚉 Vittel

WISSEMBOURG
www.ot-wissembourg.fr
This border town is one of the most charming little places in Alsace—its name means 'white castle'. You can wander through the cobbled Vieille Ville (old town), past old timber-framed houses and the 13th-century Abbatiale St-Pierre-et-St-Paul. The church, on the site of a seventh-century Benedictine monastery, has some lovely stained-glass windows. The 15th-century Maison du Sel, near the pont du Sel, has had various roles over the years, ranging from hospital to salt warehouse to abattoir. Its huge roof is an impressive sight. The local history museum, Musée Westercamp, is on the northern edge of the town, on rue du Musée (closed for refurbishment, reopening 2013). Here you'll find Gallo-Roman items, local costumes and furniture. A surviving stretch of the medieval, red-sandstone walls follows the banks of the river Lauter.

When you've explored the town, it's worth visiting the picturesque villages of northern Alsace, including Oberseebach, Hoffen and idyllic Hunspach. The rugged, forested country of the northern Vosges is to the west, with ruined medieval castles such as Fleckenstein.

This imposing fortress towers above the surrounding countryside, and was probably built in the early 12th century. It was ravaged by Louis XIV's troops in 1689, but its ruins are still well worth a detour.
✚ 467 Q4 🚹 9 place de la République, BP 120, 67163 ☎ 03 88 94 10 11 ☯ May–Sep Mon–Sat 9–12.30, 2–6, Sun 2–5.30; Oct–Apr Mon–Sat 10–12, 2–5.30 🚉 Wissembourg ❓ A mini-train tours the town, departing from the tourist office (Jun–Oct daily at 2, 3, 4, 5; Nov–May Fri–Sun at 2, 3, 4, 5)

VERDUN
www.verdun-tourisme.com
The name Verdun seems fated to be forever associated with the Battle of Verdun in World War I, during which hundreds of thousands of troops died in the trenches under German bombardment. The battlefield extends along the river Meuse, either side of this small country town, and a visit is a powerful reminder of the futility of war. Tour buses, with commentary, leave daily from the tourist office between May and the end of September.

The most evocative monuments are on the right bank, in the forest that now covers the scenes of devastation. Among them is Fort Douaumont, captured almost accidentally in February 1916 by a German platoon in the early stages of the long battle. The nearby tall, white Tower of the Dead rises over countless graves.

The Citadelle Souterraine, in avenue du 5ième R.A.P., was used as a command facility by the French during the war. You can tour the underground corridors and see reconstructions of life during the battle (Jun–Aug daily 10–6.30; Apr, May, Sep 10–6; Oct–Dec 10–5; Feb, Mar 10–1, 2–5).

In 1914, French troops heading for the front line would have passed under the arch of the 14th-century Tour Chaussée, on the left bank. The Monument aux Enfants de Verdun war memorial, across the bridge in place de la Nation, depicts one soldier from each of the five armies.

Around 10km (6 miles) northeast of the city, the Mémorial de Verdun museum (early Apr to mid-Nov daily 9–6; mid-Nov to mid-Dec 9–12, 2–6; Feb–early Apr 9–12, 2–6; closed mid-Dec to Jan) stands on the site of Fleury village, which was destroyed in battle.

Aside from its war connections, Verdun has an appealing medieval heart, a Romanesque and Gothic cathedral and pleasant riverside quays ideal for a stroll.
✚ 466 M4 🚹 Maison du Tourisme, place de la Nation, BP 232, 55106 ☎ 03 29 86 14 18 ☯ May–Sep Mon–Sat 8.30–6.30; Mar, Apr, Oct, Nov 9–12, 2–6; Dec–Feb 9–12, 2–5; also Apr–Sep Sun 9.30–5, Jan Sun 10–1 🚉 Verdun

VITTEL
www.vitteltourisme.com
Lorraine is world-famous for its water and Vittel is one of a number of luxurious spa towns in the south of the province. Relaxing is the main aim for most visitors, who soothe body and mind in the Thermes de Vittel spa or stroll and bicycle in the surrounding countryside.

In the heart of Vittel are elegant late 19th-century buildings and grand hôtels from the early 20th century. Charles Garnier, architect of Paris's lavish Opéra Palais Garnier, designed some of the buildings, including the old thermal baths. Here you'll find 'L'Eau et la Vie', a permanent exhibition focusing on the water industry (Mon–Fri 9–12, 2–5).
✚ 467 N6 🚹 Maison du Tourisme, 136 avenue Bouloumié, BP 11, 88801

ABBEVILLE AND LE TOUQUET

This drive explores the area between the rivers Somme and Canche, which includes the marshlands of the Bay of the Somme, the river valleys of the Authie and the Canche, undulating farmland broken by woodland, and the natural forest of Crécy. It follows a route rich in history, from William the Conqueror to World War II, and along the way are churches and abbeys, fortifications, seaports, resorts and villages.

THE DRIVE
Distance: 150km (93 miles)
Allow: 1 day
Start/end at: Abbeville

★ In Abbeville the great 15th-century Cathédrale St-Vulfran, has a Flamboyant Gothic facade. Houses dating from the Middle Ages to the 18th century add character, and just outside town is the miniature Château de Bagatelle.

From the middle of town, follow the D925 towards Eu and Dieppe as far as Cambron (just outside town). Turn right here onto the D3, a pretty, tree-lined road which winds alongside the canalized Somme. At a major roundabout go straight on into St-Valéry-sur-Somme.

❶ The picturesque port of St-Valéry is at the mouth of the river Somme. Fishing boats and yachts still fill the wharfs and fin-de-siècle villas overlook the beaches. The old town, with its narrow streets, is contained within ancient fortified walls.

Return a short way along the D3, and at the roundabout turn left onto the D940. Cross the Somme and follow the road as it curves around the bay. To the right is Noyelles-sur-Mer. At a small roundabout take the third exit, the D144 to Le Crotoy.

❷ Le Crotoy is an old-fashioned fishing village and resort surrounded by acres of salt marsh populated by wild birds and *pré-salé* sheep (grazed on salt marshes). It's renowned for its seafood and its literary and artistic associations.

Leave by the same route, back on the D940, following signs to Rue and Berck. Turn right off the main road to enter Rue.

❸ In the Middle Ages, Rue was a seaport but it now lies well inland. It has the 15th- and 16th-century Chapelle du St-Esprit, a masterpiece of decorative Flamboyant Gothic architecture. Nearby are timber-framed buildings and the massive medieval bell tower.

To the left of the main road you'll see a turning to the Parc Ornithologique du Marquenterre, on the D4.

❹ The Bay of the Somme is one of the best sites in Europe for seabirds and migratory species. A good place to spend a day birding is the Parc Ornithologique du Marquenterre, a huge reserve with a restaurant and places to picnic.

Continue along the D940 to Waben, then turn left towards Berck and Le Touquet, still on the D940. Follow this road past Berck, the Bagatelle Parc d'Attractions and other resorts. At a roundabout take the third exit onto the D144 into Le Touquet.

5 Built by the English as a smart resort at the end of the 19th century, and a famous social venue between the world wars, Le Touquet still has plenty of period charm, with its art nouveau seaside villas, church, covered market and restaurants.

Leave Le Touquet by the N39, cross the Canche and enter Étaples. (Turn left onto the D940 for the military cemetery.) Turn right onto the N39 to follow the Canche towards Montreuil. At the junction with the N1, turn right for Montreuil.

6 Montreuil is an inland, walled, hilltop town, which was a busy port in the Middle Ages. It has winding cobbled streets lined with 17th- and 18th-century houses, fine squares, an old citadel surrounded by ramparts and an abbey church.

From Montreuil, take the D349 Hesdin road along the southern side of the Canche valley and after 10km (6 miles) turn right onto a minor road towards Campagne-lès-Hesdin. Follow this past Campagne to Maintenay on the D130 and the D139. In the village turn right and pass the town hall. Turn left at a roundabout. Cross the river Authie by a mill, then turn left to Valloires.

7 The Abbaye de Valloires stands in a wooded setting in the Authie valley. The 18th-century buildings, in soft-pastel stone, are surrounded by attractive gardens. Founded in the 11th century, the abbey was a burial place for many of the French knights killed at the Battle of Crécy during the Hundred Years War.

From the abbey, follow the river valley on the D192 and the D224 to Argoules, Dominois, Estruval, Ponches-Estruval and Dompierre-sur-Authie. Turn right onto the D111 at Dompierre-sur-Authie towards Crécy-en-Ponthieu. Just before Crécy is the

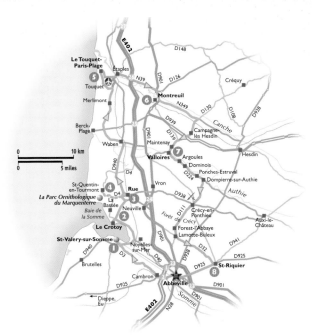

site of the battle. Go straight through Crécy, and then continue through the forest to Forest-l'Abbaye. In Forest-l'Abbaye bear left to Lamotte-Buleux and then turn left onto the D32 towards St-Riquier.

8 On the side of a steep hill, St-Riquier is an attractive small town with a Benedictine abbey at the end of a little square.

Follow the D925 back to Abbeville.

WHERE TO EAT
There are plenty of restaurants and cafés in Le Touquet.

PLACES TO VISIT
PARC ORNITHOLOGIQUE DU MARQUENTERRE
www.baiedelasomme.fr
✉ 80120 St-Quentin-en-Tourmont ☎ 03 22 25 68 99 🕐 Apr–Sep daily 10–5, mid-Feb to May, Oct to mid-Nov 10–4; mid-Nov to mid-Feb 10–3

BAGATELLE PARC D'ATTRACTIONS
www.bagatelle.fr
A theme park with mostly white-knuckle rides.
✉ 62155 Merlimont ☎ 08 26 30 20 30 🕐 Call or check website for latest times

L'ABBAYE DE VALLOIRES
www.abbaye-valloires.com
✉ 80120 Argoules ☎ 03 22 29 62 33 🕐 Guided tours only May–Aug daily 10.30, 11.30, 2.30, 3.30, 4.30, 5.30, less often rest of year

INFORMATION
TOURIST INFORMATION
www.ot-abbeville.fr
✉ 1 place de l'Amiral Courbet, 80100 Abbeville ☎ 03 22 24 27 92

Opposite *Abbaye de Valloires, in the Authie valley*
Below *Cobbles in the Vieux Ville of St-Valéry-sur-Somme*

REGIONS NORTH AND NORTHEAST FRANCE • DRIVE

FORÊT DE GÉRARDMER

Gérardmer, the pearl of the Vosges, has long attracted visitors to the shores of its magnificent lakes—Lac de Longemer, Lac de Retournemer and Lac de Blanchemer—framed by gently domed summits and pine forests crossed by numerous walking paths. This drive takes in a reminder of Charlemagne, an alpine garden, waterfalls, forests and a spectacular view of the highest mountain in the Vosges.

THE DRIVE

Distance: 120km (75 miles)
Allow: 1 day
Start/end at: Gérardmer

★ The lakeside town of Gérardmer, at an altitude of 660m (2,165ft), is in the heart of the massive Parc Naturel Régional des Ballons des Vosges (*ballons* being the rounded summits of the mountain ridge).

From Gérardmer follow the D417 towards Colmar. After only 2km (about a mile) you pass the Hôtel de la Pierre Charlemagne (Chez Dédé) on the right, and a parking area on the left signed La Cercenée, just before the roundabout where the D8 from St-Dié joins the D417. Go all the way round the roundabout and back towards Gérardmer for 25m

(27 yards) before swinging right into La Cercenée parking area (the entrance, at the roundabout end, and the exit, at the Gérardmer end, form a one-way system). Cross the D417 on the pedestrian crossing to find the Saut des Cuves.

❶ A footbridge at the Saut des Cuves gives you great views of the cascading waters through rocks and spruce trees. Children should be watched carefully as there are no safety barriers along the edges of the ravine.

Retrace your steps to the parking area, and follow the green rectangle signs on the GR533 footpath for five minutes to Charlemagne's Stone (the great ninth-century ruler hunted and fished in the area) and on to

the Pont des Fées (10 minutes), an 18th-century bridge spanning the Vologne. The path carries on to the Îles Marie-Louise (15 minutes) and the Gorge des Poitelets (25 minutes). Information panels in the parking area give details of all the walks possible from here, including, for the determined, a 39-hour route to Sarrebourg. Back in your car, at the parking area exit, turn right towards Gérardmer and immediately left alongside the Hôtel de la Pierre Charlemagne onto the C12 Route du Saut des Cuves, towards Xonrupt-Longemer. Pass through the village, joining the D67A in the direction of Longemer.

❷ Lac de Longemer and smaller Lac de Retournemer, farther along the D67, are relics from the Ice Age.

They are surrounded by meadows and forests of fir and spruce trees and are dominated by the Schlucht and Hohneck mountains. There is a large caravan and camper park on the southern shore of Longemer. Just before the Lac de Retournemer comes into sight, a short, steep climb from a path on the left (nearly opposite the well-concealed Retournemer tunnel) up the Roche du Diable offers a panoramic view over the Vologne valley.

At the junction with the D34D, turn left to rejoin the D417 at the Col de la Schlucht, a pass linking the Vosges to nearby Alsace. Turn right off the D417 along the D430 towards the high altitude Jardin d'Altitude du Haut-Chitelet, which contains more than 2,500 plant species from mountain areas around the world (open in high season only). Follow the Route des Crêtes (D430), a strategic road built during World War I to link Le Hohneck and Le Grand Ballon mountains.

❸ Le Hohneck, at 1,362m (4,467ft), is one of the most spectacular sights of this mountain ridge.

Continue along the D430 past the lovely Lac de Blanchemer to Le Markstein, a popular winter sports resort. Here the D430 bears left towards the Lac de la Lauch and Lautenbach, and the starting point of the Lac du Ballon walk (▷ 212–213). After enjoying the two-hour walk, return to Le Markstein to continue the tour along the Route des Crêtes, which now follows the D431 to Le Grand Ballon, the highest mountain in the Vosges.

❹ The view over lakes nestling in valleys, across to the Jura and the Alps, is magnificent on a clear day. Slightly below the summit of the road, the Diables Bleus (Blue Devils) monument indicates that this area saw fierce fighting during World War I. Farther along, Le Vieil Armand was another major battle front, where fighting cost 30,000 lives.

Continue to Cernay, then follow the N66 along the Thur Valley to reach Bussang.

❺ Bussang, one of the highest villages in the Vosges, is famed for the Théâtre du Peuple (People's Theatre), an experiment started in 1895 by Maurice Pottecher. His descendants have upheld the tradition, drawing crowds every summer to the theatre surrounded by forest.

Continue in the same direction on the N66 and at Le Thillot, a former mining area, take the D486 to return to Gérardmer.

WHEN TO GO
This tour can be done at most times of year, although there is likely to be snow and ice on the Route des Crêtes in winter. The route is extremely popular, so expect heavy traffic between April and October.

WHERE TO EAT
There are innumerable picturesque places for a picnic, but finding solitude, even in these vast open spaces, can be difficult. The Route des Crêtes, with excellent views along most of its length, has eateries of all sizes, to suit all wallets, and parking places are generally plentiful.

Opposite *Mist over a forest in the Vosges*
Below *A daffodil in the snow*

LAC DU BALLON

This forest trail, rocky and wild but well marked, leads to a trout-filled lake beneath the summit of Le Grand Ballon, at 1,424m (4,671ft) the highest peak in the Vosges.

THE WALK

Distance: 7km (4 miles)
Allow: 2 hours
Start/end at: approximately 10km
(6 miles) from Le Markstein on the D430

HOW TO GET THERE

This walk is in the Vosges, close to the border with Germany. The directions below describe how to get to the start point by car, driving from Le Markstein, southeast of Gérardmer (▷ 210).

★ From Le Markstein, drive along the D430 towards Lautenbach—the road descends steeply through thickly wooded hills, passing the Lac de la Lauch on the right. After about 8km (5 miles), look for a circular road sign about 500m (550 yards) farther

on the right, showing a white bicycle on a blue background and the words *Lautenbach 6.5km*. Almost concealed behind this sign is a single-track road which doubles back below the D430 for several metres.

As you turn right, two more signs become visible. One reads *La Rolle* and *Lac du Ballon*, the second, with white lettering on a brown background, indicates *Route Forestière Privée de la Rolle*. Follow the minor road uphill for 5–7 minutes, watching for a right-hand bend which reveals an orange cross-country skiing sign on the right, with parking space also on the right. The ski sign indicates *Dauvillers 4.7km* (you'll return by this track). Across the road is a path sign with a red circle on a

white background, and pinned to a tree is a small white rectangle with *64B* in black. Start the walk here, dropping below the level of the road.

❶ In the Vosges, expect to have to climb. The path is marked, although it is best to have a map with you.

Cross a stream soon and follow the arrow and the red-white-red marker pointing to the right, which indicates the way to the Cascades du Seebach and Lac du Ballon. It is uphill all the way to the lake from now on. Clear markers and directional arrows help along a very overgrown path, which could be slippery in wet weather. Continue up, and as you approach the falls, ensure you spot the correct path, which rises steeply in a zigzag on the right. If you find yourself next to the falls, you have missed the path and should retrace your steps to find it. (If you don't, you will face a hazardous climb among wet rocks up the right-hand side of the falls.)

❷ The Cascades du Seebach are a slide of convoluted rocks, with little water in a dry season, but with a restraining metal barrier to stop the foolhardy risking their lives.

As the path continues, there is a wooden walkway which is now rotten. A short distance farther on, however, the log footbridge across the main watercourse is in excellent condition. Carry on along a path up to the right which leads through woods to a few rocks arranged as steps leading up onto a broad forestry road. Turn right where a sign indicates *Lac du Ballon*. Go up this broad forestry road and as you leave the forest there is a splendid view of Grand Ballon and its hotel ahead. Take the next fork left, marked with

a red-white-red sign, which leads to steps up on to the dam wall and the lake, Lac du Ballon.

❸ Lac du Ballon lies in a small glacial hollow surrounded by pine forest. Every now and then, its mirror-like calm is ruffled by leaping trout breaking the surface. As they do so, they shatter the perfect image in the lake's waters of the wooded slopes of Le Grand Ballon looming above. A walk around the lake on the sandy shingle beach takes about 20 minutes.

Cross the dam wall, past a parking area, and turn sharp right, along a road signposted *Mordfeld* and *Lac de la Lauch*. The way is marked with both a red-white-red rectangle and a blue Latin cross on a white background. At the top of a rise, follow the Lac de la Lauch route ahead. At the next clearing, leave the blue-cross sign and double-back to the right, along a ski track marked with an orange sign and signposted

Lac de la Lauch 6km. A stream chatters along beside you in the forest to your left. A short way down this slope, the path turns sharply back on itself to the left. Soon after, the path turns right and crosses the stream. Follow a forestry road gently downhill. At a T-junction, turn right along another forestry road, which leads straight back to the start.

WHEN TO GO
This walk is best tackled between late spring and early autumn, during a dry spell, as it can be fairly muddy and slippery after rain.

WHERE TO EAT
There are no refreshments available en route, so stock up before you go. On hot days make sure you take enough water with you. The shores of Lac du Ballon provide pleasant picnic spots.

Opposite *The Vallée du Lac*
Below *Lac du Ballon*

ASPECTS OF THE SOMME

This walk explores the Somme—its landscape and architecture, and the memorials of World War I. It crosses rolling agricultural plains before descending into the wooded river valley. The field tracks can be muddy in wet weather so wear suitable shoes or walking boots.

THE WALK

Distance: 8km (5 miles)
Allow: 2 hours
Start/end at: Fouilloy, near Corbie

HOW TO GET THERE

Fouilloy is on the Somme, just east of Amiens. Park in the middle of the town square.

★ The small town of Fouilloy is virtually a suburb of Corbie. In the middle is an unusual church built in 1958, which has a facade decorated with Modernist sculptures depicting the life of St. Martin.

Start from place de la République, behind the church. Cross the main road and walk up rue Thiers, opposite the large Capsom concrete granary. Pass the school and at the end of the road turn right. At the main road, the D23, turn left. At the first fork after about 90m (100 yards), bear left, keeping a large garage and truck parking area on the right, and walk up the hill away from the town towards the tower of the Australian National War Memorial.

❶ The tall white tower of the Australian National War Memorial dominates the valley of the Somme for miles. The memorial stands high above the Somme, where the Australians, at great cost, halted the German breakthrough of the spring of 1918. Designed by Sir Edwin Lutyens, the memorial incorporates many of his preferred motifs, such as Classical entrance pavilions and furled flags in cut stone.

The road quickly becomes a track, which leads up the side of the hill to pass well to the left of the tower. Look back for fine views of the Somme valley and Corbie.

❷ A busy town beside the canalized Somme, Corbie is best known for its abbey. This was founded in 657 and housed 300 monks at the time of Charlemagne. It flourished until the Revolution, when much of it was destroyed. What remains of the complex is the 16th-century abbey church, a solid building in the heart of town.

At the first intersection, turn right along a track that runs beside the memorial's boundary fence, and follow this until it meets the road. From the memorial, turn right along the road, the D23 again, and immediately turn left along a track that goes straight across the fields. There are good views back to the memorial and across to the church of Villers-Bretonneux.

Where the track meets a road (the D168e), turn left down the hill to the crossroads and then turn right. Take the first track on the left, clearly visible from the crossroads, and follow this until it meets another track. Turn right. This is something of a dog-leg, but it avoids the road. Keep on this track across the fields, dropping steadily down into the valley. Eventually the track joins the road. Bear left along the road, which is quite busy. Cross the D1 to go straight into Aubigny, taking the pink gravel footpath, passing on the left a small military cemetery holding the remains of mostly Australian soldiers killed in the spring of 1918.

Continue to the middle of the village, where there are public toilets and benches by a bus shelter. Turn right by a large crucifix, along rue de l'Abbaye. This leads down to the canalized Somme. Turn right along the towpath and follow it past the poplars back to Fouilloy. Stay beside the river until the path meets rue Émile Zola. This street is not signed where it meets the footpath, but can be recognized by a white house with a double garage. Turn right immediately before the house, or take the direction Circuit du Bois l'Abbé (20m), marked by a wooden post just before the turning. This leads back into place de la République.

WHERE TO EAT
There are no places to eat en route. The café-bar Le Legend, in place de la République, Fouilloy, serves drinks but no food.

INFORMATION
TOURIST INFORMATION
www.mairie-corbie.fr

✉ 30 place de la République, 80800 Corbie

☎ 03 22 96 95 76

Opposite *Aubigny countryside*
Below *Graves at the Australian Memorial Cemetery at Fouilloy*

CHAMPAGNE

This drive, following the Champagne Route through the Montagne de Reims, takes you to scenic villages where you can learn about the art of champagne-making from local growers and merchants. It takes in a fantastic beech forest and includes a visit to the champagne capital, Reims.

THE DRIVE

Distance: 119km (74 miles)
Allow: Half a day
Start/end at: Reims

The chalky rock on which Reims (▷ 200–201) stands is riddled with miles of caves that provide ideal conditions for the production and storage of champagne. Although it was known as a wine as early as Roman times, it took a 17th-century Benedictine monk, Dom Perignon of Hautvillers, to invent the process that gives champagne its unique sparkle. Cellars in Reims rank among the most impressive of the champagne producers, and you can visit *caves* of such famous names as Veuve-Cliquot, Pommery and Moët & Chandon for tastings.

★ From Reims, follow the D980 southwest and turn left onto the D26 at the turning for Jouy-lès-Reims towards Chamery, a *premier cru* vineyard dominated by a 12th-century church.

❶ This type of scenery is typical of the Montagne de Reims region, a plateau of forests and tidy vineyards planted with Chardonnay, Pinot Noir and Meunier vines. The chalky soil acts as a natural regulator, providing the vines with the required amount of humidity and warmth.

Continue to Rilly-la-Montagne, an attractive town on the edge of the forest.

❷ The church at Rilly-la-Montagne has beautiful 16th-century choir stalls carved with vine motifs. For a spectacular panoramic view over Reims and the surrounding vines, hamlets and Romanesque churches, climb to the top of Mont Joli (274m/900ft).

The D26 then winds along to Mailly-Champagne where, in 1931, 23 vine growers formed a cooperative to counteract the monopoly and power of wine merchants.

❸ Verzenay, farther on, has more than 500ha (1,200 acres) of *premier cru* Pinot Noir grapes. Le Phare de Verzenay lighthouse contains the Musée de la Vigne. Nearby, Mont Sinaï, the highest point of the Montagne de Reims, (283m/928ft), offers another magnificent view over the vineyards.

❹ Farther along, the outskirts of Verzy are noted for the forest of strangely knotted beech trees, known as the Faux de Verzy, some of which are more than 500 years old. Their tangled contortions, once believed to stem from a divine curse, are now attributed to a genetic mutation. The D26 continues through the picturesque village of Ambonnay. Take the D19 to Bouzy, which produces a light red wine, then the D34 to Louvois, where Louis XIV had a château built by his architect J.H. Mansart, with gardens by Le Nôtre. Take the D9 (the second exit at the roundabout) in the direction of Avenay-Val-d'Or. Go right on the D201 to Fontaine-sur-Ay, one of the prettiest villages in the region. Farther along is Ay, a town once surrounded by ramparts. Follow the D1 in the direction of Cumières, and turn right onto the D386 towards Hautvillers, which overlooks the Marne river.

❺ After walking up the steep, narrow streets of the picturesque village of Hautvillers, with its wrought-iron signs illustrated with champagne motifs, you can visit the former Benedictine abbey. This was where Dom Perignon conducted his experiments with double fermentation and wine blending to obtain sparkling champagne. The property now belongs to a champagne house, Moët & Chandon, which has reconstructed the cellar master's workshop.

Return to the D1, which runs along the Marne river to Damery and Châtillon-sur-Marne, the latter dominated by a colossal statue of Urban II, the 11th-century pope

from Champagne who launched the First Crusade to the Holy Land. The Marne also evokes an episode from World War I, when 4,000 troops were driven up to the front in 600 Parisian taxis in 1914 to stop the German advance. From Verneuil, follow the D980 to Reims.

WHERE TO EAT
RESTAURANT DE L'ABBAYE
www.abbayehautvilliers.org
The restaurant of Hautvillers Abbey serves local and regional cuisine and has an open-air terrace.
✉ rue de l'Église, 51160 Hautvillers
☎ 03 26 59 44 79 ⏰ Closed Mon, Tue, Sun dinner; Thu and Fri by reservation only

PLACE TO VISIT
MUSÉE DE LA VIGNE
www.lepharedeverzenay.com
Constructed in 1909 by wine-merchant Joseph Goulet for advertising purposes, the lighthouse now contains a museum of viticulture.
✉ Le Phare de Verzenay, off D26 road
☎ 03 26 07 87 87 ⏰ Tue–Fri 10–5, Sat–Sun 10–5.30 💶 Adult €6, child (6–14) €3

INFORMATION
TOURIST INFORMATION
www.reims-tourisme.com
✉ 2 rue Guillaume de Machault, 51100 Reims ☎ 08 92 70 13 51 ⏰ May–Sep Mon–Sat 9–7, Sun 10–6; Apr, Oct Mon–Sat 9–6, Sun 10–6; Mar Mon–Sat 9–6, Sun 10–1; Nov–Feb Mon–Sat 9–6, Sun 10–12

Left Vineyards growing grapes for champagne, near Épernay, south of Reims
Opposite Countryside in the Montagne de Reims region

AMIENS

AÉROCLUB DE PICARDIE AMIENS MÉTROPOLE

www.aeroclub-picardie-amiens.com

This flying club lets you discover Picardie from small, motorized planes. There are also night flights and aerobatics sessions. Credit cards are not accepted.

✉ Aérodrome d'Amiens-Glisy, route de St-Quentin, 80440 Glisy ☎ 03 22 38 10 70 🕐 Throughout the year depending on the weather and reservations ✋ 30-min flight: varies according to price of fuel

COULEUR CAFÉ

Come to this exotic bar for rum cocktails. There's live music and a DJ (usually Thursday, Friday and Saturday) who plays ethnic and techno music.

✉ 8 rue des Bondes, 80000 Amiens ☎ 03 22 91 40 14 🕐 Tue–Sat 1.30pm–3am, Sun–Mon 2pm–1am

LA LUNE DES PIRATES

www.lalune.net

This rock music venue is usually a springboard for local talent but, on occasion, it also welcomes established musicians.

✉ 17 quai Bélu, 80000 Amiens ☎ 03 22 97 88 01 🕐 8.30pm–1am ✋ €10–€20

LA MÈRE L'OIE

A restaurant that offers various canned delights to take away. Alongside the goose delicacies, such as foie gras, you'll find duck foie gras, duck and cep pâté, and other meaty delights.

✉ 33 quai Belu, 80000 Amiens ☎ 03 22 22 00 00 🕐 Mon–Tue, Thu–Sat 11–3, 6–11, Sun 11–3

BERCK-SUR-MER

CLUB NAUTIQUE BERCKOIS

Choose from a range of sea activities in the beautiful bay of Authie, including motorboats, jet-skiing, waterskiing, wakeboarding, windsurfing and catamaran sailing. You can rent all the equipment you are likely to need including a wetsuit.

✉ chemin aux Raisins, BP 124, 62600 Berck-sur-Mer ☎ 03 21 84 80 53

🕐 Mid-Jun to early Sep daily on reservation; Apr–May, Oct Sat–Sun ✋ Jet-skiing €30 for 15 min

BOULOGNE-SUR-MER

CHAR À VOILE CLUB DE LA CÔTE D'OPALE

www.cvcco.com

Northern France's long, windy and sandy beaches are ideal for sand-yachting (riding a three-wheeled cycle with a sail propelled by the wind). This club offers sand yacht rental and instruction. Credit cards are not accepted.

✉ 272 boulevard Sainte-Beuve, 62200 Boulogne-sur-Mer ☎ 03 21 83 25 48 🕐 Throughout the year depending on reservations ✋ 3-hour session with an instructor, one yacht per person: €41.10

CALAIS

CALAIS VINS

www.calaisvins.com

Fully 1,000 wine vintages line the walls of this shop, plus many English beers, whiskies and ports. Some regional products complete the selection. You can try before you buy.

rue Gutenberg, 62100 Calais ☎ 03 21 36 40 40 ⏰ Mon–Sat 9–7, Sun 10–7

CITÉ EUROPE
www.cite-europe.com
This shopping mall 4km (2.5 miles) from Calais is popular with English shoppers. There's a huge hypermarket, wine merchants, clothes and shoe shops and lots of restaurants for a mid-shop break, selling everything from pizza to *moules frites*.
✉ 1001 boulevard du Kent, 62902 Coquelles ☎ 03 21 46 47 48 ⏰ Mon–Thu 10–8, Fri 10–9, Sat 10–8

LES PIRATES
This bar transports you straight to the sea. Claim a seat on a barrel in the pirate-ship interior, or venture out onto the ship's deck (terrace).
✉ 130 boulevard Jacquard, 62100 Calais ☎ 03 21 97 93 39 ⏰ Mon–Fri 9.30am–1am, Sat–Sun 9.30am–2am

COLMAR
PLANCHA BAR
www.planchabar.com
This is *the* place for cocktails and music. You can also order salads and sandwiches. There are DJs on hand every weekend to play the latest electro sounds.
✉ 5 place de la Cathédrale, 68000 Colmar ☎ 03 89 24 97 23 ⏰ Tue–Sat 10.30am–1.30am, Sun–Mon 4pm–1.30am

JENLAIN
BRASSERIE DUYCK
www.jenlain.fr
Since 1922, this family business has been brewing Jenlain, a beer that has become an emblem of Flanders.
✉ BP6, 59144 Jenlain ☎ 03 27 49 70 03 ⏰ Mon–Fri (shop only) 8–5

LILLE
CHARLES ET CHARLUS
Buy contemporary bags and other leather goods made using traditional methods at Charles et Charlus. You can choose from an extensive variety of gorgeous leathers, available in a wide range of shades.

Opposite *Shops and cafés in Boulogne*

4 rue Basse, 59800 Lille ☎ 03 20 51 01 01 ⏰ Mon–Fri 10.30–1, 2–7; Sat 10.30–7

LE KREMLIN
There's a Russian theme to this bar, including an imposing bust of Lenin. There are around 40 varieties of vodka to choose from.
✉ 51 rue Jean-Jacques Rousseau, 59800 Lille ☎ 03 20 51 85 79 ⏰ Mon–Sat 6pm–2am

MARCHÉ AUX LIVRES
A small market selling books is held inside the courtyard of the old stock exchange building, a marvel of 17th-century Flemish architecture. It's worth stopping here just to admire the surroundings, but the old books are tempting too. Credit cards are not accepted here.
✉ Cloîtres de la Vieille Bourse, 59800 Lille ⏰ Tue–Sun 1–7 🚇 Rihour

MARCHÉ DE WAZEMMES
This market is popular with locals who shop here on their Sunday stroll. Most of the stalls are set around Wazemmes church, but there is also a covered section. It's the place to buy cheap vegetables and some North African products, and there's also a small antiques section.
✉ place de la Nouvelle-Aventure, 59000 Lille ⏰ Sun, Tue and Thu 7–2 🚇 Wazemmes

N DE B HAUTE MODE
This tiny shop on a picturesque street sells unique designs in hats, bags, gloves and hair accessories to discerning but budget-conscious customers. The designs and quality are as good as haute couture, but the prices remain generally affordable. There is also a tailor-made service available.
✉ 6 rue Jean-Jacques Rousseau, 59800 Lille ☎ 03 20 42 19 79 ⏰ Tue 2–7, Wed–Sat 10.30–12, 2–7

MAROILLES
DEFROIDMONT
www.defroidmont.fr
This family has been producing regional foods since 1960 and is famed for its *flamiche au Maroilles*

(made with the cheese named after the village where it is produced). Also look for the *crottin d'Avenois* (nuggets of brioche filled with Maroilles cheese) and *tarte Vergeoise* (soft dough topped with brown sugar).
✉ 159 Grand'Rue, BP 1, 59550 Maroilles ☎ 03 27 84 65 65 ⏰ Mon–Fri 9–12, 2–6, Sat 9–12 (shop), visit by appointment

LES MAZURES
TERRE D'AVENTURES
www.ardennes-terre-aventures.com
Climbing in the high canopy of the Ardennes forest and exploring in the treetops is all part of the fun at this ecological adventure park. The rope ladders and walkways are between 2m and 23m (6ft and 75ft) from the ground. Other activities include renting a Segway (self-balancing vehicle) and exploring an adventure garden for four- to seven-year-olds.
✉ Lac des Vieilles Forges ☎ 03 24 53 18 43 ⏰ Jul–Aug daily 10–7; Sep–Jun times vary 🎫 Adults €22, child (6–14) €14

PLAILLY
PARC ASTÉRIX
www.parcasterix.com
Parc Astérix theme park is based on the characters from the famous cartoon books featuring the Gaulish heroes Astérix and Obélix. There are plenty of rides, shows and attractions. Hotel accommodation is available. Car drivers should take the A1 Paris to Lille autoroute.
✉ A1 Paris–Lille Highway, 60128 Plailly ⏰ Early Apr–Sep, school hols in Oct; mid Dec to early Jan, times vary 🎫 Adult €39, child (3–11) €29, children under 3 free 🚉 Roissy-Pôle

REIMS
LA CARTONNERIE
www.cartonnerie.fr
The city's 21st-century culture 'palace' offers large-scale salons and intimate studios, plus recording and rehearsal facilities. Performances range from shows to concerts in various genres.
✉ 84 rue du Docteur, Lemoine 51100 ☎ 03 26 36 72 40 ⏰ Ticket office: Mon–Sat 2–7

CHAMPAGNE TAITTINGER
www.taittinger.fr
Start with a tour of this impressive champagne cellar. The vaulted basement runs for miles and you can still see the vestiges of a 13th-century chapel. The guided tour includes a tasting session, to help you choose before you buy.
✉ 9 place St-Nicaise, 51100 Reims
☎ 03 26 85 45 35 ⏰ Mar to mid-Nov daily 9.30–1, 2–5.30; mid-Nov to Feb Mon–Fri 9.30–1, 2–5.30 💷 Adult €6

L'ESCALE
L'Escale is a beer-drinker's paradise, with more than 200 kinds of beer available including a dozen on tap. The interior is in the pub style, with a long bar and lots of wood.
✉ 132 rue de Vesle, 51100 Reims
☎ 03 26 88 17 85 ⏰ Mon–Thu 4pm–12.30am, Fri–Sat 4pm–1.30am, Sun 5–9

PATINOIRE BOCQUAINE
www.reims.fr
Get your skates on at this popular ice rink with a light and sound system. The rink also has theme nights and parties such as a 1980s night.
✉ 41 chaussée Bocquaine, 51100 Reims
☎ 03 26 84 07 70 ⏰ Tue–Sat 8.30pm–10.45pm, Wed, Sat–Sun 2.30–5.30, Sun 9.30–12.30 💷 Entry €4, €3.20 under 18, skate rental €2.30

LE TIGRE
This rock music venue is first and foremost a concert hall, but it also has a dance floor.
✉ 2 bis avenue Georges Clemenceau, 51100 Reims ☎ 03 26 82 64 00 ⏰ Daily 5pm–5am 💷 Varies

STRASBOURG
LA LAITERIE
Once a dairy, this building, not far from the Laiterie tram stop, is now home to underground culture, with a bar, an exhibition hall, a theatre, and a main hall with live music from reggae to rock.
✉ 13 rue Hohwald, 67000 Strasbourg
☎ 03 88 23 72 37 ⏰ Tue–Sat 7.30–11.30

MARCHÉ DES PRODUCTEURS
Vegetable growers and other food

FESTIVALS AND EVENTS

JUNE
D-DAY COMMEMORATIONS
All along the D-Day coast beaches there are marches and wreath laying ceremonies. World War II veterans mix with crowds of younger groups who dress the part and drive the carefully kept original vehicles. Enjoy the poignant moments and the fun. 6th June (and the weekend if the date falls on a Thu, Fri or Mon)

SUMMER FÊTES, LILLE
www.lilletourisme.com
There's partying in Grand' Place and free fun in the streets during weekends with National Music Day, Gay Pride and the parade of giants.
☎ 03 59 57 94 00; 0891 56 20 04 (inside France)

JUNE–AUGUST
LES FLÂNERIES MUSICALES D'ÉTÉ, REIMS
www.flanneriesreims.com
Yehudi Menuhin founded this summer season of 100 (mostly free) classical and blues concerts during June, July and August. Many concert-hall legends take part.
☎ 03 26 36 78 00

Opposite *Strasbourg Christmas market*

producers (including some organic) come from all over Alsace to this market. The closest tram stop is Langstross Grand'Rue.
✉ place du Marché-aux-Poissons, 67000 Strasbourg ⏰ Sat 7–1

PÂTISSERIE CONFISERIE KUBLER
www.kubler.fr
A winner of the prestigious confectioners' competition Meilleur Ouvrier de France, Antoine Hepp's delights include Vergers d'Alsace (Alsatian orchards), a cake that contains an apple and cinnamon mousse. Other specials include chocolate-coated gingerbread.

SEPTEMBER
BRADERIE DE LILLE
Bargain-hunters should head for the 24-hour Braderie de Lille on the first weekend of September. Nearly 200km (125 miles) of walkways are covered with bric-a-brac as the entire city sells off its second-hand goods in France's biggest yard sale.
☎ 03 59 57 94 00 (tourist information)

NOVEMBER
AMIENS FILM FESTIVAL
www.filmfestamiens.org
Now into its fourth decade, the festival accepts films from around the world from young film makers, avant-garde directors and little explored themes. Two days during the third week in November.
☎ 03 22 71 35 70

DECEMBER
CHRISTMAS MARKETS, STRASBOURG
www.ot-strasbourg.fr
The city is transformed into a Christmas wonderland of quaint wooden chalets selling home-made toys, gingerbread, gifts and mulled wine, from the Cathedral to the Christmas tree on place Kléber.
☎ 03 88 52 28 28

Take the tram to République.
✉ 29 avenue des Vosges, 67000 Strasbourg ☎ 03 88 35 22 27 ⏰ Oct–Apr Tue–Sat 7–7, Sun 7–6; May–Sep Tue–Sat 7–1

LE TOUQUET
GOLF DU TOUQUET
www.opengolfclub.com/ltq
This is one of the most famous golf clubs in France. There are two 18-hole courses: The first winds through a pine grove; the second has sand hills typical of the region. Facilities include a restaurant and hotel on site.
✉ avenue du Golf, BP 41, 62520 Le Touquet ☎ 03 21 06 28 00 ⏰ Daily 10–6 💷 €48–€92 for a round on the 18-hole course

EATING

PRICES AND SYMBOLS

The restaurants are listed alphabetically (excluding Le, La and Les). The prices given are the average for a two-course lunch (L) and a three-course dinner (D) for one person, without drinks. The wine price is for the least expensive bottle.

For a key to the symbols, ▷ 2.

AIRE-SUR-LA-LYS
HOSTELLERIE DES TROIS MOUSQUETAIRES

www.hostelleriedes3mousquetaires.com
The 'Three Musketeers' is in a 19th-century castle. Expect local rustic dishes such as stuffed pig's trotters in beer sauce and fillet of perch with potatoes and Belgian endive.
✉ Château du Fort de la Redoute, 62120 Aire-sur-la-Lys ☎ 03 21 39 01 11 🕐 Daily 12–2, 7–9. Closed mid-Dec to mid-Jan 🍴 L €30, D €50, Wine €17

AMIENS
LES MARISSONS

www.les-marissons.fr
The seasonal menu has local specials such as eels, either smoked or cooked in aromatic herbs, *pâté de canard en croûte* (duck pâté pie) and *gâteau battu* (a sugared brioche).
✉ Pont de la Dodane, Quartier St-Leu, 80000 Amiens ☎ 03 22 92 96 66

🕐 Mon–Tue, Thu–Fri 12–2, 7–10, Wed, Sat 7–10 🍴 L €25, D €46, Wine €28

ARRAS
LA FAISANDERIE

www.restaurant-la-faisanderie.com
Dine on French cuisine, traditionally prepared with sophistication. Diners can try the cep mousse with oysters followed by sautéed hare.
✉ 45 Grand'Place, 62000, Arras ☎ 03 21 48 20 76 🕐 Tue–Wed, Fri–Sat 12–2, 7–9.30, Thu 7–9.30, Sun 12–2 🍴 L €29.50, D €41, Wine €30

BOULOGNE-SUR-MER
BRASSERIE DE LA MER (AUX PECHEURS D'ETAPLES)

www.auxpecheursdetaples.fr
This huge atrium-style modern restaurant is *the* place for the freshest seafood because it's owned by the fishing cooperative from Étaples. If it's fishy, it's here! Meat eaters will find two options on the menu.
✉ 31 Grand Rue, 62200 Boulogne-sur-Mer ☎ 03 21 30 29 29 🕐 Apr–Oct daily 12–2, 7.30–10; Nov–Mar Mon–Sat 12–2, 7.30–10, Sun 7.30–10 🍴 L €30, D €40, Wine €13

CALAIS
AQUAR'AILE

www.aquaraile.com
Traditional seafood is the theme here.

Dishes on the menu may include shellfish platters and Calais sole served with lobster sauce.
✉ 255 rue Jean Moulin, 62100 Calais ☎ 03 21 34 00 00 🕐 Mon–Sat 12–3, 6.30–10; Sun 12–3 🍴 L €30, D €40, Wine €20

AU CALICE

www.lecalice.com
Dine on *flamiche au Maroille* (a quiche made with local cheese), smoked herrings or home-made cakes. In summer you can eat on the pleasant flower-filled terrace.
✉ 55 boulevard Jacquard, 62100 Calais ☎ 03 21 34 51 78 🕐 May–Sep daily 8am–2am; Oct–Mar Sun–Thu 8am–1am, Fri–Sat 8am–2pm 🍴 L €20, D €30, Wine €15

CHAUMONT-SUR-AIRE
DOMAINE DU MOULIN HAUT

www.moulinhaut.fr
The cuisine here is traditional; duck *magret* (breast) with mushrooms, pigeon flambéed in prune liqueur and scallops flambéed in aquavit. There's even a menu dedicated to the truffle alone.
✉ Route de St-Mihiel, 55260 Chaumont-sur-Aire ☎ 03 29 70 66 46 🕐 Tue–Sat 12–1.30, 7.30–9, Sun 12–1.30. Closed mid-Jan to mid-Feb 🍴 L €38, D €50, Wine €15

Opposite *Restaurants line the riverfront in Amiens*

COLMAR
LA MAISON DES TÊTES
www.la-maison-des-tetes.com
The menu has novel versions of local dishes such as home-made goose foie gras with Riesling, marmalade of apple in a Muscat jelly and basket of warm raspberries with Gewürztraminer zabaglione.

✉ 19 rue des Têtes, 68000 Colmar ☎ 03 89 24 43 43 🕐 Wed–Sat 12–2, 7–9.30, Tue 7–9.30, Sun 12–2. Closed Feb ✋ L €30, D €60, Wine €25

RESTAURANT MEISTERMANN
www.meistermann.com
Restaurant Meistermann's two dining rooms—a brasserie section and a more elegant restaurant—have separate menus featuring seafood, game and Alsatian specials. Also try the Gewürztraminer sorbet.

✉ 2a avenue de la République, 68000 Colmar ☎ 03 89 41 65 64 🕐 Tue–Sat 12–2, 7–9.30, Sun 12–2. Closed 2 weeks mid-Feb ✋ L €25, D €55, Wine €18

COURCELLES-SUR-VESLE
CHÂTEAU DE COURCELLES
www.chateau-de-courcelles.fr
In this splendid château hotel, the restaurant has a well-stocked wine cellar and serves exquisite French cuisine: grilled lobster with celery mousse, roast duck with figs and potato millefeuille.

✉ 02220 Courcelles-sur-Vesle ☎ 03 23 74 13 53 🕐 Daily 12.30–2, 7.30–9.30 ✋ L €50, D €90, Wine €35

ÉPERNAY
LES BERCEAUX
www.lesberceaux.com
Lydie and Patrick preside over this small, typically French *auberge* in the heart of Champagne country. The menu takes inspiration from the surrounding countryside using seasonal produce and, of course, you can enjoy a glass or two of the local champagne.

✉ 13 rue des Berceaux, 51200 Épernay ☎ 03 26 55 28 84 🕐 Wed–Mon 12–2, 7–9.30 ✋ L €30, D €50, Wine €18

LAON
RESTAURANT DE L'HÔTEL LA BANNIÈRE DE FRANCE
www.hoteldelabannieredefrance.com
At this 17th-century building the cuisine includes refined dishes such as poached trout with champagne and veal with morel mushroom cream sauce.

✉ 11 rue Franklin Roosevelt, 02000 Laon ☎ 03 23 23 21 44 🕐 Sun–Tue, Thu–Fri 12–2, 7–9.30, Sat 7–9.30 ✋ L €26, D €43, Wine €16.50

LILLE
À L'HUITRIÈRE
www.huitriere.fr
At this restored 18th-century house, expect classic seafood dishes, such as cod in cream with caviar from Aquitaine, and a well-stocked wine cellar. The restaurant's fish shop has mosaics and stained-glass windows depicting the sea.

✉ 3 rue des Chats Bossus, 59000 Lille ☎ 03 20 55 43 41 🕐 Mon–Sat 12–2.30, 7–9.30, Sun 12–2.30. Closed Aug ✋ L €90, D €180, Wine €25

MARLENHEIM
LE RELAIS DE LA ROUTE DU VIN
www.relais.fr
At this inn, at the gates of the Alsatian wine route, local wines are the perfect accompaniment to the traditional cuisine, which includes foie gras, smoked ham and the ubiquitous sauerkraut.

✉ 1 place du Kaufhaus, 67520 Marlenheim ☎ 03 88 87 50 05 🕐 Tue–Sun 12–2.30, 7–10 ✋ L €25, D €35, Wine €15

NANCY
CUBA FELIZ
This little corner of Cuba serves exotic dishes such as *picadillo* (beef cooked with onion, red pepper, rice and black beans).

✉ 11 rue des Maréchaux, 54000, Nancy ☎ 03 83 37 02 41 🕐 Daily 12–2, 7.30–12 ✋ L €20, D €32, Wine €16

REIMS
LE GRAND CAFÉ
www.le-grandcafe.com
They serve 13 different varieties of mussel—the most exotic infused with saffron. Large bowls of pasta, salads and cakes complete the menu.

✉ 92 place Drouet d'Erlon, 51000 Reims ☎ 03 26 47 61 50 🕐 Daily 11.30am–midnight ✋ L €20, D €30, Wine €15

STRASBOURG
À L'ANCIENNE DOUANE
www.anciennedouane.fr
Discover classic Alsace at its best in this restaurant on the bank of the river Ill. The menu has Alsatian specials—sauerkraut, *flammeküche* (a thin-crust Alsatian pizza) and Gewürztraminer wine.

✉ 6 rue de la Douane, 67000 Strasbourg ☎ 03 88 15 78 78 🕐 Daily 12–2, 7–11 ✋ L €22, D €30, Wine €12

AU CROCODILE
www.au-crocodile.com
Philippe Bohrer has been the personal chef to two Presidents at the Élysée Palace in Paris. He brings his personal touch to the French classics here at the refined Au Crocodile, where the decor and presentation ooze sophistication.

✉ 10 rue de l'Outre-France, 67060 Strasbourg ☎ 03 88 32 13 02 🕐 Tue–Sat 12–1.30, 7.30–9.30. Closed late Jul–early Aug ✋ L €60, D €115, Wine €50

OBERJAEGERHOF
At this 19th-century country house, the three dining rooms all have Alsatian touches; the menu is typically Alsatian with sauerkraut and *flammeküche*.

✉ Route de l'Oberjaegerhof, 67400 Strasbourg ☎ 03 88 39 63 84 🕐 Wed–Sat 12–1.45, 7–9.45, Sun 12–1.45, 7–11 ✋ L €20, D €36, Wine €15

TROYES
RESTAURANT LA MIGNARDISE
www.lamignardise.net
In a picturesque period building with tables also set out in a quiet cobbled courtyard during the summer, La Mignardise serves classic French cuisine using seasonal fresh produce. Take chef Didier Defontaine's suggestions for the dish of the day.

✉ 1 rue des Chats, 10000 Troyes ☎ 03 25 73 15 39 🕐 Mon–Sat 12–2, 7–10, Sun 12–2 ✋ L €40, D €60, Wine €17

REGIONS NORTH AND NORTHEAST FRANCE • EATING

223

PRICES AND SYMBOLS

Prices are the lowest and highest for a double room for one night including breakfast, unless otherwise stated. All the hotels listed accept credit cards unless otherwise stated. Note that rates vary widely throughout the year.

For a key to the symbols, ▷ 2.

COLMAR
HOSTELLERIE LE MARÉCHAL

www.hotel-le-marechal.com
This hotel is at the water's edge in the appropriately named 'Little Venice' district. There are canopied beds in most rooms. Amenities include satellite TV, power showers and whirlpool baths.

✉ place des Six Montagnes Noires, 68000 Colmar ☎ 03 89 41 60 32 💵 €105–€225, excluding breakfast (€15) 🛏 30 (3 non-smoking) 🛂

COMPIÈGNE
HOSTELLERIE DU ROYAL LIEU

www.host-royallieu.com
A 19th-century mansion set in hectares of forest, this hotel makes a comfortable base for exploring the châteaux north of the capital. There's a pretty courtyard restaurant for the summer or a bar with log fires for those chilly evenings.

✉ 9 rue de Senlis, 60200 Compiègne ☎ 03 44 20 10 24 💵 €90–€140 excluding breakfast (€14) 🛏 12 rooms, 3 suites

DOLANCOURT
MOULIN DU LANDION

In the middle of the forest outside Troyes, this converted watermill has more modern rooms than the exterior would suggest. It's a pretty waterside setting with a restaurant on site, and a heated outdoor pool

✉ 5 rue St-Keger, 10200 Dolancourt ☎ 03 25 27 92 17 💵 €65–€99 excluding breakfast (€11) 🛏 16 🌊

ÉPERNAY
LE CLOS RAYMI

www.closraymi-hotel.com
The Clos Raymi is a 19th-century mansion hotel, set in secluded gardens, with an exquisite 1930s art deco interior in shades of, principally, cream and white. The themed bedrooms, with names such as Tuscany, Colonial and Champagne, each have satellite TV and some have queen-size or multiposition beds. Rooms have a shower room or bathroom. Parking is available.

✉ 3 rue Joseph de Venoge, 51200 Épernay ☎ 03 26 51 00 58 💵 €140–€160, excluding breakfast (€14) 🛏 7

GOSNAY
CHARTREUSE DU VAL ST-ESPRIT

www.lachartreuse.com
This 19th-century castle was built on the remains of a 14th-century monastery. Bedrooms are stylish, with intriguing period furniture and moulded ceilings. Four rooms are big enough for families and the superior rooms are vast. There are two tennis courts, parking and a golf course nearby. There's even a helipad.

✉ 1 rue de Fouquières, 62199 Gosnay ☎ 03 21 62 80 00 💵 €140–€310, excluding breakfast (€15) 🛏 53 🍽

ITTERSWILLER

HÔTEL ARNOLD
www.hotel-arnold.com
An Alsatian house among the vineyards, where all the comfortable rooms have TV. The Winstub restaurant is in an old wine cellar. The hotel shop sells gifts and wines from its own vineyards.

✉ 98 route des Vins, 67140 Itterswiller ☎ 03 88 85 50 58 🤚 €85–€114, excluding breakfast (€12) 🛏 30

LILLE

HÔTEL BRUEGHEL
www.hotel-brueghel.com
Named after Flemish painter Pieter Brueghel, the interior pays homage to his style. Bedrooms are tastefully decorated.

✉ 5 parvis St-Maurice, 59000 Lille ☎ 03 20 06 06 69 🤚 €67–€130, excluding breakfast (€8.50) 🛏 66

METZ

HÔTEL DE LA CATHÉDRALE
www.hotelcathedrale-metz.fr
This historic hotel, a 17th-century town house, has welcomed visitors since 1627. The bedrooms all have satellite TV and some have wrought-iron bed frames and beamed ceilings. There is no restaurant.

✉ 25 place de Chambre, 57000 Metz ☎ 03 87 75 00 02 🤚 €75–€110, excluding breakfast (€11) 🛏 20

MONTREUIL-SUR-MER

HÔTEL DE FRANCE
www.hoteldefrance1.com
Victor Hugo wrote *Letter to Adèle* in this 16th-century building. Janie, the owner, lets her imagination run free. Vibrant fabrics, paintings and artificial flowers create a unique interior, alternating between rococo and kitsch. There is a restaurant.

✉ 2 rue Petit Coquempot, 62170 Montreuil-sur-Mer ☎ 03 21 06 05 36 🤚 €85–€120, excluding breakfast (€10) 🛏 15

OBERNAI

À LA COUR D'ALSACE
www.cour-alsace.com
All the spacious, comfortable guest rooms in this former manor house have a minibar, safe and cable TV and there is a spa. Le Caveau de Gail wine tavern and the Jardin des Remparts restaurant (with outdoor seating) serve Alsatian dishes.

✉ 3 rue de Gail, B.P. 64, 67212 Obernai ☎ 03 88 95 07 00 🌂 Closed Jan 🤚 €120–€239, excluding breakfast (€12–€18) 🛏 54 (3 non-smoking)

OSTWALD

CHÂTEAU DE L'ÎLE
www.chateau-ile.com
This hotel, only 5km (3 miles) from Strasbourg, is made up of a 19th-century château and a cluster of half-timbered houses. Bedrooms are lavishly decorated. The restaurant has three dining rooms—one has a carved wooden ceiling.

✉ 4 quai Heydt, 67540 Ostwald ☎ 03 88 66 85 00 🤚 €190–€395, excluding breakfast (€22) 🛏 62 (only 7 are in the château) 🌀 🏊 Indoor 🍴

RIQUEWIHR

HÔTEL DE LA COURONNE
www.hoteldelacouronne.com
At this hotel in a 16th-century house some of the bedrooms retain the original frescoed ceilings, while others have contemporary murals depicting flowers and fruits. There are apartments suitable for families. Parking is available.

✉ 5 rue de la Couronne, 68340 Riquewihr ☎ 03 89 49 03 03 🤚 €56–€115, excluding breakfast (€9) 🛏 40

SAINTE-PREUVE

CHÂTEAU DE BARIVE
www.chateau-de-barive.com
This 19th-century castle, set in vineyards, has bedrooms with period furniture—one also has a Jacuzzi. There's a swimming pool, sauna, tennis court and a golf course nearby. There is a restaurant.

✉ 02350 Sainte-Preuve ☎ 03 23 22 15 15 🌂 Closed Jan 🤚 €140–€235, excluding breakfast (€14) 🛏 13 🏊 Indoor

STRASBOURG

HÔTEL MAISON ROUGE
www.maison-rouge.com
This 3-star hotel set within an imposing curved facade has period furniture such as typically Alsatian Splinder marquetry. Unusually for a large establishment, rooms have a range of decor and furnishings and a safe, minibar and cable TV.

✉ 4 rue des Francs-Bourgeois, 67000 Strasbourg ☎ 03 88 32 08 60 🤚 €106–€189, excluding breakfast (€14.40) 🛏 140 🌀

TURCKHEIM

AUBERGE DU BRAND
www.aubergedubrand.com
The rooms here, named after local vintages such as Riesling and Muscat, have some antique furnishings. There is a restaurant.

✉ 8 Grand'Rue, 68230 Turckheim ☎ 03 89 27 06 10 🤚 €42–€102, excluding breakfast (€9) 🛏 9 (4 non-smoking)

Opposite *Strasbourg is a great place to stay*

Below *The concierge in hotels offers services to guests including reservations and information*

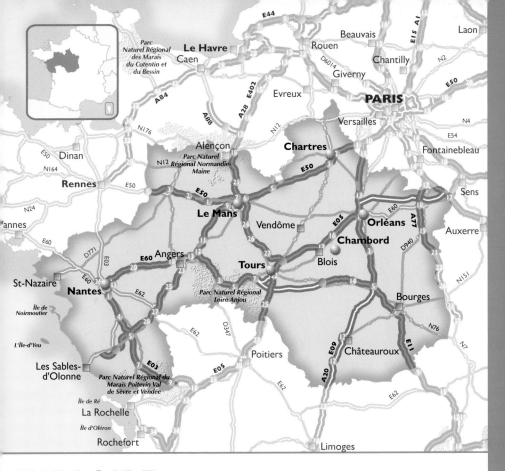

THE LOIRE

The name of France's longest river, the Loire, has become synonymous with the many opulent châteaux that stand on or near its banks; and certainly it is these palatial homes that draw most visitors to the region and keep them enthralled. With their turrets, towers, galleries, richly furnished interiors and immaculate formal gardens, Blois, Chambord, Chenonceaux, Azay-le-Rideau and other stately homes are just as impressive today as when they were built in the 16th and 17th centuries. They all stand close to each other making a tour of them easy.

Châteaux aside, the Loire and its tributary valleys, the Cher, Indre and Vienne, make up a lovely area for travellers to explore. The scenery is often lush and picturesque, and you soon realize why this area has been called 'the garden of France'.

To the west and east of the region, upstream and downstream respectively, are two historic cities, Orléans, one-time capital of France, forever associated with Joan of Arc; and Nantes, a handsome and historic port city. Midway between them is Tours, which is full of timber-framed medieval houses.

If you want to see real castles—built not to dazzle but to be defended—you have only to visit Angers, Chinon or Loches. Then there are churches. Both Chartres and Bourges are renowned for the number and variety of their medieval stained-glass windows.

In addition to its history and culture, the Loire will keep you supplied with dry white wines and entertained with the annual summer 24-hour motor race in the delightful old town of Le Mans.

ABBAYE ROYALE DE FONTEVRAUD

www.abbaye-fontevraud.com
Fontevraud Abbey is the resting place of the Plantagenet king of England Henry II, his queen, Eleanor of Aquitaine and their son Richard I (Richard the Lionheart). Established in the 12th century, the abbey originally housed nuns of the Order of Fontevraud. In 1804 the few buildings that survived the Revolution became a prison. This role ceased in 1965, and since then the abbey has undergone much restoration.

✚ 459 F7 ✉ BP 24, 49590 Fontevraud-l'Abbaye ☎ 02 41 51 73 52 🕐 Jul–Aug daily 9.30–7.30; Apr–Jun, Sep–Oct 9.30–6.30; Nov–Mar 9.30–5.30 ✋ Adult €7 (May–Oct €8.40), under 18 free 🎫 Guided tours (€4) all day 💻

ANGERS

www.angers-tourisme.com
The university town of Angers lies on the banks of the river Maine, in the area known as Black Anjou, after the local rock. The black-and-white striped walls of the Château d'Angers (2 May–4 Sep daily 9.30–6.30; 5 Sep–30 Apr 10–5.30), with its 17 drum towers, shelter a superb 14th-century tapestry series illustrating the Apocalypse of St. John the Divine.

Parts of the château may be closed while the museum is renovated following a fire in 2009. However, the tapestry is still open, and an hourly guided tour in high season (from 10.15am, adult €8, under 18 free) allows visitors to see the gardens, and an exhibition about the repairs.

The early Gothic Cathédrale de St-Maurice is surrounded by old houses, including the 16th-century Maison d'Adam.

✚ 463 F7 ℹ 7 place Kennedy, 49051 ☎ 02 41 23 50 00 🕐 May–Sep Mon 10–7, Tue–Sat 9–7, Sun 10–6; Oct–Apr Mon 2–6, Tue–Sat 10–6, Sun 10–1 🚉 Angers St-Laud

BOURGES

www.bourges-tourisme.com
Prosperous Bourges has a long history of trade and industry. Dominating the skyline is the Cathedral of St-Étienne. Stand in front of its west facade to admire the 15 wide steps leading up to five doorways, flanked by two towers. Inside are stained-glass windows dating from the 12th to the 17th centuries, and a restored astronomical clock.

The Musée des Arts Décoratifs (Jul–Aug Tue–Sat 10–12.30, 1.30–6, Sun 1.30–6; Jan–Mar 10–12, 2–5, Sun 2–5; Apr–Jun, Se–Dec Tue–Sat 10–12, 2–6, Sun 2–6), in a superb Renaissance mansion in rue Bourbonnoux, has a fine collection of art and furniture. The richly decorated Palais Jacques Cœur, in rue Jacques Cœur (Jul–Aug daily 9.30–12.30, 2–6.30; Sep–Apr 9.30–12, 2–5.15; May–Jun 9.30–12, 2–6.15), was built in the 15th century.

✚ 460 J7 ℹ 21 rue Victor Hugo, BP 126, 18000 ☎ 02 48 23 02 60 🕐 Mon–Sat 9–7, Sun 10–6

CHARTRES

▷ 230–231.

CHÂTEAU D'AZAY-LE-RIDEAU

www.monuments-nationaux.fr
This small, graceful Renaissance château was commissioned in 1518 and sits on an island in the river Indre. Highlights include the superb furniture, a portrait gallery, and French and Flemish tapestries from the 16th and 17th centuries.

✚ 459 G7 ✉ 37190 ☎ 02 47 45 42 04 🕐 Jul–Aug daily 9.30–7; Apr–Jun, Sep 9.30–6; Sep–Mar 10–12.30, 2–5.30 ✋ Adult €7.50, under 18 free 📧

CHÂTEAU DE CHAMBORD

▷ 232.

CHÂTEAU DE CHENONCEAU

www.chenonceau.com
One of the most beautiful of the Loire châteaux, Chenonceau enjoys a stunning position, built over the gentle waters of the Cher river.

The history of this elegant château is entwined with that of the several powerful women who were largely responsible for its construction, beginning with Catherine Briçonnet in the early 16th century. Henri II later gave Chenonceau to his mistress, Diane de Poitiers (▷ 35), and she laid out a fine garden and built a bridge from the château over the river Cher. Catherine de Medici, regent after Henri II's death, forced Diane out, then laid out the park, built a two-floor gallery on the bridge, and added the large outbuildings. She bequeathed the château to Louise of Lorraine, her daughter-in-law and wife of Henri III. The days of royal grandeur passed, and in the mid-19th century the château was bought by Madame Pelouze, who made it her life's work to restore it.

Today you can see the richly furnished interiors, including tapestries and some Old Master paintings, as well as the kitchen and wine cellar, where château wines are sold. A wax museum presents 'La Galerie des Dames', with historic scenes featuring the ladies. The gardens and park include a maze, and there is a floral workshop and boutique. You can view the château from the water on boat tour along the Cher, departing from Chisseaux, 2km (1 mile) upstream (La Bélandre: tel 02 47 23 98 64; Apr–Oct).

✚ 459 H7 ✉ 37150 Chenonceau ☎ 02 47 23 90 07 🕐 Jul–Aug 9–8; Jun, Sep 9–7.30; Apr–May 9–7; mid- to end Mar 9.30–7; early Feb to mid-Mar 9.30–6; Oct 9–6.30; early Nov 9–6; early Nov–early Feb 9.30–5 ✋ Adult €10.50, child (7–18) €8 🚉 Chenonceau station is a short walk from the château 🍴 Two restaurants in the outbuildings, open Mar to mid-Nov 📧

Opposite *Cathedral of St-Étienne, Bourges*
Below *Château d'Azay-le-Rideau*

INFORMATION

www.chartres-tourisme.fr
✚ 464 H5 ℹ place de la Cathédrale,
BP 289, 28005 ☎ 02 37 18 26 26
🕐 Apr–Sep Mon–Sat 9–7, Sun
9.30–5.30; Oct–Mar Mon–Sat 9–6, Sun
9.30–5 🚉 Chartres

Cathedral

🕐 Daily 8.30–7.30 🎧 Audioguide: 25
min €3.20, 45 min €4.20, 70 min €6.20

Above *Awesome Chartres cathedral,*
a Gothic masterpiece

INTRODUCTION

By the turn of the first millennium, Chartres was already attracting pilgrims and
in the 11th and 12th centuries it became known across Europe as a centre for
spiritual teaching. A sense of medieval mystery still lingers around the town,
epitomized by the teasing labyrinth laid into the floor of the magnificent Gothic
cathedral of Notre-Dame.

The cathedral's other strength is its formidable collection of stained-glass
windows, which has inspired Chartres to style itself as a sort of world capital
for stained-glass making. The International Stained Glass Centre (Mon–Fri 9.30–
12.30, 1.30–6, Sat 10–12.30, 2.30–6, Sun 2.30–6) in a medieval storehouse can
be visited as can two of the town's eight stained-glass *ateliers* (workshops)—ask
at the tourist information office.

WHAT TO SEE

CATHÉDRALE DE NOTRE-DAME DE CHARTRES

The mismatched spires of Chartres' Gothic cathedral rise above the surrounding
wheatfields of the Beauce plain. Notre-Dame de Chartres was built to house the
Virgin Mary's *sacra camisia* (tunic), a relic donated by Charles the Bald in the late
ninth century. The present cathedral dates from the early 13th century and was
built in only 25 years, after fires destroyed its five predecessors. Miraculously,
Mary's tunic survived, leading to a revival of religious enthusiasm. The lower
half of the facade survived from the earlier church and is pure 11th-century
Romanesque. The right-hand octagonal spire, crowning the south tower is 105m
(345ft) high and dates from the 12th century. The north tower, 115m (377ft) high,
was decapitated by lightning and rebuilt in the early 16th century. The choir, one
of the widest in Europe, is surrounded by a lace-like wall of stone sculpture, with
200 statues.

The 176 stained-glass windows are the glory of Chartres cathedral. Most are
13th-century, although the three set into the wall over the Royal Portal predate
the fire of 1194. They depict (from left to right) the Passion, the Incarnation and
the Tree of Jesse. The three rose windows represent the Apocalypse (south

wall), the Virgin Mary (north) and the Last Judgement (west). Chartres' stained glass has been subject to a cleaning programme since the 1970s and the extra luminosity has made a great deal of the detail more visible than hitherto.

Most of the themes are biblical texts because stained-glass windows were designed, in part, to instruct the illiterate but sometimes they also reveal glimpses of everyday medieval life. In the Prodigal Son window two men are shown gambling over a dice board. Windows were often sponsored and those who paid for them had some say in the subject matter. So, the Redemption window for instance (in the north aisle—on the corner with the transept) was donated by the guild of farriers and shows men shoeing a horse. The St-Chéron window in the ambulatory was given to the cathedral by masons and in it craftsmen are shown cutting and shaping stone.

The creation of a stained-glass window was a complex process involving a team of skilled craftsmen beginning with the glassmakers and culminating with the final expert touches of itinerant painters. Although we do not know the names of the artists who worked on the glass in Chartres, many of them can be identified by their style and technique.

The circular labyrinth on the nave floor is a unique medieval survivor. It may look at first glance like a maze but it was not made to amuse and has no deliberate tricks to it—neither dead ends nor unpredicted changes of direction. Instead, there is one traceable path from the perimeter to the centre where there was originally a copper plate (now missing). Its purpose is unknown and much speculated upon. The only thing certain is that such an elaborate geometric design could have been laid out only with consummate skill and it must have had some important function. The best suggestion is that it forms a symbolic path of pilgrimage (for people unwilling or unable to make a real pilgrimage), which could be followed by a penitent, perhaps shuffling along on his knees.

THE OLD TOWN

If you can drag your eyes away from the cathedral and from all that stained glass, spare time to explore the old district of Chartres, a delightful medieval labyrinth of streets stretching from the upper town around the cathedral to the lower town on the banks of the Eure.

The characteristic street here is the *'tertre'*, a passageway which is usually steep and often stepped. The town's finest house is the early 16th-century Maison du Saumon on place de la Poissionerie, which is adorned with sculptures. The oldest house, dating from the 12th century, is No. 29 rue Chantault. Of Chartres' other churches, the most worth visiting is the Église de St-Pierre on the square of the same name, the 11th- to 13th-century remnant of an abbey which has some remarkable 14th-century stained glass.

TIPS
» You can visit Chartres on a day trip from Paris. By car, take the A10 from the Porte de St-Cloud. Trains run from Gare Montparnasse. The journey should take around an hour.
» Save time for wandering around the town itself, with its river and historic churches.
» Visit in July and August for the Chartres International Organ Festival (▷ 251).

Below *Stained-glass windows in the cathedral*

INFORMATION

www.chambord.org

✛ 464 H7 ✉ Château et Domaine National de Chambord, Maison des Réfractaires, 41250 ☎ 02 54 50 40 00
🕐 Mid-Jul to mid-Aug 9–7.30; Apr to mid-Jul, mid-Aug to Sep 9–6.15; Oct–Mar 9–5.15 💶 €9.50, under 17 and EU nationals under 26 free; free to all first Sun of the month Oct–Mar 🚇 Mer
🚌 Guided tours in English for groups only by reservation, tel 02 54 50 50 40
🎁 Large shop for souvenirs and books

TIPS

» If you have time to visit only one château in the Loire Valley Château de Chambord is an excellent choice.
» There are plenty of picnic areas.

Below *Château de Chambord*

CHÂTEAU DE CHAMBORD

Not only is the monumental Château de Chambord the largest château in the Loire Valley, with 440 rooms, but its parkland is surrounded by the most extensive walled forest in Europe: A 32km (20-mile) wall encloses 5,440ha (13,440 acres).

The Renaissance château fires the imagination with scenes of 16th-century hunting parties, balls and banquets. King François I, who had most of the château built in the 1520s, wanted to divert the river Loire itself to run around it. The architects dissuaded him, diverting a small tributary instead, which caused sufficient flooding to fill the moats. The roof, with its extraordinary roofscape of spires, turrets, dormer windows and chimneys, originally doubled as a viewing terrace from which to observe the start and finish of hunts.

THE INTERIOR

Inside is a famous double-turn spiral staircase, by which people can ascend and descend simultaneously without meeting each other. It is believed to have been designed by Leonardo da Vinci (▷ 35). As if that wasn't enough stairs to climb, there are 14 large and 60 small staircases, although you are not allowed access to all of them. Much of the furniture and furnishings inside the château were destroyed during the Revolution, but some remarkable paintings and tapestries still remain.

Various events take place in the château, park and forest. The château is extremely popular in summer—there can be up to 8,000 visitors a day and sound and light shows run from June to September.

CHÂTEAU DE LUYNES

This château occupies an elevated position overlooking the pretty town of Luynes and offers wonderful views over the Loire Valley. It is 12km (7.5 miles) west of Tours, on the north bank of the Loire. The château has been a private residence since the 17th century and a visit here shows the grandeur in which noble Touraine families have lived. Today, you can see furniture, paintings and tapestries inside, and there are formal gardens to enjoy below the castle walls.

Opposite *A pedalo ride past the riverbank gardens of Montreuil-Bellay*

The château was originally built in the 12th century, and a warm and elegant family residence developed over the centuries. At least two kings of France are known to have been invited here for hunting and banquets. More recently, British royalty—the late Queen Elizabeth (the Queen Mother) and the Prince of Wales—has visited.

One of the lesser-known castles in the region and opened to the public only in recent years, this is a good choice for those seeking to escape the crowds. The 15th-century collegiate chapel in the château grounds is sometimes used for classical music concerts.

➕ 459 G7 ✉ 34 avenue de Clos Mignot, 37230 Luynes ☎ 02 47 55 67 55 ⏰ First weekend in Apr to Sep daily 10–12.30, 2–6 🖐 Adult €9, child (under 15) €4 🏠 Small shop

CHÂTEAU DE MONTGEOFFROY

In beautiful countryside 22km (13.5 miles) east of Angers, the 18th-century Château de Montgeoffroy is a model of proportion, elegance and harmony. The château has remained in the same family since it was built and part of it is privately occupied.

Montgeoffroy was one of the last *grandes demeures* (stately homes) to be built before the French Revolution. Designed by the Parisian architect Nicolas Barré for Maréchal de Contades, governor of Strasbourg, it was built around a chapel and two towers of a former castle. It was completed in 1776 and survived the Revolutionary years.

The interior remains unchanged and some of the furniture, furnishings and paintings are by leading craftsmen and artists of that time. The Louis XVI furniture, wood panels and wall hangings are all original. Guided tours take in some of the most beautiful rooms in the house, the magnificent kitchen and kitchen garden, the saddle room and stables, and the chapel with a stained-glass window dating from the 16th century.

➕ 464 F7 ✉ 49630 Mazé ☎ 02 41 80 60 02 ⏰ Mid-Jun to Aug daily 10–6; Mar to mid-Jun, Sep to mid-Nov daily 10–12, 2.30–6 🖐 Adult €9, child (under 15) €4.60 🚌 Daily guided tours in season

CHÂTEAU DE MONTREUIL-BELLAY

www.chateau-de-montreuil-bellay.fr

The Château de Montreuil-Bellay was built at the beginning of the 11th century by one of the most fearsome of the Anjou counts, Foulques 'the Black'. This large medieval fortress, 17km (10.5 miles) south of Saumur, later withstood attacks by the Plantagenet rulers of England. The pyramid-shaped kitchen still has its cooking utensils.

The château offers wine tastings and you can also buy estate wines.

➕ 459 F7 ✉ 49260 Montreuil-Bellay ☎ 02 41 52 33 06 ⏰ Jul–Aug daily 10–12.30, 1.30–6.30; Apr–Jun, Sep–early Nov Wed–Mon 10–12, 2–6 🖐 Adult €8, child (6–15) €4, (15–17) €6 🚌

CHÂTEAU ROYAL DE BLOIS

www.chateaudeblois.fr

Blois, on the north bank of the river, is the visitor capital of the Loire valley. Its skyline is dominated by the immense structure of the Château Royal de Blois.

The château has a blood-filled history of royal intrigue and an intriguing mix of architectural styles spanning four centuries.

From the 13th century onwards, a succession of buildings was erected around a central courtyard. The most impressive is the elegant François I Italianate wing, with its famous spiral staircase tower. The guided tour includes the royal apartments where, in 1588, Henri III orchestrated the murder of his rival for the throne, the Duc de Guise, and the duke's brother. As you walk round, look for Louis XII's royal emblem, the porcupine, and François I's symbol, the salamander, both used as decorative motifs.

A visit here is good value for money, as your ticket also includes entrance to the Musée des Beaux-Arts, the Gaston d'Orléans wing, St-Calais chapel, the gem-cutter's museum, archaeology rooms, temporary exhibitions and the St-Saturnin churchyard on the other side of the river.

A 45-minute *son et lumière* show takes place every evening in the château courtyard from the end of April to mid-September (in English on Wednesdays).

➕ 464 H7 ✉ place du Château, 41000 Blois ☎ 02 54 90 33 33 ⏰ Jan–Mar daily 9–12.30, 1.30–3.30; Apr–Jun, Oct 9–6; Jul–Aug 9–7; Sep 9–6.30; Nov–Dec 9–12.30, 1–5.30 🖐 Adult €8, child (6–17) €4

CHÂTEAU DE VILLANDRY
www.chateauvillandry.com

Local people say that the best way to appreciate Villandry is to visit at least once during each of the four seasons, and the gardens are indeed stunning all year round. Early in the morning in February, the sculpted yews have an icing-sugar dusting of frost; in April the *jardin d'amour* (garden of love) is filled with tulips; June is the month for roses; and in October, pumpkins grow in the kitchen garden. Anyone not able to make several visits can see photographs of the gardens on the excellent website or take in the slide show in the château.

The gardens are a recreation of a formal Renaissance garden *à la française* (French style). They include a water garden, hedges sculpted into the shapes of a Maltese cross and a Basque country cross, a child-friendly maze, and the Jardin de la Musique. Even the vegetable garden is sculpted to perfection, with the many crosses attesting to the fact that it was once tended by monks.

The château was built in the Italian Renaissance style by Jean le Breton (who also supervised the construction of Chambord, ▷ 232). He razed a 12th-century castle to make way for Villandry. The only part of the older structure that remains is the tower behind the courtyard.

The interior of the château dates from the 18th century and most of the rooms are open to the public. Highlights are works of art by Goya and Velázquez and a beautiful Moorish mosque ceiling. Special events include Les Nuits de Mille Feux (▷ 251), a tulip festival, art and photography exhibitions, and various classical music concerts. The terrace restaurant is good for lunch of coffee. ✚ 464 G7 ✉ 37510 Villandry ☎ 02 47 50 02 09 ⏱ Château: Jul–Aug daily 9–6.30; Apr–Jun, Sep–Oct 9–6; Mar 9–5.30; Feb, 1–11 Nov 9–5; 17–31 Dec 9.30–4.30. Gardens: open until 30 mins after the château ♿ Gardens only: adult €6, child (8–18) €3.50; château and gardens: adult €9, child (8–18) €5, under 8 free ❦ La Doulce Terrasse restaurant and salon de thé ⌂ Gift shop and gardening shop

CHÂTEAU D'USSÉ
www.chateaudusse.fr

The Château d'Ussé is promoted as Sleeping Beauty's castle and is said to have inspired Charles Perrault to write the story after a visit in the 17th century. With its multitude of turrets and spires, set against the wooded background of the Forêt de Chinon, it certainly has the most quintessential fairy-tale appearance of all the Loire châteaux.

One of few châteaux still in private hands and open to the public, it is building a reputation for its annual exhibition of period costumes, which changes as various loaned collections come and go.

Visits to the château are by guided tour only in French, and last around 90 minutes. Written translations of the commentary are available in English and six other languages.

The outside of the château is more captivating than its interior, so you may prefer simply to wander through the formal gardens designed by André Le Nôtre, who also designed the gardens at Versailles (▷ 102–103), rather than take the guided tour of the interior.

The château is compact, but be prepared to climb up and down the many stairs. It is popular with children—those under age 10 in particular will appreciate the *Sleeping Beauty* displays. ✚ 459 G7 ✉ 37420 Rigny-Ussé ☎ 02 47 95 54 05 ⏱ Apr–Aug daily 10–7; mid-Feb to Mar, Sep to mid-Nov 10–6 ♿ Adult €13, child (8–16) €4 ⌂ Gifts

CHÂTEAU DE VALENÇAY
www.chateau-valencay.com

The vast Château de Valençay is a little way off the usual Loire tourist routes, some 45 minutes' drive southwest from Blois.

It was built in the 16th century on the site of a feudal castle and is surrounded by parkland and and woods. The politician Prince Talleyrand purchased the château in 1803, on the orders of Napoleon. The Emperor held Ferdinand VII, King of Spain, prisoner here from 1808 to 1814. The building is a fine example of classic Renaissance style and has impressive roof turrets.

Today, you can enjoy various attractions on site and visit the 100-room, fully furnished interior (with a free 90-minute audioguide) and watch a historical film. Then wander through the formal gardens. There is a small farm, a play area, a picnic area and the largest maze in France, made of wooden panels. At weekends and public holidays from Easter to the beginning of November, and daily during July and August, you can watch actors in period costumes act out various tableaux around the château and the grounds, helping you to imagine former times. ✚ 459 H7 ✉ 36600 Valençay ☎ 02 54 00 15 69 ⏱ Jul–Aug daily 9.30–7; Jun 9–6.30; May, Sep 10–6; mid-Mar to Apr 10.30–6; Oct to mid-Nov 10.30–5.30 ♿ Adult €11, child (7–16) €8, child (4–6) €2.50, under 4 free ☞ Free audioguide (90 min), is available in several languages ☕ Tea room ⌂ Shop, selling various souvenirs

CHINON

www.chinon-valdeloire.com

Chinon, on the north bank of the Vienne river, is overlooked by the ruins of an imposing medieval fortress, the Château de Chinon. In the Middle Ages, the town had various links with England—the castle and surrounding area were popular with the Plantagenet kings and Henry II died here in 1189.

Joan of Arc (▷ 33) met Dauphin Charles in Chinon in 1429, reputedly assuring him of his rightful place as king of France and outlining her plans for the relief of Orléans—under siege by the English. There is a Joan of Arc museum in the Clock Tower (Apr–Sep daily 9–7; Oct–Mar 9.30–5).

Wander around the lovely old town or visit the Musée d'Art et d'Histoire, in rue Haute St-Maurice, with its statues, ceramics and local history exhibits (Jul to mid-Sep Wed–Sun 2.30–6).

For music lovers, the town offers free open-air jazz concerts on Thursdays in June. For wine buffs, the wine museum in rue Voltaire (Apr–Sep daily 10–10) includes a tasting in the entry price. From early July to mid-September, the local wine syndicate offers guided tours (with tastings) of the caves beneath the château (tel 02 47 93 30 44).

✚ 459 G7 ℹ place Hofheim, BP 141, 37501 ☎ 02 47 93 17 85

LE CROISIC

www.tourisme-lecroisic.fr

A fishing port for centuries, the pretty town of Le Croisic still has a working fleet and a renowned fish market. The picturesque huddle of streets in the old town is packed with humble, stone fishermen's cottages. Take a stroll along the quaysides among the trawlermen and yachtsmen who crowd the marina in summer—the atmosphere is busy but friendly.

The main visitor attraction is the Ocearium du Croisic, on avenue de St-Goustan (Jun–Aug daily 10–7; early Apr–Jun daily 10–6; early Feb–early Apr, Sep–late Oct, early Nov to mid-Nov, mid Dec to early Jan 10–12, 2–6; late Oct–early Nov 10–6;

mid-Nov to mid-Dec 2–6; closed last three weeks in Jan and first week in Feb). Walk through the Perspex tunnel in the vast aquarium to see sharks, rays and barracudas. There are also penguins, a coral reef display and a touch pool.

The coast of the Le Croisic peninsula is characterized by rocky inlets with small beaches, but just west of the town, the plage de Saint-Goustan offers good sands.

✚ 462 D7 ℹ place du 18 Juin 1940, 44490 ☎ 02 40 23 00 70 🌐 Jul–Aug Mon–Sat 9–7, Sun 10–5; Jun, Sep 9.30–12, 2–6, Sun 10.30–12, 2–5; Oct–Jun Mon–Sat 9.30–12, 2–6 🚆 Le Croisic

DOUÉ-LA-FONTAINE

www.journeesdelarose.com

The small town of Doué-la-Fontaine, 16km (10 miles) southwest of Saumur, has an abundance of troglodytic sites. You can visit around half a dozen, including the caves at Dénezé-sous-Doué (Apr–Oct Tue–Sun 10.30–1, 2–6.30), where you can admire some remarkable 16th-century sculptures.

The imaginatively run Zoo de Doué (Parc Zoologique), on route de Cholet (summer daily 9–7.30; otherwise varies; closed Nov to early Feb) has more than 500 animals and is a labyrinth of caves, waterfalls and tropical vegetation.

Doué-la-Fontaine has superb public rose gardens and an annual rose exhibition is held in mid-July. At Les Chemins de la Rose (mid-May to mid-Sep daily 9.30–7.30), you can stroll through the Parc de Courcilpleu, on route de Cholet, discover the history of roses in France and get advice on how to grow roses (mid-May to mid-Sep daily 9.30–7 and last two weekends in Sep).

✚ 459 F7 ℹ 30 place des Fontaines, 49700 ☎ 02 41 59 20 49

LOCHES

www.loches-tourainecotesud.com

Loches lies on the banks of the Indre river, 42km (26 miles) southeast of Tours and surrounded by the Indre-et-Loire countryside. The major sight is the medieval fortress, with

its dungeons and torture chambers, (Apr–Sep daily 9–7; Oct–Mar 9.30–5). There are also video reconstructions and computer animations depicting the keep in the 11th century.

The Logis Royal de Loches (Royal Residence) on place Charles VII contains the tomb of his mistress, Agnès Sorel, the Gothic chapel of Anne of Brittany, and Flemish tapestries (Apr–Sep daily 9–7; Oct–Mar 9.30–5). Walk around the exterior ramparts to appreciate the fortified camp as a whole.

The family home of landscape artist Emmanuel Lansyer (1835–93), on rue Lansyer, is now a museum exhibiting more than 100 of his works, (Jun–Sep Wed–Mon 10–12, 2–6; Apr, May, Oct Wed–Fri 2–5, Sat–Sun 10–12, 2–5).

✚ 459 G7 ℹ place de la Marne, BP 112, 37600 ☎ 02 47 91 82 82

Opposite *An aerial view of the Château d'Ussé*

Below *Rabelais Festival Weekend in the hillside town of Chinon*

INFORMATION

www.ville-lemans.fr

www.lemanstourisme.com

✚ 464 G6 🛈 Hôtel des Ursulines, rue de l'Étoile, 72000 ☎ 02 43 28 17 22 🕐 Jul–Aug Mon–Sat 9–6, Sun 10–12.30, 2–5; Sep–Jun Mon–Fri 9–6, Sat 9–12, 2–6, Sun 10–12 🚉 Le Mans
🎫 Guided tours are available; contact the tourist office for details

LE MANS

Motor-racing enthusiasts will love Le Musée des 24 Heures, in rue de Laigné, near the main entrance to the racetrack (Jun–Aug daily 10–7; Mar–May, Sep–Dec Wed–Sun 10–7. Closed Jan–Feb). Around 150 vehicles are on display, including motorcycles, historic racing cars including 11 that were previous winners of the 24-hour race. You can also see an art gallery, working models, and video-screen depictions of the evolution of motorized transportation.

As well as the famous 24-hour race, the 24-Hour Circuit hosts motorcycle races, a 24-hour truck race, and other trials during the year (tel 02 43 40 24 24 for race dates; tel 02 43 40 24 75 or 0892 69 72 24 or you can visit the website www.lemans.org for ticket reservations).

OLD TOWN

Le Mans' old town is within the walls of the original Roman fortress, built in AD280. The cobbled streets are packed with tastefully restored medieval timber-framed houses, which are now filled with bijoux restaurants, top-class boutiques and art galleries.

The Musée de la Reine Bérangère, covering local history, ethnography and ceramics, is in a beautiful building classed as a Historic Monument, in rue de la Reine Bérangère (Jun–Sep Tue–Sun 10–12.30, 2–6; Oct–May Tue–Sun 2–6). It is named after Queen Berangeria, wife of Richard the Lionheart, who lived nearby at the beginning of the 13th century. The St-Julien cathedral in place St-Michel (May–Sep daily 8–7; Oct–Apr 8–12, 2–7), dating from 1134, has some very early stained glass and a rose window that is almost as beautiful as the one in Chartres (▷ 230–231).

Steps to the right of the Mairie lead to the heart of the town. Here, in narrow lanes dating from Roman times, there are bakeries, restaurants and small boutiques catering for workers in the surrounding streets.

Below *Place St-Michel in the old town of Le Mans*

NANTES

Once described as the Venice of the West because of its waterways, Nantes was the historic capital of Brittany during the city's golden age in the 15th century. The town grew rich through shipbuilding and commerce and by 1704 it was the busiest port in France.

CASTLE AND CATHEDRAL

Dominating the upper (old) town is the Château des Ducs de Bretagne. This was home to the Dukes of Brittany during the reign of François II and his daughter Anne. Henri IV's Edict of Nantes, giving freedom of worship to the Huguenots, was signed here in 1598 and is now the pre-eminent artefact in the Musée d'Histoire de Nantes (Jul–Aug daily 10–7; Sep–Jun Tue–Sun 10–6), which is housed in 32 rooms in the castle. In the cathedral (daily 8.30–6.30), don't miss the beautiful Renaissance tomb of François II and Marguerite de Foix.

OTHER HIGHLIGHTS

West of the cathedral, at 10 rue Georges Clemenceau, is the Musée des Beaux-Arts, in an exceptional neoclassical building (Wed–Mon 10–6, Thu 10–8). There are rich 15th- and 16th-century collections, and the 20th-century gallery includes works by Monet, Kandinsky and Picasso.

Surrounding the heart of the old town are 18th- and 19th-century districts. Streets of fine houses are best viewed around place Graslin, where the Théâtre Graslin is one of the major performing arts venues in the city. The Musée Dobrée, on rue Voltaire, is in a palace designed by Viollet-le-Duc and has an eclectic range of items including medieval ivories, illuminated manuscripts and a gold casket said to contain the heart of Anne of Brittany (Tue–Fri 1.30–5.30, Sat–Sun 2.30–5.30).

Other sights worth visiting include the Jardin des Plantes, at the north end of rue Clemenceau, established as a botanical garden as early as 1688; Île Feydeau—for its architecture—with 18th-century mansions decorated with wrought-iron balconies; and the Musée Jules-Verne, at 3 rue de l'Hermitage, dedicated to the science-fiction author born in Nantes in 1828.

The Passage Pommeraye is a three-floor, glass-roofed arcade with wonderful neoclassical features and statuary, constructed in the early 1840s. Running between rue Santeuil and rue de la Fosse, the arcade was designated an historic monument in 1976.

INFORMATION

www.nantes-tourisme.com
✚ 458 E7 ℹ 3 cours Olivier de Clisson, 44000 ☎ 08 92 46 40 44 🕐 Mon–Sat 10–6 (Thu 10.30–6) 🚉 Nantes
🚌 Guided tours available, contact the tourist office for details 🚢 There are pleasure cruises on the Loire during the summer months

TIPS

»» Nantes tourist office sells Le Pass Touristique, which gives free entry to museums, parks, river-boat rides and public transportation, and reduced prices for zoos, cinemas and sporting activities. One-day pass: €18; two-day pass: €28; three-day pass: €36.
»» You can rent bicycles from outside the train station and at several other locations around the city.

Above *An equestrian statue of Joan of Arc in Nantes*

INFORMATION

www.ville-orleans.fr

✚ 465 H6 ℹ 2 place de l'Etape, 45040
☎ 02 38 24 05 05 🕐 Jul–Aug Mon–Sat
9–7, Sun 10–1, 2–5; Apr–Jun Mon
10–1, 2–5.30, Tue–Sat 10–1, 2–6; Mar
Mon–Fri 10–1, 2–5.30, Sat 10–1, 2–6; Sep
Mon–Sat 9.30–1, 2–6; Oct–Feb Mon–Sat
10–1, 2–5 🚆 Orléans

TIPS

» The best time to visit Orléans is at the
end of April and beginning of May, just
as the weather is getting warmer and
before the full flood of visitors arrive. You
can also enjoy the Joan of Arc festival
(7–8 May).

» Parking in town can be tricky. Electronic
signs tell you which parking areas still
have spaces.

» The Tourist Office sells Pass Châteaux
de la Loire offering reduced entry into
several châteaux west along the river.

ORLÉANS

Joan of Arc recaptured Orléans from the English in 1429 after an eight-month
siege, and the city is now strongly associated with her name. But even before
this, Orléans was the site of decisive battles. From the early days, when the city
stopped the hordes of Attila, through the Wars of Religion and the Revolution,
and finally during World War II, Orléans suffered much destruction. Its focus is
now on industry, but it is also a lively university city.

FOLLOWING IN THE FOOTSTEPS OF A SAINT

References to Joan of Arc abound in Orléans—in road names, house names,
statues and museums. You can visit the heroine's house, the Maison Jeanne
d'Arc, in place du Général de Gaulle, which is now a museum dedicated to her
life (May–Oct Tue–Sun 10–12.30, 1.30–6; Nov–Apr Tue–Sun 1.30–6). The annual
festival celebrating Joan of Arc's lifting of the siege takes place on 7–8 May, with
a medieval market, a folklore parade, concerts and fireworks.

Stained-glass windows in the dramatic Cathédrale Sainte-Croix tell the story of
St. Joan. The cathedral, overlooking the river Loire, took more than 600 years to
build and has some fine carved panels (May–Sep daily 9.15–6; Oct–Apr 9.15–12,
2–6). For more about Joan of Arc, ▷ 33.

ART AND ARCHITECTURE

Orléans was badly damaged during World War II, so many of its buildings are
relatively new. But there are still plenty of examples of impressive Renaissance
architecture and half-timbered buildings. In the Renaissance Hôtel Groslot, on
place de l'Étape (Jul–Sep Sun–Fri 9–7, Sat 5–9; Oct–Jun Sun–Fri 10–12, 2–6,
Sat 4.30–6.30), the sumptuous interior includes several remarkable pieces of
furniture. The Musée des Beaux-Arts (Tue–Sun 10–6), at 1 rue Fernand Rabier,
is also worth a visit.

PARK LIFE

To the south of the city is the Parc Floral de la Source (tel 02 38 49 30 00; Apr–
Sep daily 10–7; Oct–Mar varies). There are many attractions designed to appeal
to children here, including an outdoor play area, an animal park and a small train.

Above *The nave of Cathédrale Sainte-Croix*
Opposite *Cobbled rue Briconnet in Tours*

TOURS

This thriving city has a lively old town and excellent shopping facilities. The middle of Tours is sandwiched between the Loire and Cher rivers, with the oldest area between Pont Napoléon and Pont Wilson. Here, in the narrow pedestrian-only lanes, are several beautifully preserved timber-framed medieval buildings.

SHOPPING

Rue des Halles and rue Nationale are very popular for high-class shopping, while rue Colbert is lined with antiques shops, small restaurants and art galleries. There is a flower market on Wednesday and Saturday on the central island of boulevard Béranger. On Tuesday morning, there is a street market on boulevard Heurteloup, farther east.

ART AND ARCHITECTURE

St-Gatien cathedral, on rue Colbert, has magnificent stained-glass windows dating from the 13th to 15th centuries and, on the north side, the Psalette Cloister featuring three galleries and a remarkable spiral staircase. Next to the cathedral is the popular Musée des Beaux-Arts (Wed–Mon 9–6).

In the splendid former Archbishop's Palace, its exhibits include works by Mantegna, Rubens and Rembrandt. Spare a look for the massive 200-year-old, 30m (100ft) cedar of Lebanon in the front courtyard. Its trunk has a circumference of 7.5m (25ft). In an outbuilding opposite the main entrance you can see Fritz, a stuffed elephant who died in Tours in 1902.

INFORMATION

www.ligeris.com

✚ 464 G7 🛈 78/82 rue Bernard Palissy, BP 4201, 37042 Tours Cedex 1 ☎ 02 47 70 37 37 🕔 May–Sep Mon–Sat 8.30–7, Sun 10–12.30, 2.30–5; Oct–Apr Mon–Sat 9–12.30, 1.30–6, Sun 10–1 🚌 Tours
🚶 Guided tours: Apr–Oct; contact tourist office for details

TIP

›› Parking in the middle of town can be a problem. If you approach from the north, there are large parking areas along the south bank of the river (between the four major bridges from the northern suburbs). Alternatively, park north of the river and walk across one of the bridges.

LANGEAIS

This short walk is a pleasant tour of Langeais and the valley of the river Roumer. The route follows minor roads, tracks and footpaths and the going is easy, although there is some gentle hill-climbing.

THE WALK

Distance: 2.5km (1.5 miles)
Allow: 1 hour
Start/end at: Château de Langeais

HOW TO GET THERE

Langeais is a compact town on the north bank of the Loire, about 22km (13.5 miles) west of Tours on the N152. Langeais is best approached from the south, across the huge Gothic-style suspension bridge which was partly destroyed by a mine in 1940. It is illuminated at night.

★ Start from the Château de Langeais. The château, right in the heart of town, has a rather severe appearance and, unusually for a Loire château, was built in just four years, at the end of the 15th century. It was constructed on the site of an earlier fortress (the ruined keep is one of the oldest in France) and is where Charles VIII of France and Anne of Brittany were married in 1491.

Cross the river Roumer and walk up rue Charles VIII to the church. Pass the church and climb a flight of steps. At the top, turn right and after 50m (55 yards) turn left up another flight, the Chemin du Paradis. At the top, carry straight on into the park, and turn left in the middle. There is no clear path—just head across the grass among the trees to the park's western perimeter. Turn left and walk down towards the cemetery.

At the cemetery gates, turn right along the road. At the crossroads, go straight on along a lane marked ominously Mortvousêtes ('You are dead'), which runs along the side of a hill.

❶ Along this lane there are troglodyte houses and pleasant views over the river valley, with its allotments and gardens and the church of St-Laurent.

Follow the lane as it drops down to the D57. Cross the main road, the D57, and follow a lane, the Chemin de la Raguenière, that runs parallel to the Roumer. At the first intersection, turn left along a sandy track. Cross the river and continue to the stone bridge. Turn left at the bridge along a lane and then take the first right, la Cueille aux Prêtres. This climbs steeply uphill towards the woods, running beside the stone wall that marks the boundary of the château park. Continue to the top, past a radio mast on the right, where there is an intersection backed by a screen of pine woods. Turn left and follow the path as it winds down through the woods, taking care not to slip if it is wet.

❷ At the next intersection, there is a short detour to the right, down a steep path between stone walls. Here there is a fine view of the suspension bridge and the Loire.

The main path carries straight on, with more views of the Loire through the trees, and then ends at the top of some steps. Turn right down these, and then follow the path as it winds down among the troglodyte houses to join the main road, rue Anne de Bretagne. Turn left to return to the Château de Langeais.

WHEN TO GO

This walk can be done at any time of year. Autumn is good for the vibrant hue of the trees, but be careful of wet leaves, which may make the paths slippery.

WHERE TO EAT

There are places to eat and drink in Langeais. The walk is not long, but consider taking a drink with you, particularly if it is hot.

PLACE TO VISIT
CHÂTEAU DE LANGEAIS

www.château-de-langeais.com
✉ Fondation Jacques Siegfried, 37130
☎ 02 47 96 72 60 🕐 Jul, Aug daily 9–7; Apr–Jun, Sep to mid-Nov 9.30–6.30; Feb, Mar 9.30–5.30; mid-Nov–Jan 10–5
✋ Adult €8.20, 18–25 €7, child (10–17) €5

INFORMATION
TOURIST INFORMATION

www.tourisme-langeais.com

Below *The Château de Langeais was defended by three drum towers*
Opposite *The castle dominates Langeais*

VALLEY OF THE LOIR

The Loir is one of the least known yet most attractive of the Loire's tributaries. It winds its way through woods and quiet, undulating farmland, overlooked by ruined castles and picturesque towns and villages famous for their troglodyte houses carved out of the rocky cliffs. Leaving the Loir valley, with its close associations with the 16th-century poet Pierre Ronsard, the tour also explores the rich arable plains of the Gâtine Vendômois.

THE DRIVE

Distance: 112km (70 miles)
Allow: 1 day
Start/end at: Vendôme

Renowned for good food and wine, Vendôme is a delightful town, spread over the several branches of the Loir river. Its streets have bridges, attractive vistas and old buildings, and high on a hill is the huge ruined Château de Vendôme.

★ Start the tour at a small roundabout on the north bank of the northernmost branch of the Loir, on the D957. With the river on your left, follow signs for Le Mans and Montoire. Follow the D957 along the river's north bank at first, then continue along the D5 as it swings away west towards Villiers-sur-Loir.

❶ Surrounded by fields and vineyards, Villiers is a pleasant little village whose main attraction is the nearby Château de Rochambeau.

Continue to Le Gué-du-Loir, which is surrounded by flooded grassland and poplars. Then bear left on the D24 towards les Roches-l'Évêque, famous for its troglodyte houses. Carry on to Montoire-sur-le-Loir.

❷ The elegant town of Montoire-sur-le-Loir is full of decorative white stone buildings. The large central square leads to the river, which follows a flowery route, overlooked by the ruins of the medieval château. The Chapelle St-Gilles has remarkable wall paintings. It is locked, so ask for the key at the Mairie or at the Café de la Paix.

From Montoire, take the road west from the main square towards the château. Cross the river, turn left and drive through the woods of the Loir's south bank to Lavardin.

❸ Surrounded by woods, Lavardin is a classic medieval village, complete with winding streets of old houses, a Romanesque church with wall paintings and the spectacular ruins of a château. Just below the western edge of the church, by an entrance to the castle ruins, is a small parking area. A board here indicates a choice of three waymarked walk routes around Lavardin.

Leaving Lavardin, cross the river and return to Montoire along the more open north bank. Continue on this road, the D108, straight through

❼ The remote village of St-Laurent-en-Gâtines is known for its church, which was formerly a huge 15th-century manor, brick-built in a commanding style. Unless you arrive during a service, you won't be able to see inside.

Continue along the D766 to reach Château-Renault.

❽ On a promontory overlooking the confluence of the Brenne and the Gault, Château-Renault is a pleasant town with a ruined medieval castle, riverside mills and shops.

Leaving Château-Renault, cross the railway and turn right along the main N10, which leads you straight back to Vendôme by heading across the Gâtine Vendômois.

WHEN TO GO
This tour can be done at any time of year, although during rainy periods there may be localized flooding along the Loir valley, and in low season the sights are likely to be closed. May and June are good months to go, when Vendôme is at its loveliest, with flowers and shrubs along the banks of the river.

WHERE TO EAT
There are plenty of restaurants in the towns and villages en route.

PLACES TO VISIT
CHÂTEAU DE PONCÉ
✉ 72340 Poncé-sur-le-Loir ☎ 02 43 44 66 52 🕐 Call for latest information ✋ Adult €6.50, child (12–17) €3.50

MANOIR DE LA POSSONNIÈRE
✉ 41800 Couture-sur-Loir ☎ 02 54 72 40 05 🕐 Mid-Jun to mid-Sep Wed–Mon 10–1, 2.30–7; Apr to mid-Jun, mid-Sep to Oct Thu–Sun 2–6. Closed Nov–Mar ✋ Guided visit: adult €6, child (12–18) €4.50; garden only €4

Montoire, and follow the D917 to Trôo.

❹ Trôo is really two villages, the first a pleasant riverside settlement and the second something more extraordinary, on hills to the north. Here you'll find an old castle mound with good views over the Loir valley, a Romanesque church, the remains of fortifications and gateways and ancient stone houses. Linking the two villages is a precipitous staircase down the cliff and a mass of narrow, rocky passages connecting the houses of one of France's greatest troglodyte settlements.

The road up to the old hill town is clearly signposted soon after leaving Trôo's newer riverside quarter. From Trôo follow the same road, the D917, through Sougé, and at Pont-de-Braye proceed on the D305 towards Poncé-sur-le-Loir.

❺ Poncé-sur-le-Loir has a richly decorated Renaissance château with formal gardens. Between the railway and the river, an old paper mill houses potters and glass-blowers.

Return along the same road for 1.5km (1 mile), then turn right to cross the railway and the river on the D57 towards Couture-sur-Loir. This lovely stretch of road is flanked by steep, wooded hills.

❻ Couture-sur-Loir is a pleasant farming village of quiet streets and old houses. A short detour outside town takes you to La Possonnière, an intimate Renaissance manor house in a pretty garden. It is the birthplace of the 16th-century poet Pierre Ronsard.

Leave Couture on the D10 and go through Artins. A short while after Artins, turn right at a crossroads onto the D8 towards Ternay. Look for Ternay's unusual church that, with its detached tower, sits in a flower-filled garden. Continue on the D8 to le Berloquet and then at an intersection turn right on the D116 to les Hermites. Follow this road and the D47 to la Ferrière. In the village turn right, then follow signs to St-Laurent-en-Gâtines. At the intersection with the main road, turn left onto the D766, with St-Laurent's extraordinary church already in sight.

Opposite Castle ruins at Vendôme

CHÂTEAUX OF THE LOIRE

To visit the châteaux of the Loire is to take a step back in time to past centuries of French aristocratic life. No other stretch of river has so many noble residences—there are more than 120 fairy-tale castles and mansions along Loire's banks. This tour takes in three of the Loire's most famous châteaux (Chenonceau, Cheverny and Chambord) and passes many others en route.

THE DRIVE
Distance: 128km (80 miles)
Allow: 1 day
Start/end at: Bléré

★ The Loire, the longest river in France, flows lazily for 1,020km (630 miles) from its source in the Massif Central to the Atlantic at St-Nazaire. The drive starts from Bléré, just over 20km (12 miles) east of Tours.

From Bléré follow signs to La Croix-en-Touraine, Civray-de-Touraine and Chenonceaux. Cross the Cher and turn right in Civray-de-Touraine on the D40 to the Château de Chenonceau.

❶ Château de Chenonceau (▷ 229) is the Loire's most photographed castle. Author Gustave Flaubert said it 'floats on air and water', because of its magnificent gallery which spans the river.

Continue on the D40 along the Cher valley, passing Chissay-en-Touraine, with its late Renaissance château, now a hotel, and the crumbling medieval keep at Montrichard. From here, turn left onto the D764 in the direction of Pontlevoy. Go as far as Sambin, then fork right onto the D52 past the Château de Fougères-sur-Bièvre.

❷ Château de Fougères-sur-Bièvre is a small, fortified castle and a marvellous example of medieval architecture softened by a Renaissance gallery.

Continue on through vineyards, following signs to Cheverny, one of the Loire's finest châteaux, in magnificent grounds.

❸ Cheverny has an elaborately decorated interior with Flemish tapestries and Old Master paintings. From April to November you can see the grounds either by boat or by electric car (golfing-cart style).

From here follow signs to Chambord. Cross the D765, joining the D102 to Bracieux. Turn left onto the D120/D112 through the dense Forêt de Boulogne straight to Chambord.

❹ Chambord (▷ 232) is the largest of all the châteaux, with pinnacles, spires, domes and chimneys piercing the skyline.

Now head for Blois taking the D33 and D956.

❺ The Château Royal de Blois (▷ 233) is famous for its unusual architecture and its tales of love and intrigue.

From Blois, the N152 on the north bank of the Loire leads to Amboise, past turreted Chaumont on the south bank.

❻ Set in a spacious park planted with more than 100-year-old cedars, Chaumont is a very pretty château where Catherine de Medici lived

briefly after the death of Henri II. Have a look at the stables where the troughs are made of porcelain! From mid-June to mid-October, the château hosts an international garden festival, which has a different theme each year. The festival takes place in 25 separate gardens of the château's estate.

At Amboise, cross the river to the old town and château, one of the most visited in the Loire.

❼ Amboise has one of the truly royal châteaux of the Loire, with an interesting and blood-soaked history. Though still offering plenty to see, the castle has been much diminished over the centuries: It was abandoned by royalty after the blood-letting of the Amboise Conspiracy of 1560, and large parts were dismantled after the Revolution due to lack of funds. In the early 16th century, François I invited Leonardo da Vinci to live at Amboise; he spent the last four years of his life there (▷ 35). A museum displays models constructed from Leonardo's designs.

Take the D31 through the Forêt d'Amboise and return to Bléré.

WHEN TO GO
This route is very popular, and the major châteaux receive incredible numbers of visitors. If possible, avoid the busy tourist season of July and August, and public holidays and weekends the rest of the year. To avoid the crowds, you could choose to visit the less well-known châteaux rather than Chenonceau, Cheverny and Chambord.

Aim to arrive at any of the big châteaux half an hour before the morning opening time, at midday (if the château does not close) when many French visitors will be sitting down for lunch, or late afternoon.

WHERE TO EAT
BONNE ÉTAPE
✉ 962 quai des Violettes, 37400 Amboise
☎ 02 47 57 08 09 ⏰ Lunch and dinner

Tue–Sat and lunch Sun. Closed last 2 weeks in Dec, first week in Jan

PLACES TO VISIT
CHÂTEAU DE FOUGÈRES-SUR-BIÈVRE
www.monuments-nationaux.fr
✉ 41120 Fougères-sur-Bièvre ☎ 02 54 20 27 18 ⏰ Early May to mid-Sep daily 9.30–12.30, 2–6.30; mid-Sep to early May Wed–Mon 10–12.30, 2–5 ✋ Adult €5, under 18 and EU national under 26 free

CHÂTEAU DE CHEVERNY
www.chateau-cheverny.fr
✉ 41700 Cheverny ☎ 02 54 79 96 29 ⏰ Jul–Aug daily 9.15–6.45; Apr–Oct 9.45–5.30; Sep–Jun 9.45–5 ✋ Château and park: adult €7.50, child (7–14) €3.60, under 7 free

CHÂTEAU DE CHAUMONT
www.domaine-chaumont.fr
✉ 41150 Chaumont-sur-Loire ☎ 02 54 20 99 22 ⏰ Jul–Aug 10–7; Apr–Jun, Sep 10–6.30; Oct–early Nov 10–6; early Nov–Mar 10–5. Garden Festival: daily 10–8 (last entry at 7). ✋ Combined ticket for château and gardens: adult €15, child (12–17) €11, child (6-11) €5.50, under 6 free

CHÂTEAU D'AMBOISE
www.chateau-amboise.com
✉ 37403 Amboise ☎ 02 47 57 00 98 ⏰ Jul–Aug daily 9–7; Apr–Jun 9–6.30; Sep–Oct 9–6; Mar, 1–15 Nov 9–5.30; Feb 9–12.30, 1.30–5; 16 Nov–Jan 9–12.30, 2–4.45 ✋ Adult €9.70, child (7–14) €6.30

Opposite Gardens at the Château de Chenonceau
Below The river Loire at Blois

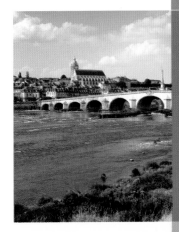

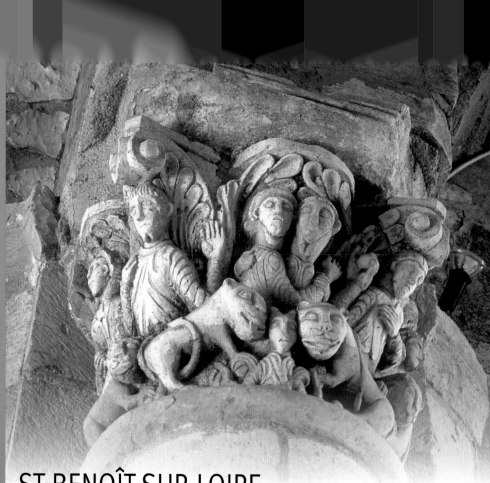

ST-BENOÎT-SUR-LOIRE

The abbey church of St-Benoît-sur-Loire is one of the most famous Romanesque buildings in France and the final resting place of St. Benedict, regarded as the father of Western monasticism. The walk takes you to a 19th-century river port, passing through flat, riverside farmland with raised 15th-century flood-protection banks. You'll also see the porch where locals used to exchange village gossip.

THE WALK

Distance: 9km (5.5 miles)
Allow: 3 hours
Start/end at: The basilica in St-Benoît-sur-Loire

HOW TO GET THERE

St-Benoît-sur-Loire is on the north bank of the river Loire, 40km (25 miles) southeast of Orléans.

★ This walk starts from the superb abbey church of St-Benoît-sur-Loire. The massive basilica, which dominates the village of the same name and the surrounding countryside, is all that remains of the Benedictine abbey of Fleury, founded in AD651.

Village life revolves around the abbey church, its services, work and religious celebrations. Six times a day the basilica is filled with the sound of Gregorian chant and prayers dedicated to St. Benedict. Between services, the monks offer guided tours of their magnificent church, with its simple, solid design, built between 1004 and 1218.

From the abbey take the chemin du Port past Hôtel du Labrador, and follow a small sign marking a bicycle path to Sully. Cross a tiny bridge onto a gravel path and turn left, then walk across open farmland until you reach a cluster of buildings (a hamlet) called the Hameau du Port.

❶ Attractive Hameau du Port, site of the Port of St-Benoît, was a landing place for river boatmen who lived in the small cottages, which date mainly from the early 19th century.

Turn right, then take the first left along the waterfront. High water levels are etched on walls and cottages, recording the years in the early to mid-1800s when severe floods had a devastating impact. Turn left just before the entrance to a campsite, along a path through woodland beside a wooden hut. After a few minutes, the trees clear at a crossing in the path above the farm. Turn right along a raised path, following the river to your right, with flat farmland to your left.

2 Such raised banks *(levées),* are common along the Loire. This one was built during the 15th century to prevent flooding.

After about 2km (just over a mile) you reach several buildings on the left-hand side. Turn left, past some farm buildings, onto the chemin de la Levée. Turn right at the T-junction, past lovely old stone buildings, and left at the next intersection back towards the abbey. Turn left again at the metal cross, proceeding across more farmland until the next crossroads. Turn right and return to St-Benoît. Cross a small bridge and take the first left into tree-shaded place du Grand Arcis, with the village

school. Cut diagonally across the small square. Rue Jean de Fleury leads to the main square.

3 At the corner of the main square is a *caquetoir* (from *caqueter*, to gossip). Parishioners gathered at this covered porch to exchange news.

Cross the main square diagonally, turning right down rue Max Jacob, and head across another small bridge. Turn immediately left down a path alongside a small *fossé* (ditch).

4 The *fossé* is bright with green weed. You will pass neat vegetable allotments and rows of private gardens, each accessed by a tiny wrought-iron bridge.

Continue along the *fossé* past a retirement home on the right. The path swings to the left and returns to the main road. Turn left towards

the heart of the village, then take the second right down the tree-lined avenue de l'Abbaye to the basilica.

WHEN TO GO
This walk can be done at any time of year. Even in mid-winter the riverscapes and views are beautiful.

WHERE TO EAT
GRAND ST-BENOÎT
✉ 7 place St-André, 45730 St-Benoît-sur-Loire ☎ 02 38 35 11 92 **$** Tue–Fri 12–2, 7.30–9, Sat 7.30–9, Sun 12–2. Closed 22 Dec–21 Jan

INFORMATION
TOURIST INFORMATION
www.tourisme-loire-foret.com

Above left *Archways in the Abbaye de St-Benoît-sur-Loire*
Above *Abbaye de St-Benoît-sur-Loire*
Opposite *Sculptured capitals in the Benedictine Abbaye de Fleury*

ANGERS

GAUMONT ANGERS MULTIPLEXE

www.gaumont.fr

This large multiplex cinema in the St-Serge district, near the university, offers first-run films, of which at least half are in English.

✉ avenue des Droits de l'Homme, 49100 Angers ☎ 0892 696 696 (premium rate) 🕐 Films start from 2pm 🖐 Adult €10.10, child (under 18) €8

AZAY-LE-RIDEAU

COOPERATIVE DE LA VANNERIE

www.vannerie.com

This is a cooperative of local artisans who produce a variety of goods, from small baskets to large outdoor benches.

✉ 1 rue de la Cheneillère, 37190 Villaines-les-Roches ☎ 02 47 45 43 03 🕐 Apr to mid-Oct Mon–Sat 9–12.30, 2–7, Sun 10–12, 2–7; Mar, mid-Oct to Nov Mon–Sat 9–12.30, 2–7, Sun 2–7; Dec–Feb Mon–Sat 9–12.30, 2–6, Sun 2–7

TOURAINE JUS DE POMMES

www.tourainejusdepommes.fr

Monsieur Robert and his staff transform the apples from their varied orchards into delicious fresh fruit juices, and brew barley from the fields into a fabulous small-batch beer. You can enjoy samples here (near the middle of the village), then

buy larger quantities in the boutique if you're impressed.

✉ Z.A. la Loge, 37190 Azay-le-Rideau ☎ 02 47 45 98 98 🕐 Mon–Fri 8.30–12.30, 2–5

BLOIS

AIR MAGIC LOIRE VALLEY

www.air-magic.com

Float into the clouds in a hot-air balloon for a breathtaking 60- or 90-minute adventure over the Loire Valley. Take-off points vary, but choices for flights include the vineyards of Amboise, Villandry or Azay-le-Rideau.

✉ 2 rue de Dionval, 28130 Saint-Piat ☎ 02 37 32 38 06 🕐 Flights all year 🖐 Starting from €130 per person

ANTEBELLUM

This antique jewellery shop in the rue St-Martin and rue du Commerce shopping area is worth a special visit for its superb selection of pieces from different periods. Browse the range of precious and semi-precious stones and fine gold and silver work.

✉ 12 rue St-Lubin, 41000 Blois ☎ 02 54 78 38 78 🕐 Tue–Sat 10–12, 2–7

AU PARADIS DES ENFANTS

For something out of the ordinary for children (and their parents), this shop offers both modern and antique toys of every possible make and kind. It is

a great stop for a birthday or just an en-route diversion.

✉ 24 rue Poite Chartraine, 41000 Blois ☎ 02 54 19 88 86 🕐 Tue–Sat 9.30–12, 2.30–7

TAPISSERIE LANGLOIS

www.langlois-blois.com

Anyone inspired by the tapestries seen in the Loire châteaux can pick up a historically accurate copy here. You'll find tapestries from many of the area's most famous châteaux with prices from €180 to €3,000 depending on the size and the amount of detail. They also do cushions, chairs, footstools and rugs, as well as kits to complete at home.

✉ 1 rue de la Voûte du Château, 41000 Blois ☎ 02 54 78 04 43 🕐 Mon–Sat 9–12, 2–7, Sun 10–12, 3–6

BOURGES

MAISON DE LA CULTURE

www.mcbourges.com

In this modern facility staging dance, classical music concerts and theatre, children's shows are on the bill during summer.

✉ place André Malraux, 18005 Bourges ☎ 02 48 67 74 74 🕐 Shows usually start at 7.30pm Mon–Sat. Closed mid-Jul to mid-Aug 🖐 Adult from €28

Above *Cycling near the Château de Chambord*

CHEVERNY
CHEVERNY GIFT SHOP
There are many château gift shops in the Loire Valley, but this is possibly the best of all. Two large showrooms have all of the usual souvenirs, as well as art, comic books, suits of armour, beautiful collectable swords and fine glassware.

✉ 41700 Cour-Cheverny ☎ 02 54 79 96 29 🕐 Jul–Aug daily 9.15–6.45; Apr–Jun, Sep–Oct 9.45–5.30; Nov–Mar 9.45–5

CHINON
ANTIQUAIRES/BROCANTEURS
Touraine is an area with rich pickings for antiques aficionados. Visit the tourist information centre in Chinon and ask for the leaflet *Antiquaires Brocanteurs et Métiers d'Art*. It lists the best of the dealers in the area, details what they specialize in, and plots the location of their shops on a map.

CHATEAU DE LA GRILLE
www.chateau-da-la-grille.com
This historic Chinon winery château, built in the 14th century and renovated in the 1740s, offers tastings of its rich red and fruitier rose wines.

✉ route des Huismes, 37500 Chinon ☎ 02 47 93 01 95 🕐 Tue–Sat 9–12, 2–6

CHOLET
CYBERPUB DU CADRAN
www.lecadran.net
Here you will find an eclectic mix of cybercafé, dance club and restaurant (offering everything from espresso to Tex-Mex cooking and Cuban mixed drinks), with theme nights and a lively atmosphere.

✉ 8 boulevard Gustave Richard, 49300 Cholet ☎ 02 41 62 26 50 🕐 Mon–Sat 4pm–2am 🖐 Cover charge some theme nights

GIEN
MUSÉE DE LA FAÏENCERIE
www.gien.com
There's a long tradition of *faïence* (glazed earthenware) in the village of Gien, with a style noted for its midnight-blue glaze and golden highlights. You can see examples at this museum, tour the factory (by prior arrangement), then buy your own piece in the shop.

✉ 78 place de la Victoire, 45500 Gien ☎ 02 38 05 21 05 (shop) 🕐 Shop: Mon–Sat 9–12, 2–6

GUERANDE
TERRE DE SEL
www.terredesel.com
Guerande is famed throughout France for the sea salt that's panned around the town. Terre de Sel offers tours of the salt flats as well as birding sessions. After a tour, visit the exhibition centre, with displays and art shows, The shop also sells prettily packaged salt grains and *fleur de sel* (salt petals) for gifts and kitchen decoration—or of course to add to food.

✉ route des Marais Salants, Pradel, 44350 Guerande ☎ 02 40 62 08 80 🕐 Jul–Aug daily 10–8; Jun, Sep 10–6; Apr–May 10–12.30, 2–6; Oct–Mar 10–12.30, 2–5

LE MANS
LA PÉNICHE EXCELSIOR
This is a unique venue south of the city heart on an old barge moored to a quay on the river Sarthe. There are events almost daily, from dances to concerts.

✉ rue de La Raterie, 72700 Allones ☎ 02 43 88 34 25 🕐 Varies according to event 🖐 €10

LE ST-FLACEAU
This bar has a terrace perched on the old Roman town wall, or you can claim a comfortable armchair in the 18th-century parquet-floored apartment, and enjoy a reasonably priced drink from the huge range on offer.

✉ 9 rue St-Flaceau, 72000 Le Mans ☎ 02 43 23 24 93 🕐 Mon–Thu 5pm–1am, Fri–Sat 5pm–2am

NANTES
BRIC-A-BRAC
If you want to bargain-hunt, head for rue Jean Jaurès, where antiques and bric-a-brac shops vie for your custom and art galleries display unrecognized masterpieces. Place Viarme is where the artists and craftsmen have their workshops, and the flea market is held here every Saturday.

☎ 02 72 64 04 79 (tourist information) 🕐 Shop opening hours vary

GAUTIER-DEBOTTÉ
www.gautier-debotte.com
This firm of confectioners is part of the heritage of Nantes—in fact, the shop is a listed national treasure. Try the 'Muscadet Nantais', a chocolate filled with a white grape that has been marinated in alcohol.

✉ 9 rue de la Fosse ☎ 02 40 48 23 19 🕐 Tue–Sat 9–7.15

LE LIEU UNIQUE
www.lelieuunique.com
This cutting-edge and ususual theatre on canal St-Félix offers all kinds of productions, from Shakespeare classics (performed at least once a year in English) to modern plays. There is a bar and restaurant open for a pre- or post-show drink or for a meal.

✉ quai Ferdinand Favre, 44013 Nantes ☎ 02 40 12 14 34 (ticket office) 🕐 Open all year 🖐 Adult from €12

RUE CREBILLON/ PASSAGE POMMERAYE
Rue Crebillon is Nantes's main shopping street, and window-shopping at the top-range stores is a popular activity. The nearby boutiques that crowd passage Pommeraye, built in 1843, are on three levels, linked together by wooden stairs, with ornate wrought-iron balconies topped by statues in a classical style.

✉ 44000 Nantes

ORLÉANS
ALAIN BESNARD
Come here if you are interested in 19th-century decorative arts. Items on offer range from small ornaments for the mantelpiece or side table to large paintings. There's also a fine range of 17th- and 18th-century furniture and art, although most pieces are probably too large to take home with you. The staff are particularly helpful.

✉ 92 rue Bannier, 45000 Orléans ☎ 02 38 53 18 02 🕐 Tue–Sat 10–12, 2–7

MARCHÉ D'ORLÉANS

This open market is known across France as one of the best in the region. The appeal lies in its bustling settings; it rotates, with a different small area of the city transformed into a village square on market day.
☻ Blossière Tue 7–12; Dauphine Tue 7–12; Munster Wed 7–12; place Dunois Thu 3–7.30; Charpenterie quai du Roi Sat 6–12.30

G. MARTIN POURET

www.martin-pouret.com
Wine vinegar has been made here by the traditional Orléans method since 1797, and it is one of the only places in the region where this is still done. The result is unique vinegar that adds a special touch to any recipe. Learn about the process and buy some in the shop.
✉ 236 Faubourg-Bannier, 45400 Fleury-les-Aubrais ☎ 02 38 88 78 49 ☻ Mon–Fri 8–12, 2–5.30

LES MUSARDISES

Jacques Desbois is the proprietor of this house devoted to blending the arts of pastry chef and chocolatier. Try the aptly named *paradis*, a blend of *crème d'orange* and a delicate chocolate mousse on meringue.
✉ 38 rue de la République, 45000 Orléans ☎ 02 38 53 30 98 ☻ Tue–Sat 8–7.30, Sun 8–12.30

PAXTON'S HEAD

Paxton's Head is a jazz club with an English pub feel and is one of the best venues for touring jazz.

✉ 264 rue de Bourgogne, 45000 Orléans ☎ 02 38 81 23 29 ☻ Daily 3pm–3am ✋ Free

ZÉNITH

www.orleans-gestion.fr/zenith/
A sleek tower of glass, the Zénith is Orléans's venue for most large cultural activities. There are pop concerts from rap to rock, as well as shows for children.
✉ 1 rue du Président Robert Schuman, 45074 Orléans ☎ 02 38 25 04 29
☻ Concerts 7.30pm, shows for children in the afternoon ✋ €40–€90

PORT ST-PÈRE
PLANÈTE SAUVAGE

www.planetesauvage.com
Planète Sauvage is one of the best safari parks in France, with more than 10km (6 miles) of roads winding through 13 separate environments. The safari village offers activities, food, drink and shopping, and there's also a serpent house here. From the D65, take the D11 in the direction of St-Mars de Coutaism and then follow the signs.
✉ 44710 Port St-Père ☎ 02 40 04 82 82 ☻ Mid-Jul to Aug daily 9.30–8; Apr to mid-Jul, Sep daily 10–7; Oct to mid-Nov daily 10–6. Closed mid-Nov to Mar ✋ Adult €19, child (4–14) €13

ST-BARTHÉLEMY-D'ANJOU
LA DISTILLERIE COINTREAU

Visit the home of the liqueur that flavours many mixed drinks. In the on-site museum, the knowledgeable staff can help you learn about the distillation process and will let you sample before you buy at this distillery just east of Angers.
✉ Carrefour Molière, boulevard des Bretonnières, 49124 St-Barthélemy-d'Anjou ☎ 02 41 31 50 50 ☻ Daily 🡒 Guided tour (in English) by appointment

TOURS
CENTRE CHORÉGRAPHIQUE NATIONAL DE TOURS

www.ccntours.com
Here Bernardo Montet directs his company in a wide range of dance. The emphasis is on modern dance, but you can sometimes see a ballet performance here.
✉ 47 rue du Sergent Leclerc, 37000 Tours ☎ 02 47 36 46 00 ☻ Check the schedule for performance times ✋ €9–€14

CENTRE MUNICIPAL DES SPORTS

This is a large leisure complex with a sports hall, two swimming pools (one of which is Olympic-sized) and an ice rink. Credit cards are not accepted.
✉ 1 boulevard Lattre de Tassigny, 37000 Tours ☎ 02 47 70 86 86; swimming pool: 02 47 70 86 20 ☻ Varies, based on holiday schedule; call for details ✋ Swimming session €2.70

LE CORSAIRE

Come aboard this central bar with an amusing nautical theme. The owners pride themselves on offering more than 400 cocktails, to be enjoyed amid the portholes and hanging lanterns.
✉ 187 avenue de Grammont, Tours 37000 ☎ 02 47 05 20 00 ☻ Mon–Sat 6.30pm–4am

MARCHÉ

Although the market, in the heart of the city, is lively at all times, Sundays are busiest. The *charcuterie* is particularly good, with a bewildering selection of fresh meats and dozens of types of sausages. The hand-crafted goods are well made.
✉ place des Halles, 37000 Tours ☻ Daily 7–2

Left *Passage Pommeraye in Nantes is lined with tempting boutiques*

MARCHÉ AUX PUCES

For those in search of value for money, the open-air flea market at place de la Victoire is the market of choice. Be prepared to have to hunt for bargains, and it's a case of 'buyer beware', especially when negotiating in a language that's not your own. Small portable souvenirs include period postcards and photos, linens, and vintage clothing.

✉ place de la Victoire, 37000 Tours
🕐 Wed, Sat 7–5

PHILIPPE BRUNEAU

A rare and beautiful collection of antique gilded wood and bronze pieces—most notably from the 17th and 18th centuries—is on offer in this quaint shop in central Tours. There's also an excellent selection of period clocks and watches.

✉ 62 rue de la Scellerie, 37000 Tours
☎ 02 47 05 25 87 🕐 Call for an appointment

LE PYMS

www.lepyms.com

This club attracts a crowd ranging from young to youthful, in a lively quarter of Tours. There are two halls, each with a different ambience. The up-to-the-minute music makes it a regional draw, and it's usually packed. Thursday is student night.

✉ 170 avenue de Grammont, Tours 37000 ☎ 02 47 66 22 22 🕐 Wed–Sun 10.30pm–4am

RUE DE BORDEAUX/ RUE NATIONALE

The largest concentration of major shops and department stores in the region stretches from the dignified 19th-century train station towards rue Nationale. On rue Nationale towards the river there are expensive boutiques and many small chain stores. Not all of the shops accept credit cards.

✉ 37000 Tours

TOURS AERO CLUB

www.toursaeroclub.fr

Take an introductory or guided flight over the Loire Valley in a training plane. Flights leave from the Tours-

MAY–SEPTEMBER
CINÉSCÉNIE

www.puydufou.com

A sound and light show lasting nearly two hours, with pyrotechnics and lasers, dancers, 50 mounted knights and a château backdrop, make this well worth a summer visit. Reservations are recommended.

✉ Château du Puy du Fou, 44190 Clisson
☎ 02 51 64 11 11 🕐 Jun–Jul Fri–Sat 10.30pm; Aug to mid-Sep Fri–Sat 10pm
✋ 1 day park and Cinescene adult €43, child (5–13) €25.50

JUNE
LE MANS 24-HOUR RACE

▷ 437.
🕐 Mid-Jun

ORLÉANS JAZZ

Features performances daily of every jazz style in venues around the city.
✉ Orléans ☎ 02 38 24 05 05 🕐 Two weeks in late Jun ✋ €24 (some concerts free)

JULY
ILLUMINATIONS AT VILLANDRY (LES NUITS DES MILLE FEUX)

www.châteauvillandry.com

For two days in early July, 2,000

Val de Loire Airport on the N152, just outside Tours.

✉ Aéroport Tours Val de Loire, 37100 Tours ☎ 02 47 51 25 68 🕐 Open all year
✋ €135 for first flight

VEIGNÉ
VAL D'INDRE CANOË-KAYAK

www.veigne.canoe.free.fr

Explore the quiet river Indre by kayak. Take a short course or a tour with a guide, or rent a kayak and go on your own. All guided trips are led by certified instructors.

✉ Moulin de Veigné-Mairie, 37250 Veigné
☎ 02 47 73 13 19 🕐 Jul–Aug daily; Apr–Jun Sat, Sun ✋ Kayak rental from €6.50 per hour

candles illuminate the gardens of the Château de Villandry (▷ 234) from sunset, and the evening finishes with a magnificent firework display (▷ shop entry on this page and also page 234).

✉ Château de Villandry, 37510 Villandry
☎ 02 47 50 02 09 ✋ Gardens €5.50

JULY–AUGUST
CHARTRES INTERNATIONAL ORGAN FESTIVAL

www.ville-chartres.fr
http://orgues.chartres.free.fr

Throughout the summer enjoy great organ music at one of France's finest cathedrals, Notre-Dame de Chartres (▷ 230–231), famous for its mismatched spires.

✉ place de la Cathédrale, 28005 Chartres
☎ 02 37 18 26 26

NOVEMBER
THREE CONTINENTS FESTIVAL

www.3continents.com

Forget Hollywood-sur-Med at the Cannes Film Festival in May. This film festival highlights the work of directors from Asia, Latin America and Africa and ticket prices are inexpensive.

✉ Nantes ☎ 02 40 69 74 14
🕐 Late Nov

VILLANDRY
CHÂTEAU DE VILLANDRY GIFT STORE

This gift store reflects the château (▷ 234) in specializing in garden products. Shelves are stocked with a variety of seeds, solidly crafted garden tools and books about the garden itself, with some in English. The store occasionally closes at lunchtime, so call in advance to check. Villandry is 10km (6 miles) from Tours on the D7 and it is clearly signed.

✉ Château de Villandry, 37510 Villandry
☎ 02 47 50 02 09 🕐 May to mid-Sep daily 9–7.30; Mar–Apr and mid-Sep to mid-Oct 9–7; mid-Oct to Feb 9–5.30

PRICES AND SYMBOLS

The restaurants are listed alphabetically (excluding Le, La and Les). The prices given are the average for a two-course lunch (L) and a three-course dinner (D) for one person, without drinks. The wine price is for the least expensive bottle.

For a key to the symbols, ▷ 2.

AMBOISE

BONNE ÉTAPE

This is a reasonably priced choice. The fish dishes served with regional sauces are particularly good. Children are made to feel welcome and their special menu costs €9.

✉ 962 quai des Violettes, 37400 Amboise ☎ 02 47 57 08 09 ⏰ Tue–Sat 12–1.45, 7.30–8.45, Sun 12–1.4. Closed last two weeks in Dec and first week in Jan
✋ L €15, D €40, Wine €15

BLOIS

AU BOUCHON LYONNAIS

www.aubouchonlyonnais.com
This good-value restaurant, headed by chef Frédéric Savy, offers a menu of regional French dishes including monkfish in pepper sauce and salmon in a paste of balsamic vinegar and roasted nuts. There is a good dessert and ice cream menu.

✉ 25 rue des Violettes, 41000 Blois ☎ 02 54 74 12 87 ⏰ Mon 7–10, Tue–Sat 12–2, 7–10 ✋ L €23, D €30, Wine €12.90

AU RENDEZ-VOUS DES PÊCHEURS

www.rendezvousdespecheurs.com
Serving fish and seafood, this restaurant's specials include crayfish flan with parsley and various lobster dishes. The children's menu is €14. Reserve ahead.

✉ 27 rue du Foix, 41000 Blois ☎ 02 54 74 67 48 ⏰ Mon 7.15–9.15, Tue–Sat 12–1.30, 7.15–9.15. Closed first 3 weeks of Aug, and Feb ✋ L €30, D €76, Wine €21

BOURGES

ABBAYE ST-AMBROIX

www.abbayesaintambroix.fr
A former chapel serving the likes of oysters and mackerel with lightly saffroned aubergine (eggplant). For dessert, try the soft chocolate wafers or ice cream made with almond milk.

✉ 60 avenue Jean Jaurès, 18000 Bourges ☎ 02 48 70 80 00 ⏰ Daily 12–1.30, 7.30–9.30 ✋ L €49, D €85, Wine €24

BOURBONNOUX

The menu of traditional dishes, designed by chef Jean-Michel Huard, is excellent value for money. Lunch might be a cucumber mint gazpacho to start, followed by a fish dish.

✉ 44 rue Bourbonnoux, 18000 Bourges ☎ 02 48 24 14 76 ⏰ Mon–Thu 12.15–1.45, 7.15–8.45, Sat 7.15–8.45, Sun 12.15–1.45. Closed mid-Aug to early Sep ✋ L €13, D €30, Wine €14

BUZANÇAIS

L'HERMITAGE

www.lhermitagehotel.com
A handsome *maison de maître* in the town centre, L'Hermitage is a lovely place to punctuate your exploration of the northern Brenne. In hunting season wild meats are on the menu.

✉ route d'Argy, 36500 Buzançais ☎ 02 54 84 03 90 ⏰ Jul–Aug daily 12–2, 7–9.30; Sep–Jun Tue–Sat 10–12, 7–9.30. Closed first three weeks in Jan ✋ L €19, D €30, Wine €14

CHAMBORD

HOTEL GRAND ST-MICHEL

www.saintmichel-chambord.com
A menu of regional dishes. Try the duck breast in a green peppercorn sauce or a local pâté. Reservations essential for Sundays and holidays.

✉ 103 place St-Louis, 41250 Chambord ☎ 02 54 20 31 31 ⏰ Daily 12–2, 7–9. Closed 12 Nov–20 Dec ✋ L €25, D €33, Wine €17

Above *Chefs preparing to serve their specialty dishes*

CHAUMONT-SUR-LOIRE
LA CHANCELIÈRE
www.restaurant-lachanceliere.fr
This is a good stop after a stroll by
the river or a visit to the Château de
Chaumont (▷ 245). The service in
the rustic dining rooms is friendly and
children are welcome. The fish dishes
are excellent.
✉ 1 rue de Bellevue, 41150,
Chaumont-sur-Loire ☎ 02 54 20 96 95
🕙 Fri–Mon 12–2, 7–9. Closed 2 weeks Nov
and 3 weeks Feb 🖐 L €21, D €35, Wine €13

CHENONCEAUX
HOSTELLERIE DE LA RENAUDIÈRE
www.chenonceaux-renaudiere.com
Here you'll find excellent and
affordable food in a simple setting.
The cuisine is regional French, and
there is a children's menu for €11.
✉ 24 rue du Docteur Bretonneau,
37150 Chenonceaux ☎ 02 47 23 90 04
🕙 Thu–Tue 7–9. Closed mid-Nov to mid-Feb
🖐 L €21, D €25, Wine €11

CHEVERNY
ROUSSELIÈRE
www.golf-cheverny.com
This old farm has a terrace and a
dining room overlooking an 18-hole
golf course. It's popular for its simple,
traditional meals such as terrines,
steak and sea bass, followed by tarte
tatin, profiteroles or cheeses.
✉ 41700 Cheverny ☎ 02 54 79 24 70
🕙 Mid-Jun to mid-Sep daily 12–3, 7–11;
mid-Sep to mid-Jun 12.15–1.44. Closed 23
Dec–5 Jan 🖐 L €22, D €31, Wine €15

FONTEVRAUD-L'ABBAYE
LA LICORNE
www.la-licorne-restaurant.com
Chef Jean-Michel Bezille cooks
prawn and basil ravioli in morel
sauce, fillet of beef with smoked pork
and shallots, and desserts such as
warm chocolate tart with pears and
lemon-butter sauce. Reservations are
essential.
✉ allée Sainte-Catherine, 49590
Fontevraud-l'Abbaye ☎ 02 41 51 72 49
🕙 Apr–Sep daily 12.15–1.30, 7.15–9, Sun
12.15–1.30; Oct–Mar Tue–Sat 12.15–1.30,
7.15–9, Sun 12.15–1.30. Closed 15 Dec–Jan
🖐 L €27, D €60, Wine €18

HAUTE GOULAINE
LE MANOIR DE LA BOULAIE
www.manoir-de-la-boulaie.fr
Laurent Saudeau is an innovative
chef. Try crab and celery ravioli or
crystalline of aubergine (eggplant)
with mascarpone-raspberry sauce.
The wine list focuses on Muscadet
and Loire wines.
✉ 33 rue de la Chapelle St-Martin, 44115
Haute Goulaine ☎ 02 40 06 15 91 🕙 Tue,
Thu–Sun 12.15–1.45, 7–9. Closed mid-Dec to
mid-Jan 🖐 L €35, D €65, Wine €16

LE MANS
LE BEAULIEU
www.restaurantlebeaulieu.com
Chef Olivier Boussard prefers
traditional cuisine: scallops roasted
in the shell and fillet of Loué
chicken with Vin Jaune (cooked in
a sherry-like wine with a creamy
tarragon sauce). Reservations are
recommended in high season.
✉ 3 place des Ifs, 72000 Le Mans
☎ 02 43 87 78 37 🕙 Mon–Fri 12.15–1.45,
7.30–10. Closed 1–10 Mar and Aug
🖐 L €29, D €51, Wine €25

NANTES
L'ATLANTIDE
www.restaurant-atlantide.net
Both the setting and the cuisine
are contemporary. Chef Jean-Yves
Gueho's open kitchen allows you to
watch him cooking. Dishes might
include Breton turbot with Cantonese
spices or fillet of bass in demi-deuil
(encrusted with truffles). For dessert
try the bananas braised in local beer.
Reservations are advised.
✉ 16 quai Ernest Renaud, 44100 Nantes
☎ 02 40 73 23 23 🕙 Mon–Fri 12–2, 8–10,
Sat 8–10. Closed Aug, 20–23 May, Christmas
🖐 L €30, D €75, Wine €21

LES CAPUCINES
www.restaurant-capucines.com
This excellent-value bistro offers a
convivial atmosphere. The carafe
wines go well with the seafood and
fish dishes.
✉ 11 bis rue de la Bastille, 44000 Nantes
☎ 02 40 20 41 58 🕙 Mon 12–2, Tue–Fri
12–2, 7.30–10, Sat 7.30–10. Closed 3 weeks
in Aug, 1 week in Feb 🖐 L €14.50, D €30,
Wine €14

ONZAIN
DOMAINE DES HAUTS DE LOIRE
www.domainehautsloire.com
Chef Rémy Giraud creates dishes
such as scallop viennoise with pears
and creamy coconut rice, and rabbit
with duck foie gras, fondue of red
chard and wasabi cream.
✉ Domaine des Hauts de Loire
Route de Herbault, 41150 Onzain ☎ 02
54 20 72 57 🕙 Wed–Sun 12.15–1.45,
7.15–9.15. Closed Dec–Feb 🖐 L €50,
D €150, Wine €22

ORLÉANS
CHEZ EUGÈNE
www.restauranteugene.fr
Chez Eugène is a popular bistro with
a taste of the south of France in its
menu. The convivial atmosphere
complements the good daily
changing menu.
✉ 24 rue Sainte-Anne, 45000 Orléans
☎ 02 38 53 82 64 🕙 Mon–Fri 12–2,
7.15–9.15. Closed 1–21 Aug, 26 Dec–6 Jan
🖐 L €35, D €50, Wine €18

LE LIEVRE GOURMAND
www.lelievregourmand.com
The pale walls of this period town
house in the centre of the city let
the food do all the talking. The
dishes on the seasonal menu are
imaginatively served with an eye to
visuals as well as taste. There's a
choice of meat and fish served with
interesting combinations including
asparagus with flaked truffles and
rhubarb and rose water.
✉ 28 quai du Châtelet, 45000 Orléans
☎ 02 38 53 66 14 🕙 Daily 12–2, 7.30–10.
Closed first two weeks in Aug 🖐 L €35,
D €45, Wine €22

LE LIFT
www.restaurant-le-lift.com
Chef Philippe Bardeau has an
excellent reputation and Le Lift
is a new project for 2010. The
contemporary dining room is
matched with dishes that change
seasonally. There's a lovely terrace for
long summer lunches or dinners and
brunch on Sunday lunchtime.
✉ place de la Loire, 45000 Orléans ☎ 02
38 53 63 48 🕙 Mon–Sat 12–2, 7.30–10,
Sun 12–3 🖐 L €30, D €55, Wine €19

ROCHECORBON
LES HAUTES ROCHES
www.leshautesroches.com
The modern cuisine at this establishment, also a hotel, has its roots in Brittany. Dishes include duck foie gras in a Vouvray terrine, a menu of lobster dishes, and stuffed tomato with crumbled crab, lemon liqueur and thyme cream.

✉ 86 quai de la Loire, 37210 Rochecorbon ☎ 02 47 52 88 88 🕐 Thu–Sun 12–1.15, Tue–Sat 12–1.15, 7.30–9.15. Closed mid-Jan to mid-Mar 🍴 L €50, D €75, Wine €25

SACHÉ
AUBERGE DU XIIÈME SIÈCLE
This is one of the best mid-range restaurants in the Loire Valley. Dishes include salad of pan-fried squab (young pigeon) and foie gras, and pan-fried perch with rhubarb. Reservations are recommended on Sundays.

✉ 1 rue du Château, 37190 Saché ☎ 02 47 26 88 77 🕐 Wed–Sat 12.15–1.30, 7.30–9.15, Sun 12.15–1.30, Tue 7.30–9.15. Closed 1 week in Jun, 1 week in Sep, 1 week in Nov, 2 weeks in Jan 🍴 L €35, D €65, Wine €15

ST-BENOÎT-SUR-LOIRE
GRAND ST-BENOÎT
www.hoteldulabrador.fr
In this restaurant, the oak-beamed ceilings contrast with the contemporary furniture. A terrace is open in summer. Seasonal and regional dishes are well prepared and beautifully presented.

✉ 7 place St-André, 45730 St-Benoît-sur-Loire ☎ 02 38 35 11 92 🕐 Tue–Fri 12–2, 7.30–9, Sat 7.30–9, Sun 12–2. Closed 22 Dec–21 Jan 🍴 L €24, D €37, Wine €18

ST-JOACHIM
LA MARE AUX OISEAUX
www.mareauxoiseaux.fr
In the marshlands close to Le Croisic, this lovely old thatched house is home to an excellent conservatory dining room spilling out onto the garden terrace. The cuisine by Eric Guérin is contemporary French gourmet with a good range of dishes.

✉ 162 lle de Fedrun, 44720 Saint Joachim ☎ 02 40 88 53 01 🕐 Mon 7.20–9.30,

Above *Dishes are well presented at the more expensive restaurants*

Tue–Sun 12–2, 7.30–9.30 🍴 L €55, D €75, Wine €22

ST-OUEN-LES-VIGNES
L'AUBINIÈRE
www.aubiniere.com
At this rustically decorated dining room, enjoy the creations of chef Jacques Arrayet, including ravioli of prawns with baby vegetables, terrines and beef entrecôte.

✉ 29 rue Jules Gautier, 37530 St-Ouen-les-Vignes ☎ 02 47 30 15 29 🕐 Tue 7–9.30, Wed–Sat 12–2, 7–9.30, Sun 12–2. Closed Feb 🍴 L €32, D €50, Wine €17

SAUMUR
AUBERGE ST-PIERRE
www.auberge-saintpierre.com
This inn, in a 15th-century monastery, has three dining rooms. The menu, which is strongly influenced by the region, is good value and the welcoming service makes this a pleasant lunch stop. The wine list has inexpensive, refreshing Loire choices.

✉ 6 place St-Pierre, 49400 Saumur ☎ 02 41 51 26 25 🕐 Daily 12–2, 7–10 🍴 L €23, D €30 Wine €17

TOURS
CHARLES BARRIER
www.charlesbarrier.fr
A quick walk across Pont Wilson brings you to this famous restaurant. The dining room is open, with lots of flowers and subtle lighting. Expect smoked salmon, *bœuf bourguignon* (beef casserole) and *blanquette de veau* (veal in cream sauce).

✉ 101 avenue de la Tranchée, 37100 Tours ☎ 02 47 54 20 39 🕐 Mon–Fri 12–2, 7.30–10, Sat 7.30–10 🍴 L €45, D €65, Wine €24

VILLANDRY
L'ORANGERIE
www.traiteur-touraine.com
This pizzeria, next to the château known for its fabulous gardens, is excellent value for money. The pizzas from the wood-fired oven are outstanding and the French cuisine is also good. It gets busy in summer with château visitors, especially at lunch. A children's menu is available.

✉ 11 rue Principale, 37510 Villandry ☎ 02 47 43 56 26 🕐 Daily 12.15–1.15, 7–8.15 🍴 L €18, D €35, Wine €16

STAYING

PRICES AND SYMBOLS

The prices given are the lowest and highest for a double room for one night including breakfast, unless otherwise stated. All hotels listed accept credit cards unless stated otherwise. Note that rates can vary widely throughout the year.

For a key to the symbols, ▷ 2.

AMBOISE
CHOISEUL

www.choiseul.com

This graceful 18th-century mansion with good-sized rooms is set in the shadow of the chateau; children under 12 stay for free. Rooms are decorated in period French style and the restaurant has views over the river. In summer breakfast is served on the terrace. There are also Italianate gardens and tennis courts.

✉ 36 quai Charles Guinot, 37400 Amboise ☎ 02 47 30 45 45 ✔ All year ✋ €133–€295, excluding breakfast (€18–€21) ❶ 28 rooms, 5 suites ✦ Outdoor

ANGERS
HÔTEL D'ANJOU

www.hoteldanjou.fr

The spacious rooms at the 19th-century Hôtel d'Anjou all have satellite TV and are soundproofed. WiFi is available for guests. There are private parking spaces for guests, massage facilities and a restaurant, La Salamandre.

✉ 1 boulevard du Maréchal Foch, 49100 Angers ☎ 02 41 21 12 11 ✋ €85–€193, excluding breakfast (€15.50) ❶ 53 ✦

AZAY-LE-RIDEAU
LA PETITE LOGE

http://lapetiteloge.free.fr

The simple, homey rooms in this small house, within 2km (1 mile) of the eponymous chateau, each have a separate entrance and a kitchen, as well as WiFi. There's a garden for post tour relaxation.

✉ 15 route de Tours, 37190, Azay-le-Rideau ☎ 02 47 45 26 05 ✔ Closed Dec–Mar ✋ €55–€65 ❶ 5

BOURGES
HÔTEL DE BOURBON

www.alpha-hotellerie.com

Hôtel de Bourbon is an 18th-century former abbey offering rooms with satellite TV. Some rooms have access for people with disabilities. For the Abbaye St-Ambroix restaurant, ▷ 252. Pets are welcome and there is parking for guests.

✉ boulevard de la République, 18000 Bourges ☎ 02 48 70 70 00 ✋ €135–€235, excluding breakfast (€15) ❶ 54 (29 non-smoking), 4 suites

CHÊNEHUTTE-LES-TUFFEAUX
PRIEURÉ

www.prieure.com

Rooms at this former priory are comfortable. In summer swimming, tennis, lawn-bowling and miniature golf are on offer. The restaurant serves Anjou-style cuisine.

✉ 49350 Chênehutte-les-Tuffeaux ☎ 02 41 67 90 14 ✋ €130–€299, excluding breakfast (€25) ❶ 19 rooms, 2 suites and 15 cottages ✦ Outdoor heated

CHENONCEAUX
HÔTEL DU BON-LABOUREUR ET DU CHÂTEAU

www.bonlaboureur.com

The small rooms at this historic inn have satellite TV, kitchenettes and a hairdryer. The restaurant is renowned for its seafood and regional dishes.

✉ 6 rue du Dr Bretonneau, 37150 Chenonceaux ☎ 02 47 23 90 02 ✔ Closed 15 Nov–15 Feb ✋ €120–€160, excluding breakfast (€14.50) ❶ 22 rooms, 4 suites (all non-smoking) ✦ 18 ✦ Outdoor

LA ROSERAIE

www.hotel-chenonceau.com

This boutique hotel combines intimacy with a warm welcome. There is a restaurant and parking.

✉ 7 rue du Docteur Bretonneau, 37150 Chenonceaux ☎ 02 47 23 90 09 ✔ Hotel: closed Dec–Feb. Restaurant: Tue–Sun 7–9, Sun 12–2 ✋ €61–€129, excluding breakfast (€10.50) ❶ 17 ✦ Outdoor

CHINON
HOTEL DIDEROT

www.hoteldiderot.com

A pretty mansion (15th to 18th centuries) is now converted into a small hotel filled with country furniture and characterful touches. The gardens are a lovely place to relax. Parking is available on site.

✉ 4 rue de Buffon, 37500 Chinon ☎ 02 47 93 18 87 ✋ €55–€79, excluding breakfast (€8.50) ❶ 20

COUR-CHEVERNY
ST-HUBERT

www.hotel-sthubert.com

This pleasant hotel has clean, bright rooms with TV. The restaurant serves local fare.

✉ 122 route Nationale, 41700 Cour-Cheverny ☎ 02 54 79 96 60 ✋ €55–€90, excluding breakfast (€8.70) ❶ 20 ✦

LE CROISIC
LE FORT DE L'OCEAN

www.hotelfortocean.com

Overlooking the ocean where the Atlantic crashes ashore is this sturdy granite hotel built in the 18th century. There's an elegant country-house feel to the interior with a well-regarded restaurant on site. Outside there are gardens and a pool.

✉ Côte Sauvage, Le Pointe du Croisic, 44490 Le Croisic ☎ 02 40 15 77 77 ✋ €190–€210, excluding breakfast (€18) ❶ 7

ST-JOACHIM
LA MARE AUX OISEAUX

www.mareauxoiseaux.com

Along with his gastronomic restaurant (▷ 254), Eric Guérin has developed a beautiful boutique hotel set amongst the watery marshlands of the Brière. Rooms are individually furnished, with natural materials and neutral shades being predominant. The best have wooden terraces with views overlooking the water.

✉ 162 Ile de Fedrun, 44720 Saint Joachim ☎ 02 40 88 53 01 ✋ €140–€160 ❶ 11

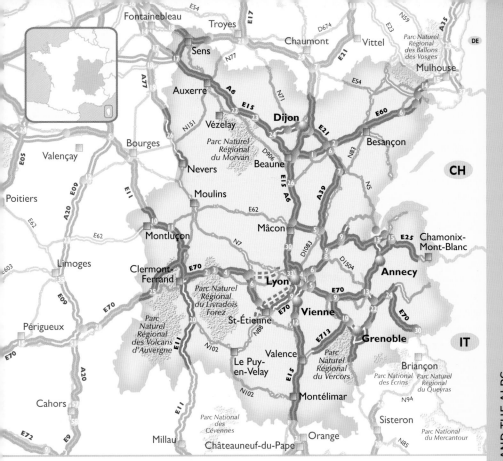

CENTRAL FRANCE AND THE ALPS

Mountains are the dominating motif of central and eastern France. The extinct volcanoes of the Auvergne in the Massif Central, grouped into the Monts Dôme, Monts Dore and Monts du Cantal, create some dramatic landscapes which are surprisingly little known. Negotiate the contours and you reach the shrine of Le Puy-en-Velay and its chapel built on a pinnacle of rock.

The Alps, in contrast, are internationally known as one great adventure playground. Shared with Switzerland (across Lake Léman/Geneva) and Italy (on the other side of Mont Blanc), they offer superb skiing in resorts such as Chamonix, Tignes and Courchevel. Grenoble is the capital of the French Alps. Annecy stands beside a lake and has a pretty old town centre. In summer, the cable cars switch to carrying hikers up to the high-altitude pastures carpeted with wildflowers. The limestone Jura mountains, to the northeast, are something of an annexe to the Alps and are more accessible. They are visited for their many cirques, gorges, caves, forests and waterfalls.

These two highland blocks are separated by the broad corridor of the Rhône valley which carries all north–south communications through the east of France. Standing astride this artery, with its central streets on a fluvial peninsula, is the country's third city, Lyon, once the Roman capital of Gaul.

North of Lyon the landscape opens out into the prosperous landscapes of Burgundy, an area renowned for its cuisine and, above all, its wines. The wealth, power and prestige that the dukes of this land once enjoyed are evident in the regional capital of Dijon, in the abbeys of Vézelay and Fontenay, and in the exquisite town of Beaune.

The mountains continue southwards from Lyon to either side of the Rhône all the way to Provence. The river Ardèche slices deep and dramatic gorges through the uplands as it crosses the border between the two regions.

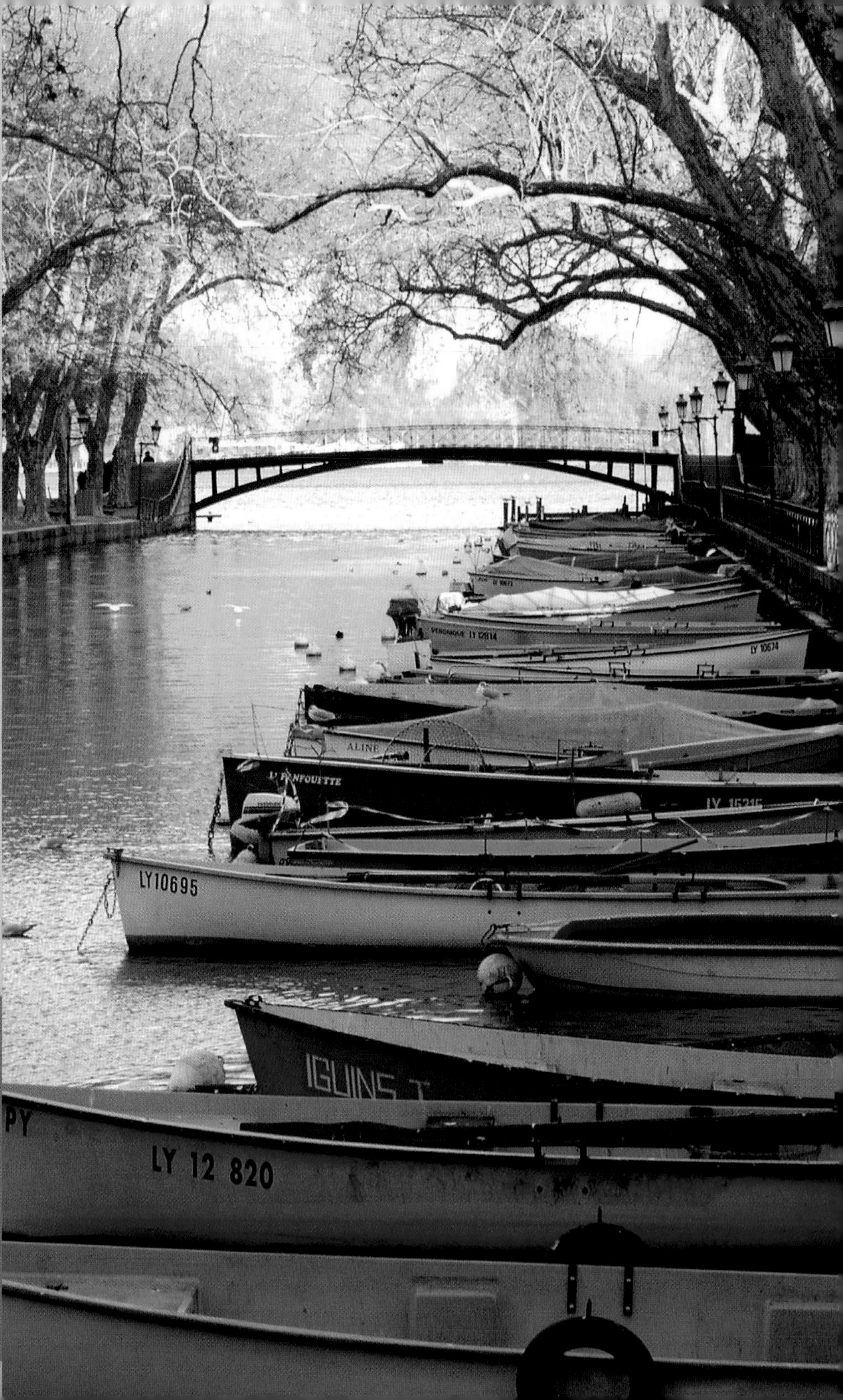
LY 10674
ALINE
LY10695
LY 12 820

ANNECY

Annecy lies at the head of a lake of the same name, flanked by gardens, villas and chic hotels. At the heart of town is a delightful canal zone, where the Thiou river flows from the lake, overlooked by the towers of the 16th-century Château d'Annecy. This ancient power base of the Counts of Geneva now houses the Musée d'Annecy (Jun–Sep daily 10–6; Oct–May Wed–Mon 10–12, 2–5). Exhibits range from anthropology to fine art. The museum's Observatoire Régional Alpin des Lacs explains the geology, flora and fauna of the region.

Cruise boats leave for lake trips from quai Perrière at the mouth of the Thiou. A one- or two-hour trip is the perfect way to enjoy more of the magnificent mountain views.

THE OLD QUARTER

The town's old quarter sits below the castle. In passage de l'Île, the Palais de l'Île (Jun–Sep daily 10.30–6; Oct–May Wed–Mon 10–12, 2–5) is Annecy's most photographed building and a symbol of the town.

Built in the 12th century on a natural islet, it was originally a prison, as well as a mint for the *genevois* currency when the area was independent. Today it houses the Centre d'Interpretation de l'Architecture et du Patrimoine, which mounts exhibitions about traditional architecture.

The narrow streets either side of the islet form the heart of old Annecy. The houses have geranium-filled window boxes and wooden balconies. On place St-Maurice is Église St-Maurice, a 15th-century former Dominican church with a splendid trompe l'oeil painting.

INFORMATION

www.lac-annecy.com

✚ 461 N9 ⓘ Centre Bonlieu, 1 rue Jean Jaurès, 74000 ☎ 04 50 45 00 33 ⓒ Jan to mid-May Mon–Sat 9–12.30, 1.45–6; mid-May to mid-Sep Mon–Sat 9–6.30; mid-Sep to Dec Mon–Sat 9–12.30, 1.45–6. For Sunday opening consult the website ⓡ Annecy

TIPS

» Go up chemin des Remparts to the Jardin des Senteurs for wonderful views over the old town.

» Cafés in rue St-Claire, rue de l'Île or the quai de l'Île are good places to enjoy an ice cream and watch the world go by.

Opposite *Boats moored in Annecy*
Below *Swans in the Thiou*

CENTRAL FRANCE AND THE ALPS • SIGHTS

REGIONS

AUTUN
www.autun.com

Autun's great treasure is the 12th-century cathedral of St-Lazare. Look for the lively carvings on the capitals inside and the wonderful tympanum. Large information panels, in several languages, guide you around the building.

The town's main museum, the Musée Rolin (Apr–Sep Wed–Mon 9.30–12, 1.30–6; Oct–Mar Mon–Sat 10–12, 2–5, Sun 2.30–5), is near the cathedral. Its Roman and medieval items shed light on the town's history. It also has a collection of contemporary and modern art.

On the eastern outskirts of town is the Plan d'Eau du Vallon, a huge lake with water sports such as windsurfing and sailing.

✚ 460 L8 ℹ 13 rue Général Demetz, 71400 ☎ 03 85 86 80 38 🕐 Mon–Sat 9–1, 2–7 🚉 Autun

AUXERRE
www.ot-auxerre.fr

Auxerre, a relaxed town on the river Yonne, was awarded 'City of Art and History' status in 1995.

You can take a cruise along the river or a leisurely stroll around the historic quarter. Head to the tourist information office in Auxerre and pick up the brochure Follow the thread of history. This guides you along an orange line on the ground that takes you past all the major sights, including the Gothic cathedral of St-Étienne, with its fine medieval frescoes, the abbey of St-Germain with its ninth-century murals, and a 15th-century clock tower.

✚ 465 K6 ℹ 1/2 quai de la République, 89000 ☎ 03 86 52 06 19 🕐 15 Jun–15 Sep Mon–Sat 9–1, 2–7, Sun 9.30–12.30, 2–6.30; 16 Sep–14 Jun Mon–Fri 9.30–12.30, 2–6, Sat 9.30–12.30, 2–6.30, Sun 10–1 🚉 Auxerre

BEAUNE
www.ot-beaune.fr

Beaune, the historic capital of Burgundy, lies in the heart of the area's most celebrated vineyards. Its manicured streets, chic boutiques and opulent cellars reflect the wealth brought to the town by trade in some of the world's most expensive wines. Learn more about the wine business at the Musée du Vin de Bourgogne, in a former mansion of the dukes of Burgundy, in rue d'Enfer (Apr–Nov daily 9.30–6; Dec–Mar Wed–Mon 9.30–7).

As the wine capital of Burgundy, it is no surprise that Beaune has 15 cellars offering tastings. The tourist office can help you arrange tours.

Beside the tourist office is the 15th-century Hôtel-Dieu, with its distinctive tiled roof. It began life as a hospital, founded in 1443 by Nicolas Rolin, Chancellor of Burgundy and an art patron. It is now a museum (mid-Mar to mid-Nov daily 9–6.30; mid-Nov to mid-Mar 9–11.30, 3–5.30), where you can see the old pharmacy, kitchens and the vaulted 70m (230ft) ward. The museum contains a polyptych of the Last Judgement.

✚ 460 M8 ℹ Porte Marie de Bourgogne, 6 boulevard Perpreuil, 21200 ☎ 03 80 26 21 30 🕐 Jun–Sep Mon–Sat 9–7, Sun 10–1, 2–6; Apr–May, Oct Mon–Sat 9–6.30, Sun 9–6; Nov–Mar Mon–Sat 9–12, 1–6, Sun 10–12.30, 1.30–5 ❓ As well as a wine festival in November, the town hosts a summer baroque festival and a three-day jazz festival in September

BESANÇON
www.besancon-tourisme.com

Capital of the Franche-Comté region, Besançon is a dignified city with handsome buildings, plenty of fountains and a 17th-century citadel. It sits on a peninsula almost encircled by the river Doubs, and you can admire the city from a different angle by taking a trip in a bâteau-mouche (sightseeing river boat).

On a hilltop 100m (300ft) above the town is La Citadelle, built in the 17th century by Louis XIV's great military engineer, Vauban. The walls of this fort enclose 11ha (27 acres) of grounds, with zoological gardens, an aquarium focusing on river life, an insectarium, a noctarium and a museum dedicated to the Resistance movement during World War II (Jul–Aug daily 9–7; Easter–Jun, Sep–Oct 9–6; Nov–Mar 10–5).

Besançon has a history of clock- and watch-making and you can learn more at the Musée du Temps, in the 16th-century Palais Granvelle (Tue–Sun 9.15–12, 2–6). The astronomical clock at St-Jean cathedral has 57 faces and gives the time in 16 places around the world. Save some time (and euros) for the boutique selling wonderful wooden clockwork toys.

The Musée des Beaux-Arts et d'Archéologie (Wed–Fri 9.30–12, 2–6, Sat–Sun 9.30–6; closes 8pm Thu), in place de la Révolution, is also well worth visiting.

✚ 461 N7 ℹ Hotel de Ville, place du 8 Septembre, 25000 Besançon ☎ 03 81 80 92 55 🕐 Mon–Sat 10–6, Sun 10–10 🚉 Viotte

BRIANÇON

www.ot-briancon.fr

Briançon is the highest town in Europe, at 1,320m (4,330ft), and is surrounded by mountain peaks. Two national parks, the Parc National des Écrins and Parc National Régional du Queyras, are in the area. The town is on the Col de Montgenèvre, one of the major Alpine passes linking France and Italy, and it grew out of a pre-Roman settlement. It now promotes itself as a ski station of the Serre Chevalier ski area, with more than 250km (155 miles) of ski runs between four villages.

At the end of the 17th century Louis XIV's military planner, Vauban, turned Briançon's old medieval town into an impenetrable walled city. Now known as Cité Vauban, this area is traffic-free and the focus of visitor interest. Go through Porte de Pignerol into Grande Rue, which has some impressive houses.

Other highlights include the Maison des Templiers (which houses the tourist information office), the 14th-century Église des Cordeliers and the Fort du Château, where 19th-century defences replaced the last vestiges of the original château, built in the 11th century. The 18th-century Collégiale (Notre-Dame de St-Nicolas) was built to Vauban's design, with its strong walls as much for protection as for worship.

✚ 461 P11 🛈 1 place du Temple, 05100 ☎ 04 92 21 08 50 🕐 Jul–Aug daily 9–7; Sep–Jun 9–12, 2–6 🚉 Briançon

CHAMBÉRY

www.chambery-tourisme.com

The historic capital of the Savoie dukedom, Chambéry has imposing historic buildings and an impressive 15th- and 16th-century old quarter.

Its most famous landmark is the amusing Fontaine des Elephants, at the base of rue du Boigne. The ancient residence of the dukes, the Château des Ducs, dominates the town; you can visit some parts (guided tours only; tel 04 79 33 42 47 for times).

Highlights include the 14th-century Tour Trésorerie, the Salles Basses and the 15th-century Sainte-Chapelle. From 1453 to 1578 this chapel housed the Holy Shroud, now in Turin. The carillon of Sainte-Chapelle is impressive with 70 bells. You can judge for yourself at the Saturday concert at 3pm.

At the foot of the château, the old quarter fans out in a series of pedestrian-only streets with elegant mansions dating from the Renaissance through to the 18th century. The 15th-century Cathédrale St-François contains a collection of trompe l'oeil paintings, and a rare 12th-century Byzantine-style ivory diptych. The Musée Savoisien, in an old Franciscan monastery, presents the history, archaeology and art of Savoie (Wed–Mon 10–12, 2–6).

✚ 461 N10 🛈 5b place du Palais de Justice, 73000 ☎ 04 79 33 42 47 🕐 Jul–Aug Mon–Sat 9–6, Sun 10–1; Sep–Jun Mon–Sat 9–12, 1.30–6 🚉 Chambéry

CHAMONIX-MONT-BLANC

www.chamonix.com

The ski resort of Chamonix-Mont-Blanc lies in the heart of the French Alps and is one of France's principal and most enduring playgrounds. It is backed by the spectacular Mont Blanc, the highest peak in Europe, at 4,808m (15,771ft). The mountain straddles the French/Italian border, with the Mont Blanc road tunnel, 22km (13.5 miles) long, connecting the two countries.

Chamonix is a chic resort, its rise dating from the time when mountaineering and skiing began to attract the wealthy crowd and further enhanced after it hosted the Winter Olympics in 1924. It provides a range of winter sports, including skiing, snowboarding, snow-shoeing, *ski de fond* (cross-country skiing) and luge, as well as hiking, mountaineering, paragliding and rafting in summer.

Chamonix's attractions for the less energetic include its casino and designer shops. For panoramic views, footpaths and a restaurant where you can enjoy the Alpine air, take the Aiguille du Midi cable car (expensive), which was upgraded in 2008. The Mont Blanc tramway, the highest in Europe, climbing to 2,372m (7,780ft), carries passengers through some exceptional landscapes and terminates at the base camp for Mont Blanc.

✚ 461 P9 🛈 85 place du Triangle de l'Amitié, 74400 ☎ 04 50 53 00 24 🕐 Daily 9–12.30, 2–6 🚉 Chamonix

Opposite *The 15th-century Hôtel-Dieu in Beaune, with its decorative tiled roof*
Left *Briançon is the highest town in Europe*
Below *Wooded hills beneath Mont Blanc*

CLERMONT-FERRAND
www.ot-clermont-ferrand.fr

Once two separate towns, industrial Clermont-Ferrand sits at the meeting point of the Auvergne and the Massif Central. The city's heart is the old Clermont, with the much smaller Montferrand to the northeast. In between, the Michelin factory is like a third town and the economic lifeblood of the city.

Much of the old town is built from dark volcanic stone quarried in the hills to the west. The Éspace Art Roman in the tourist office is a free display about the Romanesque art and architecture in the city and its environs. The most important Romanesque building is the UNESCO-listed 12th-century Notre-Dame-du-Port, in the northeast corner of the old quarter, which has an exceptional raised choir supported by finely carved pillars and elegant arches. The stained-glass windows in the choir of Cathédrale Notre-Dame-de-l'Assomption, in the heart of the town, are said to be from the same workshops as those of the Sainte-Chapelle in Paris (▷ 98).

For excellent views over the city, climb the Tour de la Bayette.

🗺 460 K10 🛈 place de la Victoire, 63000 ☎ 04 73 98 65 00 🕐 May–Sep Mon–Fri 9–7, Sat–Sun 10–7; Oct–Apr Mon–Fri 9–6, Sat 10–1, 2–6, Sun 9.30–12.30, 2–6 🚉 Clermont-Ferrand

CLUNY
www.monuments-nationaux.fr

The Cluniac order was founded in 910 by William the Pious, Duke of Aquitaine. As reformers of the Benedictine Rule, the Cluniacs' influence spread quickly and dependent houses were founded throughout Europe. Cluny Abbey's third church was built between 1080 and 1130. It was the largest and most splendid church in Christendom until St. Peter's was built in Rome. Cluny later fell into decline and was dismantled after the Revolution. Only one tower of the transept remains. The former abbey's palace is now the Musée d'Art et d'Archéologie.

Cluniac churches were designed to glorify God—and the more ornate they were, the better. Of many examples of Cluniac architecture in Burgundy, Paray-le-Monial's church, contemporary with Cluny, is almost a replica of the lost original, on a reduced scale. A chapel at Berzé-la-Ville has a series of early frescoes.

🗺 460 L8 🛈 Palais Jean de Bourbon, 71250 ☎ 03 85 59 12 79 🕐 May–Aug daily 9.30–6.30; Sep–Apr 9.30–12, 1.30–5 💶 Adult €7.50, under 18 and EU nationals under 25 free 🎫

DIJON
▷ 264.

ÉVIAN-LES-BAINS
www.eviantourism.com

Évian-les-Bains sits on the banks of Lac Léman (Lake Geneva), in the lee of Alpine hills to the south and with wonderful panoramas north across to Lausanne and the Swiss countryside. In 1789, the water of the Sainte-Catherine fountain was found to have an excellent taste and beneficial qualities. Trading on this, the town became a leading spa of the belle époque. Visitors have included Greta Garbo, Winston Churchill and the Aga Khan. Today there is a casino and a thalassotherapy facility.

The Hall d'Exposition des Eaux Minérales d'Évian (May–Sep), on rue Nationale, has information on water sources and their properties. To visit the Évian factory, 5km (3 miles) out of town, reserve ahead at the Hall (tickets include transportation).

A good way to see the area is to take a boat trip on the lake. Along the French side towards Thonon-les-Bains there are good views of the medieval village of Yvoire.

🗺 461 P8 🛈 place d'Allinges, 74501 ☎ 04 50 75 04 26 🕐 Jul–Aug Mon–Fri 8.30–12.30, 2–7, Sat 9–12, 2–7, Sun 10–12, 3–6; May–Jun, Sep Mon–Fri 9–12, 2–6.30, Sat 9–12, 2–6, Sun 10–12, 3–6; Oct–Apr Mon–Fri 9–12, 2–6, Sat 9–12, 2–5 🚉 Évian-les-Bains 🚢 Several ferries daily to and from Lausanne, in Switzerland

GORGES DE L'ARDÈCHE
www.vallon-pont-darc.com

The Gorges de l'Ardèche have been carved over hundreds of thousands of years by the power of the Ardèche river. The sheer sides of the limestone gorge reach 30m (100ft) in height and the water has sculpted cave systems, their interiors bristling with stalactites and stalagmites. The Grotte de la Madeleine and Grottes de St-Marcel are the largest, with some 40km (25 miles) of tunnels.

It's easy to admire the gorge, as the D290 runs along its northern edge. You'll get panoramic views, particularly at the Belvédères de la Haute Corniche. Just south of Vallon-Pont-d'Arc is the Pont-d'Arc, a natural bridge cut through the rock by the power of the water and one of the most photographed sights in central France. Look, too, for Aiguèze, the tiny medieval stone village on the gorge's northern bank.

An escorted kayak trip between Vallon-Pont-d'Arc and St-Martin-d'Ardèche to the southeast, lasts anything from two to five hours and takes you into the natural cathedrals of the gorge sides. If you prefer to go at your own pace, you can rent a canoe at Vallon-Pont-d'Arc and ask to be collected later from the village of Sauze, downstream.

🗺 456 L12 🛈 12 Vallon-Pont-d'Arc, place de l'Ancienne Gare, 07150 ☎ 04 75 88 04 01 🕐 Jul–Aug Mon–Sat 9.30–12.30, 3–7, Sun 9.30–12.30, 3–6; Apr–Jun, Sep–Oct Mon–Fri 9–12.30, 2–6, Sat 9.30–12.30, 2–5; Nov–Mar Mon–Fri 9–12, 2–5, Sat 9–12

GRENOBLE

Grenoble is said to be the flattest city in France—a surprising fact given that it's surrounded by mountain peaks. As an Alpine city, it draws outdoor enthusiasts year round. It also styles itself the cultural capital of the French Alps and has several major museums and many temporary exhibitions. It was the birthplace of the author Stendhal. The historic quarter of town is compact, with good shopping along the traffic-free streets around place Grenette. For good views over the city and mountains, take the gondola cable car to the 16th-century Bastille.

ART

The Musée de Grenoble (Wed–Mon 10–6.30), in a modern building in place de Lavalette, has an outstanding collection of art from the 13th to the 20th centuries. For avant-garde art, head to the Centre National d'Art Contemporain, in cours Berriat (Tue–Sun 2–7).

HISTORY

The Musée Dauphinois (Jun–Sep Wed–Mon 10–7; Oct–May 10–6), in a 17th-century convent on rue Maurice Gignoux, has two permanent exhibitions, 'People of the Alps' and 'The Great History of Skiing', plus temporary displays. To the north, the Romanesque Église St-Laurent is now the Musée Archéologique (closed to the public), incorporating a third-century AD necropolis, sarcophagi from the sixth to the eighth centuries, and the remains of a ninth-century Carolingian church and an 11th-century monastery.

INFORMATION

www.grenoble-isere.info

✚ 461 N10 ℹ 14 rue de la République, 38019 ☎ 04 76 42 41 41 ⊗ May–Sep Mon–Sat 9–6.30, Sun 10–1, 2–5; Oct–Apr Mon–Sat 9–6.30, Sun 10–1 🚉 Grenoble

TIPS

» Grenoble Pass Découverte offers entry into a choice of two (€9.90), three (€11.90) or four (€13.90) different attractions or things to do in the city. Buy it at the tourist office.

» Watch out for trams on streets that are otherwise vehicle-free—they move almost silently.

Above *Grenoble's cable car crosses the water*
Opposite *The octagonal Holy Water Tower at the Abbaye de Cluny*

INFORMATION

www.dijon-tourism.com

✚ 461 M7 ℹ cour de la Gare and 11 rue des Forges, 21000 ☎ 0892 700 558 (toll call) 🕐 Apr–Sep Mon–Sat 9.30–6.30, Sun 10–6; Oct–Mar Mon–Sat 9.30–1, 2–6, Sun 10–4 🕐 rue des Forges (for guided tours): Mon–Sat 9–12, 2–6 🚉 Dijon-Ville

INTRODUCTION

In the 14th and 15th centuries, the dukes of Burgundy rivalled the Capetian kings of France in power, wealth and prestige, and their patronage of the arts is evident from the city they built as their capital on the foundation of a Gallo-Roman *castrum*.

At the heart of the busy present-day industrial and university city is a core of picturesque medieval streets lined with historic *hôtels particuliers* (mansions) boutiques, bars, museums and galleries. There are also a surprising number of churches—'What a fair town,' remarked François I on seeing Dijon 'a town of a hundred belfries'. The centre of the city is the place de la Libération; on it stands the Palais des Ducs, the 17th-century successor to the ducal palace, now used as the town hall and Musée des Beaux-Arts.

As there are no steep slopes and most major sights are within walking distance the best way to get around on foot, backed up by use of the inexpensive bus network. But remember to take a step back and look up every now and then because Dijon has marvellous examples of Burgundy's multicoloured tiled roofs.

Dijon is a good place for shopping as well as sightseeing and the souvenir you are most likely to take home with you is either a bottle of Burgundy wine produced in the surrounding vineyards or a jar of mustard—although note that the name 'Dijon mustard' has become a generic description and much of the production is industrialized using imported seed. Both the mustard and the wine will be proudly served up in any restaurant.

WHAT TO DO
MUSÉE DES BEAUX-ARTS

www.mba.dijon.fr

The Palace of the Estates-General, an extension to the Palace of the Dukes of Burgundy next door, houses the town hall as well as this fine arts museum—

one of the oldest museums in France. Level 1 has an outstanding collection of sculpture, as well as Italian, French and Flemish paintings, mainly from the 15th to the 18th centuries. Levels 2 and 3 are devoted to modern and contemporary art, including the School of Paris and French paintings of the 19th century. Ongoing renovations of the interior mean that not all galleries will be open at all times.

✉ Palais des Ducs et des États de Bourgogne, 21000 ☎ 03 80 74 52 70 ⏰ May–Oct Wed–Mon 9.30–6; Nov–Apr 10–5. Modern and contemporary art section closed 11.45–1.45 ✋ Free

MEDIEVAL ZONE

Some of the most interesting streets behind the palace are rue Verrerie and rue des Forges, where you'll find the tourist office in Hôtel Chambellan, a pretty half-timbered building off an interior courtyard. In rue de la Chouette (Owl Street), you'll find evidence of the town's strong association with the owl. There's an owl sculpted on a side wall of the Église Notre-Dame and it is considered good luck to rub the owl with your left hand while making a wish.

PLACE DE LA LIBÉRATION

The semicircular place de la Libération was originally place Royale because it was designed to enhance a statue of Louis XIV. When the statue was melted down for cannon during the Revolution, the site was renamed place d'Armes. Most of the arches outlining the square shelter boutiques, bars and restaurants. A few have small streets or passages underneath them, such as rue Vauban, which leads to the area around the Palais de Justice, with its many old buildings.

SHOPPING

Les Halles, the immense covered market, was built in 1875 by Gustave Eiffel's company, based on the design of the former market of the same name in Paris. Markets are held here both inside and outside on Tuesdays, Thursdays, Fridays and Saturdays, and there are plenty of cafés, restaurants and food shops to choose from.

Past the triumphal arch is the start of rue de la Liberté, the town's semi-pedestrian-only main shopping street, home to the superb Moutarde Maille—a mustard-lover's dream. Pretty place François Rude, on the left, has fountains and seats, and is a good place for a coffee stop.

MORE TO SEE

CATHÉDRALE ST-BÉNIGNE

The interior of this Gothic cathedral is a delicate light gold, with straw-seated chairs. The crypt is 10th century.

✉ place St-Bénigne, 21000 ☎ 03 80 30 39 33 ⏰ Daily 9–7

ÉGLISE NOTRE-DAME

A good example of Burgundian Gothic architecture, this church has rows of grimacing monsters on its facade and a 14th-century Jacquemart—a mechanical clock on which figures strike chimes to mark the passing hours.

✉ place Notre Dame, 21000 ☎ 03 80 28 84 90 ⏰ Daily

ÉGLISE ST-MICHEL

This church is Flamboyant Gothic, with a Renaissance facade.

✉ place St-Michel, 21000 ☎ 03 80 63 17 84 ⏰ Daily

TOUR PHILIPPE LE BON

You'll get great views over the city from the top of this tower, which measures 52m (160ft) high.

✉ Palais des Ducs et des États de Bourgogne, 21000 ☎ 03 80 74 52 71 ⏰ Tours: daily every 45 min 9–12 and 1.45–5.30

TIPS

» The Jardin Botanique de l'Arquebuse, on avenue Albert 1er, about 15 minutes on foot from the middle of town, is ideal for a sandwich lunch. There's a children's play area, and the paths have been designed with wheelchair-users in mind.

» The tourist office sells a guidebook for €2.50 called *The Owl's Trail*, which gives details of the main sights along a route marked on the ground by red arrows. Information panels in French, German and English are attached to historic buildings.

Opposite top *If you tire of sightseeing, there are plenty of shops in Dijon*
Opposite bottom *A Medusa head on the gates of the Palais des Ducs*
Below *Concerts are held in the Auditorium de Dijon*

INFORMATION
www.lyon-france.com

🛉 461 M9 ℹ place Bellecour, 69002

☎ 04 72 77 69 69 🕒 Daily 9–6

Ⓜ Lyon's Métro system has four lines

🚆 There are two main stations in Lyon.
Gare de la Part-Dieu is where most TGV
services from Paris terminate, but some
trains go on to the more central Perrache
station ✈ Lyon St-Exupéry airport, 24km
(15 miles) east of Lyon

INTRODUCTION

Lyon is France's third-largest city (by population). Its Renaissance old quarter is listed as a UNESCO World Heritage Site and the city is known for its gastronomy. Geography and history have combined to give Lyon a somewhat complicated layout. The city is spread across the confluence of two of the major rivers of France, the Rhône and Saône, and its centre of gravity has shifted three times in 2,000 years. Wandering around the city, it's easy to get your rivers and bridges mixed up.

The settlement founded on Fourvière hill by Julius Caesar in 44BC became the Roman capital of Gaul. With the fall of the Roman Empire the town moved down to the riverside, to the medieval quarter which is known as Vieux Lyon. An episcopal complex was established in the fifth century and power stayed in the hands of the bishops until the 14th century, when the monarchy introduced a secular government and law courts. In the 15th century, Lyon became an important European hub for currency dealing and printing, and began hosting huge trade fairs. The silk trade came into its own at this time and the city entered a golden age, leading to the building of the Renaissance town on the narrow peninsula (the Presqu'île—'almost isle') between the two rivers.

The modern suburbs, meanwhile, spread away from the east bank of the Rhône but you are unlikely to venture this way for sightseeing.

As well as having the historical monuments and shops you would expect in a large city, Lyon enjoys the reputation of being the gastronomic capital of France with its own brand of restaurants, called *bouchons*.

WHAT TO SEE

FOURVIÈRE AND VIEUX LYON

Head across the river Saône to find Vieux Lyon, the wonderfully atmospheric old quarter. Its pedestrian-only streets cover three districts (St-Georges, St-Jean and St-Paul), lined with four-floor mansions, the whole constituting one of the most complete Renaissance towns in Europe. The main streets, rue St-Jean and rue du Boeuf, run parallel to the river, and here you'll find the typical *traboules* of Lyon—the arched galleries, courtyards and vaulted walkways that cut under the Renaissance mansions to make a warren of hidden alleyways.

This side of the river is great for browsing in antiques shops and galleries and has some of the best-value *bouchon* bistros in the city. *Lugdunum*, the Roman capital of Gaul, was set above here on top of the hill now known as Fourvière. You can walk or take the funicular to the Roman remains.

One important church, the Fourvière basilica, still stands here and is reached by funicular railway.

Opposite *Lyon's rue St-Jean at night*
Below *A puppet show*

CATHÉDRALE ST-JEAN

The cathedral anchors Vieux Lyon. Built on the site of an earlier church, the oldest part is the cloister wall, dating from the 11th century, although building went on throughout the 13th century. The resulting church is one of the finest examples of a transitional Romanesque/Gothic building. The vaults of the apse, for instance, are Romanesque at the base and topped with classic Gothic vaulting. There's some stunning stained glass, such as the rose windows in the transepts, and a rare astronomical clock dating from the 14th century. Pope John XXII was crowned here in 1316 and Henri IV married Marie de Medici here in 1600. The church received a visit by Napoleon in 1805 and was the site of the world's first recorded organ recital in 1928.

🛉 268 B3 ✉ place St-Jean, 69005 🕒 Mon–Fri 8–12, 2–7.30, Sat–Sun 8–12, 2–5

Ⓜ Vieux Lyon

LE PALAIS
St JEAN
RESTAURANT

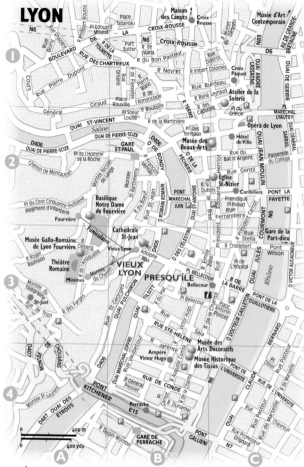

LYON

(map labels)

Maison des Canuts · Croix Rousse · Musée d'Art Contemporain · Place Tabareau · Pl Edouard Milliaud · LA · CROIX-ROUSSE · Croix-Rousse · Philibert Roussy · N6 · Rue Grognard · Rue Denfert · DE · R DE LA · TOURETTE · Parc Sutter · N6 · R de l'Alma · R du Bon Pasteur · R Diderot · D6 · AV DE GRANDE-BRETAGNE · N83 · AV DE GRANDE-BRETAGNE · BOULEVARD · RUE DES CHARTREUX · R Neyret · R Imbert Colomès · Croix Paquet · QUAI ANDRE LASSAGNE · QUAI DE SERBIE · Cours · Rue Pierre Dupont · R de Fressieus · R Pierre Blanc · R de l'Annonciade · René Leynaud · R des Capucins · Atelier de la Soierie · R du MARECHAL LYAUTEY · Ornano · Giraud · Place Rouville · Rue Burdeau · Pl du Griffon · QUAI JEAN MOULIN · Général · Pl Soeur Louise · R Bouteille · Opéra de Lyon · QUAI GENERAL SARRAIL · QUAI ST-VINCENT · R des Capucins · R TERME · Pl des Terreaux · Hôtel de Ville · Passerelle du Collège · Saône · QUAI DE PIERRE-SCIZE · R de la Martinière · Musée des Beaux-Arts · Rue du Bat d'Argent · D406 · QUAI DE PIERRE-SCIZE · O DE BONDY · GARE ST-PAUL · Rue Herriot · D406 · Pl de l'Homme de la Roche · Pl du Change · Rue Gentil · D406 · Chemin de Montauban · Montée Nicolas de Lange · Montée St-Barthélemy · R du Boeuf · PONT MARECHAL JUIN · R de la PECHERIE · R DUBOIS · Eglise St-Nizier · Cordeliers · PONT LA FAYETTE · Pl du Cent Cinquante-Huitième Régiment d'Infanterie · Basilique Notre Dame de Fourvière · Fourvière · ROMAIN · O ROMAIN · PONT LA FAYETTE · Fransisque · Pl Reaud · Rue Ferrandière · N6 · QUAI ST-ANTOINE · R Dubois · Rue Carnot · Gare de la Part-dieu · Cathédrale St-Jean · Funiculaire · Av Adolphe Max · R des Célestins · Rue Stella · R Childebert · Pont Wilson · Musée Gallo-Romaine de Lyon Fourvière · R Cléberg · Vieux Lyon · QUAI DES CELESTINS · Pl de l'hôpital · R Roger Radisson · R de l'Antiquaille · VIEUX LYON · PRESQU'ÎLE · R DE LA BARRE · Rhône · Théâtre Romaine · Minimes · Montée du Chemin Neuf · QUAI FULCHIRON · Bellecour · PONT DE LA GUILLOTIERE · St-Just · Montée du Télégraphe · Montée St-Georges · QUAI TILSITT · Pl Bellecour · Place Antonin Poncet · QUAI JULES · Rue de Trion · Rue des Farges · RUE STE-HELENE · Rue Victor Hugo · Sala · DOCTEUR GAILLETON · PONT BERNARD · Montée de Choulans · Jarente · Musée des Arts Décoratifs · D407 · QUAI MARECHAL JOFFRE · Ampère Victor Hugo · R Auguste Comte · Musée Historique des Tissus · L'UNIVERSITE · PONT DE L'UNIVERSITE · QUAI CLAUDE · RUE PASTEUR · D406 · PONT KITCHENER · Montée St-Laurent · QUAI DES ETROITS · R Général Plessier · RUE DE CONDE · R de Marseille · R Professeur Grignard · N7 · D407 · R du · cité R Duhamel · Rue Pasteur · R de Marseille · Rue de Chevreul · D487 · GARE DE PERRACHE · Perrache E15 · R Dugas Montbel · PONT GALLIENI · R Professeur Grignard

0 — 400 m / 400 yds

MUSÉE GALLO-ROMAIN DE LYON FOURVIÈRE

www.musees-gallo-romains.com

This museum, on Fourvière hill, is in an innovative subterranean building. Its 17 rooms display objects found in Lyon and the Ain and Isère regions. Highlights include the 'Claudius Tablet', part of a bronze tablet inscribed with a speech given by Emperor Claudius to the Senate in AD48, in which he put forward the rights of the native Gallic people to hold public office. Don't miss the rare mosaic portraying a typical Roman circus, along with a vivid depiction of a chariot race.

✚ 268 A3 ✉ 17 rue Cléberg, 69005 ☎ 04 72 38 49 30 🕑 Tue–Sun 10–6 💶 Adult €3.80, under 18 free; free to all on Thu

BASILIQUE NOTRE-DAME DE FOURVIÈRE

www.fourviere.org

Despite its Roman connections, Fourvière is famous for a much more modern edifice, the Basilique Notre-Dame de Fourvière, built on the site of the Roman forum and an 11th-century chapel with a white marble facade, four turrets and a rounded apse. In 1870 the people of Lyon prayed to the Virgin Mary (the city's patron) to spare their city from Prussian forces. The enemy never breached the city walls and the public donated money to build this basilica. The interior has exceptional belle-époque mosaics and vividly detailed stained glass. The church's primary treasure is a golden statue of Mary in the chapel adjoining the basilica.

Above *Detail of carving on a building in place Bellecour*
Opposite *Cathédrale St-Jean*

☩ 268 A2 ✉ Esplanade de Fourvière ☎ 04 78 25 86 19 🕐 Daily 8–7; chapel 7–7 🚇 Vieux Lyon then Funiculaire Fourvière

MUSÉE DES BEAUX-ARTS

www.mba-lyon.fr

In the Presqu'île district, the Palais St-Pierre, a former Benedictine monastery, now houses the art gallery—one of the best in France outside Paris. There are more than 1,800 paintings, shown in chronological order. Look for the fine altarpiece of *The Ascension of Christ* by Perugino from the Quattrocento, and works by 17th-century Dutch and Flemish artists including Rembrandt and Rubens. The 18th-century Italian gallery has works by Tintoretto and Veronese. The museum is particularly strong on paintings by 19th- and early 20th-century artists including Dégas, Gauguin, Manet, Monet and Picasso. There are 16 rooms devoted to ancient civilizations, with outstanding collections of Greek, Roman and Egyptian items. A further 17 rooms have varied collections, including Byzantine ivories, Limoges enamels, Islamic art and rare Japanese tea sets. The interior courtyard of the museum is now a formal garden.

☩ 268 C2 ✉ 20 place des Terreaux, 69001 ☎ 04 72 10 17 40 🕐 Permanent collections: Sat–Mon, Wed–Thu 10–6, Fri 10.30–8. Closed 1–8 May, Easter Mon, Whit Mon, Ascension Day, 14 Jul and 15 Aug. First-floor rooms closed 12–1.15; second-floor rooms closed 1.15–2.15 🚇 Hôtel de Ville ✋ Adult €7, child €4. Temporary exhibitions: adult €9, child €6

MORE TO SEE

ATELIER DE LA SOIERIE

www.atelierdesoierie.com

This is one of the few working silk workshops left in the city. Watch the material being screen-printed and made into scarves, then browse the shop.

☩ 268 C1 ✉ 33 rue Romarin, 69001 ☎ 04 72 07 97 83 🕐 Mon–Fri 9–12, 2–7, Sat 9–1, 2–6 🚇 Hôtel de Ville

ÉGLISE ST-NIZIER

This church sits on the site of a fifth-century basilica. Begun in the early 14th century, its exterior is an excellent example of Flamboyant Gothic architecture.

☩ 268 C2 ✉ place St-Nizier 🕐 Tue–Sun 10–12, 2.30–6.30, Mon 2.30–6.30

MAISON DES CANUTS

www.maisondescanuts.com

This museum recreates the old system of silk production in an original house with working handlooms. Dyeing and spinning took place on the ground floors of the tall 18th- and 19th-century houses, while the workers' families lived above.

☩ Off map 268 B1 ✉ 12 rue d'Ivry, 69004 ☎ 04 78 28 62 04 🕐 Tue–Sat 10–6 ✋ Adult €6, child (12–17) €3, under 12 free 🚇 Croix Rousse

MUSÉE D'ART CONTEMPORAIN

www.mac-lyon.com

In a spectacular building by Renzo Piano, this museum concentrates on 20th- and 21st-century art forms, mainly installations and computer-generated art.

☩ Off map 268 C1 ✉ 81 quai Charles de Gaulle, 69006 ☎ 04 72 69 17 17 🕐 Wed–Fri 12–7, Sat–Sun 10–7 ✋ Adult €8, under 18 free 🚌 4, 58

MUSÉE DES TISSUS AND MUSÉE DES ARTS DÉCORATIFS

www.musee-des-tissus.com

These museums are in the 17th-century Hôtel de Villeroy. Learn about the use of silk and other textiles in clothing and soft furnishings.

☩ 268 B4 ✉ 34 rue de la Charité ☎ 04 78 38 42 00 🕐 Musée des Tissus: Tue–Sun 10–5.30. Musée des Arts Decoratifs: Tue–Sun 10–12, 2–5.30 ✋ Adult €4.60, under 18 free for both museums

TIPS

» A Lyon City Card (€19 for one day, €28 for two days and €37 for three days), available from the tourist office, entitles you to entry to 19 museums, guided and audioguided city tours, river cruises, lunchtime classical concerts, public transportation within the city and a traditional puppet show.

» The Métro system has four lines, running from 5am until midnight. In Vieux Lyon the Métro links with a funicular to the top of the Fourvière hill.

» Parc de la Tête d'Or, by the Musée d'Art Contemporain, has plenty of places to stroll and sit in the sunshine. There's a lake, rose garden, glasshouses, playground, small zoo, *'petit train'* and mini-golf.

» River cruises with Naviginter include lunch or dinner and depart from 13 bis quai Rambaud. Tours without meals leave from quai des Célestins, where there is also a ticket office.

MÂCON

www.macon.fr
www.macon-tourisme.fr

Mâcon, on the river Saône, is one of the most important of the Burgundy wine towns, but retains a quiet atmosphere. The river's importance to the town is symbolized by the much-loved Pont St-Laurent, dating from the 11th century but altered over the years. The bridge is one of few in the area to survive World War II undamaged. Huge catfish appeared in the river during the 1970s and you can arrange fishing expeditions at the Centre de Pêche au Gros, on rue de la Liberté. If your preference is for wine, try a tasting at the Maison des Vins, on avenue de Lattre de Tassigny.

Rue Carnot is a short pedestrian-only lane lined with boutiques and old buildings, including the 16th-century Maison du Bois, overlooking the market square, place aux Herbes. Where rue Carnot meets place Poissonnière, fish designs in the ground indicate the size of the fishmongers' area.

The Musée des Ursulines, in rue des Ursulines, was a 17th-century convent and, during the Revolution, a prison. Today it exhibits wine-making antiques, sculpture and fine arts of the French and Flemish schools (Tue–Sat 10–12, 2–6, Sun 2–6). The Musée Lamartine, in rue Sigorgne, is in Mâcon's Academy of Arts, Sciences and Literature (Tue–Sat 10–12, 2–6, Sun 2–6). Mâcon-born 19th-century Romantic poet Lamartine was once president here. As well as Lamartine memorabilia, there are tapestries and 18th-century objets d'art.

🕇 461 M9 🛈 1 place St-Pierre, 71000 ☎ 03 85 21 07 07 🕐 Jul–Aug daily 9.30–12.30, 2–6.30; Jun, Sep Mon–Sat 9.30–12.30, 2–6.30; Apr–May, Oct Mon–Sat 10–12, 2–6; Nov–Mar Tue–Sat 10–12, 2–6

PALAIS IDÉAL

www.facteurcheval.com

Le Palais Idéal du Facteur Cheval (The Palace of Postman Cheval) is in Hauterives village, 50km (31 miles) south of Vienne, in hills east of the Rhône valley. It was built between 1869 and the early 1900s by the local postman with stones he collected on his daily rounds. It is now a national monument. The palace is enormous—a remarkable achievement given that it is the creation of just one man, working without formal plans (the walls are not straight). Without any training, Cheval managed to incorporate a variety of architectural features, creating, at the same time, the feel of a medieval castle, Gothic cathedral, Hindu temple and mosque. He also incorporated his own philosophical thoughts in a number of inspirational poems inscribed on plaques in the building. Both Pablo Picasso and André Breton visited the Palais Idéal, drawing inspiration for their Surrealist revolution. Classical and jazz concerts are held on summer evenings.

🕇 461 M10 ✉ Le Palais Idéal du Facteur Cheval, 26390, Hauterives ☎ 04 75 68 81 19 🕐 Jul–Aug daily 9.30–12.30, 1.30–7; Apr–Jun, Sep 9.30–12.30, 1.30–6.30; Feb–Mar, Oct–Nov 9.30–12.30, 1.30–5.30; Jan 9.30–12.30, 1.30–4.30. Closed last 2 weeks in Jan 🖐 Adult €5.50, child (6–16) €4. With audioguide: adult €7.50, child €6

PÉROUGES

www.perouges.org

Voted one of the most beautiful villages in France, Pérouges is a tiny stone settlement seemingly transported from the 15th century to the present day. It sits on a small rocky outcrop 290m (950ft) above the Ain valley and 35km (22 miles) northeast of Lyon. Perfectly preserved, it has been used in numerous period films and TV shows. It now thrives as an enclave for artists and has several small galleries. It is also known for its production of the sweet, thin biscuits called les galettes de Pérouges.

The main entrance to the village is the 11th-century Porte d'En Haut. It is marked by the Église-Forteresse (fortified church), built into the ramparts, the circle of fortified houses that form the outer layer of village buildings. The rue des Rondes follows the lines of the ramparts inside, encircling the heart of Pérouges, the place des Halles. This square is also known as place de Tilleul, and its medieval houses are now occupied by souvenir shops or cafés.

In the corner of the square is the entrance to the Musée du Vieux Pérouges (Easter–Sep daily 10–12, 2–6), where your ticket also gives admission to the remains of the old château, the Maison des Princes.

Be aware that the old, cobbled streets are exceptionally uneven—not ideal for wheelchairs or high-heels.

🕇 461 M9 🛈 Syndicat d'Initiative de Pérouges, 01800 ☎ 04 74 46 70 84 🕐 May–Aug daily 10–5; Mar, Apr, Sep, Oct Tue–Fri 10–12, 2–5, Sat 2–5; Nov–Feb Mon–Fri 2–4.30 🚉 Meximieux then 1km (0.6 mile) walk

LE PUY DE DÔME

www.puydedome.com

Le Puy de Dôme is the highest of a series of 80 ancient volcanic peaks in the southern Massif Central. The almost circular dome of laval rock rises 1,465m (4,805ft) and offers

Left Sundial in the market square, Pérouges
Opposite The imposing Puy de Dôme

wonderful views of the Auvergne national park and the city of Clermont-Ferrand (▷ 262).

Leave your car in the parking area at the foot of the *puy* and walk or take the *navette* (shuttle bus), which runs in July and August to the summit. Another *navette* leaves from the train station in Clermont-Ferrand four times a day and links with the parking area (see information below).

The visitor centre at the summit has an explanation in French and English of how the peak and other volcanic features of the surrounding Auvergne hills were formed. 'Tables d'orientation' on the terraces help you get your bearings and there are footpaths around the summit. You can also see the remains of the first-century Roman Temple of Mercury and the huge Télé de France antenna (off-limits to the public), but the stunning views alone make a trip to the top worthwhile.

You can learn more about how volcanoes work at Vulcania, 5km (3 miles) from the Puy de Dôme (tel 08 20 82 78 28; www.vulcania.com; Jul–Aug daily 9.30–7, rest of year 10–6; closed Jan–Feb, 1–11 Nov). This state-of-the-art attraction is cut out of underground volcanic basalt and is linked to Puy de Dôme by the Clermont-Ferrand *navette*.

✚ 460 K10 ✉ Off the N89, 10km (6 miles) west of Clermont-Ferrand ☎ 04 73 62 12 18; visitor centre: 04 73 62 21 46 🕔 Jun–Aug daily 7am–10pm; May, Sep, Oct 8am–9.30pm; Mar, Apr, Nov, Dec 8–7. Closed Dec–Feb 🚗 Car €6, motorcycle €4 🚌 In Jul and Aug a shuttle bus runs daily 10–6; weekends and public hols in May, Jun, Sep from 12.30–6; adult return €4, child (4–16) €1, under 4 free 🍴 🎁 Gift shop 💻 ❓ Visitors possessing disabled badges can usually travel to the summit in their own vehicles at all times. The welcome venue is wheelchair accessible, with elevators to all areas. However, until spring 2012 the transportation system at Puy de Dôme is being renovated. There will be no *navette* between the main parking area and the summit, and the main car park will be closed some of this time. Access to the summit will be by foot only, a 45 minute ascent via the chemin des Muletiers. Disabled badge

holders will not be able to reach the summit by car until the works are finished

LE PUY-EN-VELAY
www.ot-lepuyenvelay.fr
In the heart of the wooded Auvergne region, Le Puy-en-Velay is one of France's most important religious sites. During the Middle Ages it was one of the main gathering points for pilgrims en route to Santiago de Compostela in Spain. Thanks to the pilgrims, the town grew rich and the streets of the old quarter are lined with buildings dating from the 15th to the 18th centuries.

The Romanesque Cathédrale de Notre Dame is built on the site of an alleged apparition of the Virgin. Pilgrims still flock to venerate the 18th-century statue of the Black Madonna. The adjoining cloister, classed as a national monument, has a riot of Romanesque arches around the courtyard and is decorated with several frescoes inside.

The oldest and most appealing church is tiny Chapelle St-Michel d'Aiguilhe, built high on a tufa rock in the 10th century and reached by a steep stone staircase. The 16m (52ft) statue of the Virgin Mary on another tufa column was forged from 213 cannons captured at the Siege of Sebastopol during the Crimean War.

✚ 460 L11 ℹ place du Clauzel, 43000 ☎ 04 71 09 38 41 🕔 Jul–Aug Mon–Sat 8.30–7.30, Sun 10–12.30, 2–5.30; Easter–Jun, Sep Mon–Sat 8.30–12, 1.30–6.15, Sun 10–12.30, 2–5; Oct–Easter Mon–Sat 8.30–12, 1.30–6.15, Sun 10–12 🚉 Le Puy-en-Velay

SENS
www.office-de-tourisme-sens.com
Known as 'Burgundy at the gates of Paris', Sens makes a good first port of call for visitors heading southeast from the capital. The main attraction is the Cathédrale St-Étienne and its associated museums. In the Middle Ages, the cathedral held sway over a vast ecclesiastical province that included the dioceses of Paris and Chartres. Its museums, in the former Archbishop's Palace, hold a rich collection of religious items, plus

rare silks and tapestries, ivory pieces, archaeological finds and more than 800 pieces of bronze jewellery. A more recent addition is the Collection Marrey, a private collection of 19th- and 20th-century art that includes ceramics, paintings and some bronzes by Rodin. There are also Flemish and Dutch paintings from the 16th and 17th centuries (Jul–Aug daily 10–6; Jun, Sep daily 10–12, 2–6; Oct–May Wed, Sat, Sun 10–12, 2–6, Mon, Thu–Fri 2–6).

Across place de la République from the western end of the cathedral is the massive covered market (all-day market on Monday). Some of the rooms used to display art exhibitions.

Outside town to the south, the Parc du Moulin à Tan (daily 8–dusk; glasshouses daily 2.30–5.30) has 10ha (25 acres) of parkland with botanical zones, trails and animal enclosures. Vast glasshouses contain more than 1,500 species of tropical plants, including the astonishing giant waterlily, Victoria cruziana.

✚ 465 K6 ℹ place Jean Jaurès, 89100 ☎ 03 86 65 19 49 🕔 Jul–Aug Mon–Sat 9.30–1, 2–6.30, Sun 10.20–1, 2–4.30; May–Jun, Sep–Oct Mon–Sat 9.30–12.30, 2–6, Sun 10.30–1, 2–4.30; Nov–Apr Mon–Sat 9–12.30, 2–6 🚉 Sens

TANLAY

www.chateaudetanlay.fr

The Renaissance Château de Tanlay, near Tonnerre, has elegant round towers and bell-shaped domes. Inside, there are sculpted chimney pieces, period furniture and a trompe l'œil gallery. The highlight is the painted ceiling in the Tour de la Ligue, which depicts courtiers as divinities. Entry to the interior is by guided tour only. The grounds are ideal for a picnic lunch and there is a surprisingly large supermarket in the village for provisions.

The castle, surrounded by a moat, was built on the foundations of an old fortress. In 1533 the property was left to Louise de Montmorency, widow of Gaspard de Coligny. Her son, François de Coligny d'Andelot, began major reconstruction work. In the 17th century Michel Particelli d'Hémery, finance minister and associate of Cardinal Mazarin, bought Tanlay and, with the services of the architect Le Muet, completed the main château, the Petit Château, the outbuildings, stables, grounds and the moat. At the beginning of the 18th century, the château passed into the hands of Jean Thevenin, made Marquis de Tanlay by Louis XIV, and has remained in the family ever since.

⊞ 466 L6 ✉ 89430 Château de Tanlay ☎ 03 86 75 70 61 🗓 Apr–2 Nov exterior visits: Wed–Mon 10–12.30, 2.15–6. Interior: by guided tour only at 10, 11.30, 2.15, 3.15, 4.15, 5.15 👋 Guided tour: adult €8, child (12-18) €5. Gardens: €3 🚉 Tonnerre

THIERS

www.thiers-tourisme.fr

Thiers, on a hillside above the river Durolle, is in the heart of the Parc Naturel Régional Livradois-Forez. It was capital of the French knife-making industry from the Middle Ages and there are still small artisan workshops where cutlery is made by hand. In the middle of the modern town is a tiny old quarter preserving the 15th-century street-plan and architecture, including the Hôtel du Pirou, an impressive half-timbered building dating from 1410 and now home to the tourist office.

The surrounding narrow streets have fine old corbels, lintels and doorways. It's worth taking a look inside the Église St-Genès which has one of the largest Romanesque domes in France and a simple stone interior dating from 1016. St. Genès is said to have been martyred in the town and the first church erected here in 575 was allegedly on the exact site of the saint's grave.

The excellent Musée de la Coutellerie (Cutlery Museum) is at 23 and 58 rue de la Coutellerie (Jul, Aug daily 10–12.30, 1.30–7; Jun, Sep daily 10–12, 2–6; Oct–May Tue–Sun 10–12, 2–6). Number 23 concentrates on the history of the industry with demonstrations by craftsmen, while number 58 recreates a 16th-century cutler's house. Other interesting buildings on this street include the 'house of the wild man', named after the sculpture on the facade.

⊞ 460 K9 🅸 Château (Hôtel) du Pirou, 63300 ☎ 04 73 80 65 65 🗓 Jul–Aug Mon–Sat 10–7, Sun 10–12, 1–6; Sep–Jun Mon–Sat 9.30–12, 2–6 🚉 Thiers

VÉZELAY

www.vezelaytourisme.com

People visit Vézelay for its UNESCO-listed Basilique Sainte-Madeleine. The hilltop site was a major stop on the Santiago de Compostela pilgrimage route. Reminders of this past can be seen in the brass scallop shells set into rue St-Étienne as it climbs the hill.

The entrance to the basilica is impressive: A pair of immense wooden doors, each about 3.5m (11ft) wide, are left open to welcome the continual stream of visitors. The view from here along the length of the 62m (203ft) nave is stunning. The interior is sparsely furnished and bright with sunlight beaming through the high windows on the south side.

The crypt and cloister are open to visitors and you can climb the tower (200 steps) for excellent views over the village and surrounding area. In the village, there are art galleries and souvenir shops. For the more active, the Morvan countryside—Burgundy's wilderness—is ideal for walking and mountain biking.

⊞ 466 K7 🅸 rue St. Etienne, 89450 ☎ 03 86 33 23 69 🗓 Jun–Sep daily 10–1, 2–6; Oct, Easter–May Fri–Wed 10–1, 2–6; Nov–Easter Mon–Wed, Fri–Sat 10–1, 2–6

VICHY

www.vichy-tourisme.com
www.ville-vichy.fr

Vichy has been a therapeutic base since Roman times; Julius Caesar came for treatment. In the 19th century, the patronage of Napoleon III and his family led to a golden age for the spa, which continued into the early 1900s. Today, Vichy is one of France's principal spa resorts. The leading venue is the Grand Établissement Thermal, with its shimmering Oriental domes.

Historic Vichy revolves around the huge neoclassical Palais des Congrès, designed by the architect Badger at the behest of Napoleon III in 1865. In 1903 the complex was expanded when the Opéra de Vichy was added by the belle-époque architect Lecoeur. Ballet, opera and classical music concerts take place in its art nouveau interior. The Congrès is linked to the main thermal source by the Parc des Sources, which has formal gardens and wide ornate iron and glass arcades. Les Halles des Source, houses specialists in therapeutic water treatments.

Napoleon III's influence can again be seen in the park named after him, and in the neo-Gothic Église St-Louis, whose stained glass depicts members of the ruling family.

⊞ 460 K9 🅸 19 rue du Parc, 03200 ☎ 04 70 98 71 94 🗓 Jul–Aug Mon–Sat 9–7, Sun 9.30–12, 3–7; Apr–Sep Mon–Sat 9–12.30, 1.30–7, Sun 9.30–12.30, 3–7; Oct–Mar Mon–Fri 9–12, 1.30–6, Sat 9–12, 2–6, Sun 2.30–5.30 🚉 Vichy

VIENNE

Vienne, on the eastern bank of the Rhône, is not to be missed. Its Roman remains and the Romanesque architecture in its early Christian churches—including Cathédrale St-Maurice—are exceptional, and it's a wonderful place to wander. The settlement here became one of the largest towns in Roman Gaul.

ROMAN REMAINS

You can see the remains of a Gallo-Roman town at Jardin Archéolgique de Cybèle, off place François Mitterrand, but there are better remains at the Musée et Sites Archéologiques de St-Romain-en-Gal (Tue–Sun 10–6). The remains of streets, houses and public baths form an open-air exhibition. A glass and steel structure houses the main body of the museum, with excellent mosaics. The Théâtre Romain (Apr–Aug daily 9.30–1, 2–6; Sep–Oct Tue–Sun 9.30–1, 2–6; Nov–Mar Tue–Fri 9.30–12.30, 2–5, Sat–Sun 1.30–5.30) was one of the largest in the world when it was completed around AD50. Restored in 1930, it now hosts summer concerts.

MUSEUMS

The Musée des Beaux-Arts et d'Archéologie (Apr–Nov Tue–Sun 9.30–1, 2–6; Dec–Mar Tue–Fri 9.30–12.30, 2–5, Sat–Sun 1.30–5.30), in a 19th-century grain store, displays domestic items used in Roman daily life. The Musée Archéologique, in the Église St-Pierre, has a fine statue of Tutela, the Gallo-Roman goddess and guardian of Vienne.

INFORMATION

www.vienne-tourisme.com

✚ 461 M10 ℹ Cours Brillier, 38200
☎ 04 74 53 80 30 🕐 Late Jun–Sep Mon–Sat 9–6, Sun 10–6; Oct–Jun Mon–Sat 9–12, 2–6, Sun 10–12, 2–6
🔁 2-hour guided city tours throughout the year, tel: 04 74 53 80 31 🚉 Vienne

TIPS

» You can buy a multi-entry ticket to six attractions at museums or the tourist office.
» Book tickets and accommodation early if coming for the jazz festival in early June.
» A *petit train* runs through the town in summer, linking the major attractions.

Above *A tapestry in Vienne's cathedral*
Opposite *Water lilies on the moat surrounding Château de Tanlay*

CASCADES DU HÉRISSON

In the heart of the Jura mountains, the Vallée du Hérisson is known for its romantic setting, primeval forests and abundant wildlife, and the area around the Cascades du Hérisson is ideal for exploring on foot. Wear sturdy footwear and be aware that this walk is hilly in places. If time is pressing, the walk can be shortened by driving to Bonlieu, where the falls are signed down a small lane that leads to a parking area at le Saut de la Forge (see below).

THE WALK
Distance: 4km (2.5 miles)
Allow: 3 hours
Start/end at: Ilay

HOW TO GET THERE
Ilay is in the Jura, east of Lons-le-Saunier off the N78.

Hérisson is the name given to the river by a 19th-century cartographer. The original name, Yrisson, means 'sacred water' and has nothing to do with the hedgehog, the present-day translation of *hérisson*. The importance of the valley dates back to the Middle Ages, when three monastic orders fought for control of the river and the right to build various kinds of mills and forges.

The area still relies on its abundant natural resources to maintain its way of life. The Jura, one of the most wooded parts of France, is a conservation area supporting a variety of wildlife, much of which, though flourishing there, is endangered throughout the world.

★ At Ilay, there is a large parking area opposite the start of the walk, on the D39 about 100m (109 yards) from a crossroads and behind the Auberge du Hérisson. Follow the signs to Saut Girard, about 500m (550 yards) to the south, via tree-covered pathways and fields.

❶ An ironworks once stood beside the waterfall of Saut Girard; in 1811, 65 tonnes were produced in the village. Half a century later Saut Girard was a marble works.

During the Middle Ages and up to 1714, a bridge over the fall linked Lons-le-Saunier with St-Laurent-en-Grandvaux and Geneva beyond, and was used to transport salt, wine and other products.

Walk on to Saut du Moulin, beside the ruins of the mill Le Moulin Jeunet 20m (22 yards) to the right.

❷ Known as the Moulin de Frasnois in 1434, Le Moulin Jeunet fell into ruin in the 17th century after a war which devastated the lake region. It was rebuilt by Frasnois villagers in 1663. At the end of the 19th century, Séraphin-François Jeunet became the owner of the mill.

Walk on to Le Saut de la Forge, site of another former ironworks; there is a useful orientation board here. Continue walking to Le Gour Bleu, a romantic spot which is reached via a tree-covered path.

❸ The blue waters of the river are so clear that you can see right through to the gleaming river bed. Relax and enjoy the soothing sound of the waterfalls.

Cross the Hérisson river by the footbridge called Passerelle Lacuzon and climb the steep path to reach La Grotte Lacuzon, at the foot of the waterfalls of Le Grand Saut.

❹ These falls are best seen from below the towering 60m (200ft) drop. From here, after a 400m (440 yard) hike, you find yourself at the foot of Cascade de l'Éventail.

❺ This is another spectacular waterfall, with the water flowing down for 65m (215ft) over a succession of zigzag steps known as 'the Great Organ'.

❻ You can climb to the summit of l'Éventail via the Sarrazine footbridge, which takes you to the Belvédère des Tuffs and gives a fine view of the Hérisson valley and the Cascades du Hérisson.

Return the same way.

WHEN TO GO
The falls depend on local rainfall, and so reduce to a trickle in a dry summer. They are also very popular, so July and August are very busy. Spring is a good time to visit, when the falls are in full flow and woodland flowers are blooming. If the falls are in fullest flood, wet weather clothing and waterproof boots are essential.

WHERE TO EAT
AU CHALET
www.restaurant-au-chalet.com
✉ 2 routre du Lac, 39130 Bonlieu
☎ 03 84 25 57 04

INFORMATION
TOURIST INFORMATION
www.juralacs.com

Opposite *The spectacular Cascade de l'Eventail*

CANAL DE BOURGOGNE

The majestic Burgundy Canal has become one of the most popular waterways in France for boating. In summer, all types of craft jostle for position as they wait to get through the succession of locks that takes them past sleepy villages and rolling pastoral landscapes dotted with grazing cows and sheep. This drive roughly follows the canal between Tonnerre and Flavigny-sur-Ozerain, taking in châteaux, an ancient abbey and a Gallo-Roman site.

THE DRIVE

Distance: 90km (56 miles)
Allow: 1 day
Start at: Tonnerre
End at: Flavigny-sur-Ozerain

★ Tonnerre is a former Gallo-Roman settlement. Its tourist office is located inside the town's major sight, the Hôtel-Dieu, a 13th-century hospice of awe-inspiring proportions. Its immense beams were cut from local oak forests. Built by Marguerite of Burgundy, sister-in-law to Saint Louis, today's hospital still receives an income from the provisions of her will, now more than 700 years old. The building also houses the town's main museum, the Musée Marguerite de Bourgogne.

Another and more unusual sight is a spring called the Fossé Dionne, a water source emerging from a rocky escarpment and almost completely surrounded by the old wash-house. It's a charming spot, with the bluish-green water in the spring's basin overlooked by cottages, trees and the church of St-Pierre.

From Tonnerre, take the D965 to the village of Tanlay.

❶ Tanlay (▷ 272 and 278–279, walk) is an unassuming village with a beautiful Renaissance château. Built in 1550 for François de Coligny, it is surrounded by a moat and splendid gardens.

Next stop is Ancy-le-Franc. To get there continue on the D965 and turn right onto the D12. Alternatively, head back to the canal, crossing it at St-Vinnemer, and pick up the D905 to Ancy-le-Franc.

❷ The Château d'Ancy-le-Franc, built in the mid-16th century, is considered to be one of the finest examples of Renaissance architecture in Burgundy. At various times, it hosted Henri IV, Louis XIII and Louis XIV. The interior, restored and redecorated in the 19th century, is especially interesting.

Continue on the D905 through several villages and Montbard, then turn left onto the D32 to the Abbaye de Fontenay.

❸ L'Abbaye de Fontenay is one of the most beautiful abbeys in France.

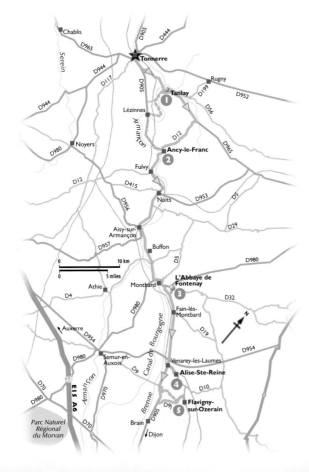

Set in a cool wooded valley and largely undamaged, it is a perfect example of a Cistercian abbey. The church, with its earthen floor, is the setting for classical concerts in the summer, and the sculpted cloister is one of the best preserved in France. The gardens are a joy, with their fountain and fish pond. The abbey, a UNESCO World Heritage Site, was once owned by the Montgolfier family, pioneers of hot-air ballooning.

Return to the D905 and follow it to Alise-Sainte-Reine.

❹ Gaulish warriors, led by Vercingetorix, retreated to Alise-Sainte-Reine after their failed attack on Julius Caesar in 52BC (▷ 30). Caesar's legions dug double trenches and fortified earthworks around the Gauls' camp to prevent them from escaping and to defend themselves from relief troops coming to save their besieged allies. After six weeks of trying to break through these barriers, Vercingetorix was forced to surrender and was later paraded through the streets of Rome, imprisoned for six years and finally strangled. An imposing statue of the Gaulish leader dominates the place.

Return to the D905 and turn left onto D9J (or D9) to Flavigny-sur-Ozerain.

❺ The tiny hilltop village of Flavigny-sur-Ozerain was once the religious base of the Auxois region. You can see the remains of an important abbey, with a Carolingian crypt. The village's old fortress gates are still standing, as are houses dating from the 13th century. *Anis de Flavigny* (aniseed sweets/candy) have been produced here since the ninth century. The film *Chocolat*, starring Juliette Binoche, was filmed here.

WHERE TO EAT
If you want to stop for a picnic, there are plenty of good places where the road runs alongside the canal. Just after Lézinnes the road crosses the river and then the canal. Turn immediately right and drive for about

Above *The Château de Tanlay*

500m (550 yards) to the Port de Lézinnes (signposted Port Fluvial). There is plenty of space to park, along with picnic tables, benches and a small see-saw for children.

PLACES TO VISIT
CHÂTEAU D'ANCY-LE-FRANC
www.château-ancy.com
✉ 89160 Ancy-le-Franc ☎ 03 86 75 14 63 ❂ Guided tours only Easter to mid-Nov Tue–Sun 👜 Adult €9, child (6–15) €6 🚍 Apr–Sep Tue–Sun 10.30, 11.30, 2, 3, 4, 5; Oct to mid-Nov 10.30, 11.30, 2, 3, 4

ABBAYE DE FONTENAY
www.abbayedefontenay.com
✉ 21500 Montbard ☎ 03 80 92 15 00 🚍 Guided tours only, lasting 1 hour. Jul–Aug 10–7; Apr–Jun, Sep–11 Nov 10–6; Oct–Mar 10–12, 2–5 👜 Adult €7.80, under 25 €3.70

CAROLINGIAN CRYPT AT FLAVIGNY-SUR-OZERAIN
www.alesia-tourism.net
❂ May–Aug daily 9–12, 2–6; Sep–Apr Mon–Tue 8.30–11.30, 2–5, Wed 8.30–11.30, 2–4, Fri 8.30–11.30, Sat–Sun 10–6 👜 Adult €1, under 12 free

INFORMATION
TOURIST INFORMATION
www.tonnerre.fr
✉ Le Cellier, place Marguerite de Bourgogne, 89700 Tonnerre ☎ 03 86 55 14 48 ❂ Jul–Aug Mon–Sat 9.30–12, 1.30–6.30, Sun 10–12.30, 1.30–6; Apr–Jun, Sep daily 9.30–12, 1.30–6. Closed Oct–Mar Wed and Sun

BOAT INFORMATION
Boats can be hired in several places along the canal: Tonnerre and other bases on the Yonne river at the northern end; Montbard near the middle; and St-Jean-de-Losne, Pont d'Ouche and Pouilly-en-Auxois at the southern end. Locks close for lunch daily, and on public holidays. Hours vary according to season, so check before setting out. The canal closes between November and March. This tour includes a section of the canal from Tonnerre to Flavigny, but there are plenty of other interesting towns and villages to visit if you have time to explore the full length of the canal.

CANALSIDE WALK

This stroll along a stretch of the Canal de Bourgogne also includes a fine example of another of Burgundy's major features, its châteaux.

THE WALK
Distance: 4.5km (3 miles)
Allow: 1 hour 30 minutes
Start/end at: Tanlay

HOW TO GET THERE
Midway between Auxerre and Dijon in Burgundy, Tanlay is east of Tonnerre on the D965. There is a small parking area between the canal and the tennis courts.

★ The walk starts at Tanlay, a village known for its fine château (▷ 272). Set off from the bridge over the Canal de Bourgogne where the

D965 approaches the village from the Tonnerre direction. Walk away from the bridge along rue du Port towards the heart of the village, then branch off to the left along the canal towpath, with the canal on the left.

❶ The Canal de Bourgogne winds through Burgundy from the Yonne to the Saône, providing a link between the Channel and the Mediterranean. It was once a major highway for freight. Now it carries holiday traffic.

At the first lock gate, cross the canal and continue along the towpath

for 1km (0.5 mile) to the next road bridge. Cross the canal here and walk into the village of Commissey.

❷ Just after crossing the canal at Commissey, look for the wash-house on the left. Turn left at the crossroads in the village to see a small church in Romanesque style, with an unusual stained-glass window in the dome above the altar.

Go straight ahead at place de la Mairie, along rue Haute, and at the crossroads just outside the village carry straight on along a minor road signed for Quincy and Rugny. Walk uphill for 300m (330 yards) to a crossroads, and turn right. Within 100m (109 yards) the surfaced road becomes a rough track.

❸ There are good views from this path into the valley of the Armançon and towards Tonnerre. The landscape is cultivated fields and woods.

Follow this track through open countryside for 400m (440 yards), and about 100m (109 yards) before it enters a wood, turn left on to another, almost invisible track. After 100m (109 yards) the track bears right over stony ground and then becomes a broad path going downhill through a lightly wooded area. Bear left where the path meets a field, and when the path forks near the edge of the wooded area, bear right and continue downhill with a wall to the right.

After another 225m (250 yards) the path meets a road. Turn right along the road and after 100m (109 yards) take the next road to the left, signed for St-Vinnemer and Lézinnes, and return to Tanlay. Opposite rue du Port, turn left into Grande Rue Basse, and after 250m (275 yards) reach the entrance to the Château de Tanlay.

❹ The Château de Tanlay (▷ 272) was built in the mid-16th century and is an excellent example of French Renaissance architecture. Surrounded by a moat, it is set in a beautiful park and was a Protestant stronghold in the Wars of Religion; tours are available.

Turn right in front of the château, following signs to Auxerre and Tonnerre, and walk along an avenue of tall trees. Just past two soccer pitches turn right on the road to Tonnerre and walk about 100m (109 yards) to the parking area.

WHEN TO GO
This walk can be done at any time of year. If you'd like to visit the château, telephone ahead to check opening hours as it may be closed in autumn and winter.

WHERE TO EAT
There are several good picnic areas along the route, including the grounds of the château, the path down through the woodland, and beside the canal when you have finished the walk.

Opposite and above *Barges and canal boats tied up in the basin of the Canal de Bourgogne, at Tanlay*
Below *The Canal de Bourgogne is a good place for a bit of peace and quiet*

MONTS DU CANTAL

Magnificent green landscapes await you on this tour of the *département* which makes up the south of the Auvergne region. Its highlight is an ascent to the summit of a volcanic peak. Before and after there are historic towns to explore. While you are in these parts, you may want to stop and buy some locally made Cantal cheese.

THE DRIVE

Distance: 91km (57 miles)
Allow: 1 day
Start at: Aurillac
End at: Salers

★ Aurillac, in the *préfecture* of Cantal, is an administrative and commercial city, with only a few pretty corners such as place St-Gérard. It can be by-passed if you are starting from elsewhere.

Leave Aurillac following the signs for Clermont-Ferrand on the D117 which runs above the suburbs and round the hillside to join the N122, the main road along the broad green pastoral Cère valley.

❶ The town of Polminhac is overlooked by the forbidding square

tower of the Château de Pesteils which stands on a rocky outcrop.

You now enter the Parc des Volcans, which covers much of the Auvergne. In Vic-sur-Cère, park in the small square to the left of the road by the newsagent's shop to take a walk in the old town.

❷ Vic-sur-Cère has some attractive streets of large old houses, which climb the hill above the road. The partly Romanesque church has an ocatagonal belfry and carved corbels beneath the eaves.

From Vic the N122 winds up through woods to the Pas de Cère, crosses and recrosses the Cère, passes by Thiézac on the left and through St-Jacques-des-Blats.

❸ If you've got a clear day, you should glimpse good views of mountains along this stretch of road. To the right is the Plomb du Cantal (1,855m/6,086ft) the highest peak in the Cantal.

As you approach the ski resort of Le Lioran, the road runs through a modern tunnel. After the tunnel it descends towards Murat, which is announced by the sight of a lonely church on a hilltop.

❹ Murat deserves a leisurely stroll around its lovely old streets which are steep and often stepped. A well-signposted route takes you around the most interesting buildings. Before you leave Murat make sure you have enough fuel to get you to Salers at the end of the route.

Leave Murat the way you came and turn right on the D3 towards Dienne and Salers. The road curves round a basalt outcrop on which stands a giant statue of the Virgin Mary. On the other side of the Col d'Entremont turn left on to the D680 towards Dienne and Salers.

After Dienne the road winds through two hamlets that come to life only between spring and autumn. Continue up the valley and fork left for the Pas de Peyrol.

❺ At 1,588m (5,210ft) the Pas de Peyrol is the highest road pass in France. In summer it is crowded with visitors, some travelling by bicycle, who come to undertake the relatively easy climb up steps to the top of Puy Mary (1,787m/5,863ft). Allow 45 minutes to walk up and down from the visitor centre.

Stay on the D680, passing the Cirque de Falgoux, a corrie (deep hollow) formed by glaciation, and descend to Salers.

❻ The end point of the route is the handsome town of Salers distinguished by its Renaissance architecture dating from its 15th-century heyday as a bailiwick of the region.

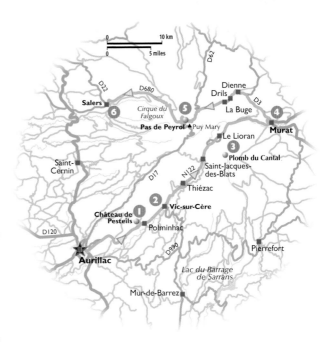

WHEN TO GO
The Pas de Peyrol is closed from October to May. In spring and autumn check that it is clear of snow before you approach it. In summer large vehicles including camping cars must follow a one-way traffic flow system over the pass.

WHERE TO EAT
Murat offers the best choice on the route with a brasserie, pizzeria, two snack bars and several restaurants.

Opposite *Salers' Renaissance architecture*
Below *Murat's houses bathed in sunlight*

ANNECY
BÂTEAUX DUPRAZ
www.bateauxdupraz.com

Take a boat trip on Lac d'Annecy in a 30-seater boat, L'Arc en Ciel ('The Rainbow'). The lake tour, lasting 30 or 50 minutes, has commentary in English and French. Board at Jardins de l'Europe opposite L'Île des Cygnes 15 minutes prior to departure.

 quai Napoléon 111, 74000 Annecy ☎ 04 50 51 52 15 or 04 50 52 42 99 🕓 Mid Jul to mid Aug 11.45, 1.15, 2.30, 3.45, 5.15, 6.30; Apr to mid-Jul, mid-Aug to mid-Nov 11.45, 2.30, 3.45, 5.15, 6.30. Closed mid-Nov to Mar ✋ Adult €12.50, child €8.50

BICYCLING
www.lac-annecy.com

A bicycle track runs from Annecy to Giez skirting Lac d'Annecy, with superb views of surrounding mountains. You can rent bicycles from various places, including Roul'mapoule (47 Avenue du Petit Port, tel 04 50 23 31 15).

 Office de Tourisme, 1 rue Jean Jaurès, 74000 Annecy ☎ 04 50 45 00 33

COURIER
www.centre-courier.com

This air-conditioned shopping mall has about 40 boutiques selling household goods, clothes, beauty products, perfume and gifts, and there's a large supermarket. Relax in a comfortable leather armchair in the brasserie with a post-shopping drink.

 65 rue Carnot, 74000 Annecy ☎ 04 50 46 46 76 🕓 Mon–Sat 9.30–7.30; supermarket Mon–Sat 8.30–9; brasserie 8am–11pm

MARKETS

A weekly food market lines rue de la République, rue Sainte-Claire, Pont Morens and quai de l'Évêché, while clothes, books and leather goods are sold on place Romains. A monthly art and antiques market is held in rue Sainte-Claire, place Sainte-Claire, quai l'Évêché, Pont Morens, rue de la République and rue de l'Isle.

☎ 04 50 45 00 33 (tourist information) 🕓 Food market: Tue 8–12; general goods: Tue 8–7; antiques: last Sat of month 8–7

TAKAMAKA
www.takamaka.fr

This outdoor-pursuit company runs a whole range of different programmes including paragliding—a wonderful way to take in the landscape. Other land activities include cross country mountain biking and free climbing, or try white-water rafting, water skiing or canyoning.

 23 Faubourg Sainte-Claire, 74000 Annecy ☎ 04 50 45 60 61 🕓 Jul–Aug Mon–Fri 9–7; Sep–Jun Mon–Fri 9–12, 2–6 ✋ Dual paraglide €85

ARBOIS
DOMAINE ROLET PÈRE ET FILS
www.rolet-arbois.com

One of the most renowned producers of Jura wines including award-winning Arbois reds, *vin jaune* and *vin de paille*, they have a shop in town, in front of the Hôtel de Ville.

 Montigny, 39600 Arbois ☎ 03 84 66 00 05 🕓 Mon–Sat 9–12, 2–6.30, Sun 2.30–6.30

BEAUNE
ATHENAEUM DE LA VIGNE ET DU VIN
www.athenaeumfr.com

The art of the table is the theme of this shop directly opposite the famed Hospices de Beaune. The shop sells fine tableware, wine, books about wine and local food and drink such as Dijon mustard, *crème de cassis* and *pain d'épices*.

 5 rue de l'Hôtel-Dieu, 21200 Beaune ☎ 03 80 25 08 30 🕓 Daily 10–7

MAISON DENIS PERRET
www.denisperret.fr

Maison Denis Perret has been here since 1973 (the Denis Perret grocery shop preceded it). Today you can find a superb range of Burgundy wines with more than 300 labels.

 place Carnot, 21200 Beaune ☎ 03 80 22 35 47 🕓 Jul–Aug daily 9–7; Jun, Sep Mon–Fri 9–12, 2–7, Sat 10–12, 2–7, Sun 10–12; Oct–May Mon–Fri 9–12, 2–7, Sat 10–12, 2–7

LA MOUTARDERIE FALLOT
www.fallot.com

The Fallot mustard mill, five minutes' walk from the heart of the historic town, is Burgundy's last independent mustard business. The one-hour interactive tour using infrared lighting

Above *Skiing in the French Alps*

and 3-D animation gives an insight into both modern and traditional manufacturing methods.

✉ 31 Faubourg Bretonnerie, 21200 Beaune ☎ 03 80 22 10 02 🕐 Jun–Aug Mon–Sat 10, 11.30, 3.30, 5; mid-Mar to May, Sep to mid-Oct Mon–Sat 10, 11.30. Closed mid-Nov to mid-Mar 💶 Adult €10, child (under 10) €8

OPÉRA NIGHT
www.operanight.net
One thing you won't find here is opera. This nightclub complex has three rooms: L'Opéra has the largest dance floor, Le Kiss plays music from the 1980s and 90s, and L'Armstrong attracts a well-dressed crowd. There's also a cocktail bar, Le Viva Café.

✉ rue de Beaumarché, Palais des Congrès, 21200 Beaune ☎ 03 80 24 10 11 🕐 Fri–Sat 11pm–6am 💶 Free Fri before midnight, €10 at other times 🚉 Beaune

LE TAST'FROMAGES
www.fromagerie-hess.com
This cheese shop sells about 120 different types including Délice de Pommard made from a ball of Brillat-Savarin (the creamy cheese from Normandy) matured in mustard seeds or blackcurrant buds. Burgundy specials include Époisses au Marc de Bourgogne and Amour de Nuits-St-Georges.

✉ 7 place Carnot, 21200 Beaune ☎ 03 80 24 73 51 🕐 Mon–Sat 8.30–12.30, 2.30–7.30, Sun 8.30–12.30

BESANÇON
LE THÉÂTRE MUSICAL DE BESANÇON
www.letheatre-besancon.fr
Franche-Comté's leading classical performing-arts venue has a varied schedule of opera, operetta, ballet and classical recitals.

✉ place du Théâtre, 25000 Besançon ☎ 03 81 87 81 97 🕐 Performances from 7.30pm 💶 Adult €10–€41

CHAMBÉRY
L'ÉCOLE DE PARACHUTISME DE SAVOIE
www.centre-parachutisme.com
This parachute school runs jumps for beginners and experienced skydivers.

Beginners can do a tandem jump with an instructor over Lake Bourget, providing wonderful views of Mont Blanc and the Alps. Those arriving by car should take the A43 from Lyon or the A41, then follow signs for the airport. The EPS offices are located next to the airport building but the activity area is next to Savoie Technolac. If you arrive by train at Chambéry's railway station you can be collected, but you need to give advance notice.

✉ Aéroport de Chambéry, 73420 Viviers du Lac ☎ 04 79 54 42 93 or 06 13 09 61 56 🕐 Daily 8am–9pm. Closed Jan, Feb 💶 First tandem jump €250

CHAMONIX-MONT BLANC
CASINO DE CHAMONIX
www.casinodefranceonline.com
You'll need your passport to get into this casino, which has French and English roulette, two blackjack tables, stud poker and slot machines. If you're hungry there's a restaurant serving Italian dishes, and there's a karaoke bar.

✉ 12 place de Saussure, 74400 Chamonix ☎ 04 50 53 07 65 🕐 Sun–Thu 8pm–2am, Fri–Sat 8pm–3am; Slot machines from 11am 💶 Free

CENTRE SPORTIF
Facilities include a swimming pool (with a slide and paddling pool), a Jacuzzi, saunas, steam rooms, a weights room, an ice rink, a climbing wall and tennis and squash courts. The restaurant and bar are next to the ice rink.

✉ 214 avenue de la Plage, 74400 Chamonix ☎ 04 50 53 09 07 🕐 Mon–Fri 12–7.30, Sat–Sun 2–7.30. Ice rink closed early May to mid-Jul 💶 Pool, ice rink or weights €5.30, squash/tennis €16, weights room €9.50

COMPAGNIE DU MONT BLANC
www.compagniedumontblanc.fr
This company arranges summer and winter sports including skiing, snowboarding and walking. It sells ski passes valid for all ski areas in Chamonix valley except Les Houches. A photo is essential for passes of four or more days. There are numerous pass options, including

beginner and family passes, which you can buy at the tourist office or at the cash desks of Compagnie du Mont Blanc. The website is useful for pre-planning.

✉ 35 place de la Mer de Glace, 74400 Chamonix ☎ 04 50 53 22 75 🕐 Open according to season and weather conditions 💶 One-day pass from €49.50, 13 days €420; family passes available

CHEVERNY
Established more than 30 years ago, Cheverny stocks high-quality kitchen gifts. You can buy items relating to Alpine cuisine, such as fondue sets, as well as Limoges porcelain, Lalique and Baccarat crystal, kitchen utensils and more everyday glassware.

✉ 126 rue Paccard, 74400 Chamonix ☎ 04 50 53 03 74 🕐 Daily 9–12, 2.30–7

REFUGE PAYOT
www.refugepayot.com
This fine food store sells local and gourmet cheeses, cold meats, wines and spirits, chocolate, honey and preserved fruit.

✉ 166 rue Vallot, 74400 Chamonix ☎ 04 50 53 18 71 🕐 Daily 8.15am–7.45pm

VOX
www.cinemavox-chamonix.com
This cinema has three screens, one with Dolby surround sound. There are several screenings of the latest movies per day, often screened in English with subtitles, and extra shows in bad weather to entertain grounded skiers and snowboarders.

✉ Cours de Bartavel, 74400 Chamonix ☎ 04 50 53 03 39 (recorded film times and info in French) 💶 Adult €8, child (under 12) €5.50, €7.50 per person for groups

CHAMPAGNE-SUR-LOUE
YVES FAILLENET
www.jurapeche.com
Professional fly fishing tuition is available here. There are one- to five-day courses on the riverbanks of the Jura.

✉ La Louve du Val d'Amour, Impasse du Rang, 39600 Champagne-sur-Loue ☎ 03 84 37 70 17 🕐 Fishing season May–Dec (for various species) 💶 1-day course €130 per person or €100 per person for 3 people

DIJON
BOUTIQUE MAILLE
www.maille.com
Maille are the masters of mustard production and have been in business since 1747. Today they also produce a fantastic range of oils, condiments and pickles. A must for your kitchen if your baggage allowance can take the weight.
✉ 32 rue de la Liberté, 21000 Dijon ☎ 03 80 30 41 02 🕐 Mon–Sat 9–7

LE FRASNOIS
ÉCURIE DES 4 LACS
www.ecuriedes4lacs.com
Go on a horseback riding holiday in the Jura with accommodation and meals included or simply go on a half-day or a full-day cross-country trail (for beginners and experienced riders). Maximum of 10 people.
✉ route des Lacs, 39130 Le Frasnois ☎ 06 86 92 01 52 🕐 Mid-Jan to Nov ✋ 2-day, 1-night packages from €230 per person

GRENOBLE
MARKETS
Grenoble's best markets include Marché place aux Herbes for food, Marché Victor Hugo for crafts and manufactured goods, and Marché de l'Abbaye for food and crafts.
ℹ Office de Tourisme, Hôtel de Ville, 11 boulevard Jean Pain, 38000 Grenoble ☎ 04 76 76 36 36 🕐 Marché place aux Herbes: Tue–Sun 6–1; Marché Victor Hugo: Mon–Sat 10–8; Marché de l'Abbaye: Tue–Sun 6–1

LA SOUPE AUX CHOUX
www.jazzalasoupe.free.fr
On the north side of the river, La Soupe aux Choux is home to the Grenoble Jazz Club. Concerts feature all types of jazz, including modern, swing, blues and New Orleans.
✉ 7 route de Lyon, 38000 Grenoble ☎ 04 76 87 05 67 🕐 Wed–Sat 8.30pm–1am. Closed Aug ✋ Varies, passes available 🚌 33

TÉLÉPHÉRIQUE DE GRENOBLE-BASTILLE
www.bastille-grenoble.com
The first aerial cable car in France, built in 1934, is a relaxing way of reaching the Bastille Fort. At the top are restaurants and a souvenir shop.
✉ quai Stéphane Jay, 38000 Grenoble ☎ 04 76 44 33 65 🕐 Téléphérique: Jul–Aug Mon 11am–12.15am, Tue–Sun 9.15am–12.15am; Jun, Sep Mon 11am–11.45pm, Tue–Sat 9.30am–11.45pm, Sun 9.30–7.25; Oct–May Mon, Tue 11–6.30, Wed, Thu, Sun 10.45–6.30, Fri, Sat 10.45am–12.15am ✋ Adult return €6.50, child (5–18) return €4.05

LYON
BERNACHON
www.bernachon.com
This heavenly chocolate shop and tea room in the 6th *arrondissement* (take Métro line A to Foch) is filled with a variety of beautifully packaged sweets (candy). Prices are high, but the quality is worth it. The tea room serves refreshments and lunch. Try the superb hot chocolate.
✉ 42 cours Franklin Roosevelt, 69006 Lyon ☎ 04 78 24 37 98 🕐 May–Jul Tue–Sat 8.30–7; Sep Tue–Sat 8.30–7, Sun 8.30–1; Oct–Nov, Jan–Apr Tue–Sat 8.30–7, Sun 8.30–5; Dec 8.30–12, 2–6.30, Sun 8.30–5. Closed late Jul–late Aug

DECITRE
www.decitre.fr
A bookworm's paradise in the heart of the city, opposite place Bellecour. Subjects include travel, cookery, language and educational material as well as maps and calendars. There is a huge section of paperback fiction in English at the shop entrance and English is spoken here. (A second Decitre shop is on the opposite, southern side of Bellecour.)
✉ 6 place Bellecour, 69002 Lyon ☎ 04 26 68 00 12 🕐 Mon–Sat 9.30–7 🚇 Lines A and D: Bellecour

LES HALLES DE LYON
www.lyon.fr
This covered market with stands, cafés and small shops offers superb food and flowers. Don't miss Bahadourian, a shop full of Asian and North African spices and foodstuffs. And look for *'Saint Marcellin affiné par la Mère Richard'*, the only cheesemaker whose name appears on local restaurant menus.
✉ 102 cours Lafayette, 69003 Lyon ☎ 04 78 62 39 33 🕐 Daily 7–12, 3–7 🚇 Line B, or tram T1 to Part-Dieu

MARCHÉ DE LA CROIX ROUSSE
www.lyon.fr
Covering almost the entire length of boulevard de la Croix Rousse, the Tuesday morning street market sells fruit, flowers and vegetables, household goods, clothes, shoes, pottery, fabric, baskets and beds. From Wednesday to Sunday the market sells only food and on Saturday morning there is also organic produce. Arrive early to avoid the crowds.
✉ boulevard de la Croix Rousse, 69001 and 69004 Lyon 🕐 Wed–Thu 6–12.30; Tue, Fri, Sat–Sun 6–1.30 🚌 13, 18

NUITS DE FOURVIÈRE
www.nuits-de-fourviere.org
The remains of Lyon's Roman amphitheatre are transformed into a spectacular concert venue each year with theatre, opera, dance, cinema and music. You sit on the stone seats of the amphitheatre, so take a cushion. Take the Métro to Vieux-Lyon station and then the funicular in the direction of St-Just. Alight at Minimes-Théâtres Romains.
✉ 1 rue Clébers, 69005 Lyon ☎ 04 72 32 00 00 (concert info and tickets) 🕐 Jun–Jul ✋ Adult €10–€45

L'OPÉRA NATIONALE DE LYON
www.opera-lyon.org
Built in 1831, the opera building was altered in 1993 by architect Jean Nouvel, who created a building around the old theatre. Inside, the Italianate auditorium has retained its original character.
✉ place de la Comédie, 69001 Lyon ☎ 0826 305 325 (toll call) 🕐 Box office: Mon–Sat 12–7 ✋ Opera €13–€90, concert €13–€53, ballet €15–€45 🚇 Lines B and C to Hôtel de Ville 🍴

PARC DE LA TÊTE D'OR
www.lyon.fr
Dating from 1856, this park includes botanic gardens, a zoo, a rose

Opposite *Lyon's market*

garden, a boating lake, children's play areas and a café/restaurant. You can walk, jog or rollerblade in the park, or rent a bicycle.

✉ 69006 Lyon ☎ 04 72 69 47 60 🌐 May–Sep daily 6.30–10.30; Oct–Apr 6.30–8.30. Zoo: mid-Apr to mid-Oct 9.30–6.30; mid-Oct to mid-Apr 9.30–4.30; botanical gardens: Apr–Sep 8–6; Oct–Mar 8–5 ✋ Free entry to the park 🚌 4, 47 🚋 Masséna

PART DIEU SHOPPING CENTRE
www.centrecommercial-partdieu.com
A huge water feature dominates this shopping mall with banks, a cinema, restaurants, tea rooms, bars, the Galeries Lafayette department store and Carrefour supermarket.

✉ 17 rue de Dr Bouchut, 69003 Lyon ☎ 04 72 60 60 62 🌐 Mon–Sat 9.30–8

LE VILLAGE DES CRÉATEURS
www.villagedescreateurs.com
This renovated *traboule* (vaulted walkway) has become a centre of fashion in the city. The space is set aside for young designers and offers workspace and retail units. More than a dozen designers are now based here with specialists in leather, accessories and ladiesware.

✉ Passage Thiaffait, 19 rue René Leynaud, 69001 Lyon ☎ 04 78 27 37 21 🌐 Shop opening hours vary

MÂCON
CHÂTEAU DE FUISSÉ
www.château–fuisse.fr
Jean-Jacques Vincent and his family produce excellent Pouilly Fuissé and Mâcon Villages wines at this *domaine*. Come to the château to taste before buying a case.

✉ 71960 Fuissé ☎ 03 85 35 61 44 🌐 Mon–Fri 10–12, 2–4

MORZINE
MATHIAS SPORTS
www.mathias.sport2000.fr
This is the perfect place to pick up summer and winter sports equipment, either to buy or rent. The shop has quality skis, boards, boots and clothing, plus a knowledgeable staff who can guide you to the best choice for your level of ability.

✉ 60 Taille de Mas du Pleney, 74110 Morzine ☎ 04 50 79 15 50 🌐 Late Oct–late Apr daily 8.30–7.30. Closed late Apr–late Oct

VICHY
LE CENTRE THERMAL DES DÔMES
www.destinationvichy.com
In this beautiful thermal spa complex, offering set or 'à la carte' treatments, choose from the thermal pool, gym, sauna, hammam (Turkish bath), Jacuzzis, Vichy showers and

massage cabins. Robes and towels are supplied, but you buy special sandals to wear around the spa. Children under 16 are not admitted.

✉ 132 boulevard des États-Unis, 03200 Vichy ☎ 08 00 30 00 63 🌐 Mon–Sat 8–12, 2.30–6. Closed Dec to mid-Feb ✋ Vary according to treatments

L'HIPPODROME
www.courses-de-vichy.fr
Horse-racing began here at Bellerive, on the opposite side of the river from Vichy, in 1875. There are both afternoon and evening meetings of flat racing and trotting. The Grand Prix de Vichy takes place in July.

✉ 2 route de Charmeil, 03700 Bellerive ☎ 04 70 30 15 50 🌐 Varies according to races ✋ From €6 🚌 Shuttle bus service (TPN) takes about 20 min from La Poste; various stops en route include train station and covered market ⛴ Free shuttle service by boat departs from La Rotunde du Lac

L'OPÉRA
www.ville-vichy.com
Built in 1901 and renovated in 1995, the opera house hosts concerts, plays and ballet as well as opera. The interior is Italian art nouveau in style and there's a bar which serves drinks.

✉ rue du Parc, 03200 Vichy ☎ 04 70 30 50 30 or 04 70 30 50 56 🌐 Open all year; box office: Tue–Sat 1.30–6.30 ✋ Tickets: €32–€68

VILLEURBANNE
ASTROBALLE
www.asvel.com
This is home to ASVEL, Villeurbanne's basketball team. The team plays in the Pro A league and the Euro league. Get tickets from Astroballe or Virgin Megastore (41 rue Eduard Herriot, 69002, Lyon).

✉ 40–44 avenue Marcel Cerdrun, 69100 Villeurbanne ☎ 04 72 14 16 70 ✋ Adult €18–€38, child €10–€18

MARCHÉ AUX PUCES DU CANAL
www.pucesducanal.com
Look closely before you buy at this huge antiques and flea market.

✉ 1 rue du Canal, 69100 Villeurbanne 🌐 Thu, Sat, Sun 8–1

JANUARY
SAINT-VINCENT TOURNANTE
www.st-vincent-tournante.fr
The brethren of the great Burgundy vineyards get together for a parade and a grand banquet to celebrate their *terroir* (land) and its bounty. At the same time they open their doors to the public and for the price of one single drinking glass (€9 in 2010), it's possible to tour the caves all day and taste their wines.
✉ Different wine village each year
☎ 03 80 26 21 30 (tourist office Beaune)
🕐 End Jan

JUNE–JULY
JAZZ À VIENNE
www.jazzavienne.com
Vienne's annual two-week summer jazz festival, attracting international performers and almost 95,000 people, is held in the Roman amphitheatre. Take a cushion and a torch as the amphitheatre is steep and dark. There are free concerts in public squares and gardens. Bars and restaurants also have live music.

✉ 21 rue des Célestes, 38200 Vienne
☎ 04 74 78 87 87 or 0892 702 007 (Théâtre Antique info line) 🕐 Jun or Jul

JULY
EUROCKÉENNES
www.eurockeennes.fr
The ultimate European rock festival—Eurockéennes—is held in Belfort each summer. This festival plays host to muddy fans enjoying the moment by the waterlogged waterside venues. In 2010 the three-day event welcomed 80,000 people to see acts like Jay-Z and Kasabian.
☎ 03 84 55 90 90 (tourist office Belfort)
✉ Belfort 🕐 First weekend in Jul

AUGUST
FESTIVAL DE BRIANÇON
www.festival-musique-briancon.com
The town welcomes classical musicians and ensembles from around the world for a series of concerts featuring the major composers.
✉ Église des Cordeliers, 05100 Briançon
☎ 06 97 91 48 33 🕐 One week early Aug

FÊTE DU LAC
www.lac-annecy.com
This annual lake festival dates back to 1860 and attracts thousands of spectators. There's a different theme each year, but attractions usually include a water pageant and music and fireworks at sunset.
✉ Le Paquier, 74000 Annecy
☎ 04 50 33 65 65
🕐 First Saturday in Aug

OCTOBER
ROCKTAMBULE
www.rocktambule.com
Jus as the winter weather approaches, bands travel from around Europe to appear live in this rare chance to play true rock music in France. Tickets are available at FNC and other major outlets
✉ Pôle Musical d'Innovation, 51 boulevard Gambetta, Grenoble ☎ 04 76 43 27 30
🕐 Ten days mid-month

Above *Fine music is on offer at L'Opéra Nationale de Lyon*
Opposite *Wheels of French cheese*

PRICES AND SYMBOLS

The restaurants are listed alphabetically (excluding Le, La and Les). The prices given are the average for a two-course lunch (L) and a three-course dinner (D) for one person, without drinks. The wine price is for the least expensive bottle.

For a key to the symbols, ▷ 2.

ANNECY
BATEAU-MS *LIBELLULE*

www.annecy-croisieres.com

Combine dinner with a boat trip on Lac d'Annecy. The mini-cruise offers lunch and dinner dances, with a commentary in French and English. ✉ 2 place aux Bois, 74000 Annecy ☎ 04 50 51 08 40 🕙 Early Jul–Aug daily 12–2.30, 8.30–10.30; end Mar–early Jul, Sep Tue–Sat 12–2.30, 8.30–10.30, Sun 12.30–2.30; Oct to mid-Nov Fri 8.30–10.30, Sat 12.30–2.30, 8.30–10.30, Sun 12.30–2.30 ✋ L €49, D €55, Wine €15, plus cruise €13.30

BRASSERIE ST-MAURICE

www.stmau.com

Fish dishes are popular here, but there are plenty of meat dishes,

plus a children's menu (€12). The brasserie is also a great place for a drink or a coffee. ✉ 7–9 rue du Collège Champuisien, 74000 Annecy ☎ 04 50 51 24 49 🕙 Tue–Sat 8am–12am; lunch 12–2, dinner 7–11 ✋ L €30, D €56, Wine €19

SHIVA

www.restaurant-indien-shiva.com

Shiva specializes in curries and tandoori dishes, and children and vegetarians are well catered for. Reservations are advisable, especially for Saturday evenings. ✉ 18 avenue de la Mandallaz, 74000 Annecy ☎ 04 50 51 76 25 🕙 Tue 7–10.30, Wed–Sun 12–2.30, 7–10.30 ✋ L €30, D €50, Wine €15

VIEUX NECY

www.levieuxnecy.com

Vieux Necy specializes in Savoyard cheese and other traditional melted cheese dishes like *raclette*. There are also grilled meat dishes. ✉ 3 rue Filaterie, 74000 Annecy ☎ 04 50 45 01 57 🕙 Tue–Sat 12–2, 7–10.30 ✋ L €25, D €35, Wine €20

ARGENTIÈRE
LA CRÉMERIE DU GLACIER

www.lacremerieduglacier.fr

This place serves filling dishes such as morel mushrooms en croute. ✉ chemin de la Glacière, 74400 Argentière ☎ 04 50 54 07 52 🕙 Thu–Sun 10am–12am, Mon–Wed 10–6 ✋ L €25, D €42, Wine €16

BEAUNE
LE CLOS DU CÈDRE

www.lecedre-beaune.com

Enjoy gastronomic fine Burgundian cuisine by the fire in winter and on the terrace in summer. ✉ 10 boulevard Maréchal Foch, 21200 Beaune ☎ 03 80 24 01 01 🕙 Mon–Fri 12–1.30, 7.30–9.30, Sat–Sun 7.30–9.30 ✋ L €32, D €50, Wine €30

LA GRILLADINE

Burgundy dishes such as *bœuf bourguignon*, poached eggs in red wine, snails, and ham with parsley. ✉ 17 rue Maufoux, 21200 Beaune ☎ 03 80 22 22 36 🕙 Tue–Wed 7–10, Thu–Sun 12–3, 7–10 ✋ L and D €25, Wine €17

BESANÇON
BERTHOD
www.berthod.fr

Berthod is a well-known wine producer and *traiteur* (delicatessen) in the town and finds many of the ingredients for the restaurant in the exceptionally well-stocked shop next door. They offer a good selection of regional dishes matched with a glass of a suitable Berthod wine, so lunch can also be a class in French cuisine. There's also a wine bar if you just want to pop in for a glass or two.

✉ 20 rue Bersot 25027 Besançon ☎ 03 81 82 27 14 ⊕ Tue–Sat 12–2.30, 7–10 ✋ L €25, D €35, Wine €15

CHAMBÉRY
CHÂTEAU DE CANDIE
www.châteaudecandie.com

This gastronomic restaurant, overseen by the Campanella brothers, was awarded its first Michelin star in August 2005. The menu is modern French using the finest ingredients.

✉ rue du Bois de Candie, 73000 Chambéry-le-Vieux ☎ 04 79 96 63 00 ⊕ Jul–Aug 12–1.30, 7.30–9.30; Sep–Jun Tue–Fri, Sun 12–1.30, Tue–Sat 7.30–9.30 ✋ L €50, D €70, Wine €23

CHAMONIX
L'ATMOSPHÈRE
www.restaurant-atmosphere.com

The menu at L'Atmosphère features local dishes including fondue and a range of fish and meat dishes; in autumn, try something from the game menu.

✉ 123 place Balmat, 74400 Chamonix ☎ 04 50 55 97 97 ⊕ Daily 12–2, 7–11 ✋ L €45, D €56, Wine €12

LA BERGERIE
www.labergeriechamonix.com

Once a farm, this restaurant is known for its quality regional cuisine. In summer dine on the terrace and in winter enjoy the log fire inside. The long and varied menu includes grilled meats, tomato and mozzarella salad and a red fruit dessert.

✉ 232 avenue Michel-Croz-Gare SNCF, 74000 Chamonix ☎ 04 50 53 45 04 ⊕ Daily 12–2, 7–10 ✋ L €28, D €35, Wine €18

LA CALÈCHE
www.restaurant-caleche.com

This restaurant serves Savoyard dishes. Try beef braised in Savoy wine, *raclette* (melted cheese dish), fondue and *tartiflette* (a baked cheese and potato dish), accompanied by Savoy wines. There's live folk music and dancing on Thursday evenings.

✉ 18 rue Paccard, 74000 Chamonix ☎ 04 50 55 94 68 ⊕ Daily 12–2, 7–11 ✋ L €38, D €50, Wine €21

LA MAISON CARRIER
www.hameaualbert.fr

Styled after an old Savoyard farmhouse, the menu here harks back to the hearty local dishes that the farmer's wife cooked up here. There is an excellent cellar of local wines.

✉ Hameau Albert I, 38 route du Bouchet, 74402 Chamonix ☎ 04 50 53 05 09 ⊕ Jul–Aug daily 12–2.30, 7.30–10; Sep–Jun Tue–Sun 12–2.30, 7.30–10. Closed first three weeks in Jun, mid-Nov to mid-Dec ✋ L €30, D €50, Wine €22

LA COURTEIX
L'OURS DES ROCHES
www.oursdesroches.com

In the heart of the Auverge, northwest of Clermont-Ferrand, the Brossard family have been serving hearty local cuisine since the late 1980s at this converted farmhouse. There are several set menus to choose from with ingredients including rabbit plus a selection of local cheeses

✉ La Courteix, 63230 Saint Ours les Roches ☎ 04 73 88 92 80 ⊕ May–Sep Tue–Sat 12–2, 7.30–9.30, Sun 12–2; Oct–Apr Wed–Fri 12–2, 7.30–9.30, Sat 7.30–9.30 ✋ L €34, D €50, Wine €19

DIJON
MAISON MILLIÈRE
www.maison-milliere.com

Here you'll find a boutique selling regional produce and gifts, a tea room and a restaurant with a garden. The restaurant has frequently changing menus and the tea room offers a choice of around 20 different teas to go with its pastries and tarts.

✉ 10 rue de la Chouette, 21000 Dijon ☎ 03 80 30 99 99 ⊕ Tea room: Tue–Sun

10–7. Restaurant: Tue–Thu 12–2, Fri–Sat 12–2, 7.30–10 ✋ L €25, D €40, Wine €14

RESTAURANT DE LA PORTE GUILLAUME
www.hotel-nord.fr

This restaurant serves Burgundy wines and dishes such as foie gras, oysters and smoked salmon with mustard and honey vinaigrette, roasted salmon, rabbit, and guinea fowl with truffles and tagliatelle.

✉ place Darcy, 21000 Dijon ☎ 03 80 50 80 50 ⊕ Daily 12–2, 7–10.45 ✋ L €30, D €40, Wine €12

RESTAURANT STÉPHANE DERBORD
www.restaurantstephanederbord.fr

The menu features Burgundy dishes such as black pudding in spiced breadcrumbs with Jura wine caramel, crayfish roasted with ginger, pineapple and red pepper compote topped with saffron sauce, and desserts such as pear caramelized in honey with nut and raisin ice cream. The prix-fixe option costs €23.

✉ 10 place Wilson, 21000 Dijon ☎ 03 80 67 74 64 ⊕ Tue–Sat 12–1.45, Mon–Sat 7.30–9.15 ✋ L €55, D €75, Wine €24

GRENOBLE
LES ARCHERS
perso.orange.fr/les.archers

This brasserie reputedly dates from the reign of King Henri IV (1589–1610). You will be spoiled for choice by the extensive menu; if you want a late meal, this is the place to come.

✉ 2 rue Docteur Bailly, 38000 Grenoble ☎ 04 76 46 27 76 ⊕ Sun–Mon 11am–1am, Tue–Sat 11am–2am ✋ L €25, D €34, Wine €12

AUBERGE NAPOLÉON
www.auberge-napoleon.fr

The dining room is air-conditioned; the menu includes regional cuisine as well as dishes like foie gras and truffles. You can reserve via the website, which also has recipes.

✉ 7 rue Montorge, 38000 Grenoble ☎ 04 76 87 53 64 ⊕ Mon–Wed 7.30–9.30, Thu–Sat 12–2, 7.30–9.30. Closed 25 Aug–7 Sep, 1–8 May ✋ L €50, D €65, Wine €23

LADOIX-SERRIGNY
LA GREMELLE
www.lagremelle.com
A lovely place for a relaxed meal during your tour of the Burgundy vineyards, La Gremelle serves excellent local beef matched by a fine wine list. Enjoy a local *digestif*, Marc de Bourgogne, after your meal.
✉ RN74, 21550 Ladoix-Serrigny ☎ 03 80 26 40 56 🕐 Daily 12–2, 7.30–9.30. Closed Feb ✋ L €35, D €55, Wine €18

LYON
L'ASSIETTE DU MARCHÉ
www.lassietedumarche.fr
A popular restaurant that's great value, so it's best to reserve. It specializes in fish and there is no formal menu, although there are always two dishes of the day (one meat, one fish), which might include tuna gratin, fish soup or pike-perch.
✉ 21 Grande Rue de Vaise, 69009 Lyon ☎ 04 78 83 84 90 🕐 Mon–Thu 12–2, Fri–Sat 12–2, 7–10 ✋ L €14.50, D €25, Wine €18

LA BRASSERIE DES BROTTEAUX
www.brasseriedesbrotteaux.com
Established in 1913, this elegant brasserie is decorated with antiques, bright tiles, glass and mirrors. The dining room is air conditioned, and you can eat outside in good weather. Opt for one of the prix-fixe menus, a salad or the Aberdeen Angus beef.
✉ 1 place Jules Ferry, 69006 Lyon ☎ 04 72 74 03 98 🕐 Mon–Fri 7.30am–midnight, Sat 10–3, 6.30–12 ✋ L €25, D €50, Wine €20 🕐

BRASSERIE GEORGES
www.brasseriegeorges.com
Founded in 1836, this is a huge restaurant with fast service. Meals include Lyonnais dishes, sauerkraut, seafood and omelettes.
✉ 30 cours Verdun, 69002 Lyon ☎ 04 72 56 54 54 🕐 Daily 11.30am–11.15pm ✋ L €30, D €40, Wine €17

RELAIS GOURMAND PIERRE ORSI
www.pierreorsi.com
Pierre Orsi and his wife preside over this temple to gastronomy. The

service is formal and impeccable and the menus are some of the most exciting in the industry.
✉ 3 place Kléber, 69006 Lyon ☎ 04 78 89 57 68 🕐 Tue–Sat 12–1.30, 8–9.30 ✋ L €45, D €80, Wine €36

NUITS-ST-GEORGES
LE ST-GEORGES
Wines from more than 100 local producers go well with local dishes such as three-fish terrine with crayfish and fresh tomato coulis, cream of cauliflower soup and white chocolate mousse with fresh figs.
✉ Carrefour de l'Europe, 21700 Nuits-St-Georges ☎ 03 80 62 00 62 🕐 Daily 12–2, 7–9.30 ✋ L €30, D €55, Wine €20

LES PRAZ DE CHAMONIX
HÔTEL EDEN RESTAURANT
www.hoteleden-chamonix.com
This hotel restaurant has exhibitions of photographs and sculptures. There's a contemporary twist to classic French cuisine from chef Charlotte Stocks. Desserts include nougat ice cream and three-chocolate terrine. There are vegetarian prix-fixe options.
✉ 35 route de Goudanys, 74400 Les Praz de Chamonix ☎ 04 50 53 18 43 🕐 Wed–Mon 7pm–10.30pm ✋ D €40, Wine €18

PULIGNY-MONTRACHET
LA TABLE D'OLIVIER LEFLAIVE
www.olivier-leflaive.com
The restaurant specializes in wine-tasting lunches, where you can have a light lunch and try labels such as Bourgogne Blanc les Setilles, St-Aubin, Puligny-Montrachet and Pommard. There's a €10 supplement for tasting *premier cru* wines and you must reserve.
✉ place du Monument, 21190 Puligny-Montrachet ☎ 03 80 21 37 65 🕐 Mon–Sat 12.30–2, 7–9.30. Closed Jan ✋ L and D €40, including wines

LE PUY-EN-VELAY
FRANÇOIS GAGNAIRE RESTAURANT
www.francois-gagnaire-restaurant.com
François Gagnaire displays his

gastronomic flair at this intimate restaurant and it's been recognized nationally with the award of the Order of Merit. The French classics are given a new twist depending on seasonal ingredients. There's a special menu for children and a range of excellent set menus.
✉ 4 avenue Clément, Charbonnier 43000 ☎ 04 71 02 75 55 🕐 Jul–Aug Wed–Sat 12–1.30, 7.30–9, Sun–Tue 7.30–9; Apr–May, Sep–Oct Tue, Thu–Sat 12–1.30, 7.30–9, Sun 12–1.30, Mon, Wed 7.30–9; Nov–Mar Tue, Thu–Sat 12–1.30, 7.30–9, Sun 12–1.30 ✋ L €36, D €70, Wine €24

RESTAURANT TOURNAYRE
www.restaurant-tournayre.com
The stone vaulted dining room dates from the 14th century, and provides a perfect setting for the traditional regional cuisine prepared by the Tournayre family. You can try foie-gras in a variety of guises.
✉ 12 rue Chênebouterie, 43000 Le Puy-en-Velay ☎ 04 71 09 58 94 🕐 Mon–Fri 12–2.30, 7.30–10 ✋ L €30, D €48, Wine €17

SERVOZ
GORGES DE LA DIOSAZ
www.hoteldesgorges.com
The menu includes salmon smoked on site, foie gras with cherry vinegar, perch with crayfish and bass fillet in a champagne butter. There are prix-fixe options and a children's menu. The restaurant uses organic fish.
✉ 74310 Servoz ☎ 04 50 47 20 97 🕐 Summer daily 12–1.30, 7–9.30; winter Tue–Sat 12–1.30, 7–9.30, Sun 12–1.30; closed Jan ✋ L €30, D €40, Wine €18

VIENNE
LES SAVEURS DU MARCHÉ
www.lessaveursdumarche.fr
Sébastien and Valérie take what's morning fresh at the market and create the menu of the day. The prix-fixe menu is excellent value with three choices of starter and main course. Dishes could include *pot-au-feu* or *brochette de boeuf*.
✉ 34 cours de Verdun, 38200 Vienne ☎ 04 74 31 65 65 🕐 Mon–Fri 12–2.30, 7.30–9.30. Closed mid-Jul to mid-Aug, late Dec–early Jan ✋ L €24, D €35, Wine €16

PRICES AND SYMBOLS

Prices are the lowest and highest for a double room for one night including breakfast, unless otherwise stated. All the hotels listed accept credit cards unless otherwise stated. Note that rates vary widely throughout the year.

For a key to the symbols, ▷ 2.

ANNECY

HÔTEL DU CHÂTEAU

www.annecy-hotel.com
At the foot of Annecy's hilltop château, this stone-built hotel has been run by the same family since it was established in 1959. It has comfortable, simple rooms in which you can have breakfast. There is parking and free internet access.
✉ 16 Rampe du Château, 74000 Annecy
☎ 04 50 45 27 66 ⊘ Closed 15 Nov–15 Dec 🖐 €55–€68, excluding breakfast (€7) 🛈 16

HÔTEL TRÉSOMS

www.lestresoms.com
Built in 1930 in Swiss-chalet style, this 3-star hotel has a superb view of Lac d'Annecy. The comfortable, well-furnished bedrooms overlook the hotel garden or the lake and have a bathroom and satellite TV. Facilities include a terrace, disabled access, private parking, an outdoor swimming pool, sauna and beauty room. The hotel restaurant has prix-fixe options.
✉ 3 boulevard de la Corniche, 74000 Annecy ☎ 04 50 51 43 84 🖐 €149–€238, excluding breakfast (€15 adults, €6 children) 🛈 49 ⌁ Outdoor 🏐

BEAUNE

HÔTEL GRILLON

www.hotel-grillon.fr
At this 19th-century house there are plenty of places to relax, including the heated outdoor swimming pool, terrace, lounge and bar. You can have breakfast in the sunny breakfast room and dinner in the Verger restaurant in the grounds.
✉ 21 route de Seurre, 21200 Beaune
☎ 03 80 22 44 25 ⊘ Closed Jan–3 Mar 🖐 €68–€120, excluding breakfast (€9.50) 🛈 17 (7 non-smoking) 🚭 ⌁ Outdoor

VILLA FLEURIE

www.lavillafleurie.fr
The interior design and furnishings of this hotel match the original style of the house, which dates from 1900. The bedrooms have a fireplace and TV. Continental breakfast is served in a breakfast room and there is a terrace, a garden and parking.
✉ 19 place Colbert, 21200 Beaune
☎ 03 80 22 66 00 🖐 €70–€100, excluding breakfast (€8.50) 🛈 10

BESANÇON

CHÂTEAU DE LA DAME BLANCHE

www.chateau-de-la-dame-blanche.fr
This elegant manor house stands in leafy grounds near Besançon. The beautifully decorated individual bedrooms have views over the park, and there is a shady terrace, where you can dine in warmer weather.
✉ 1 rue de la Goulotte, 25870 Geneuille
☎ 03 81 57 64 64 🖐 €115–€169, excluding breakfast (€12) 🛈 24

CHABLIS

HOTEL DU VIEUX MOULIN

www.larochehotel.fr
This 18th-century grain mill in the centre of town has been converted into a comfortable contemporary hotel. Rooms are airy and spacious mixing 21st-century decor with raw

Opposite *A brightly painted hotel and tea room with shuttered windows*

architectural elements. Each room has aplasma screen TV, WiFi and a large bed. There's a comfortable seating area and a restaurant on site.
✉ 18 rue des Moulins, 89800 Chablis ☎ 03 86 42 47 30 ⊗ Closed Sun and late Dec–early Feb ✋ €110–€160, excluding breakfast (€12) ☐ 7 rooms, 2 suites ✦

CHAMBÉRY
CHÂTEAU DE CANDIE
www.châteaudecandie.com
A typical 18th-century fortified Savoyard house, this hotel has been luxuriously decorated. It stands in the midst of magnificent grounds with rolling hills all around.
✉ rue du Bois de Candie, 73000 Chambéry-Le-Vieux ☎ 04 79 96 63 00 ✋ Apartment €160–€260, excluding breakfast (€20) ☐ 28 apartments and suites only ⬙ Outdoor

HÔTEL ART
www.arthotel-chambery.com
Hôtel Art is close to the station, and has soundproofed bedrooms with satellite TV, telephone and bathroom. There is no restaurant, but a cold buffet breakfast is served in the breakfast room. There is also a private garage.
✉ 154 rue Sommeiller, 73000 Chambéry ☎ 04 79 62 37 26 ✋ €53–€63, excluding breakfast (€8) ☐ 36

CHAMONIX
JEU DE PAUME
www.jeudepaumechamonix.com
This chalet in the hamlet of Le Lavancher, at an altitude of 1,250m (4,000ft), is ideal for skiing or hiking, or just for being in the mountains. Inside the extensive use of natural pine makes it feel warm and cosy, as does the log fire in the sitting room.
✉ 705 route du Chapeau, Le Lavancher, 74400 Chamonix ☎ 04 50 54 03 76 ✋ €135–€255, excluding breakfast (€15) ☐ 23

LE MANOIR
www.auberge-du-manoir.com
In a pretty Savoyard wooden chalet, this two-star hotel has a swimming pool and skiing close by. Rooms have a bathroom, satellite TV and a telephone, and many have a balcony. The hotel restaurant serves Provençal-style dishes.
✉ 8 route de Bouchet, 74400 Chamonix ☎ 04 50 53 10 77 ⊗ Closed Nov and a period in Jun ✋ €104–€194, excluding breakfast (€12) ☐ 24 ✦

CHANDOLAS
AUBERGE LES MURETS
www.aubergelesmurets.com
At the foot of the Cévennes and near the Gorges de l'Ardèche, this small hotel occupies an 18th-century stone farmhouse in its own grounds. It is well positioned for guests who choose to explore both regions. It has a good restaurant with a vaulted dining room.
✉ 07230 Chandolas ☎ 04 75 39 08 32 ✋ €65–€80, excluding breakfast (€10) ☐ 7 ⬙ Outdoor

CLERMONT-FERRAND
BEST WESTERN LAFAYETTE
www.hotel-le-lafayette.com
This hotel has modern rooms for up to four people all with satellite TV. There is private parking.
✉ 53 avenue de l'Union Soviétique, 63000 Clermont-Ferrand ☎ 04 73 91 82 27 ✋ €95–€115, excluding breakfast (€10) ☐ 48

CLUNY
LE POTIN GOURMAND
www.potingourmand.com/hotel
Le Potin Gourmand is a small hotel and restaurant in an old stone house which served as a ceramic workshop from the 12th to the 20th centuries. It has an outdoor pool and its own private parking.
✉ place du Champ de Foire, 71250 Cluny ☎ 03 85 59 02 06 ✋ €60–€120, excluding breakfast (€10) ☐ 7 ⬙ Outdoor

DIJON
HOSTELLERIE DU CHAPEAU ROUGE
www.chapeau-rouge.fr
This newly renovated 16th-century building is one of the region's most exciting boutique properties. Each room is individually furnished though they all have flat-screen TVs, air conditioning, safes and phones. Hotel facilities include a bar and a Michelin-starred restaurant serving contemporary cuisine.
✉ 5 rue Michelet, 21000 Dijon ☎ 03 80 50 88 88 ✋ €147–€229, excluding breakfast (€15) ☐ 28 rooms, 2 suites ✦

HOTEL PHILIPPE LE BON
www.hotelphilippelebon.com
This historic hotel in the middle of Dijon comprises three connected buildings from the 15th to the 17th centuries. Rooms range in size and style but have been recently decorated and upgraded.
✉ 18 rue Sainte Anne, 21000 Dijon ☎ 03 80 30 73 52 ✋ €99–€127, excluding breakfast (€13) ☐ 32

ÉVIAN-LES-BAINS
LES CYGNES
www.hotellescygnes.com
This charming, traditional hotel has brightly coloured bedrooms. It stands on the edge of Lac Leman, and there are relaxing views over the water from its leafy gardens and shady terraces. Enjoy lunch or dinner on the terraces—magical at night.
✉ 8 avenue Grande Rive, 75500 Évian-les-Bains ☎ 04 50 75 01 01 ✋ €78–€98, excluding breakfast (€13) ☐ 39 ⬙ Outdoor

GIGNY-SUR-SAÔNE
CAMPING CHÂTEAU DE L'ÉPERVIÈRE
www.domaine-eperviere.com
This small campsite has indoor and outdoor pools plus a Jacuzzi and sauna. The 16th-century château in the heart of the complex has a restaurant and a bar. You can bring your own camper van/tent or rent from the site.
✉ 71240 Gigny-sur-Saône ☎ 03 85 94 16 90 ⊗ Apr–Sep ✋ Pitch €14.50–€20 includes one person, extra person €5.70–€8.10, child (under 7) €3.50–€5.60, power €3.50–€5.40

GRENOBLE
HÔTEL GALLIA
www.hotel-gallia.com
A modern 2-star hotel offering soundproofed rooms with satellite

TV, hairdryer, safe and modem point. Parking is €6.50 per day.

✉ 7 boulevard Maréchal-Joffre, 38000 Grenoble ☎ 04 76 87 39 21 🕐 Closed mid-Jul to mid-Aug 🍴 €54–€65, excluding breakfast (€7.50) 🛏 35

IGÉ
HOTEL RESTAURANT CHATEAU D'IGÉ
www.chateaudige.net

Dominating the village of Igé, this 13th-century château offers truly monumental and strikingly decorated rooms filled with antiques. Some have four-poster beds. There's a gastronomic restaurant on site, with stone walls and tapestries, and a beautiful garden with waterside tables for an evening drink.

✉ route du Chateau, 71960 Igé ☎ 03 85 33 33 99 🍴 €95–€165, excluding breakfast (€16) 🛏 8

LADOIX–SERRIGNY EN BOURGOGNE
LA GREMELLE
www.lagremelle.com

The Gremelle is a family-run hotel with small, simple, modern rooms, all of which have their own bathroom and entrance. There is also an excellent gastronomic restaurant. It is about five minutes north of Beaune, and there is ample parking.

✉ 21550 Ladoix-Serrigny en Bourgogne ☎ 03 80 26 40 56 🍴 €54–€69, excluding breakfast (€10) 🛏 20 🏊 Outdoor pool

LYON
HÔTEL ATHENA
www.athena-hotel.com

This hotel, outside the SNCF and TGV train station—as well as near bus, Métro and tram stations—is a modern, 2-star hotel where rooms have satellite TV, telephone and radio. Parking is €9 per day.

✉ 45 boulevard Marius Vivier Merle, 69003 Lyon ☎ 04 72 68 88 44 🍴 €92–€110, excluding breakfast (€9.50) 🛏 122 🌐

HÔTEL GLOBE ET CECIL
www.globeetcecilhotel.com

A refurbished 19th-century hotel with early connections to the Vatican, the rooms are tastefully and individually

decorated, though on the compact side, and the original high ceilings and plasterwork add elegance. There are lots of shopping and dining options nearby.

✉ 21 rue Gasparin, 69002 Lyon ☎ 04 78 42 58 95 🍴 €175 🛏 60

LA REINE ASTRID
www.warwickastrid.com

In a residential area convenient for Parc Tête d'Or, this 4-star all-suite hotel is within easy walking distance of local shops and restaurants. The suites have soft furnishings in rich red, gold and dark blue and come with one or two bedrooms, bathroom, kitchen, satellite TV and internet access. There is a cocktail bar, a reading lounge with complimentary newspapers, parking and a restaurant with a terrace.

✉ 26 boulevard de Belges, 69006 Lyon ☎ 04 72 82 18 00 🍴 €134–€500, excluding breakfast (€18) 🛏 88 suites (25 non-smoking) 🌐 ♿

PÉROUGES
L'HOSTELLERIE DE PÉROUGES
www.hostelleriedeperouges.com

The rooms of this hotel are spread around the medieval cité of Pérouges, in four different buildings. All rooms are tastefully furnished.

✉ place du Tilleul, 01800 Pérouges ☎ 04 74 61 00 88 🍴 €124–€240, excluding breakfast (€16) 🛏 15

PULIGNY-MONTRACHET
LA MAISON D'OLIVIER LEFLAIVE
www.maison-olivierleflaive.com

A 17th-century town house beautifully renovated and offering well-styled accommodation. Rooms are contemporary (flat screen TV and DVD as standard) while allowing the character of the building to shine through. There's a courtyard for quiet contemplation and relaxation. Combine your stay with a scrumptious meal at Olivier's gourmet restaurant (▷ 289).

✉ place du Monument, 21190 Puligny-Montrachet ☎ 03 80 21 37 65 🕐 Closed Jan 🍴 €190, excluding breakfast (€10) 🛏 11 rooms, 2 suites 🌐

SENS
HOTEL BRENNUS
www.hotel-brennus.fr

A 19th-century house in the town centre, the Brennus is close to the cathedral. There is private parking for guests, and simple and spacious bedrooms with a shower or bath.

✉ 21 rue des Trois Croissants, 89100 Sens ☎ 03 86 64 04 40 🍴 €46–€67, excluding breakfast (€7.90) 🛏 20

VEZELAY
LE COMPOSTELLE
www.lecompostellevezelay.com

This small hotel is located in a famous medieval shrine on the pilgrimage route to Santiago de Compostela in Spain. It has an enclosed garden and bedrooms overlooking the valley.

✉ place du Champs de Foire, 89450 Vézelay ☎ 03 86 33 28 63 🍴 €49–€64, excluding breakfast (€9.50) 🛏 18

VICHY
HÔTEL DE GRIGNAN
www.hoteldegrignan.fr

The hotel is in a quiet area of town, close to Parc Napoléon III, the lake and the casino. If you fancy some spa treatments, the hotel runs special deals that combine six days of full board (with all meals) plus six days of treatments at one of the spas. The bedrooms all have bathroom, hairdryer, TV and radio. L'Abécédaire restaurant has a good prix-fixe menu.

✉ 7 place Sevigné, 03201 Vichy ☎ 04 70 32 08 11 🍴 €64–€92, excluding breakfast (€9) 🛏 100 🌐 Restaurant and communal areas

VIC-SUR-CÈRE
HOTEL BEL HORIZON
www.hotel-bel-horizon.com

A popular family hotel, the Bel Horizon is just inside the Parc des Volcans and not far from the winter sports resort of Le Lioran. It has a good restaurant with panoramic views of the Monts du Cantal from the terrace.

✉ 15800 Vic-sur-Cère ☎ 04 71 47 50 06 🍴 €45–€55, excluding breakfast (€8) 🛏 24 🏊 Outdoor

Opposite Notre-Dame de Fourvière in Lyon

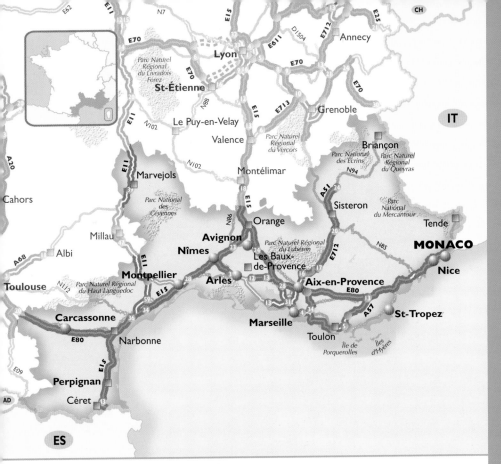

SOUTHEAST FRANCE

France's Mediterranean coast describes a lazy S-shape between the foothills of the Pyrenees on the Spanish border and the steep slopes of the Pre-Alps running across the frontier with Italy. As far as the river Rhône is the region of Languedoc-Roussillon; thereafter the almost mythical region of Provence.

Provence is the definition of the South of France, with more than its share of attractions: Everywhere you go there are stunningly beautiful landscapes, monumental ancient remains and villages that look as if they have leapt directly off postcards.

The most famous resorts of France are crammed into the extreme eastern corner of Provence, the beautiful Côte d'Azur, better known as the Riviera, which takes in St-Tropez, Cannes, Nice and the millionaire's gambling den of Monte Carlo (in the micro-state of Monaco). At the other end of the coast is the Camargue, a wetland formed by the delta of the Rhône, inhabited by flamingos, horses, bulls and a local brand of cowboy. Take this together with the magnificent cities of Aix-en-Provence, Arles, Avignon and Marseille, and landscapes such as those of the Gorges de Verdon and Mont Ventoux and it's not hard to see what drew great painters such as Van Gogh and Picasso to the colourful and luminous south.

None of which should put you off exploring Languedoc-Roussillon. It might not be as ostentatious as Provence but it has plenty of its own charms. To begin with it has one sight to dwarf almost everywhere else in France: Carcassonne, a complete, walled medieval citadel restored (some say controversially) to its original glory.

For landscapes, the two most attractive parts of the region are the austere Cévennes mountains, to the far north, and the enclave of Catalogne (French Catalonia), to the south, around Perpignan, where two towns, Céret in the hills and Collioure on the coast have successfully lured many artists of their own.

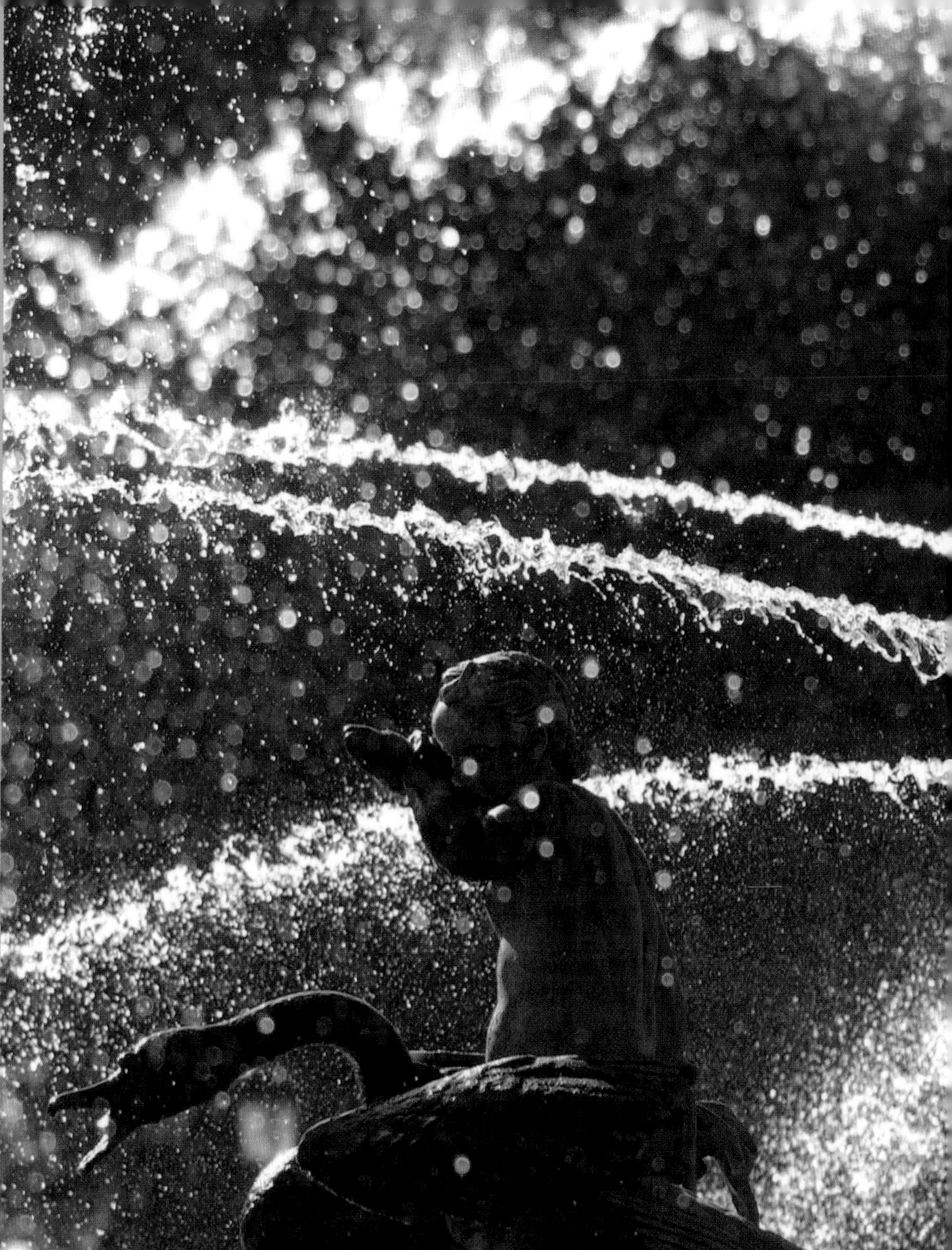

AIGUES-MORTES

www.ot-aiguesmortes.fr

When Louis IX of France took charge of the Seventh Crusade in 1245 he faced a problem: His lands did not reach the Mediterranean and he had no port from which to launch his ships. So he purchased a patch of malaria-infested swamp and built the town of Aigues-Mortes (meaning 'dead or stagnant waters') on the shore of a lagoon which was joined to the sea via a channel of the Rhône delta. To attract settlers he had to offer tax exemptions and loans.

To visit the town, park outside the walls and walk. It's impossible to get lost because Aigues-Mortes is laid out on grid pattern. The only real sight, apart from the walls, is the Tour de Constance, a tower which stands apart from the northwest corner.

➕ 456 L13 ℹ️ place Saint Louis, 30220 Aigues-Mortes ☎ 04 66 53 73 00 🕐 Jul–Aug Mon–Fri 9–8, Sat–Sun 10–8; May–Jun, Sep Mon–Fri 9–7, Sat–Sun 10–7; Oct–Apr Mon–Fri 9–12, 2–6, Sat–Sun 10–12, 2–6

AIX-EN-PROVENCE

▷ 298.

ANTIBES

www.antibesjuanlespins.com

Antibes, east of Cannes, is one of the most rewarding and important smaller towns on the Riviera. It is densely packed and attracts its fair share of millionaires, as can be seen from the size of the yachts moored in Port Vauban. The attractive historic central quarter, Vieil Antibes, is still enclosed by Vauban's 17th-century ramparts and there's a busy open-air market on Cours Masséna, in the middle of town, every morning except Monday (daily in summer).

The world-class Musée Picasso (mid-Jun to mid-Sep Tue, Thu, Sat–Sun 10–6, Wed, Fri 10–8; mid-Sep to mid-Jun Tue–Sun 10–12, 2–6) is in a striking medieval fortress on the cliff edge, once owned by the Grimaldi family, the rulers of Monaco (▷ 314–315). The gallery contains many works by Picasso (who had a studio here), and also work by Antibes-born Nicholas de Staël, as well as Fernand Léger and Joan Miró.

The Musée Archéologique, at Bastion St-André (mid-Jun to mid-Sep Tue–Sun 10–12, 2–6; mid-Sep to mid-Jun Tue–Sun 10–1, 2–5), contains many items from the area—Antibes was founded by the Greeks and went on to become a busy Roman port.

Nearby Cap d'Antibes, a promontory extending south, has some sandy beaches and seafront restaurants that are good for lunch. There's a long public beach—surprising given that this area is a haven of secluded palatial villas and expensive hotels.

➕ 457 P13 ℹ️ 11 place Général de Gaulle, 06600 Antibes ☎ 04 97 23 11 11 🕐 Jul–Aug daily 9–7; Sep–Jun Mon–Fri 9–12.30, 1.30–6, Sat 9–12, 2–6, Sun 10–12.30, 2.30–5 🚉 Antibes

Above *The 12th-century Château Grimaldi houses the Musée Picasso*
Opposite *Fountain on place de la Rotonde, Aix-en-Provence*

INFORMATION
www.aixenprovencetourism.com
✚ 457 N13 🛈 2 place Général de
Gaulle, 13100 Aix-en-Provence ☎ 04 42
16 11 61 🕔 Mon–Sat 8.30–7 (until 8pm
Apr–Sep), Sun 10–1, 2–6 🚉 Aix-en-
Provence

TIPS
» Reserve lodgings as far ahead as
possible at festival time (June and July).
» To see fine Renaissance mansions,
explore the Quartier Mazarin south of
Cours Mirabeau.
» Aix has more than 100 fountains. The
moss-covered Fontaine d'Eau Thermale is
a natural hot spring, with water pouring
out at 34°C (93°F).

AIX-EN-PROVENCE

Aix is one of Provence's most pleasing towns, with a quintessentially southern
feel. In Roman times it was known as Aquae Sextiae, a prosperous spa resort.
Later it became a place of learning, culture and art. It is famous as the home of
painter Paul Cézanne, who was born, and did most of his work, here and for its
university, founded in 1409.

COURS MIRABEAU AND VIEIL AIX

Vieil Aix, the old quarter, is enclosed by a ring of avenues and squares that
have replaced the town's ramparts. One of these avenues, the bustling Cours
Mirabeau, is Aix's main attraction. Its double row of leafy plane trees shades
hundreds of café tables on the north side; one café, Les Deux Garçons, dates
from the 1790s. Across the road are banks and offices in fine 17th- and 18th-
century *hôtels* (private mansions), some with elaborate facades, balconies
and doorways supported by huge atlantes. For more grandiose Renaissance
architecture, turn south into the quieter Quartier Mazarin.

ART

You can visit Cézanne's studio, on the avenue named after him (Jul–Aug daily
10–6; Apr–Jun, Sep 10–12, 2–6; Oct–Mar Mon–Sat 10–12, 2–5). It is preserved
as it was in the 1900s, but doesn't contain any of his work. The Musée Granet,
in place St-Jean-de-Malte (Jun–Sep Tue–Sun 11–7; Oct–May 12–6) has some
of his early paintings. The Musée des Tapisseries, in the former archbishops'
palace in place des Martyrs de la Résistance, has magnificent 17th- and 18th-
century tapestries, as well as modern pieces (Apr–Oct Wed–Mon 10–6; Nov–Mar
1.30–5).

THE CATHEDRAL

The Cathédrale St-Sauveur is an interesting mix of styles from Romanesque
to baroque, spanning the fifth to the 17th centuries. Look for the 16th-century
Flemish tapestries in the chancel, which were stolen from Canterbury Cathedral
during the English Civil War. The ancient baptistery, off the right-hand nave,
contains traces of the main street of the Roman town. There are superb pieces
of medieval art, notably Nicolas Froment's triptych of the *Burning Bush* in the
central nave, painted for King René in 1476.

Below *Aix-en-Provence's enticing fruit and
vegetable market*

ARLES

Founded by the Greeks in 600BC as a trading outpost of Massalia (Marseille), Arles was later taken over by the Romans, who built it up as a sea and river port, linked by canal to the Mediterranean.

ROMAN ARLES

At the heart of town is the spectacularly well-preserved Roman amphitheatre, Les Arènes, which held more than 20,000 spectators (May–Sep daily 9–6.30; Mar–Apr 9–6; Nov–Feb 10–5). It was converted into a medieval fortress and later into a town within a town, and is now regularly used for bullfights and other performances.

The remains of the nearby Théâtre Antique are used to stage concerts and for Arles's folk culture festival in July. Roman Arles extends to the banks of the Rhône, where you can see what remains of the vast Thermes de Constantin spa baths. On the other side of the N113 expressway is the extraordinary modern building of the Musée de l'Arles Antique (Mar–Oct daily 9–7; Nov–Feb 10–5), an airy, spacious museum displaying ancient items found at Arles.

OTHER HIGHLIGHTS

The Romanesque Église St-Trophime, on place de la République, has one of France's most beautiful cloisters (May–Sep daily 9–6.30; Mar–Apr, Oct 9–6.30; Nov–Feb 10–5). Don't miss the reliefs of the *Last Judgement* on the facade.

On rue de la République, the Museé Arlaten focuses on Provençal culture and was set up by the poet Frédéric Mistral using his 1904 Nobel Prize money (Jun–Aug daily 9.30–12.30, 2–6; Apr–May, Sep 9–12, 2–5.30; Oct–Mar Tue–Sun 9.30–12, 2–4.30).

VINCENT VAN GOGH

Van Gogh dreamed of establishing an artists' colony in Arles, and he painted several locations in and near the town. The hospital where he went to recuperate after the severed ear incident is now Espace Van Gogh, a study facility in place Félix Rey.

The Fondation Van Gogh, near Les Arènes, doesn't contain any of his paintings, but has tribute works by modern artists such as Francis Bacon (Jul–Sep daily 10–7; Apr–Jun daily 10–6; Oct–Mar Tue–Sun 11–5).

INFORMATION

www.arlestourisme.com

✚ 456 M13 ℹ Esplanade Charles de Gaulle, boulevard des Lices, 13200 Arles ☎ 04 90 18 41 20 ⏲ Apr–Sep daily 9–6.45; Oct–Mar Mon–Sat 9–4.45, Sun 10–12.45

TIPS

» A single ticket (Pass Monuments €13.50) covering all the major sights in Arles is good value if you visit more than three.

» The town's huge Saturday morning market is on boulevard des Lices. The second-hand market is on the same street on the first Wednesday of every month.

Below *The Roman amphitheatre*

INFORMATION

www.ot-avignon.fr

✚ 456 M12 ⓘ 41 cours Jean Jaurès 80400 Avignon ☎ 04 32 74 32 74
🕐 Jul–Aug Mon–Sat 9–7, Sun 9.45–5; Apr–Jun, Sep–Oct Mon–Sat 9–6, Sun 9.45–5; Nov–Mar Mon–Fri 9–6, Sat 9–5, Sun 10–12 🚉 Main station in boulevard St-Rochand; TGV station 5km (3 miles) from the middle of the city

TIPS

» The Avignon PASSion gives reductions on entry tickets to the main sights. It is free and available at museums and other attractions.
» Parking can be difficult. When spaces around the city walls are full, try parking at the train station as this has 800 parking spaces.

Above *Pont St-Bénézet (Le Pont d'Avignon)*
Opposite *Flamingoes in the wetlands of the Camargue*

AVIGNON

Massive ramparts enclose the whole of Avignon's old city, on the left bank of the Rhône. In 1309 the papal court moved here from Rome and the city grew in size and importance. The area remained in papal hands for centuries, only becoming part of France again in 1791. During its time under papal control, the city attracted a large, wealthy clerical class, but also political refugees and outcasts on the run from their own communities, who were given refuge.

Something of that dichotomy survives today—there are many luxury shops and well-to-do inhabitants but also people begging. Pont St-Bénézet (Le Pont d'Avignon) is the picturesque narrow, cobbled medieval bridge that features in the nursery rhyme. Today only a few arches survive after floods in the 17th century destroyed much of the bridge. At festival time in July (▷ 339), hundreds of thousands of visitors arrive from all over Europe.

THE PALAIS DES PAPES

The Papal Palace was the home of the popes from 1309 to 1418 and is Avignon's principal sight (Aug 9–9; Jul, early to mid Sep 9–8; mid-Mar to Jun, mid-Sep to Oct 9–7; early to mid-Mar 9–6.30; Nov–Feb 9.30–5.45). The vast, and rather bleak, fortress-like building dominates the town. Inside, it is largely unfurnished; you can visit on your own or join a guided tour in English. The Pope's Bedroom has a decorated ceiling and walls adorned with birds and golden vines on a blue background. The Grand Tinel banqueting hall has Gobelin tapestries, and there's a good view from the Terrasses des Grands Dignitaires. Across the huge, empty place du Palais is the Petit Palais (Wed–Mon 10–1, 2–6), which served as accommodation for visiting royalty and nobility and now has a collection of Gothic and Romanesque paintings and sculpture. The Rocher des Doms park, on the hill rising beside the Palais des Papes, offers dramatic views over the Rhône.

ART

The Musée Angledon (Apr–Nov Tue–Sun 1–6; Dec–Mar Wed–Sun 1–6; public hols 3–6), on rue Laboureur, has the personal collections of Jacques Doucet and Jean et Paulette Angladon-Dubrujeaud. It focuses on late 19th- and 20th-century art, including works by Cézanne and Picasso.

LES BAUX-DE-PROVENCE

www.lesbauxdeprovence.com

This stunningly picturesque medieval fortress-village is in the Alpilles hills, 25km (15 miles) south of Avignon. The village, with its atmospheric alleyways, sits dramatically on a sheer stony crag. This inaccessibility once deterred invaders but now attracts thousands of visitors.

Les Baux was originally a refuge during the eighth-century Arab raids. It became an important fortress in the Middle Ages, under the control of ambitious local lords. They claimed direct descent from the Magi king Balthazar, and to prove the point put the star of Bethlehem on their crest. The village as seen today is a narrow strip outside the original fortress, and dates largely from the 16th and 17th centuries. It has few permanent residents, having been almost entirely taken over by seasonal artists and craftspeople. Many of the restored old houses contain galleries, shops and cafés. The principal sight is the ruined walled enclosure of the medieval Citadel (the entrance is at the Musée d'Histoire des Baux). A large, bleak ruined area, known as the Ville Morte (Dead City), it offers fantastic views of the countryside.

As you walk through the streets look out, among the ice cream outlets and crêperies, for the 16th-century town hall, which has a facade of mullioned windows, a Renaissance courtyard and, inside, a museum of Nativity scene figurines (santons). There's also a 12th-century church,

Église St-Vincent, partly carved out of the rock, with a Lanterne des Morts tower (the lamp was lit when someone died) and windows designed by the 20th-century stained-glass master Max Ingrand.

Val d'Enfer, at the foot of the village, is a spectacular gorge of wild rocks and caves where you can see the Cathédrale des Images, a huge cave with a sound and light show.
✛ 456 M13 🛈 Maison du Roi, rue Porte Mage 13520 Les Baux de Provence, ☎ 04 90 54 34 39 🕒 May–Sep Mon–Fri 9–6, Sat–Sun 10–5.30; Oct–Apr Mon–Fri 9.30–5, Sat–Sun 10–5.30

BÉZIERS

www.beziers-tourisme.fr

The name of Béziers will forever be associated with the massacre that began the crusade against Cathar heresy in the Languedoc in the early 13th century. On 22 July 1209, the people of Béziers were digging in for the expected siege when the crusading army broke into the town and overran it. According to one chronicler, the Pope's Legate, Arnaud Amaury, was asked how the crusaders should distinguish the heretic Cathars from the devout Catholics of Béziers: 'Kill them all,' Amaury replied, 'God will recognize his own.' Almost the entire populace was slaughtered. Not much remains from those times except Pont Vieux, built in 1134, and three churches, St-Aphrodise, St-Jacques and the Madeleine, made of white limestone. The original cathedral of St-Nazaire

'exploded like a grenade' while Béziers was sacked by the crusaders; the building today dates from the 13th and 15th centuries.
✛ 456 K13 🛈 29 avenue Saint Saëns, 34500 Béziers ☎ 04 67 76 84 00 🕒 Jul–Aug Mon–Sat 9–6.30, Sun 10–1, 3–6; Jun, Sep Mon–Sat 9–12.30, 1.30–6; Feb–May, Oct–Nov Mon–Sat 9–12, 2–6; Dec–Jan Mon–Sat 9–12, 2–5

CAMARGUE

www.reserve-camargue.org

These picturesque wetlands in the delta of the Rhône river are home to an interesting, beautiful and fragile ecosystem in which human beings play an intimate role. Most evident are the white horses and black bulls which are rounded up by gardiens, the cowboys of the Camargue. With luck you should get a glimpse of the birdlife: A flock of flamingos is always a spectacular sight and ducks, waders and geese can also be seen with patience (and binoculars).

Arles (▷ 299) is the main access point into the Camargue. There are comparatively few roads and you might want to leave your car and strike out on foot or bicycle (▷ 326–327), or take a boat trip from the main town of Stes-Maries-de-la-Mer. There's a visitor centre at La Capeliere, south of Villeneuve, on the east shore of the largest lagoon in the Camargue, the Étang de Vaccarès.
✛ 456 L13–M13 🛈 Reserve Nationale de Camargue, Centre d'Information, La Capeliere, 13200 Arles ☎ 04 90 97 00 97 🕒 Wed–Mon 9–5

INFORMATION

www.carcassonne-tourisme.com
455 J14 28 rue de Verdun,
11890 Carcassonne 04 68 10 24 30
Jul–Aug daily 9–7; Apr–Jun, Sep–Oct
Mon–Sat 9–6, Sun 9–1; Nov–Mar
Mon–Sat 9–6, Sun 9–12 Carcassonne
Château Comtal tour: adult €8.50,
under 18 and EU nationals under 25 free

TIPS

» The roads enclosing the Ville Basse form a busy one-way system, and parking can be difficult in season, even though there are several large parking areas around the exterior.

» A good place for a walk is by the Canal du Midi—a UNESCO-listed World Heritage Site.

CARCASSONNE

The old walled city of Carcassonne (the Cité) takes your breath away. Thanks to its elevated position, if you visit late in the day, the walls and turrets are often bathed in the soft, red glow of the setting sun. The medieval Cité is the largest fortified town in Europe and never fails to amaze.

INSIDE THE CITÉ

More than 3 million visitors a year pass through the city's gates. Once inside, many people are content to stroll the narrow lanes lined with the inevitable souvenir shops interspersed with boutiques selling high-quality gifts and local produce. In the bars and restaurants around place Marcou the prices are not as high as you might expect.

The more energetic can explore the Château Comtal and the inner western ramparts (guided tour only), dating from the 12th century. In July and August, jousting displays are sometimes held in the Lices Hautes, the grassy area between the inner and outer ramparts. The Romanesque and Gothic St-Nazaire basilica has beautiful stained-glass windows and statues, and is the venue for occasional concerts.

THE LOWER TOWN

The lower town, the Ville Basse or Bastide St-Louis, has a partly pedestrian-only area, fine town houses and excellent small shops. Its central square, place Carnot, is the main meeting place and has been the site of the market (Tue, Thu, Sat mornings) since the Middle Ages. For small children there is an old-fashioned merry-go-round outside the Porte Narbonnaise.

Below The medieval Cité of Carcassonne

CANNES

www.cannes.fr
www.cannes.travel
www.festival-cannes.com

Cannes is a fairly small town with a big reputation. Its name conjures up luxury, glitz and big money, an image stemming partly from the International Film Festival held here in May, but also from its impeccable pedigree as an aristocratic winter resort. Be warned that you should make reservations a long way ahead for any hotel in Cannes, whether budget or de luxe—and don't even think about it during the film festival.

The hub of activity is the boulevard de la Croisette, a wide promenade running around the beautiful curve of the bay beside a sandy beach, most of which is divided up into pay-to-use or private sections. The latter are largely for the use of guests at the pre-war hotels on the other side of the boulevard. La Croisette begins at the Palais des Festivals et des Congrès, where you can see the handprints of film stars in the concrete of the plaza in front, although most are now a few decades old. Lined by designer shops, the promenade is attractive at night thanks to floodlighting.

Inland, rue d'Antibes is the main shopping street, with boutiques, jewellers and art specialists. West of La Croisette is a more 'real' Cannes,

with a relaxed air and lower prices. The esplanade La Pantiero, with its cropped plane trees, attracts strollers and boules players, and there are hundreds of café tables. Farther west still is Le Suquet, the small, older area of narrow lanes that was fortified by the monks of the Îles de Lérins.

✚ 457 P13 ⓘ Palais des Festivals, 1 boulevard de la Croisette, 06403 Cannes ☎ 04 92 99 84 22 ⓒ Jul–Aug daily 9–8; Sep–Jun 9–7 🚋 Cannes

CARCASSONNE
▷ 302.

CÉRET

www.ot-ceret.fr

Céret nestles close to the Spanish border, in a sheltered spot on the northern slopes of the Pyrenees. Its exceptionally mild climate produces mimosa and almond blossom in January and cherries (for which it is famous) by mid-April. The pretty town is an ideal base for hiking.

The unmissable Musée d'Art Moderne, on boulevard Maréchal Joffre (Jul to mid-Sep daily 10–7; Apr–Jun, mid- to end Sep daily 10–6; Oct–Mar Wed–Mon 10–6), was created in 1950 to collect together some of the works by artists drawn to the region on the Mediterranean light. The stunning collection now includes pieces by Matisse, Miró, Cocteau, Dalí, Picasso and Braque.

✚ 455 J15 ⓘ 1 avenue Georges Clemenceau, 66400 Céret ☎ 04 68 87 00 53 ⓒ Jul–Aug Mon–Sat 9–12.30, 2–7, Sun 10–1; Sep–Jun Mon–Fri 9–12, 2–5 (closes at 4.30pm in winter)

CÉVENNES

www.cevennes-parcnational.fr

In 1879, the writer Robert Louis Stevenson introduced the world to a little-known corner of France, the schist and granite mountains of the Cévennes, through his book *Travels with a Donkey*. The 12-day route that he followed with Modestine, the beast of burden of the title, from the Haute-Loire to Saint-Jean-du-Gard has now become the GR70 long-distance footpath and the Cévennes have become a national park with the aim of protecting the habitats of these forbidding uplands. The park's headquarters are in the château in the middle of the town of Florac, which stands at the northern end of the Gorges du Tarn (▷ 322–323). The Cévennes have a rich and rare flora with 48 endemic species of wild plants occurring within its borders.

✚ 456 L12 ⓘ Maison du Parc National des Cévennes, Château de Florac, 6 bis place du Palais, 48400 Florac ☎ 04 66 49 53 01 ⓒ Jul–Aug daily 9–6.30; Easter–Jun, Sep–All Saints (early Nov) daily 9.30–12.25, 1.30–5.30; All Saints–Easter Mon–Fri 9.30–12.15, 1.30–5.30

Above left *The famous Carlton Hotel in Cannes*
Above right *Sheep grazing in the Cévennes*

CHÂTEAUNEUF-DU-PAPE

Châteauneuf is a picture-book restored medieval fortified village, handsomely set on a riverside. The village, a popular visitor destination, is totally dedicated to producing, providing tastings of and selling its celebrated red wines. The tourist office has a list of vineyards and will be pleased to arrange tours and tastings for you.

One of the winemakers has a free museum in an old wine cellar in the heart of the village: Musée de Vins/cave Brotte-Père Anselme (daily, except 25 Dec) is all about traditional winemaking techniques, with displays of tools and equipment. At the end of your visit you can taste the wine and, of course, buy a couple of bottles to take home.

There are lovely views from the castle ruins on the hilltop.

🔠 456 M12 🚹 place Portail, 84230 Chateauneuf-du-Pape ☎ 04 90 83 71 08 🕘 Summer Mon–Sat 9.30–7, Sun 10–1, 2–6; rest of year Mon–Sat 9.30–12.30, 2–6

COLLIOURE

www.collioure.com

'In France there is no sky as blue as the one in Collioure,' said Henri Matisse, one of the founders of the Fauvist school of painting and a frequent visitor to this little fishing port. Reproductions of his work, and that of André Derain, are set up in the exact locations where they were painted, giving the modern viewer a chance to compare inspiration with the finished result. Even without its artistic heritage—it also inspired Picasso, Dufy, and Chagall—Collioure would be a attractive place. If something looks odd about the church on the waterfront it may be because its belfry is a converted lighthouse. As a complete contrast to art, Collioure is said to produce the best anchovies in France.

🔠 456 K15 🚹 place du 18 Juin, 66190 Collioure ☎ 04 68 82 15 47 🕘 Jul–Aug Mon–Sat 9–8, Sun 10–6; Apr, May, Jun, Sep Mon–Sat 9–12, 2–7; Oct–Mar Mon–Sat 9–12, 2–6

CORBIÈRES

www.corbieres-sauvages.com

Between Carcassonne and the coast, spreading south into the foothills of the Pyrenees, is this range of brooding limestone hills which reach their highest point at Pic de Bugarach (1,230m/4,035ft). Some good red wines are produced in the extensive vineyards planted in these uplands. The main reason to take the few lonely roads that wander through the hills, however, is to see the ruins of the great castles that command the heights. The best of these are Peyrepertuse, really two castles in one, and Quéribus, the final refuge of the Cathars which held out for 11 years after the castle at Montségur (▷ 365) near the Pyrenees had fallen. Also worth seeing are the small but dramatic Gorges de Galamus with its 300m (985ft) ravines.

🔠 455 J14 🚹 chemin de Padern, 11350 Cucugnan ☎ 04 68 45 69 40 🕘 Jul–Aug daily 9–7; Sep–Jun Mon–Fri 10–4

ÈZE

www.eze-riviera.com

Èze is one of the most perfect examples of a *village perché,* a fortified medieval village perched on a rocky hilltop for defensive reasons. It is also one of the easiest of all the perched villages to visit, being beside the Corniche Moyenne, midway between Nice (▷ 316) and Monaco (▷ 314–315).

The village is poised on the summit of a soaring pinnacle 430m (1,410ft) high that looks straight down onto the sea. It is exceptionally pretty, with its narrow medieval lanes and steps. Its proximity to some of the most stylish coastal towns has made Èze a chic, arty, sometimes crowded little place, yet on the whole it remains uncommercialized and rewarding to visit. There are a couple of luxury hotels in the old village.

Walk up the steep road to enter the medieval village through an imposing 14th-century fortified gateway, which takes you into a maze of old lanes dotted with flowers. The café terrace of the Eza hotel is open to the public for drinks and has wonderful views. If you head upwards, following signs to Jardin Exotique, you'll reach the ruins of a fortress, which is surrounded by an unusual cactus garden and has unforgettable views along the Riviera.

✚ 457 Q13 🚹 place Général de Gaulle, 06360 Èze (on N7 below medieval village) ☎ 04 93 41 26 00 🕙 Apr–Oct daily 9–7; Nov–Mar Mon–Sat 9–6 🚉 Èze Bord de Mer

FONDATION MAEGHT

www.fondation-maeght.com

This large and unusual art gallery in an interesting modern building has one of Europe's leading collections of 20th-century and contemporary art. It is hidden away down a country lane in Mediterranean pinewoods, outside the perched village of St-Paul-de-Vence, near Nice (▷ 316).

The gallery was launched by Marguerite and Aimé Maeght, successful art dealers, in 1964 to house their private art collection and as a memorial to their son, who died in childhood. It is still financed entirely by their foundation.

The building, designed by Catalan architect Josep-Lluis Sert, is a low, simple, mainly brick structure with a pair of strange curved shapes resting on the roof.

Several large sculptures stand in the grounds and there are quasi-natural outdoor spaces devoted to particular artists, including Giacometti, Joan Miró and Marc Chagall. These artists also feature prominently inside the building, together with Bonnard, Kandinsky, Calder and Léger, among many others. The interior is gloriously lit from above. A tiny chapel contains Georges Braque's *White Bird on a Mauve Background* in memory of the Maeghts' son.

Other highlights include the Miró *Labyrinth* with sculptures and ceramics, Chagall mosaics, and stained glass by Braque.

✚ 457 P13 ✉ 623 chemin des Gardettes, 06570 St-Paul de Vence ☎ 04 93 32 81 63 🕙 Jul–Sep daily 10–7; Oct–Jun 10–6 ✋ Adult €14, child (10–18) €9, under 10 free

Above *View of the Mediterranean from the Jardin Ezotique in Èze*
Opposite *Collioure*

FONTAINE-DE-VAUCLUSE

www.ot-delasorgue.fr

This pretty little riverside village is named after the nearby spring that has long fascinated both visitors and locals because the actual source of the water has never been located.

Water gushes from beneath a sheer cliff into a strange, still and very deep pool, surrounded by rocks and vegetation and often by a dense, dripping spray. At its height, the Fontaine-de-Vaucluse is among the world's most powerful natural flows of fresh water: 630 million cubic metres (22,260 million cubic feet) of water emerge from the source each year, then flowing down the narrow valley to become the river Sorgue.

In springtime, the water at full flow is truly spectacular. In summer, the flow is less and the number of visitors greater, so come in March, April or May for maximum effect.

To reach the spring, walk for around 15 minutes along a signposted, traffic-free lane which has several stalls selling souvenirs. On the way there's an underground museum of rocks and minerals, Le Monde Souterrain de Norbert Casteret, which deals vividly with all the efforts over the years to discover the source of the water. In the village, there's a perfectly restored traditional paper mill which, in its day, made use of the fast-flowing water.

✚ 456 M12 🚹 Chemin du Gouffre, 84800 ☎ 04 90 20 32 22 🕒 May–Sep daily 10–1, 2–6; Oct–Apr Mon–Sat 9.30–12.30, 1.30–5.30, Sun 1.30–5.30

FONTFROIDE

www.fontfroide.com

The Abbaye de Fontfroide, a 10-minute drive southwest of Narbonne (▷ 318) in Le Pays Cathar (Cathar country), is one of the largest and best preserved Cistercian abbeys in Europe. It was founded by Benedictines at the end of the 11th century in a wooded area with its own water source. The abbey was affiliated to the Cistercian order in 1145, and was a bastion of orthodoxy during the period of the Albigensian crusade against the Cathar heretics in the 13th century. It became prosperous, with 20,000 sheep and agricultural land spanning Roussillon and Catalonia.

The 12th-century abbey church of ochre sandstone stands at the end of a little road edged with scrub and cypress trees. It is as big as a cathedral and is known for its chapter house and cloister. You can explore various gardens, including the monks' kitchen garden and the *jardin des senteurs*, planted with sweet-smelling flowers. Visit between May and September to see 30,000 bushes in the rose garden in bloom.

✚ 455 K14 ✉ RD613, 11100 Narbonne ☎ 04 68 45 11 08 🕒 By guided tour only daily (also Jul, Aug Thu–Sat evening tour at 10pm) ✋ Adult €9, child (8–18) €2

FRÉJUS

www.ville-frejus.fr
www.frejus.fr

Fréjus, on the east bank of the river Argens estuary and its flood plain, is an animated and long-established little beach resort, popular with families. It is close to the Esterel hills and makes a good base for coastal excursions.

The middle of the town, 3km (2 miles) inland, consists of 17th- to 20th-century districts around an old quarter of narrow streets, many now traffic-free or with restricted traffic. At the heart of the old town is the lovely Cité Épiscopale (cathedral close), with a medieval cathedral, cloisters and fifth-century baptistery.

Nearby, there are considerable Roman ruins, including the remnants of an aqueduct, an army base, a fortified quay and a small amphitheatre, where concerts are still held.

Out of town, on the D4, there is a surprising African mosque in red stone, a perfect replica of a mosque in Mali, built by African sailors based at Fréjus in the 1920s. Other attractions out of town include a zoo and Aquatica, a huge water park on the N98.

Fréjus is big on events and festivals: As well as a market which is held on Wednesdays and Saturdays, there are special summer markets, a *bravade* (religious festival and procession) at Easter, and a grape festival in August.

✚ 457 P13 🚹 325 rue Jean Jaurès, 83600 Fréjus ☎ 04 94 51 83 83 🕒 Jul–Aug daily 9–7; Jun, Sep Mon–Fri 9–6, Sat–Sun 9.30–12.30, 2–6; Sep–May Mon–Sat 9.30–12, 2–6 🚆 Fréjus/St-Raphael

Below *An old working water wheel, at Fontaine-de-Vaucluse*

Above *Stepped and terraced buildings of the small town of Gordes*

GORDES
www.gordes-village.com

The houses appear to be built one on top of the other as they climb the steep hill on which this picturesque old village stands. Medieval Gordes, in the southern part of the Vaucluse plateau, was abandoned during the early 20th century, but was quickly discovered and restored by artists and well-to-do visitors. Now a rather chic place to have a second home, it is popular with media people. As a result, it is well served with expensive shops and restaurants.

Narrow stairways and covered passages wind steeply around the hill, which is topped by a medieval château fancifully restored by modern artist Victor Vasarely. It now contains a gallery of the work of another modern artist, Pol Mara. Around the village are numerous *bories,* windowless dome-shaped drystone dwellings, many of them centuries old. They were used as shepherds' huts, storage sheds, animal shelters and seasonal or even permanent residences; some were inhabited until the 19th century. To see a restored museum village of these structures, follow the signs to *Village des Bories,* which is off the D2, 4km (2.5 miles) from Gordes.

Also nearby is the Cistercian abbey of Sénanque.

➕ 456 M12 ℹ️ place du Château, 84220, ☎ 04 90 72 02 75 🕐 Summer daily 9–12.30, 2–6.30; rest of year Mon–Sat 9–12, 2–6, Sun 10–12, 2–6

GORGES DU VERDON
www.moustiers.eu

At the foot of the Alpes Maritime in inland Provence is one of the most spectacular natural phenomena in France, known as the Grand Canyon, mainland Europe's deepest river gorge.

Sheer cliffs rise 700m (2,300ft) above the flowing river, with panoramic views down the 21km (13-mile) length of this rocky corridor. A difficult winding road—little more than a country lane for most of the way—runs along the top of each side of the ravine. A succession of *belvédères* close to the edge provide fantastic viewpoints that give a broad look along the ravine and across the surrounding rocky terrain.

The road on the south side, the Corniche Sublime, has grander scenery and better viewpoints—the best stretch being the Balcons de la Mescla. The north side is also extremely impressive, but the road is more hair-raising and there are fewer viewpoints. At either end of the gorge are interesting small towns, Castellane and pretty Moustiers-Sainte-Marie. The drive is best undertaken outside the peak months of July and August, when nose-to-tail traffic crawls along the road. In fact, there's no great advantage in following the whole route—a short drive along the Corniche Sublime is impressive enough.

For keen walkers, there's a path running the full length of the canyon at the foot of the gorge. The river is popular for water sports.

The first survey of the gorge was carried out in 1905. The gorge was designated a Parc Naturel Régional in 1997.

➕ 457 N13 ℹ️ Maison de Lucie, place de l'Église, 04360 Moustiers-Sainte-Marie, (western edge of canyon) ☎ 04 92 74 67 84 🕐 Jul–Aug Mon–Fri 9.30–7, Sat–Sun 9.30–12.30, 2–7; Apr–Jun, Sep daily 10–12.30, 2–6.30; Mar, Oct–Nov daily 10–12.30, 2–5.30; Dec–Mar daily 10–12, 2–5

GRASSE
www.grasse-riviera.com

Grasse, about 17km (10 miles) inland from Cannes (▷ 303), is known as the 'Perfume Capital of the World', as the essences prepared here are turned into perfumes for some of the great fashion houses such as Dior and Chanel.

Although a tour of a perfume factory is why many visitors come to Grasse, the town is worth visiting in its own right and makes a good pause on the Route Napoléon. There's an evocative restored medieval quarter, with narrow traffic-free streets and many fine old mansions. The terrace at the top of the old quarter has great views of the sea andt he beautiful flower-filled Provençal countryside.

Long-established as a leather-tanning town, Grasse specialized in luxury gloves. The perfume industry arose by chance, when there was a brief fashion for scented gloves in the 16th century.

The essences for perfuming the leather were made using local jasmine, lavender and other flowers that grew abundantly around the town. Glove-making declined but the 17th and 18th centuries saw perfume-making go on to an industrial scale.

The three major perfumeries are Molinard, Galimard and Fragonard. All have tours in English, where you can learn how perfume is made.

➕ 457 P13 ℹ️ Palais des Congrès, 22 cours Honoré Cresp, 06130 Grasse ☎ 04 93 36 66 66 🕐 Jul–Aug daily 9–7; Sep–Jun Mon–Sat 9–12.30, 2–6

Above *The observatory at the summit of Mont Ventoux*
Left *The terraced gardens of Villa Sainte-Clare, overlooking Hyères*

HYÈRES

www.hyeres-tourisme.com

Hyères sits on a fertile part of the Provençal coast and is known for its vast quantities of flowering shrubs and palm trees. This has led to its alternative name, Hyères-les-Palmières. The atmospheric old quarter rises on a hill set back from the sea. A fortified Gothic gateway stands at the entrance and Italianate buildings, several with Renaissance doorways, line steep lanes. Place Massillon is the focal point, a triangular-shaped market place alongside 12th-century Tour St-Blaise. Other remnants of the medieval period include the Église St-Paul, with its Romanesque tower, and the Église St-Louis, part of a former Franciscan monastery. At the top of the hill, in Parc St-Bernard, are the vestiges of a château. Next to the park is Villa de Noailles where, in the 1920s, the Noailles family gave parties attended by illustrious guests such as Picasso and Salvador Dalí.

Southeast of the town, the Olbius Riquier tropical gardens, set around a Moorish-style villa, have palms and cacti, an animal enclosure and a greenhouse with exotic plants (May–Sep 7.30–8; Oct–Apr 7.30–5). South of town, along a narrow sandbar is Giens, where you can catch a ferry to one of the Îles d'Or (Golden Isles).

✚ 457 N14 ℹ Salle d'Honneur du Park Hotel, Ave Foch, 83400 Hyères ☎ 04 94 01 84 50 🕐 Mon–Fri 9–6, Sat 10–6 🚉 Hyères

MARSEILLE

▷ 310–311.

MENTON

▷ 330.

MINERVE

Standing on a rock outcrop at the confluence of two gorges, Minerve looks capable of withstanding any attack. But when the army of Simon de Montfort arrived in 1210 intent on dislodging the Cathar heretics within Minerve's walls the town's only weak point was exposed. Missiles from a siege engine blocked access to the only supply of fresh water and the citizens were forced to capitulate. When Minerve fell, 140 Cathar prefects chose to be burned at the stake rather than renounce their faith. The modern town is an atmospheric place to walk around. It is also the centre of an AOC wine region.

✚ 455 J13 ℹ rue des Martyrs, 34210 Minerve ☎ 04 68 91 81 43

MONACO

▷ 314.

MONTPELLIER

▷ 309.

MONT VENTOUX

www.bedoin.org

Rising high above the region, the conical summit of Ventoux makes a distinctive landmark. In spring and winter, the 1,909m (6,262ft) peak is covered in snow; at other times it is often shrouded in cloud while the rest of Provence basks in sunshine.

There is something compelling about Ventoux, and many people have wanted to get closer to this 'Giant of Provence'. The 14th-century Italian poet Petrarch was the first to write about his ascent of the mountain, which took two days. Now, there is a tarmac road all the way to the summit. The Tour de France bicycle race (▷ 27) sometimes includes this road. It is the most feared section of the race.

At the top, the winds are rarely light and the temperature is generally around 11°C (51°F) lower than at the foot of the mountain. Check the weather forecast and don't go up in stormy or windy weather, or without preparation. The view from the top takes in the Alps, the Rhône Valley, the Vaucluse plateau, the Cévennes and the Mediterranean.

✚ 456 M12 ℹ Espace Marie Louise Gravier, 84410 Bédoin ☎ 04 90 65 63 95 🕐 Mid-Jun to Aug Mon–Sat 9.30–12.30, 2–6, Sun 9.30–12.30; Sep to mid-Jun Mon–Fri 9–12.30, 2–6, Sat 9.30–12.30

MONTPELLIER

Montpellier's immediate appeal lies in the whiteness of its buildings (it is sometimes referred to as 'the white city'), the modernity of its architecture, the spaciousness of its squares, parks and walkways, and its multitude of fountains. The city is the ultimate young person's destination, offering 24-hour entertainment, especially during the hot summer days and nights, and festivals that cover cinema, dance, music and drama.

SEEING THE TOWN

People congregate around place de la Comédie in the fashionable old town, where elegant mansions and museums line narrow winding streets. The 17th- and 18th-century promenade du Peyrou is an impressive ensemble of a triumphal arch, a regal statue (of Louis XIV) and the water tower at the head of the aqueduct. The tourist office organizes guided tours that explore some sights and buildings not normally open to the public. They include a climb to the top of the triumphal arch and a visit to the university's faculty of medicine. Getting around Montpellier is easy thanks to the inexpensive, quiet and sleekly designed trams. Vélomagg has several stations throughout the city where you can rent bicycles, tandems and motorized cycles, and offers secure parking for them with 1,200 attachment points throughout the city (€1 for four hours, €2 per day). This is an excellent way to see Montpellier as there are 120km (75 miles) of bicycle routes, 11km (7 miles) of which follow the tramway. Cars are positively discouraged by high parking charges.

THE ARTS

Montpellier has a policy of making the arts available to as many people as possible, with very reasonably priced tickets. In the summer you will be spoiled for choice with the Montpellier Dance Festival in July and August, circus performers in June and the Radio France modern and classical music festival in July. The city also has an opera house, where enjoying the music is more important than dressing up. Montpellier's best art gallery, and one of the biggest in France, is the Musée Fabre, at 39 boulevard Bonne Nouvelle (Tue, Thu, Fri, Sun 10–6, Wed 1–9, Sat 11–6), with works by 16th to 18th-century painters, contemporary paintings, ceramics and sculpture.

INFORMATION

www.ot-montpellier.fr

✚ 456 L13 🛈 place de la Comédie, 30 allée Jean de Lattre de Tassigny, 34000 Montpellier ☎ 04 67 60 60 60 🕙 Jul–Sep Mon–Fri 9–7.30, Sat–Sun 9.30–5; Oct–Jun Mon, Wed–Fri 9–6.30, Tue 10–6.30, Sat 10–6, Sun 10–7 🚊 Montpellier

TIPS

» The City Card includes free museum entry, free guided tour and public transport.
» A flea market is held under the aqueduct on Saturdays.

Below *Place de la Comédie, in the stylish old town*

INFORMATION

www.marseille-tourisme.com

✚ 456 M13 ℹ️ 4 La Canebière, 13001 Marseille ☎ 08 26 50 05 00 🕐 Mon–Sat 9–7, Sun 10–5 🚉 Gare St-Charles

INTRODUCTION

France's premier port is an energetic, outward-looking city with a long history. Founded as the trading settlement of Massalia by the Greeks 2,600 years ago, it has been the western Mediterranean's main port ever since. After the Roman conquest of Provence, the port was sacked and stripped of its fleet. A period of decline followed the Saracen and other raids of the seventh century, which curtailed all Mediterranean trade. By the 11th century, however, the city had revived and continued to develop until the plague arrived in 1720, killing 50,000 residents. By the 1760s, the city was the major port trading with the Caribbean and Latin America. The republican zeal of Marseille's oppressed workers proved a backbone of the Revolution, the city giving its name to the new national anthem, *La Marseillaise,* even though it was composed in Alsace. The city sustained extensive damage during World War II.

In the second half of the 20th century, large numbers of people from France's former colonies in Africa, particularly North Africa, moved to the city giving it a distinctive mix of ethnic and cultural influences.

Today, Marseille has a population of around one million and it has the problems of any big city. While there are areas where you should be careful, on the whole the city's 'crime and drugs' image is exaggerated.

The grandly beautiful Vieux Port (Old Port) and its surrounding streets form Marseille's focal point. Here you will find bars, art galleries, music venues and scores of little restaurants. You can walk or drive the shore road a few minutes south from Le Vieux Port to the old-fashioned little harbour at Anse des Auffes, where bright fishing boats are moored in front of a choice of fish restaurants.

If you want a break from sightseeing, Marseille has several beaches within a bus or boat ride from the city centre. One interesting direction to head is south, to the wild limestone massif of Les Calanques which is named after its steep sided sea-filled inlets. Another possibility is to visit the islands of the Frioul archipelago in the Bay of Marseille.

Above *View of Marseille, looking across the port*

WHAT TO SEE

VIEUX PORT
Visitors and residents alike tend to gravitate to the large, rectangular, westward-facing Vieux Port. It is fortified, enclosed by 17th-century Italianate quays and surrounded by pale stone facades and red roofs. Thousands of boats jostle one another. Steep hillsides slope down to the waterside, overlooked on the south side by the Fort St-Nicolas defences (no entry to visitors) and the powerfully fortified Basilique St-Victor, which has a fifth-century crypt. The quai des Belges on the eastern flank is home to a fish market every morning, where seafood is sold direct off the boats. A free solar-powered ferry takes passengers from one side of the port to the other, offering a water-level view of the panorama. North of the Vieux Port, the extensive modern docks extend along the shore.

➕ 313 A2

MUSÉE D'HISTOIRE DE MARSEILLE
The fascinating Musée d'Histoire de Marseille stands alongside the Jardin des Vestiges. It sets out the complete history of the city, with a third-century Roman ship as its focal point.

The Jardin des Vestiges is an archaeological site now transformed into a garden. A walkway enables an overview of the ruins of the original Greek ramparts, traces of a roadway and parts of the dock as it was in the first century AD. Many of the items found in the excavations are now in the museum.

➕ 313 B2 ✉ square Belsunce, Centre Bourse, 13001 ☎ 04 91 90 42 22 🕐 Mon–Sat 12–7 💶 Adult €2, child (under 5) free

LE PANIER
Stepped alleys and rundown tenements with laden washing lines strung between windows climb the Panier hill from the docks. In 1943 the occupying Nazi regime destroyed 2,000 buildings here and expelled or murdered around 25,000 residents.

Among the buildings that survived is the 16th-century Maison Diamantée, so-called for a facade of stones carved into diamond-like points. It houses the Musée du Vieux Marseille (Jun–Sep Tue–Sun 11–6; Oct–May 10–5), with sections dedicated to Provençal furnishings, *santons* (Nativity scene figurines) and the esoteric playing cards called the Tarot Marseillaise. Another survival, in Grand Rue, is the 16th-century Hôtel de Cabre. After World War II, it was taken apart and rebuilt in a different street, which is why it says Rue de la Bonneterie on the wall.

At the top of the Le Panier district is the former 17th-century hospice called La Vieille Charité, a rectangle of lovely, three-tiered arcaded galleries, set around a large courtyard with a small baroque chapel. Originally a place of detention and shelter for vagrants, La Vieille Charité now hosts art exhibitions and the Musée de l'Archéologie Meditéranéenne (Jun–Sep Tue–Sun 11–6; Oct–May 10–5).

Beyond is the 19th-century neo-Byzantine Cathédrale de la Major, with its domes and striped facade. The sad, damaged little building beside it is the 12th-century Romanesque Ancienne Cathédrale de la Major (closed).

➕ 313 A2

PALAIS LONGCHAMP
This palace is home to the Musée d'Histoire Naturelle (Tue–Sun 10–5), which has a zoo behind it, and the Musée des Beaux-Arts. The latter has 16th- and 17th-century French and Italian paintings, a room devoted to local architect, sculptor and painter Pierre Puget, and another room dedicated to local artist Honoré Daumier.

➕ 313 off C2 ✉ 142 boulevard Longchamp, 13004 ☎ Palais: 04 91 14 59 50; Musée des Beaux-Arts: 04 91 62 21 17 🕐 Musée des Beaux-Arts: Closed for renovations until 2013 💶 Musée des Beaux-Arts: €2. Musée d'Histoire Naturelle: €4 🚇 Longchamp-Cinq Avenues

TIPS
» Street parking is difficult so use the big, reasonably priced parking areas. There are five in the Vieux Port area.
» The monthly *Marseille Poche* and weekly *Ventilo* list hundreds of events in the city.
» Bouillabaisse, the classic Provençal fish stew, can be made correctly only in Marseille, according to gourmets. Try it in a restaurant on the streets around the Vieux Port and see for yourself.

Below *A massive gilded Madonna crowns the belfry of the basilica of Notre-Dame-de-la-Garde*

REGIONS SOUTHEAST FRANCE • SIGHTS

CHÂTEAU D'IF

It's a 15-minute ferry journey to the island of If, with its nightmarish prison fortress, made famous by Alexandre Dumas in his novel *The Count of Monte Cristo*. The journey gives great views of the city and guided tours take you to the cells once occupied by the 'Man in the Iron Mask' and other aristocratic prisoners.

✚ 313 off A2 ☎ 04 91 59 02 30 🕐 May–Sep daily 9–6.30; Apr 9–5.30; Oct–Mar Tue– Sun 9–5.15 💶 Adult €5, under 18 free 🚢 Ferries (€10 return) leave from quai des Belges

MORE TO SEE

LA CANEBIÈRE

Leading through the city in a majestic straight line directly from the Vieux Port's quai des Belges is the broad central avenue called La Canebière. Built in the 17th century, the street was for a long time rather seedy, but today it is an inspiring sight. Most of the main shopping streets are turnings off La Canebière.

✚ 313 C2

MUSÉE CANTINI

This modern art gallery, with a good Surrealist collection and works by Matisse, Dufy, Miró, Kandinsky and Picasso, was a private home in the 17th century.

✚ 313 C3 ✉ 19 rue Grignan, 13006 ☎ 04 91 54 77 75 🕐 Jun–Sep Tue–Sun 11–6; Oct–May 10–5 💶 Adult €2, under 5 free 🚇 Estangin-Préfecture

Above *Fishermen sell their catch daily at the quai des Belges*

MUSÉE DES DOCKS ROMAINS

At the foot of the Le Panier district are several important relics and museums of the Classical period. The Musée des Docks Romains (Museum of the Roman Docks) displays a collection of first- to third-century Roman objects discovered during post-war rebuilding work. It has a good collection of Roman *dolia* (large ceramic storage jars).

➕ 313 A2 ✉ 28 place Vivaux, 13002 ☎ 04 91 91 24 62 🕐 Jun–Sep Tue–Sun 11–6; Oct–May 10–5 ✋ Adult €2, child (5–17) €1, under 5 free

NOTRE-DAME-DE-LA-GARDE

About 1km (0.6 mile) south of the old port is the hilltop Notre-Dame-de-la-Garde, a 19th-century basilica with a huge gilded Virgin, strikingly lit at night. Locals believe it gives divine protection to the city.

➕ 313 B4

QUARTIER DE L'ARSENAL

Close to the port (to the south), behind quai de Rive Neuve, is the grid of streets called the Quartier de l'Arsenal. Once a notorious shipyards area where galley slaves were housed among the workshops, it is now full of restaurants.

➕ 313 B3

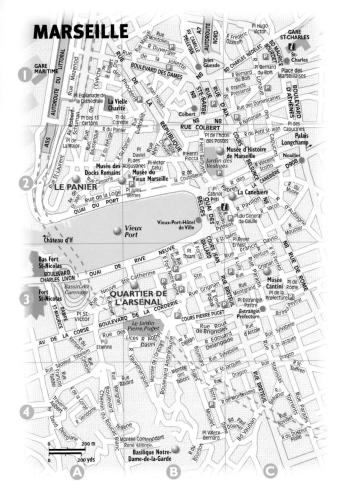

MARSEILLE

Below *Checking the condition of fishing nets in the old port*

MONACO

INFORMATION

www.visitmonaco.com

➕ 457 Q13 ℹ 2a boulevard des
Moulins, 98000 ☎ 92 16 61 16 (country
code 377) 🕐 Mon–Sat 9–7, Sun 10–12
🚉 Monaco–Monte Carlo ❓ Tourist
information kiosks are set up at the train
station and main sights in summer

Above *Flowering cacti and tropical plants
in the Jardin Exotique*
Below *A member of the royal guard*

INTRODUCTION

By a historical anomaly, this beautiful patch of rock hanging off the Provençal coast never became part of France. Instead, it has grown into a super-rich city, tax haven and millionaires' playground. It's a place that deserves to be seen, if only for the clever way it has made use of the limited space available. To accommodate the 32,000 people who live here (only 6,000 of whom are native Monégasques), the mini-state has expanded upwards in the form of skyscrapers and outwards into the sea on artificial platforms. Some streets, sitting almost on top of one another, are connected by elevators.

Monaco was originally a medieval fortified perched village, its castle a possession of Barbarossa. In the 13th century, the powerful aristocratic Grimaldi family from Genoa acquired the Rock and settled there making it their headquarters, refashioning themselves as the Princes of Monaco. Under Napoleon, most of the many independent fiefdoms of Provence were incorporated by force into France, but the Grimaldi influence in Provence and Italy was so strong that Napoleon decided to make an ally of the family instead of seizing their lands. Monaco's income had hitherto come from high taxes on its domains, but the principality found a role for itself as a refuge for the aristocracy, and in the 19th century Prince Carlo III created the glamorous zone called Monte Carlo, where the casino raised more funds for the royal family. It did so well that all taxes were eventually abolished.

Despite being just under 2sq km (0.75sq mile) in area, Monaco has several districts. Monaco-Ville is the original town on Le Rocher (the Rock); Monte Carlo is the larger new town, with a beach; La Condamine, the harbour district, lies between Monaco-Ville and Monte Carlo; on the steep slope between Monaco-Ville and the French border is the residential district Moneghetti; and Fontvieille is the area west of Monaco-Ville, which has been artificially extended into the sea.

WHAT TO SEE

MONACO-VILLE

Walk through the pretty, spotlessly clean, narrow streets, with their well-kept, pastel-shaded houses to get to Monaco's cathedral. It has a Louis Bréa altarpiece, some fine paintings and the tombs of all Monaco's past princes as well as that of Princess Grace, the former film star Grace Kelly, who died in a car accident in 1982, and Prince Rainier.

The main sight in Monaco-Ville, however, is the small but sturdily fortified 13th- to 17th-century Palais du Prince (early Apr–Oct daily 10–6), whose rooms are adorned with frescoes, tapestries and paintings. The palace also contains a museum devoted to Napoleon, with an assortment of objects, including one of his hats. In the courtyard you can watch the guardsmen in their elegant uniforms (white in summer and black in winter) perform the Changing of the Guard (daily at 11.55).

The Musée Océanographique has superb aquariums holding 350 species (Jul–Aug daily 9.30–7.30; Apr–Jun, Sep 9.30–7; Oct–Mar 10–6). There are fantastic views from the terrace.

MONTE CARLO

East of the Rock is Monte Carlo, a glitzy area of restaurants, luxurious hotels, beautifully kept palm and flower gardens, and the lavishly ostentatious belle-époque Casino. The Salons Européens and Salons Américains (daily 2pm) in the Casino have slot machines, roulette and gaming tables.

To get into the more lavish Salons Privés (Thu–Sun 2pm), which are the real Casino, not much frequented by ordinary visitors, you have to pay a fee (Casino entry fee, €10, the extra fee for Salons Privés is €10) and be appropriately dressed. A grand staircase goes down to a money-no-object nightclub. For those who have not blown all their cash at the gaming tables, there's plenty of expensive shopping around the casino and on boulevard des Moulins.

FONTVIEILLE

Fontvieille is a residential and business quarter standing on artificial platforms of rock, with a yachting marina alongside. Its Roseraie Princesse Grace is an exquisite rose garden with more than 3,500 varieties, dedicated to Princess Grace of Monaco. There are several museums here—the Musée des Timbres et des Monnaies (stamps and currency), the Musée Naval (model ships) and the Collection des Voitures Anciennes (gleaming classic cars).

TIPS

» You have to be over 18 to be admitted to the Casino, and will be required to show your passport or identity card. Entry to the Casino gardens is free.

» Law enforcement is rigorous in Monaco, with 24-hour surveillance of the entire principality, including inside public buildings. All driving laws (and most other laws), road signs and drink-driving limits are the same in Monaco as in France.

» Unless you are into motor racing, don't come during the Monaco Grand Prix in the second week in May, when tens of thousands of visitors cram into the principality and many roads are closed.

» Near the Larvotto beach area is the Jardin Japonais (daily 9am–dusk), a Shinto garden and a quiet, meditative refuge from the glitz that is Monaco.

Left Shop in the most exclusive boutiques in Monaco
Below The Grimaldi coat of arms on the Palais du Prince

INFORMATION

www.nice-coteazur.org

www.nicetourisme.com

✚ 457 Q13 🛈 5 promenade des Anglais, 06000 ☎ 08 92 707 407 ☯ Jun–Sep Mon–Sat 9–8, Sun 9–9; Oct–May Mon–Sat 9–6 🚊 Nice

TIPS

» Visit the big flower market (Tue–Sun) on cours Saleya.

» Stroll the Nice waterfront along the promenade des Anglais—a long, wide walkway edged by mimosa and palms.

» The French Riviera Pass offers free entry to a number of museums in Nice and other towns along the coast. Passes cost €24 for 24 hours, €36 for 48 hours and €54 for 72 hours.

» All municipal museums in Nice are free of charge.

Below *The Hôtel Negresco, on promenade des Anglais*

NICE

Nice was developed in stages by different peoples, including the Ligurians, Greeks and Romans. It was part of Italy until 1860, evident by the beautiful Italianate architecture of the old quarter. Artists began to arrive in the 1920s and there are several important galleries.

ART AND HISTORY

At the western end of the stony beach, a handsome 19th-century mansion contains the town's prestigious Musée des Beaux-Arts (Tue–Sun 10–6). It has extensive collections of 17th- to 19th-century French and Italian paintings and sculpture. Close by, the Kenzo Tange-designed Musée des Arts Asiatiques (May to mid-Oct Wed–Mon 10–6; mid-Oct to Apr 10–5) has magnificent examples of Chinese and other Asian pieces both ancient and modern that epitomize the artistic culture of each country.

On the Paillon promenade that divides the old town from the new, there are several galleries, including the famously avant-garde Musée d'Art Moderne et d'Art Contemporain (Tue–Sun 10–6), which has the definitive collection of works from the Nice school of the 1960s artists, including Andy Warhol's *Campbell's Soup Can*.

At the foot of Cimiez hill, the Musée Marc Chagall/Musée du Message Biblique (Jul–Sep Wed–Mon 10–6; Oct–Jun 10–5) has a phenomenal collection of Chagall's work, including stained glass, mosaics and vivid, dream-like canvases. Farther up the hill, the Musée Henri Matisse (Wed–Mon 10–6) shows the artist's exquisite line drawings and vivid gouaches. Matisse and Dufy are both buried in the cemetery nearby.

VIEUX NICE

The old quarter is a delightful tangle of picturesque narrow lanes, with bars, restaurants and little shops. There are also some interesting small baroque churches that are worth visiting.

ROMAN REMINDERS

The Cimiez hill has the ruins of a Roman city and a Musée Archéologique (Wed–Mon 10–6). The oval arena is a venue for open-air performances.

NÎMES

Nîmes and the Pont du Gard—the amazing Roman aqueduct 20km (12 miles) to the northeast (▷ 319)—are 'must-see' destinations in the southeast. On the border of Languedoc and Provence, Nîmes is large enough to offer visitors plenty to see, yet small enough, especially in the well-preserved old city, to generate a feeling of intimacy. There are excellent views over Nîmes from the Magne tower, in the beautiful Jardin de la Fontaine.

THE ROMAN AMPHITHEATRE

The top attraction is Les Arènes, one of the best preserved amphitheatres of the Roman world (Jul–Aug daily 9–8; Jun 9–7; Apr–May, Sep 9–6.30; Mar, Oct 9–6; Oct–Feb 9.30–5). Once inside, you are free to climb up and over the tiers and wonder at the scale of the 2,000-year-old monument, which could hold more than 20,000 spectators in its heyday. Today it is used for bullfighting and events such as trade fairs. In winter, a dome-shaped inflatable cover is added.

A short walk away, the Maison Carrée dates from the first century BC and is the only fully preserved temple of the ancient world (Jul–Aug daily 10–8; May–Jun 10–7.30; Apr, Sep 10–6.30; Oct 10–1, 2–6; Mar 10–6; Nov–Feb 10–1, 2–4.30). Inside, there are some beautiful examples of Roman mosaic work.

MODERN ART MUSEUM

Overlooking the temple is the Musée d'Art Contemporain (Tue–Sun 10–6). The spacious, bright Carrée d'Art (as it is known) displays art from the 1960s to the present. There are occasional touring exhibitions and an excellent third-floor bar/restaurant, with a terrace overlooking the Maison Carrée.

INFORMATION
www.ot-nimes.fr
✛ 456 L13 ℹ 6 rue Auguste, 30000,
☎ 04 66 58 38 00 🕐 Jul–Aug Mon–Fri
8.30–8, Sat 9–7, Sun 10–6; Apr–Jun,
Sep Mon–Fri 8.30–7, Sat 9–7, Sun 10–6;
Oct–Mar Mon–Fri 8.30–6.30, Sat 9–6.30,
Sun 10–5 🚃 Nîmes

TIPS
» Look out for the brass studs in the city's walkways, which bear the city symbol of a crocodile and a palm tree.
» At Les Arènes note that the topmost tier has no safety rails.

Above *Les Arènes, the Roman amphitheatre*

Above *Narbonne has a long history and a lively present*
Right *Detail of a building on place de la Loge, Perpignan*

NARBONNE

www.mairie-narbonne.fr

Narbonne is a delightful small town, with a Roman past. The Canal de la Robine, linking the town to the Canal du Midi on its north side, is a good place for a walk, with its bridges, trees and picturesque walkways.

Lanes full of shops lead off quai Dillon on the canal's right bank. On the left bank is place de l'Hôtel de Ville, the central square, where a section of the Roman Via Domitia, which linked Italy to Spain, was revealed in 1997. On the square's northern side is the Passage de l'Ancre, an entrance to the main attractions. These include the Cathédrale-St-Just-et-St-Pasteur and the Palais des Archévêques, which houses the Musée Archéologique and the Musée d'Art et d'Histoire (mid-Jul to Oct daily 10–1, 2.30–6; Apr to mid-Jul Wed–Mon 10–12, 2–5; Nov–Mar Wed–Mon 2–5). The latter has impressive collections of paintings, faïence and tapestries.

Less than an hour's drive to the south are sandy beaches, at resorts such as Gruissan-Plage, Narbonne-Plage and St-Pierre-sur-Mer. At Sigean, towards Perpignan, is the Réserve Africaine de Sigean safari park, and only a 10-minute drive away is the Cistercian Abbaye de Fontfroide (▷ 306).

✚ 456 K14 ℹ 31 rue Jean Jaurès, 11100 Narbonne ☎ 04 68 65 15 60 ◉ Apr–Sep daily 9–7; Oct–Mar Mon–Sat 10–12.30, 1.30–6, Sun 10–5 🚊 Narbonne

NICE

▷ 316.

NÎMES

▷ 317.

ORANGE

www.ville-orange.fr
www.otorange.fr

Orange became a possession of the Dutch Prince of Nassau in the 16th century, eventually giving its name to the Dutch ruling house. The town has a splendidly preserved Roman theatre, unique for its remarkable surviving backdrop wall, 103m (338ft) long. The Théâtre Antique hosts many performances during the year, including the town's world-class Chorégies, an international choral music festival. Rising behind the theatre is the Colline St-Eutrope, which gives a great view over Roman and medieval Orange. The theatre is in effect cut into the side of this hill, and many Roman objects were found here.

Near the theatre, the Musée Municipal displays some of the important Roman and medieval relics from Orange, notably a Roman land survey, carved on marble.

On the north side of town, with traffic whirling round it, is the Arc de Triomphe, a grandiose three-arched monument erected in the first century BC to mark the Romans' defeat of the local tribes.

✚ 456 M12 ℹ cours A. Briand, 84100 Orange ☎ 04 90 34 70 88 ◉ Jul–Aug

Mon–Sat 9–7.30, Sun 10–1, 2–7; Apr–Jun, Sep Mon–Sat 9–6.30, Sun 10–1, 2–6.30; Oct–Jun Mon–Sat 10–1, 2–5 🚊 Orange

PERPIGNAN

www.perpignantourisme.com

Perpignan, capital of the Roussillon region, has plenty to draw visitors: a Mediterranean climate, the region's largest shopping mall, events with a Catalan character, and an old quarter ideal for day's strolling.

Le Castillet, a small fort that has become the town's emblem, is now a museum of Catalan folk arts and traditions (Wed–Mon 9.30–12, 1.30–8). Quai Vauban is a good place for a walk along the banks of the river Basse; it passes place Arago, where you can find the busiest bars and brasseries. The Palais des Rois de Majorque is the principal historic attraction (Jun–Sep daily 10–6; Oct–May 9–5). Built on a small hill, it offers good views of the town from its ramparts and from the top of the keep. The Cathédrale St-Jean has a monumental organ and a peal of 46 bells. Behind it is Campo Santo (Apr–Jun, Sep Tue–Sun 12–7; Oct–Mar 11–5), the oldest and largest cloister cemetery in France.

✚ 455 K14 ℹ Palais des Congrès, place Armand Lanoux, 66002 ☎ 04 68 66 30 30 ◉ Mid-Jun to mid-Sep Mon–Sat 9–7, Sun 10–4; mid-Sep to mid-Jun Mon–Sat 9–6, Sun 10–1 🚌 Free minibus service follows a circular route around some of the central parking areas and pedestrian-only areas (not Sun or public hols) 🚊 Perpignan

PEZENAS

www.ot-pezenas-valdherault.com

In the 17th century, the prosperous wool town of Pézenas became the seat of the governors of Languedoc. One governor, the Prince de Conti, was determined to turn the place into a regional Versailles and himself into a patron of artists and writers. Among his protégés was the itinerant young actor Jean-Baptiste Poquelin, known by his nom de plume, Molière. Pézenas makes much of this literary connection, even though the playwright came here before he wrote any of the works that made him famous.

The old town is a handsome place to wander around, starting in the main square, place Gambetta. Nearby are many elegant medieval and Renaissance buildings, particularly old *hôtels particuliers* (mansions).

✚ 456 K13 ℹ 1 place Gambetta, 34120 ☎ 04 67 98 36 40 🕓 Jul–Aug Mon–Sat 9–7, Sun 10–7; Sep–Jun Mon–Sat 9–12, 2–6, Sun 2–5

PONT DU GARD

www.pontdugard.fr

A UNESCO World Heritage Site, this aqueduct was built in the first century BC to channel huge amounts of water to the Roman settlement at Nîmes (▷ 317). The aqueduct ran from a source near Uzès, 50km (30 miles) away, which necessitated spanning the Gardon river gorge at a height of 48m (156ft). No mortar was used, and the average drop over the entire length of the aqueduct was only 24cm (10in) per kilometre.

On the left bank, there is a huge parking area, information panels and a pathway leading to the exhibition hall, which has been designed and positioned so as not to detract from the site. The exhibition shows how water was used to enrich the civilized lifestyle of the Romans—piped supply, public baths, fountains in public areas and water-powered industry. It also deals with the geological challenges that were overcome during construction. Multimedia and interactive displays add up to an excellent facility.

Although people are no longer allowed onto the Pont itself, you can walk over the bridge that runs alongside it at the same level as the first tier of arches. By so doing you fully realize the size and weight of the building blocks used in the aqueduct's construction, but to appreciate it fully, you'll need to go up- or downstream for an unimpeded view from a distance.

✚ 456 L12 ✉ Exhibition Centre, Pont du Gard, 30210 ☎ 0820 903 330 (toll call) 🕓 Exhibition hall: Jul–Sep daily 9–7; Apr, Oct 9–6; Nov–Jun 9–5. Site: daily 7am–1am 💵 Mar–Oct €15; Nov–Feb €10 (for car and up to five people and access to museum) 🍴 🛍 🏛

ST-MARTIN DE CANIGOU

www.stmartinducanigou.org

The Pic du Canigou (2,784m/9,134ft) is sacred to the Catalans and the monastery of St-Martin du Canigou, standing in an impressive location with difficult access on its northern slopes, seems to encapsulate the spirit of the place. It is reached only by a stiff 30- to 50-minute walk uphill from the village of Casteil (ascent by 4x4 vehicle can be arranged for those who require it).

The monastery, founded in the 11th century, was damaged by an earthquake in 1428, abandoned in 1783 and later fell into ruins. In 1902 the bishop of Perpignan began its restoration and expansion. The abbey is now occupied by a small monastic community.

✚ 455 J15 ☎ 04 68 05 50 03 🚌 Guided visits (1 hour long in French): Jun–Sep daily at 10, 11, 12, 2, 3, 4, 5; Oct–May Tue–Sun at 10, 11, 2, 3, 4; check times and availability before making the ascent 💵 Adult €5, child (12–18) €3.50, under 12 free

ST-RÉMY-DE-PROVENCE

www.saintremy-de-provence.com

South of Avignon, St-Rémy-de-Provence attracts artists and art-lovers. It's a busy, well-kept, wine-making town with a small old quarter full of 16th- to 18th-century mansions, narrow streets and tree-shaded squares and fountains. There are small art galleries and

museums, including the Centre d'Art Présence Van Gogh, on rue Estrine, which displays items of memorabilia relating to the artist's time here, including letters and full-size prints of his works. Part of the house where Nostradamus was born in 1503 can be seen in rue Hoche, although it is not open to the public.

Around 1km (0.6 miles) south is the old monastery of St-Paul-de-Mausole, where Van Gogh committed himself for a year's rest and treatment after mutilating his ear. It proved to be one of the most productive periods of his life. You can visit the monastery's Romanesque church and cloisters on avenue Vincent van Gogh. Nearby is the archaeological site of the Graeco-Roman town of Glanum. For finds from Glanum, visit the Collection Archéologique in rue du Parage.

✚ 456 M13 ℹ place Jean Jaurès, 13210 ☎ 04 90 92 05 22 🕓 Jun–Sep Mon–Sat 9–12.30, 2–7, Sun 10–12; Oct–May Mon–Sat 9.30–12.30, 2–6

ST-TROPEZ

▷ 320.

SÈTE

www.ot-sete.fr

The colourful port of Sète is built around the base of Mont St-Clair, on an island between the Mediterranean and lagoon of Bassin de Thau. It was founded by royal decree in 1660 as an outlet to the sea for the Canal du Midi and it expanded in the 19th century to cater for the export of wine, wood, sulphur, cereals and iron. The tourist office organizes guided tours of the fishing harbour and visits to the auction house to watch the day's catch being sold.

In August 'nautical jousts' are staged on the Canal Royal, between teams standing on ramps protruding from the sterns of rowing boats.

✚ 456 K13 ℹ 60 Grand rue Mario Roustan, 34200 ☎ 04 67 74 71 71 🕓 Jul–Aug daily 9.30–7.30; Apr–Jun, Sep–Oct 9.30–6; Feb–Mar Mon–Fri 9.30–6, Sat–Sun 9.30–12.30, 2–5.30; Nov–Jan Mon–Fri 9.30–6, Sat 9.30–12.30, 2–5.30, Sun 9–1

INFORMATION

www.saint-tropez.st

✚ 457 P13 ⓘ 40 rue Gambetta (main part of harbourfront) ☎ 08 92 68 48 28 ⓦ Jul–Aug daily 9.30–1.30, 3–8; Apr–Jun, Sep–Oct 9.30–12.30, 2–7; Nov–Mar 9.30–12.30, 2–6

TIPS

» Don't try to drive to St-Tropez—traffic is terrible, with waits of an hour or more to get into town, and nowhere to park. Instead, use the large public parking areas at Port Grimaud and take the passenger ferry across the bay.

» If you visit in May, you'll catch the spectacular *bravades* festival, celebrating the town's resistance to invaders.

» Minutes away from the crowds of St-Tropez are the beautiful unspoiled villages of the St-Tropez peninsula.

Above *Boats and yachts moored in the bay of St-Tropez*

ST-TROPEZ

The small town of St-Tropez is world-famous—it symbolizes a certain rich, classless, glamorous but unconventional, hedonistic lifestyle. You only need to look at the luxury yachts moored along the quayside to see that the town attracts wealth and celebrities. But it is also packed with lesser mortals, who come to enjoy the atmosphere, pretend to be stars for a day, admire the enormous yachts—or maybe just enjoy St-Tropez for what it originally was and still is, a pretty, fortified harbour village.

THE OLD QUARTER

The Vieille Ville (old quarter) has managed, despite the huge numbers of visitors, to retain its charm. It has narrow streets of small old houses, with several chic boutiques. Outside the old quarter is the large main square, place des Lices, with boules players and shady plane trees. The quay curves along the edge of a beautiful blue bay with remnants of the old fortifications at one end. Beyond them is the tiny quarter called La Ponche, once a fishermen's district. The town itself has no proper beaches, so for a sandy beach head to the Cap de St-Tropez, on the peninsula.

THE CITADEL

On a hilltop to the east, clothed with pine and oleander, the Citadelle is a typical example of ruined 16th- to 17th-century defences. The fortress houses the Musée de la Citadelle, dedicated to the history of St-Tropez, with a good section on the 1944 Allied invasion (daily 10–12.30, 1.30–5.30).

SISTERON

www.sisteron.fr

In Provence's mountainous interior, Sisteron is an unusual fortified town that once marked the border between Provence and the Dauphiné. Its curious setting is a clue to its defensive role, a narrow valley edged by high, almost vertical cliffs, dramatically scored with the hues of various geological strata.

The old quarter is a labyrinth of stepped alleys, narrow streets and covered passageways called *andrônes*, where you'll find Notre-Dame des Pommiers, a 12th-century Romanesque church. A signposted route leads past some fine houses, ending up in place de l'Horloge, where there's a market on Wednesday and Saturday mornings.

Sisteron's gaunt citadel, narrowing as it follows a rocky ledge, stands 500m (1,600ft) above the waters of the Durance, on a high ridge overlooking the town. It survived until World War II, when the Germans used it as a garrison, strategic base and prison, but it was destroyed by Allied bombers in August 1944. Now it's a mere shell of ramparts enclosing the former fortress site, although the remaining gates, towers and 12th-century keep are impressive, as is the view.

🔢 457 N12 🚹 Hôtel de Ville, 04200 ☎ 04 92 61 36 50 🕐 Mid-Jul to mid-Aug Mon–Sat 9–7, Sun 10–12, 2–7; Jun to mid-Jul, Sep Mon–Sat 9–7, Sun 10–5; Apr–May, Oct Mon–Sat 9–12, 2–6; Nov–Mar Mon–Sat 9–12, 2–5 🚋 Sisteron

Right Matelot *dolls, handmade locally and sold in Toulon*
Below *Roman ruins in the town of Vaison-la-Romaine*

TOULON

www.toulontourisme.com

France's second-largest naval port, Toulon is often bypassed for more glamorous locations farther east. The city was transformed into a naval base soon after Provence became part of France in 1481, and under Louis XIV it became the strategic base for the Mediterranean fleet, a role that it maintains today. The port's surroundings (a huge natural harbour backed by a ring of hills) and Toulon's lively atmosphere make it worth a visit if you are nearby.

The Atlantes figures by the baroque sculptor Pierre Puget, on either side of the old town hall doorway, are powerful figures, based on stevedores Puget had seen unloading ships in Marseille. Boats leave regularly for trips around the harbour from quai Stalingrad and, for those interested in maritime history, there's the Musée National de la Marine on quai de Norfolk (Jul–Aug daily 10–6; Sep–Jun Wed–Sun 10–6; closed Jan). The excellent Musée d'Art de Toulon (Tue–Sun 12–6) has an extensive collection of more than 500 Provençal paintings from the 17th century onwards. The cours Lafayette is the setting every morning for Toulon's well-known Marché de Provence, a huge market selling some of the best produce that Provence has to offer.

🔢 457 N14 🚹 12 place Louis Blanc, 83000 ☎ 04 94 18 53 00 🕐 Late Jun–Sep Mon, Wed–Sat 9–7, Tue 10–7, Sun 9–1; Oct–late Jun Mon, Wed–Sat 9–6, Tue 10–6, Sun 9–1 🚋 Toulon

VAISON-LA-ROMAINE

www.vaison-la-romaine.com

In northeast Vaucluse, close to Mont Ventoux (▷ 308), this small town has a spectacular setting with the Dentelles peaks rising behind. Visitors come for the exceptional Roman ruins. The town also has an interesting medieval area on the other side of the Ouvèze river, across a Roman bridge. The Ville Haute (Upper Town) is a picturesque area of lanes and alleys, overlooked by the ruined château, built in the 12th century and redesigned in the 15th. There's a street market on Tuesdays.

The Roman town is partly exposed in two sites. In the Quartier du Puymin (Jun–Sep daily 9.30–6.30; Apr, May 9.30–6; Mar, Oct 10–12.30, 2–5.30; Nov to mid-Feb 10–12, 2–5; closed Jan to early Feb) are streets, walls, patches of fresco, mosaics, statuary and a restored theatre. The smaller Quartier de la Villasse (Jul–Sep daily 10–12, 2.30–6.30; Apr–May 10–12, 2.30–6; Mar, Oct 10–12.30, 2–5.30; Nov to mid-Feb 10–12, 2–5; closed Jan and early Feb) has a remarkable street of shops and fine mosaic floors. The Musée Archéologique (Jul–Sep daily 9.30–6.30; Apr, May 9.30–6; Mar, Oct 10–12.30, 2–5.30; Nov to mid-Feb 10–12, 2–5; closed Jan and early Feb) is easy to follow.

🔢 456 M12 🚹 place Sautel, 84110 (between the Roman sites) ☎ 04 90 36 02 11 🕐 Jul–Aug daily 9–12.30, 2–6.45; Apr–Jun, Sep to mid-Oct Mon–Sat 9–12, 2–5.45, Sun 9–12; mid-Oct to Mar Mon–Sat 9–12, 2–5.45

GORGES DU TARN

The gorge of the river Tarn is one of the most beautiful areas in France. This drive explores both the Gorges du Tarn and the Gorges de la Jonte. The route is an arduous one, with narrow, winding roads, the occasional steep section and, in the Tarn gorge, too much traffic if you are there on the wrong day. However, it is a rewarding route with magnificent scenery.

THE DRIVE
Distance: 110km (68 miles)
Allow: 1 day
Start/end at: Florac

★ Florac is a delightful little town, sitting below the towering cliffs of the Rocher de Rochefort. Its picturesque setting belies its violent history. Occupying a strategic position on the edge of the Causse Méjean, Florac, a local capital, was constantly fought over. Its castle was destroyed and rebuilt several times. The present 17th-century building, now the office of the Parc National des Cévennes, houses displays about the park and its wildlife.

From the middle of Florac, head south, but not by the main N106 that crosses the river. At a roundabout go straight over to take the D907, signed Meyrueis, Barre-des-Cévennes and St-Jean-du-Gard. After 5km (3 miles) take a right fork signed Vebron, Meyrueis, St-André-de-Vigne and Mont Aigoual, and drive for 10km (6 miles) through a lovely valley to reach les Vanels. Take the D996 to the right, signed for Fraissinet-de-Fourques, Meyrueis, Mont Aigoual and Grotte de Dargilan. There follows a long climb to the Col de Perjuret. At the top go straight on, following signs to Meyrueis to descend from the col into Meyrueis.

❶ Meyrueis is a popular visitor destination, not least because, at 700m (2,300ft), it is relatively cool in the heat of summer. It has managed to remain a quiet place, as a stroll under the old plane trees on quai Sully or around the narrow streets will show. Look for Maison Belon, with its elegant Renaissance windows. Southwest of Meyrueis, off the D39, the magnificent Grotte de Dargilan is the largest cave in the Cévennes and Causses. It has huge underground caverns, immense calcium carbonate deposits and crystalline lakes. After a visit to the cave, you emerge on a cliff face with views of the Gorges de la Jonte.

To leave Meyrueis, return to the D996 at the intersection with the main street and turn left, signed for Millau and Gorges de la Jonte. Take this narrow road out of town, following the road to right and left into the gorge. The gorge itself is attractive and easy to follow. At Belvédère des Vautours visitors can watch the comings and goings of a colony of vultures, live on video camera.

Continue to the western end of the gorge, where there is the tiny village of Le Rozier.

❷ Le Rozier is where the Jonte and Tarn rivers meet. The Grand Hôtel de la Muse et du Rozier, a rather strange but interesting building, stands right beside the river. Close to Le Rozier, but separated from it by the river, is Peyreleau, a prettier village, grouped around a modern church and an old tower, the last remnant of a medieval castle.

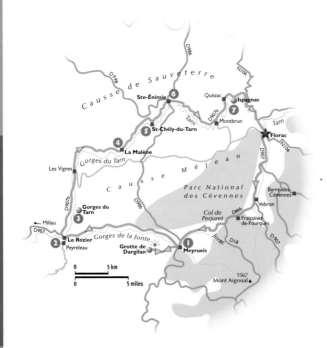

REGIONS · SOUTHEAST FRANCE · DRIVE

Continue through Le Rozier, bearing right on a short one-way street and then left onto a bridge across the Tarn. On the other side, turn immediately right onto the D907 signed Les Vignes, Sainte-Énimie, Gorges du Tarn and La Muse (this sign indicates the D907, but subsequent signs along the road indicate D907b). Follow the road through the Gorges du Tarn.

❸ The Gorges du Tarn is 50km (30 miles) long and can be followed by car (the easiest), by boat (the most exciting) or on foot (hard but rewarding). The Tarn has no tributaries, but is fed by the water of more than 40 resurgent springs, with much of the water flowing in as waterfalls. The gorge is never more than 500m (545 yards) wide. Occasionally it narrows to just 30m (33 yards), with sides that are sometimes vertical and overhanging and dotted with greenery.

From Les Vignes, the views become even more beautiful as the road leads to La Malène.

❹ Beyond Les Vignes, the gorge enters its narrowest, most spectacular section. Here are the Pas de Souci, where the Tarn flows over and under huge blocks created by the collapse of part of the gorge walls, and les Détroits, sheer cliffs that are 400m (1,300ft) high. The best way to see these is by boat, which you can take from La Malène.

Next comes a series of tunnels, then a 1.5km (1 mile) stretch of open road and a final twin tunnel controlled by traffic lights. Take the next (very sharp) turning to the right, signed for St-Chély-du-Tarn. Access to St-Chély-du-Tarn may be difficult in high season when traffic is heavy, as the right turn off the gorge is too tight for medium or large cars unless they swing out into oncoming traffic. The turn will be impossible for anyone towing a caravan or trailer. The road to the village is about 500m (550 yards) long and very narrow.

❺ St-Chély is a pretty little village on the left bank of the Tarn. The bridge over the Tarn is believed to date from Roman times and the church has an external stairway to its attractive bell tower. Equally charming sights are the old village houses with their Renaissance chimneys.

Retrace the route to the gorge road and turn right (no sign). Follow signs to Ispagnac and Florac to reach Sainte-Énimie.

❻ The village, with its cobbled lanes and old square, is named after St. Énimie, a seventh-century princess and hermit. Legend has it that her leprosy was cured when she bathed in the village's Fontaine de Burle.

Beyond Sainte-Énimie, the gorge opens up slightly. There are châteaux to be seen on each side of the route as it nears Ispagnac.

❼ As the route approaches the end of the gorge, look for the 16th-century Château de Charbonnières to the right near Montbrun. You also pass Quézac, a village with a Gothic bridge over the Tarn. Delightful Ispagnac has a 12th-century church.

Continue through Ispagnac and turn right at the N106, signed for Alès and Florac. This road takes you straight back to Florac.

WHEN TO GO
The prime consideration on this tour is the narrowness of the road in places, especially the D907b from Le Rozier to Sainte-Énimie. The sides of the gorge are steep so the road can be uncomfortably narrow for caravans and camper vans. For this reason, driving this extremely popular route in July and August may result in very slow progress.

If you are going in winter, check with the tourist office at Florac that the Col de Perjuret is passable, as this high point receives heavy snowfall, and watch for ice on the roads.

WHERE TO EAT
Le Rozier has a choice of bars and restaurants for lunch.

Below *A typical French church in the Gorges du Tarn*

SOUTHEAST FRANCE • DRIVE

REGIONS

THE HEART OF PROVENCE

This drive starts in Aix-en-Provence and takes in the Montagne Sainte-Victoire, which inspired many works by the painter Paul Cézanne, before turning south towards the Massif de la Sainte-Baume, where you'll have a view to Marseille. The roads are narrow in places and hilly in others, but this makes the drive interesting rather than arduous.

THE DRIVE

Distance: 135km (84 miles)
Allow: 1 day
Start/end at: Aix-en-Provence

★ The heart of Aix-en-Provence (▷ 298) is the cours Mirabeau, a wide boulevard planted with a double row of plane trees that provide welcome shade from the summer sun. North of here lies Vieil Aix, the oldest and most charming section of the city.

Leave Aix-en-Provence on the D10, signed for St-Marc-Jaumegarde and Vauvenargues, to reach the Barrage du Bimont after about 8km (5 miles), a short detour off the route.

❶ The lake behind the Barrage du Bimont dam provides water for local towns.

Continue on the D10 to Vauvenargues.

❷ The attractive village of Vauvenargues is famous for its Renaissance château, inherited by Pablo Picasso in 1958. The artist died here in 1973, and is buried within the extensive park. The park and château are not open to the public.

Rejoin the D10 by driving straight through the village (there is only one road). The D10, now signed for Jouques and Rians, runs along

the northern flank of the Montagne Sainte-Victoire.

❸ Cézanne loved this mountain and it inspired many of his works.

Bear right at the next intersection, following the D223, signed for Rians. This road becomes the D233 at the departmental border. The road narrows and climbs, offering good views. At the next intersection, turn left onto the D23. This road ends at a T-junction with the D3. Take a right turn, signed for Ollières and St-Maximin-la-Sainte-Baume. Approaching St-Maximin, turn left at the traffic lights, then right and left again as you traverse St-Maximin.

4 The basilica in St-Maximin-la-Sainte-Baume is the best example of Gothic architecture in Provence. It was built on the site of a sixth-century church that was, according to local legend, the resting place for the remains of St. Mary Magdalene. Construction of the new basilica started in 1295 and continued until the 16th century, although no belfry was ever built and the west front was unfinished.

Leave town on the N560 signposted Aubagne, Marseille and St-Zacharie. The road goes under the railway bridge and then there is a major fork left with signs to the A8 autoroute. Carry on towards St-Zacharie. A short distance farther on, cross the canal and just after this turn left on the D83 signposted Rougiers. After 7km (4.5 miles), cross the D1 road to reach Rougiers centre.

Go through the village. The D83 is even narrower on the far side. The road goes uphill towards a ruin and a church that you'll see on top of the hill ahead. It then bears sharp left and

goes through an open barrier, before continuing up the valley. Go over a crest and down to an intersection. Turn right onto the D95 heading east towards Plan-d'Aups. Go past signs warning of deer, and continue to the Hôtellerie at la Sainte-Baume.

5 The Hôtellerie is a 19th-century restoration of a Dominican friars' pilgrim hostel, dating from medieval times. It has now become an international base for spiritual studies, reached by a stiff hike.

Continue on the D80 through Plan-d'Aups, after which the road widens a little. At the next intersection, turn right onto a road signed for Auriol, which joins the D45a to make a long, twisty descent around many hairpin bends. When you reach the roundabout at the A560 go directly ahead (across the roundabout). At the next crossroads, take a right turn, signed for Moulin de Redon, onto the very narrow D45, going towards St-Zacharie. Turn left in the heart of the village onto the D85, following signs for Trets and Col du Petit Galibier.

Stay on this road and up the D12, which has fine views, to reach Trets.

6 Originally Roman, much of the existing town of Trets dates from the Middle Ages. You can see the remains of medieval walls, some square 14th-century towers, a castle that is 100 years older, and a 15th-century church.

In the middle of the town, turn left onto the D6, signed Aix and Marseille. At the roundabout on the outskirts of town take the D908 signed Peynier.

7 The tiny village of Peynier has a pleasant Romanesque church.

Continue on the D980 through Peynier, and climb up into the foothills of the Montagne de Regagnas that lies to the east. Take the D46c to the right, signed for Belcodène, and go through the village, following signs for Fuveau (the road number changes to D46b). Go over the autoroute and enter Fuveau. Turn left and right into the main square, then almost immediately, take the first turning on the left, which is the road D46 to Gardanne. At a roundabout with a central fountain, take the exit signed for Aix and continue to the N96. Turn right and follow this road and the N7 to Aix.

WHERE TO EAT
There are many restaurants and brasseries in St-Maximin-la-Sainte-Baume.

INFORMATION
✉ Hôtellerie la Sainte-Baume, outside the village of Plan-d'Aups ☎ 04 42 04 54 84

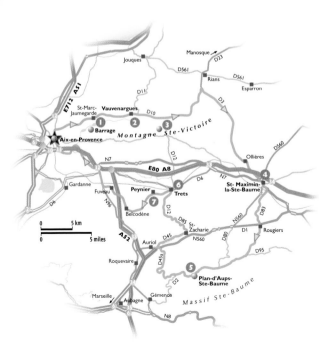

Opposite Eating alfresco on the cours Mirabeau, in Aix-en-Provence

THE CAMARGUE BY BICYCLE

Bicycling is a good way to explore the flat, sometimes blustery, distances of the Carmargue. This circular route is 20km (12.5 miles) and makes an excellent bicycle tour. It begins at Stes-Maries-de-la-Mer, where you'll find several places to rent bicycles. The tourist office on avenue Van Gogh has a list. The route takes in the Parc Ornithologique du Pont de Gau, which is perfect for birding.

THE TOUR

Distance: 20km (12.5 miles)

Allow: 1 hour 30 minutes to 4 hours, depending on how long you spend at the bird reserve and if you do the extra 10km (6 mile) detour to the Château d'Avignon.

Start/end at: Stes-Maries-de-la-Mer

★ The village of Stes-Maries-de-la-Mer is named after the three Marys (Mary Magdalene, Mary Salome and Mary Jacobe) who were said to have sailed from the Holy Land and landed here with Sarah, their Egyptian servant. Sarah is the patron saint of gypsies and there is a festival in her honour in May. In the crypt of the fortified Romanesque church is the black statue of Sarah, often draped in chiffon.

Leave Stes-Maries on the D85A, a minor road that runs between the Réserve Départementale des Impériaux et du Malagroy on your right and the Étang de Ginès on the left. After 4km (2.5 miles) the road bears left (there's a good view east here near the Mas de Cacharel), while an alternative route branches off right to Méjanes. After 6km (4 miles) the D85A joins the D570, the main road, at Pioch-Badet. For a longer trip, turn right and cycle 5km (3 miles) to the Château d'Avignon, which has a rich collection of 19th-century furniture. Heading south back towards Stes-Maries will bring you past the Centre d'Information de Ginès and the Parc Ornithologique du Pont de Gau.

The Camargue is a haven for birds, including pink flamingos, ducks, egrets, herons, cranes, geese and swans. For a guaranteed bird sighting, visit Parc Ornithologique du Pont-de-Gau.

To return along the Petit-Rhône after the Parc Ornithologique, turn right onto the D85 just before the Musée de Cire (wax museum) and left onto the D38, which loops back into Stes-Maries-de-la-Mer around the Étang des Launes.

WHERE TO EAT
HOSTELLERIE DU PONT DE GAU
www.pontdegau.camargue.fr
Small hotel with a good, moderately priced restaurant.
✉ Route d'Arles, 13460 Stes-Maries-de-la-Mer ☎ 04 90 97 81 53

PLACES TO VISIT
CHÂTEAU D'AVIGNON
☎ 04 90 97 58 60 🕐 Guided tours only: Wed–Mon 10–5 🖐 Adult €3, 16–25 €1.50
🎫 Tours every hour from 10am

PARC ORNITHOLOGIQUE DU PONT-DE-GAU
www.parcornithologique.com
☎ 04 90 97 82 62 🕐 Apr–Sep daily 9–dusk; Oct–Mar 10–dusk

INFORMATION
TOURIST INFORMATION
www.saintesmaries.com
✉ 5 avenue Van Gogh, 13460 Stes-Maries-de-la-Mer ☎ 04 90 97 82 55 🕐 Jul–Aug

daily 9–8; Apr–Jun, Sep 9–7; Mar, Oct 9–6; Nov–Feb 9–5

Above *You can take a boat tour from Stes-Maries-de-la-Mer*
Opposite top *The shore of Étang de Vaccarès*
Opposite bottom *Church bells in Stes-Maries-de-la-Mer*
Below *Bicycling is a fun way to see the picturesque wetlands of the Camargue*

VALLÉE DES MERVEILLES

The Vallée des Merveilles is in the eastern part of the Parc National du Mercantour, in the Alpes-Maritimes region of the Provençal Alps. With the adjoining Parco Naturale dell'Argentera in Italy, it shelters Alpine and Mediterranean flora and fauna. At least 25 of its plant species are not found anywhere else in the world and at least half of all France's flower species are represented. With some of the loveliest scenery in France, it is aptly named the Valley of Marvels. This hike, for which you should be well prepared, takes you past glacial boulders with images of animals and weapons carved by ancient peoples.

BE PREPARED

The only way to reach the Vallée des Merveilles is on foot—not only are there no real roads, but private vehicles are banned from this section of the park because it is a protected zone. (Some four-wheel-drive visitor vehicles are allowed on the first section to the Refuge des Merveilles.) Allow at least a day for this hike and start early in the morning.

If you want to stay in the area overnight, options include the shelters (refuges; Refuge des Merveilles at Lac Long or Refuge de Valmasque at Lac Vert) or one of the hotels at the winter ski resort of

Castérino, although not all are open year round. Camping is not allowed. Be aware of sudden storms, plan your hike with the park office in Tende by taking their map with you, wear suitable walking boots, and take food and drinks.

THE WALK

Distance: 30km (18.5 miles)
Allow: 1 day
Start/end at: Parking area at Lac des Mesches

HOW TO GET THERE

St-Dalmas-de-Tende is in the far southeast of France near the Italian border, off the N204 south of Tende.

★ The gateway to the Vallée des Merveilles is the little village of St-Dalmas-de-Tende. To reach the start of the walk, drive up the D91 towards Lac des Mesches, passing through woods with the heights of Cime de la Nauque to the left. At the lake there is a car parking area.

Follow the footpath towards Lac Long, which will take several hours. At first the walking is pleasant and easy, winding through wooded slopes, but then the path begins to rise steeply.

❶ Pines surround Lac Long's chilly shores and in spring the area is a

Above, right and opposite *Expect beautiful scenery and varied wildlife if you go walking in the Parc National du Mercantour*

wonderful sight as wild flowers bloom. All around is the stony mass of mountains, with Mont Bégo looming to the north. This is the southern end of the Vallée des Merveilles and here is the Refuge des Merveilles. The valley can be sinister in dull light, with the rocks a threatening dark shade.

At this point you join GR52 (GR stands for *Grandes Randonnées* or long-distance path). Climb until you reach Mont des Merveilles, where you can look for the carvings. As there are few obvious landmarks to describe where they are, refer to the maps from the park offices.

❷ Despite their huge number (more than 100,000), it is easy to miss these ancient carvings, especially in winter, when many are covered in snow. It is thought that the oldest date from about 1800BC, with others added in Roman times.

No one knows why these intriguing images were carved, although one theory is that Mount Bégo (sometimes called the Magic Mountain) was a sacred site, and the images were etched into the rocks as votive offerings by prehistoric pilgrims. The drawings were not

properly studied until the 1890s, when naturalist Clarence Bicknell excavated and catalogued them. He showed how the diagrams of hunting weapons, daggers, animals and symbols provide an insight into the Ligurian culture.

The footpath continues past a string of lakes through the heart of the valley towards Lac du Basto. Although difficult to find, engravings are littered all along the path, some of them close by and others towards the slopes of the mountains. Before Lac du Basto, GR52 heads off to the left, while your path continues towards Valmasque.

❸ There is a *refuge* at Valmasque, near Lac Vert, a lovely place where Mont Sainte-Marie looks down from its imposing height of 2,738m (8,981ft).

Here the path turns northeast for the homeward run. After Mont Peracouerte farther on, turn right and head south to Castérino.

❹ Castérino is a tiny resort in an attractive setting on the D91. If you're feeling tired at this point, taxis cover the final 3km (2 miles) to the car park at Lac des Mesches.

WHEN TO GO
Spring is the best time to come for the wild flowers. It is possible to do the hike all year round, although the *refuges* are not always open. Always book ahead if you are planning to stay or eat in one of the refuges.

WHERE TO STAY
REFUGE DES MERVEILLES
www.tendemerveilles.com/merveilles
www.cafnice.org
www.cafresa.org
☎ 04 93 04 64 64 🕓 Mid-Jun to Sep daily; Oct to mid-Jun weekends and French school hols

REFUGE DE VALMASQUE
www.cafresa.org
☎ 04 93 62 59 99 for reservations (before Jun only) 🕓 Mid-Jun to Sep

WHERE TO EAT
You can have meals at the *refuges* if you book ahead. There are seasonal cafés and auberges at Castérino.

INFORMATION
MAISON DU PARC NATIONAL
www.mercantour.eu
✉ Chalet de Casterino, 06430 Tende
☎ 04 93 04 89 79

CÔTE D'AZUR AND
THE PARC NATIONAL DU MERCANTOUR

There could hardly be a greater contrast than that between the Côte d'Azur coast and the Parc National du Mercantour. One is glitter and bustle, the other peace and unspoiled beauty. This driving tour combines the two, starting in Menton, one of the most pleasant of the Côte d'Azur towns, and then heading north into the hills of Haute-Provence, the foothills of the Alpes-Maritimes. Be aware that the roads to the north of the Côte d'Azur tend to be winding and slow.

REGIONS   SOUTHEAST FRANCE • DRIVE

THE DRIVE

Distance: 150km (93 miles)
Allow: 1 day
Start/end at: Menton

★ Menton claims to be the warmest town on the Côte d'Azur. It is a picturesque Italianate town, on the French side of the border. The Musée Jean-Cocteau, at the southern corner of the port, has a collection of works by the artist.

From the middle of town, take the road signed Autoroute (Nice, Italia) and Sospel. Follow signs for Sospel on the D2566, going under the A8 and passing through Castillon-Neuf. At Sospel, go over the railway crossing and then turn left, following signs for Moulinet and Col de Turini.

❶ The bridge in the pretty village of Sospel is of 11th-century design, complete with a central tower, but of 20th-century vintage, as the original was destroyed in World War II.

Bear left at a bend onto the D2204, signposted l'Escarène, and climb up to Col St-Jean, from where there are superb views back down to Sospel. Go over Col de Braus (1,002m/3,287ft) and descend around hairpin bends almost into l'Escarène. Just after a railway bridge take a right turn, continuing on the D2566 signed for Lucéram and Peïra-Cava.

❷ Drive through Lucéram, a haphazard collection of medieval alleys. At the next intersection, which is isolated and on a steep hill, bear left, following signs for Turini. The road climbs around 16 hairpin bends and passes through Peïra-Cava.

❸ Peïra-Cava is one of the best viewpoints on the route, with a superb panorama to the Parc National du Mercantour.

Continue to the Col de Turini.

❹ At an altitude of 1,607m (5,271ft), the Col de Turini has fine views in good weather. There is a hotel, café and restaurant.

Turn left onto the D70, signed for la Bollène-Vésubie and Nice, carefully descending the long, winding road from the pass. After about 10km (6 miles), look for a chapel on the left (on a bend) just after the Chapelle-St-Honorat tunnel.

5 There is a parking place here, from where there are superb views over La Bollène-Vésubie.

Continue through La Bollène. At a T-junction turn left onto the D2565, signed for Nice and St-Martin-Vésubie, to reach a valley bottom. There, follow signs for Lantosque and Nice, going straight on at first, then turning left along the main road. After 1km (half a mile) you can either go right and drive through Lantosque village, or take the bypass. The road through the village rejoins the main road; if you go that way turn right (signed for Nice).

Continue through St-Jean-de-la-Rivière. About 1km (half a mile) beyond St-Jean take the left fork, the D19, signed *Nice par Levens*—be sure to follow this sign since both directions are signed for Nice. The road narrows and climbs up the side of the Vésubie valley. After you leave the tunnel just before Duranus, there is a viewpoint to the right, the Saut des Français, above sheer cliffs. Continue along the road into Levens.

6 The attractive main square at Levens has shady gardens and good views to the south. The late 18th-century friary Chapelle des Pénitents Blancs stands on the north side, and the Chapelle des Pénitents Noirs, with a fine baroque facade, on the east side. The Maison du Portal gateway is all that is left of the castle. There is a viewpoint at the World War I memorial.

Leave Levens on the D19, signed for Nice. Continue for about 16km (10 miles), passing Tourrette-Levens. Just after St-André you'll pass under the A8. Take a left turn at the traffic lights here, signed for Sospel, cross a river and go straight over at the next set of traffic lights and go back under the A8. Take the next right turn, signed for Route de Turin, crossing the river and a level crossing (grade crossing). Take a left turn at the traffic lights, signed for La Trinité and Drap, and at a roundabout take the road signed

for La Turbie and Laghet. Follow the D2204a up a winding valley to the sanctuary at Laghet. There a hairpin bend takes the road sharply to the right. Pass under the A8 again, and turn left at the next intersection (an autoroute slip road, signed for Menton). Turn left again at the next intersection onto a road signed for La Turbie and Monaco. Continue to La Turbie.

7 The ancient village of La Turbie is on the Via Julia, a Roman road built by Julius Caesar to link Genoa with Cimiez, on the northern outskirts of Nice. The triumphal arch, the Trophée des Alpes, was built by Augustus Caesar in about 6BC to celebrate his local supremacy.

Drive through La Turbie and bear left past a hotel, following signs for Roquebrune and Menton, and then go downhill. At the bottom, take a right turn at the traffic lights, signed for Nice and Beausoleil. Take a left turn at the next set of traffic lights, signed for Cap Martin. As it leaves the heart of the village, the road veers sharp left. Go straight ahead here, on the road signed for Mayerling and

Cap Martin. This road soon reaches the sea. Park here for the start of the Cap Martin Coast walk, ▷ 332–333.

Follow the coast road back to Menton.

WHEN TO GO
The route can be treacherous in winter. Roads in the area are closed in late January for the Monte Carlo Rally (check exact dates with the tourist office).

WHERE TO EAT
There are several bars and restaurants in Sospel.

LES TROIS VALLÉES HOTEL-RESTAURANT
www.les3vallees-turini.fr
✉ Col de Turini ☎ 04 93 04 23 23

PLACE TO VISIT
MUSÉE JEAN-COCTEAU
✉ Le Bastion, Port de Menton, quai Napoléon III, 06500 Menton ☎ 04 93 35 49 71 🕐 Wed–Mon 10–12, 2–6 💷 Free

Opposite *Cows grazing on the hills in the park*

REGIONS SOUTHEAST FRANCE • DRIVE

331

CAP MARTIN COAST

This coastal walk visits what many consider to be the most attractive section of the Côte d'Azur. A long linear walk (you return by train), it is best done in the afternoon, after the heat of the day has passed and the sun is at the best angle for the views. The walk takes you past rhododendrons, cascades of honeysuckle and huge cactus plants to the right, with the turquoise sea to the left and coastal towns ahead. You can extend the walk by continuing into Monaco.

THE WALK

Distance: 6km (4 miles)
Allow: 1 hour 30 minutes (longer if you continue to Monte Carlo)
Start at: Cap Martin
End at: Cabbé or Monte Carlo

HOW TO GET THERE

Cap Martin is to the east of Monaco, in the southeast of France, close to the Italian border.

★ The thrusting headland of Cap Martin has long been a lookout point—the ruined tower at its heart was once a fortified medieval watchtower. At the base of the tower are the remains of an 11th-century priory. Legend has it that the prior had an agreement with the local folk that if the tower's bell rang, they would all hurry to the site to defend the monks. One night, just to test the system, the prior rang the bell and was very pleased with the speedy response. The local people were less pleased and a few nights later, when the bell rang again, they did not bother to turn out. But this time it was no trial run, and the priory was sacked by pirates and all the monks were killed.

Today Cap Martin is a rich suburb of Menton (▷ 330), its fine mansions set idyllically among sweet-smelling mimosas and olive trees.

Start from the parking area at the seaward end of avenue Winston Churchill on Cap Martin. Walk back in the direction in which you drove, then pass to the left of the hotel entrance, along a wide footpath at the edge of the sea. The path is marked at its start by a sign for Ville de Roquebrune-Cap Martin, and a list of times for walks. Follow the path skirting the edge of gardens and chic hotels. The path heads west along the edge of Cap Martin. There is a superb view of Monaco ahead and the sea to the left.

1 The path along Cap Martin is named Promenade Le Corbusier after the highly influential architect of the 1920s, who is connected with this stretch of coast through his association with artist and designer Eileen Gray. Her imaginative house above the shore was designated a historic monument in 1998. The house, hidden from view, lies below the path that continues up the western side of the Cap. Here the path is very close to the rail line.

In several places, steps lead up to the Cap, but the best route continues into Cabbé, from where trains run back into Carnolès. From Carnolès station, head seaward and follow the coastal path back to the car parking area.

To extend the walk, you can follow the path into Monte Carlo.

2 The principality of Monaco (▷ 314–315) has distinct areas, including the commercial hub—La Condamine—and Monte Carlo with its famous casino, hotels, marina, exclusive shops and restaurants. You don't have to be a wealthy player at the gaming tables to appreciate Monte Carlo, as the parks and gardens are a delight and the waterfront and views over the Mediterranean are superb.

Trains from here also serve Carnolès. This longer walk has the advantage of a glorious entrance to Monaco, but the disadvantage is that the route occasionally strays onto roads.

WHEN TO GO
Before you set off, check there is a suitably timed train from Cabbé to take you back to Carnolès.

WHERE TO EAT
There are expensive, high-quality restaurants in Cap Martin, and less expensive places in Cabbé.

Opposite Menton's busy marina, with the terraced buildings of the old town rising up the steep hillside
Above *Swimming in the Lido at Monte Carlo*
Below *Casino de Monte Carlo, Monaco*

AGDE

CENTRE INTERNATIONAL DE TENNIS

Pine trees surround this renowned tennis club which boasts 23 outdoor courts and 8 indoor courts and courses for all age groups. Other facilities within the complex include badminton and squash courts, beach volleyball, a sauna, a gym and an outdoor swimming pool. There's also a café and salad bar on site, and a golf course nearby.

✉ avenue de la Vigne, 34300 Cap d'Agde ☎ 04 67 01 03 60 ✋ Membership €178, 5 days' tuition €150

AIX-EN-PROVENCE

CINÉMA LE RENOIR

www.lescinemasaixois.com

This cinema has three auditoriums, one with a giant screen and THX sound. Most films shown are art house, but there are also some box-office hits. All films are shown in their original language.

✉ 24 cours Mirabeau, 13100 Aix-en-Provence ☎ 08 92 68 72 70 ⏲ Daily 2–9 ✋ Adult €9.30

CONFISERIE ENTRECASTEAUX

This is the place to buy *calissons* (marzipan, almond and glacé fruit), an Aix special. Made according to a family recipe for four generations, they come in a distinctive diamond-shaped box, reproducing the original shape of the *calisson*. Other treats on offer include glacé fruit, nougat and chocolate.

✉ 2 rue Entrecasteaux, 13100 Aix-en-Provence ☎ 04 42 27 15 02 ⏲ Mon–Sat 8–12, 2–7

HAPPY DAYS

On the liveliest square in town, this yellow-painted bar is popular with the fashionable crowd. The interior is funky, with yellow and burgundy walls and furniture.

✉ place Richelme, 13100 Aix-en-Provence ☎ 04 42 21 02 35 ⏲ Mon–Sat 8am–2am

ANTIBES

BALADE EN FRANCE

You can buy virgin olive oils from around France here, plus a range of Provençal foodstuffs such as tapenade. The basement of the shop sells a selection of anis and pastis bottled by small producers plus absinthe—the drink beloved of artist Vincent van Gogh, which has recently been reintroduced to the French public. Try a drop, mixed with water, at the absinthe bar before deciding to buy a bottle.

✉ cours Massena 25, 06600 Antibes ☎ 04 93 34 93 00 ⏲ Daily 9–8

MARINELAND

www.marineland.fr

One of France's longest-standing marine parks with whale, dolphin and sea lion shows plus a shark pool with a walk-through transparent tunnel and lots of Mediterranean sealife in the seawater tanks.

✉ R.N. 7, 06600 Antibes ☎ 04 93 33 49 49 ⏲ Hours vary by season. Closed Jan ✋ Adult €36, child (3–12) €28

LA SIESTA

On the seafront road, this club is packed all summer thanks to a great

Above You can go hiking in the ochre quarries of Roussillon in Provence

variety of entertainment, including several dance floors, a swimming pool, restaurant, casino and access to the beach.

✉ Route du Bord de Mer, 06600 Antibes-Juan-les-Pins ☎ 04 93 33 31 31 🕔 Mid-Jun to mid-Sep daily 11pm–5am; mid-Sep to mid-Jun Fri–Sat only ✋ Varies

ARLES
BIJOUX DUMONT
This family business has been making reproductions of original Provençal jewellery since 1967. Most are made using 18-carat gold, silver or semi-precious stones and they incorporate emblems of the region. Choose from cicada brooches, Provençal crosses or Les Saintes-Maries-de-la-Mer cross pendants.

✉ 3 rue du Palais, 13200 Arles ☎ 04 90 96 05 66 🕔 Tue–Sat 9–12, 2.30–7

LA CABANO DIS EGO
www.cabano-dis-ego.com
Horses and bulls are bred here and activities include traditional horseback riding, French cowboy games and hot-air balloon flights.

✉ Le Sambuc, 13200 Arles ☎ 04 90 97 20 62 🕔 All year ✋ Varies, but day viewing cowboy activities plus lunch, adult €38, child (5–12) €19

AURIBEAU
ALPES AZUR EVASIONS
www.alpesazurevasions.com
Pascal Genoud is a professional mountain guide and offers bespoke walking and hiking routes in the Côte d'Azur and Alpes-Maritimes regions. You can tailor the morning, day or multiple days to your ability and interest—perhaps flowers, birding or photography.

✉ 740 chemin Pierrenchon, 06810 Auribeau ☎ 08 73 35 57 50 🕔 All year ✋ Call for details

AVIGNON
CHAPELIER MOURET
www.chapelier.com
This hat shop is worth visiting for the interior alone. The same family has been making hats here since 1860, following methods passed from father to son. There's a great

collection of panamas and *capelines* (wide-brimmed hats that are typical of the region).

✉ 20 rue des Marchands, 84014 Avignon ☎ 04 90 85 39 38 🕔 Tue–Sat 10–12.30, 2–7

DISTILLERIE MANGUIN
www.manguin.com
This distillery produces *eau de vie* according to traditional methods. The fruit, grown on the distillery's own land, is saturated with sugar before it is marinated in alcohol.

✉ Île de la Barthelasse, 84000 Avignon ☎ 04 90 82 62 29 🕔 Mon–Sat 9–12, 2–6

PALAIS ROYAL
www.palaisroyal.net
On Fridays and Saturdays this former printing works hosts dinner theatre in the cabaret tradition, with dancers and fine food. Thursday is set aside for vocalists, while Sunday has a theme night. The rest of the week it's a fine food restaurant

✉ 10 bis rue Peyrollie, 84000 Avignon ☎ 04 90 14 02 54 🕔 Fri, Sat (and other show nights) 8pm–3am. Closed Aug ✋ Dinner/cabaret €42–€48, concert from €10

RED ZONE BAR
www.redzonebar.com
Here you'll find salsa on Tuesday night, live music on Wednesday, student night on Thursday and dancing on Friday and Saturday. The crowd is eclectic but always manages to be fashionable.

✉ 25 rue Carnot, 84000 Avignon ☎ 04 90 27 02 44 🕔 Daily 9pm–3am

BÉZIERS
CHARME D'INTÉRIEUR
www.charmedinterieur.com
Crammed with all the knick-knacks that make a house a home, this interior design shop on the edge of town, near Rond Point Vincent Bach, has plenty of small, lightweight items, such as textiles, lighting and ornaments, that can be easily packed and taken home as souvenirs. Styles range from traditional Mediterranean to contemporary. Other branches are at Montpellier and Perpignan.

✉ Voie Domitienne, 34500 Béziers ☎ 04 67 31 01 12 🕔 Mon–Sat 8–7

CANNES
AÉROCLUB D'ANTIBES
www.aeroclub-antibes.com
This flying club, just west of Cannes, organizes tours that fly over a variety of landscapes including the bay of St-Tropez, the Alps and the cliffs of Bonifacio in the south of Corsica.

✉ Aérodrome de Cannes Mandelieu, avenue Francis Tonner, 06150 La Bocca, Cannes ☎ 04 93 47 64 43 🕔 On reservation ✋ €72–€135 for 30 min

ALEXANDRE III
www.theatrecannes.com
The Alexandre is an old cinema turned theatre which has kept its retro interior and stages plays, including the classics as well as modern interpretations.

✉ 19 boulevard Alexandre, 06400 Cannes ☎ 04 93 94 33 44 🕔 All year

LE FESTIVAL
www.lefestival.fr
Between two luxury hotels and facing the sea, the bar's terrace, which is open all year round, is a popular place for people-watching and admiring the beautiful expanse of blue to the horizon.

✉ 52 La Croisette, 06400 Cannes ☎ 04 93 38 04 81 🕔 Daily 9am–midnight. Closed mid-Nov to late Dec

JACQUES LOUP
www.jacques-loup.com
In addition to its own collection, this shoe shop carries the hottest designs for men and women, and a range for children, from international shoemakers such as Bottega Veneta, Rossi, Church's and Tod's. It also stocks clothes for men and women from Prada, Marni, Lanvin and Miu Miu. An institution for every fashionista in Cannes.

✉ 21 rue d'Antibes, 06400 Cannes ☎ 04 93 39 28 35 🕔 Mon–Sat 9.30–8

PALAIS DES FESTIVALS ET DES CONGRÈS
www.palaisdesfestivals.com
This venue hosts the Festival du

Film every year. At other times, it welcomes international exhibitions, various performances in the Lumière auditorium and plays, ballets and concerts in the Théâtre Debussy.

✉ 1 boulevard de la Croisette, 06400 Cannes ☎ 04 93 39 01 01 🕐 Varies according to performance

CASTELLANE
ABOARD RAFTING
www.aboard-rafting.com
Experience the thrill of white-water rafting through the gorges of Verdon, or if you prefer, see the waterfalls and pools by canoe. Alternatively, rent a mountain bike.

✉ 8 place de l'Église, 04120 Castellane ☎ 04 92 83 76 11 🕐 Apr–Sep daily 9–7 ✋ Half a day's rafting from €55, guided 2-hour airboat trip €33

CAVAILLON
LE GRENIER À SONS
www.grenier-a-sons.org
This dynamic 350-seat concert hall stages jazz, rock, blues, reggae and more, by established musicians and budding talents. There's also a bar.

✉ 157 avenue du Général-de-Gaulle, 84301 Cavaillon ☎ 04 90 06 44 20 🕐 Ticket office Tue–Fri 2–6.30 ✋ Approximately €13

CHÂTEAU ARNOUX ST-AUBAN
LE CINÉMATOGRAPHE
www.cinefil.com
This cultural complex has two cinema auditoriums, a library and an exhibition space. The cinema shows box-office hits, films for children and some art-house offerings all screened in their original language. There's also parking and a café.

✉ Centre Culturel Simone Signoret, route de Manosque, 04160 Château Arnoux St-Auban ☎ 0892 680 128 (toll call) 🕐 Films every evening and Wed, Sat, Sun afternoons ✋ Adult €8.50

COUSTELLET
GARE DE COUSTELLET
www.aveclagare.org
Formerly a train station, this is now a 280-seat venue with a bar hosting live music, ranging from jazz to hard rock. Painting and photography

exhibitions are also held. Credit cards are not accepted.

✉ 105 quai des Entreprises, 84660 Coustellet ☎ 04 90 76 84 38 🕐 Fri–Sat 9pm–2am ✋ Concerts €15

DIGNE-LES-BAINS
TRAIN DES PIGNES
www.trainprovence.com
Since 1891, a single steam-powered carriage has chugged along a track linking the Alps to Provence. The train, with old-fashioned wooden benches, is a stylish way to see Provence's mountain scenery.

✉ Éspace Pierre Ferrié, 04000 Digne-les-Bains ☎ 04 97 03 80 80 🕐 Daily from 7.29am (more trains May–Oct) ✋ From €17.65 (a round-trip ticket to Nice is €68)

ÈZE
VERRERIE D'ART
At the heart of the picturesque village of Èze, this glass workshop produces beautiful pieces from small figurines to imposing sculptures. You can watch the craftspeople who use traditional methods to heat the glass before they shape it.

✉ place du Général-de-Gaulle, 06360 Èze ☎ 04 93 41 16 74 🕐 Summer daily 9.30–6; winter Fri–Mon 9.30–1, 2–6

FORCALQUIER
PIANO BAR LE SAXO
Three rooms accommodate a piano bar, a bar and a restaurant with a rustic wood interior throughout. In winter there's live music and pizza, in summer themed party nights.

✉ 13 boulevard Latourette, 04300 Forcalquier ☎ 04 92 75 00 30 🕐 Apr–Oct daily 9pm–2am; Nov–Mar Fri–Sat 5pm–2am

GORGES DU VERDON
AVENTURES ET NATURE
www.aventuresetnature.com
Pascal Faudou, a certified hiking instructor, leads various activities in the Verdon gorges. Try canyoning, hiking or 'aqua rando' (walking and swimming). He also runs five-day intensive training sessions. Credit cards are not accepted.

✉ 04120 La Palud sur Verdon ☎ 04 92 77 30 43 🕐 Mar–Nov on reservation ✋ Half a day's canyoning from €45

GRASSE
FRAGONARD
www.fragonard.com
World-renowned as the perfume capital, Grasse is home to many perfumeries, of which Fragonard, dating back to the 18th century, is one of the oldest. It is also the most prestigious. Visit the perfume museum before shopping for home fragrances, perfumed soaps and fragrances for men and women.

✉ 20 boulevard Fragonard, 06130 Grasse ☎ 04 93 36 44 65 🕐 Factory and museum: Feb–Oct daily 9–6; Nov–Jan 9–12.30, 2–6

GRÉOLIÈRES
GRÉOLIÈRES LES NEIGES
www.greolieres.com
The ski resort at Gréolières is a mere hour's drive from Cannes at an altitude of 1,400m–1,800m (4,600ft–5,900ft) with 21 slopes and 14 ski lifts in winter. In summer, skiing is replaced by hiking, mountain biking and horseback riding.

✉ 06620 Gréolières les Neiges ☎ 04 93 59 70 12 (snow report); tourist office 04 93 24 10 79 🕐 Ski resort: Christmas to mid-Mar ✋ Ski pass €22–€24 per day

ISOLA
ISOLA 2000
www.isola2000.com
At an altitude of 2,000m (6,500ft), this ski resort offers 50 tracks and one snow park with heli-skiing, snow scooters and an ice rink. In summer outdoor activities continue with hiking and horseback riding. You can take the cable car to 2,320m (7,610ft) for spectacular views.

✉ Tourist Office, Immeuble Le Pévelos, 06420 Isola ☎ 04 93 23 15 15 🕐 Ski resort: Dec–Apr, depending on snowfall ✋ Ski pass €28.80 per day

JUAN-LES-PINS
HYDRO AERO CONCEPT
Touring the Rade du Golfe on a hybrid of a super-light plane and a boat provides a unique bird's-eye view of islands and lighthouses. Juan-les-Pins is near Antibes.

✉ Ponton Hollywood, 06160 Juan-les-Pins ☎ 04 93 67 05 11 🕐 Jun–Oct daily 10–8 ✋ €100 for 1-hour

LAURIS
CAP RANDO
www.caprando.com
Discover Provence on horseback with this equestrian facility. There are several different trails to follow including the Parc Naturel Régional du Lubéron trail, a lavender route from Lubéron to Verdon and on to Nice, and one crossing the Provençal Alps. The venue also offers carriage tours. Accommodation is provided on two-day packages.
✉ Mas de Recaute, 84360 Lauris ☎ 04 90 08 41 44 🕐 All year by appointment 🖐 Two-day (one night) packages €235

MANOSQUE
LE LIDO
www.cinemovida.com
This cinema shows the latest Hollywood blockbusters, dubbed in French, on its four screens.
✉ 2 avenue St-Lazare, 04100 Manosque ☎ 0892 687 514 (toll call) 🕐 Daily 2–9.15 🖐 Adult €8

MARSEILLE
BAR DE LA MARINE
Facing the old harbour, this local bar is evocative of scenes described by Provençal author Marcel Pagnol. It's fashionable with a cool atmosphere and a soundtrack of acid jazz.
✉ 15 quai de Rive-Neuve, 13007 Marseille ☎ 04 91 54 95 42 🕐 Daily 7am–2am

BAR DE LA SAMARITAINE
www.la-samaritaine-marseille.fr
Remaining true to its quintessential 1930s character, this bar is a local institution. Its terrace, facing the picturesque old harbour, becomes a piano bar from Thursday to Saturday.
✉ 2 quai du Port, 13002 Marseille ☎ 04 91 90 31 41 🕐 Jul–Aug daily 6am–midnight; Sep–Jun 6am–10.30pm

CENTRE DE LOISIRS DES GOUDES
www.goudes-plongee.com
This company will take you diving in the bay of Marseille, around the Rioux archipelago, where caves and old wrecks are host to extraordinary flora and fauna. Some packages include all meals, use of kayaks and mountain bikes.
✉ 2 boulevard Alexandre Delabre, 13008 Marseille ☎ 04 91 25 13 16 🕐 Summer only daily 8am–10pm 🖐 €212 for a weekend 🚌 19 to Les Goudes

LE PELLE-MÊLE
France's greatest jazz musicians have played here on the small stage. The leather and wood interior creates a warm atmosphere and an intimate setting for gigs.
✉ 8 place aux Huiles, 13100 Marseille ☎ 04 91 54 85 26 🕐 Tue–Sat 6pm–3am 🖐 Varies according to performance

MÈZE
FIL D'AIR–CENTRE DE KITESURF
www.fildair.com
The vast salt lake of the Bassin de Thau is a great place to participate in the exciting sport of kiteboarding. Fil d'Air offers instruction for all levels of ability, from an hour-long introductory lesson to a seven-day schedule.
✉ 52 rue de la Méditerranée, 34140 Mèze ☎ 06 10 25 22 58 🕐 Apr–Oct 🖐 One-day lesson €150–€60 🚌 21, 24

MONACO
CASINO DE MONTE-CARLO
www.montecarlocasinos.com
The rich and famous flock to this grand belle-époque gambling temple decorated with frescoes and paintings and featured in several movies. The dress code is smart and you must be over 18 and show your passport or identity card.

Below Jacques Loup shop in Cannes

✉ place du Casino, 98000 Monaco ☎ 377 98 06 21 21 🕐 Café de Paris (slot machines) opens at 10am 🖐 Entry €10 and a further €10 to enter the Salóns Privées

OPÉRA DE MONTE-CARLO
www.opera.mc
Since its inauguration by the actress Sarah Bernhardt in 1879, this belle-époque opera house has welcomed the world's greatest voices to perform on its stage. The architect here, Charles Garnier, also designed the famous Opéra Garnier in Paris.
✉ place du Casino, 98000 Monaco ☎ Box office: 377 98 06 28 28 🕐 Ticket office: Tue–Sat 10–5.30 🖐 Varies according to performance

MONTPELLIER
CAFÉ JOSEPH
This is the ideal bar in which to get a real taste of Montpellier's livelier side: waiters with attitude, fashion-conscious youth and just the right amount of chic. Take the tram to place de la Comédie.
✉ 3 place Jean Jaurès, 34000 Montpellier ☎ 04 67 66 31 95 🕐 Mon–Sat 11am–2am

L'OPÉRA COMÉDIE
www.opera-montpellier.com
This grandiose 19th-century opera house takes pride of place in the heart of town. It plays host to some of the biggest stars, particularly in the summer.
✉ 11 boulevard Victor Hugo, 34000 Montpellier ☎ 04 67 60 19 80 🕐 All year 🖐 Adult from €19

MOUSTIERS-STE-MARIE
ATELIER ST-MICHEL
www.faience-moustiers.fr

Moustiers-Ste-Marie is famous for its faience and has many makers of fine ceramics. Particularly striking are the Martial and François Baudey reproductions of pieces from the city's faience museum. These include beautiful 18th-century rectangular plates, pot-holders and bowls with painted birds, flowers and scenes of country life. You can also order personalized china.

✉ avenue de Lerins, 04360 Moustiers-Ste-Marie ☎ 04 92 74 67 73 ⏰ Summer daily 9.30–6; winter Mon–Sat 9.30–12, 2–6

NICE
AUDITORIUM DU CONSERVATOIRE NATIONAL DE RÉGION
www.crr-nice.org

Operating under the name Les Lundis Kosmas, Regional Academy of Music students open their rehearsals every Monday evening. Established more than 20 years ago in honour of the composer Kosma, the event is an institution.

✉ 127 avenue de Brancolar, 06364 Nice ☎ 04 97 13 50 00 ⏰ Mon 6pm but closed during school hols. Call to check schedule ⏰ Free

L'F
On the liveliest street in town, this café has one of Nice's best terraces–and it's even heated during colder spells. Inside is a 1930s and 1940s interior with banquette seating and a black-and-white squared floor.

✉ 6 place Charles-Félix, 06300 Nice

☎ 04 93 85 74 10 ⏰ Daily 7.30am–2.30am. Kitchens close 11.30pm

GRAND CAFÉ DE LYON
www.cafedelyon.fr

This art nouveau-style bistro is a Nice institution. It's a brasserie at lunchtime, a tea room in the afternoon and later, a good place for a drink.

✉ 33 avenue Jean Médecin, 06000 Nice ☎ 04 93 88 13 17 ⏰ Daily 7am–11pm

MARCHÉ SALEYA D'ARTISANAT D'ART
Take a stroll through Nice's evening arts and crafts market after a drink at a nearby bar. You'll find Provençal handicrafts (pottery, glasswork, olive wood kitchenware), plus crafts from other regions of the world.

✉ Cours Saleya, 06300 Nice ⏰ Jun–Sep daily 6pm–12.30am

ODYSSÉE VERTICALE
www.odysseeverticale.com

Head to the great outdoors with this company who operate guided sports and activities including trips along the Via Ferrata and overnight hikes in the Vallée des Merveilles, along with skiing and canyoning. For the less active you can try photo safaris or boules.

✉ 14b rue de France, 06000 Nice ☎ 04 93 86 71 99 ⏰ All year ⏰ Varies

NÎMES
LES ARÈNES
www.arenes-nimes.com

Major events from bullfights to the biggest pop concerts are held in Nîmes's stunning 24,000-seat Roman amphitheatre, which is open to the public during the day (▷ 317).

✉ Les Arènes, 30000 Nîmes ☎ 04 66 28 40 20 ⏰ All year but check for concerts and events ⏰ Adult from €40

ORANGE
THÉÂTRE ANTIQUE
www.theatre-antique.com

This is probably the best-maintained ancient Roman theatre, and home since 1869 to the annual Chorègies, a world-famous opera and classical music festival. During the rest of the year it sees a varied schedule of circus, dance and concerts.

✉ rue Madeleine Roch, 84100 Orange ☎ 04 90 51 17 60 ⏰ Jun–Aug daily 9–7; Apr, May, Sep 9–6; Mar, Oct 9.30–5.30; Jan–Feb, Nov–Dec 9.30–4.30 ⏰ Adult €8

PAULHAN
MIEL ROUQUETTE
www.miel-rouquette.fr

Honey-lovers should definitely pay this place a visit. The shop is part of a working bee farm between Agde and Lodève. As well as selling an extensive range of honey, it sells a host of honey-based products, including nougat and honey vinegar. Sample the honey, visit the hives or go on the interesting, and free, 90-minute tour.

✉ 43 rue des Lavandes, 34230 Paulhan ☎ 04 67 25 04 40 ⏰ Mon–Sat 10–12, 2–7

PORQUEROLLES
PORQUEROLLES PLONGÉE
www.porquerolles-plongee.com

One of the three Îles d'Hyères, Porquerolles has rocky bays which host an extraordinary array of sea flora and fauna. Some dives are onto wrecks, including cargo ships and even a submarine.

✉ Zone Artisanale 7, 83400 Porquerolles ☎ 04 98 04 62 22 ⏰ Apr to mid-Nov daily dawn–dusk; mid-Nov to Mar by appointment ⏰ PADI Open water training and certification €403

ROBION
VELO LOISIR EN LUBERON
www.veloloisirluberon.com

This 78km (48-mile) bicycling route winds through the villages surrounding Forcalquier and the Montagne de Lure. You can stay at guest houses and eat at roadside restaurants en route.

✉ 203 rue Oscar Roulet, 84440 Robion
☎ 04 90 76 48 05

ROUSSILLON
SENTIER DES OCRES
www.roussillon-provence.com
Former ochre quarries have created a site of breathtaking beauty, known as Provence's 'little canyon', the setting for a 45-minute hike.

✉ Village de Roussillon, 84220 Roussillon
☎ 04 90 05 60 25 (tourist office)
🕐 Jul–Aug daily 9–7.30; Sep–Jun Mon–Fri 9–6, Sat–Sun 9–6.30 ✋ Entry €2.50

ST-ÉTIENNE DE TINÉE
AURON ST-ÉTIENNE DE TINÉE
www.auron.com
This ski resort in the Alpes-Maritimes, at an altitude between 1,600m (5,250ft) and 2,400m (7,900ft), has 39 tracks and 27 ski lifts. Ski, snowboard or choose from hang-gliding, sledge tours, ice-skating, quads and snow scooters. From Nice take the A8 exit at St-Isidore, then the RN 202 towards Digne/Grenoble.

✉ Tourist Office: Maison du Mercantour, 06660 St-Étienne de Tinée ☎ 04 93 23 02 66 🕐 Ski resort open Dec–Apr ✋ Ski pass €28.50 per day

ST-TROPEZ
CAFÉ DE PARIS
www.saint-tropez.com/cafe-de-paris
St-Tropez is one of the places to people-watch and the terrace of the Café de Paris is the best place to do it. Come here for pre- and after-dinner drinks, and celebrity spotting.

✉ Le Port, 83990 St-Tropez ☎ 04 94 97 00 56 🕐 Daily 10am–12am

RONDINI
www.rondini.fr
Since 1927, this family business has been making Tropézienne, a Roman-style sandal worn by Picasso. The sandals are still handmade today and now come in various styles.

✉ 16 rue Clémenceau, 83990 St-Tropez

FESTIVALS AND EVENTS

FEBRUARY
FÉTE DU CITRON
www.feteducitron.com
France's most easterly coastal town celebrates its citrus crop with majestic floats decorated with lemons and oranges.

✉ Menton ☎ 04 92 41 76 76 (tourist office for general info) or 04 92 41 76 95 for tickets to the stands 🕐 Late Feb

NICE CARNIVAL
www.nicecarnaval.com
The Riviera celebrates Mardi Gras with two weeks of parades. Huge papier-mâché floats proceed through the town to be set alight at sea on the final night. Pay to sit in the stands or look out of your hotel window for free.

✉ Nice ☎ 0892 707 407 (toll call) tourist office

MAY
FILM FESTIVAL
www.festival-cannes.fr
May means Hollywood comes to the Riviera as starlets are photographed along the Croisette and the steps of the Palais des Festivals. All the biggest screenings and parties are invitation only, but there are some public screenings.

✉ Cannes ☎ 01 53 59 61 00

☎ 04 94 97 19 55 🕐 Summer daily 10–12.30, 3–7; winter Mon–Sat 9–12, 2–6.30

LA TARTE TROPÉZIENNE
www.tarte-tropezienne.com
In 1955, while he was catering for the actors and crew of the film *And God Created Woman*, confectioner Alexandre Micka created a cake filled with butter cream. It was a great success, and one of the stars, Brigitte Bardot, christened it *Tarte Tropézienne*, and the name has stuck.

✉ 36 rue Georges Clémenceau, 83990 St-Tropez ☎ 04 94 97 71 42
🕐 Daily 10–7.30. Closed Nov–Jan

GRAND PRIX
www.monaco-tourism.com
Monte Carlo's annual weekend in the spotlight, when the city becomes a race track, with Formula One cars screeching through the streets around the casino.

✉ Monaco ☎ 377 92 166 116 (tourist office)

JULY
AVIGNON FESTIVAL
www.festival-avignon.com
Provence becomes the world capital of culture in July when the biggest names in theatre, dance and music flock to the walled city for a season of spectacular performances against a stunning backdrop. There's also plenty of free street entertainment.

✉ Avignon ☎ 04 90 14 14 14

AUGUST
FÊTE ST. LOUIS
To celebrate the feast of the patron saint of the town the fishermen dress in traditional costumes and indulge in jousting contests with ornate boats in the harbour.

✉ Sete ☎ 04 99 04 71 71 🕐 18–24 Aug

STES-MARIES-DE-LA-MER
PROMENADE DES RIÈGES
www.promenadedesrieges.com
Discover the magical scenery of the Camargue's inland waters, beaches and wildlife on a horseback-riding excursion. The stables have the white horses for which the Camargue is known, and use locally made saddles. The website has information about the level of experience needed. There are weight restrictions. Credit cards are not accepted.

✉ route de Cacharel, 13460 Les Stes-Maries-de-la-Mer ☎ 04 90 97 91 38 🕐 All year by appointment ✋ 2-hour excursion €30, day-long excursion from €65

PRICES AND SYMBOLS

The restaurants are listed alphabetically (excluding Le, La and Les). The prices given are the average for a two-course lunch (L) and a three-course dinner (D) for one person, without drinks. The wine price is for the least expensive bottle.

For a key to the symbols, ▷ 2.

AIX-EN-PROVENCE
LE CLOS DE LA VIOLETTE
www.closdelaviolette.com
Elegant modern dining is the byword here. The interior is understated and contemporary while the menu, by Jean Marc Banzo, is guided by the best Provençal ingredients and changes seasonally. Staples include *rouget* (red mullet) and local pigeon.
✉ 10 avenue de la Violette, 13100 Aix-en-Provence ☎ 04 42 23 30 71 🕐 Tue–Sat 12–2, 7.30–9. Closed first three weeks in Aug ✋ L €75, D €90, Wine €15

ANTIBES
LE BRÛLOT
www.brulot.com
There's exposed stone, an antique baker's oven and a basement room with vaults dating from the 12th century in this restaurant. The cuisine makes good use of the wood oven: grilled steak with Provençal herbs and grilled scampi flambéed with pastis (a local aniseed spirit). Alongside these traditional offerings, there are specials some days of the week such as couscous on Thursdays and ham on the bone on Fridays.
✉ 3 rue Frédéric Isnard, 06600 Antibes ☎ 04 93 34 17 76 🕐 Thu–Sat 12–2.30, 7.30–10, Mon–Wed 7.30–10 ✋ L €25, D €40, Wine €14

ARLES
LA GUEULE DU LOUP
The cuisine in this small restaurant, though true to the traditions of the Camargue and Provence, bears owner/chef Jean-Jacques Allard's personal touch. For example, eels from the Camargue are served with a leek and chicory fondue in a red wine sauce. The crème brulée is well-regarded.
✉ 39 rue des Arènes, 13200 Arles ☎ 04 90 96 96 69 🕐 Tue–Sat 12–1.30, 7.30–9.30; Mar–Sep Mon 7–9.30. Closed Jan ✋ L €40, D €50, Wine €15

LA MAMMA
www.lamammaarles.com
This restaurant has a rustic feel, and a massive pizza oven. Expect Italian and regional cuisine such as sautéed beef with olives, crudités with anchovy sauce and, of course, a range of pizzas.
✉ 20 rue de l'Amphithéâtre, 13200 Arles ☎ 04 90 96 11 60 🕐 Tue–Sat 12–2.30, 7–10.30, Sun 12–2.30 ✋ L €25, D €32, Wine €13

LA PAILLOTTE
This charmingly decorated Provençal-style restaurant lies in the heart of Arles, very close to the place du Forum. It specializes in regional cuisine using creatively cooked local produce. Try the *magret de canard* (duck breast) or the caramelized lamb with almonds. It has a terrace for al fresco dining.
✉ 28 rue du Docteur Fanton, 13200 Arles ☎ 04 90 96 33 15 🕐 Fri–Tue 12–1.30, 7–9.30, Thu 7–9.30. Closed two weeks in Jan and Feb ✋ L €25, D €30, Wine €18

Above *The terrace at elegant Hostellerie le Phebus in Gordes*

AVIGNON
CHRISTIAN ÉTIENNE
www.christian-etienne.fr

In a 14th-century palace, which was once the home of the Marshal of the Roman court, the dining room of this restaurant bears traces of this rich history, with beautiful painted ceilings and frescoes; the rest is pure Provençal. Christian Étienne, former sous-chef at the luxury Ritz Hotel in Paris, creates exquisite regional dishes with truffles and tomatoes his preferred ingredients—the black truffle omelette is a house specialty.

✉ 10 rue de Mons, 84000 Avignon
☎ 04 90 86 16 50 ⏰ Tue–Sat 12–1.15, 7.30–9.15 🖐 L €75, D €105, Wine €25

LE SIMPLE SIMON
This place is a piece of old England in the heart of Avignon. Inside there are decorative plates hanging on the walls, a collection of teapots on the shelves and a cakes and desserts display. During the afternoon it's a great place to enjoy a cup of tea and a scone. At lunchtime, a dish of the day is served.

✉ 26 rue Petite-Fusterie, 84000 Avignon
☎ 04 90 86 62 70 ⏰ Tue–Sat 12–7
🖐 L €23 (lunch only)

LES BAUX-DE-PROVENCE
HOSTELLERIE DE LA REINE JEANNE
www.la-reinejeanne.com

With superb views from the dining room, this restaurant is a meeting point for ramblers. It stands at the entrance of the village, overlooking the Val d'Enfer and the Vallon de Baumanière. It serves traditional and Provençal specialties such as fondue de noix de Saint-Jacques (scallop fondue) and pieds et paquets Provençaux (a stew of sheep's feet and tripe with Provençal vegetables).

✉ Grand Rue, 13520 Les Baux-de-Provence
☎ 04 90 54 32 06 ⏰ Daily 12–2.30, 7–9.30. Closed late Nov–late Dec and mid-Jan to mid-Feb 🖐 L €20, D €28, Wine €20

OUSTAÙ DE BAUMANIÈRE
www.oustaudebaumaniere.com

The Oustaù de Baumanière combines a 16th-century Provençal country-house restaurant coupled with a four-star hotel. Here you can enjoy exquisite dishes such as truffle and leek ravioli, pan-fried foie gras with a wine reduction and 'blue' lobster with a herb salad.

✉ 13520 Les Baux-de-Provence ☎ 04 90 54 33 07 ⏰ Apr–Oct daily 12–2, 7–9; mid-Feb to mid-Mar, Nov, Dec Fri–Tue 12–2, 7–9, Thu 7–9. Closed Jan to mid-Feb 🖐 L €140, D €175, Wine €55

BÉZIERS
OCTOPUS
www.restaurant-octopus.com

Bright, modern decor and a young team supply the background elements at Octopus. The regional ingredients, including lamb from the Aveyron hills, are brought to life with fresh sauces in dishes such as gaspacho cerise et gingembre, gambas nacrée (prawns) or filet de rouget (red mullet) and emulsion de coquillages (shellfish).

✉ 12 rue Boieldieu, 34500 Béziers ☎ 04 67 49 90 00 ⏰ Tue–Sat 12.15–2, 7.10–10 🖐 L €45, D €60, Wine €26

CANNES
LA POTINIÈRE DU PALAIS
www.lapotiniere.fr

The palais (palace) refers to the Palais des Festivals, where major events in Cannes, including the film festival, take place. The renovated 1948 bistrot inside, decorated in pale shades of yellow and green, was once frequented by Pablo Picasso and Maurice Chevalier, among other celebrities. But there's more to this restaurant than just a choice location; it serves contemporary Provençal cuisine. The cooking is exceptionally good and the menu includes many fish dishes and classics such as grilled steak and roast chicken.

✉ square Mérimée, 06400, Cannes
☎ 04 93 39 02 82 ⏰ Mon–Sat 12–2.30, 7.30–10 🖐 L €50, D €75, Wine €20

CARCASSONNE
LA COTTE DE MAILLES
www.cottedemailles.com

This small, family-friendly restaurant is set on a narrow alleyway in the heart of the citadel. You'll find a range of local dishes on the menu including the filling cassoulet and confit de canard (duck confit).

✉ 2 rue Saint Jean, La Cité, 11000 Carcassonne ☎ 04 68 72 36 24
⏰ May–Oct daily 12–2.20, 7.30–10.30; Nov–Apr Fri–Wed 12–2.30, 7.30–10.30 🖐 L €23, D €30, Wine €13

LE PARC FRANCK PUTELAT
www.leparcfranckputelat.com

The finest gastronomic restaurant near the château, Franck Putelat is knocking at the door of the very top flight with his Michelin stars. The dishes are a delight and the service suitably formal. The carte prices are high but there are good value tasting menus at lunchtime.

✉ chemin des Anglais, 11000 Carcassonne
☎ 04 68 71 80 80 ⏰ Tue–Fri 12–1.30, 7.30–9, Sat 7.30–9, Sun 12–1.30. Closed early Nov 🖐 L €80, D €120, Wine €50

CASSIS
LA VILLA MADIE
www.lavillamadie.com

Overlooking the coastline in the lee of the red rocks of the Calanques, this smart eatery offers excellent cuisine with all the tastes and colours of Provence. There's an expansive terrace, Le Bar Bleu, to make the most of the weather, offering light meals. The lunch-only Le Petit Cuisine offers a less expensive bistro-style cuisine.

✉ avenue Revestal, Anse de Corton, 13260 Cassis ☎ 04 96 18 00 00 ⏰ Daily 12–1.30, 7.30–9 🖐 L €45, D €65, Wine €22

CHEVAL-BLANC
L'AUBERGE DE CHEVAL BLANC
www.auberge-de-chevalblanc.com

Chef Hervé Perrasse prepares the great classics of Provençal cuisine, including the escabèche millefeuille (anchovies in puff pastry) and Provençal cake made with fresh, local herbs and white wine. The beamed dining room has displays by local artist Christine Darellis.

✉ 481 avenue de la Canebière, 84460 Cheval-Blanc ☎ 04 32 50 18 55 ⏰ Jul–Aug daily 7.30–9.30, Sun 12–1.30; Sep–Jun Tue–Fri 12–1.30, 7.30–9.30, Sat 7.30–9.30, Sun 12–1.30 🖐 L €28, D €38, Wine €20

COLLIOURE
LE NEPTUNE
www.leneptune-collioure.com
With a view of the coast from it shady terrace, this restaurant excels in the cuisine of this corner of southern France, combining tastes from land and sea. Collioure is renowned for its anchovies. Otherwise try the *galinette de méditerranée farcie* (stuffed fish) or lamb brought in from the Aveyron.
✉ 9 route de Port Vendres, 66190 Collioure ☎ 04 68 82 02 27 🕓 Daily 12–1.30, 7–9.30 🖐 L €60, D €50, Wine €20

ÈZE
CHÂTEAU DE LA CHÈVRE D'OR
www.chevredor.com
Set in a medieval castle atop the fortified village of Èze, the views from the terrace are among the finest in the Côte d'Azur—so the food has to be special to compete. You won't be disappointed—this hotel restaurant is a gastronome's delight with the finest ingredients and service to match. It has two Michelin stars.
✉ rue de Barrie, 06360 Èze ☎ 04 92 10 66 60 🕓 Mon–Thu 7.30–9.30, Fri–Sun 12–1.30, 7.30–9.30. Closed late Nov–early Mar 🖐 L €120, D €200, Wine €48

FRÉJUS
L'ABRI-COTIER
www.labri-cotier.com
Comfortable wall-seating, a superb view of the harbour and a heated terrace contribute to the feel-good nature of this restaurant. The food is outstanding, with dishes such as sea bass in a champagne sauce and bay prawns mingling on the menu with simple meals such as pizzas, salads and risottos. There's a basic children's menu.
✉ Quai Marc Antoine, 83600 Fréjus ☎ 04 94 51 11 33 🕓 Jul–Aug Mon–Tue, Thu–Fri, Sun 12–11, Wed, Sat 7.30–10; Sep–Jun Mon–Tue, Thu 12–6, Fri–Sun 12–10 🖐 L €35, D €42, Wine €15

GORDES
HOSTELLERIE LE PHEBUS
www.lephebus.com
Chef Xavier Mathieu's sophisticated regional cuisine includes fillet of sole pan-fried in salt butter with tangy jasmine and vanilla sauce or farmhouse duck foie gras. You can sit in the elegant dining room, which has beamed ceilings, or you may prefer the terrace and its fantastic views.
✉ route de Mur Joucas, 84220 Joucas-Gordes ☎ 04 90 05 78 83 🕓 Fri–Mon 12.30–2, 7.30–9.30, Tue–Thu 7.30–9.30. Closed mid-Oct to Mar 🖐 L €75, D €100, Wine €24

HYÈRES
LA COLOMBE
www.restaurantlacolombe.com
Chef Pascal Bonamy likes to innovate, mixing the finest ingredients. His sea bass dish comes with asparagus and pearl onions, and he uses peppers from Espelette, in the Basque country. The interior, with yellow and blue tones and cane chairs, betrays a regional influence.
✉ route de la Bayorre, 84360 Hyères ☎ 04 94 35 35 16 🕓 Jul.–Aug Wed–Fri, Sun 12.30–1.30, 7.30–9.30, Tue, Sat 7.30–9.30; Sep–Jun Tue–Fri 12–1.30, 7.30–9.30, Sun 12–1.30 🖐 L €38, D €50, Wine €20

LAURIS
LA TABLE DES MAMÉES
www.latabledesmamees.com
There are exposed stone vaulted ceilings and a large fireplace in this 14th-century country house. The cuisine is also full of character, with dishes such as duck with olives, garlic and courgettes (zucchini) and traditional fish soup. The cellar contains plenty of local wines.
✉ 1 rue du Mûrier, 84360 Lauris ☎ 04 90 08 34 66 🕓 Tue–Sat 12–2.30, 7.30–10, Sun 12–2.30. Closed Mar 🖐 L €33, D €45, Wine €18

MARSEILLE
LES ARCENAULX
www.arcenaulx.oxatis.com
Books line the walls of Marseille's majestic former arsenal, which has a beamed ceiling and long red wall seats. Sophisticated regional cuisine is on the menu, with dishes such as honey and lemon duck served with citron-scented courgette (zucchini) gratin. In the afternoons, Les Arcenaulx is a tea room.
✉ 25 cours Estienne d'Orves, 13001 Marseille ☎ 04 91 59 80 40 🕓 Mon–Sat 12–2, 8–11 🖐 L €45, D €50, Wine €20

CHEZ FONFON
www.chez-fonfon.com
The lively fishing port, now a conservation area, is the place to try bouillabaisse, the Mediterranean fish soup for which Marseille is famous. Here you are in a different world, far from the touristy restaurants of the city's old port. Chez Fonfon is an institution in town and has been run by the same family for more than 50 years. It has an elegant, Mediterranean interior with green basket-weave chairs, a tiled floor and Provençal fabrics.
✉ 140 rue du Vallon des Auffes, 13007 Marseille ☎ 04 91 52 14 38 🕓 Apr–Oct Mon 7.15–9.45, Tue–Sat 12–1.45, 7.15–9.45; Nov–Mar Tue–Sat 12–1.45, 7.15–9.45 🖐 L €45, D €50, Wine €20

MONACO
LE LOUIS XV
www.alain-ducasse.com
The height of luxury, this restaurant is within the majestic Hôtel de Paris, which was built in 1864. Here in this Alain Ducasse restaurant, Franck Cerutti practises his art. The Mediterranean-inspired menu changes with the seasons and is in themes, including the kitchen garden, hunting, the farm, the sea and rivers. The luxurious Louis XV-style interior provides the backdrop to a feast fit for a king. Jackets and ties are the dress code.
✉ Hôtel de Paris, place du Casino, 98000 Monaco ☎ 377 98 06 88 64 🕓 Thu–Mon 12.15–1.45, 8–9.45; Wed dinner in Jul and Aug. Closed Nov–Dec, late Feb to mid-Mar 🖐 L €170, D €170, Wine €90

MONTPELLIER
LES BAINS
www.les-bains-de-montpellier.com
This stylish restaurant is named after the public baths that used to occupy the building. It serves a range of modern and traditional Mediterranean dishes with an emphasis on seafood. You can eat outside on the expansive terrace

or in the stylish dining room. The restaurant also serves afternoon tea.
✉ 6 rue Richelieu, 34000 Montpellier ☎ 04 67 60 70 87 🕐 Mon 8–11, Tue–Sat 12–2, 8–11 🖐 L €25, D €40, Wine €20

BRASSERIE DU THÉÂTRE
Opposite the opera house, on a summer evening you can sit out on the terrace and hear the music from performances drifting in. The restaurant specializes in seafood, but also has meat and poultry on the menu. The €14 prix-fixe option, of two courses and wine, is excellent value. The interior is a little lifeless, so opt for the terrace if the weather is fine. Service is good.
✉ 22 boulevard Victor Hugo, 34000 Montpellier ☎ 04 67 58 88 80 🕐 Mon–Sat 12–3, 7–12am 🖐 L €28, D €35, Wine €15

MOUSTIERS-SAINTE-MARIE
LA BASTIDE DE MOUSTIERS
www.bastide-moustiers.com
This quality hotel/restaurant is run by a protégé of renowned chef Alain Ducasse. The renovated stone *bastide* (country house) has a relaxed feel and you can dine on the shaded terrace or in one of several intimate dining rooms. The set menu changes almost daily, taking into account the seasons. It blends Provençal cuisine with modern touches.

✉ chemin de Quinson, 04360 Moustiers-Sainte-Marie ☎ 04 92 70 47 47
🕐 Tue–Sun 12–2, 7.30–9.30. Restaurant closed mid-Nov to 1 Dec, mid to late Jan and Mon–Wed Feb–Mar 🖐 L €50 D €70 Wine €45

FERME SAINTE-CÉCILE
www.ferme-ste-cecile.com
The restaurant is in a former 18th-century farm set close against the hillside and there's a lovely shady terrace for alfresco dining. The menu makes the most of the local produce: Dishes include lamb in a spicy crust, or foie gras served with a thyme and courgette (zucchini) marmalade.
✉ route des Gorges du Verdon, 04360 Moustiers-Saint-Marie ☎ 04 92 74 64 18
🕐 Tue–Sun 12–2, 7–9. Closed mid-Nov to Dec and two weeks in Feb 🖐 L €28, D €38, Wine €15

NARBONNE
LE PETIT COMPTOIR
www.petitcomptoir.com
An unimposing facade gives way to a surprisingly lavish dining room decorated with period mirrors and plenty of flowers. It's not easy to predict what you'll find on the menu in this small restaurant (it changes every week according to what is available in the local market), but pasta, casserole and pastry dishes are sure to be on offer.

✉ 4 boulevard du Marèchal-Joffre, 11100 Narbonne ☎ 04 68 42 30 35 🕐 Tue–Sat 12–10 🖐 L €33, D €45, Wine €15

LA TABLE SAINT CRESCENT
www.la-table-saint-crescent.com
Located in a medieval oratory, and offering a splendid vine-surrounded terrace, this restaurant serves creative cuisine accompanied by a wide selection of Languedoc-Roussillon wines. Specialities include *ravioles d'huîtres à l'infusion de fenouil séché* (oyster ravioli with an infusion of dried fennel), *cabillaud poché en aïgo boulido* (cod poached in herbs and oil) and *pommes de terre écrasées à l'huile d'olive* (potatoes crushed in olive oil).
✉ 68 avenue du Général Leclerc, 11100 Narbonne ☎ 04 68 41 37 37 🕐 Tue–Fri 12–1.30, 7.30–9.30, Sat 7.30–9.30, Mon 12–1.30 🖐 L €45, D €57, Wine €20

NICE
L'ÂNE ROUGE
www.anerougenice.com
Chef Michel Devillers likes to cook fish, and his creations are tantalizing: succulent scallops roasted with chorizo, fresh and dried tomatoes with thyme flowers. The warm, elegant interior has beamed ceilings, colourful pictures hung on ochre

Below *Le Brûlot in Antibes*

walls, comfortable high-back padded chairs and a large fireplace. The flower-filled terrace has a view of the harbour.

✉ 7 quai des Deux-Emmanuel, 06300 Nice ☎ 04 93 89 49 63 🌐 Mon–Tue, Fri–Sun 12–2.30, 7.30–10, Thu 7.30–10 👋 L €64, D €64, Wine €24

AU RENDEZ-VOUS DES AMIS
www.rdvdesamis.fr

A bright and lively family-run restaurant with a very pleasant terrace, this is only a short distance from the centre of Nice. It serves a generous Provençal cuisine. Among the specialties are *raviolis à la niçoise*, *mijoté de gigot d'agneau au pistou* (roast leg of lamb with basil and garlic paste), or *fricassée de lapins à la crème de moutarde* (rabbit in mustard cream sauce). For dessert try *clafoutis aux prunes et amandes* or *fondant au chocolat* (a baked plum and almond dessert) or *mousse de marscapone* or an ice cream.

✉ Aire Saint-Michel, 176 avenue Rimiez, 06100 Nice ☎ 04 93 84 49 66 🌐 Thu–Tue 12–1.30, 7.30–9.30. Closed Tue Sep–Jun, 20 Oct–20 Nov and 2 weeks in Feb 👋 L €30, D €40, Wine €14

CHEZ SIMON

Five generations of the same family have run this establishment, once a coaching inn. Beamed ceilings, basket-weave chairs and a plough-wheel candelabrum set the traditional character of the dining room. The traditional Provençal cuisine includes dishes such as stuffed mutton tripe.

✉ St-Antoine-de-Ginestière, 06200 Nice ☎ 04 93 86 51 62 🌐 Daily 12.30–2, 7.30–10 👋 L €45, D €56, Wine €16

NISSA SOCCA

This small café on one of Nice's most atmospheric old-town streets is a city institution offering masses of the traditional *socca* (pancakes made from chick-pea flour) and Niçoise pizza, along with plates of fresh pasta and young wine by the carafe.

✉ 5 rue Ste-Réparate, 06000 Nice ☎ 04 93 80 18 35 🌐 Mon–Wed, Fri–Sat 12–2, 7–9.30, Thu 7–9.30 👋 L €20, D €35, Wine €15

RESTAURANT BOCCACCIO
www.boccaccio-nice.com

There are no fewer than six dining rooms here, all of which have a marine theme. One has a large aquarium, another with a vaulted wooden ceiling is reminiscent of the interior of a caravel (a historic small ship), and model boats carry on the nautical theme. The menu has Mediterranean seafood dishes such as bass in a salty crust, bouillabaisse and seafood platters.

✉ 7 rue Masséna, 06000 Nice ☎ 04 93 87 71 76 🌐 Daily 12–2.30, 7–11 👋 L €50, D €60, Wine €24

L'UNIVERS DE CHRISTIAN PLUMAIL
www.christian-plumail.com

This restaurant in the old port has been receiving excellent reviews. It's the domain of Christian Plumail, a young and innovative chef who mixes modern recipes with traditional ingredients to put a new twist on classic French cuisine.

✉ 54 boulevard Jean Jaurès, 06300 Nice ☎ 04 93 62 32 22 🌐 Mon 7.30–10, Tue–Fri 12–2, 7.30–10, Sat 7.30–10 👋 L €44, D €70, Wine €24

NÎMES
AUX PLAISIRS DES HALLES
www.auxplaisirsdeshalles.com

A fine city restaurant that serves exquisite cuisine with good value fixed-price menus. Attention to detail is everything here. Regional dishes of meat, fish and poultry are served alongside good seafood. The resident patisserie chef, Yannick Rico, creates fantastic desserts that are a feast for the eyes as well as the lips. The courtyard makes a lovely outdoor venue. The wine list is extensive.

✉ 4 rue Littré, 30000 Nîmes ☎ 04 66 36 01 12 🌐 Tue–Sat 12–2.30, 7.30–10. Closed late Oct–early Nov, mid-Feb to Feb 👋 L €45, D €60, Wine €17

NOVES
LA MAISON DE BOURNISSAC
www.lamaison-a-bournissac.com

This hotel (▷ 348) and restaurant is in a renovated 16th-century country house close to St-Rémy, on a hill overlooking Ventoux. It has a patio where you can have a dinner by candlelight, and a terrace for lunches. Try *pigeon fermier rôti sur coffre cuisse* (roast free-range pigeon) or the wild mushrooms.

✉ Montée d'Eyragues, 13550 Noves ☎ 04 90 90 25 25 🌐 Daily 12–1.30, 7–9.30 👋 L €60, D €85, Wine €28

PEILLON
AUBERGE DE LA MADONE
www.auberge-madone-peillon.com

Set just outside the walls of the medieval citadel of Peillon inland above the Côte d'Azur, this is an ideal spot for a relaxing summer lunch during a tour of the area. The family-owned establishment has an excellent reputation for its classic French menu. If you like the area, you could stay in one of the auberge's pretty rooms.

✉ 2 place Auguste Arnulf, 06440 Peillon ☎ 04 93 79 91 17 🌐 Mon–Tue, Thu–Sun 12–2.30, 7.30–9.30. Closed mid-Nov to Jan 👋 L €35, D €62, Wine €24

ST-CHAMAS
LE RABELAIS
www.restaurant-le-rabelais.com

The menu changes every six weeks in this restaurant in a 17th-century grain mill with vaulted stone ceilings standing in a Provençal village with cave houses. The garden is planted with olive trees.

✉ 8 rue Auguste Fabre, 13250 St-Chamas ☎ 04 90 50 84 40 🌐 Tue, Thu–Sat 12–1.30, 8–9.30, Sun, Wed 12–1.30 👋 L €40, D €55, Wine €20

ST-PAUL-DE-VENCE
LE SAINT PAUL
www.lesaintpaul.com

One of the prettiest and most renowned restaurants along the Riviera whether you eat on the attractive terrace of the refurbished stone *mas* (farmhouse) or in the Provençal dining room. The cuisine is classical French, the service polite and professional. A great place for a splash-out lunch or romantic dinner.

✉ 86 rue Grand, 06570 St Paul-de-Vence ☎ 04 93 32 65 25 🌐 Daily 12.45–1.45, 7.45–9.30 👋 L €60, D €80, Wine €45

ST-RÉMY-DE-PROVENCE
AUBERGE SANT ROUMIERENCO
www.auberge-santroumierenco.com
In a beautiful country house with stone walls and a beamed ceiling, this hotel and restaurant stands in its own grounds. Reliable choices on the menu are *magret au miel des Alpilles* (honeyed duck), lamb with garlic cream and the *coquillles Saint-Jacques* (scallops) with saffron. Regional wines are served and the desserts are home-made.

✉ route de Noves, 13210 St-Rémy-de-Provence ☎ 04 90 92 12 53 🕐 Daily 12–1.30, 7–9.30 🍴 L €25, D €35, Wine €18

LE BISTROT DES ALPILLES
www.lebistrotdesalpilles.com
This regional bistro is an institution in town and has large paintings of toreadors, comfortable wall seats and wooden chairs. There is a terrace for fine-weather dining. The brasserie food betrays a southern accent. Try aubergine (eggplant) and goat's cheese terrine, Mediterranean tuna with a vegetable reduction and tapenade or the grilled beef. For dessert, don't miss the lavender, thyme, apricot tart, chocolate mousse and rose sorbets. A short children's menu is available.

✉ 15 boulevard Mirabeau, 13210 St-Rémy-de-Provence ☎ 04 90 92 09 17 🕐 Daily 12–2, 7.30–10 🍴 L €28, D €40, Wine €20

ST-TROPEZ
LE CAFÉ
www.lecafe.fr
Some think the soul of the real St-Tropez lies within these four walls. It's on a square in the heart of the town and has one of the best terraces. Enjoy Provençal cuisine while watching the activity of the market or a game of boules. To start, you could try monkfish soup with garlic mayonnaise cream or marinated salmon with ginger and coriander (cilantro), then follow with beef in vintage port with baby carrots. Desserts include pastry nougat glacé.

✉ place des Lices, 83990 St-Tropez ☎ 04 94 97 44 69 🕐 Daily 12–2.30, 7.30–11 🍴 L €30, D €45, Wine €20

Above *It is the fresh ingredients that make Mediterranean dishes so appetizing*

SALON DE PROVENCE
LE MAS DU SOLEIL
www.lemasdusoleil.com
A pretty, small hotel and restaurant with its own garden specializing in Provençal cuisine. Try, for instance rabbit terrine and then follow with the *épaule d'agneau confite et son jus au thym* (preserved shoulder of lamb with thyme). Finish your meal with Frenh cheeses with walnut bread.

✉ 38 chemin Saint-Côme,13300 Salon de Provence ☎ 04 90 56 06 53 🕐 Tue–Sat 12–2, 7.30–9.30, Sun 12–2 🍴 L €45, D €65, Wine €20

SAUSSET LES PINS
LES GIRELLES
www.restaurant-les-girelles.com
While gazing out at superb views of the sea, what else can you eat but Provençal-style fish and seafood, especially bouillabaisse and roast lobster. The chef bakes his own bread. There is a wide selection of wines.

✉ rue Frédéric Mistral, 13960 Sausset les Pins ☎ 04 42 45 26 16 🕐 Tue–Sun 12–2. Closed Jan 🍴 L €40, Wine €20

SISTERON
LA CITADELLE
www.hotel-lacitadelle.com
This is a great place to try local dishes, including stuffed tripe, Sisteron lamb and other dishes such as sea bass with garlic mayonnaise. In season, there is also a game menu.

✉ 126 rue Saunerie, 04200 Sisteron ☎ 04 92 61 13 52 🕐 Summer daily 12–2.30, 7.30–10; winter Mon–Sat 12–2.30, 7.30–10, Sun 12–2.30 🍴 L €15, D €25, Wine €12

TOULON
LE GROS VENTRE
www.legrosventre.net
The country house-style dining room makes a relaxing backdrop to the delicious French cuisine at this long-established Toulon restaurant. The menu veers more towards seafood than meat, though filet is served in many guises including *en croûte* and with foie gras.

✉ 279 littoral Frédéric Mistral, Le Mourillon-Plages, 83000 Toulon ☎ 04 94 42 15 42 🕐 Sat–Tue 12–2.30, 7.30–10.30, Fri 7.30–10.30 🍴 L €55, D €75, Wine €25

PRICES AND SYMBOLS

Prices are the lowest and highest for a double room for one night including breakfast, unless otherwise stated. All the hotels listed accept credit cards unless otherwise stated. Note that rates vary widely throughout the year.

For a key to the symbols, ▷ 2.

AIX-EN-PROVENCE
HÔTEL LE PIGONNET

www.hotelpigonnet.com
Le Pigonnet is a former country house that is now a 4-star hotel. It's right in the middle of town at the end of a tree-lined avenue. From the hotel there's a wonderful view of Montagne Sainte-Victoire. Inside is refined elegance with antiques and objets d'art. You can have dinner in the gastronomic restaurant Riviera, soothe your anxieties at the spa and wellness centre, or take a stroll through the gardens.
✉ 5 avenue du Pigonnet, 13090 Aix-en-Provence ☎ 04 42 59 02 90 ✋ €115–€365, excluding breakfast (€21) 🛏 49, 1 suite ≈ Outdoor

ALET-LES-BAINS
L'EVÉCHÉ

www.hotel-eveche.com
This historic hotel, in a renovated 14th-century bishop's palace, stands in its own grounds a short distance from the pretty medieval town of Alet-les-Bains. The restaurant serves local specialties such as *cassoulet au confit de canard* (traditional duck cassoulet)
✉ 11580 Alet-les-Bains ☎ 04 68 69 90 25 ✋ €60–€64, excluding breakfast (€9.50) 🛏 30

LES ARCS-SUR-ARGENS
LOGIS DU GUETTEUR

www.logisduguetteur.com
This 3-star hotel is in a restored 11th-century castle. You can have dinner in the vaulted basement, or by the pool in fine weather. The bedrooms are traditional in style.
✉ place du Château, 83460 Les Arcs-sur-Argens ☎ 04 94 99 51 10 ✋ €130–€185, excluding breakfast (€17) 🛏 13 😊 ≈ Outdoor

ARLES
HÔTEL CALENDAL

www.lecalendal.com
The 17th-century building that houses this 2-star hotel is near the Roman arenas. The interior is Provençal in style with a tiled floor, wrought iron and warm tones. In fine weather, you can have a buffet-style breakfast and light meals in the garden.
✉ 5 rue Porte-de-Laure, 13200 Arles ☎ 04 90 96 11 89 😊 Closed Jan ✋ €109–€159, excluding breakfast (€12) 🛏 38 😊

HOTEL JULES CESAR

www.hotel-julescesar.fr
A former Carmelite convent has here been transformed into a hotel-restaurant, with elegant antiques set off by its stone walls. Bedrooms are spacious; there is a beautiful Provençal garden; and the former chapel is now a conference room.
✉ 9 boulevard des Lices, 13631 Arles ☎ 04 90 52 52 52 ✋ €160–€250, excluding breakfast (€14.50) 🛏 55, 3 suites 😊 ≈

LA MAS DE PEINT

www.masdepeint.com
Set on a farm that offers 'cowboying' experiences and exploration of the Camargue, this is as far away from a roughing-it experience as you can get. Spacious and well furnished in modern-country style, it's a wonderful place to relax and there's an excellent restaurant on site. You don't need to ride horses to enjoy staying here!
✉ Le Sambuc, 13200 Arles ☎ 04 90 97 20 62 ✋ €235–€295, excluding breakfast (€22) 🛏 8 rooms, 3 suites 😊 ≈ Outdoor

Above *Stay in rustic surroundings in an auberge*

AVIGNON
HÔTEL DE L'HORLOGE
www.hotel-avignon-horloge.com
Set in the heart of the city, this refurbished hotel has a modern and stylish feel and makes a comfortable retreat after sightseeing. Rooms, each with private facilities, have wrought-iron furniture and most have full-size French windows. There's a pleasant restaurant set in a light conservatory. The delights of Avignon are just on your doorstep. Private parking is available for an extra fee.

✉ 1 rue Félicien David, 84000 Avignon ☎ 04 90 16 42 00 ✋ €85–€195, excluding breakfast (€12.30) 🛏 66

LES BAUX-DE-PROVENCE
LE MAS D'AIGRET
www.masdaigret.com
Nestled against a cliff, this 3-star hotel has some surprising interiors— the breakfast room, bar, lounge and some of the guest rooms have been carved out of the rock and still display the exposed rockface. The bedrooms are simply but tastefully decorated. There is a restaurant.

✉ 13520 Les Baux-de-Provence ☎ 04 90 54 20 00 ✋ €95–€235, excluding breakfast (Apr–Oct €14.50; Nov–Mar €9) 🛏 16 ♿ ≋ Outdoor

BORMES LES MIMOSAS
LE BELLEVUE
www.bellevuebormes.fr.st
This small hotel in pretty medieval Bormes les Mimosas (which claims to be one of the most beautiful villages of France) offers simple and good-value accommodation. It boasts a very pleasant terrace where you can sit and enjoy the sea breeze. The restaurant serves Provençal dishes.

✉ 14 place Gambetta, 83230 Bormes les Mimosas ☎ 04 94 71 15 15 🕐 Closed Dec ✋ €42–€68, excluding breakfast (Apr–Sep €9; Jan–Mar €8.50) 🛏 12 ♿

CARCASSONNE
HÔTEL DE LA CITÉ
www.hoteldelacite.com
Queen Elizabeth II has stayed at this super-sumptuous hotel. It has one of the few gardens within the old city. Suites have themes ranging from warm Provençal to neo-Gothic.

✉ place Auguste-Pierre Pont, 11000 Carcassonne ☎ 04 68 71 98 71 🕐 Closed Dec–15 Jan ✋ €425–€535, excluding breakfast (€28) 🛏 40 rooms, 21 suites ♿ ≋ Outdoor

LE MONTSEGUR
www.hotelmontsegur.com
An old *hôtel particulier,* in its own grounds which include an enclosed parking area for guests. Bedrooms are decorated in classical French style and have modern amenities, including WiFi internet access. The hotel is well located, only a short distance from the *cité.*

✉ 1 avenue Bunau Varilla, 11000 Carcassonne ☎ 04 68 25 31 41 ✋ €82–€118, excluding breakfast (€10) 🛏 21 ♿

COUIZA
CHÂTEAU DES DUCS DE JOYEUSE
www.châteaudesducs.com
This is a renovated 16th-century castle with its own park on the banks of the Aude river. Some bedrooms are in the towers and have four-poster beds and fireplaces. The restaurant serves local specialities.

✉ Allée du Château, 11190 Couiza ☎ 04 68 74 23 50 ✋ €90–€135, excluding breakfast (€13) 🛏 23 rooms, 12 suites

LA CROIX-VALMER
CHÂTEAU DE VALMER
www.château-valmer.com
This château lies at the heart of 5ha (12 acres) of grounds, with its own private beach, tennis court and a large swimming pool. The bedrooms are upholstered using Provençal fabrics, and are complemented with marble bathrooms. Some have a canopy bed and certain suites can accommodate up to four people. All rooms have satellite TV. Mediterranean cuisine is served at La Pinède Plage restaurant. There is private parking.

✉ route de Gigaro, 83420 La Croix-Valmer ☎ 04 94 55 15 15 🕐 Closed mid-Nov to 1 Dec, mid- to late Jan and Mon–Wed Feb–Mar 20 ✋ €210–€540, excluding breakfast (€27) 🛏 20 ♿ ≋ Outdoor

FORCALQUIER
AUBERGE CHAREMBEAU
www.charembeau.com
This 2-star country inn has been developed from a restored 18th-century farmhouse. Some rooms can accommodate up to four people and have a kitchenette, while some rooms have a balcony and others have a terrace. There's also a tennis court and pool.

✉ route de Niozelles, 04300 Forcalquier ☎ 04 92 70 91 70 🕐 Closed mid-Nov to Feb ✋ €58–€100, excluding breakfast (€9) 🛏 23 ≋ Outdoor

FRÉJUS
L'ARÉNA
www.arena-hotel.com
This charming three-star hotel has a terracotta facade. There are palm trees in the garden, wooden furniture in the bedrooms and a restaurant that serves Mediterranean cuisine. Private parking is available.

✉ 145 rue Général de Gaulle, 83600 Fréjus ☎ 04 94 17 09 40 🕐 Closed mid-Dec to mid-Jan ✋ €85–€150, excluding breakfast (€11.40) 🛏 39 ♿ ≋

HYÈRES
HÔTEL PROVENCAL
www.provencalhotel.com
On a promontory at the southern tip of the Giens Peninsula, and in the centre of the village, this hotel has panoramic views of the Hyères islands. Outside there is a garden and a tennis court. The restaurant serves Mediterranean cuisine on a splendid terrace.

✉ place Saint-Pierre, Giens, 83400 Hyères ☎ 04 98 04 54 54 ✋ €111–€216, excluding breakfast (€14) 🛏 41 ≋ Outdoor, open Jun–Sep

MARSEILLE
HOTEL ALIZE
www.alize-hotel.com
Conveniently located, in the historic centre of old Marseille, this hotel, in a renovated 18th-century building, has views of the Old Port. Rooms have all the modern amenities.

✉ 35 quai des Belges, 13001 Marseille ☎ 04 91 33 66 97 ✋ €73–€96, excluding breakfast (€8) 🛏 39

HÔTEL LE CORBUSIER
www.hotellecorbusier.com
The hotel is in a block of 300 apartments designed by Le Corbusier. It comes complete with play areas, shops, a cinema, a bar and a library. The bedrooms are very simple. There is private car parking.
✉ 280 boulevard Michelet, 3rd floor, 13008 Marseille ☎ 04 91 16 78 00 ✋ €65–€118, excluding breakfast (€9) ① 21

HÔTEL HERMÈS
www.hotelmarseille.com
This 2-star hotel is by the Vieux Port and was refurbished in 2006. The soundproofed bedrooms are light and have a TV; some have a balcony.
✉ 2 rue Bonneterie, 13002 Marseille ☎ 04 96 11 63 63 ✋ €79–€100, excluding breakfast (€8) ① 28

MONACO
HÔTEL HERMITAGE
www.montecarloresort.com
This belle-époque luxury hotel faces the sea and has a panoramic restaurant, Le Vistamar, where breakfast is served under a glass ceiling designed by Gustave Eiffel. There is access to Les Thermes Marins de Monaco spa.
✉ square Beaumarchais, 98000 Monaco ☎ 377 98 06 40 00 ✋ €535–€1,050, excluding Continental breakfast (€31), buffet breakfast (€38) ① 280 rooms, 60 suites
Outdoor

MONTPELLIER
LE GUILHEM
www.leguilhem.com
This small hotel in a renovated 16th-century building in the historic centre of Montpellier has views over gardens and of the 12th-century School of Medicine. The bedrooms are all different and some have vaulted stone ceilings.
✉ 18 rue Jean-Jacques-Rousseau, 34000 Montpellier ☎ 04 67 52 90 90 ✋ €96–€192, excluding breakfast (€12) ① 35

HÔTEL LE JARDIN DES SENS
www.jardindessens.com
The large, minimalist rooms at this hotel were designed by Philippe

Starck. Most overlook the gardens and pool and one suite has its own pool. The acclaimed restaurant serves superlative cuisine.
✉ 11 avenue St-Lazare, 34000 Montpellier ☎ 04 99 58 38 38 ✋ €170–€280, excluding Continental breakfast (€15), buffet breakfast (€22) ① 15 rooms, 2 suites
Outdoor

MOUSTIERS-SAINTE-MARIE
LA BASTIDE DE MOUSTIERS
www.bastide-moustiers.com
This 4-star inn houses one of leading chef Alain Ducasse's restaurants (▷ 343) with suggested lunch and dinner menus. The 12 bedrooms are named after local produce and each is decorated according to its name.
✉ chemin de Quinson, 04360 Moustiers-Sainte-Marie ☎ 04 92 70 47 47
🕐 Hotel closed mid-Nov to 1 Dec, mid- to late Jan and Mon–Wed Feb–Mar ✋ €190–€400, excluding breakfast ① 12
Outdoor

NARBONNE
DOMAINE DE SAINT DOMINGUE
www.domaine-saint-domingue.fr
An old mas (farmhouse), set in 5ha (12 acres) close to the city, this is more a grand country house than a hotel—there's no restaurant on site for instance, although they do serve a light breakfast. But you can enjoy the facilities—the pool, the resident ducks, the pond-life and the vineyards. Rooms are spacious and well furnished with contemporary bathrooms.
✉ chemin de Boutes, 11000 Narbonne ☎ 04 68 40 72 21 🕐 Closed Jan ✋ €115–€185 ① 5 Outdoor

NICE
HÔTEL DE LA BUFFA
www.hotel-buffa.com
This 2-star hotel has an inviting but unpretentious interior. Bedrooms feature Provençal fabrics and have satellite TV. The street-facing rooms have double glazing and there's private car parking.
✉ 56 rue de la Buffa, 06000 Nice ☎ 04 93 88 77 35 ✋ €65–€95, excluding breakfast (€7) ① 13

HÔTEL NEGRESCO
www.hotel-negresco-nice.com
Built in 1912, this palace and its signature black dome have been given landmark status. The interior is an ode to fine art from the Renaissance to the modern: In the Salon Royal, Niki de Saint-Phalle's Nana, an oversized sculpture of a woman, sits happily next to classical portraits. The hotel has its own private beach.
✉ 37 promenade des Anglais, 06000 Nice ☎ 04 93 16 64 00 ✋ €247–€617 ① 117 rooms, 24 suites

HÔTEL SUISSE
www.hotel-nice-suisse.com
Set below the peak of the château and a few minutes' walking distance from the beach and the delights of Nice, this beautiful ochre coloured 19th-century building has elegant refurbished rooms with a bright Mediterranean feel. Some have balconies with fantastic views over the Baie des Anges and the old town.
✉ 15 quai Raubà–Capéù, 06000 Nice ☎ 04 92 17 39 00 ✋ €153–€194, excluding breakfast (€14) ① 42

NOVES
LA MAISON DOMAINE DE BOURNISSAC
www.lamaison-a-bournissac.com
A pretty country mansion renovated with an eye for the colours and spirit of the surrounding countryside. Rooms are well furnished with many rustic wooden pieces and the garden is filled with fig trees and lavender. The gourmet restaurant on site (▷ 344) is the icing on the cake.
✉ Montee d'Eyrages, 13550 Noves ☎ 04 90 90 25 25 🕐 Closed mid-Jan to Mar ✋ €145–€240, excluding breakfast (€17)
Outdoor

PERPIGNAN
HÔTEL DE LA LOGE
www.hoteldelaloge.fr
This small, 2-star, family-run hotel is in a 15th-century mansion. The comfortable rooms have TV and private bathroom. There is a small bar, but no restaurant.

✉ 1 rue Fabriques d'en Nabol, 66000 Perpignan ☎ 04 68 34 41 02 ✋ €47–€70, excluding breakfast (€7) ❶ 21

ROUSSILLON
LE CLOS DE LA GLYCINE
www.luberon-hotel.com
This pretty, renovated house is in the heart of an atmospheric Provençal hill village. Local colours from the ochre hills predominate, matched by rustic furnishings. Each room is individually furnished and they vary in size. Some have a small balcony. The restaurant has large windows with good views.

✉ place de la Poste, 84220 Roussillon ☎ 04 90 05 60 13 ✋ €125–€175, excluding breakfast (€13) ❶ 7 rooms, 1 suite

ST-ANDIOL
LE BERGER DES ABEILLES
This 2-star hotel is in a Provençal cottage. Some of the bedrooms have antique furniture. There's parking and a garden where you can have dinner.
✉ RD 74E, 13670, St-Andiol-en-Provence ☎ 04 90 95 01 91 🕐 Closed Jan to mid-Mar ✋ €95–€118 ❶ 8

STES-MARIES-DE-LA-MER
HÔTEL DE CACHAREL
www.hotel-cacharel.com
The hotel lies in a tranquil, watery location at the heart of a nature reserve, and has its own stables and there are horseback rides daily. There's a large fireplace, tiled floor and fine furniture in the bedrooms, but no TV. There is no restaurant, but you can order a dinner platter of cold meats and cheese with wine.
✉ route de Cacharel, 13460 Les Stes-Maries-de-la-Mer ☎ 04 90 97 95 44 ✋ €128, excluding breakfast (€11) ❶ 16 🌊 Outdoor

LA LAGUNE
www.lalagune.net
A small rural hotel which makes an ideal base for exploring the Camargue. The bedrooms are in a regional style but with modern conveniences. Animals are accepted at extra charge. Bicycles can be rented to explore the local area. The restaurant serves good local cuisine.
✉ route d'Arles, 13460 Les-Stes-Maries-de-la-Mer ☎ 04 90 97 84 34 ✋ €78–€118, excluding breakfast (€12) ❶ 20 🌊 Outdoor

ST-RÉMY-DE-PROVENCE
DOMAINE DE VALMOURIANE
www.valmouriane.com
This estate in the Alpilles de Provence region is surrounded by olive trees and vineyards. Rooms are bright and warmly decorated. Facilties include an English bar with piano and fireplace, a billiards room, a library and a restaurant with terrace. Massage and beauty treatments are available for guests.
✉ Petite route des Baux (D27), 13210 St-Rémy-de-Provence ☎ 04 90 92 44 62 ✋ €145–€280, excluding breakfast (€18) ❶ 13 🌊 Outdoor

ST-TROPEZ
HÔTEL BYBLOS
www.byblos.com
This palace has true luxury in a Provençal style. The sophisticated interior is decorated with local materials, and furnished with antiques, local fabrics and ceramic or wrought-iron artwork.
✉ avenue Paul Signac, 83990 St-Tropez ☎ 04 94 56 68 00 🕐 Closed Nov to mid-Apr ✋ €395–€724, excluding breakfast (€35) ❶ 52 rooms, 43 suites 🌊 Outdoor

VILLEFRANCHE-SUR-MER
HÔTEL WELCOME
www.welcomehotel.com
The Hôtel Welcome is in a modern building overlooking the bay. The bright bedrooms all have balconies. There is no restaurant.
✉ 3 quai Admiral Courbet, 06230 Villefranche-sur-Mer ☎ 04 93 76 27 62 🕐 Closed mid-Nov to Christmas ✋ €98–€2228, excluding breakfast (€11) ❶ 35

Below Monaco's Hôtel Hermitage

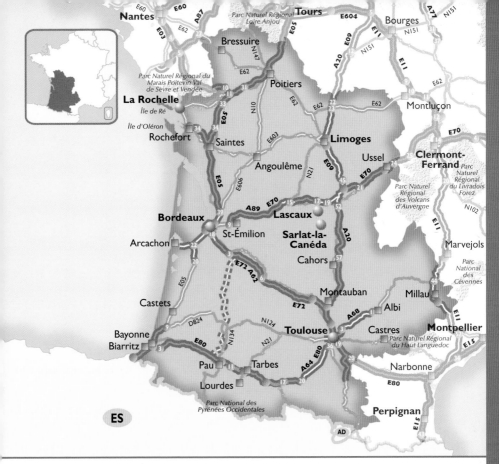

SOUTHWEST FRANCE

A clear watershed separates the climate of the southwest, influenced by the Atlantic, from the drier, Mediterranean climate of the Languedoc and Provence. This is still the Midi and the sun shines more often than not; but thanks to precipitation falling on the Pyrenees and Massif Central, and feeding the rivers Charente, Dordogne, Lot, Tarn, Garonne and Adour, the landscapes are predominantly green. The four regions that make up the southwest—Aquitaine, Limousin, Midi-Pyrénées and Poitou-Charentes—are quintessentially rural, with few large cities and little heavy industry. More typically, you will find yourself in patchwork countryside composed of pastures, woods, orchards, fertile river plains growing maize, and rolling hills planted with sunflowers.

If modern civilization often seems far away, ancient civilization is often close at hand. The southwest has an abundance of caves adorned with prehistoric paintings and drawings. Those of Lascaux are merely the most well known; but there are many others.

Southwest France is backroads country *par excellence*. Toulouse, Bordeaux, Poitiers and Limoges are all worth visiting, but more enticing are the innumerable small towns and villages with porticoed squares and streets of half-timbered buildings. Such places may stand in picturesque locations and many treasure a historic monument: a Romanesque church or a château. Such places can be linked up on endlessly varied itineraries. In the same day, you can easily cross a high Pyrenean pass, meander through a string of beautiful towns and have dinner at an outdoor table on the waterfront of Biarritz with the sound of breakers in the background.

Life is less hurried here than in the north of France, and you'll be well advised to take your time to try or buy the local produce which includes foie gras, oysters, truffles, Bordeaux wine and Cognac.

AINHOA AND SARE

www.sare.fr

The French Basque Country covers a small territory but one which is more often than not extremely picturesque. Everywhere around it are well-kept examples of the Basque farmhouse, or *etxe,* a large white construction in which the timbering is painted dark red—once it would have been stained with ox-blood—or dark green.

The two prettiest villages of the Basque Country are Ainhoa and Sare, clusters of immaculate houses close to the Spanish border. Ainhoa is little more than a single street but it has some magnificent 17th- and 18th-century houses. Beside a small lane outside Sare is the Musée du Gâteau Basque, where the secrets of the perfect *gâteau basque*, a local delicacy, are explained.

From the low pass of Col de St-Ignace, between Sare and Ascain, an old-fashioned cog railway ascends to the summit of La Rhune (905m/3,000ft) where a few steps take you across an international frontier to three Spanish bars. If you don't want to take the train, you can climb to the top of the mountain on foot but it's a stiff hike.

✚ 454 E13 🚹 place de Fronton, 64310 Sare ☎ 05 59 54 20 14 🕓 Mon–Fri 9.30–12.30, 2–6 (1.30–5.30 out of season), Sun 10–12.30

ALBI

www.albi-tourisme.fr

This pleasantly untouristy town has lovely pink-brick architecture, superb shopping choices and views. The magnificent river Tarn adds a quiet grace to the buildings.

The tourist office has a useful, free brochure in English, which gives routes for three cultural heritage walks, as well as details of religious heritage sites and the town's arts and crafts shops.

The Cathédrale Sainte-Cécile (Jun–Sep daily 9–6.30; Oct–May 9–12, 2–6.30) has an austere, fortress-like Gothic exterior which belies the sumptuous Renaissance decoration of the interior. In the 16th century, Italian artists covered the walls and

ceiling of the nave with frescoes, and on the west wall is a huge, grisly 15th-century mural depicting *The Last Judgement*.

Beside the tourist office, the former archbishop's palace, the Palais de la Berbie, is now the Musée Toulouse-Lautrec. The museum is undergoing refurbishment, but some galleries remain open (Jul–Aug daily 9–6; Jun, Sep daily 9–12, 2–6; Apr–May daily 10–12, 2–6; Mar, Oct Wed–Mon 10–12, 2–5.30; Nov–Feb Wed–Mon 10–12, 2–5).

✚ 455 J12 🚹 Palais de la Berbie, place Sainte-Cécile, 81000 ☎ 05 63 49 48 80 🕓 Jul–Aug Mon–Sat 9–7, Sun 10–12.30, 2.30–6.30; May–Jun, Sep Mon–Sat 9–12.30, 2–6.30, Sun 10–12.30, 2.30–5; Oct–Apr Mon–Sat 9–12.30, 2–6, Sun 10–12.30, 2.30–5 🚊 Albi

ARCACHON

www.arcachon.com

The Bassin d'Arcachon, a huge natural bay 90km (55 miles) in circumference, is ideal for families seeking seaside holidays. Its sandy beaches and calm waters are protected from the waves that pound the Atlantic coast just beyond Cap Ferret. It's a great place for outdoor activities such as sailing, canoeing, kayaking, surfing, parasailing, bicycling and walking. The only drawback is that parking in high season can be difficult.

In town, the Observatoire Sainte-Cécile (Le Belvédère; daily 10–6), built by the young Gustave Eiffel, is a spiral staircase suspended on cables inside a metal lattice tower, which sways as you ascend. Although only 15m (50ft) high, it gives a good view over the town, the surrounding villas and the Bassin d'Arcachon.

The best way to see the bay is on a boat trip. Aim for a trip that visits both the Île aux Oiseaux and several of the small oyster-fishing ports around the bay.

Eleven kilometres (7 miles) south of Arcachon, the energetic can hike up Europe's largest sand dune, the Dune du Pilat, nearly 3km (2 miles) long and 110m (360ft) high. There are superb views from the top.

✚ 454 E11 ✉ esplanade Georges Pompidou, 33311 ☎ 05 57 52 97 97 🕓 Mon–Sat 9–6, Sun 10–1, 2–5 🚊 Arcachon

AVEN ARMAND

www.aven-armand.com

In 1897 locksmith Louis Armand lowered himself through a hole in a great funnel-shaped depression in the plateau of Causse Mejean and found himself in a vast sloping cavern reaching 112m (367ft) at its highest point. It contained a 'forest' of tree-like stalagmites, including the largest stalagmite in the world at 30m (almost 100ft) tall. Most modern visitors enter by means of an inclined tunnel and a funicular railway but, if you prefer, you can be lowered into the original swallowhole by rope, accompanied by a speleologist.

Even if you choose the easier access, the cave of the Forêt Vierge is still an awesome echoing place.

✚ 456 K12 🚹 48150 Meyrueis ☎ 04 66 45 61 31 🕓 Jul–Aug daily 9.30–6; Mar–Jun, Sep–Nov 10–12, 1.30–5 🖐 Adult €9.10, child (5–15) €6.20

Opposite *Albi's cathedral*
Below *Oyster beds in Arcachon*

REGIONS SOUTHWEST FRANCE • SIGHTS

9–7, Sun 10–1; Sep–Jun Mon–Fri 9–6.30, Sat 10–6 🚃 Bayonne

BAYONNE

www.bayonne-tourisme.com

The unofficial capital of the French Basque country (you may well hear the Basque language, Euskara, spoken), Bayonne sits on the confluence of the Adour and Nive tidal rivers and makes a good half-day trip from Biarritz.

In the 18th century the town was a major port, with whaling, shipbuilding, cod fishing and trade with the West Indies bringing in wealth. It also had a reputation for fearless pirates *(corsaires)*. You can see the results of that wealth in the magnificent town houses overlooking the rivers, and the arcaded traffic-free shopping streets, such as rue du Port-Neuf, with its many chocolate boutiques.

There are two good museums, both in the 'Petit Bayonne' area. The Musée Bonnat (May–Oct daily 10–6.30; Nov–Apr Wed–Mon 10–12.30, 2–6), on rue Jacques-Laffitte, has a nationally recognized art collection, with works by El Greco, Delacroix, Goya and Degas. The Musée Basque, on the quai des Corsaires, covers Basque culture, from its earliest history to modern times, and includes a history of the town (Jul–Aug daily 10–6.30; Sep–Jun Tue–Sun 10–6.30).

The town's festival, in the first week of August, has everything from bull fighting and carnivals to Basque music and dancing.

➕ 454 E13 ℹ️ place des Basques, 64108 ☎ 08 20 42 64 64 🕐 Jul–Aug Mon–Sat

BIARRITZ

www.biarritz.fr

In 1854 Empress Eugénie persuaded her husband Napoleon III to holiday here. He built Villa Eugénie for her and the rest of Europe's glitterati soon followed, turning Biarritz into the most stylish seaside resort in southwest France. This is testified by the town's streets, many of which are named after famous visitors. Biarritz built a reputation for balls and banquets, and casinos, golf courses, chic restaurants, boutiques and exquisite food shops followed. Most visitors come to Biarritz for its three beaches: the Grande Plage, the most fashionable; the small beach in the Port-Vieux, popular with locals; and the Plage de la Côte des Basques, beloved of surfers.

Other attractions include the Musée de la Mer (Jun, Sep daily 9.30–7; Jul–Aug daily 9.30–midnight; Apr–May, Oct daily 9.30–12.30, 2–6; Nov–Mar Tue–Sun 9.30–12.30, 2–6. Open extended hours during French school holidays), where you'll find an aquarium, shark tank, and seals, with feeding times at 10.30 and 5. The nationally important Asiatica, Musée d'Art Asiatique, on rue Guy-Petit, has more than 1,000 works of art from India, China, Nepal and Tibet (Jul–Aug daily 10.30–6.30; Sep–Jun 2–6). For chocoholics, the Planète Musée du Chocolat (Jul–Aug daily 10–6; Sep–Jun 10–12.30, 2–6.30), on avenue Beaurivage, offers tastings. For shopping, try Les Halles covered market (mornings only).

➕ 454 D13 ℹ️ square d'Ixelles, 64200 ☎ 05 59 22 37 00 🕐 Jul–Aug daily 8–8; Sep–Jun Mon–Sat 9–6, Sun 10–5 🚃 Biarritz–La Négresse

BORDEAUX

▷ 356–359.

CAHORS

www.mairie-cahors.fr
www.tourisme-cahors.com

Cahors has a beautiful setting, on a south-facing isthmus, formed by a loop in the river Lot. The town is known for its dark red wine from the vineyards on the steep terraces to the south and west. The heart of the town splits into two parts, with the main street, boulevard Gambetta (named after Léon Gambetta, one of France's most admired republicans, a native of Cahors), running between the medieval quarter on the east side and the newer streets and buildings on the west. The English besieged Cahors during the Hundred Years War, and the old town bears this legacy, with ramparts, battlements, barbicans and fortified towers.

In the west is the symbol of the town, Pont Valentré. The curious proportions of this medieval bridge are emphasized by three pointed towers from which missiles could be fired. In the old town, the 12th-century Cathédrale St-Étienne is a mix of styles, with Périgord-style Byzantine domes, a fine, carved north doorway and frescoes. Near the cathedral is the Maison de Roaldès, a mansion belonging to Henri IV.

➕ 455 H12 ℹ️ place François Mitterrand, 46000 ☎ 05 65 53 20 65 🕐 Mon–Sat 9–12.30, 1.30–6 🚃 Cahors

CANAL DU MIDI

Even with the aid of modern equipment it would take a major engineering and logistical feat to stretch a canal halfway across the width of France, but for it to have been done in the 17th century is extraordinary. The Canal du Midi, from Toulouse to the Mediterranean, was built because of the tenacity of one man, Pierre-Paul Riquet (1604–80), who paid a third of the cost himself but managed to convince Colbert, Louis XIV's Comptroller-General of Finances, to pay for it as well.

Beginning in 1666, a 12,000-strong workforce took 14 years to dig the 240km (149-mile) long channel and construct the 328 locks, bridges and aqueducts necessary to even out the gradients. The greatest obstacle was the Seuil de Naurouze, a low pass from which the water flows east and west. An ingenious hydraulic system at this point keeps the canal supplied with water running off the slopes of the Montagne Noir. Riquet died in 1680, six months before the canal was complete, having given his life and energy to it.

A 19th-century canal beside the Garonne river effectively extends the waterway to connect the Mediterranean with the Atlantic, and together these two canals are called the Canal des Deux Mers. Although commercial traffic no longer uses this cross-country route, the canals are immensely popular with leisure sailing, and the towpaths are perfect for walking or cycling along. Barges can be rented in the major towns along the canals.

🖶 455 K13

CASTRES

www.ville-castres.fr

Castres is a pleasant town with something of a Venetian feel. It makes an ideal stop on the route between Albi (▷ 353) and Toulouse (▷ 372–375) (once you have passed the extensive industrial estates that surround the town and negotiated the busy approach roads).

The small historic part of town is easily explored in an hour or two, and you can see an impressive collection of Spanish paintings in the Musée Goya (Jul–Aug daily 10–6; Sep–Jun Tue–Sat 9–12, 2–6, Sun 10–12, 2–4). This is the town's top sight and has France's second-most important collection of Spanish paintings outside the Louvre in Paris. The works range from the Middle Ages to the present day, and include three Goya paintings and an important series of his engravings. The collection is in the beautiful Hôtel de Ville, the former bishop's residence, designed by Mansart. The small but exquisite garden was designed by André Le Nôtre.

Ask at the tourist office for a leaflet detailing 11 sights that can be easily seen on a walking tour using the easy-to-follow map.

The walls of the old houses along the eastern bank of the Agout descend directly into the water on either side of ancient stairwells, and the river contains many fish.

From May to the end of October, a passenger barge, *Le Coche d'Eau*, makes a 45-minute round trip between the quay opposite the tourist office and La Gourjade park.

🖶 455 J13 🛈 2 place de la République, 81100 ☎ 05 63 62 63 62 🌐 Jul–Aug Mon–Sat 9.30–6.30, Sun 10.30–12, 2–4.30; Sep–Jun Mon–Sat 9.30–12.30, 1.30–5.30 🚇 Castres

COGNAC

www.tourism-cognac.com

Cognac's old town still retains its medieval layout and several references to the salt trade on which its economy once depended. In its narrow streets, half-timbered buildings jostle for position alongside some fine 15th- to 17th-century stone town houses. The Tour St-Jacques, on rue du Château, a solid fortified gateway, is all that remains of the ramparts. You can also admire the 15th-century rose window in the Église du Prieuré St-Léger (tel 05 45 82 05 71; times vary).

Smart shops and cafés radiating from place François I represent the Cognac of today: Lively and prosperous, it is a hub of commerce, gastronomy and tourism and the heart of the global cognac business. Telltale black stains on pale stonework reveal the places where barrels of the famous spirit are ageing. The vast cellars of the Château François I (birthplace of the king who acceded to the throne in 1515) are now the home of Otard cognac (guided tours Jul–Aug daily 11, 2, 3, 4, 5, 6; Apr–Jun, Sep–Oct 11, 2, 3.30, 5; Nov–Dec Mon–Fri 11, 2, 4. Closed Jan–Mar). Among the cognac houses you can visit are Camus, Martell, Hennessy and Rémy Martin.

🖶 458 F10 🛈 16 rue du 14 Juillet, 16100 ☎ 05 45 82 10 71 🌐 Jul–Aug Mon–Sat 9–7, Sun 10–4; May, Jun, Sep Mon–Sat 9.30–5.30; Oct–Apr Mon–Sat 10–5 🚇 Cognac

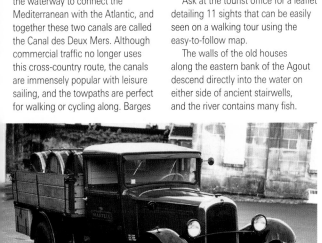

Left *An old van carries barrels of Martell cognac*
Opposite left *A café in Bayonne*
Opposite right *Pont Valentré, at Cahors*

INTRODUCTION

Bordeaux, one of France's oldest trading ports, is an elegant city whose wealth has been built on wine. The Romans were among those who took advantage of the city's position on the broad estuary of the river Garonne and later its proximity to plentiful vineyards helped its growth. When the marriage of Eleanor of Aquitaine and the future King Henry II of England brought the western half of France under English rule in the 12th century, the city enjoyed a vast upsurge in revenue. Many wine merchants became wealthy and their legacy lives on in the elegant mansions and palaces they built.

The 18th century, in particular, sealed the city's reputation and many of the great monuments date from that time. Like Paris only a century earlier, the city was rationalized with the creation of wide boulevards, public gardens and the colonnaded Grand Théâtre. During this time, wealth was also boosted from trade with the colonies in sugar, spices and coffee.

The principal sights are relatively close together and most are easily reached from the magnificent Grand Théâtre or from the huge central square, Esplanade des Quinconces. If it is your first visit to Bordeaux, be sure to walk out onto the Pont de Pierre, Bordeaux's oldest bridge, for great views of the Porte de Bourgogne and the stone buildings lining the quayside. If the sun is shining, it will be obvious why the city was often called Bordeaux la Blonde.

WHAT TO SEE

GRAND THÉÂTRE

www.opera-bordeaux.com

This striking venue, with its 12 lofty Corinthian columns topped by statues of the nine Muses and three goddesses, dominates place de la Comédie. It was built between 1773 and 1780 by Victor Louis, the restorer of Chartres cathedral (▷ 230–231), and is almost 90m (295ft) long and 50m (165ft) wide. Restored to its original glory in 1991, its auditorium is known for its exceptional acoustics and the tiered boxes drip with gold leaf. The sweeping grand staircase was a model for Garnier's lobby in the Opéra Palais Garnier in Paris (▷ 96). You won't be able to see inside if a rehearsal is under way, so it's worth checking earlier in the day for any scheduled break in rehearsals later.

➕ 359 C3 ✉ place de la Comédie ☎ 05 56 00 85 95; tours 05 56 00 66 00 🕐 Visits Wed, Sat 3, 4, 5

CATHÉDRALE ST-ANDRÉ AND TOUR PEY-BERLAND

This 1,000-year-old cathedral, whose delicate twin spires can be seen from all over the city, is a UNESCO World Heritage Site. The nave is said to be where Eleanor of Aquitaine married the future Henry II of England in 1152. The north and south doors of the transept, the choir and the Porte Royale on the north wall are decorated with medieval sculptures and scenes from the Last Judgement.

Next to the cathedral is the 15th-century Tour Pey-Berland. On its pinnacle, 50m (165ft) up, is the statue of Notre-Dame-d'Aquitaine. The view from the top is tremendous, as is the noise if you're up there when the 11-tonne bell, Ferdinand-André, is tolling.

➕ 359 B4 ✉ place Pey-Berland ☎ 05 56 52 68 10 🕐 Mon 2–6, Tue–Fri 7.30–6, Sat 9–7, Sun 9–6 🎧 Guided tours Sat and first Sun of the month at 2.30 and 5.50pm

MUSÉE DES BEAUX-ARTS

The fine arts museum is in the gardens of the Palais Rohan. Its permanent collection covers the main art movements from the Renaissance to World War II. Temporary exhibitions are held in the Galerie des Beaux-Arts opposite. Although

INFORMATION

www.bordeaux-tourisme.com

➕ 359 F11 ℹ 12 cours 30 Juillet, 33080 Bordeaux ☎ 05 56 00 66 00 🕐 Jul–Aug Mon–Sat 9–7.30, Sun 9.30–6.30; May–Jun, Sep–Oct Mon–Sat 9–7, Sun 10–12, 1–3; Nov–Apr Mon–Fri 9.30–12.30, 4–6 🚉 Gare St-Jean

Opposite *Detail of a horse in the fountain at esplanade des Quinconces*
Below *A Bacchus head on the fountain*

TIPS

» Ask at the information office for details about vineyard tours or follow the route of the vineyard drive (▷ 376–377). Everything you want to know about Bordeaux wines is at www.vins-bordeaux.fr

» On the last Friday of each month, in-line skaters take over the allée de Bristol, on the north side of esplanade des Quinconces, for La Nuit du Roller.

» Explore the city with a bicycle that comments on the main sights in English—contact the tourist office for information.

Above *The imposing Grand Théâtre stands in place de la Comédie*
Below *Pont St-Pierre, spanning the Garonne river*

relatively small, the museum's collection includes works by masters such as Titian, Van Dyck, Delacroix, Rubens and Matisse.

⊞ 359 A4 ✉ 20 cours d'Albret ☎ 05 56 10 20 56 ◉ Wed–Mon 11–6 ♿ Free to permanent galleries 🎫 Guided tours Wed 12.30 and other times by arrangement

ÉGLISE NOTRE-DAME

Once associated with the nearby Dominican convent, this imposing church was completed in 1707 by Pierre Michel, an architect already engaged to construct the nearby fortress. The elaborate decoration of the church contrasts with the simplicity of its construction. The central nave, flanked by a series of small side chapels, extends beyond two ornate gilded wrought-iron gates to a baroque altar. On the west wall, an elaborate bas-relief depicts St. Dominic's vision of the Virgin Mary handing him a rosary.

⊞ 359 B3 ✉ place du Chapelet ☎ 05 56 81 44 21 ◉ Mon 2.30–7, Tue, Thu 8.30–12, 2.30–6.30, Fri 8.30–1, 2.30–6.30, Sat 8.30–12, 2.30–7.30, Sun 10–12, 6–7.30

BASILIQUE ST-SEURIN

St-Seurin church was granted the title of basilica by the Pope in 1873, because of its significance to the Christian faith. It is also a UNESCO World Heritage Site, with origins dating back to Gallo-Roman times. You'll find an eclectic collection of styles and forms from the 11th to the 18th centuries, with both austere and lavish types of decoration. Excavations in 1910 revealed a huge Christian burial ground dating from the fourth century.

⊞ 359 off A2 ✉ place des Martyrs de la Résistance ☎ 05 56 48 22 08 ◉ Wed–Sat 8.30–11.45, 2–7.45, Sun 9–12.45, 6–8.15. Crypt: daily 2–6 ♿ Crypt €2.50 🎫 Guided tours Sat 2.30–5.30

MORE TO SEE

BASILIQUE ST-MICHEL

This triple-naved Flamboyant Gothic basilica, now a UNESCO-listed site, became a focal point for pilgrims throughout the Bordeaux area. Its freestanding bell tower gives a wonderful panorama of the city and river.

⊞ 359 off C4 ✉ place Meynard ☎ 05 56 94 30 50 ◉ Thu 2.30–5.30, first and third Sun of the month 2.30 and 5.30

CAPC—MUSÉE D'ART CONTEMPORAIN

A 19th-century converted warehouse is now a multimedia exhibition space, with cutting-edge exhibits and lively temporary exhibitions.

⊞ 359 C1 ✉ 7 rue Ferrère ☎ 05 56 00 81 50 ◉ Tue–Sun 11–6 (also Wed 6–8pm) ♿ Free 🎫 Guided tours Sat, Sun 4pm; rest of year by appointment

ÉGLISE SAINTE-CROIX

Outside, there are 12th-century sculptures above the main door. Inside, look for the baroque organ and an unusual collection of 17th-century religious paintings.

⊞ 359 off C4 ✉ place Pierre Renaudel ☎ 05 56 94 30 50 ◉ Thu 10–12

ESPLANADE DES QUINCONCES

This huge tree-lined space, on the site of the 15th-century Château de Trompette, is said to be the largest centrally located square of any city in Europe.

⊞ 359 B2

MAISON DU VIN
(CONSEIL INTERPROFESSIONNEL DU VIN DE BORDEAUX)

The best way to get to know the wines of the Bordeaux region is to have a drink at the wine bar in the headquarters of the official regulatory body, which occupies a handsome 18th-century building in the form of the prow of a ship. Each wine served has its own personalized information card and if you have any more questions, simply ask the sommelier.

🕂 359 B2 ✉ 3 cours du XXX Juillet ☎ 05 56 00 43 47 🕔 Mon–Sat 11–10

MUSÉE D'AQUITAINE

The history of Bordeaux from prehistoric times to today is covered in this museum, on the site of a convent. Objects from foreign cultures underline the city's role in exploration and trade.

🕂 359 B4 ✉ 20 cours Pasteur ☎ 05 56 01 51 00 🕔 Tue–Sun 11–6 ✋ Free

PLACE DE LA BOURSE

A sculpture of Neptune symbolically opening the road to trade stands in front of this elegant semicircular sweep of golden buildings which look out over the quayside.

🕂 359 C3

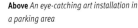

Above *An eye-catching art installation in a parking area*

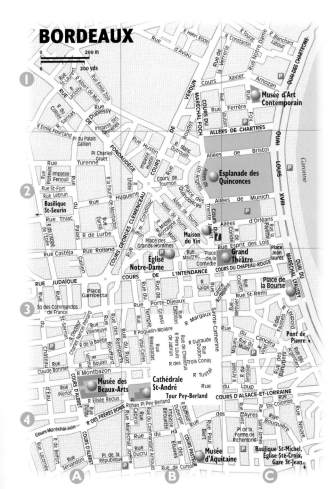

COLLONGES-LA-ROUGE

www.collonges-la-rouge.fr
www.ot-pays-de-collonges-la-rouge.fr
Collonges-la-Rouge is grouped with a dozen nearby villages with the title Le Pays de Collonges-la-Rouge. It is full of delightful buildings made from red sandstone. The Maison de la Sirène bears the figure of a mermaid, there are whimsical turrets on the Hôtel de la Ramade de Friac, and the Castel de Vassinhac has mullioned windows, watchtowers and loopholes for firing missiles. Ask at the tourist office for a map showing the main buildings, with an itinerary in French. To the south, there is a 20-minute circular walk through countryside, giving good views of the village.

➕ 459 H11 ℹ place de la Halle, Meyssac, 19500 ☎ 05 55 25 32 25 ⏰ Jul–Aug daily 10–1, 2–7; Apr–Jun, Sep 10–12, 2–6; Oct–Mar Mon–Sat 2–5

CONQUES

www.tourisme-conques.fr
This medieval village in the hills above the Lot valley is an important stop on the pilgrimage route to Santiago de Compostela in Spain. The houses gather around the three spires of the Abbatiale Sainte-Foi, a Romanesque abbey dedicated to the martyr St. Faith, whose relics were brought here in the ninth century. The church principally dates from the 12th century and has a famous west-door tympanum which is considered a masterpiece of Romanesque art. Best seen with the afternoon sun on it, it impresses the consequence of the Last Judgement on pilgrims ancient and modern. On the outer edge of the archivolt are the *curieux de Conques*—faces peeping inquisitively out of the stonework. The highlight of the abbey's treasury is the 10th-century reliquary statue of the saint.

➕ 455 J11 ☎ 05 65 72 85 00 ⏰ Apr–Sep daily 9.30–12.30, 2–6.30; Oct–Mar 10–12, 2–6

CORDES-SUR-CIEL

www.cordesurciel.eu
Because Cordes-sur-Ciel stands apart from the main routes of modern communication it has changed little since its heyday in the 14th century when its craftsmen and merchants grew rich from leather working and weaving. It is now populated by craftspeople and the place lives largely on tourism.

The town centre is closed to cars and parking is restricted. It's best to park at the bottom of the hill and walk up through one of the gateways, the Porte des Ormeaux (west) or the Portail Peint (east), which lead on to the main street, the Grand Rue Raymond VII. Halfway along the Grand Rue is the Maison Fonpeyrouse which accommodates the tourist information office. Almost opposite is the Maison du Grand Veneur (a restaurant) which has a sculpted facade. On the same side of the street, the Maison du Grand Ecuyer (a hotel-restaurant) also has a decorated facade. From place de la Bride, there is a view over the countryside.

➕ 455 J12 ℹ place Jeanne Ramel-Cals, 81170 ☎ 05 63 56 00 52 ⏰ Jul–Aug daily 9.30–1, 2–6.30; Apr–Jun, Sep Mon 2–6, Tue–Sat 10.30–12.30, 3–6, Sun 10.30–1, 2–5; Oct Mon, Tue–Fri, Sat 2–6, Sun 10.30–12.30, 2–6; Nov–Dec Tue–Sat 1.30–5.30, Sun 2–5; Jan–Mar Tue–Sat 2–5.30, Sat 10.30–12.30, Sun 2–5

DOMME

www.ot-domme.com
Clinging to a clifftop, Domme is a neat *bastide* (fortified medieval town), with narrow, flower-filled streets and stone buildings. Views from the terrace on the Belvédère de la Barre are exceptional, with the Dordogne river weaving through the landscape far below.

Domme is clustered around its old market hall and the handsome Maison du Gouverneur built, like the rest of the village, from stone that glows gold in sunlight. Below the village lies the largest stalactite-filled cave in the Périgord Noir (Feb–11 Nov, ask at the tourist office for tickets and tours). Domme's

population often took shelter here during wars. In 1307, an assembly of Knights Templar, falsely accused of heresy, were imprisoned in the Porte des Tours, part of Domme's still-visible defences. The graffiti they scratched into the stonework of the Prison des Templiers, including Christ in Majesty and scenes of Paradise and Crucifixion, are a moving testimony to their faith.

On place de la Halle, the small Musée d'Arts et de Tradition Populaire uses everyday objects and scenes to tell the story of local customs and culture (Apr–Sep daily 10.30–12.30, 2.30–6).

⊞ 459 H11 ⓘ place de la Halle, 24250 ☎ 05 53 31 71 00 ⓒ Feb–Jun, Sep, Oct Mon–Fri 10–12, 2–6; Nov–Jan Mon–Fri 10–12, 1.30–4.30. Closed first week of Jan

LES EYZIES

www.leseyzies.com

Caves in the limestone cliffs surrounding the village of Les Eyzies-de-Tayac-Sireuil provided shelter for humans as far back as 400,000BC. The cave-dwelling people who settled here were resourceful, intelligent and exceptional craftsmen, decorating their caves with paintings and carvings of great artistry. Bison, deer, horses and cattle gallop across the stone surfaces. Les Eyzies (now with UNESCO World Heritage status) is one of the densest concentrations of such sites anywhere in the world and hundreds of thousands of people visit each year, with summer the most popular, and crowded, time to visit.

The best place to start is the Musée National de Préhistoire (Jul–Aug daily 9.30–6.30; Jun, Sep Wed–Mon 9.30–6; Oct–May Wed–Mon 9.30–12.30, 2–5.30). In an old château, built under the cliff face, this remarkable museum exhibits flint axes, bone carvings, body ornaments, hunting weapons and domestic tools.

Of the various caves, Abri du Poisson offers a rarity—the first conclusive proof that Cro-Magnon people were adept at fishing—a superb, life-sized fish engraved in the ceiling vault. The Grotte des Combarelles, dating from around 13,000BC, has more than 600 wall engravings depicting ibex, mammoth, reindeer and cattle, as well as enigmatic symbols and human figures, while the Grotte du Font de Gaume contains polychrome paintings ranked among the true masterpieces of prehistoric art.

⊞ 459 G11 ⓘ 19 rue de la Préhistoire, 24620 ☎ 05 53 06 97 05 ⓒ Mid-Jun to mid-Sep Mon–Sat 9–7, Sun 10–12, 2–6; Apr to mid-Jun Mon–Sat 9–12, 2–6, Sun 10–12, 2–5; mid-Sep to Oct Mon–Sat 9–12, 2–6; Nov–Mar Mon–Fri 9–12, 2–6, Sat 10–12, 2–5 ❓ You must reserve ahead for Grotte du Font de Gaume, Grotte des Combarelles and Abri du Poisson ⓡ Les Eyzies-de-Tayac

FIGEAC

www.tourisme-figeac.com

This delightful old town on the banks of the river Célé grew up around an abbey, the only remnant of which is the Église Saint-Saveur. It prospered in the 11th and 12th centuries, especially because of its location on the pilgrimage routes to Rocamadour (▷ 378–379) and Santiago de Compostela in Spain. In 1302 Figeac came into the possession of the French crown and it was granted the privilege of minting its own money—as recalled by the name of the building housing the tourist information office, the Hôtel de la Monnaie, although the actual mint was elsewhere.

A marked walking route leads visitors around the town's old streets of 14th- and 15th-century half-timbered houses. Look for the signs into the concealed square of place des Écritures which is paved with a large reproduction of the Rosetta Stone in black African granite. Figeac was the birthplace of Jean-Francois Champollion (1790–1832), who deciphered the scripts on the stone. A nearby museum celebrates his life and work.

⊞ 455 H11 ⓘ Hôtel de la Monnaie, place Vival, 46102 ☎ 05 65 34 06 25 ⓒ Jul–Aug daily 9–7; May, Jun, Sep Mon–Sat 9–12.30, 2–6, Sun 10–1; Oct–Apr Mon–Sat 9–12.30, 2–6

FUTUROSCOPE

www.futuroscope.com

Constantly evolving, this leisure park, 11km (7 miles) north of Poitiers (▷ 366), now offers 22 different attractions based on the moving image and high-tech visual effects.

The architecture shouts for attention, with forms ranging from the weird to the wonderful, or just plain wacky. These extraordinary structures house attractions such as huge semicircular 3-D screens, seats moving in synchronization with the images, or 360-degree panoramas. the films include images from space, landscapes from around the planet plus computer-generated visuals that stimulate the senses and provide an alternative view of the world around us.

The park also has interactive water fountains, children's play areas and a lake which children can ride boats armed with water cannons. In summer, the lake is lit to form a backdrop to spectacles and shows.

⊞ 459 G8 ✉ Parc Futuroscope, BP 2000, 86130 Jaunay-Clan ☎ 05 49 49 30 80 ⓒ Apr–Aug daily 10–dusk; Sep to mid-Nov 10–6 (hours may vary). Closed Jan–early Feb 🎟 Adult 1-day ticket: €35, child (5–16) €26, under 5 free; adult 2-day ticket: €66, child (5–16) €47, under 5 free. Prices depend on season 🚌 From Poitiers station (routes 9 and E) 🚉 On-site station served by TGVs from Paris 🏧 🖥 🍽

Above *St-Martin-de-Ré on the Île de Ré*

GOUFFRE DE PADIRAC
www.gouffre-de-padirac.com
There are many caves to visit in southwest France, but this one between Rocamadour and the Dordogne river is especially worth a visit. You begin by taking the stairs or lift to the bottom of a gigantic, 100m (330ft) deep pothole where you enter the cave proper and board one of the punts waiting for you at the subterranean quay. Down river, deep underground, you disembark on the shore of the Lac de la Pluie and the visit continues on foot to the Lac Supérieur and the Salle du Grand Dôme, the largest of the cave's chambers. The visit covers about 2km (1.5 miles) underground and takes 90 minutes.
➕ 459 H11 ☎ 05 65 33 64 56 ⏰ 2–29 Aug daily 8.30–6.30; 5 Jul–1 Aug 9.30–6; 3 Apr–4 Jul 9.30–5; 30 Aug–7 Nov 10-5 (dates vary each year). Closed rest of year ✋ Adult €9.20, child (4–12) €6

GROTTE DE NIAUX
www.sesta.fr
The caves of Niaux, near Tarascon-sur-Ariège, were painted by hunters in the Pyrenean foothills during the Magadalenian period. They have been kept open thanks to a strict control of visitor numbers which preserves a stable temperature of 12°C (54°F) and protects the paintings. There are only 11 guided

tours per day, lasting 45 minutes, with a maximum of 20 people per visit. The entire cave is 2km (1.5 miles) long but some galleries are not open to the public. The highlight of the visit is the Salon Noir where there are six 'panels' depicting animals in black pigment with a striking sense of realism.

Foix, north of Tarascon and Niaux, is the capital of the Ariège *département*. It is dominated by the slim silhouettes of the castle of the counts of Foix who once controlled a large area of the southwest.
➕ 455 H14 ☎ 05 61 05 10 10 ⏰ Guided tours approx. every 45 min, some in English, 10.30 to 4.15; reservations essential ✋ Adult €9.40, child (13–18) €7, (5–12) €5.70

ÎLE DE RÉ
www.iledere.fr
Long, narrow Île de Ré extends 30km (19 miles) into the Atlantic and is linked to the mainland by an elegantly curved bridge. The south side is made up of a succession of long beaches; the north, sheltered from direct ocean winds, provides safe berths for yachts in several small ports. A gentle climate and the Île de Ré gastronomy—potatoes and wine from the land, fish and oysters from the sea—are two of the attractions of this beautiful and much-loved island.

Even in summer, when the main roads can be busy, it is possible to find a quiet spot, though you may have to seek it on foot or by bicycle—there are more than 100km (60 miles) of official bicycle tracks to explore.

Each of the villages has its unique character. Watch yachts riding quietly at anchor in front of whitewashed houses on the quayside at La Flotte, or visit its superb medieval market hall. Ars, one of the prettiest villages in France, hosts a wonderful market with a range of high-quality produce. There are exceptional views from the church tower in St-Martin-de-Ré (for opening times contact the local tourist office, tel 05 46 09 20 06).
➕ 458 E9 ℹ Île de Ré Tourisme, BP 28, 17580 Le Bois-Plage-en-Ré (also tourist offices in each of the main villages) ☎ 05 46 09 00 55 🚊 La Rochelle on mainland (approximately 14km/9 miles east of Rivedoux-Plage). Regular bus service from La Rochelle train station to Île de Ré 🚌 Various guided tours—contact the tourist office for details

LANDES
www.tourismelandes.com
France's second largest *département*, Les Landes, is known for two features. One is an immense managed forest of maritime pine trees planted in the 19th century to stabilize the sand dunes and marshes. Along the rim of the forest runs the Landes' other natural treasure: a single beach stretching 160km (100 miles) from the Bay of Arcachon to the Basque Country.

Tourist sights in the Landes are spread out. They include the thermal spa town of Dax, on the Adour river; the village museum in Brassempouy (in the south of the *département*) which displays the oldest carved human head in the world; and, to the north of the capital Mont-de-Marsan, the large nature reserve of the Parc Naturel Régional des Landes de Gascogne.
➕ 454 E12 ℹ 6 place Général Leclerc, 40011 Mont de Marsan ☎ 05 58 05 87 37 ⏰ Mid-Jun to Aug Mon—Sat 9–6; Sep to mid-Jun Mon, Sat 9–7, Tue–Fri 9–12.30, 2–6

LASCAUX

The original Lascaux cave system was discovered in 1940 by local schoolboys after their dog disappeared down a pothole. What they encountered underground was one of the world's most significant Palaeolithic sites, its walls alive with uniquely vibrant cave paintings around 17,000 years old.

PRESERVING THE ORIGINAL PAINTINGS

The magnificent original cavern, a short distance southeast of the town of Montignac, is sadly no longer open to the public. The carbon dioxide-laden breath of countless visitors was destroying the paintings and a film of greenish micro-organisms was creeping steadily across the walls. Using sophisticated 3-D plotting techniques, and new advances in resin and ferro-cement technology, experts created a perfect replica some 200m (220 yards) away, and Lascaux II is what today's visitors experience. The whole recreated cave structure looks, and even feels, authentic.

PAINTING TECHNIQUES

During your visit you can learn more about the techniques used by the original artists as they worked by the light from fat burning on stone lamps. They mixed mineral pigments such as haematite and kaolin to achieve the desired shades and often allowed the natural contours of the rockface to accentuate the forms of the animals depicted. Speckled effects were achieved by blowing diluted pigment through plant stems to create gradations of tone.

SPECTACULAR EFFECT

Even if the original intent behind the pictures remains a mystery, the overall effect is superb. Horses, antelope and bulls—many of them life-size—swirl around the walls and roof of the caves with undiminished exuberance. It is no surprise that Lascaux has been called 'The Sistine Chapel of Prehistory'.

INFORMATION

www.lascaux.culture.fr
www.tourisme-lascaux.fr

✚ 459 H11 ✉ Lascaux II, Montignac (enquiries via Semitour Périgord, BP 1024, 24001, Périgueux) ☎ 05 53 05 65 65 🕐 Jul–Aug daily 9–7; Apr–Jun, Sep 9–6; Oct–early Nov 10–12.30, 2–6; early Nov–Mar 10–12.30, 2–5.30 💵 Adult €8.80, child (6–12) €6, under 6 free 🚉 Le Lardin (12km/8 miles north) or Sarlat-la-Canéda (25km/15 miles south) 🚌 Guided visits approximately every hour, depending on the number of people. Tours are mainly in French, but English tours are available in Jul and Aug ❓ Pushchairs (strollers) and mobile phones are not permitted. It is advisable to wear a light sweater when venturing underground 🎁 Gift shop

Above *A cave painting of a horse at Lascaux II*

LIMOGES

www.ville-limoges.fr
www.tourisme-limoges.com

The name Limoges is inextricably linked with fine porcelain. The city was originally renowned for exquisite *champlevé* enamels, and it was only in 1768, with the discovery of kaolin deposits nearby, and new firing techniques, that porcelain manufacture took off. The so-called 'arts of fire' still flourish. The tourist office has details of manufacturers and retail outlets while the Musée National de la Porcelaine Adrien Dubouché (Wed–Mon 10–12.25, 2–5.40) has a comprehensive collection charting the development of the craft.

In the Middle Ages, Limoges was made up of two adjoining settlements—the old Cité, on a mound around the cathedral and bishop's residence, and the administrative and commercial hub, to this day known as Le Château. At the heart of the historic quarter, the Gothic Cathédrale St-Étienne (summer daily 10–6; winter 10–5), on place St-Étienne, looks out over a distinct medieval village, once the domain of the bishops.

Exhibits at the Musée des Beaux-Arts, in place de la Cathédrale, (after restoration due to reopen in 2011) include a priceless display of enamels and several Impressionist paintings, including works by Renoir, who was born in Limoges in 1841.

For a thought-provoking account of World War II experiences, head to the Musée de la Résistance et de la Déportation (Jun to mid-Sep Wed–Mon 10–12, 2–6; mid-Sep to May Wed–Mon 2–5).

➕ 459 H9 ℹ️ 12 boulevard de Fleurus, 87000 ☎ 05 55 34 46 87 🕐 Mid-Jun to mid-Sep Mon–Sat 9–7, Sun 10–5.30; early May to mid-Jun, late Sep–early Oct Mon–Sat 9–7; early Oct–early May Mon–Sat 9.30–6 🚆 Limoges 🚌 The tourist office arranges a variety of guided tours on subjects of general and specific interest

LOURDES

www.lourdes-france.com

Lourdes is famous worldwide as a place where people seek healing. It all began when a young country girl, Bernadette Soubirous, saw the Virgin Mary here on 11 February 1858, and on 17 subsequent occasions.

Today, Lourdes attracts more than 5 million visitors each year, including around 100,000 volunteers who help people with illnesses and disabilities during their stay. The town's places of worship are known collectively as Les Sanctuaires Notre-Dame de Lourdes. They vary from small and intimate to a cavernous underground basilica accommodating over 20,000 people.

The information office near the Sanctuaires issues a map listing times of Masses, blessings of the sick and torchlight processions. The guided tour 'In the footsteps of Bernadette' includes the Museum of St. Bernadette (Sat–Sun 10–12, 2.30–5; French school hols daily 10–12, 2.30–5), a free video about her life, her birthplace (Easter–Oct daily 9–12.15, 2.15–7), the house where she lived at the time of the visions (daily 9.30–12, 2–7.30), the Church of the Sacred Heart (daily 8.30–7) and the Hospice of St. Bernadette (May–Sep daily 9–12, 3–7).

➕ 454 F14 ℹ️ place Peyramale, 65101 ☎ 05 62 42 77 40 🕐 Early Jul–early Sep Mon–Sat 9–7, Sat 10–6; early Apr–early Jun, early Sep–early Oct Mon–Sat 9–6.30, Sun 10–12.30; early Oct–early Apr Mon–Sat 9–12, 2–6 ❓ Les Sanctuaires Notre-Dame de Lourdes: tel 05 62 42 78 78

MARAIS POITEVIN

www.ville-coulon.fr
www.marais-poitevin.com

When Henri de Navarre, the future king Henri IV, rode through this marshland, he described it as 'a great, green, natural Venice'. The name stuck, and La Venise Verte (the Marais Poitevin) continues to attract visitors seeking peace and quiet. There are stretches of narrow waterways lined with irises and cowslips, and life moves at a much slower pace.

The Marais Poitevin is a paradise, but a man-made one. Hundreds of years ago local inhabitants—mainly fishermen, farmers and Benedictine monks from the nearby abbey of Maillezais—began to drain and reclaim the land, and Dutch engineers in the 16th century continued the process.

Today there are two distinct landscapes. Nearer the Vendée coast, the 'dry marshes', the Marais Déssechés, peter out in a wind-scoured canvas of huge skies, fields of wheat and bleached salt pans, home to purple herons and black kites. Inland, enclosed and inaccessible without a boat, lie the Marais Mouillés, the secretive wetland area criss-crossed by narrow channels leading to tiny, poplar-lined fields and low, whitewashed houses. This is where the area's tourist industry has developed, with opportunities for walking, bicycling, fishing, canoeing and punting. In Coulon you can hire a punt *(une plate)* and oar *(une pigouille),* with or without a boatman.

➕ 458 E9 ℹ️ 31 rue Gabriel Auchier, 79510 Coulon ☎ 05 49 35 99 29 🕐 Mid-Jun to mid-Sep daily 10–7; mid-Sep to mid-Jun Mon–Sat 10–12, 2–5.30

Above *A waterway in Marais Poitevin, dubbed La Venise Vert*
Opposite *Tour de France sculpture by Jean Bernard Metais, in Pau*

MILLAU VIADUCT
www.leviaducdemillau.com
Few motorway bridges are iconic architecture but the great viaduct by which the A75 bypasses Millau and crosses the Tarn river has become a tourist attraction in its own right since its opening in 2004. It was designed by Norman Foster and is the world's tallest road bridge. If it were placed next to the Eiffel Tower it would project 20m (65ft) above it. The bridge is 2.5km (1.5 miles) long, curved and gently sloping. Millau tourist office operates minibus tours and there's an information centre at Cazalous motorway service area.

A short way southeast of Millau is La Couvertoirade, a well-preserved town built by the Knights Templar. At Roquefort, southwest of Millau, you can visit the caves where France's favourite blue cheese is made.

✚ 456 K12 ℹ Viaduc Espace Info, aire des Cazalous, on the D992 5 min from Millau heading towards Albi 🕒 May–Sep daily 10–7; Oct–Apr 10–5 👋 Free

MOISSAC
www.moissac.fr
It's easy to be put off by the rest of Moissac, a rather messy modern town on the north bank of the lower Tarn, but right in the centre is what remains of an important abbey and a gem of Romanesque stone carving. The south portal of the abbey church, the Église St-Pierre, which was affiliated to Cluny in the 11th century, has a magnificent

tympanum depicting the Vision of the Apocalypse According to St. John. Christ sitting in judgment presides over the middle of the composition. Below him the 24 elders sit craning their necks to look at him. Nearby, the abbey cloisters, with some rich sculptures, are entered through the tourist information office.

✚ 455 H12 ✉ 6 place Durand de Bredon, 82000 Moissac ☎ 05 63 04 01 85 🕒 Jul–Aug daily 9–7; Sep daily 9–6; Apr–Jun, Oct Mon–Fri 9–12, 2–6, Sat–Sun 10–12, 2–6; Nov–Mar Mon–Fri 10–12, 2–5, Sat–Sun 2–5

MONTSÉGUR
www.montsegur.fr
The ruined castle on a 1,207m (4,000ft) peak above Montségur is an atmospheric place to visit even if you don't know its history.

This is where the Cathars of 13th-century Languedoc—who had been declared heretics by the pope—made their last stand. The castle held out for almost 11 months against besiegers sent by the Inquisition until a trebuchet (siege catapult) managed partly to destroy the eastern tower which was then abandoned by the garrison.

On 2 March 1244 the inhabitants of the fortress agreed to surrender but asked for a fortnight's grace before abandoning it. On 16 May, the Inquisition gave the Cathars a last chance to recant or face the flames. More than 200 of those who had taken refuge in Montségur refused to renounce their faith. They were taken down the mountain in chains and burned on a giant pyre on the plain below.

✚ 455 H14 ✉ 09300 Montségur 🕒 Jul–Aug daily 9–7.30; Apr–Jun daily 10–6.30; Sep 9.30–6.30; Oct 10–6; Mar 10.30–5.30; Nov 10.30–5, Dec, Feb 11–4.30. Closed Jan 👋 Adult €4, child (8–13) €2.10

PAU
www.pau-pyrenees.com
Pau was the birthplace of the popular king Henri IV in 1553, and became a cosmopolitan resort in the 19th century thanks to its mild winters. Development into a high-class spa

and casino town soon followed. But Pau has managed to retain plenty of green space. Just about everything grows well, including bamboo, American sequoias, cedars of Lebanon and Mexican cacti.

Pau has been called 'the town of a thousand palm trees', many of which can be seen from the boulevard des Pyrénées, which runs along the southern edge of the town between the château and Parc Beaumont. The terrace here overlooks the Gave de Pau (a river) and provides a memorable view of the snow-capped Pyrenees to the south. A free funicular railway operates between the terrace and the lower level, where both the railway and river run.

The Musée National du Château de Pau has a rich collection of Gobelin tapestries (mid-Jun to mid-Sep daily 9.30–12.15, 1.30–5.45; mid-Sep to mid-Jun 9.30–11.45, 2–5).

✚ 454 F13 ℹ place Royale, 64000 ☎ 05 59 27 27 08 🕒 Jul–Aug Mon–Fri 9–6.30, Sat 9–6, Sun 9.30–1, 2–6; Sep–Jun Mon–Sat 9–6, Sat 9.30–1 🚉 Pau

PECH MERLE
www.pechmerle.com
The prehistoric paintings in a cave at Pech Merle—the only one of several painted caves in the hills above Cabrerets which is open to the public—were discovered by two teenage boys in 1922. They are best known for a frieze of two horses adorned with black spots, one of which demonstrates a skilful use of the contours of the rock to evoke the head.

What distinguishes Pech Merle from other caves is the eclectic subject matter: As well as other animals depicted on the walls including bison, mammoths and aurochs, there is a rare drawing of a fish, and human figures, especially one known as 'the wounded man'. On the cave floor there are fossilized prehistoric footprints.

✚ 455 H12 ✉ 46330 Cabrerets ☎ 05 65 31 27 05 🕒 Early Apr–early Nov daily 9.30–12, 1.30–5; visitor numbers limited, reservations advised 👋 Adult €8, child (5–14) €4.50

PÉRIGUEUX

www.ville-perigueux.fr
www.tourisme-perigueux.fr

Truffles, foie gras, walnuts and Périgord pâtés epitomize the cuisine of Périgueux, and you can find them all in the town's legendary markets. They fill the ancient streets and squares of what was once Vesunna, a Gallo-Roman settlement astride the river Isle. In the old quarter, the town's medieval history is tangible in place de la Clautre, place du Coderq and rue Limogeanne. To find traces of the town's earlier history, you can follow rue des Gladiateurs to the Roman arena, where there are vestiges of an early settlement dating from the first and second centuries AD, or examine the prehistoric items in the Musée du Périgord, on cours Tourny (Apr–Sep Mon, Wed–Fri 10.30–5.30, Sat–Sun 1–6; Oct–Mar Mon, Wed–Fri 10–5, Sat–Sun 1–6).

As you wander around the town, admire the half-timbered medieval houses, redeveloped waterfront, Renaissance *hôtels*, and—on place de la Clautre—the strangely Levantine Cathédrale St-Front. This is a UNESCO World Heritage Site, with Byzantine domes and spiky finials (daily 9–12, 2.30–7). The town hosts fêtes and festivals for everything from mime to mushrooms.

🚩 459 G10 ℹ️ 26 place Francheville, 24070 Périgueux ☎ 05 53 53 10 63 🕐 Jul–Aug Mon–Sat 9–7, Sun 10–1, 2–7; Jun, Sep Mon–Sat 9–7, Sun 10–1, 2–6; Oct–May Mon–Sat 9–12.30, 2–6 🚉 Périgueux

POITIERS

www.mairie-poitiers.fr
www.ot-poitiers.fr

Perched on a plateau between the rivers Clain and Boivre, lively Poitiers has a rich artistic and historical heritage and is home to one of the oldest universities in France.

Often acclaimed as 'the town with 100 bell towers', Poitiers has more than 70 listed buildings around its inner maze of narrow streets. Romanesque sights include the Église Notre-Dame-la-Grande (Mon–Sat 9–7, Sun 12–7), on place Charles de Gaulle. It has a barrel-vaulted nave and superb 12th-century frescoes over the choir. In summer, short but spectacular *Polychromies* shows bathe the western facade in light, reproducing the church's appearance in the Middle Ages and highlighting the artistry of the stonemasons (Jul–Aug from 10.30pm; Sep from 9.30pm; consult tourist office for exact time; lasts 15 mins). The tiny jewel of the Baptistère St-Jean, on rue Jean-Jaurès (Apr–Sep Wed–Mon 10.30–12.30, 3–6; Oct–Mar Wed–Mon 2.30–4.30) retains several ancient sarcophagi and a superb collection of frescoes.

Other buildings to look out for in the old town include half-timbered merchant properties, Renaissance town houses, medieval artisan dwellings and 18th-century mansions. Modern additions, like the state-of-the-art Médiathèque François Mitterrand, strike a distinctive new note, but don't conflict with the town's heritage.

🚩 459 G8 ℹ️ 45 place Charles de Gaulle, BP377, 86009 Poitiers ☎ 05 49 41 21 24 🕐 2 Jun–17 Sep Mon–Sat 10–10, Sun 10–6, 7–10; 18 Sep–1 Jun Mon–Sat 10–6 🚉 Poitiers

LES PYRÉNÉES

www.parc-pyrenees.com

The Pyrenees form a continuous barrier for more than 400km (250 miles), from the Basque Country on the Bay of Biscay to Catalonia on the Mediterranean. They have little by way of foothills on the northern side and dip from the heights only at the two extremes. Although rarely passable—in the middle of the range there are only seven roads across—the Pyrenees are nonetheless easily accessible and they offer a wide variety of attractions for the visitor. Walking and climbing are popular activities and each year many determined people spend up to two months following the GR10 footpath from ocean to seashore. Perhaps surprisingly, the Pyrenees are a favourite among bicyclists, too, who can get a passport stamped as they cross each mountain pass.

If you are not that energetic, you can still take in some of the best views by car. Natural amphitheatres have been scooped out by glaciation—particularly the Cirque de Gavarnie (▷ 382–383)—and fast-flowing streams *(gaves)*, tumble in waterfalls before becoming sedate rivers. The central part of the range is protected by the Pyrenees National Park which harbours rare endemic flowers and protects the few brown bears that survive in remote habitats. You can take the cable car from the ski resort of La Mongie to the observatory on the Pic du Midi de Bigorre (2,872m/9,423ft) but it's a pricey trip (Jun–Sep daily 9–4.30; Oct–May 10–3.30; departures every 15 minutes). If you miss the last cable car down you can spend the night on the mountain top.

🚩 454–455 F14–H14 ℹ️ Parc National des Pyrénées, 2 rue du IV Septembre, 65007 Tarbes ☎ 05 62 54 16 40 🕐 Check website

LA ROCHELLE

The seaport of La Rochelle is sophisticated, lively and modern, but retains reminders of its long history. A stroll around La Rochelle's quiet, arcaded walkways reveals evidence of a past based on fishing and shipbuilding. Medieval half-timbered houses, ornamented Renaissance *hôtels* and graceful 18th-century mansions sit in harmony around an attractive harbour.

Around 1,000 years ago, Rochela was a fishing village. It became wealthy and influential in the 12th century, under the patronage of Eleanor of Aquitaine, and was renamed La Rochelle.

Today, the Port des Minimes marina, where vast numbers of sailing craft tie up, is the largest on the Atlantic seaboard and is boosted by international sailing races and boat shows.

THE OLD PORT

At the heart of La Rochelle, the Vieux Port is constantly busy and a great place to watch boats come and go. The entrance to the harbour is policed by two towers of unequal height. The upper lookout post of the Tour St-Nicolas (Apr–Sep daily 10–6.30; Oct–Mar 10–1, 2.15–5.30) provides a splendid view. Opposite stands the Tour de la Chaine, which, as its name suggests, used to secure the other end of a chain stretched across the mouth of the harbour at night.

The Aquarium (Jul–Aug daily 9–11; Apr–Jun, Sep 9–8; Oct–Mar 10–8), south of Le Gabut, at the Bassin des Grands Yachts, brings you face to face with the flora and fauna of the ocean.

THE CITY CENTRE

The 15th- to 18th-century Port de la Gross-Horloge marks the separation between the port and the rest of the city centre. Sights worth seeing here include the Hôtel de la Bourse, an 18th-century stock exchange, and the Maison Henri II, a grand 16th-century Renaissance facade with little depth behind it.

INFORMATION

www.ville-larochelle.fr
www.tourisme-larochelle.com
⊞ 458 E9 🛈 Le Gabut, 17025 ☎ 05 46 41 14 68 🕒 Jul–Aug Mon–Sat 9–8, Sun 10.30–5.30; Jun, Sep Mon–Sat 9–7, 10.30–1.30, Sun 10.30–5.30; Apr–May Mon–Sat 9–6, Sun 10.30–5.30; Oct–Mar Mon–Sat 10–12.30, 1.30–6, Sun 10–1 🚉 La Rochelle

TIPS

» To get around La Rochelle quickly and inexpensively, try one of the town's yellow bicycles, reserved for visitors. It's free for the first two hours, and around €1 per hour after that. Contact Autoplus (tel 08 10 17 18 17; www.rtcr.fr), on place de Verdun.

» Getting across the Vieux Port or to the yacht marina is easy with Le Passeur Autoplus or the Bus de Mer, a fast service from the Vieux Port jetty to the Port des Minimes. Both are ideal for the Aquarium.

Opposite *Dinner on place St-Louis, in the old part of Périgueux*
Below *La Rochelle's Vieux Port*

Above *The fortress at La Roque-Gageac was built into the rockface*

ROCAMADOUR

www.rocamadour.com

Set on a granite pinnacle above the gorge of the River Alzou and surrounded by forest, this fortified village is one of the prettiest in France. Named after St. Amadour, it's been a place of pilgrimage since medieval times and the noble sanctuary occupies the highest point in the town.

The church of Notre-Dame, dating from the 1470s, houses the wooden statue of the Black Madonna whose miracles were written about as early as the 11th century. Rocamadour was also a popular stopover for pilgrims on the route to Santiago de Compostella in northern Spain.

West of the town, the Gouffre de Padirac is a soaring cavern carved by water flowing through the fissures in the limestone that blankets this region. Remains of Neanderthal man found at Fieux close by, prove human existence has had a long history here.

➕ 455 H11 ✉ L'Hospitalet, 46500 Rocamadour ☎ 05 65 33 22 00 🕐 Early Jul–Aug daily 9.30–7; late Apr–early Jul, Sep daily 10–12.30, 1.30–6; Mar–late Apr

daily 10–12.30, 2–6; Oct Mon–Fri 1–12, 2–5; Nov–late Mar Mon–Fri 10–12, 2–5

ROCHEFORT

www.paysrochefortais-tourisme.com
www.ville-rochefort.fr

Louis XIV commissioned Colbert, minister of finance and the navy, to create a fine naval arsenal here, assembling in one place every craft and trade required to build, arm and fit out a huge succession of warships. Today the restored dockyard still evokes the spirit of distant discovery.

You can visit the beautifully preserved Corderie Royale, at the Centre International de la Mer (Jul–Aug daily 9–7; Sep–Jun 10–12.30, 2–6). Once Europe's longest factory, it produced the vast quantities of rope and sail needed by France's navy. The 65m (212ft) frigate *L'Hermione,* at the Arsenal Maritime, has been recreated using 18th-century techniques (Jul–Aug daily 9–7; Apr–Jun, Sep 9–7; Sep–Mar 10–12.30, 2–6).

The elegant Hôtel de Cheusses, on place de la Galissonnière, is home to the Musée National de la Marine

(May–Sep daily 10–8; Feb–Apr, Oct–Dec 1.30–6.30; closed Jan). It contains a collection of naval items, including model ships, figureheads and navigation instruments.

The Musée des Commerces d'Autrefois (Jul–Aug daily 10–8; Apr–Jun, Sep–Oct 10–12, 2–7; Nov–Dec, Feb–Mar Mon–Sat 10–12, 2–6; closed Jan), housed in a turn-of-the-20th-century department store, features re-creations of an old grocer's, butcher's, barber's and bistro to show what a town street looked 100 years ago.

The Jardin des Retours, by the river Charente, is ideal for a walk.

➕ 458 E9 ℹ 9 L'avenue Sadi-Carnot, 17300 Rochefort ☎ 05 46 99 08 60 🕐 Jul–Aug Mon–Sat 9.30–7; Apr–Jun, Sep 9.30–12.30, 2–6.30; Oct–Mar 9.30–12.30, 2–6. Closed Sun and public hols 🚉 Rochefort ℹ Another tourist office is at the Porte d'Arsenal

LA ROCHELLE
▷ 367.

LA ROQUE-GAGEAC

www.cc-perigord-noir.fr

This pretty village has been inhabited since prehistoric times and occupies a dramatic position beside the Dordogne river. The Hundred Years War and the 16th-century Wars of Religion turned the village's troglodytic fortress into an impregnable stronghold (Apr to mid-Nov daily 10.30–1, 2–6). Created in the 12th century, the fortress incorporated ingenious devices, using caves in the limestone, to defy attempts to scale the rockface.

The village's position between the cliffs and the river gives it almost Mediterranean weather patterns, and vegetation thrives. Alongside the small church, perched high up, you'll find the Jardin Exotique (open all year), home to exotic plants, trees and shrubs. Another garden worth a visit is the Jardin de la Ferme Fleurie (daily 10–12, 2–6).

➕ 459 H11 ℹ rue Tourny, BP 114, 24203 Sarlat ☎ 05 53 31 45 45 🕐 Jul–Aug Mon–Sat 9–7, Sun and public hols 10–12, 2–6; Sep–Jun Mon–Sat 9–12, 2–6

ST-BERTRAND DE COMMINGES

www.cathedrale-saint-bertrand.org

The Romans built a settlement on the plains beneath the present site of St-Bertrand around 72BC; the ruins have been excavated and left exposed. In the 11th century work began on a cathedral in a defensive position uphill, the Ville Haute, which was named in honour of its founder St. Bertrand de l'Isle. This massive, church, a Romanesque structure, stands proud of the rest of the town. Beside it is a peaceful cloister with one open side giving good views.

✚ 455 G14 🛈 Parvis de la Cathédrale, 31510 ☎ 05 61 95 44 44 🕙 May–Sep Mon–Sat 9–7, Sun 2–6; Feb–Apr, Oct Mon–Sat 10–12, 2–6, Sun 2–6; Nov–Mar Mon–Sat 10–12, 2–6, Sun 2–5

ST-CIRQ-LAPOPIE

www.saint-cirqlapopie.com

This golden-stone village, huddled on wooded limestone cliffs 80m (262ft) above the river Lot, has medieval houses with half-timbered walls and brown roof tiles, packed together in narrow lanes. There is no vehicular access for visitors. The narrow road (CD8) from the Lot valley up to St-Cirq hugs the rockface on the left, passes the bulk of the village on the right, and continues up to a parking area, from where there's a rather steep walk back to the village. For good views, climb the castle ruins. Next to the ruins, the Gothic Église de St-Cirq juts out from the rockface to survey a dizzying sweep of the Lot and Cère valley. The village was once a wood turners' colony and you can still buy various wooden items.

✚ 455 H12 🛈 place Sombral, 46330 ☎ 05 65 31 29 06 🕙 Jul–Aug 10–1, 2–7.30; Jun, Sep daily 10–1, 2–7; Oct–Jun Wed–Sat 10–1, 2–6, Sun 2–6

ST-ÉMILION

www.saint-emilion-tourisme.com

A UNESCO World Heritage Site, St-Émilion has mellow golden stonework and is home to some celebrated wines. Clinging to a rocky outcrop, it is effectively an open-air museum, with ramparts, seven medieval town gates and winding, narrow streets. The steepest, called *escalettes*, run from west to east, following the hillside's contours. Wine runs through the town's veins: Vineyards stretch to every horizon, shops sell wine and every accessory for its enjoyment, and the legendary, wallet-denting vintages await in dark, cool cellars. The Romans planted vines here, but it wasn't until after the Revolution that disciplined wine monoculture was developed. The town has three underground sights, all near place des Crénaux: the Église Monolithe, the Catacombs and the eighth-century Hermitage, all accessible by guided tour only. These take place every 45 mins daily from 10–2. Above ground, visit the 13th-century Chapelle de la Trinité (guided tour only, see below) and the Église Collégiale (behind the tourist office; summer daily 9–7.30; winter daily 9–6), founded in the 11th century. You'll get some wonderful views from the Tour du Roy, between rue Sainte-Marie and rue du Couvent.

✚ 459 F11 🛈 place des Crénaux, 33330 ☎ 05 57 55 28 28 🕙 Mid-Jul to mid-Aug daily 9.30–8; early Jul, late Aug 9.30–7; Jun, Sep–Oct Mon–Thu 9.30–12.30, 1.30–6.30, Fri 9.30–12.30, 1.30–7, Sat 9.30–7, Sun 9.30–6.30; May daily 9.30–12.30, 1.30–6.30; Mar–Apr daily 10–12.30, 2–6; Nov–Dec daily 9.30–12.30, 2–5.30; Jan–Feb daily 10–12.30, 2–5 🚉 St-Émilion 🚌 Various guided tours—contact the tourist office for details

Below *A street café in St-Émilion*

ST-JEAN-DE-LUZ

www.saint-jean-de-luz.com

Corsaires from St-Jean-de-Luz once raided the offshore coast for ships and booty. Later, fishermen plied a more law-abiding but still dangerous trade sailing to Newfoundland and Spitsbergen to catch cod and whale. Nowadays, the fleet lands the tuna, anchovies and sardines which supply the town's many restaurants. St-Jean is also a holiday resort with a heyday in the early 20th century, and it has a little history to impart.

In 1660, the year after France and Spain settled their common border through the Basque region and the mountains by the Treaty of the Pyrenees, Louis XIV came to St-Jean-de-Luz to marry a Spanish princess, Maria Teresa. The wedding took place in the Église St-Jean Baptiste and, when it was done, the door that the couple had left the church by was sealed up so that commoners wouldn't be able to use it.

Across the harbour, reached by a bridge, is Ciboure, where the composer Maurice Ravel (1875–1937) was born. His Dutch-style house stands by the waterfront.
✚ 454 D13 ℹ 20 boulevard Victor Hugo, 64500 Saint-Jean-de-Luz ☎ 05 59 26 03 16 🕐 Mon–Sat 9–12.30, 2–6

ST-LIZIER

www.ariege.com/stlizier

Although now a mere village with a population of just over 1,500, St-Lizier has two cathedrals. A bishopric was installed here in the fifth century and abolished only during the Revolution. By then most of the population had drifted down to the larger, more accessible town of St-Girons below, leaving a redundant but monumental architectural assembly behind on the hill.

St-Lizier is dominated by the former bishop's palace, built in the 17th century, to which one of the cathedrals, Notre Dame de la Sède, is attached (both buildings are currently closed for restoration).

The other cathedral in St-Lizier, sometimes referred to as the church, contains 11th-century frescoes

and there is a superb Romanesque cloister beside it.

Another building in St-Lizier, the Hôtel Dieu (now a retirement home) contains an 18th-century pharmacy. The tourist office organizes guided tours of the monuments of St-Lizier in summer, and by arrangement out of season.
✚ 455 H14 ℹ place de l'Église, 09190 St-Lizier ☎ 05 61 96 77 77 🕐 Daily 10–12, 2–6

SAINTES

www.ot-saintes.fr

Saintes, a historic port on the Charente, is the tourist hub of Saintonge. The town was capital of Aquitania under the Romans and became an early convert to Christianity. Today, visitors come to enjoy its Roman and religious monuments, shops and riverside.

The old town is set back, below and behind the main boulevards. On the riverbank is the Arch of Germanicus, erected in AD19, while the fascinating Musée Archéologique, in esplanade André Malraux, offers an insight into the life of the town in Gallo-Roman times (Apr–Sep Tue–Sat 10–12.30, 1.30–6, Sun 1.30–6; Oct–Mar Tue–Sun 2–5). A first-century chariot is among the exhibits. There is more classical heritage in the Amphitheatre in rue Lacurie (daily), built in AD40.

Churches worth a look include St-Eutrope, in rue St-Eutrope (daily 9–7). Compare the Romanesque delicacy of the bell tower on the Abbaye-aux-Dames (Apr–Sep daily 10–12.30, 2–7; Oct–Mar daily 2–6) with the heavy-handed Gothic treatment of the roof of the Cathédrale St-Pierre (daily 9–7).
✚ 458 F10 ℹ place Bassompierre, 17100 Saintes ☎ 05 46 74 23 82 🕐 Jun to mid-Sep Mon–Sat 9–1, 2–6 (also 6–7pm Jul–Aug); Jul to mid-Sep Sun 10–1, 2–6; mid-Sep to May Mon–Sat 9.30–12.30, 2–6 (closes earlier in winter) 🚆 Saintes

Below *Looking through the Arch of Germanicus in Saintes*

SARLAT-LA-CANÉDA

This beautifully restored golden-stone town is now one of the most popular places in the Dordogne. Sarlat, in the heart of the Périgord Noir area, is renowned for its gastronomy, and devotees of foie gras and other delicacies make regular pilgrimages to the town's specialist suppliers and restaurants. But the town itself is also an attraction.

PHOTOGENIC BUILDINGS

Apart from the fairly nondescript rue de la République, Sarlat looks much as it must have done in its Renaissance heyday, with narrow winding alleys and passages wriggling between well-preserved town houses. La Maison d'Étienne de La Boétie, birthplace in 1530 of the eponymous philosopher and poet, is one of the most photographed buildings in Sarlat, with its fine Renaissance mullions and gables.

SARLAT'S GOLDEN AGE

At the end of the Hundred Years War Sarlat was eventually returned from English to French rule, and was granted special privileges to reward its loyalty to the king. It entered a golden age, as a new merchant class brought wealth to the area and created many of the fine stone houses that survive today. Sarlat became a pearl of the French Renaissance. It fell on harder times at the end of the 18th century but this was a blessing in disguise, as it meant the town escaped wholesale redevelopment. The Loi Malraux, passed in 1962 to help preserve France's older towns, ensured it remained that way.

INFORMATION

www.ot-sarlat-perigord.fr
➕ 459 H11 ℹ️ rue Tourny, BP 114, 24203 ☎ 05 53 31 45 45 🕐 Jul–Aug Mon–Sat 9–7, Sun 10–12, 2–6; May, Jun Mon–Sat 9–6, Sun 10–1, 2–5; Sep Mon–Sat 9–1, 2–7, Sun 10–1, 2–5; Apr, Oct 9–12, 2–6, Sun 10–1; Nov Mon–Sat 9–12, 2–5, Sun 10–1; Dec–Mar Mon–Sat 9–12, 2–5 🚉 Sarlat-La-Canéda

TIPS

» If you can't decide which delicacies to buy, visit Moulin de Moreau-Traditions du Périgord on rue de la Liberté, and see them all—foie gras, chestnuts, mushrooms, walnuts, truffles.

» Sarlat's Saturday market (8.30–6) is one of the best known in France.

» Parking can be very difficult so it is best to use the parking areas around the edge of town.

Above *Place de la Liberté in Sarlat*

INFORMATION

www.ot-toulouse.fr

⊕ 455 H13 ℹ Donjon du Capitole,
31080 Toulouse ☎ 05 61 11 02 22
🕐 Jun–Sep Mon–Sat 9–7, Sun 10.30–
5.15; Oct–May Mon–Fri 9–6, Sat 9–12.30,
2–6, Sun 10–12.30, 2–5 🚇 Toulouse

INTRODUCTION

Toulouse has always been one of France's least known and, its admirers would say, under-appreciated cities. Built largely of brick—for which it is known as *la ville rose* (the pink city), and standing on both the Garonne river and the Canal du Midi, it is distinctly southern in its climate and lifestyle, making it especially popular with young people who make up a large student population.

Until the crusade against the Cathars brought 'foreign' invaders from northern France to the south, the counts of Toulouse enjoyed great independence and prestige, ruling over lands stretching from English-held Aquitaine to Provence. Toulouse was the de-facto capital of the *langues d'oc*—the lands where Occitan rather than French was spoken.

In the 15th and 16th centuries Toulouse earned its living from the woad industry and many private mansions were built on the proceeds of this widely used blue dye.

In recent decades, Toulouse has been busy re-inventing itself as a centre for hi-tech industries. A space research institute and the national space museum are located here and beside the airport is the assembly plant for the European aircraft consortium, Airbus.

WHAT TO SEE

PLACE DU CAPITOLE

This spacious square, lined by bars and restaurants and with a *croix occitane* (the symbol of Midi-Pyrénées region) inlaid in the middle, is the city's heart. Its east side is dominated by the imposing facade of the neoclassical Capitole (town hall, open normal office hours). Inside, you can climb the monumental staircase to visit a suite of first-floor reception rooms—unless they are in use for a wedding or official function. The main room, overlooking the square, is the Salle des Illustres, which is hung with paintings depicting the history of the city. At one

Above *Shuttered buildings in Toulouse*

end there is a large canvas by Jean-Paul Laurens of the defence of Toulouse against the troops of Simon de Montfort during the Cathar period.
373 B1

BASILIQUE ST-SERNIN

The largest Romanesque church in France and an important stop on the pilgrimage route towards Santiago de Compostela in Spain, St-Sernin was begun in 1080 and completed in the 14th century. From the outside its distinguishing feature is a superb octagonal belltower rising through five storeys. Inside, it is the sheer volume of the place that most impresses. In the ambulatory there are carved wooden altars and 11th-century marble bas-reliefs of God, a seraph, a cherub, angels and two of the apostles.

Below is a hexagonal crypt which contains the 13th-century reliquary of St. Saturninus, martyred by bulls around 250AD, after whom the church is named.
373 B1 ✉ place Saint-Sernin, 31000 ☎ 05 61 21 70 18 🕐 Jul–Sep Mon–Sat 8.30–6.30, Sun 8.30–7.30; Jun, Oct Mon–Sat 8.30–12.30, 2–6.30, Sun 8.30–12.30, 2–7.30; Nov–May Mon–Sat 8.30–12, 2–6, Sun 8.30–12.30, 2–7.30 ✋ Church free; ambulatory and crypt €2

CITÉ DE L'ESPACE

www.cite-espace.com

On the northern perimeter of the city is the Cité de l'Espace, an educational adventure park dedicated to space exploration. Attractions include a life-size Ariane rocket, a planetarium and an audiovisual presentation charting life on Earth. You can also see the Mir space station.
373 off C2 ✉ avenue Jean Gonord, 31506 ☎ 0820 377 223 (toll call) 🕐 Opens daily at 9.30 with closing times between 5.30 and 7.30 depending on season. Closed Jan and Mon Sep–Dec ✋ Adults Jul–Aug €22; Sep–Jun €19.50, child (5–15) Jul–Aug €15.50; Sep–Jun €14

ENSEMBLE CONVENTUEL DES JACOBINS

www.jacobins.mairie-toulouse.fr

Toulouse's second most impressive church, west of place du Capitole, is a masterpiece of southern French Gothic style. It has supremely elegant fan vaulting supported on a palm-tree-like column, and modern stained-glass windows by Max Ingrand. The church was built as the first Dominican monastery and contains the remains of St. Thomas Aquinas, who died in Italy in 1274. A doorway from the church leads into the restored cloister, for which there is an admission fee.
373 B1 ✉ rue Lakanal, 31000 ☎ 05 61 22 21 92 🕐 Daily 9–7 ✋ Church free; cloister €3

Above *Inside Le Couvent des Jacobins*

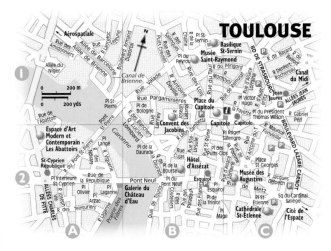

TIPS

» If you've come to shop, the narrow lanes between place du Capitole and rue de Metz have bijou boutiques, while larger shops can be found along the rue d'Alsace.

» Shaded by trees, the UNESCO-listed Canal du Midi (▷ 355) is the perfect place for a walk, jog, boat trip or meal in a barge restaurant.

» Get free entry to certain museums and discounts on other attractions with the Carte Privilège Toulouse en Liberté pass, which you can buy at the tourist office.

MUSÉE DES AUGUSTINS

www.augustins.org

This 14th- to 15th-century monastery makes a splendidly atmospheric museum. It is chiefly of interest for its collection of carved Romanesque capitals but it also has Gothic sculpture and paintings from the 17th to 19th centuries.

✚ 373 C2 ✉ 21 rue de Metz, 3100 ☎ 05 61 22 21 82 ⏰ Daily 10–6 🖐 €3, under 18 free

MUSÉE SAINT-RAYMOND

www.saintraymond.toulouse.fr

This archaeological museum can be found next to St-Sernin. It is especially rich in works of Roman art including mosaics and sculptures in white marble.

✚ 373 B1 ✉ place Saint-Sernin, 31000 ☎ 05 61 22 31 44 ⏰ Daily 10–6 🖐 €3, under 18 free

MORE TO SEE

LES ABATTOIRS

www.lesabattoirs.org

Devotees of modern art will want to head for this contemporary exhibition space in the old abattoir buildings across the river from the city centre. Also on the left bank, at the southern end of Pont Neuf, the city's oldest bridge, is a photography gallery, Le Château d'Eau (1 place Laganne, 31300; tel 05 61 77 09 40; www.galeriechâteaudeau.org; Tue–Sun 1–7; €2.50), in the old water tower.

✚ 373 A1 ✉ 76 allées Charles de Fitte, 31300 ☎ 05 62 48 58 00 ⏰ Wed–Fri 10–6, Sat–Sun 11–7 🖐 Adult €7 child (4–17) €3

AÉROSPATIALE (AIRBUS)

www.taxiway.fr

You'll need to reserve for either of the 90-minute tours around the two Airbus factories beside Toulouse airport. Watch the construction of the A380 double-decker passenger plane. Another option is a visit to the first Concorde ever built.

✚ 373 off A1 ✉ Village Aéroconstellation, rue Frantz Joseph Strauss, 31700 Blagnac ☎ 05 34 39 42 00 ⏰ French school hols Mon–Sat; rest of year Wed, Sat 🏷 Guided tours in French (in English according to demand) 🖐 Adult €14, child (6–18) €11. Extra charge for Concorde: adult €4.50, child (6–18) €3

Below The striking neoclassical facade of the Capitole town hall

Above *Basilique St-Sernin, distinguished by its superb octagonal belltower*

BÂTEAU-MOUCHE

www.toulouse-croisieres.com

Pleasure trips on the Garonne sail from the sunken riverside garden of place de la Daurade and last for 75 minutes. Buy your ticket on board at least 10 minutes before departure.

➕ 373 B2 ✉ 7 Port Saint-Sauveur, 31000 ☎ 05 61 25 72 57 🕐 Jul to mid-Sep daily 10.30, 3.15, 4.45, 6.15; Apr–Jun, mid-Sep to Oct Tue–Sun 10.30, 3.15, 4.45 ✋ Adult €8, child (3–14) €5

CATHÉDRALE ST-ÉTIENNE

After seeing St-Sernin, Toulouse's cathedral can be a disappointment. The 13th-century bishop, Bertrand de L'Isle, had plans to restructure the building but he died having completed only the choir which was out of line with the original nave. The cathedral does, however, have a few redeeming qualities such as the 14th- and 15th-century stained glass.

➕ 373 C2 ✉ place St-Étienne 🕐 Daily 9–7 ✋ Free

FONDATION BEMBERG (HÔTEL D'ASSÉZAT)

www.fondation-bemberg.fr.

This Renaissance mansion was built in the 16th century for Pierre d'Assézat, a woad merchant. It now contains a collection of art including Impressionist, Pointillist and Fauvist works, Renaissance bronzes and rare books.

➕ 373 B2 ✉ place d'Assézat, rue de Metz, 31000 ☎ 05 61 12 06 89 🕐 Tue–Sun 10–12.30, 1.30–6 ✋ €5

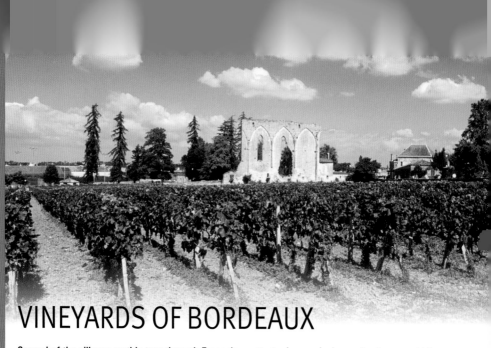

VINEYARDS OF BORDEAUX

Several of the villages on this tour through France's greatest wine-producing region have world-famous names. The drive takes in the beautiful old town of St-Émilion and crosses the river Garonne, which flows through Bordeaux, a thriving city and the wine capital of France.

THE DRIVE

Distance: 120km (75 miles)
Allow: 1 day
Start/end at: Langon

★ Langon, on the banks of the Garonne, is known for its sweet dessert wines. There's a partly Romanesque church with 12th-century frescoes, and 28 menhirs (standing stones), said to be 28 girls turned to stone for missing Mass.

Leave Langon on the N113, signed for Libourne. Just outside the town, turn right after the railway viaduct running parallel with the road, towards St-Macaire.

❶ St-Macaire, a medieval town built on limestone rock, with the impressive church of St-Sauveur, is named after a sixth-century bishop.

Leave St-Macaire by following the N113 northeast for about 500m (quarter of a mile) before turning left onto the D672 towards Sauveterre-de-Guyenne. Pass through le Pian-sur-Garonne and St-André-du-Bois.

❷ In St-André-du-Bois, the Château de Malromé was the final home of the artist Henri de Toulouse-Lautrec before his death in 1901, at the age of 37. It contains a rare collection of his drawings. The artist is buried in Verdelais, just southwest of St-André.

Carry on along the D672. Where the main road takes a detour right around Palay, take the scenic but steep route through the hamlet, rejoining the D672 farther north to continue towards Sauveterre-de-Guyenne.

❸ Sauveterre-de-Guyenne, an interesting small *bastide* (fortified town), has four large gateways and a castle built by Edward I of England.

Leave Sauveterre-de-Guyenne, following signs to Libourne on the D670, and pass the small town of Le Puch. Continue on the same road, whose sweeping bends demand constant vigilance, and pass through St-Jean-de-Blaignac. Cross the river Dordogne, and go through Lavagnac. Continue through Merlande and Vignonet, arriving at a roundabout on the D936. Carry straight on (signed Libourne and St-Émilion). About 4km (2.5 miles) farther on, at St-Laurent-des-Combes, take the right turn for St-Émilion.

❹ Medieval St-Émilion (▷ 369) perches on a hilltop overlooking the Dordogne valley. The village is famous throughout the world for its wine and locally for its macaroons. St-Émilion's other attractions include its unique monolithic church carved out of solid rock, its catacombs, the medieval Tour du Roi and the delightful frescoes in the simple, elegant Chapelle de la Trinité.

Leave St-Émilion on the same road as you entered by. Cross straight over the D670 onto the D122 (signed for Branne), a narrow, winding road with crumbling edges. After 4km (2.5 miles) turn left onto the D19/D122, signed for Branne, and follow the road over the metal Dordogne bridge into Branne. Leave Branne on the D936, signed Cadillac and Bordeaux. Just under 1km (half a mile) farther on, bear left towards Bordeaux, staying on the D936.

Turn left off the D936 onto the D11, for Targon and Cadillac. Cross over the D128 near Grézillac, continuing on the D11. After about 9km (5.5 miles), turn right onto the main road, the D671, and then immediately left, back onto the D11 following signs to Targon throughout. Go through Targon, leaving town on the D11 towards Cadillac, following signs to Escoussans. After 6km (4 miles) bear right at the fork on the D11 for Cadillac and then pass through Escoussans. After 2km (just over a mile), at the T-junction, take a right turn for Cadillac and Bordeaux, staying on the D11 which winds downhill through woodland towards Cadillac.

5 Cadillac is a small fortified town on the banks of the Garonne. It has an impressive 17th-century château with vaulted basement rooms once used by tapestry weavers. When the Duc d'Epernon started its construction, Henri IV, realizing how rich and ambitious the duke was, encouraged him wholeheartedly, hoping the distraction would make him less dangerous. The town was also the home of the Chevalier de Lamothe de Cadillac, founder of the city of Detroit, in the US.

As you come into Cadillac follow the signs for the D10 and Bordeaux. After 100m (109 yards), turn left at the traffic lights, still on the D10 (now signed for the A62 autoroute), and go over the bridge across the Garonne. Continue to Cérons.

6 Cérons is an ancient port on the Garonne, with a Romanesque church that has lovely carvings on the doorway. The village has its own

appellation for dessert wines, as does nearby Cadillac. In the fishing season, you'll see signs advertising the sale of *alose*, a large freshwater fish abundant along this stretch of the river.

Follow signs to Illats and the A62. Around 2km (just over a mile) after Cérons, where the approach to the A62 veers off to the left, bear right onto the D117, signed for Illats, Landiras and St-Symphorien. The road goes over the autoroute. Pass through Illats and stay on the D11, signed for Landiras and St-Symphorien. Go through Artigues and continue to Landiras, where you turn left onto the D116, signed for Pujols-sur-Ciron and Langon. After 3.5km (2 miles) turn right onto the D118 towards Budos. In Budos, bear round to the left onto the D125, towards Sauternes, crossing the river Ciron and following this pleasant, if winding, road through vines and woods to Sauternes.

7 The Maison du Vin, in the village square at Sauternes, has wine-tasting. Just outside Sauternes,

on a hilltop to the north, is the 12th-century Château d'Yquem (not open to the public). It is known for producing one of France's most prestigious white wines.

In Sauternes, follow signs for Roaillan and Langon. At the next intersection, turn left onto the D8 to Langon. After 1km (0.5 miles), bear right, on the D8 to return to Langon.

WHERE TO EAT
AMELIA CANTA
www.ameliacanta.com
✉ St-Émilion ☎ 05 57 74 48 03 ⏰ Daily. Closed Dec–Jan

PLACES TO VISIT
MAISON DU SAUTERNES
www.maisondusauternes.com
✉ 14 place de la Mairie, Sauternes ☎ 05 56 76 69 83 ⏰ Mon–Fri 9–7, Sat–Sun 10–7

CHÂTEAU DE MALROMÉ
www.malrome.com
✉ 33490 St-André-du-Bois ☎ 05 56 76 44 92 ⏰ Château closed to the public. Open by reservation only

Opposite *A vineyard in St-Émilion*

ROCAMADOUR

Perched high on the rocky plateau known as the Causse du Quercy, Rocamadour (▷ 368) seems to defy gravity, occupying an almost vertical site on three main levels. The site of the oldest pilgrimage in France, and a major stop on the pilgrim trail to Santiago de Compostela, it continues to astonish its many visitors with its setting. This walk starts from the top of the village, and includes a stroll in the town as well as a circular walk in the Alzou valley, haunt of eagles and other birds of prey, through the surrounding countryside. Owing to the precipitous setting, you should expect some steep ascents and descents.

THE WALK

Distance: Village walk: 1km (half a mile); country walk: 8km (5 miles)
Allow: Village walk: 1 hour 30 minutes; country walk: 3 hours
Start/end: Rocamadour
Parking: There are free parking areas at the top and bottom of the town

HOW TO GET THERE

Rocamadour can be approached from the parking areas on two levels: via the D673 from the upper plateau, on foot or by elevators; or from the Alzou valley below, on foot or by a miniature train. Both approaches offer some spectacular views.

THE VILLAGE WALK

According to legend, the religious origins of this rocky site go back to the hermit Amadour, whose perfectly preserved body was discovered in the 12th century. From that time on, miracles began to occur, and crowds of up to 30,000 pilgrims would attend the site on certain holy days.

★ From the parking area near the château, a coin-operated barrier (€2.50 per person) allows access to the ramparts for an unforgettable panorama of the site and its rocky setting. Afterwards, go down the steeply winding chemin de Croix,

with the Stations of the Cross at each turn of the pathway. You will pass through a tunnel under the basilica to arrive in the Cité Religieuse which has seven chapels.

❶ Chapelle de Notre-Dame, to the left of the basilica, contains the small, much-revered statue of the Black Madonna, blackened by centuries of candle smoke.

❷ You can also visit the Musée d'Art Sacré Francis Poulenc, dedicated to the composer (1899–1963), who had a vision during a visit to the town in 1936 and subsequently composed *Litanies à la Vierge Noire* de Rocamadour. The museum has a collection of sacred art and artefacts.

❸ Walk down the 223 steps of the Grand Escalier to visit the village at the lower level.

Turn left along the main street (lined with souvenir shops) to pass the tourist office, next to the Hôtel de Ville. Just before one of the old town gates, Porte Salmon, turn right down the lane, then descend one of the flights of steps. Go towards the lower car park by the river.

THE COUNTRY WALK
★ This is marked with an image of a dragonfly *(libellule)* and has a signpost to Fouysselaze at the start.

Cross the river Alzou by the stone bridge, and take the lane on the left. After about 150m (170 yards), a little path on your right leads to the Fontaine de la Fillole. Climb the hill among hazel and oak trees. Once on the plateau, continue between drystone walls past the farm of Fouysselaze on your right.

❶ On the farm of Fouysselaze, farmers make the delicious goat's milk cheeses known as *cabécou*.

When the path meets the tarmac road, turn right and follow the road past the entrance to the farm and a wall on the right where a sheep passage has been made. Skirt the large hollow on your right, known as Le Cloup de Magès.

❷ To the left is a dolmen (megalithic tomb), at least 4,000 years old.

Leave the road and take the GR46 footpath to Rocamadour, crossing the D32 and following the sign for the Fontaine de Berthiol. There are magnificent views of the village through the trees. Cross the Alzou by the little bridge near the Moulin de Roquefraîche, go straight over the small crossroads, and enter the village by Porte Basse, then pass through Porte Hugon.

❸ If you can't face the Great Staircase, take the elevator and funicular through the rock, up to the plateau where the walk started.

WHEN TO GO
Rocamadour can be crowded in high season. In late spring its environs are carpeted with meadow flowers.

WHERE TO EAT
There are bars and restaurants in the lower level of Rocamadour.

INFORMATION
TOURIST INFORMATION
www.rocamadour.com
✉ L'Hospitalet, 46500 Rocamadour
☎ 05 65 33 22 00

GETTING AROUND
A *petit train* (miniature road train) runs from the beginning of April until the end of September, carrying visitors to and from the lower parking areas to the shops and restaurants (adult return €3.50, child return €2). There is also a 30-minute evening tour of floodlit Rocamadour (adult €5, child €2.50). A funicular lift *(ascenseur incliné)* between the top parking area and the religious citadel costs €4 return (under 8 free). Another lift *(ascenseur de Rocamadour)* goes between the citadel and the shops and restaurants (€3 return, under 8 free). Opening times for the lifts vary according to season.

Opposite *Rocamadour is one of France's top sights and attracts crowds of visitors*
Below *Rocamadour is perched on a rocky plateau*

BASQUE HILL COUNTRY

Forest and pasture-clad hills paint the Basque Country in vivid shades of green. This drive explores some of the best of its scenic delights, with broad vistas and a preview of the Pyrenean peaks marking the French-Spanish frontier. You cross several cols (mountain passes), mostly by good but narrow roads, and with gradients that are generally not too steep.

THE DRIVE
Distance: 116km (72 miles)
Allow: 1 day
Start/end at: St-Jean-Pied-de-Port

★ An attractive town on the river Nive, St-Jean-Pied-de-Port was formerly the capital of Basse Navarre and a meeting point for pilgrims making their way to the shrine of Santiago de Compostela in Spain.

The old part of St-Jean is contained within the 15th-century fortified walls, while the Citadelle owes its sturdiness to the design of Vauban, Louis XIV's great military engineer. A walk along the ramparts gives good views over the town's narrow streets and alleyways.

Leave St-Jean-Pied-de-Port, following directions for St-Palais and Mauléon on the D933. After 4.5km (3 miles), turn right in St-Jean-le-Vieux onto the D18, signed for Ahaxe and Mendive. Follow the D18 to begin the long climb to a series of cols, waymarked regularly for bicyclists (with Col d'Iraty, the height reached, and the remaining distance). On a green crest about 1km (0.5 mile) beyond Col d'Haltza, just out of sight on the left of the road, stands the Chapelle St-Sauveur.

Chapelle St-Sauveur, locked when not in use, is the setting for an annual Corpus Christi pilgrimage. It is barn-like in size and appearance and at first glance would seem to

belong to a hill farm. Surrounding it are 13 small crosses, and a larger stone pedestal with a crucifix stands nearby. A plaque fixed to one wall remembers with gratitude the help given by the Basques of Iraty to Belgian forces in World War II.

Continue to climb among beech woods until you reach Col de Burdincurutcheta (1,135m/ 3,723ft), which is 13km (8 miles) from Mendive. Descend for 2.5km (1.5 miles) to a pastureland basin and a small tarn where the road forks. This is an ideal spot for a picnic, with a snack bar on the left open in season. Bear left onto the D19 and shortly afterwards enter the Forêt d'Iraty.

One of the great forests of the Pyrenees, the Forêt d'Iraty has mainly beech and yew with some pine. In previous centuries, large quantities of Iraty timber were used for shipbuilding. Today the forest has leafy trails winding through it and picnic areas alongside the Burdincurutcheta-Bagargui road. It is also a great place for cross-country skiing in winter.

Climbing once again through the forest, continue for 7km (4 miles), through les Chalets d'Iraty, until you arrive at Col Bagargui (1,327m/4,353ft).

During the autumn migrations, millions of birds cross the Basque country. In October, the Col Bagargui is a fine vantage point for viewing a variety of birds such as honey buzzards, storks, cranes and kites.

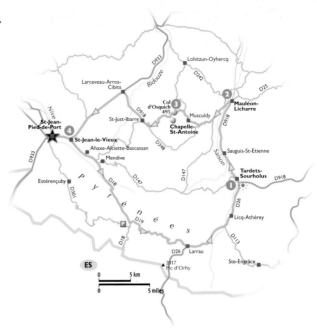

Descend the eastern side of the col (with some tight hairpin bends) to Larrau (13km/8 miles). Turn left on the D26, then 2.5km (1.5 miles) farther on, cross a bridge and pass the buildings of Logibar to the right of the road beside the river. In a little under 15km (9 miles) from Logibar, the D26 meets the D918 at a T-junction. Turn left to reach Tardets-Sourholus.

❶ Tardets is a small town with fine, long views to the frontier mountains. It is a focus of Basque folklore and there is a pilgrimage here twice a year. The Chapelle de la Madeleine stands on a peak high above the valley to the north.

Continue on the D918 for 13km (8 miles) to Mauléon.

❷ Mauléon and Licharre stand on opposite banks of the river Saison, downstream from Tardets. Mauléon is an old medieval town clustered beneath the ruins of its 15th-century castle. On the corner of

rue de la Navarre, on the left bank, is a Renaissance château with an impressive roof.

Leave Mauléon on the D918, signed for Col d'Osquich and St-Jean-Pied-de-Port. At a small roundabout 500m (quarter of a mile) later, turn left again and begin a gentle ascent for 13km (8 miles) to Col d'Osquich.

❸ Col d'Osquich (495m/1,624ft) marks the border between Basse Navarre and the Soule district and offers wonderful views.

Cross the col. At the summit, a small pedestrian track from the lay-by (turnout) on the left leads off to the Chapelle St-Antoine, also known as the Chapelle de la Paix, at a height of 706m (2,316ft). You can see the chapel to the left, high on the skyline, from the road as it descends from the col. Pass by St-Just and Cibits to reach Larceveau. Turn left at the small roundabout and follow the D933 for 11.5km (7 miles) to St-Jean-le-Vieux.

❹ In the Middle Ages the town of St-Jean-le-Vieux was on the Santiago

pilgrimage route, and beside the road in nearby Aphat-d'Ospital you can see the near-derelict 12th-century Chapelle St-Blaise, a tiny place of worship used by the pilgrims.

Continue for another 4.5km (3 miles) to return to St-Jean-Pied-de-Port.

WHEN TO GO
This drive climbs over two cols that are well over 1,000m (3,300ft), so avoid the winter, when the area is covered in snow. Lingering patches of snow can still make driving conditions difficult in spring. July and August are best, but make sure you're not planning to go during the Tour de France cycle race in July, when the roads will be closed to traffic (▷ 27).

WHERE TO EAT
HÔTEL-RESTAURANT MENDY
www.hotel-mendy.com
✉ 64220 St-Jean-le-Vieux ☎ 05 59 37 11 81 🕐 Lunch and dinner Tue–Sat, lunch Sun

CIRQUE DE GAVARNIE

The Cirque de Gavarnie is a massive, natural amphitheatre of semicircular precipices in three towering limestone tiers, with caves, ice bridges, rivers of scree, glaciers and waterfalls. This walk in the Parc National des Pyrénées starts in Gavarnie, and includes a strenuous route up into the forest high above the valley path taken by most visitors to the cirque and its 423m (1,387ft) waterfall. Apart from signposts at major path junctions, the route is not waymarked, but the main path is easily discernible: Do not deviate from it. If you prefer not to risk the steep parts of the walk, stay in the valley and go to Hôtel du Cirque.

THE WALK

Distance: 10km (6 miles)
Allow: 1 day
Start/end at: Gavarnie village
Parking: Park on the lower outskirts of Gavarnie, near the Route de Boucharo

HOW TO GET THERE

At 1,350m (4,430ft), Gavarnie is the highest village in the Hautes-Pyrénées. It lies at the end of the D921, south of Lourdes and Argelès-Gazost and close to the border with Spain.

Gavarnie was originally a hamlet inhabited by shepherds. During the Middle Ages, the Knights Templar protected the Boucharo Pass on the pilgrim route to Santiago de Compostela. The knights' headquarters later transformed into a church, which contains an unusual 12th-century statue of the Virgin Mary holding a pilgrim's flask.

★ From the parking area, walk up to the heart of the village, with its Maison du Parc and church. Continue through the village with the Gave de Gavarnie stream on your left, then follow the track up the valley. At the first bridge, bear left, cross the Gave and turn immediately right. After about 250m (275 yards), you'll see a path on the left next to a small stream, marked with a signpost indicating Parc National 1 hour, Refuge des Espuguettes 2 hours, Hourquette d'Alans 3 hours 15 minutes, and Barrage des Gloriettes 5 hours 30 minutes.

❶ Take this path, the Chemin des Espugues, which rises steeply in a series of zigzags through rocks and bushes, eventually entering the forest. Continue climbing until the path begins to level out and another signpost appears.

This signpost indicates Refuge des Espuguettes 1 hour to the left, Parc National 250m and Cirque de Gavarnie 1 hour to the right. Take the right-hand path, and cross a small wooden bridge across a tumbling stream. This is an idyllic spot for a picnic, with patches of lush meadowland shaded by trees, and tantalizing glimpses of Gavarnie far below.

❷ A few metres farther on, pass the Refuge du Pailha on your left and follow the path through forest until it enters the national park (via an unusual kind of wooden gate).

From here the path follows the contours of the rock face, which rises and sometimes overhangs on the left, with views to the right down through trees to the track on the valley floor.

❸ The path leads eventually down to the Hôtel du Cirque, where, from the terrace, the full magnificence of the cirque's panorama is revealed. An orientation table describes (in French) the origins of the cirque and names the peaks and features. In recent years, the site has developed into one of France's main rock-climbing bases.

Follow the path towards the cirque for about 100m (110 yards), then

Above *Walking along the waterside path to the Cirque de Gavarnie*
Opposite *Typical scenery on the way to the Cirque de Gavarnie*

take the path on the left to go into the cirque.

The limestone rockfaces are nearly 1,500m (5,000ft) high, making the highest peak, Le Marboré, more than 3,000m (10,000ft) above sea level. The main waterfall, La Grande Cascade, is five times the height of the Eiffel tower, and the highest in Europe.

Crossing several streams, continue to the base of La Grande Cascade. Return to the Hôtel du Cirque along the same path. Back at the Hôtel, take the track on the left and follow it down through woods and clearings. At a stream, cross the bridge and then you will pass an information panel on your left. Some 100m (109 yards) farther on, where the path forks, take the left fork and cross the Gave de Gavarnie over another bridge. Follow the path until it reaches a disused bridge across wetland. Take the path that rises on the right and walk across open ground towards the *gave* (stream), which is now running on your right and below you.

❹ As the path bends to the left, on rising ground to the left is the tomb of Franz Schrader (d1924), a geographer and landscape painter, who mapped the Massif de Gavarnie, as well as capturing it on canvas.

Continue to follow the path along the left bank of the *gave* to take you back to Gavarnie.

WHEN TO GO
This walk is possible from mid-May through to mid-November, although the waterfall loses its allure as the summer progresses, sometimes reducing to a trickle by autumn. The route most visitors take, which leads directly from the village to the cirque, is walkable at almost any time if you are properly equipped. Weather conditions for the following 24 hours are posted in the window of the tourist information office, or you can ask at the Maison du Parc.

INFORMATION
MAISON DU PARC GAVARNIE
www.parc-pyrenees.com
☎ 05 62 92 42 48 ⏱ Call ahead for opening times

THE TÉNARÈZE

Gers *département* — Gascony of old — has an abundance of pretty medieval villages, castles and other historic sights separated by rolling hills and vineyards. This tour offers a selection of the best the region has to offer. The route mostly runs along quiet, traffic-free roads which are equally good for cycling and driving.

THE DRIVE
Distance: 66km (41 miles)
Allow: 1 day
Start/end at: Condom

★ Condom is an attractive town on the river Baïse. Despite the meaning of its name in English, it has nothing to do with prophylactics. Particularly worth seeing is the maginificent Flamboyant Gothic cathedral.

Leave Condom heading south towards Auch on the D930. Just before you reach Valence-sur-Baïse turn right for the Abbaye de Flaran on the D142. Cross the bridge over the green river and park beneath plane trees where indicated.

❶ The Abbaye de Flaran is one of the best preserved Cistercian monasteries in southwest France. It was founded in 1151 but the present buildings largely date from the 17th and 18th centuries. It is now used for arts and concerts.

Turn right out of the abbey car park and resume the route on the D142 which runs past a stately gate house, and over rolling hills to Cassaigne. At the crossroads outside the village go straight over and down the drive to the château.

❷ The Château de Cassaigne stands in an estate of vineyards growing grapes to make Armagnac, a brandy said by connoisseurs to rival the more famous Cognac. There are free guided tours.

Leaving the château, turn right and then almost immediately right again through the village of Cassaigne on the D142, signposted for Lauraët. Turn left at the main road and shortly afterwards take the right turn on the D142 for Lauraët. Crossing three consecutive smalls stone bridges you reach Vopillon.

❸ The tiny village of Vopillon has a squat stone Romanesque church that looks as if it has been cut in half. The structure is all that is left of a long-vanished monastery.

Continue across country, stilll on the D142 towards Montréal. Join the D113 2km (1.5 miles) before the town and follow the signs into the main square.

❹ Montréal is one of many *bastides* in Gascony: new towns founded in the Middle Ages which are identifiable by their geometrically planned streets converging on an arcaded square.

Leave the square of Montréal beside the church on the route marked *'toutes directions'* and at the

Map showing Lannes, Osse, Fourcès, D117, D114, D29, Larroque-sur-l'Osse, Montréal, D15, D254, D142, Séviac, D29, Condom, D15, Larressingle, Caussens, Vopillon, Château de Cassaigne, Mouchan, D931, Cassaigne, Gondrin, D35, Auzoue, D229, Valence-sur-Baïse, Abbaye de Flaran, D930, Courrensan, Osse, D112

⑦ Larressingle is a cross between a village and a castle, partly preserved but largely unprettified. It was built in the 13th century by the abbots of Condom as a refuge from the wars raging between the French and the English.

Take the D15 back into Condom.

WHERE TO EAT
L'AUBERGE

Informal bar serving snacks or full meals during normal dining hours.
✉ Fourcès ☎ 05 62 29 40 10
🕐 Restaurant: May–Oct daily 12–2.30, 7–9.30; Nov–Apr Wed–Mon 12–2.30, 7–9.30, Tue 7–9.30. Bar: May–Oct daily 9.30am–11.30pm; Nov–Apr Thu–Mon 9.30am–11pm, Tue 9am–5pm

PLACES TO VISIT
ABBAYE DE FLARAN

www.gers-gascogne.com
✉ 32310 Valence-sur-Baïse ☎ 05 62 28 50 19 🕐 Jul–Aug 9.30–7; Sep–Jun 9.30–12.30, 2–6

CHÂTEAU DE CASSAIGNE

www.château decassaigne.com
☎ 05 62 28 04 02 🕐 Mid-Jun to mid-Sep 9–12, 2–7; mid-Sep to mid-Jun Tue–Sun 9–12, 2–6 ▶ Free guided tours last 1 hour

SEVIAC VILLA GALLO-ROMAINE

www.seviac-villa.com
✉ Montréal-du-Gers ☎ 05 62 29 48 57 🕐 Jul–Aug daily 10–7; Mar–Jun, Sep–Nov 10–12, 2–6. Closed Dec–Feb

Opposite *The river running through Condom*
Below *Barrels of Armagnac brandy*

T-junction on the edge of town turn right, downhill, for *'Villa romaine de Séviac'*. Cross the bridge below the town, turn left and then quick right, still following signs for the villa. A last right turn over the crest of the hill brings you to Séviac.

⑤ The remains of the Gallo-Roman villa of Séviac, with their extensive mosaic floors, stand in a peaceful and picturesque hilltop spot.

Return down the hill, cross the bridge back towards Montréal and turn left on to the D29 for Fourcès.

⑥ Fourcès is unusual for a *bastide* town because it is laid out on a circular plan. Although it is small, it is a delightful place to stroll around.

Cross the bridge out of Fourcès and go over the staggered junction on to the D114 towards Larroque, Condom and Larressingle. Turn off right after 4km (2.5 miles) on to the D254 through Larroque-sur-l'Osse on a very pretty road past vineyards and arable fields to strike the D15. Turn left towards Condom, cross the river Osse and take the right turn to visit Larresingle.

ALBI
L'ARTISAN CHOCOLATIER
Owner Michel Belin has been judged among the ten best chocolate-makers in France– he even has a chocolate creation meant to smell of Havana cigars. In addition to chocolate, he also makes delicious cakes and pastries. Credit cards are accepted for purchases over €15.
✉ 4 rue du Docteur Camboulives, 81000 Albi ☎ 06 63 54 18 46 ⏰ Mon–Sat 9–12.30, 2.30–7.15

ANGOULÊME
CHOCOLATERIE LETUFFE
www.chocolaterie-letuffe16.com
This chocoholics' heaven is known throughout France and beyond for its chocolate artistry, from the humblest nougat to delights such as *guinettes* (cherry and cognac) and *marguerites d'Angoulême* (chocolate and orange).
✉ 10 place Francis-Louvel, 16000 Angoulême ☎ 05 45 95 00 54 ⏰ Mon–Fri 9–12, 2–7, Sat 9.30–12, 2–6.30

ARCACHON
ACADÉMIE DE TENNIS FRANCK LEROUX
www.tennisleroux.com
This tennis academy is one of the best in the country and offers professional coaching to all age groups but specializes in training for children and teenagers. There are 22 outdoor courts and the centre is only 200m (220 yards) from the majestic sandy beaches around Arcachon.
✉ 7 avenue du Parc, 33120 Arcachon ☎ 06 19 56 01 45 ⏰ All year 👐 2 hours' coaching: adults €170, under 17s €150; 5–day inclusive package for youth €4,460

HIPPODROME DU BEQUET
www.hippodrome-lateste.com
The racecourse at La Teste-de-Buch, southeast of Arcachon, past the Dune du Pilat, makes for a fun day out. Bet on a horse, watch a race or hang out in one of the many bars and restaurants on site.
✉ route de Cazaux, La Teste-de-Buch, 33260 Arcachon ☎ 05 56 54 19 90 or 05 56 54 74 26 ⏰ Various race days May–Sep; call ahead to check 👐 Varies according to meeting

VOL LIBRE DU PYLA
Among the adrenalin sports you can do off the Dune du Pilat near Arcachon are hang-gliding (*deltaplane*) and paragliding (*parapente*). You'll need to reserve in advance and bring some identification with you. Training is provided. You get here by taking a train to Arcachon (from Bordeaux).

There are also several Citram buses which operate from Bordeaux daily.
✉ 14b avenue de la Belle Étoile, 33270 Bouliac ☎ 05 56 20 59 44 ⏰ Mid-Jun to mid-Sep daily 10–6 👐 Varies according to activity

VSM ÉCOLE DE PLONGÉE
www.oceana.fr
This well-known diving school along the A660 from Bordeaux (there's another another dive school at Cazaux) gives one-to-one tuition or group lessons.
✉ 1 quai Capit Allègre, 33120 Arcachon ☎ 05 56 83 98 95 ⏰ Various dive times (call ahead), Jun–Aug 👐 From €26

AUBUSSON
POINT CENTREPOINT
www.point-centrepoint.com
www.veroniquedeluna.com
The town of Aubusson is famed for the huge tapestries that hang in historic châteaux all across France. Veronique de Luna keeps this tradition alive with her traditional and modern hand-crafted designs. The gallery displays a good range of work in all sizes. Veronique also holds classes and can supply a whole range of patterns and threads so that you

Above *Enjoy a day at the races in Arcachon*

can set about making your own.
✉ 46 Grand Rue, 23200 Aubusson ☎ 01
43 36 43 17 🕓 May–Sep Tue–Sat 10–1,
3–7; rest of year by reservation

BAYONNE
BOUCHERIE CODEGA
www.boucherie-charcuterie-codega.com
For the best in Bayonne's famous
ham, other charcuterie and top-
quality meat head to this family-
owned enterprise. They can supply
items for a picnic or a ham that, if
stored correctly, will last for months.
✉ chemin d'Arans, Quartier St-Léon 84100
☎ 05 59 63 36 13 🕓 Mon–Sat 6.30–1,
3–8

BIARRITZ
CENTRE CHORÉGRAPHIQUE NATIONAL
www.ville-biarritz.fr
www.balletbiarittz.com
Choreographer Thierry Malandain
runs this dance venue, with creative,
touring and educational activities. It is
home to Ballet Biarritz.
✉ Gare du Midi, 23 avenue Foch, 64200
Biarritz ☎ 05 59 24 67 19 🕓 Performances
all year 💰 From €10

LAGOONDY SURF CAMP
www.lagoondy.com
You can either reserve lessons by the
hour or rent surf equipment here,
but the most fun is to take a whole
package of unlimited lessons with
professional instructors, equipment
rental, full board at the campsite plus
accommodation in a tent or chalet.
There's entertainment in the evenings
and the beach is close.
✉ 64201 Biarritz ☎ 05 59 24 62 86
🕓 Early May–Sep 💰 1.5-hour lesson €35

BORDEAUX
BAILLARDRAN
www.baillardran.com
Come here to try cannelé, a small
cake produced according to an old,
not-so-secret recipe. It has a creamy
inside hidden beneath a caramelized
outer crêpe-like layer infused with
rum, orange-flower water and vanilla.
✉ Galerie des Grands Hommes, 33000
Bordeaux ☎ 05 56 79 05 89 🕓 Mon–Sat
10–7.30

BRADLEY'S BOOKSHOP
www.bradleys-bookshop.com
This is the place to come for English-
language books in Bordeaux. It
has the full range of guidebooks,
phrasebooks and holiday reading,
plus a large selection of original-
language videos and DVDs.
✉ 8 cours d'Albret, 33000 Bordeaux
☎ 05 56 52 10 57 🕓 Mon 2–7, Tue–Sat
9.30–7

ESPACE CULTUREL DU PIN GALANT
www.lepingalant.com
You'll find this modern venue near
Bordeaux's Mérignac airport. There's
an extensive schedule, with events
ranging from opera, musicals,
classical and modern concerts, to
jazz, dance and theatre. Reserve your
seats in advance.
✉ 34 avenue du Maréchal de Lattre de
Tassigny, 33698 Mérignac ☎ 05 56 97 82 82
🕓 Performance times vary 💰 Varies

GALERIE DES REMPARTS
www.galeriedesremparts.com
The gallery and art shop are
dedicated to the promotion of a
selection of international painters,
such as Loilier and Dubuc, with a
focus on contemporary artists. The
gallery holds exhibitions and offers a
resale and valuation service. The staff
are highly knowledgeable.
✉ 63 rue des Remparts, 33000 Bordeaux
☎ 05 56 52 22 25 🕓 Tue–Sat 10.30–1,
2.30–7

GOLF DE BORDEAUX-LAC
Close to gardens and the Bordeaux
woods are two 18-hole golf courses
and a covered driving range with 25
posts. Group lessons and courses
are available and there's a golf shop.
Credit cards are not accepted.
✉ avenue de Pernon, 33000 Bordeaux-Lac
☎ 05 56 50 92 72 🕓 Daily 8–6 💰 Entry
free, but call ahead to reserve a time slot

LE GRAND THÉÂTRE
www.opera-bordeaux.com
This neoclassical building, home
to the National Opera of Bordeaux,
is worth a visit for the architecture
alone. There are guided tours when

rehearsals and performances allow.
Performances take place most days,
with matinées on Saturdays (▷ 357).
✉ place de la Comédie, 33000 Bordeaux
☎ 05 56 00 85 95 ☞ Tours organized by
the tourist office

IN-LINE SKATING
www.assoair.com
Downtown Bordeaux is a pedestrian-
only zone and attracts large numbers
of bicyclists, walkers and in-line
skaters. There is a regular skating
night when more than 500 bladers
take over the heart of the city.
🕓 First Sun of the month, times vary
💰 Free

L'INTENDANT
This extraordinary wine shop is
housed in a circular tower, climate-
controlled to protect the 15,000
bottles of wine that line the walls,
with the top floor reserved for the
oldest vintages.
✉ 2 allées de Tourny, 33000 Bordeaux
☎ 05 56 48 01 29 🕓 Mon–Sat 10–7.30

MARCHÉ BIOLOGIQUE
This organic market is a fairly recent
addition to Bordeaux's market
scene and one not to be missed. It
is held opposite warehouse No. 5 on
the quayside.
✉ quai des Chartrons, 33000 Bordeaux
☎ 05 56 00 66 00 (tourist information)
🕓 Thu 6am–4pm

MARCHÉ CAPUÇINS
www.marchedescapucins.com
This is one of Bordeaux's most typical
markets, where you will find fresh
flowers and local delicacies such as
foie gras, caviar, cheeses and the
locally made cake called cannelé. The
market also frequently hosts cultural
events and shows.
✉ place des Capucins, 33080 Bordeaux
☎ 05 56 00 66 00 (tourist information)
🕓 Daily 7am–1pm. Covered market closed
Mon.

MARCHÉ ST-MICHEL
The St-Michel flea market is a busy
Sunday morning market, with goods
ranging from furniture to crockery,
paintings, dolls, bicycles and retro

REGIONS SOUTHWEST FRANCE • WHAT TO DO

REGIONS SOUTHWEST FRANCE • WHAT TO DO

clothes. On the second Sunday of March, June, September and December the market swells to become the Grand Déballage de Brocante—a bric-a-brac market.

✉ place St-Michel, 33000 Bordeaux
☎ 05 56 00 66 00 (tourist information)
🕐 Sun 7–4

VILLAGE NOTRE-DAME
www.villagenotredame.com
An enormous two-floor building in the Chatrons district that houses about 30 antique dealers selling furniture in all styles. There is also a maintenance and restoration specialist. This is a great place to find out about smaller regional antique fairs and exhibitions.

✉ 61–67 rue Notre-Dame, 33000 Bordeaux
☎ 05 56 52 66 13 🕐 Mon–Sat 10–12.30, 2–7, Sun 2–7 (Oct–Apr only)

CAHORS
MARCHÉ TRADITIONNEL
Classed as one of the 100 most beautiful markets in France, this open-air market has real character. The classification comes from its generous supply of gastronomic ingredients, from goat's cheese to foie gras and tasty breads to fresh seasonal vegetables. At certain times of the year you can also buy locally produced wines.

✉ place de la Cathédrale, 46000 Cahors
☎ 05 65 53 20 65 (tourist information)
🕐 Wed, Sat 7.30–12.30

CAUTERETS
CONFISERIE AUX DÉLICES
www.berlingots.com
Eric Lestable still follows his grandmother's recipe for *berlingots* (boiled candy), a centuries-old tradition in Cauterets. Watch it being made by hand in this old village shop, then have a free taste.

✉ place de la Mairie, 65110 Cauterets
☎ 05 62 92 07 08 🕐 Daily 9–12.30, 2–7

FOIX
ÉCOLE DE PARAPENTE GYPAÈTES
www.gypaetes.com
This paragliding school offers flights with instructors for beginners,

equipment rental for experienced gliders and courses of up to five days. Flights go over the Pyrenees and, in winter, they leave from ski resorts. Make sure you reserve at least a week ahead in summer and note that credit cards are not accepted.

✉ BP05, 09001 Foix ☎ 06 78 55 39 26
🕐 All year 🖐 €60 for a flight of 15–20 min with an instructor; €120 for a half-day course

GRADIGNAN
THÉÂTRE DES QUATRE SAISONS
www.t4saisons.com
With reasonably priced family theatre, dance and musical events, from classical concerts to acrobatic circus displays, this refurbished space is a great addition to live events in the Gironde.

✉ Parc de Mandavit, 33170 Gradignan
☎ 05 56 89 98 23 🕐 Performances daily all year; call for times 🖐 Varies

GUERET
LES LOUPS DE CHABRIÈRES
www.loups-chabrieres.com
As part of a European-wide effort to save the wolf, this sanctuary houses packs of these rare animals in large natural enclosures where their behaviour can be watched by scientists and the public.

✉ St-Vaury, Monts de Guéret 23000
☎ 05 55 81 23 23 🕐 May to mid-Sep daily 10–8; Feb–Apr, mid-Sep to Dec daily 1.30–6. Closed Jan 🖐 Adult €8.50, child (4–12) €7

LACANAU-OCÉAN
LACANAU SURF CLUB
www.surflacanau.com
The area has long been a popular weekend retreat for the Bordelais, but it is now frequented by visitors who come for the surfing. This club runs courses for novices through to advanced surfers. If you're here in August, you can watch Europe's surfing championships. Ouest Aquitaine buses run from Bordeaux and if you are driving, follow signs to Lacanau-Océan, Côte d'Argent.

✉ Maison de la Glisse, 17 boulevard de la Plage, 33680 Lacanau-Océan ☎ 05 56 26 38 84 🕐 May–Aug Mon–Fri 9–12, 2–6,

Sat–Sun 9–7 🖐 2-hour discovery session €33.50, five 2-hour sessions €120

LIMOGES
BRASSERIE MICHAUD
On one of the liveliest squares in the city, Brasserie Michaud is one of a rare breed, brewing its lager-style beers on site. Interior tables are set around the traditional copper tanks. You can try dark and unfiltered brews along with the standard amber—but they don't sell other types of alcoholic beverage, so you need to be a beer-lover. You can buy bottles and gift packs.

✉ place Denis Dessoubs, 87000 Limoges
☎ 05 55 79 37 98 🕐 Daily 3pm–11pm

PARC DU REYNOU
www.parczooreynou.com
Part zoo (35ha/6 acres), part country park (10ha/24.7 acres), the grounds here surround a classical 18th-century château. You can stroll around the lake or the forest and then visit the 110 species in the zoo. These range from exotic species such as monkeys and giraffes to numerous farm animals in the petting area.

✉ Domaine du Reynou, 87110 Le Vigen
☎ 05 55 00 40 00 🕐 Apr–Sep daily 10–8 (ticket office closes 6pm); Oct, Mar Wed, Sat–Sun 10–7 (ticket office closes 4pm); Nov–Feb Wed, Sat–Sun 12.30–5.30 (ticket office closes 4pm) 🖐 Adults €12.80, child (3–12) €9.20

MARTILLAC
LES SOURCES DE CAUDALIE
www.sources-caudalie.com
This unique spa, a 15-minute drive south of Bordeaux, offers vinotherapy, where wine and wine by-products form the basis for a range of treatments. They include Sauvignon massages, Merlot wraps, crushed Cabernet scrubs and the Premier Grand Cru facial.

✉ Chemin de Smith Haute Lafitte, 33650 Bordeaux-Martillac ☎ 05 57 83 82 82
🕐 Daily 10–7 🖐 50-minute facial €100

MARTRES TOLOSANE
RENAISSANCE ARTISANALE
Just below the church, this shop is one of many *faïence* (earthenware

glazed with opaque colours) producers in the village. You can browse and buy lamps, vases, dinner services and decorative items. To arrange a tour of the workshop you will need to call in advance. If you plan to arrive by car, the facility is about 70km (43 miles) from Toulouse off the A64.

✉ 2b avenue des Pyrénées, 31220 Martres Tolosane ☎ 05 61 98 89 31
🕐 Sat–Thu 10–12, 3–6

MILLAU
L'ATELIER DU GANTIER
www.atelierdugantier.fr
Monsieur and Madame Canillac produce handmade gloves in the Millau tradition for €70–€140. Call in advance to arrange a tour of the workshop or provide measurements for a pair of custom-made gloves.
✉ 21 rue Droite, 12100 Millau ☎ 05 65 60 81 50 🕐 Mon–Sat 9–12, 2–7

MONTBRON
MAISON DU CANOË DE MONTBRON
The river Tardoire winds its way around Angoulême and through the gorges of Chambon. Maison du Canoë, just 30km (19 miles) from Angoulême, off the D939, offers guided canoe trips and canoe rental for a water-level view. The gorges take a full day. Note that credit cards are not accepted.
✉ route de Vouthon, 16220 Montbronn ☎ 05 45 23 93 58 🕐 Jul–Sep daily 9–6; Oct–Jun by prior arrangement only
🚶 Varies according to distance 12.5km (8 miles) is €20

MONTSÉGUR
LE MONTSÉGURIEN
Stop at this delicatessen for its wonderful wild boar pâté and stock up for a picnic. Many of its meat products (dried sausage, salami, pâtés and cured ham) are made on the premises.
✉ 115 rue Principale, 09300 Montségur ☎ 05 61 01 54 46 🕐 Tue–Thu, Sat–Sun 9–12.30

MORNAC-SUR-SEUDRE
CELODINE
This pretty little boutique is a bit of a surprise in the tiny port village. It stocks the best in seasonal fashion and accessories at reasonable prices. The owner personally chooses the stock so you can be sure care is put into the range whatever time of year you shop.
✉ 40 rue du Port ☎ 05 46 05 51 64
🕐 Jul–Aug daily 10–7; May–Jun, Sep Wed–Fri 2–7, Sat–Sun 10–7; Oct–Apr Sat–Sun 10–7

PÉRIGUEUX
MARKETS
Périgueux's markets are a rich source of the region's delicacies. Stock up on foie gras and other foods produced from fattened geese and ducks (*confit*, gizzards, terrines, breast fillets), and truffles. Outside the truffle season (November to the end of March), you can buy the precious fungus preserved in small jars. Drivers can take either the N21 or D939 to get here.
✉ place du Coderc and place de la Clautre, 24000 Périgueux ☎ 05 53 53 10 63 (tourist information) 🕐 Wed, Sat 8–12.30

PRÉCHAC
CENTRE D'ACTIVITÉS ET DÉCOUVERTES DE LA TRAVE
Basse Nautique belongs to the French Federation of Canoeing and Kayaking and leads guided trips and a number of different descents on the Ciron. This tributary of the Garonne is particularly beautiful around here.
✉ La Trave, 33730 Préchac ☎ 05 56 65 27 16 🕐 Apr–Sep daily 9–7; Oct–Mar Mon–Fri 9.30–12.30, 1.30–5.30 🚶 Varies according to activity

RIBÉRAC
MARKETS
Cheese-makers, bakers and florists gather in the market square on Friday morning. You can pick up great picnic food, pottery or even local paintings from the various stalls. On Fridays in October and November there's a walnut market (picked when they are fresh) and there are night markets in July and August (days vary, call ahead to the tourist office for information).
✉ place du Marché, 24600 Ribérac ☎ 05 53 90 03 10 (tourist information) 🕐 Fri 9–12

LA ROCHELLE
MARKET
Between rue Thiers, rue Gambetta and rue St-Yon, the busy market is frequented by Rochelais and residents from miles around who are aware of the quality of the goods. Items on sale include fresh seafood and other products ranging from glassware to electronics, all in a charming, lively setting. Come early on a Sunday for the best atmosphere.
✉ place du Marché, 17000 La Rochelle
🕐 Daily 7–1

LA ROCHELLE AQUARIUM
www.aquarium-larochelle.com
A large, well-run aquarium with a global cross-section of ocean environments. Café Tropical offers the chance for a snack. If you arrive by car, head to the train station, and follow signs.
✉ quai Louis Prunier, 17002 La Rochelle ☎ 05 46 34 00 00 🕐 Jul–Aug 9am–11pm; Apr–Jun, Sep daily 9–8; Oct–Mar 10–8
🎫 Adults €13, child (3–17) €10, under 3 free

ROQUEFORT-SUR-SOULZON
FROMAGERIES PAPILLON
www.roquefort-papillon.com

The Papillon cheese-maker is one of the smaller producers of Roquefort but its tour is free. You watch a short film about production, take the guided tour through the cellars, taste the finished product and, if you like it, buy some for your next picnic lunch.

✉ 8 bis avenue de Lauras, 12250 Roquefort-sur-Soulzon ☎ 05 65 58 50 00 🕐 Jul–Aug daily 9.30–6.30; Oct–Mar 9.30–11.30, 1.30–4.30; Apr–Jun, Sep 9.30–11.30, 1.30–5.30

ST-ÉMILION
CVS
St-Émilion is not short of wine shops, with most of them displaying a vast selection of Bordeaux wines. This shop, on the main square, is a good choice for tasting before deciding what you want to buy.

✉ 1 place Marché, 33330 St-Émilion ☎ 05 57 24 63 00 🕐 Mon–Sat 10–1, 2–6

SARLAT-LA-CANÉDA
MARKETS
The Saturday market in the heart of the town has local products with an emphasis on fresh fruit and vegetables. Wednesday sees a smaller, fresh-produce market in place de la Liberté, and there are covered markets every day except Monday at the Ancienne Église Sainte-Marie from May to the end of October. Sales of foie gras are held in place Boissarie on Saturday mornings, and of truffles in the same square on Saturday mornings from December to February.

☎ 05 53 31 45 45 (tourist information) 🕐 Main market Sat 8.30–6, Wed market 8.30–1

ROUGIÉ SARLAT
www.rougie.com

Rougié has been producing and selling foie gras and other local delicacies since 1875. This traditional delicatessen is popular with locals and is an easy way to discover and appreciate the best of the local goose and duck produce. Because most

products are canned, they make easily transportable gifts.

✉ avenue du Périgord, 24200 Sarlat-la-Canéda ☎ 05 53 31 72 00 🕐 Mon–Sat 10–1, 2.30–7, Sun 10–1

TOULOUSE
AU PÈRE LOUIS
For a real sense of Toulouse history, visit the oldest wine bar in town. It has an extensive wine list, exotic aperitifs and serves traditional bistro food from noon.

✉ 45 rue des Tourneurs, 31000 Toulouse ☎ 05 61 21 33 45 🕐 Mon–Sat 8.30–2.30, 5–11

MARCHÉ ST-SERNIN
A popular morning event with locals and visitors, this flea market is diverse. The location provides a stunning backdrop to browsing. Goods range from the exotic—African jewellery, dyed fabrics, Spanish leather—to the ordinary and practical, such as stockings, thread and pottery.

✉ Around Basilique St-Sernin, 31000 Toulouse ☎ 05 61 11 02 22 🕐 Sun 8–2

MARCHÉ VICTOR HUGO
The biggest covered market in Toulouse is on the ground floor of a car park. The high-quality fresh produce includes excellent duck, cold meat, fish and cheese. The restaurants on the upper level maintain the lively atmosphere.

✉ place Victor Hugo, 31000 Toulouse ☎ 05 61 11 02 22 (tourist information) 🕐 Tue–Sun 8–1

PILLON
www.maison-pillon.fr

With its traditional shopfront, this is one of the most popular confectioners and bakeries in the city, valued for the superior quality of its chocolates. Pillon have four shops, two selling chocolates, the others selling pastries. Here you can watch chocolates being made and buy the house special, le pavé du Capitole (a delicious orange-scented chocolate).

✉ 23 rue du Languedoc, 31000 Toulouse ☎ 05 61 55 03 08 🕐 Mon–Sat 9–7.30, Sun 9–1

THÉÂTRE DU CAPITOLE
www.theatre-du-capitole.org

Part of Toulouse's impressive central square, this theatre with a grand interior, hosts operas, ballet, recitals and classical music. The bar is open on performance nights.

✉ 1 place du Capitole, 31000 Toulouse ☎ 05 61 63 13 13 🕐 All year Tue–Sun; box office: Mon, Sat 10–1, 2–5.45; Tue–Fri 9–6 ✋ Varies €12–€93

XAVIER
www.fromages-xavier.com

Experts in traditional cheeses, this shop deals with small local farmers and dairy farmers producing cheeses made from unpasteurized milk. Try the various goat's cheeses. The shop also offers foreign cheeses, and some extras such as truffles and home-made bread.

✉ 6 place Victor Hugo, 31000 Toulouse ☎ 05 34 45 59 45 🕐 Closed Mon early Jul–Aug

VALLON-PONT-D'ARC
BASE NAUTIQUE DE PONT D'ARC
www.canoe-ardeche.com

The Ardèche Gorge is one of the most spectacular places for canoeing, with majestic scenery and is not a particularly difficult route. The base here rents out equipment or operates a schedule of guided runs lasting from half a day to several days.

✉ 07150 Vallon-Pont-d'Arc ☎ 04 75 37 17 79 🕐 Apr–Oct ✋ One day down the river: adult €29, child (7–12) €12

VICDESSOS
MONTCALM AVENTURE
www.montcalm-aventure.com

The team here offers courses in canyoning, climbing and potholing, and they can take you hiking in the mountains. For children under the age of six, there's an adventure park. Take the N20 south from Foix and the D8 from Tarascon.

✉ Centre Village, 09220 Vicdessos ☎ 05 61 05 19 37 🕐 Daily 9.30–7 ✋ €50 half-day activity

Opposite Eymet has an annual oyster and wine festival in August

FESTIVALS AND EVENTS

MAY
BORDEAUX INTERNATIONAL FAIR
www.foiredebordeaux.com
A 10-day annual event established more than 80 years ago, with cultural events alongside main exhibitions dedicated to interior design, the environment and agriculture. It is the largest such fair in France, with exhibitors from more than 50 countries. It's about a 15-minute bus ride from place des Quinconces, or follow signs to *Bordeaux lac* (there is free parking).
✉ Parc des Expositions, Bordeaux-Lac, 33300 Bordeaux ☎ 05 56 11 99 00
🕐 Daily 9.30–7 💷 Adult €7.70, child (6–11) €5.70

JUNE
BORDEAUX PRIDE
www.lgpbordeaux.net
Bordeaux's annual gay and lesbian festival offers a range of intellectual events (lectures, discussions), as well as a parade through the city followed by a legendary party.
🕐 Jun 2pm–dawn 💷 Free

JULY
BLUES PASSIONS FESTIVAL
www.bluespassions.com
This combination of world-class blues and the rich visual and culinary offerings of Cognac make this festival worth attending.
✉ Cognac Blues Passions, 1 rue du Port, 16100 Cognac ☎ 05 45 36 11 81 🕐 End of Jul 💷 Day tickets (to 3 concerts) €30–€45

JULY–AUGUST
FÊTE DE BAYONNE
For five days in summer Bayonne is transformed into one of the biggest party venues in France. The ceremonial 'King of Bayonne' opens the proceedings and the communal singing of the traditional hymn *Pobre de mi* closes the festivities.
✉ Town Hall square and surrounding streets ☎ 0820 42 64 64 (tourist information) 🕐 First week in Aug

MIMOS INTERNATIONAL FESTIVAL OF MIME
www.mimos.fr
This is the only major international festival dedicated to the art of mime. Performances run during the first week in August, with many artists performing in the street.
✉ Nouveau Théâtre de Périgueux, 1 avenue d'Aquitaine, 24000 Périgueux ☎ 05 53 53 18 71 🕐 End Jul to early Aug

WHITE WINE AND OYSTER FESTIVAL
This is the highlight of the summer in the Dordogne town of Eymet, south of Bergerac. Proceedings begin in the town square soon after dawn, when oyster and wine producers from all over the region set up their stalls. Wine sampling gets going surprisingly early—some people start at 6am. It makes sense to arrive early as after mid-morning supplies of some of the finer products can run low.
✉ 24500 Eymet ☎ 05 53 23 74 95 (tourist office) 🕐 15 Aug

SEPTEMBER
ST-ÉMILION FÊTES DES VENDANGES
Every September, St-Émilion celebrates the start of the all-important grape harvest with spectacular ceremonies in the town's Collegiate Church of the Cordeliers. The day culminates in the announcement of the start of the harvest, which is made to the crowds from the top of the Tour du Roy.
✉ place Pierre Meyrat, 33330 St-Émilion ☎ 05 57 55 50 50 (Syndicat Viticole); 05 57 55 50 55 (Maison du Vin) 🕐 Third Sun in Sep

DECEMBER
CHRISTMAS REGATTA
www.srr-sailing.com
Just before Christmas, boats set sail from Port des Minimes in La Rochelle for a winter's race on the high seas. Get a free view of the race from the quayside and toast the victor in the town's bars.
✉ 17000 La Rochelle ☎ 05 46 41 14 68 (tourist information)

REGIONS SOUTHWEST FRANCE • WHAT TO DO

EATING

PRICES AND SYMBOLS

The restaurants are listed alphabetically (excluding Le, La and Les). The prices given are the average for a two-course lunch (L) and a three-course dinner (D) for one person, without drinks. The wine price is for the least expensive bottle.

For a key to the symbols, ▷ 2.

ALBI
L'ESPRIT DU VIN

One of Albi's better known restaurants, 'the Spirit of Wine' is in an old building in the centre of the city. It serves dishes which marry tradition with creative flair. Wine is available by the glass.

✉ 1 quai Choiseul, 81000 Albi ☎ 05 63 54 60 44 ❸ Tue–Sat 12–2, 7.30–9.30 ✋ L €45, D €60, Wine €28

Above *Southwest France is foie gras and confit de canard country*

AUCH
LA TABLE D'OSTE

www.table-oste-restaurant.com
There's a small terrace outside this restaurant near the cathedral when the weather allows alfresco dining. The cuisine is based on regional recipes using ingredients sourced from local farmers. Reliable dishes to order are beef and duck.

✉ 7 rue Lamartine, 32000 Auch ☎ 05 62 05 55 62 ❸ May–Sep Mon 7–9.30; Tue–Fri 12–1.30, 7–9.30, Sat 12–1.30; Oct–Apr Mon 7–9.30, Tue–Sat 12–1.30, 7–9.30 ✋ L €25, D €35, Wine €15

BAGNÈRES DE BIGORRE
LE SAINT-VINCENT

Le Saint-Vincent is a hotel-restaurant five minutes' walk from the spa facilities of a small town in the Pyrenean foothills. Most of the dishes are derived from regional traditions. Used to spa customers,

the restaurant is willing to cater for people with special diets as long as it is informed in advance.

✉ 31 rue Maréchal Foch, 65200 Bagneres de Bigorre ☎ 05 62 91 10 00 ❸ Daily 12–2, 7.30–9.30 ✋ L €28, D €40, Wine €16

BELVES
LE BELVEDERE

www.hotel-restaurant-perigord.com
Traditional dishes of the region, such as grandmother's onion terrine and foie gras grilled with apples, are the staples of the restaurant, in the middle of this medieval town.

✉ avenue Paul Campel, 24170 Belves ☎ 05 53 31 51 41 ❸ Daily 12–2, 7.30–9.30 ✋ L €30, D €45, Wine €15

BIARRITZ
CHEZ ALBERT

www.chezalbert.fr
Set on the quayside in the port, this airy dining room with its tables

sprawling out across the towards the water specializes in the freshest seafood, not surprising since the fisherman could throw their catch from the boats to the kitchen.

✉ allée Port des Pêcheurs, 64200 Biarritz
☎ 05 59 24 43 84 ⏰ Jul–Aug Mon–Fri 12.15–2, 7.30–10, Sat–Sun 12.15–2, 7.30–11; Sep–Jun Mon–Tue, Thu–Fri 12.15–2, 7.30–10, Sat–Sun 12.15–2, 7.30–11 🍴 L €30, D €50, Wine €20

BORDEAUX
LE FRANCHOUILLARD
www.lefranchouillard.com
This restaurant has France à la carte, with a menu that changes every few weeks so you can sample the cuisine of different regions of the country; it's reasonably priced.

✉ 21 rue Maucoudinat, 33000 Bordeaux
☎ 05 56 44 95 86 ⏰ Mon–Sat 12–3, 6pm–1am 🍴 L €25, D €345, Wine €14

RESTAURANT DE FROMAGES BAUD ET MILLET
www.baudermillet.fr
This restaurant serves up a selection of more than 200 cheeses, an all-you-can-eat cheese platter as well as cheese-based dishes including *tartiflette* (a baked cheese and potato dish) and *raclette* (melted cheese with potatoes, pickles and pearl onions).

✉ 19 rue Huguerie, 33000 Bordeaux
☎ 05 56 79 05 77 ⏰ Mon–Sat 10am–11.30pm 🍴 L €28, D €40, Wine €12

LA TUPINA
www.latupina.com
This old-style bistro has been open since the 1960s and concentrates on regional dishes served with panache. It's won numerous accolades and awards for the quality of its locally sourced ingredients. The *charcuterie*, pork and foie gras dishes are particularly good.

✉ rue porte de la Monnaie, 33800 Bordeaux ☎ 05 56 91 56 37 ⏰ Mon–Fri 12–1.30, 7.30–9; Sat 7.30–9, Sun 12–1.30 🍴 L €35, D €50, Wine €20

BOULIAC
LE CAFÉ DE L'ESPÉRANCE
www.cafe-esperance.com
There's a traditional bistro

atmosphere and its reputation is well deserved. The wine list is first class.

✉ 10 rue de l'Esplanade 33270 Bouliac
☎ 05 56 20 52 16 ⏰ Daily 12.20–3.30, 7.30–11 🍴 L €28, D €40, Wine €17

BRANTÔME
AU FIL DE L'EAU
www.fildeleau.com
The set menus are not extensive but concentrate on the best local ingredients and dishes including some freshwater fish choices. A beautiful place for lunch or dinner.

✉ 21 quai Bestin, 42310 Brantôme
☎ 05 53 05 76 65 ⏰ Apr–Oct 12–2, 7.30–9.20 🍴 L €24, D €29, Wine €17

CADILLAC
AU FIN GOURMAND
This restaurant offers regional cuisine to suit all tastes and budgets. Traditional dishes include foie gras and pigeon in red wine, and entrecôte with shallots.

✉ 6 place de la République, 33410 Cadillac
☎ 05 56 62 90 80 ⏰ Tue–Sat 12–3.30, 7–9, Sun 12–3 🍴 L €22, D €30, Wine €12

CAHORS
LE MARCHÉ
www.restaurantlemarche.com
Chef Hervé transforms ingredients sourced from around the Lot region into dishes that delight the eyes as well as the mouth. The menu is not extensive but it changes with the seasons, and the quality to price ration here is exceptional. The ambience is modern contemporary rather than rustic.

✉ 27 place Chapou ☎ 05 65 35 27 27
⏰ Mon–Fri 12–2, 7.30–10, Sat 7.30–10
🍴 L €28, D €36, Wine €19

CASTRES
LE VICTORIA
www.restaurant81-levictoria.fr
The atmospheric cellars of a 17th-century convent near the town's Musée Goya are the setting for this restaurant which specializes in regional cuisine.

✉ 24 place 8 Mai 1945, 81100 Castres
☎ 05 63 59 14 68 ⏰ Mon–Fri 12–2.30, 7.30–10.30, Sat 7.30–10.30 🍴 L €28, D €38, Wine €17

COGNAC
LES PIGEONS BLANCS
www.pigeons-blancs.com
This old *relais de poste* is now a charming small hotel and gastronomic restaurant. The welcoming dining room is crisp and bright and the menu mixes seafood, such as lobster and sea bass, from the nearby coast with ingredients from the land—so there's a good choice of classical dishes.

✉ 11 rue Jules Brisson, 16100 Cognac
☎ 05 45 82 16 36 ⏰ Mon 7.30–9, Tue–Sat 12–2, 7.30–9, Sun 12–2 🍴 L €25, D €45, Wine €17

EUGÉNIE-LES-BAINS
LES PRÈS D'EUGÉNIE
www.michelguerard.com
This restaurant run by Michel Guerard, one of the stars of French cuisine, has a 3-star Michelin rating. Expect the most innovative cuisine, impeccable service plus a fine wine list. The tasting menu La Dinette de Marthe-Alice Pouypoudat is excellent value. Reserve well in advance.

✉ 40320 Eugénie-les-Bains ☎ 05 58 05 05 05 ⏰ Tue–Fri 7.30–9.30, Sat–Sun 12.30–2.30, 7.30–9.30 🍴 L €160, D €190, Wine €40

FIGEAC
LA BELLE ÉPOQUE
www.domainelabelleepoque.com
This restaurant 6km (4 miles) outside Figeac forms part of a rural holiday complex consisting of three gîtes, a campsite and a swimming pool. Traditional regional food is served with an accent on dishes made with local duck.

✉ Le Coustal Camboulit, 46100 Camboulit
☎ 05 65 40 04 42 ⏰ Daily 12–2, 7.30–9.30 🍴 L €30, D €35, Wine €15

FRANCESCAS
LE RELAIS DE LA HIRE
www.la-hire.com
This delightful 18th-century manor house stands in its own grounds (which have a children's playground), 13km (8 miles) from Condom and Nérac. It serves regional cuisine with a creative touch. As well as an ample selection of wines it has an

'Armagnacothéque': a 'library' of Armagnac brandies.

✉ 11 rue Porte Neuve, 47600 Francescas ☎ 05 53 65 41 59 🕐 Tue, Thu–Sat 12–2, 7.30–9.30, Sun, Mon, Wed 12–2 🍴 L €35, D €50, Wine €15

LIMOGES
LES PETITS VENTRES
www.les-petits-ventres.fr
This restaurant serves typical Limousin cuisine with local steaks, lamb and sausage, plus more unusual dishes such as pig's ears or trotters. Set meals are exceptionally good value.

✉ 20 rue de la Boucherie, 87000 Limoges ☎ 05 55 34 22 90 🕐 Tue–Sat 12–2, 7.30–10 🍴 L €22, D €30, Wine €18

MONPAZIER
PRIVILÈGE DU PÉRIGORD
www.privilegeperigord.com
There's a patio and terrace here for outdoor dining when the weather permits and there are jazz concerts on some summer evenings. The menu leans towards tradition, making the best of seasonal produce and herbs, but with an added Italian touch. The restaurant is located near the Porte de Notre-Dame.

✉ 60 rue Notre-Dame, 24540 Monpazier ☎ 05 53 22 43 98 🕐 Daily 12–2, 7.30–9.30 🍴 L €30, D €35, Wine €15

MOSNAC
MOULIN DU VAL DE SEUGNE
www.valdeseugne.com
The menu concentrates on local specialities including a *menu du terroir* foie gras. The wine cellar features Bordeaux *crus*, local Pineau de Charante and aged Cognacs. Set menus suit various budgets.

✉ Marcouze, 17240 Mosnac ☎ 05 46 70 46 16 🕐 Daily 12–2, 7.30–9.30. Closed Jan 🍴 L €30, D €40, Wine €14

OSSES
MENDI ALDE
www.hotel-mendi-alde.fr
Local country cuisine, ham, *confit* and *charcuterie* is served with home-baked bread and pâtisseries.

✉ place de l'Eglise, 64780 Osses ☎ 05 59 37 71 78 🕐 Jun–15 Sep daily 12–2,

7.30–9.30; 16 Sep–Nov, 21 Jan–May Wed–Sun 12–2, 7.30–9.30, Mon 12–2; closed Dec–20 Jan 🍴 L €22, D €30, Wine €13

PÉRIGUEUX
LE CLOS SAINT-FRONT
www.leclossaintfront.com
The specialties of this restaurant in a 16th-century building in the middle of the city include foie gras, risotto of wild mushrooms.

✉ 5–7 rue de la Vertu, 24000 Périgueux ☎ 05 53 46 78 58 🕐 May–Sep daily 12–2, 7.30–9.30 ; Oct–Apr Tue 7.30–9.30, Wed–Sat 12–2, 7.30–9.30 🍴 L €46, D €60, Wine €20

PUJOLS
LA TOQUE BLANCHE
www.latoqueblanche-pujols.com
Restaurant La Toque Blanche serves wonderfully delicate duck dishes, ranging from grilled with preserved pears to traditional foie gras.

✉ 47300 Pujols ☎ 05 53 49 00 30 🕐 Aug daily 12–3.30, 7–11; rest of year Wed–Sat 12–3.30, 7–11, Sun 12–3.30, Tue 7–11 🍴 L €30, D €45, Wine €16

ROCAMADOUR
BEAUSITE
www.bestwestern-beausite.com
There are views over the Alzou valley from the terrace of this hotel-restaurant in the centre of Rocamadour. Among the gourmet dishes served are duck foie gras terrine with quince chutney, fillet of roast gilt-head with aniseed flavoured sauce and slice of venison with cranberries, celery chips and roasted fig. The wine to choose here is the local Cahors.

✉ Le Bourg, 46500 Rocamadour ☎ 05 65 33 63 08 🕐 Daily 12–2, 7.30–9.30pm 🍴 L €40, D €50, Wine by the glass from €3.50

ROCHEFORT-SUR-MER
LA CORDERIE ROYALE
www.corderieroyale-hotel.com
There's a variety of seafood, meat and poultry dishes on the menu here, including duck with pan-fried foie gras, clams filled with parsley butter, pan-fried skate with citrus fruit and beef in chanterelle cream.

✉ rue Audebert, 17300 Rochefort-sur-Mer

☎ 05 46 99 35 35 🕐 Easter–Oct daily 12–2.30, 7–10; Nov–Easter Tue–Sat 12–2.30, 7–10, Sun 12–2.30. Closed mid-Dec to mid-Jan 🍴 L €50, D €65, Wine €20

LA ROCHELLE
LA MARÉE
www.la-maree.fr
Reserve ahead, as this seafood restaurant is very popular. There are three dining areas with more than a dozen types of shellfish on offer, plus a choice of fish dishes, depending on what's in season.

✉ 1 avenue de Colmar, 17000 La Rochelle ☎ 05 46 41 19 92 🕐 Daily 12–2, 7–10 🍴 L €23, D €30, Wine €12

LA MARINE
www.brasserie-lamarine.com
There's a choice of brasserie cuisine and local seafood dishes at La Marine. Specialities are the oysters and *tarte du jour*.

✉ 30 quai Duperre, 17000 La Rochelle ☎ 05 46 41 08 68 🕐 Daily 11.30am–2am 🍴 L €25, D €33, Wine €12

ST-JEAN-PIED-DE-PORT
LES PYRÉNÉES
www.hotel-les-pyrenees.com
Imaginative uses of local produce, from truffles and Pyrenean lamb to anchovies, sardines, cod and tuna from the Bay of Biscay.

✉ 19 place du Général-de-Gaulle, 64220 St-Jean-Pied-de-Port ☎ 05 59 37 01 01 🕐 Jul–Sep daily 12–3, 7–12; Apr–Jun Wed–Mon 12–3, 7–12; Oct–Mar Mon 12–3, Wed–Sun 12–3, 7–12 🍴 L €45, D €95, Wine €26

ST-MARTIN-DE-RÉ
LA BALEINE BLEUE
www.baleinebleue.com
The cool and comfortable dining room is bettered by the terrace in summer, with views out over the busy yacht marina in the heart of the town. Christophe Rouillé presides over a kitchen that produces contemporary cuisine. There are wine suggestions on the menu. This is a wonderful place for a leisurely lunch.

✉ quai Launay Razilly, 17410 St-Martin-de-Ré ☎ 05 46 09 03 30 🕐 Tue–Sun 12–2.30, 7.30–2am 🍴 L €28, D €38, Wine €18

SAINTES
LE BISTROT GALANT
www.lebistrotgalant.com
The eclectic menu changes regularly and has meat dishes such as sirloin steak with spicy pepper sauce.
✉ 28 rue St-Michel, 17100 Saintes
☎ 05 46 93 08 51 🕐 Tue–Sat 12–1.45, 7.15–9 🖐 L €25, D €30, Wine €18

TOULOUSE
AU POIS GOURMAND
www.pois-gourmand.fr
This restaurant on the bank of the Garonne river specializes in duck and other regional dishes, and also serves good seafood and fish. It has a good wine list.
✉ 3 rue Emile Heybrard, 31300 Toulouse
☎ 05 34 36 42 00 🕐 Tue–Fri 12–2, 7.30–9.30, Mon 7.30–9.30, Sun 12–2. Closed one week mid-Aug 🖐 L €50, D €70, Wine €16

LA BOHÈME
www.la-boheme-toulouse.com
Conveniently located in a street near place du Capitole, this restaurant specializes in Toulouse's favourite stew, cassoulet, but also offers other regional dishes of the southwest including *magret aux cèpes* (duck with ceps), *confit de canard* (preserved duck) and oysters.
✉ 3 rue Lafayette, 31000 Toulouse ☎ 05 61 23 24 18 🕐 Mon–Fri 12–2, 7.30–10, Sat 7.30–10 🖐 L €30, D €40, Wine €15

LE COLOMBIER
www.restaurant-lecolombier.com
Fine local dishes include cassoulet. *Confit de canard* (preserved duck) and snails also appear on the menu.
✉ 14 rue Bayard, 31000 Toulouse
☎ 05 61 62 40 05 🕐 Mon, Sat 7.15–10, Tue–Fri 12–2, 7.15–10 🖐 L €21, D €36, Wine €16

TRÉMOLAT
BISTROT D'EN FACE
www.vieux-logis.com
This bistro is part of a luxury hotel which was formerly a tobacco farm. The open kitchen allows you to watch the food being prepared. On a warm evening, you can eat on the terrace under the linden trees. It would be hard to find better food or service at this price and the desserts, such as the enormous portion of delicious chocolate mousse, are amazing. There is also a small gift shop with food from the Dordogne region. Reservations are essential.
✉ 24510 Trémolat ☎ 05 53 22 80 06 🕐 Wed–Sun 12–1.30, 7.30–9 🖐 L €23, D €30, Wine €12

Above *Try fresh crabs at one of the many seafood restaurants in the southwest of France*

PRICES AND SYMBOLS

The prices are the lowest and highest for a double room for one night including breakfast, unless otherwise stated. All hotels listed accept credit cards unless otherwise stated. Note that rates can vary widely throughout the year.

For a key to the symbols, ▷ 2.

AGEN
CHÂTEAU DE LASSALLE

www.châteaudelassalle.com

This stylish hotel has stone houses around a courtyard. Each spacious bedroom is decorated with antiques. The restaurant is excellent.

✉ Château de Lassalle, Brimont, 47310 Laplume ☎ 05 53 95 10 58 ✋ €99–€149, excluding breakfast (€13) ① 13 rooms, 4 suites 🔄 🏊 Outdoor

ALBI
HÔTEL LA RÉGENCE GEORGE V

www.laregence-georgev.fr

This small hotel is near the station.

The spacious, bright rooms have the benefit of high ceilings and are decorated in simple style.

✉ 29 avenue Maréchal Joffre, 81000 Albi ☎ 05 63 54 24 16 ✋ €50–€60, excluding breakfast (€8.50) ① 9

BEAULIEU
MANOIR DE BEAULIEU

www.manoirdebeaulieu.com

This excellent hotel/restaurant is on the banks of the Dordogne river. The rooms are simple, the restaurant welcoming and there's a rustic bar.

✉ 4 place du Champs de Mars, 19120 Beaulieu ☎ 05 55 91 01 34 ✋ €81–€109, excluding breakfast (€12) ① 25

BELVES
LE BELVEDERE

www.hotel-restaurant-perigord.com

This hotel occupies a restored Périgordine-style town house in a pretty medieval village. The Belvedere has a recommended restaurant attached (▷ 392).

✉ 1 avenue Paul Campel, 24170 Belves ☎ 05 53 31 51 41 ✋ €45–€58, excluding breakfast (€7.50) ① 15

BIARRITZ
HÔTEL MAISON GARNIER

www.hotel-biarritz.com

A small family-run hotel, in a quiet part of town in a restored 19th-century town house. The rooms have cable TV, shower room and internet.

✉ 29 rue Gambetta, 64200 Biarritz ☎ 05 59 01 60 70 ✋ €100–€170, excluding breakfast (€10) ① 7

BORDEAUX
HÔTEL DE FRANCE

www.hotel-france-bordeaux.fr

This basic but clean hotel is a great choice for those on a budget. All the rooms have a private bathroom; the hotel's position makes it easy to get to the city's many attractions.

✉ 7 rue Franklin, 33000 Bordeaux ☎ 05 56 48 24 11 ✋ €66, excluding breakfast (€8) ① 20 🔄

Opposite *The town of Albi*

LES 4 SOEURS
www.hotel-bordeaux-centre.com
A characterful hotel with a great location. Some of the rooms are small and basic, but there are a few larger rooms overlooking the square. Some bedrooms sleep up to five people, making them a good choice for families.
✉ 6 cours du 30 Juillet, 33000 Bordeaux
☎ 05 57 81 19 20 🛏 €95, excluding breakfast (€10) 🚪 34 ♿

BOULIAC
HÔTEL ST-JAMES
www.saintjames-bouliac.com
This hotel was designed by architect Jean Nouvel to be in harmony with the environment. Bedrooms have top-of-the-range audio-video equipment, electric blinds and views over the heated swimming pool. There are three restaurants, ranging from bistro to formal, and all are renowned.
✉ 3 place Camille Hostein, 33270 Bouliac
☎ 05 57 97 06 00 🛏 €185–€310, excluding breakfast (€25) 🚪 15 rooms, 3 suites ♿ 🏊 Outdoor

BRANTÔME
CHABROL
www.lesfrerescharbonnel.com
This charming hotel and excellent restaurant (Les Frères Carbonell) is on the banks on the river Dordogne. There are great views from the hotel. Bedrooms are spacious and light.
✉ 57 rue Gambetta, 24310 Brantôme
☎ 05 53 05 70 15 🕐 Closed Sun eve and Mon; 15 Nov–15 Dec and Feb 🛏 €60–€80, excluding breakfast (€12) 🚪 19

CADILLAC
CAMPING MUNICIPAL DE CADILLAC
This 2-star campsite is on the banks of the river Garonne. Plenty of shady pitches and a play area make it ideal for families. A swimming pool, snack bar and cinema are nearby.
✉ rue du Port, 33410 Cadillac ☎ 05 56 62 72 98 🕐 Closed Oct–May 🛏 €7.20 per person, a tent and a car; caravan €3; electricity €3.10 🚪 28 pitches 🍴

CASTERA-VERDUZAN
HÔTEL RESTAURANT DES THERMES
www.hotel-des-thermes.fr
As well as a bar and lounge this 39-bedroomed spa hotel, set in the countryside of the Gers south of Condom, features an entertainment room and a library for the guests' use. The restaurant serves regional Gascon cooking.
✉ Aux Fontaines, 32410 Castera-Verduzan
☎ 05 62 68 13 07 🛏 €68–€103, excluding breakfast (€8) 🚪 39

CASTRES
LE CASTELET
www.lecastelet.fr
This charmingly decorated bed-and-breakfast, with a *table d'hôte* restaurant, stands among oak trees. At the end of a private road outside the small village of St-Hippolyte, the Castelet is located near the town of Castres.
✉ St-Hippolyte, 81100 Castres
☎ 05 63 35 96 27 🛏 €100–€130 🚪 5 🏊 Outdoor

CHAMPAGNE-DE-BELAIR
LE MOULIN DU ROC
www.moulinduroc.com
On the bank of the river Dronne this 17th-century mill was once used to produce walnut oil. Today it is a small, stylish hotel that looks out over an expansive park where you can swim, go boating, fish or play tennis. Other activities such as golf, go-carting, canoeing and horseback riding are all nearby. The restaurant serves local produce.
✉ 24530 Champagne-de-Belair
☎ 05 53 02 86 00 🕐 Closed Dec–early May 🛏 €170–€250, excluding breakfast (€16) 🚪 10 rooms, 2 suites, 1 apartment ♿ 🏊 Outdoor

CONDOM
LE LOGIS DES CORDELIERS
www.logisdescordeliers.com
Have breakfast beside the pool, relax, then take a stroll around the delightful town of Condom. Alternatively you could use this hotel as a base for exploring the *département* of the Gers.

✉ 2 bis rue de la Paix, 32100 Condom
☎ 05 62 28 03 68 🛏 €48–€71, excluding breakfast (€8) 🚪 21

CORDES-SUR-CIEL
CHÂTEAU DE LABORDE
www.châteaudelaborde.com
There are only five rooms in the château itself—built in the 19th century—but more in the *métairie* (small farm), which stands in the grounds. The latter are cheaper, reflecting the difference in atmosphere.
✉ 81170 Cordes-sur-Ciel ☎ 05 63 56 35 63 🛏 €58–€65, excluding breakfast (€8) 🚪 5 in château, 25 in *métairie*

DOMME
LES QUATRE VENTS
www.hotel-dordogne-perigord.fr
Five of the rooms here are four-person duplexes making this a good choice for families. The best of the double rooms has a private balcony and a view over the valley.
✉ 24250 Domme ☎ 05 53 31 57 57 🛏 €55–€70, excluding breakfast (€8) 🚪 26 🏊 Outdoor

FIGEAC
CHÂTEAU DU VIGUIER DU ROY
www.château-viguier-figeac.com
Antiques and four-poster beds furnish this renovated château which partly dates from the 14th century. It has a courtyard, cloister and garden.
✉ rue Droite (Emile Zola), 46100 Figeac
☎ 05 65 50 05 05 🛏 €179–€299, excluding breakfast (€19) 🚪 16 rooms, 3 suites 🏊 Outdoor

ÎLE D'OLÉRON
THALASSA OLÉRON ST-TROJAN
www.novotel.com
Just outside the town of St-Trojan-les-Bains, the Novotel has both ocean and forest views. There's a spa, a heated saltwater pool, exercise facilities, and an excellent restaurant, Le Pertuis. You can also use the complimentary bicycles to travel round the island.
✉ Plage de Gatseau, 17370, St-Trojan-les-Bains ☎ 05 46 76 02 46 🛏 €115–€175, excluding breakfast (€15) 🚪 109 ♿ 🏊 Indoor 🍴

REGIONS | SOUTHWEST FRANCE • STAYING

397

IRLEAU LE VANNEAU
LE PARADIS CHAMBRES D'HÔTE
www.gite-le-paradis.com
This bed-and-breakfast is in a beautiful old house in its own grounds where you can fish or take a boat out on the private lake. Each bedroom has a shower room, there's a communal kitchen and a terrace.
✉ 29 Sainte-Sabine, 79270 Irleau le Vanneau ☎ 05 49 35 33 95 🕔 Closed mid-Nov to Mar ✋ €50–€80 🛏 5

MAGESQ
RELAIS DE LA POSTE
www.relaisposte.com
Set in 7ha (17 acres) in the heart of the Landes, this luxury retreat has a Michelin-starred gastronomic restaurant and a spa. Rooms are spacious and well furnished and the expansive grounds really allow you to escape from the bustle of surrounding towns.
✉ 24 avenue de Maremme, 40140 Magesq ☎ 05 58 47 70 25 ✋ €220–€250 🛏 2 🏊 Outdoor heated

MARGAUX
LE PAVILLON DE MARGAUX
www.pavillonmargaux.com
This family-run hotel is excellent value for money. The rooms (nine superior and five standard) are all named after different wine estates, with bottles of that vineyard's wine in the room. The restaurant is well priced, although the wine list can be expensive.
✉ 3 rue Georges Mandel, 33460 Margaux ☎ 05 57 88 77 54 ✋ €75–€125, excluding breakfast (€12) 🛏 14 🚭

MONPAZIER
EDWARD I
www.hoteledward1er.com
Some of the rooms in this comfortable 19th-century small château have views over the hills of Périgord. Others look on to the delightful medieval village of Monpazier. All rooms are stylishly furnished.
✉ 5 rue St-Pierre, 24540 Monpazier ☎ 05 53 22 44 00 ✋ €68–€126, excluding breakfast (€12) 🛏 12

PAU
HÔTEL LE POSTILLON
www.hotel-le-postillon.com
A traditional, family-run hotel, decorated in French provincial style. Rooms, which all have a shower room, are comfortable and a few have a balcony. Rates do not change for the high season, so advance reservations are advised. There is no restaurant on site.
✉ place de Verdun, 10 cours Camou, 64000 Pau ☎ 05 59 72 83 00 ✋ €51–€58, excluding breakfast (€6.50) 🛏 28 🚭

PAUILLAC
CHÂTEAU CORDEILLAN-BAGES
www.cordeillanbages.com
This 4-star hotel is next to the Château Lynch Bages vineyard. The spacious rooms are comfortable, and the restaurant, which has a huge wine list, serves regional cuisine. The estate has wine tasting courses at the école du Bordeaux, plus access to the nearby swimming pool, tennis court or golf course.
✉ route des Châteaux, 33250 Pauillac ☎ 05 56 59 24 24 🕔 Closed mid-Dec to mid-Feb ✋ €199–€292, excluding Continental breakfast (€20), buffet breakfast (€28) 🛏 24 rooms and 1 suite 🚭

PÉRIGUEUX
BRISTOL
www.bristolfrance.com
The historic sights of the city centre are easily accessed from this functional but comfortable modern hotel. The rooms have free WiFi internet access.
✉ 37 rue Antoine Gadaud, 24000 Périgueux ☎ 05 53 08 75 90 ✋ €56–€78, excluding breakfast (€8) 🛏 29

LA ROCHELLE
HOTEL CHAMPLAIN FRANCE ANGLETERRE
www.hotelchamplain.com
Once a private residence, this hotel has superbly furnished and spacious rooms. There is a bar, but no restaurant. Parking is available.
✉ 20 rue Rambaud, 17000 La Rochelle ☎ 05 46 41 23 99 ✋ €75–€140, excluding breakfast (€12) 🛏 36 rooms (6 non-smoking), 4 suites 🚭

ST-JEAN-DE-LUZ
LE PARC VICTORIA
www.parcvictoria.com
This hotel is in an unusual 19th-century building with light and airy rooms. The suites are great for families and have their own garden. The restaurant has an inventive menu. Nearby there is a spa and the chance to go diving in the Atlantic.
✉ 5 rue Cepe, 64500, St-Jean-de-Luz ☎ 05 59 26 78 78 🕔 Closed 15 Nov–15 Mar ✋ €175–€330, excluding breakfast (€20) 🛏 8 rooms, 11 suites 🚭 🏊 Outdoor

ST-MARTIN-DE-RÉ
HOTEL LA JETÉE
www.hotel-lajetee.com
This small stylish hotel is set in the heart of this chic resort with its many restaurants and boutiques. Rooms are colourful—either with red or blue themes—and minimalist in style. There's an interior courtyard for relaxing outside, and a bar but no restaurant on site. The hotel has a small number of parking spaces (at extra cost).
✉ quai Georges Clémenceau, 17410 St-Martin-de-Ré ☎ 05 46 09 36 36 ✋ €96–€125, excluding breakfast (€12) 🛏 24

ST-PREUIL
LE RELAIS DE ST-PREUIL
This collection of traditional buildings in the countryside close to Cognac has been renovated to create a comfortable maison d'hôte. Furnished throughout with period pieces, there's a cosy yet stylish feel, and the pool and terrace tempt you to leave your sightseeing for another day. There's a good restaurant on site.
✉ Lieu-dit Chez Rivière, 16130 St-Preuil ☎ 05 45 80 80 08 ✋ €120–€140, excluding breakfast (€13) 🛏 5 rooms, 2 suites 🏊 Outdoor

SARLAT
HOTEL COMPOSTELLE
www.hotel-compostelle-sarlat.com
This hotel, named for its proximity to the Santiago de Compostela pilgrimage route, has been run by the same family for three generations. Rooms can be reserved online.

✉ 64–66 avenue de Selves, 24200 Sarlat ☎ 05 53 59 08 53 🌐 Closed Dec and Jan ✋ €74–€92, excluding breakfast (€9) 🛏 23

PLAZA MADELEINE

www.hoteldelamadeleine-sarlat.com

Behind the expansive period facade, the Madeleine has been renovated and refurbished in contemporary style with good bathrooms featuring granite and marble. There's a gastronomic restaurant on site and a wood-panelled bar that has the feel of an old Victorian gentlemen's club.

✉ 1 place de la Petite Rigaudie, 24200 Sarlat ☎ 05 53 59 10 41 ✋ €85–€130, excluding breakfast (€11) 🛏 39 🏊

🌳 Outdoor

TOULOUSE

HÔTEL DES BEAUX-ARTS

www.hoteldesbeauxarts.com

An intimate 3-star hotel in an 18th-century building. Bedrooms have satellite TV and minibar. Dine in the nearby Dix-Neuf restaurant, owned by the same group.

✉ 1 place du Pont Neuf, 31000 Toulouse ☎ 05 34 45 42 42 ✋ €130–€230, excluding breakfast (€18) 🛏 19 🏊

🍴 Esquirol

ST-CLAIRE

www.stclairehotel.fr

You can start your day with a shiatsu massage (reserved in advance) in this central hotel, rustic French in style but Feng Shui in spirit. Rooms have flat-screen TVs and WiFi.

✉ 29 place Nicolas Bachelier, 31000 Toulouse ☎ 05 34 40 58 88 ✋ €85–€129, excluding breakfast (€9.50) 🛏 16 🏊

VALENCE-SUR-BAISE

HÔTEL LA FERME DE FLARAN

www.fermedeflaran.com

A small rural hotel in a 17th-century building near the Abbaye de Flaran, this establishment lies within easy reach of both Auch and Condom. Rooms are simply furnished. The restaurant is highly rated.

✉ Bagatelle, Maignaut Tauzia, 32310 Valence-sur-Baise ☎ 05 62 28 58 22 🌐 Closed Mon Apr, Jun, Sep, Sun and Mon Oct–Mar ✋ €56–€66, excluding breakfast (€7) 🛏 15 🌳 Outdoor

VITRAC

LE DOMAINE DE ROCHEBOIS

www.rochebois.com

Facilities at this 4-star, neoclassical-style hotel include a nine-hole golf course, swimming pool, fitness area, billiards room and tennis court on site and ballooning and canoeing nearby. The restaurant is run by chef Christophe Ochler.

✉ Route de Montfort, 24200 Vitrac ☎ 05 53 31 52 52 🌐 Closed Nov–Mar ✋ €165–€350, excluding breakfast (€15) 🛏 34 rooms, 6 suites 🏊 🌳 Outdoor

Below *Treat yourself by staying in a luxury hotel with a spa*

REGIONS | SOUTHWEST FRANCE • STAYING

CORSICA

Three qualities draw visitors across the Ligurian Sea from mainland France to Corsica (Corse in French): superb sandy beaches lapped by transparent water perfect for swimming; a mid-Mediterranean climate offering reliable sunshine, blue skies and brilliant light; and the extraordinary variety and attractiveness of Corsica's landscapes. This last ingredient comes as a delight to first-time visitors. More than 1,000km (600 miles) of rocky, indented coastline offer some tremendous views over cliffs, coves and islets. Head inland and you gain altitude immediately: Although you are rarely more than 50km (30 miles) from the sea, the highest parts of the island reach 2,600m (almost 9,000ft).

Almost everywhere Corsica is a green island, with a breathtaking range of vegetation from tangled masses of Mediterranean shrub to forests of chestnut trees. A thin population distributed among villages and hamlets adds to the sense of peace and wildness.

Culturally, there is a strong hint of Italian influence throughout the island, not least in the local language which is sometimes used in place of French. In the early Middle Ages the island was ruled by the state of Pisa and many Tuscan-style churches were built. Genoa then assumed control over Corsica but in the mid-18th century it was confronted by an independence movement led by Pascal Paoli, still revered as a heroic figure in Corsican history for his defence of the principle of self-determination before it became fashionable elsewhere in Europe and in the USA. The bankrupt Genoans were forced to appeal to the French for military help and the island was effectively sold to Louis XV in 1768. Had Corsica's most famous son, Napoleon Bonaparte, been born a year earlier he would not have been born French. Under the Second Empire, Corsica became an integral part of metropolitan France and today it is divided into two *départements*.

Corsica is a joy to explore but you will need a car to see most of it: Either rent one when you arrive or bring your own. Car ferries from Marseille, Toulon and Nice call at various ports on the island.

AJACCIO

Ajaccio is a scenic port on the west coast of the island, framed by mountains. The streets are great for strolling, with plenty of bars, restaurants and shops, while the pastel shades of the old town are easy on the eye. The main street, cours Napoléon, runs north of place du Général de Gaulle for almost 2km (about a mile) alongside the Golfe d'Ajaccio. Place du Général de Gaulle is the heart of the new town, a large, undistinguished square. In contrast, place Foch, in the middle of the old town, is green with palm trees and lined with shops and cafés.

NAPOLEON

Ajaccio delights in its links with Napoleon (▷ 38–39), who was born here in 1769. Statues, plaques and monuments dedicated to the Bonaparte family can be seen at every turn. South of place Foch, in rue St-Charles, is Maison Bonaparte, the house where Napoleon was born and lived until he was nine (Mon 2–6, Tue-Sat 9–12, 2–6; closed Mon Oct–Mar). On the first floor is the sofa where he was born and at the end of the long gallery is the Trapdoor room, where his mother Letizia and her children escaped from the forces of Pascal Paoli (leader of the island's independence movement) in 1793.

The Musée Napoléonien, in the town hall on place Foch (mid-Jun to mid-Sep daily 9–11.45, 2–5.45; mid-Sep to mid-Jun Mon–Fri 9–11.45, 2–4.45) has a copy of Napoleon's death mask. The Chapelle Impériale, next to the Palais Fesch, contains the bodies of several members of the Bonaparte family. Napoleon himself is buried in Les Invalides in Paris (▷ 84). In June there's a festival dedicated to him.

ART

Joseph Fesch, Cardinal of Lyon and Napoleon's uncle, amassed an extraordinary collection of paintings. See them in the Musée Palais Fesch (Jul–Aug Mon, Wed, Sat 10.30–6, Thu–Fri 12–8.30, Sun 12–6; May–Jun, Sep Mon, Wed, Sat 10.30–6, Thu–Fri, Sun 12–6; Oct–Apr Mon, Wed–Fri, Sat 10–5, Sun 12–5), in rue Cardinal Fesch. Works include *Portrait of a Gloved Man* by Titian, *Leda and the Swan* by Veronese and a *Virgin and Child* by Botticelli.

INFORMATION

www.ajaccio.fr
www.ajaccio-tourisme.com
✚ 457 R15 ℹ 3 boulevard du Roi Jérôme, 20181 ☎ 04 95 51 53 03
🕐 Jul–Aug Mon–Sat 8–8, Sun 9–1, 4–7; Apr–Jun, Sep–Oct Mon–Sat 8–7, Sun 9–1; Nov–Mar Mon–Fri 8–12.30, 2–6, Sat 8–12, 2–5 🚊 Ajaccio

TIPS

» For one of the best sights in Corsica, take a 2-hour boat trip (mid-Apr to Oct) to see the Îles Sanguinaires, deserted islands which turn a deep red as the sun sets.
» Every morning except Monday a farmers' market in square Campinchi sells fresh produce from around the island.
» For a break from sightseeing, shop on rue Cardinal Fesch, then head to boulevard Lantivy and boulevard Pascal Rossini, which are behind the beach, close to the Citadelle. They have magical sea views and are lined with bars and restaurants.

Opposite *Ajaccio at night*
Below *The fishing port, surrounded by pastel-shaded buildings*

INFORMATION
www.bastia-tourisme.com
✚ 457 S14 ℹ rue José Luccioni, 20200
☎ 04 95 54 20 40 🕓 Mon–Sat 8–8,
Sun 8–1, 3–7 🚉 Bastia

TIPS
» There's a flea market every Sunday morning in place St-Nicolas.
» Head south of town for sandy beaches and the bird reserve at l'Étang de Biguglia.

BASTIA

Bastia is at the southern end of Cap Corse (▷ 405), a vast mountainous peninsula in the north of Corsica. The Genoese made it the island's base of government in the 15th century and built the *bastiglia* (fortress) that gave the town its name. They exported wine to Italy from here, bringing prosperity.

THE OLD QUARTER

Bastia is still Corsica's commercial heart, although the original town, the Terra Vecchia, is untouched by modern business. This old quarter exudes charm, with winding streets and beautiful baroque churches.

Place St-Nicolas, an immense square more than 300m (300 yards) long, with a statue of Napoleon, is the perfect point to start your tour of Bastia. Boulevard Paoli and rue César Campinchi run parallel to the square and are great for shopping. The Terra Vecchia, with the best of Bastia's historic sights, lies to the south of place St-Nicolas. Farther south along the quai du Sud is the citadel, Terra Nova.

On rue Napoléon, you'll find the Oratoire de l'Immaculée Conception, with a sumptuous interior of crimson velvet, gilt and glittering chandeliers. In the Terra Nova, by place du Donjon, is the Moorish-looking 14th-century Palais des Gouverneurs, built at the height of Genoese power. This contains the Musée d'Ethnographie Corse, which focuses on the history of Corsica from prehistoric times to the present day.

In the baroque interior of the Oratoire Sainte-Croix, in rue de l'Évêché, is a holy relic, the Christ des Miracles—a crucifix found in 1428 floating in the sea bathed in a mysterious glow.

Above *Bastia's harbour*

BONIFACIO

www.bonifacio.fr

On Corsica's southern tip, Bonifacio offers views of Sardinia over the turquoise water of the Mediterranean.

The town has a citadel, built by the Genoese which is perched on sculpted limestone cliffs 70m (230ft) above the sea. The old town, enclosed within the ramparts, is one of the island's best sites and gets very crowded in the high season. Look for the high houses, once accessible only by retractable ladders, and the flying buttresses used for collecting rainwater.

The steps of Montée Rastello are quite a climb, but worth it for the view from the old town. At the top, cross avenue de Gaulle to Montée St-Roch for the spectacular view of the limestone cliffs and the Grain de Sable, an enormous piece of cliff face that plunged into the sea 800 years ago. In rue du Palais de Garde is the 14th-century church of Sainte-Marie Majeure. This contains a fragment of the True Cross rescued from a shipwreck. The relics of St-Boniface are kept in the church in an ivory casket.

If you want to take to the water, several companies offer boat trips around the coast and to the Lavezzi islands, and the area also has some excellent diving.

Bonifacio is a place of legends, reputedly the setting for Ulysses' encounter with the Lestrygon giants in the *Odyssey*, and home to the 'Staircase of the King of Aragon', supposedly built during the course of one night by Aragonese soldiers in a siege in 1420.

➕ 457 S15 ℹ️ 2 rue Fred Scamaroni, 20169 ☎ 04 95 73 11 88 🕐 Jul–Aug daily 9–8; Sun, Sep daily 9–7; Oct–May Mon–Fri 9–12, 2–6

CALVI

www.tourisme.fr/calvi

Calvi, on the northwest coast of the island, is dominated by a Genoese citadel on a rocky promontory. Inside its walls, the pretty baroque church of St-Jean Baptiste contains the *Christ des Miracles*, an ebony statue said

by locals to have deterred the Turks besieging the town in 1553, when it was carried through the streets. Also inside the citadel is the St-Antoine oratory, which has frescoes from the 15th and 16th centuries.

South of the citadel, in the lower town, is the baroque church of Sainte-Marie-Majeure, with its pink door. Farther south is a beautiful bay, with a sandy beach that is 4km (2.5 miles) long and backed by pines.

There is plenty to do in and around Calvi, including water sports such as sailing and diving, or taking boat trips to the Scandola coast (▷ 407). You can drive or take the train to the seaside resort of l'Île Rousse to the north. This is a pleasant place to spend an afternoon and browse in the excellent covered market in a 19th-century building.

West of Calvi, the Revellata peninsula has a sandy beach and beautifully clear water.

➕ 457 R14 ℹ️ Port de Plaisance, 20260 ☎ 04 95 65 16 67 🕐 Mid-Jun to mid-Sep daily 9–1, 2.30–7; May to mid-Jun, mid-Sep to Oct daily 9–12, 2–6; Nov–Apr Mon–Sat 9–12, 2–6 🚆 Calvi

CAP CORSE

www.visit-corsica.com

This island within an island has mountains, tiny fishing villages, Romanesque churches, vineyards and sandy coves.

Cap Corse is a mountainous peninsula with a central ridge more than 1,000m (3,300ft) high. At Corsica's northeastern extremity, it points like a finger, 40km (25 miles) long and 15km (9 miles) wide, towards Italy's Ligurian coast.

On the Cap's western coast, white villages and Genoese watchtowers cling to the top of rugged cliffs. On the east side, smoothed by the lava from ancient volcanoes, there are sandy coves and little ports.

Cap Corse was once intensively cultivated but is now covered in *maquis*, the scrubland vegetation typical of Corsica. The *capcorsins* (residents of Cap Corse) traditionally ventured farther than people from other parts of the island. They

became skilful sailors and merchants, going to Italian, French and African ports to trade wine, oil, cork and fish.

On the west coast, the ancient settlement of Nonza clings to the cliffs 150m (500ft) above a distinctive black beach and is topped by the remains of a Genoese watchtower. Its fine 16th-century church is dedicated to St. Julie and has an impressive marble altar. On the east coast, Macinaggio has beautiful white beaches, and just north is the Réserve Naturelle des Îles Finocchiarola, a nature reserve of little islands.

Farther south, towards Bastia, is the village of Erbalunga, with its small port. It was once popular with French artists. Many people from Cap Corse who emigrated to South America returned to this area and built spectacular houses with the money that they made there. You can still see some of these *palazzi americani* — Renaissance-style palaces and colonial mansions — in the small villages of Sisco and Cannelle.

➕ 457 S14 ℹ️ Port de Plaisance, 20248 Macinaggio ☎ 04 95 35 40 34 🕐 Mid-Jun to mid-Sep daily 9–12, 3–7.30; mid-Sep to mid-Jun Mon–Fri 9–12, 2–5

Below *Cap Corse*

CORTE

www.centru-corsica.com

Corte is surrounded by the mountain peaks of the Parc Naturel Régional de Corse and is home to the island's only university, with around 4,000 students. The town is built on a rocky outcrop, and, like many other Corsican towns, has a 15th-century citadel, which stands high above. Inside the citadel is the Musée de la Corse, which focuses on Corsican society and culture.

For spectacular panoramic views of the Restonica and Tavignano valleys, climb up to the Belvédère viewing platform.

This region is excellent for walking and Corte is a popular stop-off with walkers. To get to the Niolo region—a plateau surrounded by the island's highest peaks—take the Scala di Santa Regina, a stunning mountain pass northwest of town.

✚ 457 S15 ℹ️ La Citadelle, 20250 Corte ☎ 04 95 46 26 70 🕐 Jul–Aug daily 9–8; Jun, Sep Mon–Sat 9–6; Oct–May Mon–Fri 9–12, 2–6 🚉 Corte

FILITOSA

www.filitosa.fr

Filitosa, an easy day trip from Propriano, is a prehistoric site inhabited from the neolithic period to Roman times. Finds reveal that people lived in the caves here as early as 5,000 years ago.

The most impressive items on the site are the megalithic standing stones (or menhirs) with their carved faces. It is not known why they were placed here.

There is also a small museum, and the location in the Tavaro Valley makes this an ideal spot for a picnic.

✚ 457 S16 ℹ️ On the D57 north of Propriano ☎ 04 95 74 00 91 🕐 Easter–end Oct 8–dusk 🎫 Adult €5

LA PORTA

This small village is notable for some fine Corsican baroque religious architecture and is set among chestnut groves and rolling hills in the heart of the Castagniccia area, nearly 40km (25 miles) northeast of Corte. The region is named after the Corsican word for chestnut, *castagnu*. The nuts that were harvested here formed part of the staple diet of many Corsicans.

In previous centuries, La Porta saw battles against the Romans, the Vandals, the Arabs, the Genoese and the French. Today it is a peaceful village of narrow streets, with tall buildings with painted shutters.

La Porta is a good place for walks, as many paths lead from here into the hills and mountains of La Castagniccia.

In Piazza di un Piano locals sit on the benches chatting and watching visitors who come to see the Église St-Jean-Baptiste, an ochre-and-white 17th-century church. Its facade is ornately decorated with pinnacles and scrolls, and its 18th-century campanile is thought to be the finest baroque bell tower on the island. Inside, the church has a magnificent Italian organ, built by a monk in 1780, a fine painted ceiling and a 17th-century figure of Christ painted on wood.

✚ 457 S14

PORTO

www.porto-tourisme.com

The Gulf of Porto, on Corsica's west coast, is a UNESCO World Heritage Site, while the town of Porto is a popular seaside resort, especially busy in summer. The focal point is the Genoese tower (Jun–Aug 9–9; Apr–May, Sep–Oct daily 11–7), which stands at the front of the port and which is a perfect viewing point for the beautiful sunsets for which the town is famous. Built in the second half of the 16th century, it is unusual in being square rather than circular, like most of the other Genoese towers on the island. Inside, there is a museum with an exhibition about the towers.

In the summer, you can take a boat trip to see the flora and fauna in the nearby Réserve Naturelle de Scandola (▷ 407), or to *les calanches de Piana*, rocky inlets with sides hundreds of metres high.

The aquarium at the marina (Jun–Aug daily 9–8; Sep 9–7; Oct–May 9–5) is in a former Genoese warehouse and has species from the Gulf and in the Scandola nature reserve. Expect to find grouper, moray eels and octopus. For those who prefer their marine life in the sea, experience the superb diving in the Golfe de Porto, where coral, tuna, lobster and even barracuda are among the species you may see.

✚ 457 R15 ℹ️ place de la Marine, 20150 ☎ 04 95 26 10 55 🕐 Jun–Sep Mon–Sat 9–7, Sun 9–1; May Mon–Sat 9–5; Oct–Apr Mon–Fri 9–5

Below left *Corte clings to the hillsides*
Below right *Porto's sheltered sandy beach*

Above left *Sartène, in the southwest of Corsica, is proud of its long history*
Above right *The beautiful Réserve Naturelle de Scandola*

RÉSERVE NATURELLE DE SCANDOLA

This nature reserve was created in 1975 and is part of the Parc Naturel Régional de Corse. The site covers 1,900ha (4,700 acres), of which 900ha (2,200 acres) are land and 1,000ha (2,500 acres) are sea. The whole area is a UNESCO World Heritage Site. There are no paths to the reserve, so the only way to get there is by boat—companies in Calvi, Porto, Cargèse and Ajaccio run boat tours.

The reserve is popular with scientists and visitors because of the varying geology, flora and fauna, and there are even some Roman remains. There are jagged and sheer cliffs (some of the distinctive red cliffs are up to 900m/3,000ft high), with caves and grottoes and stacks left by wave erosion.

Animal spotters and birders will have a great time, as the reserve is home to peregrine falcon, osprey, puffins, bearded vultures, Audouin gulls and dolphins. With such a rich variety of wildlife and marine life, activities such as fishing, diving and camping are prohibited.

Nearby Girolata (not part of the reserve although part of the UNESCO site) can be reached only by foot or boat as there is no access road..

✚ 457 R15

ST-FLORENT

www.visit-corsica.com

St-Florent, a pretty port in the Nebbio region in the northeast of the island, is a popular holiday spot because of its beaches and Moorish-style Genoese citadel, which overlooks the harbour. At its heart is place des Portes, a good place to sit with a drink and watch the local action. The main sight here is the 12th-century Pisan Cathédrale de Nebbio, to the east, on the site of the old Roman city. St-Florent's main beach, Plage de la Roya, is to the south of the town.

For the energetic, a path goes west along the Agriates coast, past the beautiful beaches of Lodo and Saleccia and the protected Désert des Agriates. For those who prefer to take things easy, boats leave for the beaches from the marina.

Patrimonio, some 6km (4 miles) northeast of St-Florent, produces red, white, rosé and dessert wines. The area has long been recognized as a producer of some of the best wines in Corsica. Patrimonio exported wine to Italy during the Middle Ages, and it is recorded that Cap Corse muscat was drunk at papal tables during the Renaissance.

✚ 457 S14 ℹ️ Centre Administratif, 20217 ☎ 04 95 37 06 04 🕐 Summer only Mon–Fri 9–12, 2–5, Sat 9–12

SARTÈNE

www.visit-corsica.com

Sartène, in the southwest of the island, is proud of its traditions, dating back to the Middle Ages. On Good Friday, the Catenacciu procession takes place, during which a penitential citizen wearing a red hooded robe, with his feet wrapped in chains, carries a heavy cross through the town.

The rest of the year, the cross and chains can be seen in the Église Sainte-Marie in the old town, a maze of very narrow streets. The Santa Anna quarter, with its cobbled streets, is worth exploring. The Musée Départemental de la Préhistoire Corse, in a former prison, displays items from prehistoric sites in Corsica (closed for renovations).

There are interesting prehistoric sites with menhirs (standing stones) to the south of Sartène, reached via quiet roads that take you into the countryside. Once you have parked your car, there is usually a walk to the stones.

About 15km (9 miles) south are the menhirs at Cauria and the Fontanaccia dolmen. Off the D48 are the Palaggio menhirs, one of the best collections of megalithic standing stones in the Mediterranean.

✚ 457 S16 ℹ️ cours Soeur Amélie, 20100 ☎ 04 95 77 15 40 🕐 Jul–Aug Mon–Sat 9–12.30, 3–7; Sep–Jun Mon–Fri 9–12, 2–6

BONIFACIO

Bonifacio (▷ 405), poised above the Mediterranean on white limestone cliffs, is the best-sheltered port in Corsica. Its imposing citadel and fortified old town tower above the active port. Lying in a vast, bare region, Bonifacio is distinct from the rest of Corsica in its customs and its geography. The town has given its name to the narrow, treacherous straits that separate Corsica from Sardinia and controls many of the strategic routes in the western Mediterranean. This one-day walk is in two parts; it starts with a stroll around the town followed by a ramble along the coast, taking in churches, beaches, a lighthouse and impressive views of the citadel and even Sardinia.

THE WALK
Distance: 10km (6 miles)
Allow: 1 day
Start/end at: Bonifacio

HOW TO GET THERE
Bonifacio, in the south of Corsica, is served by Figari-Sud Corse airport, 20km (12 miles) to the north. The main coastal roads, the N196 and N198, both finish in the town. In high summer the lack of parking is apparent and traffic jams do occur.

THE TOWN WALK
Bonifacio (▷ 405) was founded by the Tuscans but was seized by Genoa in the 12th century. The indigenous population was expelled and replaced by colonists, who built a new town to a geometric plan.

The massive citadel, occupying the western end of the promontory, is set back from the cliffs, but the old town sits precariously on the precipice. Enclosed within the ramparts, the old town has narrow, shady streets with high houses, built as individual fortresses and once accessible only by retractable ladders. Each house had its own courtyard, oven, cistern, olive press, cellar, granary and sometimes a stable. The flying buttresses over the streets are gutters for collecting precious rainwater.

★ Park near the port and walk to Église St-Érasme.

❶ Take the paved ramp to the left of the church up to the Col St-Roch. Continue up a second paved ramp towards the Porte de Gênes and pass through the gate into place d'Armes. From place d'Armes, enter rue des Deux-Empereurs.

❷ Habsburg Emperor Charles V (1500–58), who was also Charles I of Spain, had a lifelong struggle against France. He passed through Bonifacio in 1541, and a plaque in rue des

Above *Bonifacio's citadel and harbour*

Deux-Empereurs commemorates his visit. It also celebrates the fact that Napoleon Bonaparte, Corsica's most famous son and the Emperor of France, stayed in a house in the street for a few weeks in 1793.

❸ Take the third street on the left, to visit the 13th-century Église Sainte-Marie-Majeure.

Then take rue Archivolto to the Maison du Podestat, also 13th century. Continue to place Montepagano and pass beyond the citadel walls onto the peninsula, by way of rue St-Dominique and the 13th-century Oratoire Sainte-Croix and the Gothic Église St-Dominique. At the far west end of the peninsula, next to a desolate area known as the Bosco, is the marine cemetery.

❹ This is a spectacular place with its white mausolea, each topped by a crucifix, leaning together like little houses by the sea. The town-like atmosphere is heightened by an orderly grid of streets which takes you from one end to the other. From here you can look over the Mediterranean to Sardinia.

Return to the citadel, passing Église St-Dominique on your right, to visit the limestone steps of the Escalier du Roi d'Aragon, via place Carrega.

❺ The 187 steps of the Escalier du Roi d'Aragon, hewn from the limestone cliff, lead down to the sea. Although the stairway was no doubt an escape route if the port was blocked, legend says that it was cut overnight by Aragonese invaders trying to capture the city in 1420.

❻ Return to place Montepagano by rue des Pachas and take rue Doria to place Manichella and place du Marché, 65m (215ft) above the sea, with a breathtaking vista. Take ruelle de la Madonnetta to place d'Armes, then return to the port.

THE COAST WALK

★ From the port, leave the town and head north along the N196 towards the Site Préhistorique de l'Araguina. Before the campsite, after the garage, turn left and take the hidden path towards plage de l'Arinella. Continue for about 750m (820 yards) towards a small bay with a beach (Plage de la Catena) opposite the citadel of

Bonifacio. Just above the beach, the path forks. Take the path on the right that leads away from the sea. Continue westwards for about 1.6km (1 mile). The path makes a sharp turn to the left and heads towards the Anse de Fazzio. (The other path continues to Plage Paraguano.)

❶ About 200m (220 yards) farther on, the path reaches Plage de Fazzio, opposite a small island.

The path continues around the eastern side of the bay.

❷ Follow the coast road to the lighthouse, Phare de la Madonetta.

❸ At the Grotte Marine du Sdragonato sea cave, the path leaves the shoreline for about 100m (109 yards), then rejoins it in a bay.

Follow the marked path around the two small bays approached earlier (Plage de l'Arinella and Plage de la Catena) back to the port.

Above *Bonifacio is perched on cliffs*

AJACCIO
U TRINIGHELLU
The direct translation of the name of this railway is 'the trembler' because the old carriages (cars) are slow and creaky, but U Trinighellu is one of the most scenic rail journeys in Europe. The routes travel through the heart of the island, passing mountains, gorges and forests.

✉ Gare (Train Station), 20090 Ajaccio ☎ 04 95 23 11 03 🕙 Schedules: 3 or 4 trains daily linking Ajaccio with Corte, Bastia and Calvi

BONIFACIO
BONIFACIO WINDSURF
www.bonifacio-windsurf.com
This school offers courses in windsurfing and kite surfing, ranging from introductory to advanced. You can also rent equipment by the hour, the day or longer.

✉ Hameau de Pianterella, 20169 Bonifacio ☎ 04 94 73 52 04 🕙 May–Sep daily 9–8 🖐 Instruction for beginners €140, Level 3 €150, 1-week's instruction and board rental €290, board rental €25 per hour

CALVI
PLONGÉE CASTILLE
www.plongeecastille.com
This diving school offers introductory sessions and a range of courses leading to initial or higher level qualifications. For qualified divers the school organizes guided dives.

✉ Port de Calvi, 20260 Calvi ☎ 04 95 65

14 05 🕙 Office: May–Sep 9–12.30, 3.30–7 🖐 Introduction to diving €50, PADI course €380

GHISONACCIA
CAVE ST-ANTOINE
www.cavesaintantoine.com
The vineyard produces a range of labels mixing local grape varieties with the varieties used in mainland wines. You can enjoy a tasting and, if you're impressed, buy.

✉ 20240 Ghisonaccia ☎ 04 95 56 61 00 🕙 Mon–Fri 8–12, 2–5

PORTICCIO
INSTITUTE OF THALASSOTHERAPY
www.sofitel.com
The most prestigious spa on the island has a range of treatments including massage, hydrotherapy, aromatherapy, algae baths and facials. Packages are available that include a room at the hotel.

✉ Hôtel Sofitel, Domaine de la Pointe, Golfe d'Ajaccio, 20166 Porticcio ☎ 04 95 29 40 40 🕙 Daily 8am–10pm

PORTO-VECCHIO
CASA DI L'ARTE
You'll find an excellent range of local art and ceramics here. The shop specializes in Terraghia pottery, paintings and wooden objects.

✉ 10 rue Jean Jaurès, 20137 Porto-Vecchio ☎ 04 95 70 12 58 🕙 Mon–Sat 9.30–12.30 3–7 (also summer Sun 10–12.30, 3–5)

CORSICA MOUNTAIN QUAD
Enjoy the countryside quad-bike-riding on day-long exploration routes with a guide, or simply book half an hour of fun.

✉ L'Ospedale–direction Zonza, 20137 Porto-Vecchio ☎ 04 95 70 68 08 🕙 Daily 10–6 by appointment only. Reserve in advance 🖐 €55 for 1.5 hours, €65 for 2 hours, €85 for 3 hours

PONTE LECCIA
LANA CORSA
www.lana-corsa.com
This small cooperative takes the raw wool of native Corsican sheep and creates unique garments. Only natural products and dyes are used in the process.

✉ U Salgetu, 20218 ☎ 04 95 48 43 79 🕙 Apr–Oct Mon–Sat 9–7; Nov–Mar Mon–Fri 9–6, Sat 9–2

ST-FLORENT
ALTORE
www.altore.com
This organization offers training and guides for a range of extreme sports and activities including paragliding, mountaineering, skiing and trekking, with a multilingual qualified team of guides and instructors.

✉ 20214 St-Florent ☎ 06 88 21 49 16 🕙 Mid-May to mid-Oct

Above *Corsica is good for outdoor activities*
Opposite *Fish is on every menu*

PRICES AND SYMBOLS

The restaurants are listed alphabetically (excluding Le, La and Les). The prices given are the average for a two-course lunch (L) and a three-course dinner (D) for one person, without drinks. The wine price is for the least expensive bottle.

For a key to the symbols, ▷ 2.

AJACCIO
PALM BEACH

The best tables here are at the water's edge, taking in the majestic vista. Chef Simon Andrews enhances nature's bounty with a seasonal menu using the finest French ingredients including Charolais beef and veal raised on milk.

➕ route des Iles Sanguinaires, 20000 Ajaccio ☎ 04 95 52 01 03 ⊙ Tue–Sat 12–1.30, 7.30–9.30, Sun 12–1.30. Closed Nov to mid-Feb ✋ L €60, D €89, Wine €25

BASTIA
LE PRESSOIR

www.restaurantlepressoir.com

This rustic-style restaurant on two levels and with stone walls is near the town centre and faces Toga port. It serves Italian cuisine, including cannelloni, ravioli and excellent pizzas cooked over a wooden fire. Try, for instance, the *calzone du pizzaiolo* (pizza chef's calzone) or, to finish, *tiramisù banane chocolat* (banana and chocolate tiramisu). For an alternative, there are roasted meats from the rôtisserie.

✉ Sortie Port de Commerce, Toga, 20200 Bastia ☎ 04 95 32 34 96 ⊙ Mon–Sat 12–2, 7.30–10 ✋ L €30, D €40, Wine €14

BONIFACIO
U CAPU BIANCU

www.ucapubiancu.com

In this hotel and restaurant with lovely views over the bay, the Senegalese chef, El Hadji Gadio, playfully mixes elements of Corsican cuisine with African influences. For dessert try the symphony of strawberries. The main restaurant is open only in the evenings—for lunch there is a more informal beach restaurant—and you are recommended to reserve 24 hours in advance. Children are not welcome.

✉ Route Canetto, 20169 Bonifacio ☎ 04 95 73 05 58 ⊙ Daily 7.30–10.30 ✋ D €160, including wine

CALVI
LE BELGODERE

www.lebelgodere.com

Enjoy good views at this beach restaurant specializing in fish. There are also 13 different salads, as well as crêpes, panini and sandwiches. On some summer evenings in summer the restaurant organizes dinner-dances with African or Latino bands.

✉ La Plage, 20260 Calvi ☎ 04 95 65 08 56 ⊙ All day, but meal service 8.30–10.30, 12–2, 7.30–10 ✋ L €25, D €30, Wine €15

LA SIGNORIA

www.hotel-la-signoria.com

If you want somewhere exclusive to try Corsican cuisine, try this elegant restaurant in an 18th-century house (part of a 4-star luxe hotel), standing in its own large park of pine trees, palm trees and vines, and with a view of the Cirque de Bonifato.

✉ route de la Forêt de Bonifato, 20260 Calvi ☎ 04 95 65 93 00 ⊙ Daily 12–2, 7.30–10.30 ✋ L €70, D €100, Wine €35

CENTURI
LE VIEUX MOULIN

www.le-vieux-moulin.net

This restaurant is *the* place to sample locally caught seafood. There's a large terrace with lovely views out into the little fishing boats moored in the rocky bay.

✉ Le Port, 20238 Centuri ☎ 04 95 35 60 15 ⊙ Mar–Oct daily 12–2.30, 7.30–9.30 ✋ L €40, D €60, Wine €20

CORTE
AUBERGE DE LA RESTONICA

www.aubergerestonica.com

Traditional Corsican cuisine is on the menu at this restaurant. From June to September you can also enjoy pizzas and a range of snacks at lunchtime.

✉ route de Restonica, 20250 Corte
☎ 04 95 46 09 58 🕐 Jul–Aug daily
12–2.30, 7.30–9.30; Sep–Jun Tue–Fri
12–2.30, 7.30–9.30, Sat 7.30–9.30
✋ L €35, D €45, Wine €15

CUTTOLI
AUBERGE U LICETTU
www.u-licettu.com
Home-produced ingredients are
the forte of this delightful rustic
restaurant only 15 minutes from
Campo dell'Oro airport. Vegetables
come from the garden and the
cheeses, terrines and *charcuteries* are
all prepared here.
✉ Plaine de Cuttoli, 20167 Cuttoli
☎ 04 95 25 61 57 🕐 Tue–Sat 12–2,
7.30–10, Sun 12–2; reservations essential
✋ L €40, D €40, including wine

L'ÎLE ROUSSE
L'ÎLE D'OR
In the Hôtel Agilla (▷ 414), in the
town centre close to the church, this
restaurant is a friendly, family place
with a large selection of dishes and
an attentive service. It specializes in
local cuisine and, above all, fish.
✉ rue d'Agilla, 20220 L'Île Rousse
☎ 04 95 60 12 05 🕐 Daily 12–2, 7.30–10
✋ L €28, D €38, Wine €13

MONTICELLO
A PASTURELLA
www.a-pasturella.com
Local dishes are combined with
French classics here. The short
menu changes seasonally, taking
into account what's market fresh. In
season the sea urchins are delicious.
✉ 20220 Monticello ☎ 04 95 60 05 65
🕐 Mon–Sat 12–1.30, 7.30–9.30, Sun
11–1.30 ✋ L €26, D €35, Wine €17

PORTICCIO
LE PIANO – RESTAURANT
CHEZ TOINOU
www.restaurant-piano.com
Chef and host Zizou has been in
business for more than 20 years. He
mixes local seafood with ingredients
from the Corsican heartland in dishes
that are definitely classical French.
✉ Les Candilelli, 20166 Porticcio ☎ 06 78
92 66 81 🕐 Mon–Tue 7.30–9.30, Wed–Sun
12–2, 7.30–9.30 ✋ L €35, D €55, Wine €14

PORTO-VECCHIO
LE BELVÉDÈRE
www.hbcorsica.com
With its calm atmosphere, rustic
decoration and lovely terrace looking
out to sea, this is a good place to
explore Corsican culinary traditions
and those of the Mediterranean in
general. In summer there is a grill
where you can eat fish, vegetables
and seafood *a la brasa* (grilled).
✉ route de Palombaggia, 20137 Porto-
Vecchio ☎ 04 95 70 54 13 🕐 Daily 12–2,
7.30–10 ✋ L €85, D €105, Wine €25

CASA DEL MAR
www.casadelmar.fr
Dress smartly to dine in this luxury
restaurant where Italian chef
Davide Bisetto serves up a gourmet
cuisine inspired by Mediterranean
traditions. Try the *foie gras de canard
a la chataigne* (terrine of duck with
chestnuts), the langoustines or the
lobster.
✉ route de Palombaggia, 20538 Porto-
Vecchio ☎ 04 95 72 34 34 🕐 Daily
8pm–1.30am ✋ D €150, Wine €30

ST-FLORENT
LA RASCASSE
With an emphasis on locally caught
fish and seafood, this gourmet
restaurant specializes in creative

contemporary cuisine. It has a
panoramic terrace where film stars
come to eat. Chef Jean-Michel
Querci's lobsters are among the
specialities as are the *ravioles de
moules* (ravioli with mussels), *soupe
de poissons émulsion safran* (fish
soup with saffron), the foie gras
carpaccio and, for dessert, the
whisky baba.
✉ quai d'Honneur, Port de Plaisance,
20217 St-Florent ☎ 04 95 37 06 99
🕐 Daily 12–3, 7–12. Closed Oct and Mon
Nov–Mar ✋ L €45, D €60, Wine €19

SAN NICOLAU
U CATAGNU
This restaurant on Corsica's Costa
Verde has a pleasant terrace and
specializes in inventive Mediterranean
cuisine incorporating influences
from world cuisine including Asiatic
touches. It is particularly good at
grilled fish and meat. Two dishes
to try are the *gratin de fuits de mer*
(seafood gratin) and the *millefeuilles
de fraises* (strawberry pastry). The bar
has a good selection of cocktails.
✉ Moriani Plage, 20230 San Nicolau
☎ 04 95 38 52 24 🕐 Daily 12–2, 7.30–10
✋ L €25, D €35, Wine €16

Below *On this Mediterranean island, seafood
and fish are always fresh and popular*

PRICES AND SYMBOLS

The prices are the lowest and highest for a double room for one night including breakfast, unless otherwise stated. All hotels listed accept credit cards unless otherwise stated. Note that rates can vary widely throughout the year.

For a key to the symbols, ▷ 2.

AJACCIO
CAMPO DEL L'ORO

www.hotel-campodelloro.com
This modern complex, including a restaurant and a bar, has views over the Gulf of Ajaccio. Rooms are comfortably furnished with a minimalist feel reflecting a recent renovation. Its grounds are planted with palm trees and bougainvillea.
✉ plage du Ricanto, 20189 Ajaccio
☎ 04 95 22 32 41 🖐 €101–€210 🛈 138
🏊 Outdoor

BARBAGGIO
U CASTELLU PIATTU

www.chez.com/castellupiattu
The rooms at this Modernist stone bed-and-breakfast all have a bathroom and independent access.

Above *Popular places to stay in Corsica are family-run inns, specialist holiday villages and gîtes*

There is also a restaurant. The expansive pool and terrace offer panoramic views.
✉ Pezzo Brietta, 20253 Barbaggio
☎ 04 95 37 28 64 or 06 24 33 18 32
🖐 €80–€96 🛈 5 🏊 Outdoor

BASTIA
BONAPARTE

www.hotel-bonaparte-bastia.com
A small hotel in the town centre, in close proximity to the main tourist sights, the Bonaparte is decorated in a cheerful and rather eclectic mixture of styles. Secure private parking is available for guests for an additional charge.
✉ 45 boulevard Général Graziani ☎ 04 95 34 07 10 🖐 €85–€95, excluding breakfast (€7) 🛈 23

BONIFACIO
U CAPU BIANCU

www.ucapubiancu.com
A luxury hotel situated in the south of the island, this place has magnificent views. The hotel has its own private beach and a gourmet restaurant. There is an outdoor pool. Bonifacio's medieval citadel is only 10 minutes' away.
✉ Domaine de Pozzoniello, 20169 Bonifacio
☎ 04 95 73 05 58 🖐 €247–€642, excluding breakfast (€22) 🛈 43 🏊 Outdoor

CALENZANA
LA MAISON D'HÔTES

In this bed-and-breakfast, rooms all have a bathroom. *Table d'hôte* is available if you reserve.
✉ Route de Calvi, 20214 Calenzana
☎ 04 95 60 15 53 or 06 86 44 88 34
🖐 €65–€95 🛈 4 🏊 Outdoor

CALVI
HÔTEL LA VILLA

www.hotel-lavilla.com
The rooms at this luxury hotel are in four traditional stone residences. The hotel has several swimming pools and a gastronomic restaurant.
✉ chemin Notre-Dame-de-la-Serra, 20260 Calvi ☎ 04 95 65 10 10 🖐 €200–€596, excluding breakfast (€30) 🛈 52 🏊 Outdoor

SAINT-CHRISTOPHE

www.saintchristophecalvi.com
Within easy reach of the centre of Calvi, the beach and the marina, Saint-Christophe has a restaurant with sea views. Parking and a motorbike garage are available.
✉ place Bel'Ombra, 20260 Calvi ☎ 04 95 65 05 74 🖐 €97–€147 🛈 48 🎱 🏊

LA SIGNORIA

www.hotel-la-signoria.com
A luxury Corsican *domaine* among vines and pine trees is decorated

with great style and elegance. It has beautiful gardens and a private beach.
✉ route de la Fôret de Bonifato, 20260 Calvi ☎ 04 95 65 93 00 ✋ €310–€650, excluding breakfast (€30) 🚪 24 ⛱ Outdoor

ERBALUNGA
HÔTEL CASTEL BRANDO
www.castelbrando.com
At this family-owned 3-star hotel the rooms are comfortable, although they vary in size. The main building was a family home when built in the middle of the 19th century. There's a spacious pool and terrace and some good leisure facilities on site.
✉ 20222 Erbalunga ☎ 04 95 30 10 30 ✋ €105–€225, excluding breakfast (€13) 🚪 27 🛎 ⛱ Outdoor 🛥

L'ÎLE ROUSSE
AGILLA
www.hotel-agilla.com
In the pedestrian area of L'Île Rousse old town, not far from the beach, this small hotel offers simple and comfortable accommodation. For those on a tight budget this is one of the best value places to stay on the island.
✉ rue d'Agilla, 20220 L'Île Rousse ☎ 04 95 60 12 05 ✋ €35–€70, no breakfast 🚪 6 🛎

LUCCIANA
LA MADRAGUE
www.hotel-lamadrague.com
This modern two-storey hotel with a nice garden, bright bedrooms and a relaxing swimming pool is on the northeast coast of the island, conveniently located five minutes' from Bastia airport,
✉ Route de Pineto, 20290 Lucciana ☎ 04 95 30 02 50 ✋ €75–€182, excluding breakfast (€9–€10; mid-Jul to mid-Aug breakfast is included in room price) 🚪 32 ⛱ Outdoor

MONTICELLO
A PASTURELLA
www.a-pasturella.com
This hotel-cum-restaurant is in a little village set back from Île Rousse bay, 4km (2.5 miles) from the sea. The sober but tasteful bedrooms have views of the countryside.

✉ 20220 Monticello ☎ 04 95 60 05 65 ✋ €75–€102, excluding breakfast (€11) 🚪 14

MURO
CASA DE THEODORA
www.a-casatheodora.com
This 16th-century palazzo has been tastefully restored while retaining lots of period character, including majestic frescoes in the public rooms and some of the bedrooms. The hotel has a luxury feel but rooms do vary in size. There's a pretty courtyard garden and an indoor pool.
✉ piazza u Duttora, 20225 Muro ☎ 04 95 61 78 32 🕐 Closed Dec–Mar ✋ €140–340, excluding breakfast (€8) 🚪 5 🛎 ⛱ Indoor

PIANA
LES ROCHES ROUGES
www.lesrochesrouges.com
The restaurant of this charming 1912 hotel is listed as a historic monument. It has a large terrace and marvellous views of the Gulf of Porto.
✉ 20115 Piana ☎ 04 95 27 81 81 ✋ €114–€129, excluding breakfast (€12) 🚪 30

PORTO
HÔTEL LE LONCA
www.hotel-lelonca.com
This is an air-conditioned hotel within walking distance of the beach. It offers single, double, triple and quadruple rooms and has a car park. The decor is a little dated but is clean and offers good value for money.
✉ Vaita, 20150 Porto ☎ 04 95 26 16 44 ✋ €65–€120, excluding breakfast (€8) 🚪 28 🛎

PORTO-VECCHIO
BELVÉDÈRE
www.hbcorsica.com
Some of the spacious bedrooms are on the ground floor with access directly into the garden at this luxury hotel. There is a gourmet restaurant on the beach, with a backdrop of pine, eucalyptus and palm trees.
✉ route de Palombaggia, 20137 Porto-Vecchio ☎ 04 95 70 54 13 🕐 Mar–Dec ✋ €100–€420, excluding breakfast (€20) 🚪 15 ⛱ Outdoor

GRAND HÔTEL CALA ROSSA
www.cala-rossa.com
Grand 4-star property with a spa plus a private beach. The whitewashed walls accented with stone, wood and colourful artworks reflect the warmth and energy of the Mediterranean region.
✉ 20137 Porto-Vecchio ☎ 04 95 71 61 51 ✋ €340–€1,165 🚪 42 🛎 ⛱ Outdoor and indoor

QUENZA
SOLE ET MONTI
A small, modern but warm mountain hotel with a pleasant terrace and gardens lies at the foot of the Fourches de Bavella in the central-south part of the island. Its restaurant is highly rated.
✉ 20122 Quenza ☎ 04 95 78 62 53 🕐 May–Sep ✋ €80–€190 excluding breakfast (€10) 🚪 20

ST-FLORENT
HÔTEL DE LA ROYA
www.hoteldelaroya.com
This small hotel, situated on the beach, is of modern design and has a swimming pool. There's a garden, and it's close to the beach.
✉ plage de la Roya, 20217 St-Florent ☎ 04 95 37 00 40 ✋ €140–€270 🚪 30 (suites and villas) ⛱ Outdoor

SARTENE
LILIUM MARIS
www.lilium-maris.com
Although belonging to Sartene, Tizzano beach is 15km (9 miles) from town in an untrampled part of the southwest coast. The hotel is modern but tastefully decorated.
✉ Plage de Tizzano, 20100 Sartene ☎ 04 95 77 12 20 ✋ €75–€165, excluding breakfast (€9) 🚪 29

SUARTONE
LA RONDINARA
www.rondinara.fr
A campsite on the N198 that is close to a beach with water sports.
✉ 20169 Suartone ☎ 04 95 70 43 15 🕐 Closed Oct to mid-May ✋ Adult Jul–Aug €7.60, rest of opening time €5.90; caravan Jul–Aug €4.70, €3.70 rest of opening time; electricity €3.60 ⛱ Outdoor

PRACTICALITIES

Practicalities gives you all the important practical information you will need during your visit, from money matters to emergency phone numbers.

PRACTICALITIES FRANCE

WEATHER
CLIMATE

» Paris has cool winters and warm summers. The longest days are in June, when you're likely to find comfortable temperatures and the most sunshine. August can be hot, muggy and stormy.

» The northwest, affected by the Atlantic, is often rainy, with mild winters and cool summers.

» The southwest has hot summers.

» In the mountains, altitude is the main factor which affects the weather. The Vosges are hot in summer, the Massif Central is stormy and the southern Massif is dry. In contrast, the Cévennes get a lot of rain and the northern Massif can become very hot.

» The south of France has hot, dry summers and warm, wet winters. Summer winds are cooling but the colder and fiercer Mistral, from the north, can swirl around for days, particularly in March and April.

» For weather information, look up www.meteofrance.com.

WHEN TO GO

» Spring is a good time to visit Paris, with blossom on the trees and the weather warming up. August is quiet, as many Parisians flee to other parts of France to escape the muggy heat. Some restaurants close for the whole month and there are fewer cultural activities. Autumn can be pleasant but hotel rooms may be hard to find as the trade-fair season is in full swing. If you don't mind cooler winter weather, December can be magical, with the streets sparkling with Christmas lights.

» For other parts of France, what you plan to do when you're there will determine the best time to go. January, February and March are the months to go skiing in the Alps; sun-lovers should head to the Mediterranean in July and August; Strasbourg's huge Christmas market is popular; car fanatics go to Le Mans in June for the 24-hour endurance race.

» Tourist office websites (▷ 430) list festivals and activities.

PARIS
TEMPERATURE

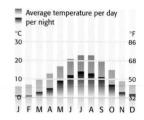

RAINFALL

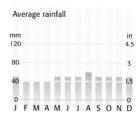

BORDEAUX
TEMPERATURE

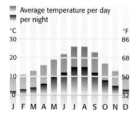

RAINFALL

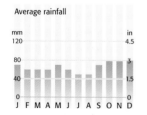

LYON
TEMPERATURE

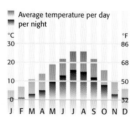

RAINFALL

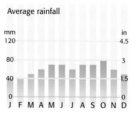

MARSEILLE
TEMPERATURE

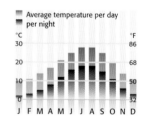

RAINFALL

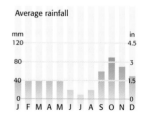

TIME ZONES

City	Time difference	Time at 12 noon
French time		
Amsterdam	0	12 noon
Berlin	0	12 noon
Brussels	0	12 noon
Chicago	-7	5am
Dublin	-1	11am
Johannesburg	+1*	1pm
London	-1	11am
Madrid	0	12 noon
Montréal	-6	6am
New York	-6	6am
Perth, Australia	+7*	7pm
Rome	0	12 noon
San Francisco	-9	3am
Sydney	+9*	9pm
Tokyo	+8*	8pm

Clocks in France go forward one hour on the last Sunday in March, until the last Sunday in October.

* One hour less during Summer Time.

CUSTOMS

From another EU country

Below are the guidelines for the quantity of goods you can bring to France from another EU country, for personal use:

» 800 cigarettes

» 400 cigarillos

» 200 cigars

» 1 kg of smoking tobacco

» 110 litres of beer

» 10 litres of spirits

» 90 litres of wine (of which only 60 litres can be sparkling wine)

» 20 litres of fortified wine (such as port or sherry)

From a country outside the EU

You are entitled to the allowances shown below only if you travel with the goods and do not plan to sell them.

» 200 cigarettes or
100 cigarillos or
50 cigars or
250gms of tobacco

» 60cc/ml of perfume

» 250cc/ml of eau de toilette

» Cash worth the equivalent of €10,000 must be declared on entry to the country

» 4 litres of still table wine

» 1 litre of spirits or strong liqueurs over 22% volume;

» or 2 litres of fortified wine, sparkling wine or other liqueurs

» Arriving by means other than maritime transport €430, by maritime transport €300 of all other goods

» 16 litres of beer

» Many monuments and museums in France close on 1 January, 1 May, 1 November, 11 November and 25 December.

» Bus and train services are reduced on all national holidays (▷ 429).

DOCUMENTS

PASSPORTS AND VISAS

» Entry requirements differ depending on your nationality and also may be subject to change without notice.

» Prior to your visit, check with the French tourist office (www.franceguide.com) or the French Embassy (www.ambafrance-uk.org or www.consulfrance-newyork.org).

» UK, US and Canadian visitors are required to have a valid passport, but not a visa, for stays of up to three months. You should have at least six months' validity remaining on your passport. Citizens of some EU countries that have National Identity cards need either a passport or National Identity card.

» Before you travel, check visa and passport regulations since these are subject to change.

» Take a photocopy of the information pages of your passport and keep a separate note of your passport number in case of loss or theft.

LONGER STAYS

» US and Canadian visitors need a *Carte de séjour* and a visa. For information call the Immigration Department of the French Consulate (▷ below).

TRAVEL INSURANCE

» Make sure you have full health and travel insurance before you set off.

» EU nationals receive reduced-cost health treatment if they present their European Health Insurance Card (EHIC; ▷ 420), but full health and travel insurance is still advisable. For other visitors, full health insurance is essential. Before heading to France, check that your insurer has a 24-hour helpline.

FRENCH EMBASSIES AND CONSULATES ABROAD

COUNTRY	ADDRESS	WEBSITE
Australia	6 Perth Avenue, Yarralumla, ACT 2600 Tel (02) 6216 0127	www.ambafrance-au.org
Canada	1501 McGill College, Bureau 1000, Montreal, Quebec H3A 3M8 Tel 514 878-4385	www.consulfrance-montreal.org
Ireland	36 Ailesbury Road, Ballsbridge, Dublin 4. Tel 1 277 5000	www.ambafrance.ie
New Zealand	34–42 Manners Street, Wellington, 12th floor, PO Box 11-34 Tel 4 384 25 55	www.ambafrance-nz.org
UK	58 Knightsbridge, London SW1 7JT. Tel 020 7073 1000	www.ambafrance-uk.org
US (Los Angeles)	10390 Santa Monica Boulevard, Suite 410, Los Angeles, CA 90025 Tel 310/235-3200	www.consulfrance-losangeles.org
US (New York)	934 Fifth Avenue, New York, NY 10021. Tel 212/606-3600	www.consulfrance-newyork.org

MONEY

THE EURO

» France is one of 16 European countries that has adopted the euro as the official currency. Euro notes and coins were introduced in January 2002, replacing the former currency, the French franc.

BEFORE YOU GO

» It is advisable to use a combination of cash, traveller's cheques and credit cards rather than relying on only one means of payment during your trip.

» Check with your credit or debit card company that your card can be used to withdraw cash from Automated Teller Machines (ATMs) in France.

TRAVELLER'S CHEQUES

» Traveller's cheques are a safer way of bringing money with you than cash as you can claim a refund if they are stolen—but commission can be high when you cash them, particularly in hotels and shops.

ATMS

» ATMs are common in France, often with on-screen instructions in a choice of languages. Among the cards accepted are Visa, MasterCard and Diners Club. You'll need a four-digit PIN, comprising numerals only.

» Your card issuer may charge you for withdrawing cash.

BANKS

» Hours vary, but usual opening hours are Monday to Friday 8.30 or 9 to 12 and 2 to 5, although some city banks may not close for lunch.

» In smaller towns and villages banks sometimes close on Mondays but open on Saturday mornings instead.

» Banks close on a national holiday. Only banks with *change* signs change traveller's cheques or foreign currency and you'll need your passport to do this.

BUREAUX DE CHANGE

» Bureaux de Change have longer opening hours than banks, but the exchange rates may not be so good. You'll find them across Paris and in all of the major cities.

» Avoid changing large amounts of traveller's cheques at hotels as the rates may not be competitive.

CREDIT CARDS

» Most restaurants, hotels and shops accept credit cards, but some have a minimum spending limit.

» Before you travel, it's worth finding out how much your card issuer will charge you to withdraw cash from an ATM and the emergency number to call if your card is stolen.

TAXES

» Non-EU residents can claim a sales tax refund *(détaxe)* of 12 per cent on certain purchases, although you must have spent more than €175 in one shop, at one time. Ask the store for the relevant forms, which the trader should complete and stamp. Give these forms to customs when you leave the country, along with the receipts, and they will be stamped. Post the forms back to the shop and they will either refund your credit card account or send you a cheque.

» Remember that you may have to show the goods to Customs when you leave France, so keep them within easy reach.

» Exempt products include food and drink, medicine, tobacco, unset gems, works of art and antiques.

» The company Global Refund offers a reimbursement service (800 32 11 11 11; www.globalrefund.com).

WIRING MONEY

» In an emergency, you can have money wired to you from your home country, but this can be expensive (as agents charge a fee for the service) and time-consuming.

» You can send and receive money via agents such as Western Union (www.westernunion.com) and Travelex (www.travelex.com/fr).

» Money can be wired from bank to bank, which takes up to two working days, or through Travelex and Western Union, which is normally faster.

CONCESSIONS

» If you are a student or teacher, apply to the International Student Travel Confederation (www.isic.org) in your own country for an International Student Identity Card (ISIC). This entitles you to various reductions during your visit.

» Seniors often get reduced-rate tickets on public transportation and on admission to museums and sights by showing a valid identity card or passport.

» Small children frequently have free entry to sights.

» EU national under the age of 26 have free access to some museums in France.

POST OFFICES

» Most post offices have ATMs.

» Cards accepted are listed on each dispenser and instructions are available in English.

» Money can be wired, through Western Union (▷ above), via most post offices, and generally takes only a few minutes to receive.

» International Money Orders can be sent from all post offices (a charge is applied).

» Most larger post offices offer exchange services in the following currencies: American, Australian and Canadian dollars, Japanese yen, British pounds sterling, Swiss francs, Swedish kronor and Danish and Norwegian kroner.

TIPPING GUIDE	
Restaurants (service included)	Change *
Hotels (service included)	Change *
Cafés (service included)	Change *
Taxis	10 per cent
Tour guides	€1–€1.50
Porters	€1
Hairdressers	€1
Cloakroom attendants	30c
Toilets	Change
Usherettes	30c
* Or more if you are impressed with the level of service	

TIPS

» Try to avoid using higher denomination notes when paying taxi drivers and when buying low-cost items in smaller shops.

» Never carry money or credit cards in back pockets, or other places that are easy targets for thieves.

» Keep your spare money and traveller's cheques in your hotel safe *(coffre-fort)* until you need them.

» Check the exchange rates for traveller's cheques and cash offered in post offices as well as in banks, as banks do not always offer the best exchange rate.

» In France, MasterCard is sometimes known as Eurocard and Visa is known as Carte Bleue.

» Some smaller hotels and inns don't accept credit cards, so find out before you check in.

PRICES OF EVERYDAY ITEMS (PARIS)

Takeout sandwich		€2.20–€3.20
Bottle of mineral water	(from a shop, 0.5 litres)	€0.30–€0.50
Cup of coffee	(from a café, espresso)	€2–€2.25
	(crème, larger cup with milk)	€2–€3.50
Beer	(un demi, half a litre)	€2–€3
Glass of house wine		€2–€3.50
French national newspaper		€1–€1.20
International newspaper		€1.50–€2.30
Litre of fuel (gas)	(98 unleaded)	€1.25
	(diesel)	€1.08
Métro ticket	(single)	€1.60
	(per ticket, if you buy a carnet)	€1.16
20 cigarettes	(on average)	€3.50

HEALTH

BEFORE YOU GO

» EU citizens receive reduced-cost healthcare in France with the relevant documentation. This is the European Health Insurance Card (EHIC), which has replaced the E111. Full health insurance is still strongly advised. For all other countries full insurance is essential.

» Make sure you are up to date with anti-tetanus boosters. Bring any medication you need with you and pack a first-aid kit. In summer always bring sun-protection cream.

IF YOU NEED TREATMENT

» The French national health system is complex. Any salaried French citizen who receives treatment by a doctor or public hospital can be reimbursed by up to 70 per cent. The same is true if you are an EU citizen and have a valid EHIC card.

» If you are relying only on your EHIC, rather than travel insurance, make sure the doctor you see is part of the French national health service *(a conventionné)*, rather than the private system, otherwise you may face extra charges. In any case, you will have to pay up front for the consultation and treatment. To reclaim part of these costs, send the *feuille de soins* (a statement from the doctor) and your EHIC to the Caisse Primaire d'Assurance-Maladie (state health insurance office) before you leave the country. Call 0845 606 2030 or visit www.ehic.org to find the nearest office. You should also attach the labels of any medicine you have to buy.

» If you have to stay overnight in a public hospital, you will have to pay 25 per cent of the treatment costs, as well as a daily charge *(forfait journalier)*. These fees are not refundable. It is far better to have full health insurance than to rely solely on the EHIC.

» Citizens of non-EU countries must have full health insurance.

» If you are hospitalized and have insurance, ask to see the *assistante sociale* to arrange reimbursement of costs directly through your insurers.

» In an emergency, dial 15 for the Service d'Aide Médicale d'Urgence (SAMU) unit (ambulance). They work closely with hospital emergency units and are accompanied by trained medical personnel.

» If you are able to get yourself to a hospital, make sure it has a casualty or emergency department *(urgences)*.

FINDING A DOCTOR

» You can find a doctor *(médecin)* by asking at the local pharmacy or at your hotel. Appointments are usually made in advance, but few doctors will refuse an emergency case.

» Emergency house calls (24-hours) can be arranged in the Paris area by calling SOS Médecins (tel 36 24). Otherwise call 15 for emergencies or SOS Help (tel 01 46 21 46 46; www.soshelpline.org) for help in English.

FINDING A HOSPITAL

» Hospitals are listed in the phone book under *Hôpitaux* and round-the-clock emergency services are called *urgences*.

» Private hospitals are more expensive than public and treatment is not necessarily better. If you choose a private hospital, check that you are covered for the costs before receiving treatment.

» For ease of communication, English-speakers in Paris may prefer The American Hospital (63 boulevard Victor Hugo, 92200 Neuilly; 01 46 41 25 25; www.american-hospital.org) or The Hertford British Hospital (3 rue Barbès, 92300 Levallois-Perret;

USEFUL NUMBERS

Emergency medical aid/ambulance
15
General emergencies
112
Police
17
Fire (Pompiers)
18
Anti-Poison Centre in Paris
01 40 05 48 48
FACTS (HIV/Aids
advice in English.
Mon–Fri 11am–2pm)
01 44 93 16 16
SOS Help (English crisis information hotline).
Daily 3pm–11pm
01 46 21 46 46

01 46 39 22 22; www.british-hospital.
org). Both are private hospitals.

DENTAL TREATMENT

» EU citizens can receive reduced-
cost emergency dental treatment
with the EHIC, although insurance is
still advised. The reclaim procedure is
the same as medical treatment.
» Other visitors should check
that their insurance covers dental
treatment. It's a good idea to have a
dental check-up before your visit.

PHARMACIES

» A pharmacy *(pharmacie)* will have
an illuminated green cross outside.
Most are open Mon–Sat 9–7 or 8,
but they usually post details on the
door of a pharmacy that is open later
(called the *pharmacie de garde)*.
» Pharmacists are highly qualified
and provide first aid, as well as
supplying medication (some drugs
are by prescription, or *ordonnance,*
only). But they cannot dispense
prescriptions written by doctors
outside the French health system,
so bring sufficient supplies of any
prescribed drugs you need.
» Some pharmacists speak English
and can direct you to local doctors
or specialists.
» They also sell a range of health-
related items, although items such
as soap, toothbrushes and razors are
less expensive at a supermarket.
» Some commonly used medicines
sold in supermarkets at home (such
as cold remedies) can be bought only
in pharmacies in France.

TAP WATER

» Tap water is safe to drink and
restaurants will often provide a carafe
of water, although most French
people opt for bottled water.
» In public places look for the sign
eau potable (drinking water). Don't
drink from anything marked *eau
non potable*.

SUMMER HAZARDS

» The sun can be strong in any part
of the country between May and
September, so pack a high-factor sun
block. You may also like to take an

insect repellent, although the insect
bites you get in France are more
likely to be irritating than dangerous.
» If you are planning high altitude
walks take plenty of water, warm
clothing and check weather reports
before you go, as sudden changes in
weather are not unknown.
» Recent hot dry summers have led
to forest fires in some areas in the
south of France. If you are concerned
about this, ask at the nearest tourist
information office whether the area
you intend to visit is at risk.
» Lyme disease exists in France. After
walking in woodland and country
areas check for tick bites.

» If you are visiting France from the US, Australia or New Zealand, you may be concerned
about the effect of long-haul flights on your health. The most widely publicized concern is
deep vein thrombosis, or DVT. Misleadingly named economy-class syndrome, DVT occurs
when a blood clot forms in the body's deep veins, particularly in the legs. The clot can move
around the bloodstream and could be fatal.
» Those most at risk include the elderly, pregnant women and those using the contraceptive
pill, smokers and the overweight. If you are at increased risk of DVT see your doctor before
departing. Flying increases the likelihood of DVT because passengers are often seated in a
cramped position for long periods of time and may become dehydrated.
To minimize risk:
Drink water (not alcohol).
Don't stay immobile for hours at a time.
Stretch and exercise your legs periodically.
Do wear elastic flight socks, which support veins and reduce the chances of a clot forming.
» Other health hazards for flyers are airborne diseases and bugs spread by the plane's
air-conditioning system. These are largely unavoidable, but if you have a serious medical
condition seek advice from a doctor before setting off.

EXERCISES

1 Ankle Rotations	2 Calf Stretches	3 Knee Lifts
Lift feet off the floor. Draw a circle with the toes, moving one foot clockwise and the other counterclockwise.	Start with heel on the floor and point foot upward as high as you can. Then lift heels high keeping balls of feet on the floor.	Lift leg with knee bent while contracting your thigh muscle. Then staighten leg pressing foot flat to the floor.

OPTICIANS

It's always a good idea to pack a spare pair of glasses or contact lenses and your prescription, in case you
lose or break your main pair.

NAME	WEBSITE
Opticiens Krys	www.krys.com
Lissac Opticien	www.lissac.com
Alain Afflelou	www.alainafflelou.com
Optical Center	www.optical-center.com
Optic 2000	www.optic2000.fr

ALTERNATIVE MEDICAL TREATMENT

» Alternative medicine, such as
homoeopathy, is generally available
from the majority of pharmacies.
» Alternative treatment is available
and is on the increase, although
chiropractics and reflexology are
not widespread. Useful websites
include www.chiropratique.org
(the Association Française de
Chiropratique), www.acupuncture-
france.com (Association Français
d'Acupuncture) and www.
naturosante.com (a site relating to
alternative medical treatments and
their benefits).

BASICS

ELECTRICITY

» Voltage in France is 220 volts. Sockets take plugs with two round pins. UK electrical equipment will need an adaptor plug, which you can buy at airport and Eurostar terminals. American appliances using 110–120 volts will need an adaptor and a transformer. Equipment that is dual voltage should need only an adaptor.

LAUNDRY

» There are two options if you need a laundry service—a *laverie automatique* (laundrette) and a *pressing/nettoyage à sec* (dry-cleaners). Dry-cleaners are easier to find, but are more expensive. Some have an economy service, but this is not recommended for your best silk jacket.

MEASUREMENTS

» France uses the metric system. Road distances are measured in kilometres, fuel is sold by the litre and food is weighed out in grams and kilograms.

TOILETS

» Today's modern unisex public toilets are a vast improvement on previous facilities. Coin-operated and self-cleaning, you can find them in Paris and most large cities.

» In smaller towns and villages, free public toilets can normally be found by the market square or near tourist offices, although cleanliness varies.

» The two most reliable options are to take advantage of facilities in museums or other visitor attractions (almost always a good standard) or in restaurants and cafés, though you should be a customer to use the facilities, so be sure to buy a drink.

» Ask for *les toilettes* or WC (pronounced 'vay say').

SMOKING AREAS

» Smoking is banned in public places such as cinemas, buses, Métro stations, and bars and restaurants.

» Some taxis may display a no-smoking sign.

CHILDREN

» The French autoroute system has a good network of service stations at approximately 40km (25-mile) intervals, which sell food and have recreation areas. At intervals of about 10km (6 miles), there are *aires*, stopping areas with toilets and recreation areas but no food or fuel—good for restless children to run around.

» Most restaurants welcome children, although not many have high chairs and children's menus are not common outside family-friendly tourist resorts, so it's probably best to aim for family-style bistros where facilities are better and the staff are more helpful.

» If you need special facilities in your hotel, such as a cot, or a child seat in your rented car, make sure you reserve them in advance.

» For baby-changing facilities while you are out and about, try the restrooms in department stores and the larger museums.

» Supermarkets and pharmacies sell nappies (diapers) and baby food, although supermarkets are often closed on a Sunday so make sure you stock up.

» Entrance to museums is often free to young children.

» For babysitting services, you could try www.babysittingservices. com. Inter-Service Parents (tel 01 44 93 44 93) gives out information on babysitting agencies and children's activities in Paris.

VISITORS WITH DISABILITIES

» France has made great headway in recent years in providing access and facilities for visitors with disabilities. All new buildings must take the needs of people with special requirements into account, and, where possible, existing buildings such as town halls, airports and train stations must be adapted with ramps and automatic doors.

» However, some visitor offices, museums and restaurants that are in historic, protected buildings are still not fully accessible. A telephone call before going to a restaurant is a good idea to organize a more easily accessible table.

» The Association des Paralysés de France (13 place de Rungis, 75013 Paris; 01 53 80 92 97; www. apf.asso.fr) provides information on wheelchair access. For other organizations which give advice to people with disabilities, ▷ 66.

CAR RENTAL

» Driving is a good way to explore the villages and countryside of France, although driving in Paris is not recommended.

» It is best to reserve a car in advance, making sure that full insurance is included in the package. You can also arrange car rental through some travel agents when you book your travel arrangements.

» For information on driving, ▷ 51–55.

PLACES OF WORSHIP

» Some of the most magnificent buildings in France are the great Gothic cathedrals found in the major cities and the tiny parish churches and chapels in towns and villages. They have become so popular as visitor attractions that it's easy to forget that they are still active places of worship. As such, it's important to respect these churches and worshippers by dressing appropriately. Men should wear long trousers rather than shorts and should avoid sleeveless shirts. Women should keep their knees and shoulders covered and men should remove hats on entering the building.

» Take photos only if it is permitted and don't forget to turn off your mobile phone.

LOCAL WAYS

» Greetings are often quite formal in France. Offer to shake hands when you are introduced to someone, and use *vous* rather than *tu*. It is polite to use Monsieur, Madame or Mademoiselle when speaking to people you don't know. For very young women and teenage girls use Mademoiselle, otherwise always use Madame.

» The Continental kiss is a common form of greeting between friends, and the number of times friends kiss each other on the cheek varies from region to region.

» Address waiting staff as Monsieur, Madame or Mademoiselle when you are trying to attract their attention.

» Communicating in French is always the best option, even if you can manage only *bonjour, s'il vous plaît* and *merci*. The French are protective of their language and your efforts to speak it will be appreciated. If your knowledge of French is limited, ask the fail-safe *Parlez-vous anglais?* and hope the answer is *oui*. See also Words and Phrases ▷ 447–451.

» Remember that in France it is traditional to say hello as you enter a shop, bar or café, particularly in small towns and villages, and that you are greeting your fellow customers as

well as the proprietor. For a mixed audience, a *bonjour, messieurs, dames* is the appropriate phrase. When it is your turn to be served, greet your server with *Bonjour, Madame* or *Bonjour, Monsieur*, and then don't forget to say *merci* and *au revoir* or *bonne journée* as you leave.

CONVERSION CHART

From	To	Multiply by
Inches	Centimetres	2.54
Centimetres	Inches	0.3937
Feet	Metres	0.3048
Metres	Feet	3.2810
Yards	Metres	0.9144
Metres	Yards	1.0940
Miles	Kilometres	1.6090
Kilometres	Miles	0.6214
Acres	Hectares	0.4047
Hectares	Acres	2.4710
Gallons	Litres	4.5460
Litres	Gallons	0.2200
Ounces	Grams	28.35
Grams	Ounces	0.0353
Pounds	Grams	453.6
Grams	Pounds	0.0022
Pounds	Kilograms	0.4536
Kilograms	Pounds	2.205
Tons	Tonnes	1.0160
Tonnes	Tons	0.9842

CAR RENTAL COMPANIES INCLUDE:

NAME	TELEPHONE	WEBSITE
Avis	08 21 23 07 60	www.avis.fr
Easycar	08 26 10 73 23	www.easycar.com
Europcar	08 25 358 358	www.europcar.fr
Hertz	08 25 86 18 61	www.hertz.fr
Rent-a-Car	08 91 70 02 00	www.rentacar.fr
Sixt	08 20 00 74 98	www.sixt.fr

COMMUNICATION

TELEPHONING

French numbers

All numbers in France have ten digits. The country is divided into five regional zones, indicated by the first two digits of the phone number (▷ 425). You must dial these two digits even if you are calling from within the zone.

International Calls

» To call France from the UK dial 00 33, then drop the first zero from the 10-digit number. To call the UK from France, dial 00 44, then drop the first zero from the area code.
» To call France from the US, dial 011 33, then drop the first zero from the 10-digit number. To call the US from France, dial 00 1, followed by the number.

Call Charges

For calls within France, peak period is from 8am to 7pm, Monday to Friday. You'll save money if you call outside this time. Numbers beginning with 08 have special rates. 0800 numbers are free. 081 and 086 numbers are charged at local rate. Other 08 numbers cost more than national calls—sometimes considerably more. Watch for the prefixes 0893, 0898 and 0899, which are particularly expensive.

PAYPHONES

» Nearly all public payphones in France use a phone card *(télécarte)*, with 50 or 120 units, rather than coins. You can buy these at post offices, *tabacs* (tobacconists) and France Télécom shops. Some phones also accept certain credit cards, although this may make the calls more expensive. Calls to an emergency number are free.
» The phone gives instructions in various languages—press the flag button to select your choice. If the phone displays the blue bell sign, you can receive incoming calls.
» Public phones in cafés and restaurants use cards, coins or need to be switched on by staff and you pay after the call. They tend to be more expensive than public payphones. Check the rates for hotel phones, as they can be much higher than from a public payphone.

MOBILE PHONES

You can usually use your own mobile, but there are a few points to check before leaving:

USEFUL TELEPHONE NUMBERS

Directory Enquiries (national)	118008
(international)	www.pagesjaunes.fr/ annuairedumonde

» Contact your Customer Service department to find out if you have any restrictions on making calls from France.
» Check if you need an access code to listen to your voice mail.
» Make sure the numbers memorized in your directory are in the international format.
» Check the call charges, which can rise dramatically when you use your phone abroad.

COUNTRY CODES FROM FRANCE	
Australia	00 61
Belgium	00 32
Canada	00 1
Germany	00 49
Ireland	00 353
Italy	00 39
Monaco	00 377
Netherlands	00 31
New Zealand	00 64
Spain	00 34
Sweden	00 46
UK	00 44
US	00 1

PREFIXES	
00	International
01	Île-de-France (including Paris)
02	Northwest France
03	Northeast France
04	Southeast France
05	Southwest France
06	Mobile telephone numbers
0800	Toll-free
08	Special-rate numbers

SENDING A LETTER

» You can buy stamps *(timbres)* for a letter *(lettre)* or a postcard *(carte postale)* at post offices and *tabacs.* Write *par avion* (by air) on the envelope or postcard.

» If you want registered post, ask at the post office for the letter to be sent *recommandé.* For a parcel *(colis),* you can choose either *prioritaire* (priority) or the less expensive, but slower, *économique.*

» Mailboxes are yellow. In Paris, some have two sections, one for Paris and the suburbs *(Paris–Banlieue),* and another for national and international mail *(autres départements/étranger).* Mail sent from France should take between two and five days to arrive, but can take longer.

POST OFFICES

» Post offices *(bureaux de poste)* are well signposted. The postal service is known as La Poste.

» Opening hours are generally Monday to Friday 8–5 or 6, Saturday 8–12. Some branches close for lunch and some stay open longer. Queues tend to be worst during lunch hours, in the late afternoon and market day.

» Facilities may include phone booths, photocopiers, fax *(télécopieur)* and access to the Minitel directory service. Poste Restante services are also available for a fee.

» Money can be wired through Western Union (▷ 418) via most post offices and international money orders can be sent from post offices (a charge is payable). Many also have exchange services in the following currencies: American, Australian and Canadian dollars, Japanese yen, British pounds sterling, Swiss francs, Swedish kronor and Danish and Norwegian kroner.

INTERNET ACCESS

» Internet cafés are popular in Paris and major towns, although they are quite expensive. Some hotels and libraries have internet terminals, as do many post offices. Some rural towns have free internet access hotspots and these are becoming more common.

LAPTOPS

» Most hotels of two stars and above provide modem points. You can easily connect to the internet providing this service is supported by your ISP (Internet Service Provider).

POSTAGE RATES	
Within France	€0.55
To Western Europe	€0.65
To rest of the world	€0.85

Local telephone charges will apply. Remember that you may need a modem plug adaptor (▷ 422).

» An increasing number of hotels, particularly in towns, provide WiFi internet connection.

TIP

» When reserving show tickets by telephone or calling for tourist information, bear in mind that you may be calling a higher-rate telephone number. This is usually indicated by the prefix 089.

GUIDE PRICES		
Type of call	Initial charge	Each further minute
Local, peak	€0.091 (1 min)	€0.033
Local, off-peak	€0.091 (1 min)	€0.018
National, peak	€0.112 (39 sec)	€0.091
National, off-peak	€0.112 (39 sec)	€0.061
Calling the UK, off-peak	€0.11 (15 sec)	€0.12
Calling the US, off-peak	€0.11 (27 sec)	€0.15

FINDING HELP

Most visits to France are trouble-free, but make sure you have adequate insurance to cover any health emergencies, thefts or legal costs that may arise (▷ 417). If you do become a victim of crime, it is most likely to be at the hands of a pickpocket, so always keep your money and mobile phones safely tucked away.

PERSONAL SECURITY

» Take a note of your traveller's cheques numbers and keep it separate from the cheques themselves, as you will need it to make a claim in case of loss.
» Don't keep wallets, purses or mobile phones in the back pockets of trousers, or anywhere else that is easily accessible to thieves. Money belts and bags worn around the waist are targets, as thieves know you are likely to have valuables in them. Always keep an eye on your bags in restaurants, bars and on the Métro, and hold shoulder bags close to you, fastener inwards, when you are walking in the streets.
» Thieves and pickpockets are especially fond of crowded Métro trains, airports, the Gare du Nord Métro station in Paris, markets, tourist hotspots and the south coast, particularly the Côte d'Azur. Beware if someone bumps into you—it may be a ploy to distract you while someone else snatches your money.
» If you are the victim of theft, you must report it at the local police station *(gendarmerie)* if you want to claim on your insurance. Keep hold of the statement the police give you. You must also contact your credit card company as soon as possible to cancel any stolen cards.
» Keep valuable items in your hotel safe *(coffre-fort)*.
» Theft of cars and theft from cars are significant problems in France, even in country areas. When you park your car, don't leave anything of value inside. It's risky leaving anything in view that may attract a thief. Carry your belongings with you or leave them in your hotel.

» On trains, try to keep your luggage where you can see it.

LOSS OF PASSPORT

» Always keep a separate note of your passport number and a photocopy of the page that carries your details, in case of loss or theft. You can also scan the relevant pages of your passport and then email them to yourself at an email account that you can access anywhere (such as www.hotmail.com).
» If you do lose your passport or it is stolen, report it to the police and then contact your nearest embassy or consulate (▷ below).

POLICE

» There are various types of police officer in France. The two main forces are the Police Nationale, who are under the control of the local mayor,

and the Gendarmerie Nationale, who you often see at airports.
» You are likely to encounter the armed CRS riot police only at a demonstration.
» In Paris each *arrondissement* has several police stations.
» In France, the police have wide powers of stop and search. It is wise to carry your passport in case a police officer stops you and requests your ID.

FIRE

» The French fire department deals with a number of emergencies in addition to actual fires. These range from stranded cats to road accidents and gas leaks. They are trained to give first aid.

HEALTH EMERGENCIES
▷ 420–421.

EMBASSIES AND CONSULATES IN PARIS		
Country	Address	Website
Australia	4 rue Jean-Rey, 75015. Tel 01 40 59 33 00	www.france-embassy.gov.au
Canada	35 avenue Montaigne, 75008. Tel 01 44 43 29 00	www.amb-canada.fr
Germany	13–15 avenue Franklin Roosevelt, 75008 Tel 01 53 83 45 00	www.paris.diplo.de
Ireland	12 avenue Foch, 75116. Tel 01 44 17 67 00	www.embassyofireland.fr
Italy	51 rue de Varenne, 75007 Tel 01 49 54 03 00	www.ambparigi.esteri.it
Spain	22 avenue Marceau, 75008 Tel 01 44 43 18 00	www.amb-espagne.fr
UK	35 rue du Faubourg-St-Honoré, 75008 Tel 01 44 51 31 00	//ukinfrance.fco.gov.uk/en
US	2 avenue Gabriel, 75008 Tel 01 43 12 22 22	//france.usembassy.gov

MEDIA

TELEVISION

» France has five non-cable television stations: the nationally owned and operated channels 2 and 3, the privately owned 1 and 6, and the Franco-German ARTE (channel 5). Almost all the programmes are in French. There are advertisements on all terrestrial channels except ARTE.

» TF1 has news broadcasts, recent films, soaps and shows.

» France 2 has news, recent French and foreign films, soaps, shows and documentaries.

» France 3 has news, regional shows, documentaries, mostly French films and, once a week, a film in its original language.

» ARTE is a Franco-German channel operating from 7pm every evening with programmes in French and German. International films are shown in their original language and there are also cultural documentaries.

» M6 shows a lot of low-budget films and past American sitcoms and soaps. There are also some interesting documentaries.

» Digital television (TNT) offers more than 100 channels, either through satellite or cable.

» If the TV listings mention VO (version originale), the show or film will be in the language in which it was made, with French subtitles (Channel 3 usually screens a film in VO every Sunday at midnight).

» French television channels do not always keep exactly to schedule.

» Most hotels have a cable service, which is likely to include BBC World and CNN. Cable channels offer multilingual versions of some programmes. Ask at your hotel how to use this option.

» The commercial-free ARTE usually offers a choice between French and German for its cultural shows.

RADIO

» French radio stations are available mainly on FM wave lengths, with a few international stations on LW. All FM stations are in French. Stations (Paris frequencies) include:

» Chérie FM: 91.3 FM; French mainstream pop, news, reports.

» France Infos: 105.5 FM; news bulletins every 15 minutes.

» France Musique: 91.7 FM; classical and jazz music, concerts, operas.

» NRJ: 100.3 FM; French and International pop, techno, rap, R'n'B.

» Radio Classique: 101.1 FM; classical music.

» Skyrock: 96 FM; hip-hop, R'n'B.

» BBC Radio 4 198 kHz MW; news, current affairs, drama.

» BBC Five Live 909 kHz MW; news and sport.

» BBC World Service 648 kHz LW.

NEWSPAPERS

» In tourist areas, you can buy the main English dailies, sometimes a day old, at a price premium.

» *The Economist, USA Today* and *The Wall Street Journal* can be found at newsstands in cities, along with *The European*, which presents a pan-European perspective in English, and the *International Herald Tribune*, which reports international news from a US standpoint.

» You may find only an international edition of your preferred paper.

» Most French cities and regions have their own newspapers, such as *Le Progrès* in Lyon, *Breton Ouest-France* in Brittany or *Le Populaire* in central France.

NEWSPAPERS
French daily newspapers have clear political leanings.
Le Monde
This stately paper, left-of-centre, refuses to run photos and uses illustrations.
Libération
This lively youth-focused paper is more clearly leftist.
L'Humanité
Left wing.
Le Figaro
Mainstream conservative daily.
Le Parisien
This tabloid paper is written at a level of French that makes it fairly easy for non-native readers to understand.
Journal du Dimanche
Sunday newspaper.

» Major cities also produce listings of live performances, exhibitions and cinema. In the capital there's *Pariscope*, Lyon has *Lyon Poche* and in Nantes there is *Les Mois Nantais*. Free listings publications can be picked up at tourist offices.

» Weekly news magazines include *Le Nouvel Observateur, Le Point* and *L'Express*.

» For women's fashions, options include *Elle, Vogue, L'Officiel* or *Marie Claire*.

» For celebrity gossip and pictures, buy *Paris Match, Voici* or *Gala*.

CABLE TV	
Depending on what cable option your hotel has, you may have some of the following channels:	
BBC Prime	With a mix of BBC shows, old and new
Canal+	Shows recent films (some in the original language)
MTV	Contemporary music channel
MCM	The French version of MTV
Eurosport or Infosport	For major sporting events
Planète	Nature and science documentaries
RAI Uno	Italian
TVE 1	Spanish
Euronews	A European all-news channel
LCI	All news in French
Canal Jimmy	Shows some British and American shows like *Friends* and *NYPD Blue* in English or multilingual versions
Paris Première	A cultural channel with some films in English
Canal J	With children's shows until 8pm
Téva	A women's channel that runs some English-language shows such as *Sex and the City*

FILMS, BOOKS AND MAPS
FILMS

» Watching a French film is a good way to get the feel of the place before you visit.

» For a classic, try *Les Enfants du Paradis* (1945) directed by Marcel Carné. For *nouvelle vague* (new wave) cinema—often filmed with a hand-held camera—try *Jules et Jim* (1962), directed by François Truffaut and starring Jeanne Moreau, or *À Bout de Souffle* (1959), directed by Jean-Luc Godard. The surreal *Belle de Jour* (1967), starring Catherine Deneuve, caused a scandal at the time due to its erotic subject matter. The 1987 weepie *Au Revoir les Enfants* is the story of a Jewish boy in occupied France in World War II.

» No reference to French movies would be complete without mentioning Gérard Depardieu, the actor who conquered France and then Hollywood. His best-known films include *Cyrano de Bergerac* (1990) and *Jean de Florette* (1986). The sequel to this, *Manon des Sources* (1986), stars Emmanuelle Béart, one of France's leading actresses.

» Jean-Pierre Jeunet's *Delicatessen* (1991) turns the controversial subject of cannibalism into a black comedy.

» For a French feel with a Hollywood budget, watch a film directed by Luc Besson, such as *The Fifth Element* (1997) or *Léon* (1994), known for the fine performance of Jean Reno.

» The quirky and hugely successful *Amélie* (2001), starring Audrey Tautou (pictured above), is set in Montmartre, Paris. *Les Rivières Pourpres* (*The Crimson Rivers*; 2000) is directed by Matthieu Kassovitz, the actor who played the love interest in *Amélie*. It's an action thriller set in the French Alps, worth watching for the atmospheric scenery alone, and starring two of the best French actors of the moment, Jean Reno and Vincent Cassel.

» If you're looking for beautiful countryside, *French Kiss* (1995), with Hollywood's Meg Ryan is a good start, as is *A Good Year* (2006) starring Russell Crowe. Another English-language movie set in France is *Chocolat* (2000), starring Juliette Binoche.

» Cannes hosts Europe's most prestigious film festival in May. It attracts top international actors, directors and producers, as well as hundreds of starlets and self-promoting wannabes whose antics contribute much to the atmosphere of the festival. Millions of euros of business is conducted during the 12 days of the festival. For more details, look up www.festival-cannes.fr.

BOOKS

» For those who prefer to find their atmosphere on the page, there is no shortage of choice.

» Books written from a foreigner's perspective range from Charles

Dickens' view of the French Revolution in *A Tale of Two Cities* (1859) to Peter Mayle's experiences in the southeast of France in *A Year in Provence* (1989). English actress Carol Drinkwater recounts her Provençal experiences in *The Olive Farm* (2001) and *The Olive Season* (2003).

» Classic literature set in Paris includes Victor Hugo's *The Hunchback of Notre Dame* (1831) and George Orwell's *Down and Out in Paris and London* (1933), which describes the difficulties of surviving penniless in the capital in the 1930s. Adam Gopnik's essays in *Paris to the Moon* (2000) provide one American's view of life in the French capital in the 21st century. Ernest Hemingway's *A Moveable Feast* (published in 1964) and Gertrude Stein's *The Autobiography of Alice B. Toklas* (1933) describe a more romantic era in the early 20th century, when a young couple could live on $5 a day and an art collector could snap up works by Pablo Picasso and Henri Matisse for a song.

MAPS

The Automobile Association (UK) produces a French road atlas and touring atlas, as well as 16 regional road sheet maps of France. To order a copy, look up www.theAA.com.

OPENING TIMES AND TICKETS

TICKETS

» Tourist information offices in French cities often sell a pass that gives entry to the main sights at a reduced rate. For example, the Lyon City Card entitles you to entry to 21 museums, guided and audio city tours, river cruises, lunchtime classical concerts, public transportation within the city and a 10 per cent discount on purchases at Galeries Lafayette. It's worth investing in one of these if you plan on spending a few days in one city.

» For information on transportation tickets, ▷ 56–66.

» Students with an International Student Identity Card (ISIC) and seniors get reduced-price entry at some museums.

» For information on show and concert tickets, ▷ 435.

» The Paris Pass costs just €28 and gives several benefits, including unlimited travel on public transportation within the capital, free entry to more than 50 of Paris's top museums and galleries as well as major attractions. Visit the website www.parispass.com for full details.

NATIONAL HOLIDAYS

France has 11 national holidays *(jours fériés)*, when train and bus services are reduced and banks and many museums and shops close. The most steadfastly respected are 1 January, 1 May, 1 November, 11 November and 25 December. If you're in France during a national holiday, it's a good idea to ring ahead to see if the sight you want to visit is open.

1 January	New Year's Day
March/April	Easter Monday
1 May	Labour Day
8 May	VE Day
A Thursday in May	Ascension Day
May/June	Whit Monday
14 July	Bastille Day
15 August	Assumption Day
1 November	All Saints' Day
11 November	Remembrance Day
25 December	Christmas Day

OPENING TIMES

Banks	Usual opening hours are Monday to Friday 9–12, 2–5, but these can vary.	Banks close at noon on the day before a national holiday, as well as on the holiday itself.
Shops	Food shops are open Tuesday to Friday 7 or 8am–6.30 or 7.30pm.	Some close all day Monday while others will open in the afternoon only. On Saturday and Sunday they may open mornings only. Smaller shops tend to close at lunchtime from 12–2. Bakers *(boulangeries)* open on Sunday mornings and super-markets and hypermarkets are open six days a week and have long business hours, opening at about 9am and staying open until 9 or 10pm, but closing on Sundays. Some also remain closed on Monday mornings.
Museums	In Paris, most national museums close on Tuesdays—the Musée d'Orsay is a notable exception, closing on Mondays. Municipal museums in Paris usually close on Tuesdays.	Entrance to some museums is free on the first Sunday of the month, although this can lead to crowds. If you plan to travel a long distance to see a particular museum, call in advance as opening hours can be idiosyncratic (some museums open on public holidays and some do not and the renovation craze has not helped).
Restaurants	Lunch is generally served 12–2 or 2.30 and dinner 7.30–10 or 11.	Brasseries tend to serve food all day. Some restaurants in Paris close for the whole of August for staff to have their annual vacation. Some restaurants on the coast close from November to Easter.
Post offices	These generally open Monday to Friday 8–5, 6 or 7 weekdays and 8–12 on Saturday.	Small branches may close for lunch.
Pharmacies	Most are open Monday to Saturday 9–7 or 8.	They all display a list of local pharmacies that open later and on a Sunday.

TOURIST OFFICES

IN PARIS

» The Paris tourist office (www. parisinfo.com) in rue des Pyramides is a handy source of information on anything from sightseeing and accommodation to exhibitions and children's activities. You can also buy the Paris Museum Pass and the Paris Visite bus and Métro pass and the Paris City Passport.

» In the summer there are also information kiosks at various sites around the city.

» The regional tourist office, the Comité Régional du Tourisme—Paris Île-de-France, has offices at the Carrousel du Louvre and Disneyland® Resort Paris. It covers the whole of the Île de France, including Versailles and Fontainebleau.

TOURIST OFFICES

BORDEAUX
✉ 12 cours du 30 Juillet, 33080 ☎ 05 56 00 66 00 🕐 May–Jun, Sep–Oct Mon–Sat 9–7, Sun 10–12, 1–3; Jul–Aug Mon–Sat 9–7.30, Sun and public hols 9.30–6.30; Nov–Apr Mon–Fri 9.30–12.30, 4–6

DIJON
✉ cour de la Gare and 11 rue des Forges, 21000 ☎ 08 92 70 05 58 🕐 Both offices: Apr–Sep Mon–Sat 9.30–6.30, Sun 10–6; Oct–Mar Mon–Sat 9.30–1, 2–6, Sun 10–4

LILLE
✉ Palais Rihour, place Rihour, 59002 ☎ 03 59 57 94 00 (outside France), 08 91 56 20 04 (within France) 🕐 Mon–Sat 9.30–6.30, Sun 10–12, 2–5

LYON
✉ place Bellecour, 69002 ☎ 04 72 77 69 69 🕐 Daily 9–6

MARSEILLE
✉ 4 La Canebière, 13001 ☎ 08 26 50 05 00 🕐 Mon–Sat 9–7, Sun 10–5.

MONACO
✉ 2a boulevard des Moulins
☎ 92 16 61 16 (country code 377)
🕐 Mon–Sat 9–7, Sun 10–12

NICE
✉ 5 promenade des Anglais, 06000 ☎ 08 92 70 74 07 🕐 Jun–Sep Mon–Sat 9–8, Sun 9–6; Oct–May Mon–Sat 9–6

PARIS
www.paris-touristoffice.com
✉ 25–27 rue des Pyramides, 75001 ☎ 08 92 68 30 00 (€0.34 per minute) 🕐 Daily 9–7 🚇 Pyramides

REIMS
✉ 2 rue Guillaume de Machault, 51100 ☎ 08 92 70 13 51 🕐 May–Sep Mon–Sat 9–7, Sun 10–6; Apr, Oct Mon–Sat 9–6, Sun 10–6; Mar Mon–Sat 9–6, Sun 10–1; Nov–Feb Mon–Sat 9–6, Sun 10–12

RENNES
✉ 11 rue St-Yves, 35064 ☎ 02 99 67 11 11 🕐 Jun–Sep Mon–Sat 9–7, Sun 11–1, 2–6; Oct–May Mon 1–6, Tue–Sat 10–6, Sun 11–1, 2–6

ROUEN
✉ 25 place de la Cathédrale, BP 666, 76008 ☎ 02 32 08 32 40
🕐 May–Sep Mon–Sat 9–7, Sun and public hols 9.30–12.30, 2–6; Oct–Apr Mon–Sat 9.30–12.30, 1.30–6, Sun and public hols 10–1

STRASBOURG
✉ 17 place de la Cathédrale, 67082 ☎ 03 88 52 28 28 🕐 Daily 9–7

TOULOUSE
✉ Donjon du Capitole, 31080 ☎ 05 61 11 02 22 🕐 Jun–Sep Mon–Sat 9–7, Sun 10.30–5.15; Oct–May Mon–Fri 9–6, Sat 9–12.30, 2–6, Sun 10–12.30, 2–5

FRENCH TOURIST OFFICES

The French Tourist Office, Maison de la France, has a useful website—www.franceguide.com. Some of its offices abroad are listed below.

AUSTRALIA
✉ Level 20, 25 Bligh Street, Sydney, NSW 2000 ☎ (02) 9231 5244; email: info.au@franceguide.com

CANADA
✉ 1800 avenue McGill College, Suite 1010, Montréal, H3A 2W9 ☎ (514) 876 9881; email: canada@franceguide.com

GERMANY
✉ Zeppelinallee 37, D-60325 Frankfurt am Main
☎ 0900 157 0025 (€0.49 per min); email: info.de@franceguide.com

IRELAND
15 60 235 235;
email: info.ie@franceguide.com

ITALY
✉ Via Tiziano 32, 20145 Milano
☎ 899 199 072 (€0.52 per min); email: info.it@franceguide.com

SPAIN
✉ Plaza de España 18, Torre de Madrid 8a Pl. Of. 5, 28008 Madrid
☎ 807 11 71 81 (€0.35 per min); email: es@franceguide.com

UK
✉ Lincoln House, 300 High Holborn, London W1V 7JH
☎ 09068 244123 (60 pence per min); email: info.uk@franceguide.com

US (NEW YORK)
All requests for information and brochures are only accepted through the website: www.franceguide.com

USEFUL WEBSITES

www.aeroport.fr
Information on all of France's airports.
(French)

www.fodors.com
A comprehensive travel-planning site that lets you research prices, reserve air tickets and put questions to fellow visitors.
(English)

www.franceguide.com
Practical advice from the French Tourist Office on everything from arriving in France to buying a property. The site also has features on holidays and attractions. (French, English, German, Spanish, Italian, Dutch, Portuguese)

www.francetourism.com
The official US website of the French Government Tourist Office.
(English)

www.intermusees.com
The organization that runs the Carte Musées-Monuments pass for Paris.
(French and English)

www.lemonde.fr
Catch up on current events on the site of *Le Monde* newspaper.
(French)

www.meteofrance.com
Weather forecasts for France.
(French, English and Spanish)

www.monuments-nationaux.fr
Find out more about some of France's most historic monuments, on the site of the Centre des Monuments Nationaux.
(French and English)

www.parisdigest.com
An independent site that guides you to the best Paris has to offer, whether you want to sightsee, shop or eat out.
(English)

www.pagesjaunes.fr
France's telephone directory, online.
(French and English)

www.parisinfo.com
The website of the Paris Tourist Office is packed with information on sights, restaurants, shops, hotels, transportation and events. It also has useful links to other sites.
(French and English)

www.radio-france.fr
News, music and sport.
(French)

www.ratp.fr
The site of Paris's Métro and bus operator, with lots of information about getting around in Paris.
(French and English)

www.skifrance.fr
Search for a resort, find out the latest snow conditions and see the slopes in real time via webcam.
(English and French)

www.theAA.com
The AA website contains a route planner, helpful if you are driving in France. You can also order maps of the country.
(English)

www.tourisme.fr
Lists details of every tourist information office in France.
(French)

Other websites are listed alongside the relevant sights and towns and On the Move (▷ 45–66).

KEY SIGHTS QUICK WEBSITE FINDER		
SIGHT/TOWN	**WEBSITE**	**PAGE**
Aix-en-Provence	www.aixenprovencetourism.com	295
Arles	www.arlestourisme.com	299
Avignon	www.ot-avignon.fr	300
Battlefields of Picardie	www.somme-tourisme.com	187
Bordeaux	www.bordeaux-tourisme.com	356–359
Caen	www.ville-caen.fr	129
Colmar	www.ot-colmar.fr	190
Corsica	www.visit-corsica.com	400–414
Dijon	www.visitdijon.com	264–265
Disneyland® Resort Paris	www.disneylandparis.com	81
Lille	www.lilletourisme.com	194–197
Lyon	www.lyon-france.com	266–269
Marseille	www.marseille-tourisme.com	310–313
Monaco	www.visitmonaco.com	314–315
Mont St-Michel	www.monuments-nationaux.fr	140–143
Montpellier	www.ot-montpellier.fr	309
Musée d'Orsay	www.musee-orsay.fr	93
Musée du Louvre	www.louvre.fr	90–91
Nice	www.nicetourisme.com	316
Reims	www.reims-tourisme.com	200–201
Rennes	www.tourisme-rennes.com	146–147
Rouen	www.rouentourisme.com	148–149
St-Malo	www.saint-malo-tourisme.com	154
Strasbourg	www.ot-strasbourg.fr	202–205
Toulouse	www.ot-toulouse.fr	372–375
Tour Eiffel	www.tour-eiffel.fr	100–101
Versailles	www.châteauversailles.fr	102–103

ESSENTIAL INFORMATION

PRACTICALITIES

SHOPPING

Shopping is one of the joys of a visit to France. The French are demanding and discerning consumers, whether shopping for their daily bread or for haute couture. France is renowned for food, wine, porcelain and crystal. Prices are often as high as at home, but in one category—wines and spirits—British visitors can take advantage of the lower levels of duty. Non-EU visitors can reclaim VAT on certain purchases.

FOOD

It's not surprising that in the country that gave us foie gras, champagne and haute cuisine, food has always been taken very seriously, with quality and freshness high on every shopper's list of priorities.

Food stores (other than supermarkets) are specialists, usually selling only one type of product. You are most likely to see the *boulangerie* (bakery), *pâtisserie* (pastry/cake shop), *fromagerie* (cheese shop), *boucherie* (butcher's shop), *charcuterie* (delicatessen), *poissonnerie* (fishmonger's) and *caviste* (wine shop).

INDIVIDUAL BOUTIQUES

The predominance of the specialist shop also carries through to the non-food sector. France has seen less ingress of chain stores than other countries, so there are individual boutiques selling fashion (*prêt-à-porter*), lingerie, shoes and items such as china and kitchenware. In larger cities, the department store (*grand magasin*) brings all these specialists under one roof.

MARKETS

The *marché* (market) is a French institution. Large cities hold at least one daily market, and smaller towns have a weekly market. They start around 7am and finish at noon. This is where to find the freshest seasonal produce, including fruit, vegetables, regional foodstuffs and cheeses, and other products from basketware to pottery.

Other forms of market are advertised in the local press or by flyers attached to posts in the area. *Foires artisanales* bring together potters, sculptors and other artists, and are held once or twice a year at historical locations such as medieval villages or châteaux.

Marchés aux puces (flea markets) can be found in some of the larger cities. *Brocante* refers to items that fall between genuine antiques and flea-market goods—anything from furniture to china. *Vide grenier* is the French equivalent of a British car-boot sale.

MODERN STORES

On the outskirts of every big town or city, supermarkets and hypermarkets (*hypermarchés* or *grandes-surfaces*) have sprung up; the main names include Carrefour, Auchan, Champion and E. Leclerc. Here you will find the specialist *boulangerie*, *boucherie* and *charcuterie* under one roof.

Often the *hypermarchés* are surrounded by other stores, for example DIY and sports stores, in a *centre commercial*.

CHIC SHOPPING

Paris is the hub of *la mode française*, but away from the capital, French style at its best can be found in chic resorts: Nice or Cannes in the southeast, Biarritz in the southwest, La Baule in the northwest and Chamonix in the Alps.

WINES AND SPIRITS

Hypermarchés sell an excellent range of French wines and spirits but it is more fun to buy from the vineyards (*domaines*) themselves. You can taste the youngest bottled wine of the finest producers in Bordeaux, Burgundy or Champagne but you will be expected to buy at least one bottle in return.

If you are not sure your budget will stretch to fine wines then many areas have cooperatives where you can sample local AOC (*Appellation d'Origine Contrôlée*) wines or *vins de pays* (country wines) for less.

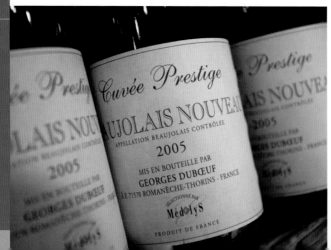

REGIONAL SHOPPING

Modern transportation and commerce mean that the best-known products of the regions, for long a trademark of France and once obtainable only from their source, can now usually be bought all across the country. However, there is a particular pleasure in buying your souvenirs from their place of origin, or seeking out local producers for food and wine to take home as a taste of France.

NORTHWEST FRANCE AND THE LOIRE

Brittany is known for its lace, but the handmade variety is rare and expensive. Pottery is much more common. The best is from Quimper, although imitations crowd souvenir shops around the region. Local food items of the northwest are farm-produced Camembert cheese, honey or salt from the coastal flats at Guérande. Drinks include excellent cider, Calvados (apple brandy) and crisp Muscadet wine, the best of which is produced *sur lie*—where the newly fermented wine remains in contact with the lees (sediment). The towns of Auray and Honfleur are artists' enclaves.

NORTH, NORTHEAST FRANCE AND THE ÎLE DE FRANCE

The north's principal lure is the champagne produced around Reims, but Alsace-Lorraine has interesting white wines in Riesling and Gewürztraminer. Head north for beer too. Soft, creamy Brie is the principal cheese of the region, produced in the Île de France, east of Paris. Mustard from Meaux is another excellent buy.

CENTRAL FRANCE AND THE ALPS

Natural products made by hand from the raw materials of the area are very much in vogue today: bone-bladed knives, wooden walking sticks, items made of slate, even fur —all items that have been produced here for centuries.

Coming up to date, look for winter and summer sportswear and adventure equipment from snowboards to mountain bikes.

Preserved foods such as jams and *charcuterie* (dried and prepared meats) also make good purchases.

Burgundy equals Bordeaux in its reputation for wine, with sublime reds and whites, the best of which are produced along the Côte d'Or near Beaune. *Eau-de-vie* (a clear spirit) and *marc* (local brandy), made from distilled grape skins, are the main after-dinner drinks. Dijon is synonymous with mustard.

Moving down the Saône valley through the Beaujolais vineyards brings you to Lyon with its centuries of experience in silk production. Today you can still buy hand-produced silk items. South of Lyon you will find the Rhône valley, with its world-famous wines.

Thiers has been France's main producer of cutlery for several centuries and some is still made by hand here.

SOUTHWEST FRANCE

This region's tasty food includes truffles, *cèpes* (ceps mushrooms) and foie gras (goose or duck liver).

Bordeaux needs no introduction as a wine-producing area and some of the finest names in the business have châteaux in the region, including Margaux and Pomerol.

You can taste and buy fine French brandies around Cognac and in the Armagnac region.

Porcelain and enamel from Limoges have long been renowned, while the town of Aubusson has supplied the châteaux of France with tapestries since the Middle Ages.

SOUTHEAST FRANCE AND CORSICA

Several staple foodstuffs grown in the southeast include dried wild herbs, virgin olive oil (best around Nyons) and strings of garlic. Head to Castelnaudary or Toulouse (both towns claim to be its true home) for authentic cassoulet. The slow-cooked dish is made from sausage and duck or goose with beans, and you can take some home in tins.

In addition to the aroma of wild herbs, the air in the south is heavy with the scent of flowers, particularly around Grasse, famous for its perfumes. *Savon* (soap) *de Marseille* is known for its quality, and other soap in the region is often made with a base of olive oil. Nothing of the olive tree is wasted: The wood is carved into items, from salad bowls to coasters. Terracotta pottery is also widespread.

In Corsica, pick up local cheeses and wines, ceramics and hand-carved wood items.

France has a rich cultural heritage in the performing arts. Paris has the richest selection of performances, but more than 300 music festivals are held around the country each year, plus an abundance of live performances at Maisons de la Culture or Maisons d'Animation Culturelle in the provinces. Listings magazines are the best source of information. There are great contrasts in nightlife throughout France. Large swathes of countryside might as well be desert for those seeking nightlife, other than an alfresco dinner followed by a few pages of summer reading. The major cities, of course, are a different matter. Paris leads the way, with a worldwide reputation as a party city. Lyon, Marseille, Nantes, Toulouse, Montpellier and other cities have a thriving nightlife and the youth base of many university towns ensures that there is a vibrant club scene. In addition to the geographical divide, there is the seasonal schism. The resorts of the Alps are buzzing during the ski season, but close down in the summer. This is the time of year when there's a mass exodus from the cities to the coast. It is then that Côte d'Azur clubs come into their own.

BALLET AND CONTEMPORARY DANCE

The Opéra National de Paris (Palais Garnier, 8 rue Scribe, 75009, Paris; tel 08 92 89 90 90; www.operadeparis.fr) is more than 300 years old; its reputation reached its zenith under the direction of the Russian dancer Rudolf Nureyev in the late 1980s.

Several other major cities have their own ballet companies. The best known of these companies include Lyon (www.opera-lyon.com), Biarritz (www.balletbiarritz.com) and Monte Carlo (www.balletsdemontecarlo.com).

Modern and contemporary dance are popular. In Paris, the Centre Georges Pompidou (www.centrepompidou.fr) leads the way with performances by French and international companies. Montpellier's Centre Choréographique National (www.mathildemonnier.com) is regarded as a focus of excellence for contemporary dance.

CLASSICAL MUSIC

Paris has no world-renowned orchestra, and live classical music has a lower profile here than in some European capitals. However, several ensembles, such as the Orchestre de Paris (www.orchestredeparis.com), have an annual schedule and autumn is the main classical music season.

Classical recital seasons held in important historical venues are a popular addition to arts calendars across France. Two of these are the Grandes Eaux Musicales at Versailles (www.châteauversaillesspectacles.fr) and the International Organ Festival at Chartres cathedral (http://orgues.chartres.free.fr).

JAZZ

Paris is one of Europe's leading jazz venues, with a plethora of small clubs including Le New Morning (▷ 111) catering for an army of aficionados. Jazz is also the focus

for many festivals, including the autumn Festival du Jazz in the capital, festivals in Nice, Antibes and at the Roman amphitheatre in Vienne in July, and the Grenoble festival in March.

OPERA

One of the capital's finest examples of modern architecture, the Opéra Bastille, opened in 1989 (www.operadeparis.fr) and has a regular schedule of performances. There are 12 regional opera companies around the country including those in Lyon (www.opera-lyon.com) and Toulouse (www.theatre-du-capitole.fr).

THEATRE

The founding of Paris's Comédie Française (www.comedie-francaise.fr) in 1680 kick-started a national love of the theatre. Paris continues to stage a wealth of classical, avant-garde and foreign-language plays. The Comédie, which performs mainly at the Palais Royal in Paris, still concentrates on the classics, and the great French dramatists (Molière, Racine, Victor Hugo) are revisited each season.

Every major French city has a theatre. Almost all productions are in French, but with some knowledge of the language, a visit to the theatre can still be enjoyed. In most auditoriums in France smoking is not permitted.

BOOKING TICKETS

Most theatre box offices sell tickets for their own performances and will accept telephone bookings with payment by credit card. FNAC stores (www.fnac.com) are ticket agents; for rock, pop or jazz concerts try Virgin Megastore (www.virginmega.fr), or for multi-venue arts festivals try the tourist office.

Matinée performances are often less expensive than evening shows, and same-day tickets (if available) are also sold at a price reduction.

In Paris, the Kiosque Théâtre sells reduced-price tickets for the day of the performance for most Paris theatres. There are outlets at 15 place de la Madeleine and at Gare Montparnasse.

DRESS CODES

Evening orchestral, operatic and theatre performances require smart but not necessarily formal clothing, although you can dress up without feeling overdressed. For other types of performance, casual clothing is perfectly acceptable.

CABARET

Revues are a peculiarly Parisian form of entertainment, and although Toulouse-Lautrec might be disappointed, today's leg-shows still display a substantial amount of flesh.

The Moulin Rouge (▷ 111) is the Grande Dame of the genre, and its 100-artiste costumed spectacles continue to enthuse new audiences, particularly since the eponymous movie blockbuster in 2001. For a more intimate, and perhaps more titillating performance, try Crazy Horse (▷ 110).

THE CAFÉ-BAR

The inextricably linked café-bar is the lifeblood of French nightlife. Even the most humble village will have at least one place to meet over a few drinks. In country areas French bars have multiple personalities—they are a place for teenagers to hang out around the slot machine or over a game of pool, and somewhere for farmers to meet to discuss the latest subsidy controversy. In the cities, and especially in the resorts, bars are more sophisticated—diners drop in for an aperitif before dinner or a coffee and *digestif* afterwards.

Every French bar worth its salt will have tables outside during the summer, and the most popular are those where the clientele can watch the world go by as evening turns to night.

A PMU bar is a branch of the French tote system where you can bet on horse races and often watch meetings live on TV. However, these venues are not always used to welcoming visitors.

In cities, bars may open at 7am to serve breakfast and stay open until the early hours of the morning. There are no set licensing hours, though a late-night permit is needed to serve drinks after midnight. Out of season and out of the cities, bars may close as early as 9pm.

Unaccompanied children under 16 are not allowed into bars and the legal age for drinking is 16.

CASINOS

Not necessarily just for James Bond types, a night at a casino is part entertainment, part spectator sport, and provided you don't go totally over the top and lose your shirt, a great place to mix with European high rollers.

You'll find casinos in all the grand belle-époque resorts or spas, although the doyenne has to be Monte Carlo (www.montecarlocasinos.com). *Grands Casinos* are the epitome of elegance, and you should be too if you want to get past the doormen. The tables open around 10pm and close around 4am.

CLUBS

All major urban areas have a lively club scene, particularly in the university towns. Flyers at tourist offices, record stores or fashionable cafés will point you in the right direction. Clubs open around 9pm but don't really get started until around 11pm, then partying continues until the early hours.

GAY AND LESBIAN SCENE

Paris is an excellent destination, particularly the Marais district, which has a wealth of gay hotels, bars, clubs and businesses. Other hotspots are in the south around St-Tropez and along the Côte d'Azur.

To find out more check the regional listings magazines.

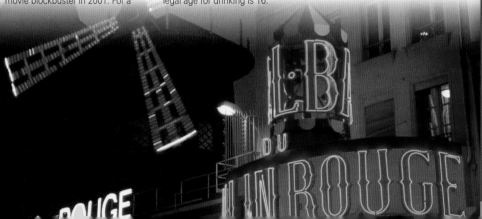

SPORTS AND ACTIVITIES

Whatever the season there's a full schedule of sporting action in France, and, surprisingly, many of the premier events don't cost a cent to watch. With its magnificent landscapes—snow-covered alpine peaks, hillsides festooned with wild flowers, magnificent rivers and Atlantic, Channel and Mediterranean coastlines—it would be surprising if the French did not enjoy outdoor activities. But enjoy is perhaps too bland a word: They have a great enthusiasm for sporting activities, and indeed have had a pivotal influence on several modern technical sports. Think of the Montgolfier brothers for ballooning, Blériot for flying or Jacques Cousteau for scuba-diving. If you can climb it, jump from it, ski down it, sail on it, swim under it, ride on it or slither through it, the French do it—and there will be an association to organize and publicize the activity.

GENERAL INFORMATION

Each district in France has some form of sporting facility, be it a simple *boules* (bowling) pitch, sports hall, swimming pool *(piscine)*, tennis court or golf course. Information about these facilities appears in tourist information publications under *loisirs* (leisure). Most regional tourist organizations publish booklets relating to leisure facilities.

The various associations (see below) can provide extra information about their particular sports. However, the French Government Tourist Office (▷ 430) also produces some excellent brochures on leisure and sporting activities.

AIR SPORTS

Most regions of France have at least one airfield where a variety of clubs meet to practise flying *(vol)*, gliding *(vol à voile)* or launching themselves out of planes *(parachutisme)*. These are privately run members' clubs that generally welcome foreign members. They also offer introductions *(baptêmes)* to the sport for beginners, with prices starting at €50 for a flight, €300 for parachute training and €220 for a tandem parachute jump.
Fédération Française de Vol Libre: www.ffvl.fr
Fédération Française de Vol à Voile: www.ffvv.org

BICYCLING/MOUNTAIN BIKING

Bicycling *(cyclisme)*, either off or on road, is a popular pastime, as well as a serious sport. It is easy to rent bicycles in towns and at more than 200 train stations (around €15 per day). Some cities have cut-price bicycle rental schemes to try to reduce the number of motor vehicles. For beginners, the flat areas of the Landes in Aquitaine are ideal. Experienced riders with mountain bikes *(vélo touts terrain—VTT)* could head for the Alps or the Massif Central.
Fédération Française de Cyclisme: www.ffc.fr

The Tour de France is arguably the most important sporting event in France. The three-week-long event crosses the country in July, with the last stage and dramatic climax in Paris with the push for the line at the end of the Champs-Élysées.

You don't need a ticket to see the Tour de France. Simply find a suitable spot along the route. You'll need to arrive early as the roads are closed

at least a couple of hours before the race is due to pass by.
www.letour.fr

CLIMBING

The Alps have some of the most challenging climbs in the world and Mont Blanc is Europe's highest mountain. It's also possible to climb in the Pyrenees and the Massif Central.

The Club Alpin Français (www.ffcam.fr) has information about climbing schools and lessons, or equipment rental for experienced climbers. Instructional courses with an accompanying guide cost between €100 and €200

DOWNHILL SKIING

The European ski season kicks off each year with the Premier Neige men's downhill race on the first Sunday in December at Val d'Isère, in the Alps. Large crowds gather in the finish area at La Daille to cheer on their preferred skier and drink mulled wine (vin chaud). You don't even need a ticket for this event.

The Val d'Isère tourist office has details of the race dates: BP 228, 73155 Val d'Isère (tel 04 79 06 06 60; www.valdisere.com).

FISHING

France's 240,000km (150,000 miles) of rivers, 120,000ha (300,000 acres) of lakes and 4,800km (3,000-mile) coastline are perfect for a spot of fishing. However, on rivers and lakes, some of which are private, you will require a licence (visit www.encyclopeche.com for details of the nearest Federation de Pêche) to cast your line.

FRENCH OPEN TENNIS

The second Grand Slam tournament of the season is on the clay courts of Roland-Garros Stadium in Paris at the end of May/beginning of June.

You'll need to apply for tickets for set dates by the end of February. For a booking form contact: FFT, Billeterie, 2 avenue Gordon Bennett, 75016 Paris, tel 08 26 65 00 00 (www.rolandgarros.fr).

Any unsold tickets go on sale at the stadium a few days before the tournament begins. Ticket prices range from €20 to €80.

GO-KARTING

You can take to the track at specially built go-karting venues across the country. All the equipment is provided, plus an introduction to the go-karts if required. Prices start at €15 for 10 minutes of track time. During peak times track time is limited.

GOLF

Although France was somewhat left behind as golf mania swept through the UK and North America, it has been catching up fast, with hectares of new greens springing up. Some of the best courses are linked to venerable French resorts—Dinan, Nice and Vichy, to name just three—where the golf course is seen as an extension of the experience of spa and casino. You can take to the course for around €50 per round. Fédération Française de Golf: www.ffgolf.org

HORSE-RACING

Horse-racing is a popular sport in France, and the most popular flat race for owners and betters takes place in October at Longchamps in the Bois de Boulogne, outside Paris. The Prix de l'Arc de Triomphe is an opportunity for ladies to don their hats, drink champagne and cheer on their horse. Hippodrome de Longchamps: Route des Tribunes, Bois du Boulogne, 75116 Paris (tel 01 44 30 75 00; www.prixarcdetriomphe.com).

HORSEBACK RIDING

Horseback riding (équitation/randonnée équestre), or perhaps a little riding instruction, is available throughout France but is more concentrated in holiday areas during the summer months. Some of the most spectacular yet undemanding routes are on the flat marshes of the Camargue in the southeast, the Marais Salants in the northwest, or

the dry pine forests of the Landes in the southwest. A day-long guided ride with picnic costs around €75. One hour starts at €12.
Fédération Française d'Équitation: www.ffe.com

KAYAKING

Many of France's waterways offer excellent opportunities for kayaking, including the Gorges de l'Ardèche or the Lot or Dordogne rivers. You can rent equipment on site by the hour, the day or longer, or you can take a day group kayak ride for around €30. Fédération Française de Canöe-Kayak: www.ffck.org

MOTOR SPORTS

The first contender for highlight of the motor-racing calendar is the Le Mans 24-hour rally, where the cars test their endurance around this part racing circuit, part road track. General entry tickets cost €62 and a pit walk is €460. Order from the Ticket Office (Billetterie), Circuit des 24 Heures du Mans, 72019 Le Mans Cedex 2 (tel 08 92 69 72 24; www.lemans.org).

The most glamorous Formula One race is at Monte Carlo in Monaco, where the cars twist and turn through the narrow streets. The presence of the jet set turns Monaco into much more than a Grand Prix, but if you simply want to watch the racing, prices for hillside viewing start at €70, with stand seats costing from €70 to €409 (www.grand-prix-monaco.com).

The Monte Carlo Rally takes place in the mountains above the principality in January. Spectators don't need to pay a fee, but take warm clothes and make sure you arrive in plenty of time because the police close the roads.

PARAPENTE

The parapente is a little like a parachute but more controllable, and you don't need to take a plane ride—a running jump from any high point launches you into the air. Pioneered in France, it is a popular sport. Obviously mountainous

areas—the Alps, the Massif Central and the Pyrenees—are the best places to try it. Training courses cost around €360, or try a tandem flight for €120.
Fédération Française de Vol Libre: www.ffvl.fr

RUGBY

There is a strong rugby following in France and the high point of the season (Sep–end May) is the international Six Nations Tournament. Teams scrum down at the Stade de France: ZAC du Cornillon Nord, 93216 St-Denis La Plaine Cedex (tel 01 55 93 00 00; ticketline 08 92 70 09 00; www.stadefrance.fr).

SKIING AND SNOWBOARDING

Skiing and snowboarding are the main sports of the winter season, with as many resorts as there are snowy days of the year, each offering options for the beginner, intermediate or expert.

You can mix with the European glitterati at chic Courchevel or Chamonix, or go for off-piste action at Argentière. There's also good

skiing in the Pyrenees and in the Massif Central at Le Mont-Dore.

You will need to buy a ski pass (up to €44.50 per day in Val d'Isère). You can rent equipment for around €180 per week. Lessons in English are available in a group (one morning €48, five mornings €230, one-morning private lessons (maximum four people) €190). Contact the École du Ski Français: www.esf.net or Club Alpin Français: www.ffcam.fr

SOCCER

Soccer is one of the premier sports in France. Tickets for the top matches (season Aug–end May) are like gold dust. Top clubs include:
Olympique Lyonnais: Siège de l'Olympique Lyonnais, 350 avenue Jean Jaurès, 69361, Lyon (ticketline 3969 premium rate; www.olweb.fr).
A.S. Monaco: Stade Louis II, avenue des Castelans, 9814 Monaco (tel 00 377 92 05 74 73; www.asm-fc.com).

WALKING AND HIKING

France has more than 30,000km (18,600 miles) of footpaths, with a series of *Grandes Randonnées*

(long-distance footpaths) and *Petites Randonnées* that are included on maps published by the Institut Géographique National (IGN, Éspace IGN rue La Boétie, 75008 Paris; www.ign.fr).

The premier *Grandes Randonnées* routes are GR34 around the coast of Brittany and GR20 across the rugged interior of Corsica. These take at least two weeks to complete depending on fitness orthe weather.

To supplement this network, every *département* (region) and local *communes* (districts) have shorter walks: footpaths signposted around lakes, along riverbanks or linking historical monuments. Most tourist offices have plenty of information about walks in their area, and town halls usually have free maps.

WINDSURFING

There are usually perfect conditions for windsurfing along the southwest coast from Biarritz up past Arcachon in the Landes and north into the Loire Atlantique. However, windsurfing schools and board rental can be found all around the French coastline and on the major lakes. Renting a board will cost from €25 an hour.

HEALTH AND BEAUTY

What the rest of the world has discovered in the last 10 years the French have known for centuries—pampering is good for everyone.

SPAS

France is dotted with natural water sources, which over time developed into therapeutic spas. In the 18th century spas became places for pleasure as well as health, with Vichy leading the way. During the latter part of the 19th century, coastal resorts such as Dinard and Biarritz joined the pampering business. Today France's spas are some of the finest in the world, with high standards of training and cleanliness, plus a genteel clientele. Spa towns usually also offer high-class shopping and dining for a total package of enjoyment.

THALASSOTHERAPY

The French invented thalassotherapy—the use of seawater in a variety of therapeutic techniques. Venues, often linked with health spas, are dotted all along France's coastline—almost equally distributed between the Mediterranean, Atlantic and northern coasts. Treatments are also available in spas —locations include Paris and Aix-les-Bains.

VINOTHERAPY

France is synonymous with wine, so it should come as no surprise that it was the French who would combine wellbeing with one of the country's greatest crops.

Les Sources de Caudalie, just a 15-minute drive outside Bordeaux, pioneered the use of grape skins and wine in beauty treatments. Along with the treatments was a dietary regime that included a glass or two each day—to improve a client's *bien être*. It's now turned into a worldwide phenomenon.

For more information see www.sources-caudalie.com.

FOR CHILDREN

Although France is brimming with highbrow attractions—museums, châteaux, art galleries and the like—you're never far from something that the children will want to do. Any tourist office will point you in the direction of sights and activities to interest or excite them and often it's possible to find a sight that appeals to the whole family.

BEACHES

There is an excellent range of beaches along France's 4,800km (3,000 miles) of coastline. These have areas where children can play or explore for hours.

FESTIVALS AND FAIRS

These are held throughout France in the summer and are perfect for children of all ages.

SPORTS

France has a comprehensive range of sports. The level of training and supervision is usually very high, so children can try a new sport or simply enjoy one in which they are already proficient—from horseback riding to bicycling or windsurfing to snowboarding.

THEME PARKS

Disneyland® Resort Paris (▷ 81) needs little introduction. Other theme parks include Parc Astérix (▷ 198, 219) and Planète Sauvage safari park (▷ 250). Futuroscope (▷ 361) and Vulcania (▷ 271) are high-tech choices.

FESTIVALS AND EVENTS

Whenever and wherever France celebrates, one thing is certain—you are unlikely to go hungry or thirsty. Even in cities the atmosphere is more family party than public event. Whatever the theme, glasses and plates are filled and refilled, and visitors get to see the true identity of a town or village, reflecting as much the history and traditions of the region as of France itself. For France's national holidays, ▷ 429.

RELIGIOUS

In the east, St. Nicolas parades through town on 6 December, offering children sweets and gingerbread. Provence focuses on Nativity scenes: Craftsmen make *santon* figurines and shepherds lead their flocks to church on Christmas Eve.

Easter sees Corsican processions of penitents. Other saints' day festivities range from Burgundy's bacchanalia to celebrate St. Vincent, patron of the vine, to Brittany's portside blessings.

ARTS

The Cannes Film Festival in May has the highest profile, but summer nights are filled with the sound of dying sopranos as countless Mimis and Violettas warble their last in open-air operas across Provence. These are big-money events, whereas Avignon has a lively fringe where you can enjoy the off-beat on a budget. Cultural serendipity is served best at events such as classical concerts in churches.

Jazz is France's adopted art form, with top artists appearing in unlikely settings, including Normandy's apple orchards.

FOOD AND DRINK

In October, France celebrates a week of food festivals, street fairs and cookery contests. However, the eating continues year-round.

Wine country produces some excellent combination festivals, with chestnuts—roasted, puréed and baked—served alongside local wines in Rhône, and figs, olives and goat's cheeses served at November's *primeur* wine launches in Languedoc. Delicacies in the north include cider, crêpes and apple tarts.

TRADITIONAL

Traditional is sometimes a euphemism for off-beat. With origins lost in the mists of time, events such as the Soufflaculs parade in Nontron, Aquitaine (▷ 15), have to be seen to be disbelieved. Here, villagers walk through town in their nightshirts, pumping bellows to ward off evil spirits. A few villages celebrate the Day of the Donkey in lieu of Bastille celebrations on 14 July.

EATING

France loves its food—and appreciates its top chefs as it does its famous artists and musicians. Even an office cafeteria will take pride in the quality of the food it serves, and any French citizen with a napkin on their lap and a fork in their hand expects fine ingredients, well prepared. Regional cuisine is seen as a reflection of each corner of the country and while Paris may have the big names and bigger spenders, dinner in a provincial town can eclipse a meal in the capital.

The celebrity chefs, such as Alain Senderens, Paul Bocuse and Joel Robuchon, are the standard-bearers of haute cuisine. They and their colleagues Alain Ducasse and Jacques and Laurent Pourcel dictate the food fads of tomorrow. Garlanded with Michelin rosettes and Gault et Millau *toques* (France's highest culinary awards), they have introduced the concepts of world and fusion foods to the nation. In recent years, a move to lighter dishes and simpler techniques has, belatedly, acknowledged vegetarian tastes, although France's concept of vegetarianism is a little hazy, sometimes involving beef stock, chicken and bacon.

France also has numerous inexpensive North African, Lebanese and Vietnamese restaurants in most large towns.

Wherever you dine, remember that fast food is not indigenous. Be prepared to take time over your meal—good food is a way of life and meals are something to be enjoyed, rather than rushed.

RESTAURANTS
Every large town has its respected restaurants, quite different from the bistros and brasseries for everyday eating. In these, you'll find a more refined setting, with starched linen, polished glass and silverware and a sense of hushed reverence for the gastronomic offerings to come. Here, families celebrate birthdays and First Communions, promises are whispered and business deals settled over something even more important than a handshake. Remember to dress smartly and

reserve in advance. You can find quality regional food in the dining rooms of Logis de France hotels (▷ 446) and there are Michelin-starred establishments across the country, with Paul Bocuse in Lyon, the Pourcel twins in Montpellier and the legacy of the late Bernard Loiseau in Burgundy. The menu *dégustation*, which is found only in the finest restaurants, is a prix-fixe menu offering a sample of the finest dishes accompanied by a selection of appropriate wines. Best value are the midweek set menus at lunchtime, bringing a meal at even the most stellar establishments down to a realistic price.

BRASSERIES AND BISTROS
Brasseries were once brewery bars that served meals. Today, they are friendly informal restaurants that open long hours. Enjoy local specialty dishes, as well as standards such as steak-frites and *choucroute* (sauerkraut). Bistros are often small, independent or family-run restaurants serving traditional cooking, with a modest wine list. In Paris and across France, top chefs are opening bistro annexes to their flagship restaurants. The Pourcels' Jardin des Sens in Montpellier has spawned satellites in other cities, such as Avignon.

CAFÉS AND BARS
Cafés and bars serve coffee, soft drinks, alcohol, snacks and often herbal and traditional teas too. They open from breakfast time until late in the evening and you can expect to pay a little more for your drink if you sit at a table or on the

outdoor terrace. You'll notice the locals tend to stand at the bar. Bars often have newspapers and you can linger over your cup of coffee people-watching.

CUTTING COSTS
If you are on a budget, have your main meal at lunchtime, when most restaurants serve a *menu du jour*, or menu of the day, of two or three courses with a glass of wine for around 50 per cent of the cost in the evening. Many restaurants have prix-fixe meals in the evening, too, with three, four or more courses, the best of which is the *menu gastronomique*.

OPENING TIMES
Most restaurants and bistros keep strict serving times. Restaurants open at 12, close at 2.30, then reopen at 7.30. Except in the bustling heart of a lively city, restaurants stop taking orders between 10pm and 11pm. Many restaurants close Saturday and Monday lunchtimes and on Sunday evenings. Some Paris restaurants may close during July and August, and establishments on the coast often close completely between November and Easter.

ETIQUETTE
Most restaurants include service in the price of dishes, indicated by *service compris* or s.c. If the service is exceptional you may like to leave a tip. Although it is only the very top restaurants that may have a dress code, it is usual to dress up when dining in a smarter venue. Address staff as *Monsieur, Madame* or *Mademoiselle*. By law all restaurants are non-smoking.

MENU READER

THE MEDITERRANEAN

... **à la languedocienne:** with tomatoes, aubergines (eggplant), *cèpes* (cep mushrooms) and garlic.

... **à la niçoise:** with olive oil, garlic, tomatoes, onion, herbs, olives, capers, anchovies and tarragon.

... **à la provençale:** with olive oil, garlic, tomatoes, onion and herbs.

Bouillabaisse: fish stew served with *aïoli* (garlic mayonnaise) or *rouille* (chilli and garlic mayonnaise).

Brandade de morue: paste of salt cod mixed with milk, garlic and olive oil.

Cagoularde: stew of snails in wine.

Cassoulet: a thick stew of haricot beans and meat, such as goose and pork sausage.

Daube: meat stewed in wine.

Foie gras à la toulousaine: goose liver in pastry.

Pistou: sauce made of ground garlic, basil and cheese bound with olive oil.

Ratatouille: tomatoes, onions, courgettes (zucchini) and aubergines (eggpant) slow-cooked in garlic and olive oil.

Salade niçoise: tomatoes, French beans, anchovies, olives, peppers and boiled egg.

Soupe de poisson: a soup of puréed mixed fish.

THE PYRENEES AND THE SOUTHWEST

...**à la basquaise:** meat served with Bayonne ham, *cèpe* mushrooms and potatoes.

...**à la bordelaise:** with red wine sauce and mixed vegetables.

...**à la landaise:** dishes cooked in goose fat with garlic.

...**à la périgourdine:** accompanied by a truffle or foie gras sauce, or stuffed with truffles or foie gras.

Confit de canard: pieces of duck that are salted, cooked and then preserved in their own fat.

Foie gras: the enlarged liver of maize-fed geese or ducks, cooked and served in slices hot or cold.

Lièvre à la royale: hare boned and stuffed with bacon, cooked in wine and served with a truffle sauce.

Magret de canard: boned duck breast, grilled or fried.

BRITTANY, NORMANDY AND THE LOIRE

Agneau des prés-salés: lamb raised on the salt marshes.

Beurre blanc: butter whipped with white-wine vinegar and shallots.

Châteaubriand: a thick cut of tenderloin steak for two people with shallot, herb and white wine sauce.

Coquille St-Jacques: scallop served hot in its shell in a cream sauce topped with melted cheese or toasted breadcrumbs.

Cotriade: fish stew.

Crêpes or galettes: pancakes with either sweet or savoury fillings.

Far: a thick, sweet tart with prunes, similar to a flan.

Homard à l'armoricaine: lobster served flambéed in a cream and wine sauce.

Moules marinière: mussels in a white wine, shallot and parsley sauce.

Noisette de porc aux pruneaux: loin of pork with prunes.

Plat (assiette or plateau) de fruits de mer: seafood platter consisting of mixed crayfish *(langouste),* oysters *(huîtres),* prawns/shrimps *(crevettes),* mussels *(moules),* crab *(crabes)* and whelks *(bulots),* served on ice.

Sauce normande: made with cider and cream.

Tarte tatin: upside-down apple tart.

THE NORTH AND ALSACE-LORRAINE

Bäeckeoffe: mixed meat cooked in wine with potatoes and onions.

Carbonnade flamande: beef slow-cooked in beer and spices.

Choucroute garnie: pickled cabbage cooked in wine with pork, sausage and smoked ham, served with boiled potatoes.

PRACTICALITIES EATING

Chou rouge à la flamande: red cabbage cooked with apples in vinegar and sugar.

Jambon en croûte: ham in a pastry case.

Quiche Lorraine: egg custard tart with bacon, onion and herbs.

Salade de cervelas: cold sausage in vinaigrette sauce.

Waterzooi: a soup originating from Belgium, made of a vegetable and cream stew, with either chicken or freshwater fish.

THE JURA AND THE ALPS

Diots: pork sausages.

Fondue: there are two different types: *au fromage,* cubes of bread dipped into molten cheese mixed with wine (and sometimes kirsch); or *bourguignonne:* cubes of meat cooked in oil, then dipped into sauces.

Gratin dauphinois: sliced potatoes baked in milk with nutmeg.

Gratin savoyard: sliced potatoes with cheese cooked in stock.

BURGUNDY AND THE NORTHERN RHÔNE

Andouille: tripe and pork sausage served cold.

Andouillette: tripe and pork sausage served hot.

Boeuf bourguignon: beef slow-cooked with onions and mushrooms in red wine.

Boudin: blood pudding/sausage.

Coq au vin: chicken with mushrooms and onions stewed in red wine (traditionally Chambertin).

Escargots à la bourguignonne: snails in garlic and parsley butter.

Jambon persillé: ham and parsley in jelly served cold in slices.

Pommes à la lyonnaise: fried sliced potatoes and onions.

Poulet de Bresse: chicken from Bourg en Bresse (considered the best in France).

Poulet (or jau) au sang: chicken in a blood-thickened sauce.

Quenelles de brochet (pike): individual fish mousses with cream sauce.

Saladier à la lyonnaise: cooked sheep's feet and pig's trotters, ox

tongue and calf's head served with vinaigrette dressing.

CORSICA

Aziminu: a type of *bouillabaisse* (▷ 442, The Mediterranean).

Brocciu: a sheep's cheese made in Corsica.

Fiadone: cheesecake with lemon.

Fritelles de brocciu: fried doughnuts of cheese and chestnut flour.

Oursins: sea urchins, a local delicacy.

Piverunta: lamb stew with red (bell) peppers.

Raffia: a skewer of roasted lamb offal.

Sanglier: wild or semi-wild boar.

Tianu di fave: pork stew with haricot beans.

SAUCES

Béchamel: a classic sauce of flour, butter and milk. Often a base of other sauces such as Mornay, with cheese.

Béarnaise: egg yolk, vinegar, butter, white wine, shallots and tarragon.

Chasseur: hunter-style, with wine, mushrooms, shallots and herbs.

Demi-glace: brown sauce of stock with sherry or Madeira wine.

Diane: cream and pepper sauce.

...à la meunière: a method of serving fish, fried in butter then served with lemon juice, butter and parsley.

HOW TO ORDER STEAK

The French taste is for meat to be lightly cooked. Lamb will automatically come rare (unless you demand otherwise). If you order steak, you will be asked how you would like it cooked. Options are:

Bleu: blue, the rarest steak, warm on the outside but uncooked and cool in the middle.

Saignant: bloody, or rare, the steak is cooked until it starts to bleed and is warm in the middle.

À point: literally 'at the point'. The meat is cooked until it just stops bleeding. Many restaurants serve steak *à point* with some blood in the middle. If you want a warm pink middle but no visible blood, ask for steak *plus à point*. It's not an official French term, but good restaurants should oblige.

Bien cuit: 'well cooked', served with only a narrow pink middle. If you want no pink to remain, ask for it *bien bien cuit,* although your waiter may not be impressed.

FOOD AND DRINK

The French don't just love consuming good food and drink, they love talking about it almost as much. If you want to start a conversation anywhere in France, just ask someone to tell you about the produce of their *terroir* (local area). Express even the mildest interest in a dish put in front of you and the waiter or manager is likely to tell you about its origins, how the ingredients have been selected and the cooking method used.

Food is clearly far more than a means of sustenance; it's not going too far to say that it is a key part of national identity. When president Sarkozy proposed that soufflé, foie gras and other French delicacies should be given protected World Heritage status by UNESCO in the same way as the abbey of Mont St-Michel he might have raised a few chuckles abroad but his countrymen understood just what he meant.

For the visitor to France, the reverence shown towards eating and drinking can be bewildering and fascinating in turn. However, there is no denying that an exquisitely prepared and presented three-course lunch in the middle of a day of sightseeing can be as memorable as a morning spent in the Louvre. And a tour of the vineyards of Champagne or Bordeaux can be a good way to get to know the culture of a region in its broadest sense.

REGIONAL PRODUCTS

To talk about 'French cuisine' as if it were all one is to begin with a misunderstanding. Even to sum up food and wine region by region is simplistic but it's certainly one way to appreciate the complexity of the subject.

Provençal cooking is characterized by its extensive use of olive oil, tomatoes and herbs, and Gascony by its use of duck and goose.

It is much more accurate, however, to identify specific sources, and France's great culinary legacy to the world is certainly the *appellation d'origine controllée* (AOC), a guarantee with the force of law

that a product has been produced in delimited area according to certain standards. The denomination AOC is most used for wine but there are 43 classified cheeses and AOCs covering meat, shellfish, butter, fruit and olive oil.

VEGETARIAN FOOD

There are very few vegetarians in France and vegetarian restaurants are usually found only in big cities and trendy towns full of craftspeople. Restaurateurs rarely think of including meat- and fish-free dishes on their menus. The best option is to choose a salad and be prepared to quietly remove any meat or fish from it.

If you are a vegetarian, and especially if you are a vegan, you will need to plan your trip ahead and you might want to telephone a restaurant before you arrive to see if it can cater for you.

EXOTIC CUISINE

Even the French occasionally crave something different from their national cuisine. France's back-up menu hints at the country's colonial past and the source of its recent immigrants. All cities and some large towns have restaurants serving Vietnamese food and couscous from the Maghreb countries.

US-style fast food, burgers, chicken and so forth, is as popular as anywhere else in the world but sometimes it is adapted to French taste with more fresh ingredients included.

WINE

Winemaking in France predates the Roman occupation and while some New World winemakers are convinced that not much has changed since then, the industry does evolve.

The French consume less wine each year—partly as a result of much stricter laws on drinking and driving—and this, coupled with increasing global competition has caused crises in areas which have got used to churning out cheap table

wines. But while some vineyards are taken out of production, new ones are planted elsewhere and traditional wine regions which have specialized in quality rather than quantity are holding their own.

The French wine industry is divided into 13 regions, some highly regimented and with subdivisions famous in their own right; others have been newly created to promote less-well-known styles of wine.

The regions and their official websites are:

Alsace www.vinsalsace.com
Beaujolais www.beaujolais.com
Bordeaux www.bordeaux.com
Burgundy (Bourgogne)
www.bourgogne-wines.com
Champagne www.champagne.com
Charentes www.pineau.fr
Corsica (Corse)
www.vinsdecorse.com
Jura-Savoie www.jura-vins.com
Languedoc-Roussillon
www.languedoc-wines.com,
www.vinsderoussillon.com,
www.vindepaysdoc.com
Provence
www.vinsdeprovence.com
Southwest (Sud-Ouest)
www.vins-du-sud-ouest.com
Val de Loire
www.vinsvaldeloire.com
Vallée de Rhone
www.vins-rhone.com

OTHER DRINKS

France's favourite everyday aperitif is pastis, an aniseed-flavoured liqueur which is mixed with water to make a long cloudy drink. A more elegant aperitif is *kir*: a mixture of white wine and *crème de cassis* (blackcurrant liqueur). Marseillan in the south produces the vermouth Noilly Prat. Cognac and Armagnac are both brandies valued by connoisseurs. Calvados and Benedictine are liqueurs made in different parts of Normandy, and Chartreuse is made near the monastery in which it originated. The north of France—Lille and Alsace—makes extremely good beers and cider is made and drunk in Brittany.

From palaces through to farmyards, the range of places to stay in France depends as much on your taste as on your budget. The high-quality international hotel chains are found everywhere, although the more 'French' option may be a campsite, gîte or family-run auberge.

Hotels are inspected regularly and classified into six categories: no star, 1 star, 2 star, 3 star, 4 star and 4 star L (Luxury). They must display their rates (including tax) both outside the hotel and in the rooms, and charge per room and not per person. You generally have to pay extra for breakfast and for any additional beds you may want in your room.

There are two ways to get hotels beyond your budget without paying more than you can afford: In Paris and major cities, booking a package with a major tour operator will often allow you to stay in a better class of hotel than you might otherwise consider affordable. The other deal, in several towns and cities (but not Paris), is through the Bon Weekend en Ville promotion. This offers two nights for the price of one at a range of hotels and includes other discounts. It's available from participating tourist offices. Other tourist offices may have their own special packages.

The number of low-cost air fares to regional French airports from the UK and other European cities has widened the possibilities for arranging your own holiday package.

LUXURY

If you are looking for a luxury hotel, then France is the right place for you. The traditional haunts of the rich and famous include the fabulous belle-époque hotels on the Riviera, which offer the full-luxury treatment, and the glitz of the Paris Ritz. These have been joined by new designer hotels such as the Hi-Hotel in Nice, where concept rooms involve rock pools and high-tech plasma screens. Smaller, but no less expensive, are the boutique hotels, with no more than a couple of dozen rooms styled by fashion gurus. For true luxury (that's truly French), stay at one of the country's many châteaux— former aristocratic and royal residences which now offer paying guests a taste of another era. For more information, look at the website of Relais et Châteaux (www.relaischâteaux.com).

In most of the luxury options, health and beauty treatments are provided in state-of-the-art spas.

ON A BUDGET

Budget hotels may be something of a surprise. Independent city hotels are often quite stylish, although some are dated and draughty. Bland international chain hotels and motels are the easy option, and while these may be useful overnight stops on long journeys south, there are far more interesting options available at similar prices.

Best of all are the Logis de France hotels—you can get a full list from the French Tourist Office (▷ 430). These are small, family-run inns and hotels offering a good standard, from basic and comfortable to quaint and charming. Most have their own restaurants, offering traditional local dishes of a high quality. All are regularly inspected and listed on the website www.logishotels.com. Some have themed breaks which promote winter sports, fishing or hiking. Some hotels, particularly in more remote areas, offer deals including dinner or all meals. Make sure you check whether room rates include breakfast. In many city hotels, €8–€12 for a croissant and coffee may seem expensive, when the café-bar at the corner offers the same for less.

BED-AND-BREAKFAST

Chambre d'hôte is France's answer to the traditional bed-and-breakfast, and local tourist offices have lists of families who offer rooms to visitors. However, the best *chambres d'hôte* are affiliated to the Gîtes de France organization (see opposite). Graded

with one to four ears of corn *(épis)*, depending on comfort and facilities, each region's selection is published in a dedicated brochure. Often housed in converted farm buildings or restored watermills, they offer a slice of French life. Breakfast usually includes fresh home-made croissants and jams. Since many are run by farmers' wives and vineyard owners, it is worth taking the *table d'hôte* option and dining with the family. In Paris, B&B in private homes is available through www.bed-and-breakfast-in-paris.com.

A de luxe option is bed-and-breakfast with the nobility. Princes and countesses offer rooms in their family châteaux in the Loire and western France. Brochures are available from Bienvenue au Château (Centre d'Affaires Les Alizés, La Rigourdiène, 35510 Cesson Sevigue; www.bienvenueauchâteau.com).

SELF-CATERING

While plenty of holiday companies sell package deals at self-contained holiday parks—with the obligatory kids' club, face-painting and live entertainment in season, a popular alternative is to rent a gîte. These are self-contained cottages, houses and apartments, often with swimming pools, in small towns and country areas, and are generally promoted through Gîtes de France or Clévacances (www.clevacances.com). You can rent gîtes by the week or fortnight, and the accommodation is usually simple and decent (bring your own linen or rent on-site), but with a certain rustic charm. Graded from the simple to the very comfortable, the properties are listed in national and regional guides, and may also be found through local tourist offices. For accredited gîtes see www.gites-de-france.fr.

CAMPING

More than 9,000 fully equipped campsites, officially graded from 0 to 4 stars, and 2,300 farm campsites are regularly inspected and graded as carefully as the nation's hotels. Most have excellent facilities, with

mobile homes and pre-pitched tents ready for occupation. Visitors with their own caravans and tents can find inexpensive sites offering electricity, showers and toilets. In high season (in the north from May to September, and in the south from April to October) it is important to reserve ahead; you may not park your motorhome or put up your tent beside the beach or at the roadside. Police stations have addresses of local campsites in an emergency. Many towns and villages have places set aside for motorhomes to park for one or two days for free.

Contact the National Federation of Campsites 01 42 72 84 08 or www.campingfrance.com.

TIPS

» The Loisirs Acceuil desk at tourist offices arranges themed breaks in local hotels, gîtes and *chambres d'hôtes*. These may include extras such as fishing or truffle-hunting with your hosts, farmhouse cookery lessons and craft workshops.
» Paris hotels often charge lower rates during July and August, and provincial and seaside hotels may reduce prices after mid-September.
» If you are planning a winter sports holiday, after Christmas hotels offer discounts during school term-time.
» For a little extra, hotels will often put another bed in your room—ideal for families on a budget.
» If you are planning a hiking tour of a region, you can arrange to have your luggage transported between Logis de France hotels by prior arrangement. In some regions the hotel may even have donkeys to carry your bags.

Even if you're far from fluent, it is always a good idea to try to speak a few words of French while in France. The words and phrases on the following pages should help you with the basics, from ordering a meal to dealing with emergencies.

CONVERSATION

What is the time?
Quelle heure est-il?

When do you open/close?
À quelle heure ouvrez/fermez-vous?

I don't speak French.
Je ne parle pas français.

Do you speak English?
Parlez-vous anglais?

I don't understand.
Je ne comprends pas.

Please repeat that.
Pouvez-vous répéter (s'il vous plaît)?

Please speak more slowly.
Pouvez-vous parler plus lentement?

What does this mean?
Qu'est-ce que ça veut dire?

Write that down for me please.
Pouvez-vous me l'écrire, s'il vous plaît?

Please spell that.
Pouvez-vous me l'épeler, s'il vous plaît?

I'll look that up (in the dictionary).
Je vais le chercher (dans le dictionnaire).

My name is...
Je m'appelle ...

What's your name?
Comment vous appelez-vous?

This is my wife/husband.
Voici ma femme/mon mari.

This is my daughter/son.
Voici ma fille/mon fils.

This is my friend.
Voici mon ami(e).

Hello, pleased to meet you.
Bonjour, enchanté(e).

I'm from ...
Je viens de ...

I'm on holiday.
Je suis en vacances.

I live in ...
J'habite à ...

Where do you live?
Où habitez-vous?

Good morning.
Bonjour.

Good evening.
Bonsoir.

Goodnight.
Bonne nuit.

Goodbye.
Au revoir.

See you later.
À plus tard.

How much is that?
C'est combien?

May I/Can I...?
Est-ce que je peux ... ?

I don't know.
Je ne sais pas.

You're welcome.
Je vous en prie.

How are you?
Comment allez-vous?

I'm sorry.
Je suis désolé(e).

Excuse me.
Excusez-moi.

That's all right.
De rien.

USEFUL WORDS

Yes	**Oui**
No	**Non**
There	**Là-bas**
Here	**Ici**
Where	**Où**
Who	**Qui**
When	**Quand**
Why	**Pourquoi**
How	**Comment**
Later	**Plus tard**
Now	**Maintenant**
Open	**Ouvert**
Closed	**Fermé**
Please	**S'il vous plaît**
Thank you	**Merci**

SHOPPING

Could you help me, please?
(Est-ce que) vous pouvez m'aider, s'il vous plaît?

How much is this?
C'est combien?/Ça coûte combien?

I'm looking for ...
Je cherche ...

When does the shop open/close?
À quelle heure ouvre/ferme le magasin?

This isn't what I want.
Ce n'est pas ce que je veux.

This is the right size.
C'est la bonne taille.

Do you have anything less expensive/smaller/larger?
(Est-ce que) vous avez quelque chose de moins cher/plus petit/plus grand?

I'll take this.
Je prends ça.

Do you have a bag for this?
(Est-ce que) je peux avoir un sac, s'il vous plaît?

Do you accept credit cards?
(Est-ce que) vous acceptez les cartes de crédit?

I'd like ... grams please.
Je voudrais ... grammes, s'il vous plaît.

I'd like a kilo of ...
Je voudrais un kilo de ...

What does this contain?
Quels sont les ingrédients?/ Qu'est-ce qu'il y a dedans?

I'd like ... slices of that.
J'en voudrais ... tranches.

Bakery	**Boulangerie**
Bookshop	**Librairie**
Chemist	**Pharmacie**
Supermarket	**Supermarché**
Market	**Marché**
Sale	**Soldes**

NUMBERS

1	un
2	deux
3	trois
4	quatre
5	cinq
6	six
7	sept
8	huit
9	neuf
10	dix
11	onze
12	douze
13	treize
14	quatorze
15	quinze
16	seize
17	dix-sept
18	dix-huit
19	dix-neuf
20	vingt
21	vingt et un
30	trente
40	quarante
50	cinquante
60	soixante
70	soixante-dix
80	quatre-vingts
90	quatre-vingt dix
100	cent
1000	mille

POST AND TELEPHONES

Where is the nearest post office/ mail box?
Où se trouve la poste/la boîte aux lettres la plus proche?

How much is the postage to...?
À combien faut-il affranchir pour ...?

I'd like to send this by air mail/ registered mail.
Je voudrais envoyer ceci par avion/en recommandé.

Can you direct me to a phone?
Pouvez-vous m'indiquer la cabine téléphonique la plus proche?

What is the number for directory enquiries?
Quel est le numéro pour les renseignements?

Where can I find a telephone directory?
Où est-ce que je peux trouver un annuaire?

Where can I buy a phone card?
Où est-ce que je peux acheter une télécarte?

Please put me through to...
Pouvez-vous me passer ..., s'il vous plaît?

Can I dial direct to ...?
Est-ce que je peux appeler directement en ...?

Do I need to dial 0 first?
Est-ce qu'il faut composer le zéro (d'abord)?

What is the charge per minute?
Quel est le tarif à la minute?

Have there been any calls for me?
Est-ce que j'ai eu des appels téléphoniques?

Hello, this is ...
Allô, c'est ... (à l'appareil)?

Who is speaking please ...?
Qui est à l'appareil, s'il vous plaît?

I would like to speak to ...
Je voudrais parler à ...

DAYS

Monday	lundi
Tuesday	mardi
Wednesday	mercredi
Thursday	jeudi
Friday	vendredi
Saturday	samedi
Sunday	dimanche

MONTHS

January	janvier
February	février
March	mars
April	avril
May	mai
June	juin
July	juillet
August	août
September	septembre
October	octobre
November	novembre
December	décembre

SEASONS

spring	printemps
summer	été
autumn	automne
winter	hiver

HOLIDAYS

holiday	vacances
Easter	Pâques
Christmas	Noël

BASICS

morning	matin
afternoon	après-midi
evening	soir
night	nuit
today	aujourd'hui
yesterday	hier
tomorrow	demain
day	le jour
month	le mois
year	l'année

AT THE AIRPORT

Airport
Aéroport

Airline
Compagnie aérienne

Aeroplane
Avion

Terminal
Aérogare

Arrivals
Arrivées

Luggage
Bagages

Luggage claim
Livraison des bagages

Carry-on luggage
Bagages à main

Luggage trolley
Chariot

Checked-in luggage
Bagages enregistrés

Passport
Passeport

Customs
Douane

To declare
Déclarer

Departures
Départs

Buy a ticket
Acheter un billet

Make a reservation
Faire une réservation

One-way ticket
Billet simple

Plane ticket
Billet d'avion

Return ticket
Billet aller-retour

Check-in
L'enregistrement

Stopover
Escale

Check in luggage
Enregistrer les bagages

Boarding pass
Carte d'embarquement

Security check
Contrôle de sécurité
Duty-free
Boutique hors taxes
Flight
Vol
Gate
Porte
Early
En avance
Late
En retard
Shuttle bus
Navette

HOTELS
Do you have a room?
(Est-ce que) vous avez une chambre?
I have a reservation for ... nights.
J'ai réservé pour ... nuits.
How much each night?
C'est combien par nuit?
Double room.
Une chambre pour deux personnes/
double.
Twin room.
Une chambre à deux lits/ avec lits
jumeaux.
Single room.
Une chambre à un lit/pour une
personne.
With bath/shower/toilet.
Avec salle de bain/douche/WC.
**Is the room air-conditioned/
heated?**
(Est-ce que) la chambre est
climatisée/chauffée?
**Is breakfast/lunch/dinner included
in the cost?**
(Est-ce que) le petit déjeuner/le
déjeuner/le dîner est compris dans
le prix?
Is there an elevator in the hotel?
(Est-ce qu')il y a un ascenseur à
l'hôtel?
Is room service available?
(Est-ce qu')il y a le service en
chambre?
When do you serve breakfast?
À quelle heure servez-vous le petit
déjeuner?
May I have breakfast in my room?
(Est-ce que) je peux prendre le petit
déjeuner dans ma chambre?
Do you serve evening meals?
(Est-ce que) vous servez le repas du
soir/le dîner?

I need an alarm call at...
Je voudrais être réveillé(e) à...heures.
I'd like an extra blanket/pillow.
Je voudrais une couverture/ un
oreiller supplémentaire, s'il vous plaît.
May I have my room key?
(Est-ce que) je peux avoir la clé de ma
chambre?
**Will you look after my luggage
until I leave?**
Pouvez-vous garder mes bagages
jusqu'à mon départ?
Is there parking?
(Est-ce qu')il y a un parking?
Where can I park my car?
Où est-ce que je peux garer ma
voiture?
Do you have babysitters?
(Est-ce que) vous avez un service de
babysitting/garde d'enfants?
When are the sheets changed?
Quand changez-vous les draps?
The room is too hot/cold.
Il fait trop chaud/froid dans la
chambre.
Could I have another room?
(Est-ce que) je pourrais avoir une
autre chambre?
I am leaving this morning.
Je pars ce matin.
**What time should we leave our
room?**
À quelle heure devons-nous libérer la
chambre?
Can I pay my bill?
(Est-ce que) je peux régler ma note,
s'il vous plaît?
May I see the room?
(Est-ce que) je peux voir la chambre?
Swimming pool.
Piscine.
No smoking.
Non fumeur.
Sea view.
Vue sur la mer.

GETTING AROUND
Where is the information desk?
Où est le bureau des
renseignements?
Where is the timetable?
Où sont les horaires?
Does this train/bus go to...?
Ce train/bus va à ...?
Do you have a Métro/bus map?
Avez-vous un plan du Métro/des
lignes de bus?

**Please can I have a single/ return
ticket to...?**
Je voudrais un aller simple/ un aller-
retour pour ..., s'il vous plaît.
I'd like to rent a car.
Je voudrais louer une voiture.
Where are we?
Où sommes-nous?
I'm lost.
Je me suis perdu(e).
Is this the way to...?
C'est bien par ici pour aller à ...?
I am in a hurry.
Je suis pressé(e).
Where can I find a taxi?
Où est-ce que je peux trouver un
taxi?
How much is the journey?
Combien coûte le trajet?
Go straight on.
Allez tout droit.
Turn left.
Tournez à gauche.
Turn right.
Tournez à droite.
Cross over.
Traversez.
Traffic lights.
Les feux.
Intersection.
Carrefour.
Corner.
Coin.
No parking.
Interdiction de stationner.
Train/bus/Métro station.
La gare SNCF/routière/la station de
Métro.
Do you sell travel cards?
Avez-vous des cartes d'abonnement?
Do I need to get off here?
(Est-ce qu')il faut que je descende ici?
Where can I buy a ticket?
Où est-ce que je peux acheter un
billet/ticket?
Where can I reserve a seat?
Où est-ce que je peux réserver une
place?
Is this seat free?
(Est-ce que) cette place est libre?

CAR RENTAL
I'd like to rent a car.
Je voudrais louer une voiture.
I'd like an automatic car.
Je voudrais une voiture avec
transmission automatique

I'd like a compact car.
Je voudrais une voiture compacte.

I'd like a mid-range car.
Je voudrais une voiture intermédiaire.

I'd like a large car.
Je voudrais une voiture luxe.

I'd like a convertible car.
Je voudrais une voiture décapotable.

I'd like a 4x4 car.
Je voudrais un quatre quatre.

Is insurance included?
L'assurance est-elle comprise?

Can I return it to Nice/Lyon.
Puis-je la rendre a Nice/Lyon?

I'd like a street map.
Je voudrais un plan.

MONEY

Is there a bank/currency exchange office nearby?
(Est-ce qu')il y a une banque/un bureau de change près d'ici?

Can I cash this here?
(Est-ce que) je peux encaisser ça ici?

I'd like to change sterling/dollars into euros.
Je voudrais changer des livres sterling/dollars en euros.

Can I use my credit card to withdraw cash?
(Est-ce que) je peux utiliser ma carte de crédit pour retirer de l'argent?

What is the exchange rate today?
Quel est le taux de change aujourd'hui?

COLOURS

brown	marron/brun
black	noir(e)
red	rouge
blue	bleu(e)
green	vert(e)
yellow	jaune
white	blanc
pink	rose

RESTAURANTS

I'd like to reserve a table for ... people at ...
Je voudrais réserver une table pour ... personnes à ... heures, s'il vous plaît.

A table for ..., please.
Une table pour ..., s'il vous plaît.

What time does the restaurant open?
À quelle heure ouvre le restaurant?

We'd like to wait for a table.
Nous aimerions attendre qu'une table se libère.

Could we sit there?
(Est-ce que) nous pouvons nous asseoir ici?

Is this table taken?
(Est-ce que) cette table est libre?

Are there tables outside?
(Est-ce qu')il y a des tables dehors/à la terrasse?

Where are the toilets?
Où sont les toilettes?

Could you warm this up for me?
(Est-ce que) vous pouvez me faire réchauffer ceci/ça, s'il vous plaît?

Do you have nappy-changing facilities?
(Est-ce qu')il y a une pièce pour changer les bébés?

We'd like something to drink.
Nous voudrions quelque chose à boire.

Could we see the menu/ wine list?
(Est-ce que) nous pouvons voir le menu/la carte des vins, s'il vous plaît?

Is there a dish of the day?
(Est-ce qu')il y a un plat du jour?

What do you recommend?
Qu'est-ce que vous nous conseillez?

This is not what I ordered.
Ce n'est pas ce que j'ai commandé.

I can't eat wheat/sugar/salt/ pork/beef/dairy.
Je ne peux pas manger de blé/sucre/ sel/porc/bœuf/ produits laitiers.

I am a vegetarian.
Je suis végétarien(ne).

I'd like...
Je voudrais ...

Could we have some more bread?
(Est-ce que) vous pouvez nous apporter un peu plus de pain, s'il vous plaît?

How much is this dish?
Combien coûte ce plat?

Is service included?
(Est-ce que) le service est compris?

Could we have some salt and pepper?
(Est-ce que) vous pouvez nous apporter du sel et du poivre, s'il vous plaît?

May I have an ashtray?
(Est-ce que) je peux avoir un cendrier, s'il vous plaît?

Could I have bottled still/ sparkling water?
(Est-ce que) je peux avoir une bouteille d'eau minérale non-gazeuse/gazeuse, s'il vous plaît?

We didn't order this.
Nous n'avons pas commandé ça.

The meat is too rare/overcooked.
La viande est trop saignante/trop cuite.

The food is cold.
Le repas/Le plat est froid.

Can I have the bill, please?
(Est-ce que) je peux avoir l'addition, s'il vous plaît?

The bill is not right.
Il y a une erreur sur l'addition.

I'd like to speak to the manager, please.
Je voudrais parler au directeur, s'il vous plaît.

The food was excellent.
Le repas/Le plat était excellent.

FOOD AND DRINK

Breakfast	Petit déjeuner
Lunch	Déjeuner
Dinner	Dîner
Coffee	Café
Tea	Thé
Orange juice	Jus d'orange
Apple juice	Jus de pomme
Milk	Lait
Beer	Bière
Red wine	Vin rouge
White wine	Vin blanc
Bread roll	Petit pain
Bread	Pain
Sugar	Sucre
Wine list	Carte/liste des vins
Main course	Le plat principal
Dessert	Dessert
Salt/pepper	Sel/poivre
Cheese	Fromage
Knife/fork/spoon	Couteau/ Fourchette/Cuillère
Soups	Soupes/potages
Vegetable soup	Soupe de légumes
Chicken soup	Soupe au poulet
Lentil soup	Soupe aux lentilles
Mushroom soup	Soupe aux champignons
Sandwiches	Sandwichs
Ham sandwich	Sandwich au jambon
Dish of the day	Plat du jour
Fish dishes	Les poissons

Prawns	Crevettes roses/bouquet
Oysters	Huîtres
Salmon	Saumon
Haddock	Églefin
Squid	Calmar
Meat dishes	Viandes
Roast chicken	Poulet rôti
Casserole	Plat en cocotte
Roast lamb	Gigot
Mixed cold meat	L'assiette de charcuterie
Potatoes	Pommes de terre
Cauliflower	Chou-fleur
Green beans	Haricots verts
Peas	Petits pois
Carrots	Carottes
Spinach	Épinards
Onions	Oignons
Lettuce	Laitue
Cucumber	Concombre
Tomatoes	Tomates
Fruit	Les fruits
Apples	Pommes
Strawberries	Fraises
Peaches	Pêches
Pears	Poires
Fruit tart	Tarte aux fruits
Pastry	Pâtisserie
Chocolate cake	Gâteau au chocolat
Cream	Crème
Ice cream	Glace
Chocolate mousse	Mousse au chocolat

TOURIST INFORMATION

Where is the tourist information office, please?
Où se trouve l'office du tourisme, s'il vous plaît?

Do you have a city map?
Avez-vous un plan de la ville?

Where is the museum?
Où est le musée?

Can you give me some information about...?
Pouvez-vous me donner des renseignements sur ...?

What are the main places of interest here?
Quels sont les principaux sites touristiques ici?

Please could you point them out on the map?
Pouvez-vous me les indiquer sur la carte, s'il vous plaît?

What sights/hotels/restaurants can you recommend?
Quels sites/hôtels/restaurants nous recommandez-vous?

We are staying here for a day.
Nous sommes ici pour une journée.

I am interested in...
Je suis intéressé(e) par ...

Does the guide speak English?
Est-ce qu'il y a un guide qui parle anglais?

Do you have any suggested walks?
Avez-vous des suggestions de promenades?

Are there guided tours?
Est-ce qu'il y a des visites guidées?

Are there organized excursions?
Est-ce qu'il y a des excursions organisées?

Can we make reservations here?
Est-ce que nous pouvons réserver ici?

What time does it open/close?
Ça ouvre/ferme à quelle heure?

What is the admission price?
Quel est le tarif d'entrée?

Is there a discount for seniors/ students?
Est-ce qu'il y a des réductions pour les personnes âgées/les étudiants?

Do you have a brochure in English?
Avez-vous un dépliant en anglais?

What's on at the cinema?
Qu'est-ce qu'il y a au cinéma?

Where can I find a good nightclub?
Où est-ce que je peux trouver une bonne boîte de nuit?

Do you have a schedule for the theatre/opera?
Est-ce que vous avez un programme de théâtre/d'opéra?

Should we dress smartly?
Est-ce qu'il faut mettre une tenue de soirée?

What time does the show start?
À quelle heure commence le spectacle?

How do I reserve a seat?
Comment fait-on pour réserver une place?

Could you reserve tickets for me?
Pouvez-vous me réserver des places?

ILLNESS AND EMERGENCIES

I don't feel well.
Je ne me sens pas bien.

Could you call a doctor?
(Est-ce que) vous pouvez appeler un médecin/un docteur, s'il vous plaît?

Is a doctor/pharmacist on duty?
(Est-ce qu')il y a un médecin/docteur/ une pharmacie de garde?

I feel sick.
J'ai envie de vomir.

I need to see a doctor/dentist.
Il faut que je voie un médecin/ docteur/un dentiste.

Please direct me to the hospital.
(Est-ce que) vous pouvez m'indiquer le chemin pour aller à l'hôpital, s'il vous plaît?

I have a headache.
J'ai mal à la tête.

I've been stung by a wasp/bee/ jellyfish.
J'ai été piqué(e) par une guêpe/ abeille/méduse.

I have a heart condition.
J'ai un problème cardiaque.

I am diabetic.
Je suis diabétique.

I'm asthmatic.
Je suis asmathique.

I'm on a special diet.
Je suis un régime spécial.

I am on medication.
Je prends des médicaments.

I have left my medicine at home.
J'ai laissé mes médicaments chez moi.

I need to make an emergency appointment.
Je dois prendre un rendez-vous d'urgence.

I have bad toothache.
J'ai mal aux dents.

I don't want an injection.
Je ne veux pas de piqûre.

Help!
Au secours!

I have lost my passport/wallet/ purse/handbag.
J'ai perdu mon passeport/ portefeuille/porte-monnaie/sac à main.

I have had an accident.
J'ai eu un accident.

I have been robbed.
J'ai été volé(e).

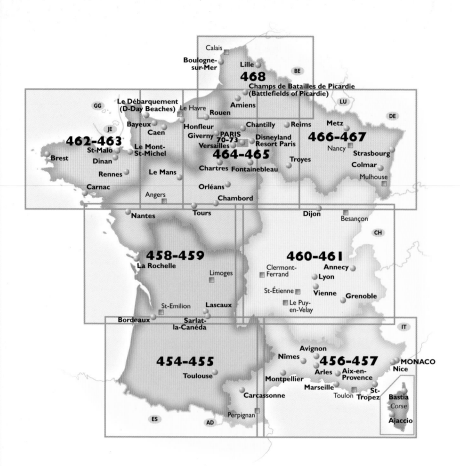

Calais
Boulogne-sur-Mer
Lille
BE
468
Champs de Batailles de Picardie
(Battlefields of Picardie)

GG
Le Débarquement
(D-Day Beaches)
Le Havre
Amiens
LU
DE
Bayeux
Honfleur
Chantilly
Reims
Metz
JE
Caen
Giverny
PARIS
70-73
Disneyland
Resort Paris
Nancy
Strasbourg
462-463
Le Mont-
St-Michel
Versailles
Troyes
Colmar
St-Malo
Brest
Dinan
Chartres
Fontainebleau
464-465
Mulhouse
Rennes
Le Mans
Carnac
Orléans
Angers
Chambord
Nantes
Tours
Dijon
Besançon
CH

458-459
La Rochelle
Limoges
460-461
Clermont-Ferrand
Annecy
Lyon
St-Étienne
Vienne
Grenoble
Le Puy-en-Velay
St-Emilion
Lascaux
Bordeaux
Sarlat-la-Canéda
IT

Avignon
Nîmes
456-457
MONACO
Nice
454-455
Arles
Aix-en-Provence
Toulouse
Montpellier
Marseille
St-Tropez
Toulon
Bastia
Carcassonne
Corse
ES
Perpignan
Ajaccio
AD

| 454-468 | 0 | 20 km |
| | 0 | 15 miles |

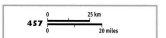

| 457 | 0 | 25 km |
| | 0 | 20 miles |

▬▬	Toll motorway (Turnpike)	●	Featured place of interest
═══	Motorway (Expressway)	■	City / Town
❷ ●	Motorway junction with and without number		Built-up area
⇒	National road		National park / Area of outstanding natural beauty
⇒	Regional road	✈	Airport
───	Railway	⚓	Port / Ferry route
▓▓▓	International boundary	621 ▲	Height in metres
─ ─	Administrative region boundary	⇌	Mountain pass

MAPS

Map references for the sights refer to the atlas pages within this section or to the individual town plans within the regions. For example, Toulouse has the reference ✚ 455 H13, indicating the page on which the map is found (455) and the grid square in which Toulouse sits (H13).

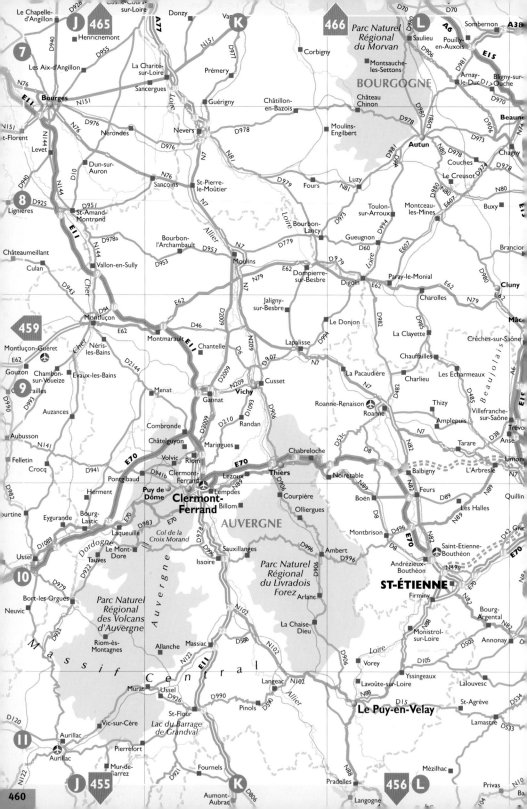

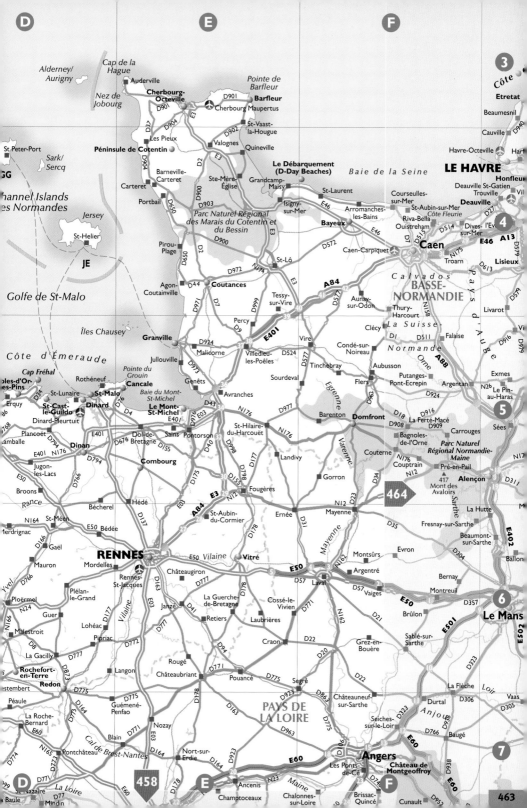

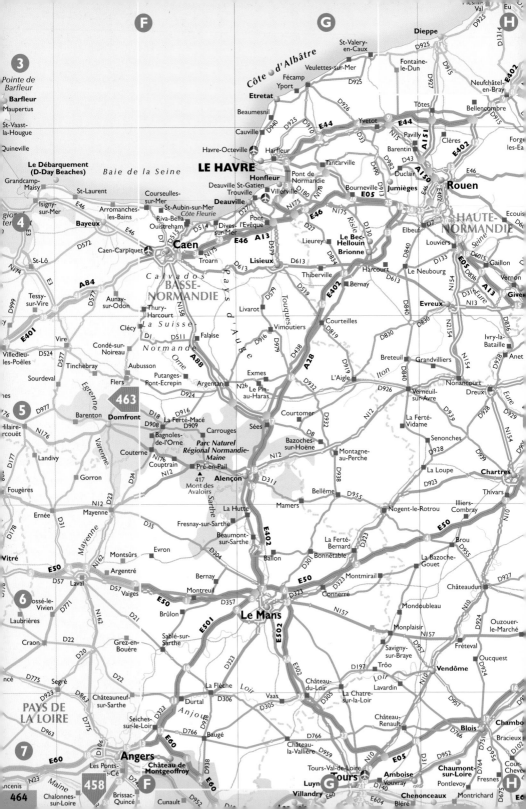

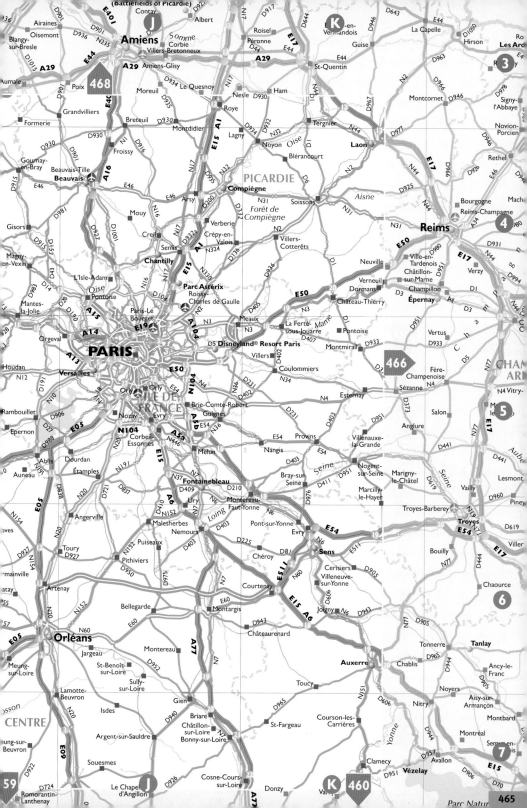

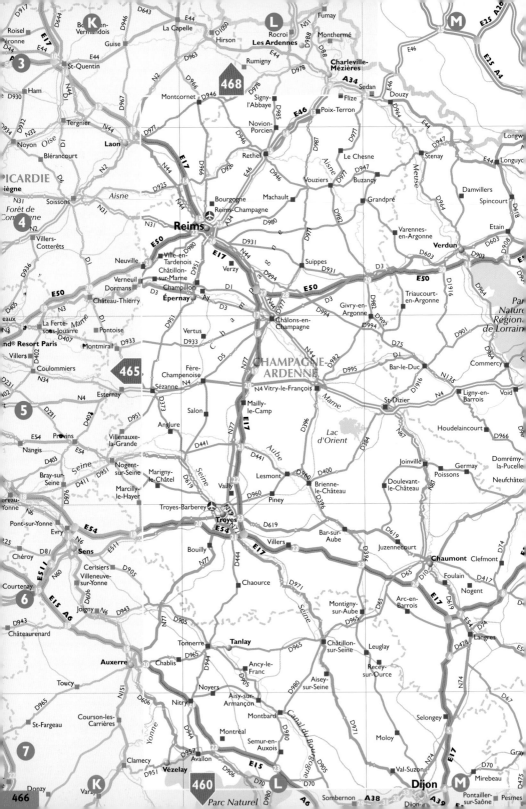

Place	Map	Grid
Abbaye de Fontfroide	455	K14
Abbeville	468	H3
Ablis	465	H5
Abreschviller	467	P5
Accous	454	F14
Agay	457	P13
Agde	456	K13
Agen	455	G12
Agon-Coutainville	463	E4
Aigrefeuille-sur-Maine	458	E7
Aiguebelle	457	P14
Aiguebelle	461	N10
Aigues-Mortes	456	L13
Aiguillon	454	G12
Ailefroide	461	P11
Aime	461	P10
Airaines	468	H3
Aire-sur-l'Adour	454	F13
Airvault	459	F8
Aisey-sur-Seine	466	L6
Aisy-sur-Armançon	466	L7
Aix-en-Provence	457	N13
Aixe-sur-Vienne	459	H10
Aix-les-Bains	461	N10
Aizenay	458	E8
Ajaccio (Corse)	457	R15
Alban	455	J13
Albert	468	J3
Albertville	461	N10
Albi	455	J12
Alençon	464	G5
Alès	456	L12
Allanche	460	K10
Allevard	461	N10
Allos	457	P12
Altkirch	467	P6
Alzon	456	K12
Amance	467	N6
Ambérieu-en-Bugey	461	M9
Ambert	460	K10
Amboise	459	G7
Amiens	468	J3
Amou	454	E13
Amplepuis	460	L9
Ancenis	458	E7
Ancy-le-Franc	466	L6
Andernos-les-Bains	458	E11
Andrézieux-Bouthéon	460	L10
Anet	464	H5
Angers	463	F7
Angerville	465	J6
Anglet	454	E13
Anglure	466	K5
Angoulême	459	G10
Aniche	468	K2
Annecy	461	N9
Annemasse	461	N9
Annonay	460	M10
Anse	460	L9
Antibes	457	P13
Apt	456	M12
Aramits	454	E14
Arcachon	454	E11
Arc-en-Barrois	466	M6
Archiac	458	F10
Ardentes	459	H8
Arès	458	E11
Argelès-Gazost	454	F14
Argelès-sur-Mer	456	K15
Argentan	464	F5
Argentat	459	H11
Argenton-Château	458	F8
Argenton-sur-Creuse	459	H8
Argentré	463	F6
Argent-sur-Sauldre	465	J7
Arlanc	460	K10
Arles	456	M13
Armentières	468	J2
Arnay-le-Duc	460	L7
Arracourt	467	N5
Arreau	454	G14
Arrens-Marsous	454	F14
Arromanches-les-Bains	463	F4
Ars-en-Ré	458	E9
Arsy	465	J4
Artenay	465	H6
Arudy	454	F14
Arzacq-Arraziguet	454	F13
Asco (Corse)	457	S14
Aspet	455	G14
Astaffort	455	G12
Aubagne	457	N13
Aubenas	456	L11
Aubeterre-sur-Dronne	459	G10
Auboué	467	N4
Aubusson	459	J9
Aubusson	463	F5
Auch	455	G13
Auderville	463	E3
Audierne	462	B6
Audressein	455	G14
Aullène (Corse)	457	S15
Ault	468	H3
Aumale	468	H3
Aumont-Aubrac	456	K11
Aunay-sur-Odon	463	F4
Auneau	465	H5
Aups	457	N13
Auray	462	C6
Aurignac	455	G14
Aurillac	460	J11
Auterive	455	H13
Autun	460	L8
Auxerre	465	K6
Auxi-le-Château	468	J3
Auzances	460	J9
Availles-Limouzine	459	G9
Avallon	466	L7
Avesnes-sur-Helpe	468	L3
Avignon	456	M12
Avranches	463	E5
Ax-les-Thermes	455	H14
Ay	466	L4
Azay-le-Ferron	459	H8
Azay-le-Rideau	459	G7
Baccarat	467	P5
Badonviller	467	P5
Bagnères-de-Bigorre	454	F14
Bagnères-de-Luchon	455	G14
Bagnoles-de-l'Orne	464	F5
Bagnols-les-Bains	456	K12
Bagnols-sur-Cèze	456	L12
Bailleul	468	J2
Bains-les-Bains	467	N6
Baix	456	M11
Balbigny	460	L9
Ballon	464	G6
Bangor	462	C7
Bapaume	468	J3
Baraqueville	455	J12
Barbezieux-St-Hilaire	459	F10
Barentin	464	G4
Barenton	463	F5
Barfleur	463	E3
Barjols	457	N13
Bar-le-Duc	466	M5
Barneville-Carteret	463	E4
Barr	467	P5
Barre-des-Cévennes	456	K12
Barrême	457	N12
Bar-sur-Aube	466	L6
Bastia (Corse)	457	S14
Batz-sur-Mer	458	D7
Baugé	464	F7
Baume-les-Dames	461	N7
Bayeux	463	F4
Bayonne	454	E13
Bazoches-sur-Hoëne	464	G5
Beaucaire	456	M13
Beaulieu-sur-Dordogne	459	H11
Beaumesnil	464	G3
Beaumont-de-Lomagne	455	G13
Beaumont-sur-Sarthe	464	G6
Beaune	460	M8
Beaupréau	458	E7
Beaurepaire-en-Bresse	461	M8
Beauvais	465	J4
Beauvoir-sur-Mer	458	D8
Bécherel	463	D5
Bédée	463	D6
Beg-Meil	462	B6
Bélâbre	459	H8
Belfort	467	P6
Bellac	459	H9
Bellegarde	456	L13
Bellegarde	465	J6
Bellegarde-sur-Valserine	461	N9
Belle-Île	462	C7
Bellême	464	G5
Bellencombre	464	H3
Belleville-sur-Vie	458	E8
Belley	461	N9
Belvès	455	G11
Benfeld	467	P5
Bénodet	462	B6
Berck-Plage	468	H2
Bergerac	459	G11
Bergues	468	J1
Bernay	464	F6
Bernay	464	G4
Berre-l'Étang	456	M13
Besançon	461	N7
Bessines-sur-Gartempe	459	H9
Béthune	468	J2
Beuillsola	457	P12
Beynac-et-Cazenac	459	H11
Béziers	456	K13
Biarritz	454	D13
Bias	454	E12
Bias	455	G12
Bidart	454	D13
Billom	460	K10
Binic	462	D5
Biscarrosse-Plage	454	E12
Blain	463	E7
Blangy-sur-Bresle	468	H3
Blaye	458	F11
Blérancourt	465	K4
Bléré	459	G7
Blériot-Plage	468	H1
Bligny-sur-Ouche	460	L7
Blois	464	H7
Boëge	461	N9
Boën	460	L10
Bohain-en-Vermandois	468	K3
Bollène	456	M12
Bonifacio (Corse)	457	S16
Bonlieu	461	N8
Bonnétable	464	G6
Bonneval-sur-Arc	461	P10
Bonny-sur-Loire	465	J7
Bordeaux	458	F11
Bort-les-Orgues	460	J10
Bouilly	466	L6
Boulogne-sur-Gesse	455	G13
Boulogne-sur-Mer	468	H2
Bourbon-Lancy	460	K8
Bourbon-l'Archambault	460	K8
Bourbonne-les-Bains	467	N6
Bourbriac	462	C5
Bourg	458	F11
Bourganeuf	459	H9
Bourg-Argental	460	L10
Bourg-en-Bresse	461	M9
Bourges	460	J7
Bourg-Lastic	460	J10
Bourgogne	466	L4
Bourgoin-Jallieu	461	M10
Bourgueil	459	G7
Bourneville	464	G4
Boussens	455	G14
Bouxwiller	467	P5
Bozel	461	P10
Bracieux	464	H7
Brancion	460	M8
Branne	459	F11
Brantôme	459	G10
Bray-sur-Seine	465	K5
Breil-sur-Roya	457	Q12
Bressuire	458	F8
Brest	462	B5
Bretenoux	459	H11
Breteuil	464	G5
Breteuil	465	J3
Briançon	461	P11
Briare	465	J7
Brie-Comte-Robert	465	J5
Brienne-le-Château	466	L5
Brignoles	457	N13
Brionne	464	G4
Brioux-sur-Boutonne	459	F9
Brissac-Quincé	458	F7
Brive-la-Gaillarde	459	H11
Broons	463	D5
Brou	464	H6
Brûlon	464	F6
Bruniquel	455	H12
Bubry	462	C6
Bucquoy	468	J3
Buis-les-Baronnies	456	M12
Burie	458	F10
Bussang	467	P6
Buxy	460	L8
Buzancy	466	M4
Cabrerets	455	H12
Cadillac	454	F11
Caen	464	F4
Cagnes-sur-Mer	457	P13
Cahors	455	H12
Calacuccia (Corse)	457	S15
Calais	468	H1
Calenzana (Corse)	457	S14
Calignac	454	G12
Callac	462	C5
Calvi (Corse)	457	R14
Camarès	455	K13
Camaret	462	B5
Cambo-les-Bains	454	E13
Cambrai	468	K3
Campan	454	F14
Cancale	463	E5
Cancon	455	G11
Canet-Plage	456	K14
Cannes	457	P13
Capbreton	454	E13
Cap Corse (Corse)	457	S14
Capestang	456	K13
Cap Ferret	454	E11
Caraman	455	H13
Carantec	462	B5
Carbère	456	K15
Carbon-Blanc	458	F11
Carcans	458	E11
Carcassonne	455	J14
Carcès	457	N13
Cargèse (Corse)	457	R15
Carhaix-Plouguer	462	C5
Carling	467	N4
Carnac	462	C7
Carpentras	456	M12

MAPS FRANCE

Place	Map	Ref
Pau	454	F13
Pauillac	458	F10
Pavilly	464	G4
Péaule	463	D7
Peira-Cava	457	Q12
Pellegrue	454	F11
Percy	463	E5
Périgueux	459	G10
Péronne	468	K3
Pérouges	461	M9
Perpignan	455	K14
Perros-Guirec	462	C5
Pertuis	457	N13
Pesmes	461	M7
Pézenas	456	K13
Piana (Corse)	457	R15
Piedicroce (Corse)	457	S15
Pierre-de-Bresse	461	M8
Pierrefort	460	J11
Pierrefort	467	N5
Pierroton	454	E11
Piney	466	L5
Pinols	460	K11
Pipriac	463	D6
Pirou-Plage	463	E4
Pithiviers	465	J6
Plabennec	462	B5
Plage-en-Ré	458	E9
Plancoët	463	D5
Plélan-le-Grand	463	D6
Pleumartin	459	G8
Pleyben	462	B5
Ploërmel	463	D6
Plouay	462	C6
Ploudalmézeau	462	B5
Plouescat	462	B5
Plougasnou	462	C5
Plougastel-Daoulas	462	B5
Plouha	462	C5
Plouigneau	462	C5
Ploumanac'h	462	C5
Plouray	462	C6
Pluvigner	462	C6
Poissons	466	M5
Poitiers	459	G8
Poix	468	J3
Poix-Terron	466	L3
Pompey	467	N5
Pons	458	F10
Pontailler-sur-Saône	461	M7
Pont-à-Mousson	467	N5
Pontarlier	461	N8
Pont-Aven	462	B6
Pontcharra	461	N10
Pontchâteau	463	D7
Pont-Croix	462	B6
Pont-d'Ain	461	M9
Pont-de-Roide	461	N7
Pont-de-Vaux	461	M8
Pont du Gard	456	L12
Pontgibaud	460	J9
Pontivy	462	C6
Pont-l'Abbé	462	B6
Pont l'Evêque	464	G4
Pontlevoy	459	H7
Pontoise	465	J4
Pontoise	465	K5
Pontorson	463	E5
Pontrieux	462	C5
Pont-sur-Yonne	465	K6
Pornic	458	D7
Porquerolles	457	N14
Portbail	463	E4
Port-de-Bouc	456	M13
Port-Grimaud	457	P13
Porticcio (Corse)	457	S15
Port-Joinville	458	D8
Port-Louis	462	C6
Port-Manech	462	B6
Port-Navalo	462	C7
Porto (Corse)	457	R15
Porto-Vecchio (Corse)	457	S16
Port-sur-Saône	467	N6
Pouancé	463	E6
Pouilly-en-Auxois	460	L7
Pouyastruc	454	F13
Pradelles	460	L11
Prahecq	458	F9
Prats-de-Mollo-la-Preste	455	J15
Préchac	454	F12
Pré-en-Pail	464	F5
Prémery	460	K7
Preuilly-sur-Claise	459	G8
Privas	456	L11
Propriano (Corse)	457	S16
Provins	465	K5
Prunete (Corse)	457	S15
Puget-Théniers	457	P12
Puiseaux	465	J6
Putanges-Pont-Ecrepin	464	F5
Puy de Dôme	460	K10
Puy-l'Evêque	455	H12
Questembert	463	D6
Quiberon	462	C7
Quillan	455	J14
Quillins	460	M10
Quimper	462	B6
Quimperlé	462	C6
Quineville	463	E4
Quingey	461	N7
Quissac	456	L12
Rabastens-de-Bigorre	454	F13
Rambervillers	467	N5
Rambouillet	465	H5
Randan	460	K9
Raon-l'Etape	467	P5
Réalmont	455	J13
Recey-sur-Ource	466	M6
Redon	463	D6
Reignier	461	N9
Reims	466	L4
Remiremont	467	N6
Rémuzat	456	M12
Rennes	463	E6
Réquista	455	J12
Rethel	466	L4
Retiers	463	E6
Reuilly	459	J7
Rhinau	467	Q5
Rians	457	N13
Ribérac	459	G10
Rieumes	455	H13
Rieux	455	H13
Rignac	455	J12
Riom	460	K9
Riom-ès-Montagnes	460	J10
Riquewihr	467	P6
Riscle	454	F13
Riva-Bella	464	F4
Rivedoux-Plage	458	E9
Rivesaltes	455	K14
Roanne	460	L9
Rocamadour	459	H11
Rochechouart	459	G9
Rochefort	458	E9
Rochefort-en-Terre	463	D6
Rochervière	458	E8
Rocroi	468	L3
Rodez	455	J12
Rogliano (Corse)	457	S14
Rohan	462	D6
Roisel	468	K3
Romans-sur-Isère	461	M11
Romorantin-Lanthenay	459	H7
Ronchamp	467	N6
Roquebillière	457	Q12
Roquefort	454	F12
Roquefort-sur-Soulzon	456	K12
Rosans	457	M12
Roscoff	462	B5
Rosporden	462	B6
Rostassac	455	H11
Rostrenen	462	C5
Rothéneuf	463	D5
Roubaix	468	K2
Rouen	464	H4
Rougé	463	E6
Rougemont	467	N7
Roussillon	456	M12
Rouvres-en-Xaintois	467	N5
Royan	458	E10
Roybon	461	M10
Roye	465	J3
Royère-de-Vassivière	459	H9
Rue	468	H2
Ruelle-sur-Touvre	459	G10
Rue	461	N9
Rumigny	468	L3
Sables-d'Or-les-Pins	463	D5
Sablé-sur-Sarthe	464	F6
Sabres	454	E12
Saillagouse	455	J15
Sains	463	E5
St-Agrève	460	L11
St-Amand-Montrond	460	J8
St-Aubin-du-Cormier	463	E6
St-Aubin-sur-Mer	464	F4
St-Avold	467	N4
St-Benoît-sur-Loire	465	J6
St-Brieuc	462	D5
St-Cast-le-Guildo	463	D5
St-Cirq-Lapopie	455	H12
St-Claude	461	N8
St-Denis-d'Oléron	458	E9
St-Dié	467	P5
St-Dizier	466	M5
Ste-Enimie	456	K12
Sainte-Lucie-de-Tallano (Corse)	457	S16
Ste-Mère-Église	463	E4
St-Émilion	459	F11
Saintes	458	F10
Stes-Maries-de-la-Mer	456	L13
St-Étienne	460	L10
St-Étienne-de-Tinée	457	P12
St-Fargeau	465	K7
St-Florent (Corse)	457	S14
St-Florent	459	J8
St-Flour	460	K11
St-Guénolé	462	B6
St-Hilaire-du-Harcouët	463	E5
St-Jean-d'Angely	458	F9
St-Jean-de-Luz	454	D13
St-Jean-Pied-de-Port	454	E14
St-Laurent	463	F4
St-Lizier	455	H14
St-Lô	463	E4
St-Lunaire	463	D5
St-Macaire	454	F11
St-Malo	463	D5
St-Martin-d'Ardèche	456	L12
St-Maximin-la-Ste-Baume	457	N13
St-Méen	463	D6
St-Nazaire	458	D7
St-OmerArras	468	J2
St-Palais	454	E13
St-Paul	457	P13
St-Pierre-le-Moûtier	460	K8
St-Pierre-sur-Mer	456	K14
St-Pol-de-Léon	462	B5
St-Pol-sur-Ternoise	468	J2
St-Quay-Portrieux	462	D5
St-Quentin	468	K3
St-Rémy-de-Provence	456	M13
St-Riquier	468	J3
St-Savin	459	G8
St-Symphorien	454	F12
St-Thégonnec	462	B5
St-Tropez	457	P13
St-Vaast-la-Hougue	463	E3
St-Valery-en-Caux	464	G3
St-Valery-sur-Somme	468	H3
Saissac	455	J13
Salernes	457	N13
Salies-de-Béarn	454	E13
Sallanches	461	P9
Salles	454	E11
Salon	466	L5
Salon-de-Provence	456	M13
Salviac	455	H11
Samatan	455	G13
Samoëns	461	P9
Sancergues	460	K7
Sancoins	460	K8
Santa Severa (Corse)	457	S14
Sarlat-la-Canéda	459	H11
Sarralbe	467	P4
Sarrebourg	467	P5
Sarreguemines	467	P4
Sarron	454	F13
Sartène (Corse)	457	S16
Sarzeau	462	C7
Saucats	454	F11
Saujon	458	E10
Saulieu	460	L7
Sault	456	M12
Saumur	459	F7
Sauternes	454	F11
Sauveterre-de-Béarn	454	E13
Sauveterre-de-Guyenne	454	F11
Sauxillanges	460	K10
Sauzon	462	C7
Saverdun	455	H14
Saverne	467	P5
Savigny-sur-Braye	464	G6
Scaër	462	C6
Seclin	468	K2
Sedan	466	M3
Séderon	457	N12
Sées	464	G5
Segonzac	459	F10
Segré	463	F6
Seiches-sur-le-Loir	464	F7
Sélestat	467	P5
Selongey	466	M7
Semur-en-Auxois	466	L7
Senlis	465	J4
Sennecey-le-Grand	461	M8
Senonches	464	H5
Senonens	467	P5
Sens	465	K6
Sérent	462	D6
Serres	457	N12
Sète	456	K13
Seurre	461	M8
Seyne	457	N12
Sézanne	466	K5
Sierentz	467	P6
Sigean	456	K14
Signy-l'Abbaye	466	L3
Siorac-en-Périgord	459	G11
Sisco (Corse)	457	S14
Sisteron	457	N12
Six-Fours-les-Plages	457	N14
Soissons	465	K4
Solenzara (Corse)	457	S15
Sombernon	460	L7
Sommières	456	L13
Sospel	457	Q12

MAPS | FRANCE

PICTURES

The Automobile Association would like to thank the following photographers, companies and picture libraries for their assistance in the preparation of this book. Abbreviations for the picture credits are as follows: (t) top; (b) bottom; (l) left; (r) right; (AA) AA World Travel Library.

4 AA/T Souter;
5 AA/R Moss;
6 AA/B Toms;
7 AA/M Short;
8bl AA/P Kenward;
8br AA/C Sawyer;
9 AA;
10 AA/I Dawson;
11tl AA/R Moore;
11tr AA/R Strange;
12t AA/M Jourdan;
12b AA/T Teegan;
13 AA/C Sawyer;
14 AA/I Dawson;
15bl Nicolas José/Photolibrary Group;
15tr AA/A Baker;
16 AA/Y Levy;
17bl ©Rebecca Johnson/Alamy;
17br AA/B Smith;
18 AA/K Paterson;
19tr AA/K Blackwell;
19bl AA/R Strange;
20 AA/J Tims;
21tr AA/J Tims;
21cr AA/J Edmanson;
21bl AA/C Sawyer;
22 AA/B Smith;
23bl AA/K Blackwell;
23br AA/R Moore;
24 CRT des Pays de la Loire;
25t AA/D Noble;
25b AA/M Jourdan;
26 Alamy ©Jordan Weeks;
27bl AFP/Getty Images;
27br Haymarket Publishing;
28tl Sipa Press/Rex Features;
28tr AA/C Sawyer;
29 AA/B Smith;
30 AA/C Sawyer;
31t AA/A Baker;
31b AA/R Strange;
32 AA;
33t AA/J Edmanson;
33br AA;

34 AA/R Moore;
35t Louvre, Paris, France, Giraudon / The Bridgeman Art Library;
35b AA/C Sawyer;
36 AA/D Noble;
37t Chateau de Versailles, France, Lauros / Giraudon / The Bridgeman Art Library;
37b AA/B Rieger;
38 AA/D Noble;
39bl AA/M Jourdan;
39br AA;
40 AA/A Baker;
41t AA/C Sawyer;
41b Bibliothèque-Musée Forney, Paris, France, Archives Charmet / The Bridgeman Art Library;
42 Action Press/Rex Features;
43bl AA;
43br AA/R Moore;
44 AA/K Blackwell;
45 AA/J Wyand;
46 AA/N Setchfield;
48 AA/C Sawyer;
49 AA/C Sawyer;
50 AA/R Strange;
52 AA/P Kenward;
53(i) K Glendenning;
53(ii) AA/J Wyand;
53(iii) AA/A Baker;
53(iv) AA/R Strange;
53(v) AA/N Setchfield;
53(vi) AA/R Moore;
53(vii) AA/C Sawyer;
53(viii) K Glendenning;
53(ix) AA/A Baker;
55 AA/S Day;
57 AA/P Bennett;
58 AA/C Sawyer;
59 AA/K Paterson;
60 AA/C Sawyer;
61 AA/C Sawyer;
62 AA/M Jourdan;
63bl AA
63br AA/C Sawyer;
64 Cintract Romain/Photolibrary Group;
65 AA/A Baker;
67 AA/J Edmanson;
68 AA/M Jourdan;
76 Gavin Hellier/Photolibrary Group;
77 Brigitte Merle/Photononstop/ Photolibrary Group;
78 AA/M Jourdan;
79 AA/M Jourdan;
80 AA/T Souter;
81 © Disney;

82 K Glendenning;
83 AA/K Paterson;
84 AA/K Paterson;
85tl AA/M Jourdan;
85tr AA/T Souter;
86 AA/M Jourdan;
87 AA/M Jourdan;
88 AA/M Jourdan;
89 AA/K Paterson;
90 AA/J Tims;
91bl AA/M Jourdan;
91br Louvre, Paris, France, Giraudon / The Bridgeman Art Library;
92 AA/K Paterson;
93 AA/P Enticknap;
94tl AA/M Jourdan;
94tr AA/M Jourdan;
95 AA/M Jourdan;
96 AA/M Jourdan;
97 AA/M Jourdan;
99 AA/T Souter;
100 AA/T Souter;
101bl AA/J Tims;
101br AA/J Tims;
102 AA/M Jourdan;
103 AA/D Noble;
104 AA/T Souter;
106 AA;
107 AA/J Tims;
108 AA/C Sawyer;
110 AA/P Enticknap;
112 AA;
113 Photodisc;
114 AA/C Sawyer;
117 AA/C Sawyer;
118 AA/C Sawyer;
120 AA/C Sawyer;
122 AA/R Strange;
124 AA/R Moore;
125 AA/I Dawson;
126 AA;
127 AA/A Kouprianoff;
128bl AA/A Kouprianoff;
128br AA/A Kouprianoff;
129 AA/I Dawson;
130 AA/J Tims;
131 AA/I Dawson;
132 AA/I Dawson;
133 AA/I Dawson;
134 AA/S Day;
135t AA/A Baker;
135b AA/R Moore;
136 AA/R Moore;
137 AA/I Dawson;
138 AA/I Dawson;
139 AA/I Dawson;
140 AA/C Sawyer;

309 AA/N Setchfield;
310 AA/C Sawyer;
311 AA/A Baker;
312 AA/C Sawyer;
313 AA/C Sawyer;
314t AA/A Baker;
314b AA/R Strange;
315bl AA/C Sawyer;
315br AA/R Strange;
316 AA/R Moore;
317 AA/A Baker;
318tl World Pictures/Photoshot;
318tr AA/N Setchfield;
320 AA/A Baker;
321bl AA/A Baker;
321br AA/B Smith;
323 AA/N Setchfield;
324 AA/C Sawyer;
326t AA/C Sawyer;
326b AA/C Sawyer;
327t AA/C Sawyer;
327b AA/C Sawyer;
328 AA/C Sawyer;
329l AA/C Sawyer;
329r AA/C Sawyer;
330 AA/C Sawyer;
332 AA/A Baker;
333t AA/A Baker;
333b AA/A Baker;
334 AA/A Baker;
337 AA/C Sawyer;
338 AA/C Sawyer;
340 AA/C Sawyer;
343 AA/C Sawyer;
345 AA/J Tims;
346 AA/C Sawyer;
349 AA/C Sawyer;
350 Mike Herringshaw/Photolibrary
Group;
352 Michel Viard/Photononstop/
Photolibrary Group;
353 AA/N Setchfield;
354tl AA/N Setchfield;
254tr AA/N Setchfield;
355 AA/N Setchfield;
356 AA/N Setchfield;
357 AA/N Setchfield;
358t AA/N Setchfield;
358b AA/N Setchfield;
359 AA/N Setchfield;
360bl AA/T Oliver;
360br Robert Harding/Photolibrary
Group;
361 AA/B Smith;
362 J P De Manne/Photolibrary
Group;
363 AA/A Baker;

364 Alain Even/Photononstop/
Photolibrary Group;
365 AA/N Setchfield;
366 AA/B Smith;
367 AA/N Setchfield;
368 Jon Arnold/Photolibrary Group;
369 AA/N Setchfield;
370 AA;
371 Ruth Tomlinson/Photolibrary
Group;
372 Alan Copson/Photolibrary Group;
373 AA/N Setchfield;
374 AA/N Setchfield;
375 WYSOCKI Pawel/Photolibrary
Group;
376 AA/N Setchfield;
378 AA/N Setchfield;
379 AA/N Setchfield;
380 AA/P Bennett;
382 AA/D Halford;
383 AA/N Setchfield;
384 Bruno Barbier/Photolibrary
Group;
385 Soleil Noir/Photolibrary Group;
386 Photodisc;
389 AA/C Sawyer;
391 AA/N Setchfield;
392 AA/B Smith;
395 AA/R Strange;
396 AA/N Setchfield;
399 AA/J Holmes;
400 World Pictures/Photoshot;
402 Camille Moirenc/Photononstop/
Photolibrary Group;
403 World Pictures/Photoshot;
404 World Pictures/Photoshot;
405 AA/R Moore;
406bl AA/B Toms;
406br AA/B Toms;
407tl World Pictures/Photoshot;
407tr World Pictures/Photoshot;
408 Robert Harding/Photolibrary
Group;
409 Tristan Deschamps/Photolibrary
Group;
410 AA/R Moore;
411 AA/R Moore;
412 AA/C Sawyer;
413 AA/R Moore;
415 AA/C Sawyer;
417 AA/P Kenward;
419 AA/J Tims;
420 AA/R Strange;
422 AA/C Sawyer;
423 AA/Y Levy;
424 AA/I Dawson;
425 AA/C Sawyer;

426 AA/N Setchfield;
428 © Miramax/Everett/Rex
Features;
432 AA/C Sawyer;
433 AA/J Tims;
434 AA/B Rieger;
435 AA/T Souter;
436 AA/T Mackie;
438tl AA/T Teegan;
438tr AA/J Tims;
439 AA/M Jourdan;
440 AA/S Montgomery;
442bl AA/R Moore;
442br AA/B Smith;
443 AA/M Short;
445t AA/A Baker;
445b AA;
446t AA/R Moore;
446b AA/P Kenward
453 AA/R Strange.

Every effort has been made to
trace the copyright holders, and
we apologise in advance for any
accidental errors. We would be
happy to apply the corrections in the
following edition of this publication.

CREDITS

Series editor
Sheila Hawkins

Project editor
Bookwork Creative Ltd

Design
Low Sky Design Ltd

Cover design
Chie Ushio

Picture research
Liz Allen

Image retouching and repro
Sarah Montgomery

Mapping
Maps produced by the Mapping Services
Department of AA Publishing

Main contributors
Lindsay Bennett, Colin Follett, Kathryn Glendenning,
David and June Halford, Cathy Hatley, Nicholas Inman,
Isla Love, Michael Nation, Lyn Parry, Laurence Phillips,
Alwyn Sambrook, Andrew Sanger, The Content Works

Updater
Lindsay Bennett

Indexer
Marie Lorimer

Production
Lorraine Taylor

See It France
ISBN 978-1-4000-0552-9
Fourth Edition

Color separation by AA Digital Department
Printed and bound by Leo Paper Products, China
10 9 8 7 6 5 4 3 2 1

A04411
Maps in this title produced from: Map data © Tele Atlas N.V. 2011.   Tele Atlas
© IGN France. Mapping © ISTITUTO GEOGRAFICO DE AGOSTINI S.p.A., NOVARA 2008
Transport map © Communicarta Ltd, UK
Weather chart statistics © Copyright 2004 Canty and Associates, LLC.